Systematic Instruction of the Moderately and Severely Handicapped

MARTHA E. SNELL, editor
University of Virginia

Charles E. Merrill Publishing Co.
A Bell & Howell Company
Columbus   Toronto   London   Sydney

Dedication

For all the "first and second priority" individuals—those who are not yet served and those for whom services are still inadequate—their current teachers, and their teachers-to-be.

And for my mentors, Ed Keller and Don Burke.

Published by Charles E. Merrill Publishing Company
A Bell and Howell Company
Columbus, Ohio 43216

This book was set in Helvetica and Univers.
The production editor was Jan Hall.
The cover was prepared by Will Chenoweth.

Library of Congress Catalog Card Number: 77-93413

International Standard Book Number: 0-675-08390-7

Printed in the United States of America

1 2 3 4 5 6 7 8 9 10/ 85 84 83 82 81 80 79 78

Preface

The purpose of this text is to set forth empirically based guidelines and models for teaching the moderately and severely handicapped. Readers of this book may be those preparing to be teachers, new teachers, or experienced teachers already in the service of schools, institutions, group homes, and workshops. The text covers a range of curricula relevant for teaching the severely handicapped—from the cognitive beginnings of visual tracking and mutual imitation to more advanced instructional targets in functional academics and vocational preparation. Therefore it also should serve as a resource for parents, classroom teaching assistants, program administrators, and the supplementary professional staff who work closely with the classroom.

The common philosophy of the contributors to this volume is a behavioral one. Sidney Bijou (1976) expresses well the value we place upon applied behavior analysis.

> The application of behavior principles to the teaching of retarded children is not another educational fad, and those who might stand around patiently waiting for it to pass will be disappointed. Since it is the end product of 50 years of experimental research and theory construction, it is likely that with continued support of basic and applied research, it will become even more effective (p. 7)

Such an orientation means that you, the reader, must feel quite comfortable with measuring the behavior of your students and that you automatically turn to an analysis of performance data when evaluating the effect of a particular instructional program at each stage of learning. This is part of what is meant by "systematic instruction."

Another characteristic of systematic instruction is your moment-by-moment awareness of what is happening during a teaching interaction. This includes the antecedent conditions you, the environment, and the student's peers provide in the form of instruction, materials, and prompts to direct the learner's attention to the relevant aspects of a learning task. It includes observation of the quality of the learner's response to the antecedent stimuli (the speed and accuracy of the performance in light of the amount of assistance provided); and finally it includes an awareness of the consequences you intentionally and unintentionally provide the learner for a particular performance.

Systematic instruction also applies to your curriculum—its daily intensity, its match to the learner's immediate instructional needs, and its range and degree of relevance for the learner's future.

> Teachers must abandon their traditional concepts of curriculum if they are to be successful with severely and profoundly retarded students. They must be trained to deal with a whole range of behaviors that have rarely been the concern of the public schools. The traditional three Rs are simply not enough here. Teachers must be prepared to help their students learn to survive in the world from the moment they wake up in the morning until they go to bed at night.
>
> Active parent participation is more than an ingredient in this approach—it is a must. Without it, there is little hope that behaviors acquired in the classroom will be maintained. (Bijou, NARC Publication, 1976, p. 7)

What other skills will you need in your repertoire to fill the position of teacher for a group of severely handicapped students? First, you will need a knowledge of the characteristics and causes of severe handicapping conditions—a body of information that grows constantly, an awareness of the parameters by which we describe and define this population, their learning characteristics, their legal rights, and the laws that protect those rights. Next, you will need facility with behavioral observation and measurement, learned through a combination of study and repeated application with severely handicapped individuals. And you will benefit from having a firm foundation in normal growth patterns and the early developmental sequences. However, since normal developmental maps do not supply the sole guides for teaching this population, you must be aware of the critical functional ingredients that need to be added to a curriculum based upon normal developmental sequences. That is, mental and developmental ages furnish only rough indicators of instructional content. A 20-year-old man with a measured mental and adaptive age of 3 years is *not* a 3-year-old. His experience, his learning history, and his current needs and interests are starkly different. While a curriculum suited to his developmental age will incorporate what we know about the normal order and content of learning, ingredients must be added to his curriculum to ensure that he will acquire a set of functional, generalized skills enabling some degree of self-sufficiency.

The population you are preparing yourself to teach or are presently teaching is one many other professionals essentially have given up on. Philip Roos, executive director of the National Association for Retarded Citizens, succinctly emphasizes this point.

We are dealing with the most severely handicapped members of the human race—individuals whose nervous systems have been seriously damaged, or never developed properly. The severely and profoundly retarded include approximately the lowest 5% of the retarded population. More than 99% of all persons learn more easily than they do. Many have IQs that may be termed "unmeasurable."

When these children enter school they may exhibit a wide variety of social and developmental handicaps. Still, all of these children are human beings—all have a right to learn, to develop and to be treated as individuals. (Bijou, NARC publication, 1976, p. 5)

Although you, as the classroom teacher (or house parent, institutional program staff, or workshop instructor), are not alone in the task, the primary responsibility for systematic, relevant instruction of the severely handicapped will be or already is yours.

Reference

Educating the twenty-four hour retarded child. Arlington, Tex.: National Association for Retarded Citizens, 1976.

Acknowledgments

Thanks must be extended to the Department of Special Education at the University of Virginia for allowing some release time in the spring of 1977, for providing the support of graduate and undergraduate students, for the extended, patient secretarial assistance of Ms. Sharron Hall, and for the continued encouragement from my colleagues.

Acknowledgment must be made to the many publishers and authors who have granted permission to quote their work and reprint their illustrations. This same gratefulness is extended to the parents who granted permission for photographs of their children to be printed in this text.

Contributors

Diane D. Bricker, Mailman Center for Child Development, University of Miami

G. Thomas Bellamy, Specialized Training Program, Center on Human Development, University of Oregon

Linda K. Bunker, Department of Physical Education, University of Virginia

Susan Campbell, Project MESH, Bureau of Child Research, University of Kansas

Peggy Coyne, Madison Public Schools, Madison, Wisconsin

Terry DeBriere, Project MESH, Bureau of Child Research, University of Kansas

Laura Dennison, Mailman Center for Child Development, University of Miami

Clarence J. DeSpain, Madison Public Schools, Madison, Wisconsin

Rebecca F. DuBose, Child Study Center, George Peabody College for Teachers

Robert W. Flexer, Research and Training Center in Mental Retardation, Texas Technical University

Marc W. Gold, Institute for Child Behavior and Development, University of Illinois at Urbana-Champaign

Sue Hamre-Nietupski, Madison Public Schools, Madison, Wisconsin

Cynthia Harris, Project MESH, Bureau of Child Research, University of Kansas

Robert H. Horner, Specialized Training Program, Center on Human Development, University of Oregon

Donna Jarboe, Project MESH, Bureau of Child Research, University of Kansas

Fran Johnson, Madison Public Schools, Madison, Wisconsin

Jaci McDaniel Marks, Madison Public Schools, Madison, Wisconsin

Andrew S. Martin, Research and Training Center in Mental Retardation, Texas Technical University

David Pomerantz, Department of Special Education, State University College at Buffalo

Ian Pumpian, Madison Public Schools, Madison, Wisconsin

Cordelia C. Robinson, Meyer Children's Rehabilitation Center, University of Nebraska Medical Center

Jacques H. Robinson, Special Education Department, Kent State University

Nancy Schuerman, Madison Public Schools, Madison, Wisconsin

Deborah D. Smith, Department of Special Education, University of New Mexico

James O. Smith, Department of Special Education, University of New Mexico

Martha E. Snell, Department of Special Education, University of Virginia

Charles Spellman, Project MESH, Bureau of Child Research, University of Kansas

Jacalyn Stengert, Madison Public Schools, Madison, Wisconsin

Barbara Swetlik, Madison Public Schools, Madison, Wisconsin

Ann P. Turnbull, Division of Special Education, University of North Carolina at Chapel Hill

Jill D. Wheeler, Madison Public Schools, Madison, Wisconsin

Wes Williams, Center for Special Education, University of Vermont

Robert York, Center for Special Education, University of Vermont

Contents

Systematic Instruction of the Moderately and Severely Handicapped

Introduction to Chapter 1

Who are the severely handicapped? Are they simply a small group of individuals situated one standard deviation between the moderately and profoundly handicapped? Are they a new disability category that encompasses the lower functioning mentally retarded, the seriously emotionally disturbed, the deaf-blind, and those demonstrating serious multiple handicapping conditions? What about those classified as *trainable* or *developmentally young*—where do they fit? As you read this first chapter by Rebecca DuBose, you will be exposed to a variety of answers and rebuttals presented by psychologists and special educators over the past one hundred years. Presently we are still striving for clarification in our classification system.

As emphasized recently by Sontag, Smith, and Sailor (1977), the term *severely/profoundly handicapped* erroneously implies, as does any classification label, homogeneous functioning among its members. Yet individuals in this group are widely divergent, not only in their impairments (severe mental retardation, serious emotional disturbance, blindness, deafness, and/or immobilizing orthopedic conditions), but also in their functional retardation, their special service needs, and their ultimate potential. Sontag et al. (1977) suggest not a new category, but that special education be remodeled into three global areas: early childhood education, general special education, and severely handicapped education. While general special education would focus upon preacademic and academic instruction of individuals possessing any of a variety of disability labels, severely handicapped education would emphasize basic skills development which precedes academic instruction. These basic skills center around language acquisition, self-care abilities, and the building of early cognitive, motor, perceptual, and social skills. Early childhood education would serve those children requiring both basic skill development and preacademic instruction. Teacher

training would be characterized by the development of competencies in these corresponding areas.

McDowell and Sontag (1977) note that this model places emphasis upon the educational framework rather than upon the number of debilitating characteristics a pupil possesses. Additionally, the reorganization dictated by the model "would not only facilitate the progressive inclusion of the low-incidence population into the school and community, but would also cut across disability areas and create a programmatic and need-centered model of service delivery for all handicapped children" (p. 3).

Inherent to this view of special education—severely handicapped education, early childhood education, and general special education—are different but overlapping curricular emphases for each population of learners: basic skill development, preacademic remediation *and* basic skill development, and preacademic-academic remediation. When you consider the moderately and severely handicapped group upon which this text focuses and scan the table of contents, it becomes clear that competencies in two curricular emphases are necessary: basic skill development (Chapters 4 through 8) and preacademic remediation (Chapters 9 through 12). Your job as teachers of the moderately and severely handicapped will be a complex one—only outsiders are fooled by the small number of students you have in comparison to regular classrooms. The range of skills you must be ready to teach will range widely from visual tracking and toilet training to functional reading and employment skills; the members of your immediate teaching team will vary as much as the handicaps displayed by your students.

Accurate educational identification of this group of individuals is undeniably a more lengthy and tedious task than mere identification. This will necessitate that you and your colleagues carefully, systematically, and repeatedly measure your students' behavior in the classroom and, as both Wes Williams and Marc Gold emphasize in later chapters, in the actual settings in which the skills must be utilized. Rebecca DuBose describes in this first chapter some wide-range instruments that will assist you in narrowing the "teachable" levels of performance. Later chapters will provide more finely sequenced assessment devices for specific curricular areas as well as guidelines for constructing your own informal tests.

Finally Chapter 1 builds the case for public education of the severely handicapped. Regardless of the size of your community, the total of seriously handicapped infants, children, adults, and even senior citizens will add up to a very small group—approximately the lowest functioning 5% of those already identified as mentally retarded, seriously emotionally disturbed, or as multiply handicapped (individuals possessing a combination of *intense* physical, mental, and emotional problems) (National Association for Retarded Citizens, 1976). The population of severely handicapped has always been small but has never been served adequately. Luckily parents and special educators have been vocal and Public Law 94–142 is a response to their cries. However, despite the services this law will facilitate, you will need to promote and even defend the implementation of this law—the call for special classrooms integrated into regular school buildings, adequate materials, classrooms, psychological and ancillary services, and regular monitoring of the quality of instruction actually provided.

You may be called upon to describe the causes and variety of severe handicaps, to predict the educational and vocational potential of this group, and to argue in dollars and cents figures in defense of the exorbitant costs of this education. In order to fill this role you will find it necessary to read far beyond the introductory purpose of this chapter and seek references on law and special education (Abeson, Bolick, & Hass, 1975; Ballard, Nazzaro, & Weintraub, 1976; Friedman, 1976; Kindred, Cohen, Penrod, & Shaffer, 1976; Weintraub, Abeson, Ballard, & LaVor, 1976); on the characteristics of mental retardation (Balthazar & Stevens, 1975; Grossman, 1973; MacMillan, 1977; Robinson & Robinson, 1976); on the characteristics of emotional disturbance (Achenbach, 1974; Kauffman, 1977; Lovaas, 1977; Ross, 1974); and on physical handicapping conditions (Bigge, 1976; Bleck & Nagel, 1975; Cruickshank, 1976).

The task is extensive and the time is limited, so let us begin.

References

Abeson, A. A., Bolick, N. , & Hass, J. *A primer on due process.* Reston, Va.: Council for Exceptional Children, 1975.

Achenbach, T. M. *Developmental psychopathology.* New York: Ronald Press, 1974.

Ballard, J., Nazzaro, J. N., & Weintraub, F. J. *P.L. 94–142, the Education for All Handicapped Children Act of 1975.* Reston, Va.: Council for Exceptional Children, 1976.

Balthazar, E. E., & Stevens, H. A. *The emotionally disturbed, mentally retarded: A historical and contemporary perspective.* Englewood Cliffs, N. J.: Prentice-Hall, 1975.

Bigge, J. L. *Teaching individuals with physical and multiple disabilities.* Columbus, Ohio: Charles E. Merrill, 1976.

Bleck, E.E., & Nagel, D. A. *Physically handicapped children: A medical atlas for teachers.* New York: Grune & Stratton, 1975.

Cruickshank, W. (Ed.). *Cerebral palsy: A developmental disability.* Syracuse, N. Y.: Syracuse University, 1976.

Friedman, P. R. *The rights of mentally retarded persons.* New York: Avon Books, 1976.

Grossman, H. J. (Ed.). *Manual on terminology and classification in mental retardation.* Washington, D.C.: American Association on Mental Deficiency, 1973.

Kauffman, J. M. *Characteristics of children's behavior disorders.* Columbus, Ohio: Charles E. Merrill, 1977.

Kindred, M., Cohen, J., Penrod, D., & Shaffer, T. (Eds.). *The mentally retarded citizen and the law.* New York: Free Press, 1976.

Lovaas, O. I. *The autistic child: Language development through behavior modification.* New York: Irvington Publishers, 1977.

MacMillan, D. L. *Mental retardation in school and society.* Boston: Little, Brown & Co., 1977.

McDowell, F. E., & Sontag, E. The severely and profoundly handicapped as catalysts for change. In E. Sontag, J. Smith, & N. Certo (Eds.), *Educational programming for the severely and profoundly handicapped.* Reston, Va.: Council for Exceptional Children, 1977.

National Association for Retarded Citizens. *Educating the twenty-four hour retarded child.* Arlington, Texas: NARC, 1976.

Robinson, N. M., & Robinson, H. B. *The mentally retarded child* (2nd ed.). New York: McGraw-Hill, 1976.

Ross, A. O. *Psychological disorders of children.* New York: McGraw-Hill, 1974.

Sontag, E., Smith, J., & Sailor, W. The severely and profoundly handicapped: Who are they? Where are we? *Journal of Special Education,* 1977, *11,* 5–11.

Weintraub, F. J., Abeson, A., Ballard, J., & LaVor, M. L. (Eds.). *Public policy and the education of exceptional children.* Reston, Va.: Council for Exceptional Children, 1976.

Identification

This chapter was written by **Rebecca F. DuBose,** Child Study Center, George Peabody College for Teachers.

From our earliest recorded literature we can find references to people who differed substantially from the majority of the community. These individuals were described as being "possessed by demons," "afflicted," or "mad." Most frequently they were objects of neglect, ridicule, and torture. The nineteenth century brought concern for humane treatment. With that concern came the need to identify and classify these individuals, which led to the development of procedures for measuring mental ability and adaptive behavior. Once these procedures were available, demands were made for more definitive information, directly applicable to educational programming and daily activities. This chapter provides an overview of the identification and classification of moderately, severely, and profoundly handicapped individuals, procedures for determining their needs, and current views in establishing educational goals for this population.

Identifying and Classifying Handicapped Persons

Mentally retarded individuals

Prior to the nineteenth century, an individual demonstrating unusual behavior that could not be explained was thought to possess an alien spirit or to be under the control of an outside force. Hence the person was classified as an *idiot* or *insane.* The development of the biological sciences during the nineteenth century permitted neurological and etiological anomalies to constitute a more refined classification system (Down, Note 1; Ireland, 1898; Seguin, 1866). In the United States the use of an intelligence quotient (IQ) or mental ratio was being used to divide *aments,* an early term for the mentally retarded, into administrative grades. In 1920 the American Association for the Study of the Feebleminded defined an *idiot* as a mentally defective person having a mental age of not more than 35 months, or, for a child, an IQ of less than 25. The *imbecile* was defined as having a mental age between 36 and 83 months inclusive, or, for a child, an

IQ between 25 and 49. The *moron*, according to the American standards, had a mental age between 84 and 143 months, IQ 50 to 74 (Tredgold, 1937).

A major step in the expansion of this inadequate classification system occurred in 1959 with the American Association of Mental Deficiency's publication of a manual designed to provide for uniformity in the medical and behavioral classification terminology of mental retardation. This standard (Heber, 1959) included a medical classification system subdivided into eight sections denoting mental retardation associated with diseases and conditions due to (1) infection, (2) intoxication, (3) trauma or physical agent, (4) disorders of metabolism, (5) new growths, (6) unknown prenatal influence, (7) uncertain cause with structural reactions manifest, and (8) uncertain (or presumed psychological) cause with functional reaction alone manifest. The 1959 standard emphasized current level of functioning and limited the term *mental retardation* to those individuals whose disability was apparent during the developmental period. The standards were widely accepted and used in program implementation through the 1960s.

The 1961 AAMD *Manual on Terminology and Classification in Mental Retardation* defined *mental retardation* as "subaverage general intellectual functioning which originated during the developmental period and is associated with impairment in adaptive behavior" (Heber, 1961, p. 3). "Subaverage intellectual functioning" was any score greater than one standard deviation below the population mean of the age group on measures of general intellectual functioning. Given an IQ test such as the *Wechsler Intelligence Scale for Children* (Wechsler, 1974) with a standard deviation of 15, Heber's defi-

nition stated that IQ scores less than 85, one standard deviation below the mean IQ for the population, warranted the label of mental retardation. The 1961 manual introduced three classification systems: a medical system, an intelligence system, and an adaptive system. The intelligence system reflected five levels of retardation. As noted in Table 1.1, the level increments decreased by one standard deviation below the mean for a specific age group for a particular test. Standard deviations vary from test to test and from age to age.

"Adaptive behavior" referred to the effectiveness with which the individual adjusted to the natural and social demands of his environment—a characteristic related to maturation, learning, and social adjustment. The adaptive system of categorizing mental retardation included four levels ranging from mild (level one) to complete lack of adaptation (level four). No precise, objective measures of adaptive behavior were noted; however, the *Vineland Social Maturity Scale* (Doll, 1965) was suggested as the best single measure of adaptive behavior. The inclusion of aberrant adaptive behavior as a necessary criterion for determining the existence of mental retardation reflected the growing awareness of the importance of one's adjustment to societal demands as a viable measure of human behavior.

The numerous changes in the field of education during the sixties necessitated a new manual that would reflect current thinking. A revision, *Manual on Terminology and Classification in Mental Retardation* (Grossman, 1973), included a definition of *mental retardation* which deleted the borderline category and defined it as follows: ". . . significantly subaverage general intellectual functioning existing concurrently with deficits in adaptive behavior, and

TABLE 1.1   *Heber and Grossman AAMD levels of mental retardation in SD units and IQ ranges*

Performance Term	Range in SD Units	Corresponding IQ Range for Stanford-Binet (LM) Tests (SD = 16)	Corresponding IQ Range for the Wechsler Scales (SD = 15)
	1961 (Heber)		
Borderline Retardation*	1.01 to 2.00	68–84	70–85
Mild Retardation	2.01 to 3.00	52–67	55–69
Moderate Retardation	3.01 to 4.00	36–51	40–54
Severe Retardation	4.01 to 5.00	20–35	25–39
Profound Retardation	<5.01	<20	<25

*1973 (Grossman) classification system corresponds to the 1961 classification except for the deletion of the Borderline Level, a range of subnormal intelligence not included within mental retardation.

manifested during the developmental period" (p. 5). Although at first Grossman's definition appears quite similar to Heber's definition in 1961, the phrase "significantly subaverage" referred to performance which was more than *two* standard deviations below the mean on a standardized intelligence test, thereby eliminating the borderline group from classification as mentally retarded. The phrase "existing concurrently" denoted the importance of measured deficits in intelligence and adaptive behavior occurring simultaneously. Table 1.1 reflects the intelligence classification system as defined in the 1973 manual. The 1973 definition delineated more precisely and narrowly the population of individuals falling into the retarded range. To be considered retarded, the individual must show a measured intelligence score below 70 *and* exhibit adaptive behaviors inappropriate for his age and cultural group. This implied that an individual could have a measured intelligence quotient of below 70 and not be classified as retarded if he possessed appropriate adaptive skills expected for his age group.

Grossman defined mildly retarded individuals as those who are "educable" (EMR). As children, they can usually master basic academic skills and, as adults, can maintain themselves independently or semi-independently in the community. Moderately retarded individuals are considered "trainable" (TMR) and learn self-help, communication, social and simple occupational skills, but acquire only limited academic or vocational skills. Severely mentally retarded individuals also regarded as TMR require continuing and close supervision but may perform self-help and simple work tasks under supervision. Profoundly retarded individuals require continuing and close supervision but some may be able to perform self-help tasks. These individuals frequently possess additional handicaps and require total life-support systems for maintenance.

The 1973 manual elaborated upon the meaning and implications of adaptive behaviors for different age groups. Expectations during infancy and early childhood center on sensorimotor, communication, self-help, and socialization skills. During childhood and early adolescence, desirable adaptive behaviors include the application of basic academic skills in daily activities, the use of appropriate reasoning and judgment in mastering the environment, and the demonstration of proper social skills including participation in group activities. The relevant adaptive behaviors during later adolescence and adult life include vocational performance and social responsibilities.

Baumeister and Muma (1975) provide a highly critical review of the AAMD definition and classification system offered by Heber (1961) and later by Grossman (1973) and his associates. Citing the widespread and uncritical acceptance of the 1961 manual, they question the validity of that definition and highlight the damaging implications of its use. Baumeister and Muma note that the definition is behavioral and in no way leads to the extensive medical classification contained in the manual. Furthermore, the classification, although based on "well established authority" (p. 296), is neither valid nor functional. A second concern of Baumeister and Muma is that "the AAMD definition implicitly adopts one theory of intelligence to the exclusion of others" (p. 296). It is based on the general ability theory, which assumes a single dimension or underlying continuum of intelligence. This allows the single IQ score or one of its alternatives to become an entity and sole gauge upon which a person's intelligence is based. If the ultimate goal is to change behavior, the IQ score is probably the most trivial bit of information available about a person. By excluding other theories of human adaptation and learning, cultural, motivational, and physiological factors known to account for variability in performance are ignored.

According to Baumeister and Muma the phrase "developmental period," included in the definition, lacks clarity. The intent here is to eliminate from the label all individuals whose deviant behavior becomes apparent after their eighteenth year. Baumeister and Muma remind the reader that chronological age is not an operational referent of behavior. Its relevancy for programming is not apparent.

The inclusion of the popular, yet vague and ill-defined, term *adaptive behavior* is the subject of severe criticism, not only from Baumeister and Muma but others (Adams, 1973; Cleary, Humphreys, Kendrick, & Wesman, 1975; McIntosh & Warren, 1969). Baumeister and Muma point out that "it is a problem in adaptive behavior that first brings the child to the attention of those responsible for labeling him" (p. 302). The responsible agent will probably use the *Vineland Social Maturity Scale* as the criterion for verifying that the problem exists. Investigating the role played by the *Vineland* in the classification of the level of mental retardation and its relationship to measured intelligence, Adams (1973) found a statistically significant relationship between IQs and social quotients (SQs), indicating they are not independent measures but aspects of the same behavior. Furthermore, his findings support his hypothesis that physicians were more likely to use IQs than SQs when classifying individuals with mental retardation. Baumeister and Muma comment that "adaptive behavior scales often turn out to be a poor man's intelligence test, and they generally enjoy such high correlations with standardized intelligence tests as to suggest that these are functionally redundant measures" (p. 303).

Confusion over the meaning and measurement of adaptive behavior, as it is now applied, arises because the definition is so broad as to be minimally meaningful. Skills that allow one to function adequately in a narrow, restrictive environment are likely to be poorly correlated with the ability to cope in other settings (Cleary et al., 1975). However, the need to include a measure of adaptive behavior has been emphatically demonstrated by Mercer (1975) in her studies of individuals from ethnic minorities and lower socioeconomic backgrounds. Mercer states that such an instrument would need to be a multicultural pluralistic assessment with multiple normative frameworks. The instrument would describe performance in nonacademic settings, provide information on an individual's social-role performance as perceived by that individual's own sociocultural peers, identify persons whose problems are school-specific, provide information on the individual's abilities in a variety of different roles and social settings, and identify competencies. Mercer and her associates are in the process of developing such an instrument.

Baumeister and Muma (1975) advocate a similar position based on "a theory-guided approach to the definition of human adjustment that focuses upon the developing organism and its interactions with a dynamic environment" (p. 305). Variables would include personal, social, and environmental elements viewed in a hierarchical and interdependent system. No such label as *mental retardation* would exist. Rather a continually changing profile would allow for the entire spectrum to be included in the system.

Severely handicapped individuals

The definitions and classification systems thus far elaborated have been limited to those directly related to the mentally retarded. The focus of this book is not limited to the retarded but embraces all moderately and severely handicapped persons. It has been generally recognized by the professional community that individuals possessing severe, profound, or multiple handicaps can be grouped under the umbrella of severely handicapped. Paul Thompson (1974), director of Programs for Severely Handicapped Children and Youth, Bureau for the Education of the Handicapped, U.S. Office Education, defines the severely handicapped child as

one who, because of the intensity of his physical, mental or emotional problems or a combination of such problems, needs educational, social, psychological, and medical services beyond those which have been offered by traditional, regular, and special educational programs, in order to maximize his full potential for useful and meaningful participation in society and for self-fulfillment. (p. 73)

Thompson goes on to emphasize the multiple learning problems faced by these children and suggests the target population would include

those classified as seriously emotionally disturbed, schizophrenic and autistic, profoundly and severely mentally retarded, and those with two or more serious handicapping conditions, such as the mentally retarded-deaf and mentally retarded-blind. (p. 73)

It should be clear from these delineations that a totally deaf or blind person with no other handicapping condition would not be included in the catchall term *severely handicapped*.

Focusing upon the possible range of "pre-treatment," maladaptive behavior, Sontag, Burke, and York (1973) provide a perspicuous description of the severely and profoundly handicapped as those

who are not toilet trained; aggress toward others; do not attend to even the most pronounced social stimuli; self mutilate; ruminate; self stimulate; do not walk, speak, hear, or see; manifest durable and intense temper tantrums; are not under even the rudimentary forms of verbal control; do not imitate; manifest minimally controlled seizures; and/or have extremely brittle medical existences. (p. 21)

In synthesizing these descriptions for purposes of this book, the target population will include: (1) all moderately, severely, and profoundly mentally retarded individuals; (2) all severely and profoundly emotionally disturbed persons; (3) all moderately to profoundly retarded or disturbed individuals who have at least one additional impairment (i.e., deafness, blindness, crippling condition).

It should be apparent from these descriptions that additional handicaps do not have an additive effect on the child; the effect is multiplicative. The person's severe handicaps in one area can not be measured or treated in isolation of their impact on skill development. For example, the inability to see interferes with the acquisition of fine and gross motor skills, and the inability to express oneself in ways that others understand can interfere with social development or bring on behavior management problems.

No attempt has been made here to devise a classification system encompassing all handicapped persons. It is to be hoped that systems of the future will focus on different aspects from those of the past. The identification and classification of individuals whose behavior is different from the majority were initiated with the intention of providing individuals the services and help they needed. Today the intent remains the same; the problem continues to be in the procedures for determining who needs what services and how these services can be delivered most effectively.

The number of individuals identified as mentally retarded has been difficult to specify because of changes in the definition and the difficulties inherent in prevalence studies. The President's Committee on Mental Retardation (1970) estimates that 3% of the population is mentally retarded. The 3% incidence rate would break down into 2.3% mild, 0.6% moderate, and 0.1% severe-profound (Kauffman & Payne, 1975). The U.S. Office of Education reports 2.3% of the school-age population as mentally retarded with 0.8% falling into the moderate and severe range and 1.5% considered mildly retarded. Others (Mercer, 1973; Tarjan, Wright, Eyman, & Keeran, 1973), strictly adhering to the criteria of significantly subaverage intelligence and impaired adaptive behavior, cite a much lower figure, about 1.0% of the population. It can be concluded that the population of severely handicapped is greater than these figures cited for the retarded population because such estimates do not include individuals with severe emotional disturbance. Phillip Roos, in a recent publication for the National Association for Retarded Citizens (1976), remarks upon the size of this population:

We are dealing with the most severely handicapped members of the human race—individuals whose nervous systems have been seriously damaged, or never developed properly. The severely and profoundly retarded include approxi-

mately the lowest 5% of the retarded population. More than 99% of all persons learn more easily than they do. Many have IQs that may be termed "unmeasurable." (p. 5)

The Measurement of Mentation

The classification systems described in the previous section grew out of a need for homogeneity within large groups of individuals. Individual variability was regarded as a form of error. In the late 1800s a few experimental psychologists began conducting psychological experiments involving an individual's reaction time to sensory stimuli. Alfred Binet, a Frenchman, felt these early tests were too largely sensory and focused unduly on simple abilities. In order to tap the complex functions that identified individual differences, Binet's opinion was that functions such as memory, imagination, attention, comprehension, suggestibility, and aesthetic appreciation must be tested. Binet felt that tests, rather than providing an absolute measure of ability, should rate persons with respect to each other (Binet, 1898). In 1905, with Theophile Simon, Binet published the first Binet-Simon scales which in 1908 were revised to include the concept of mental age. The Binet-Simon tests were quickly adapted and translated into many languages and within a few years were recognized as the first major tests of intelligence. In the United States a revision by L. M. Terman at Stanford University became known as the *Stanford-Binet* (Terman, 1916). After 10 years of research, the second revision appeared in 1937. It consisted of two equivalent forms, L and M (Terman & Merrill, 1937). In an attempt to eliminate obsolete items and to adjust items because of cultural and time changes, the authors published a third revision in 1960 which combined forms L and M into a single (L-M) form.

David Wechsler has developed a number of intelligence scales for purposes similar to those of the Binet scales. These scales are grouped into subtests arranged in increasing order of difficulty. Subtest grouping allows for the computation of verbal and performance IQs. Wechsler has developed three scales: one for adults, *Wechsler Adult Intelligence Scale (WAIS)* (Wechsler, 1955); one for school-age children, *Wechsler Intelligence Scale for Children (WISC)* (Wechsler, 1949) and *Revised Edition (WISC-R)* (Wechsler, 1974); and one for preschool and primary levels, *Wechsler Preschool and Primary Scale of Intelligence (WPPSI)* (Wechsler, 1967).

In some cases, scales of infant intelligence have been given to severely handicapped children. The scales most commonly used are the *Infant Intelligence Scale* (Cattell, 1940), a downward extension of the 1937 *Stanford-Binet,* and the *Bayley Infant Scales of Development* (Bayley, 1969). The value of infant tests has been seriously questioned by Lewis (1976). Correlations of infant test scores with later scores over long periods of time are negligible. However, when the tests are given to children with clearly identified handicaps, the IQs from infant tests have proven to be highly predictable of later performance (Bierman, Connor, Vaage, & Honzik, 1964; DuBose, 1977; Illingsworth, 1961; Werner, Honzik, & Smith, 1968). The value of these measures appears to be in identifying moderately, severely, and profoundly handicapped youngsters for whom additional educational services will be needed.

The individual mental measures described continue to be the measures most frequently used to assess handicapped children. The data from mental measures can be valuable if carefully analyzed for the purpose of identifying the developmental stages of mental operations observed during this isolated behavior sample. Unfortunately the format and content of most tests were not designed to permit this item analysis. The careful scrutiny required to derive such information from the data is seldom undertaken by psychologists and diagnosticians. A case in point is the *Columbia Mental Maturity Scale* (Burgmeister, Blum, & Lorge, 1972). The test cards sample mental operations along several dimensions, yet this information is not available to the user. If the cards were clearly classified as to the mental operation assessed, then the examiner could identify possible developmental differences in the acquisition of mental operations.

Some of the more recently published tests have been designed to provide clearer indications of the skills assessed and perhaps will lead to reports containing more specific information concerning the individual's cognitive development. Refinement of instruments containing tasks tapping specified mental operations will take time. For example, factor analytic studies on the *Illinois Test of Psycholinguistic Abilities* (Kirk, McCarthy, & Kirk, 1968) produced data questioning the validity of the operational factors the authors thought they were measuring (Sedlak & Weener, 1973). Whenever psychological and educational measures are used to assess human behavior, a large portion of variance may be accounted for by a cognitive factor.

Only when these factors are identified and analyzed can programming for skill development of cognitive structures lead toward an understanding of the tested individual's specific behavior and a means to influence this behavior.

The Measurement of Adaptation

While some psychologists worked to refine tests of mental measurement, others sought ways to measure behaviors used in everyday experiences. These latter measures grew out of the need to classify the behavior of individuals already in institutions for the retarded. Henry Goddard, director of research at the Vineland Training School in New Jersey, found "amazing correspondence" between scores obtained when he examined 400 children using the Binet test and scores resulting from extended evaluations by teachers (Goddard, 1910). This represented an early effort to evaluate children's abilities to function in classroom and institutional settings by a means other than standardized tests. As a continuation of Goddard's evaluations, Edgar Doll of the Vineland School proposed the *Vineland Social Maturity Scale* in 1935. The scale was revised in 1936 and was published by the school along with a manual containing administration instructions and standardization information. The scale used the interview technique to determine the individual's abilities in motor skills, social development, language, and the activities of daily living. The *Vineland* was revised again in 1953, translated into several languages, and has become widely used throughout the world.

The need to help handicapped persons move toward independent living and self-management was the impetus for more formal assessment of adaptive behavior. The new behavioral technologies of the 1960s (Glaser, 1965) introduced to the educational community the procedures permitting psychologists and special educators to accomplish the following: formulate procedures for analyzing the minute operations involved in skill acquisition, determine steps leading to mastery, assess individual behavioral repertoires, identify procedures that lead to the acquisition of new steps, and evaluate performance. Haimowitz (1973) succinctly summarized this approach to measurement: "When we observe a child's current level of mastery in the developmental sequence, we can usually tell what he will next achieve, although we can tell nothing of his age nor how soon he will develop the next level of skill" (p.

96). Such an approach is the cornerstone for systematic instruction of the moderately, severely, and profoundly handicapped. With significance removed from such factors as mental ages and IQs, attention is focused on the learner, environment, materials, situation demands, the consequences of behavior, and the rate of acquisition. The interaction of these factors can be evaluated, altered, and renegotiated to produce a successful instructional program. This approach unites testing with teaching. No longer are they separate entities, but both are part of the same process, with the legitimate goal of teaching the individual to be able to master the test.

The early endeavors in this direction focused on the acquisition of self-care skills (Bensberg, 1965; Hart & DuBose, Note 2; Larsen & Bricker, 1968). Later instruments were broadly based and included all essential living skills (communication, socialization, cognition-adaptation, movement), with emphasis on the sequential steps in the acquisition of these basic skills, and were limited primarily to competencies usually acquired before the introduction of academic training. More recently, measures have included skills necessary for independent and community living more appropriate for handicapped adults. Table 1.2 overviews several of the new tools used to identify, assess, and program for moderately, severely, and profoundly handicapped persons.

These newer measures of assessment are far more functional for everyone. Their content was arrived at by going into the community and determining what skills were necessary in order to live and work outside the bounds of stigmatizing institutions and total-care environments. Once these skills were identified, they became the assessment items. Many of the authors recognized that individuals can accomplish part, but not all, of some tasks or perhaps complete the task but at a slower rate. The rating or scoring systems allow for this needed flexibility. Another advantage to the newer tests is that the emphasis is placed on particular skills or competencies and not on global ability scores that are likely to result in labels or demeaning classifications. Perhaps the most exciting advantage of the functional, environmentally based tools is the ease with which an instructional program can be formulated from the assessment data. An example is the *TARC* system. A computer program is arranged to formulate instructional objectives by scanning the biographical data sheet for interfering factors such as "severe vision loss," scanning the profile to de-

termine the rank order of the six lowest areas. Once this information is fed into the computer, it is compared with percentage data from the standardization sample norms and a ranking of the objectives and their specific behavioral components is produced (Sailor & Horner, 1976).

Assessment of handicapped children can produce positive or negative effects. If the results are simply scores used to label the individual, then negative connotations are a probable byproduct. On the other hand, positive effects can result if assessment data detail what an individual needs to learn and how he may best acquire learning behavior within the constraints of his milieu. To facilitate this approach, a new model for classifying and educating handicapped individuals is essential.

Systematizing a Functional Analysis of Human Behavior for Planning Educational Services

Debilitating definitions of mental retardation and assignment of classificatory levels of retardation have led to the stigmatization and placement of individuals in programs accentuating their deficiencies and attenuating their chances of tapping their full potential to acquire the complex physical, mental, and social schemata of their age mates. The enervating effects of such misfortunes were forewarned as early as 1905 by the father of the testing movement, Binet, who said, "It will never be to one's credit to have attended a special school" (Binet & Simon, 1905). Perhaps more devastating than attendance in special schools or classes has been participation in a potpourri of programs negatively stereotyping the children into a homogeneous group rather than recognizing their heterogeneity and carefully constructing learning environments conducive to the development of each individual's potential.

Classification of exceptional individuals is now and will continue to be a necessity. The classification schema provides services from federal, state, local, and private agencies. To refuse to classify such individuals is to fail to serve them, but to classify them according to currently recognized methodologies may do them far more harm than good. Stigmatizing labels carrying metaphorical implications are known to be damaging to the child (Mercer, 1974); however, the far more devastating effects of participation in a specialized program can dissolve individuality and shape the child into the

TABLE 1.2   *Instruments for assessing the moderately, severely and profoundly handicapped*

Test	Appropriate Age	Behavior Assessed	Type of Measurement
AAMD Adaptive Behavior Scale (Nihira, Foster, Shellhaas, & Leland, 1969, 1975)	Preschool through independent living (moderately, severely, and profoundly retarded)	Part One: Independent functioning, physical development, economic activity, language, number and time, domestic and vocational activity, self-direction, responsibility, socialization	Norm-referenced
		Part Two: Measures of maladaptive behaviors related to personality and behavior disorders in 14 domains	
AAMD Adaptive Behavior Scale, Public School Version (Lambert, Windmiller, Cole, & Figueroa, 1975)	Grades two through six (regular and special classes)	95 items assessing appropriate school behavior; Parts One and Two as described above	Norm-referenced
Balthazar Scales of Adaptive Behavior, I and II (Balthazar, 1971a, b)	Preschool through independent living (severely and profoundly retarded)	Scale I: Self-help skills	Criterion-referenced
		Scale II: Coping behaviors, maladaptive and adaptive behaviors	Criterion-referenced
Behavioral Characteristics Progression (1973)	Infant through independence (including multiple handicaps)	59 behavioral strands including assessment for severe physical and sensory impairments	Criterion-referenced
Cain-Levine (Cain, Levine, & Freeman, 1963)	Preschool to adolescence (trainable mentally retarded)	Self-help, social, communication, initiative	Norm-referenced
Callier-Azusa (Stillman, 1974)	Infant through preschool	Motor, activities of daily living, communication, cognitive	Norm-referenced
Camelot Behavior Checklist (Foster, 1974)	Preschool through independence (mentally retarded)	Self-help, physical development, home duties, vocational behavior, economic behavior, numerical skills, communication skills, social behaviors, responsibility	Criterion-referenced
			Norm-referenced
Developmental Profile (Alpern & Boll, 1972)	Infant through 12½ years	Physical, activities of daily living, communication, cognitive	Norm-referenced

TABLE 1.2 *(Continued)*

Test	Appropriate Age	Behavior Assessed	Type of Measurement
Devereaux Social Scale (Spivack & Spotts, 1966)	8 through 12 years (emotionally disturbed)	17 strands covering broad developmental areas with emphasis on social-emotional behavior	Norm-referenced
Learning Accomplishment Profile (Griffin, Sanford, & Wilson, 1975)	Infant through preschool	Motor, cognitive, language, activities of daily living	Norm-referenced
Lexington Developmental Scale (Irwin, Ward, Deen, & Greis, 1973)	Infant through 6 years	Screening of sensory, motor, language, personal-social, cognitive, emotional behavior	Norm-referenced
Pennsylvania Training Model Individual Assessment Guide (Somerton & Turner, 1975)	Infant through self-care (severely, profoundly retarded, multihandicapped)	Sensory, motor, activities of daily living, communication, perceptual-cognitive, social and emotional development	Criterion-referenced
Portage Guide to Early Education (Shearer, 1972)	Infant through self-care	Motor, activities of daily living, communication, cognitive, social	Criterion-referenced
Project Memphis (Quick, Little, & Campbell, 1973)	Infancy through preschool	Personal-social, gross and fine motor, language, and perceptual-cognitive	Norm-referenced
Student Progress Record (Note 3)	Preschool to adolescence (trainable retarded)	Motor, physical fitness, self-care, academic, language	Criterion-referenced
TARC Assessment System (Sailor & Mix, 1975)	Infant through independence (retarded and severely handicapped)	Self-help, motor, communication, social	Norm-referenced
T.M.R. Performance Profile for Severely and Moderately Retarded (DiNola, Kaminsky, & Sternfeld, 1963)	Preschool through independent living (moderately and severely retarded)	Social, self-care, communication, basic knowledge, practical skills, body usage, health	Criterion-referenced
Vineland Social Maturity Scale (Doll, 1965)	Infant through adulthood	Motor, occupation, communication, social relations, self-help, self-direction	Norm-referenced
Y.M.E.R. Performance Profile for the Young Moderately and Mildly Retarded (DiNola, Kaminsky, & Sternfeld, 1967)	Preschool to independent self-care (mildly and moderately retarded)	Social behavior, self-help, safety, communication, motor, manipulation, perceptual, intellectual, academic, imagination, emotional	Criterion-referenced

11

stereotyped person the classification system tells him to be (Hobbs, 1975).

The familiar etiological-categorical classification system must be replaced by a functional, flexible, qualitative system that depicts immediate needs and strategies for meeting those needs given the child's ecological system. The outcome of such a system is individualization, defined by Walker, Tucker, Lucro, and Mirro (Note 4) to be

a decision-making process which follows a systematic sequence of events beginning with identification of needs and identification of environmental elements which may affect these needs, progresses to coordination of elements to meet these needs, provides evaluation to insure that what is planned is actually occurring, and utilizes evaluation results to change both the presence and coordination of elements. (p. 32)

The formation of the described classification system can be accomplished through systematizing a functional analysis of human behavior for planning educational services.

Before planning a functional classification system, some prior assumptions regarding human life goals must be stated. The first assumption concerns the human need to participate in a societal system. Within any given societal system a heterogeneous population exists which promotes both individualization and communalization on various levels depending upon the givens of the individuals and the ecological system. DesLauriers and Carlson (1969) have expressed this as the need to have the pleasurable satisfaction of being a human surrounded by humans and welcomed into the world.

A second assumption is that human behavior can be altered. The degree to which changes can occur is limited by the individual's present level of functioning, the rate at which he can acquire new skills, and the opportunities and demands of his ecological system.

A third assumption is that the handicapped individual's interests can best be attended through proper consideration of the individual and all the aspects of his life. Such an assumption recognizes the importance of diagnosis, prognosis, prescription, and measurement in evaluating the interactions between the child and tangential elements around him.

To fulfill the classification system's intent, certain general principles merit consideration in its construct. The system must recognize the sequential

acquisition of human behaviors and be based on a developmental model rather than a model of deviancy (Blatt, 1972). The classification system must be comprehensive, reflecting what the individual can and cannot do across multiple factors. Factors would include domains of social, self-care, motor, language, cognition, adaptation, academic, and, when appropriate, vocational skills. Preferred learning styles would be reflected, as well as conditions for optimal skill acquisition. The system should recognize people important in the individual's life as well as the effects of various settings on his performance. This is a dynamic, ever-changing system because of several factors: the transactions between the individual and what he brings to the situation (competencies he possesses and outcomes he desires), the significant others, the settings in which interactions take place, the demands or expectations of him in the situation, the consequences provided in his environment for his behavior, the consistency of those consequences, and his perceptions of the consequences for various behaviors. The frequent changes required in this system prevent lasting categorization of past models and allow for fluidity that marks an individual's growth and development.

The classification system must indicate the services needed by the handicapped individual. The only criterion for admission to a service is that a need exists. The amount or extent of service needed will depend on the importance of that particular service at a given point in time. A classification system must generate data demonstrating effective delivery of services leading each individual toward a more productive and satisfying life (Martin, 1972). Effective service is a classification system's only *raison d'être*.

Figure 1.1 illustrates how the identification-classification system might be conceptualized for an individual. Needs, ecological agents, intervention strategies, and evaluation procedures would be identified, classified, and ranked. Following each evaluation, the cycle would be altered to include new elements determined as necessary by the evaluation, then repeated. For each need, the ecological agents most likely to assist in meeting that need also vary. The intervention strategies to be used by the various ecological agents also change, depending on the specific needs and the interactions among the other variables. Evaluation is directed toward determining whether the need has been met, given the acceptable criteria. It is quite possible that a need would not be completely met yet could

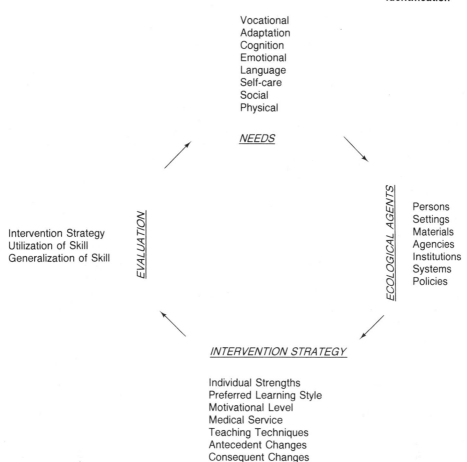

Vocational
Adaptation
Cognition
Emotional
Language
Self-care
Social
Physical

NEEDS

ECOLOGICAL AGENTS

Persons
Settings
Materials
Agencies
Institutions
Systems
Policies

EVALUATION

Intervention Strategy
Utilization of Skill
Generalization of Skill

INTERVENTION STRATEGY

Individual Strengths
Preferred Learning Style
Motivational Level
Medical Service
Teaching Techniques
Antecedent Changes
Consequent Changes

FIGURE 1.1   *Identification-classification paradigm*

be reordered. The system coordinates to meet many needs at the same time; however, the demands a need places on the system at any given time remain a function of the priority of that need. The success of the system in meeting that need is dependent upon the agents and the appropriateness of the intervention strategies. This paradigm, based on a functional analysis of human behavior, is applicable to all individuals for whom needs can be determined.

Educating the Moderately, Severely, and Profoundly Handicapped

In one of the significant court cases in educational history, *Mills* v. *Board of Education of the District of Columbia* (1972), Judge Joseph C. Waddy declared that the District of Columbia shall provide each child of school age "a free and suitable publicly-supported education regardless of the degree of the child's mental, physical, or emotional disability or impairment" (Abeson, 1973, p. 3). The courts have intervened on behalf of seriously handicapped individuals and claimed for them their right to educational services. Children previously denied educational opportunities, because they fell between the cracks of a categorical service delivery system, are now recognized as full participants regardless of the number of constraints or their impairments. Educational provisions for moderately, severely, and profoundly handicapped persons are no longer options available in selected public school settings; programs must be provided wherever the need exists. The 24-hour retarded child has come to school.

Two questions confront the responsible educational agent: What are the needs? How shall these needs be met?

The educational needs of severely and profoundly handicapped children are disparate from needs commonly met in public educational programs. The impact of what it means to provide for this population confronted one supervisor when she decided to personally oversee the first day of school for a group of severely and profoundly handicapped youngsters whom she had assigned to the special education program. When the bus arrived, she saw *no* happy clean faces of neatly dressed children eagerly anticipating their first day in school. *Rather* she saw only silent children waiting to be carried off the bus. It became apparent immediately that toilet skills were *not* in their repertoires. The school and its staff were *not* prepared. The supervisor hastily called the superintendent and exclaimed, "Forget that order of pencils, paper, scissors, and paste. Within the next hour, send me *Pampers*—big ones, plastic bags, wash cloths, floor mats, and *Hogg* chairs." The red tape of purchase orders in that particular school system has never been cut so quickly as it was on that day: the impact of providing educational services to severely handicapped children had been felt.

Individual assessment will determine the educational goals. One or more of the assessment devices previously described can be used to identify the skills in the child's repertoires, those emerging and those not currently operable. From this data behavioral objectives can be formulated. A review of assessment devices and curricular materials quickly identifies some of the key target areas in which programming will be expected. These areas will include motor skill development (gross, fine, and perceptual), language development (receptive, expressive, and inner), social development (self-occupation, student-adult, student to student, student to group), self-care development (eating, dressing, toilet skills, grooming, home management), cognitive-adaptive development (sensorimotor schemata, memory, problem solving, association, and relationships). These skills will be spread over a continuum from initial skill acquisition to independent levels. Educators defeat the purpose of individualized programming if they design one curriculum for severely handicapped and another for moderately handicapped. We can expect moderately impaired persons to move beyond the basic objectives of self-care, simple communication, and motor competencies usually terminal for severely handicapped persons. For some moderately handicapped individuals the focus will be on functional reading, writing, and math, self-expression, self-management, and vocational skills.

Curriculum development is costly and complex, particularly when procedures must include adaptation for a wide array of handicapping conditions. Fortunately the Bureau of Education for the Handicapped has supported projects for the development of appropriate curricula (Altman & Meyen, 1976). Available are a number of curricula guides outlining these skills and training procedures in detail. Among those frequently used are the following: "Developmental Pinpoints" as outlined in *Teaching the Severely Handicapped* (Cohen, Gross, & Haring, 1976); *The Right-to-Education Child* (Myers, Sinco, & Stalma, 1973); *The Portage Guide to Early Education* (Shearer, 1972); *Guide to Early Developmental Training* (Tilton, Liska, & Bourland, 1972); University of Wisconsin and Madison Public School's cooperatively developed curricula (Notes 5, 6, and 7); *Education and Care of Moderately and Severely Retarded Children* (Alpern & Boll, 1971); and *Teaching the Moderately and Severely Handicapped* (Vols. 1, 2, 3) (Bender & Valletutti, 1976). Procedures to teach many of the identified skill needs can be found within the curricula cited.

Some educators will prefer to generate a behavioral-remedial approach for the training of certain skills. An example of this is the structured training curriculum developed at the Kansas Neurological Institute (Guess, Sailor, & Baer, 1977). These authors postulate that "severely handicapped children can be taught a variety of rule-governed speech skills, and that the techniques used in training can be effective for a large number of linguistic deficits" (p. 364). The program makes "no assumptions that the development of certain linguistic skills is necessarily dependent on the prior existence of other prerequisite behaviors" (p. 364).

Williams and Gotts (1977) have declared that curriculum development for the severely handicapped is currently "an art rather than a science" (p. 221). To be effective a curriculum for severely handicapped persons must be entirely flexible to meet the very diverse needs of individuals who have a large range of sensory, physical, mental, and emotional handicaps. The critical element appears to be the application of behavior technology in the training of skill sequences.

The critical question of how to teach moderately, severely, and profoundly handicapped persons to gain the competencies they need remains open-ended. Educators agree that the skills will not come to the severely handicapped person from simple exposure to those who have the skills. Williams, Brown, and Certo (1975) describe the basic components of an instructional program to include the following:

1. What *skill does a teacher intend for the student to perform (What does a teacher intend to teach the student)?*
2. Why *does a teacher want the student to perform a specific skill?*
3. How *does a teacher intend to teach the student to perform a skill?*
4. How *can a teacher empirically verify that the skill of concern is being or has been taught?*
5. Can *the student perform the skill at a situationally acceptable rate?*
6. What *does a teacher intend to use as vehicles (instructional materials) for the skill to be acquired and performed?*
7. Can *the student perform the skill across the following: a. Person; b. Places; c. Instructional Materials; d. Language Cues?*
8. Can *the student perform a skill without directions to do so from persons in authority? (pp. 165–166)*

The format described is a systematic approach to teaching handicapped individuals. *Precise, systematic instruction is the procedure found to be most effective in directing the learning of severely impaired persons.* Within this procedure, task analysis, targeting objectives, modeling, shaping, time out, overcorrection, reinforcement schedules, and performance evaluation are a few of the components that will be used.

A word of caution is needed. The rapid advances in the technology of skill training during the last decade have led educators to focus on the acquisition of specific and, at times, isolated units of behavior. For some individuals and some behaviors, this procedure has proven overwhelmingly successful: those who made only a few sounds now imitate words; those who wet their pants now use toilets; those who ate with their hands now use spoons. However, many of the procedures are still in primitive stages and must undergo rigorous evaluation. Altman and Meyen (1976) succinctly outline research questions that must be addressed if the needs of the severely and profoundly handicapped are to be met. Insight into what apparently has happened to some individuals occurred to this writer

when a recent graduate student naively asked: "Why does Sally refer to everything she sees as, 'This is a . . .'?" Within a generation of handicapped children there are some who have acquired an exceptional bag of splinter skills that are functional in certain situations and under certain conditions. They can label pictures and objects, but only by using the stimulus-response paradigm on which they were trained; they read, but cannot converse about what they have read; they recognize and write numbers, but cannot evaluate; they traverse the balance beam, but fail to use that skill to master the neighborhood curbing; they replicate exquisite block designs, but cannot begin to assemble a simple model airplane; they complete complicated picture puzzles and never realize there is meaning in the picture. These are marked children, reflecting the instructional technology of their times—its strengths and its weaknesses.

The training of their teachers must be dramatically restructured (Brown & York, 1974; Meyen, 1975; Sontag, Burke, & York, 1973) to meet the very special needs of severely handicapped persons; watered-down curricula for the teachers or for their students simply will not suffice. Brown, Nietupski, and Hamre-Nietupski (1976) voiced concern over classroom instructional strategies and suggested the need for serious and scientific investigation before these are accepted as valid procedures for instructing severely handicapped persons. They questioned the relative value of one-to-one instructional arrangements as the preferred methodology for all interactions. One-to-one instruction is expensive in terms of time, money, and personnel; more importantly, it trains the student to respond to teacher-cued stimuli, thus minimizing the opportunities for self-initiated skills to emerge. Additionally, such teacher-cued interaction impedes the development of adaptive interstudent interactions. These findings, based on the authors' extensive experience with severely handicapped youngsters, have led Brown and his associates to recommend "that students also receive a substantial amount of instruction in group and clustered individualized arrangements and in arrangements that allow them to teach and learn from each other (p.11)." Recommendations are also made for systematic instructional strategies that stress generalization.

Each time a student is taught a functional skill or game, it might be required that the skill be performed: (a) in reaction to, or in the presence of at least three different persons; (b) in at least three different natural settings; (c) in response to at least three different sets of instructional materials; and (d) to at least three different appropriate language cues. (p. 10)

In attempting to help each individual develop the specific skills that have been identified as target objectives, the concomitant factors that help the student understand what he is learning, why he should learn it, how he can use the skill, and when to use it have not been carefully researched. If the systematic procedure recommended by Williams, Brown, and Certo (1975) and the suggestions of Brown, Nietupski, and Hamre-Nietupski (1976) are followed, then this problem should not recur.

Education is more than the acquisition of stated skills; it is the ownership of concepts intuitively discovered by the individual while acting upon his world. Rather than educating an individual to be the passive recipient of behavioral objectives set, trained, and evaluated by others, the challenge of the educator is to create a responsive learning environment that motivates the handicapped learner to be the actor in his world, setting his own objectives, determining his own acquisition methodology, and evaluating his own performance.

References

Abeson, A. (Ed.). *A continuing summary of pending and completed litigation regarding the education of handicapped children.* Arlington, Va.: Council for Exceptional Children's State-Federal Information Clearinghouse for Exceptional Children, 1973, pp. 1–5.

Adams, J. Adaptive behavior and measured intelligence in the classification of mental retardation. *American Journal of Mental Deficiency,* 1973, *78* (1), 77–81.

Alpern, G., & Boll, T. *Education and care of moderately and severely retarded children.* Seattle: Special Child Publications, 1971.

Alpern, G., & Boll, T. *Developmental profile.* Indianapolis: Psychological Development Publishers, 1972.

Altman, R., & Meyen, E. Public school programming for the severely/profoundly handicapped: Some researchable problems. *Education and Training of the Mentally Retarded,* 1976, *11* (1), 40–45.

Axelrod, S., Hall, R. V., Weis, L., & Rohrer, S. Use of self-imposed contingencies to reduce the frequency of smoking behavior. In M. J. Mahoney & C. E. Thoresin (Eds.), *Self-control: Power to the person.* Monterey, Calif.: Brooks/Cole, 1974.

Balthazar, E. *Balthazar scales of adaptive behavior I: The scales of functional independence.* Champaign, Ill.: Research Press, 1971a.

Balthazar, E. *Balthazar scales of adaptive behavior II: Scales of social adaptation.* Palo Alto: Consulting Psychologists Press, 1971b.

Baumeister, A. A., & Muma, J. R. On defining mental retardation. *Journal of Special Education,* 1975, *9*(3), 293–306.

Bayley, N. *Bayley infant scales of development.* New York: Psychological Corp., 1969.

Behavioral Characteristics Progression. Palo Alto, Calif.: Vort Corp., 1973.

Bender, M., & Valletutti, P. *Teaching the moderately and severely handicapped* (Vols. 1, 2, 3). Baltimore: University Park Press, 1976.

Bensberg, G. *Teaching the mentally retarded: A handbook for ward personnel.* Atlanta: Southern Regional Education Board, 1965.

Bierman, J. M., Connor, A., Vaage, M., & Honzik, M. P. Pediatricians' assessment of the intelligence of two-year-olds and their mental test scores. *Pediatrics,* 1964, *34,* 680–683.

Binet, A. La mesure en psychologie individuelle. *Revue Philosophique,* 1898, *46*(2), 113–123.

Binet, A., & Simon, T. Sur la necessite d'etabur undiagnostic scientific des estats inferieurs de l'intelligence. *Annee Psychologique,* 1905, *11,* 1–28.

Blatt, B. Public policy and the education of children with special needs. *Exceptional Children,* 1972, *38,* 537–545.

Brown, L., Nietupski, J., & Hamre-Nietupski, S. The criterion of ultimate functioning and public school services for severely handicapped students. In M. A. Thomas (Ed.), *Hey don't forget about me: Education's investment in the severely, profoundly, and multiply handicapped.* Reston, Va.: Council for Exceptional Children, 1976.

Brown, L., & York, R. Developing programs for severely handicapped students: Teacher training and classroom instruction. *Focus on Exceptional Children,* 1974, *6*(2).

Burgmeister, B., Blum, L. H., & Lorge, I. *Columbia mental maturity scale.* New York: Harcourt Brace Jovanovich, 1972.

Cain, C., Levine, S., & Freeman, E. *Cain-Levine social competency scale.* Palo Alto: Consulting Psychologists Press, 1963.

Cattell, P. *Infant intelligence scale.* New York: Psychological Corp., 1940.

Cleary, T. A., Humphreys, L. G., Kendrick, S. A., & Wesman, A. Educational uses of tests with disadvantaged students. *American Psychologist,* 1975, *30*(1), 15–41.

Cohen, M., Gross, P., & Haring, N. G. Developmental pinpoints. In N. G. Haring & L. J. Brown (Eds.), *Teaching the severely handicapped* (Vol. 1). New York: Grune & Stratton, 1976.

DesLauriers, A. M., & Carlson, C. F. *Your child is asleep: Early infantile autism.* Homewood, Ill.: Dorsey, 1969.

DiNola, A. J., Kaminsky, B. P., & Sternfeld, A. E. *T.M.R. performance profile for the severely and moderately retarded.* Ridgefield, N.J.: Reporting Service for Children, 1963.

DiNola, A. J., Kaminsky, B. P., & Sternfeld, A. E. *Y.M.E.R. performance profile for the young moderately and mildly retarded.* Ridgefield, N.J.: Reporting Service for Children, 1967.

Doll, E. A genetic scale of social maturity. *American Journal of Orthopsychiatry,* 1935, *51,* 180–188.

Doll, E. *The Vineland scale of social maturity.* Circle Pines, Minn.: American Guidance Services, Inc., 1965.

DuBose, R. F. Predictive value of infant intelligence scales with multiply handicapped children. *American Journal of Mental Deficiency,* 1977, *81,* 388–390.

Foster, R. W. *Camelot behavioral checklist.* Bellevue, Wash.: Edmark Associates, 1974.

Goddard, H. H. Four hundred feebleminded children classified by the Binet method. *Journal of Psycho-Asthenics,* 1910, *15,* 17–30.

Glaser, R. (Ed.). *Teaching machines and programmed learning, II: Data and direction.* Washington, D. C.: National Education Association of the United States, 1965.

Griffin, P., Sanford, A., & Wilson, D. *Learning accomplishment profile* (Diagnostic ed.). Winston-Salem, N.C.: Kaplan School Supply Corp., 1975.

Grossman, H. J. (Ed.). Manual on terminology and classification in mental retardation. *American Journal of Mental Deficiency Special Publication,* Series No. 2, 1973.

Guess, D., Sailor, W., & Baer, D. A behavioral-remedial approach to language training for the severely handicapped. In E. Sontag, J. Smith, & N. Certo (Eds.), *Educational programming for the severely and profoundly handicapped.* Reston, Va.: Council for Exceptional Children, 1977.

Haimowitz, N. R. Development patterns: Birth to five years. In M. R. Haimowitz & N. R. Haimowitz (Eds.), *Human development: Selected readings* (3rd ed.). New York: Thomas Y. Crowell Co., 1973.

Heber, R. F. (Ed.). A manual on terminology and classification in mental retardation. American Journal of Mental Deficiency, 1959, *64.* Monograph Supplement.

Heber, R. F. (Ed.). A manual on terminology and classification in mental retardation. (Rev. ed.) American Journal of Mental Deficiency Monograph, 1961, *64.*

Hobbs, N. (Ed.). *Issues in the classification of children* (Vol. 1). San Francisco: Jossey-Bass, 1975.

Illingsworth, R. S. The predictive value of developmental tests in the first year with special reference to the diag-

nosis of mental subnormality. *Journal of Child Psychology and Psychiatry,* 1961, *2,* 210–215.

Ireland, W. W. *The mental affections of children: Idiocy, imbecility, and insanity.* London: J. Churchill, 1898.

Irwin, J. V., Ward, M. W., Deen, C. C., & Greis, A. B. *Lexington developmental scale.* Lexington, Ky.: Child Development Center of UCPB, 1973.

Kauffman, J. M., & Payne, J. S. (Eds.). *Mental retardation: Introduction and personal perspectives.* Columbus: Charles E. Merrill, 1975.

Kirk, S. A., McCarthy, J. J., & Kirk, W. D. *The Illinois test of psycholinguistic abilities* (Rev. ed.). Urbana, Ill.: University of Illinois Press, 1968.

Lambert, N., Windmiller, M., Cole, L., & Figueroa, R. *AAMD adaptive behavior scale, public school version* (1974 rev.). Washington, D.C.: American Association on Mental Deficiency, 1975.

Larsen, L., & Bricker, W. A manual for parents and teachers of severely and moderately retarded children. *IMRID Papers and Reports No. 22,* 1968.

Lewis, M. (Ed.). *Origins of intelligence.* New York: Plenum Press, 1976.

Martin, E. W. Individualism and behaviorism as future trends in educating handicapped children. *Exceptional Children,* 1972, *38,* 517–525.

McIntosh, E. I., & Warren, S. W. Adaptive behavior in the retarded: A semi-longitudinal study. *Training School Bulletin,* 1969, *66,* 12–22.

Mercer, J. R. The myth of 3 percent prevalences. In R. K. Eyman, C. E. Myers, & G. Tarjan (Eds.), *Sociobehavioral studies in mental retardation.* American Association on Mental Deficiency Monograph, 1973, *1.*

Mercer, J. R. A policy statement on assessment procedures and the rights of children. *Harvard Educational Review,* 1974, *44* (1), 125–141.

Mercer, J. R. Psychological assessment and the rights of children. In N. Hobbs (Ed.), *Issues in the classification of children* (Vol. 1). San Francisco: Jossey-Bass, 1975.

Meyen, E. L. *Preparing personnel for the severely and profoundly mentally retarded.* Paper presented at the Conference on Education of Severely and Profoundly Retarded Students, New Orleans, April 1975.

Mills v. Board of Education. Civil Action No. 1939–71 (District of Columbia), August, 1972.

Myers, D. G., Sinco, M. E., & Stalma, E. S. *The right-to-education child (A curriculum for the severely and profoundly mentally retarded).* Springfield, Ill.: Charles C Thomas, 1973.

National Association for Retarded Citizens. *Educating the twenty-four hour child.* Arlington, Tex.: NARC, 1976.

Nihira, K., Foster, R., Shellhaas, M., & Leland, H. *Adaptive behavior scales: Manual.* Washington, D.C.: American Association on Mental Deficiency, 1969.

Nihira, K., Foster, R., Shellhaas, M., & Leland, H. *Adaptive behavior scale: Manual.* (1975 Rev.) Washington, D.C.: American Association on Mental Deficiency, 1975.

President's Committee on Mental Retardation. *The six hour retarded child.* Washington, D.C.: U.S. Government Printing Office, 1970.

Quick, A. D., Little, T. L., & Campbell, A. A. *Project Memphis.* Belmont, Calif.: Fearon Publishers, 1973.

Sailor, W., & Horner, R. D. Educational assessment strategies for the severely handicapped. In N. G. Haring, & L. J. Brown (Eds.), *Teaching the severely handicapped.* New York: Grune & Stratton, 1976.

Sailor, W., & Mix, B. J. *The TARC assessment system.* Lawrence: Kans.: H & H Enterprises, Inc., 1975.

Sedlak, R. S., & Weener, P. Review of research on the Illinois Test of Psycholinguistic Abilities. In L. Mann & D. A. Sabatino (Eds.), *The first review of special education* (Vol. 1). Philadelphia: Buttonwood Farms, 1973.

Seguin, E. *Idiocy and its treatment by the physiological method.* New York: Brandow, 1866.

Shearer, D. *The Portage guide to early education.* Portage, Wis.: Cooperative Educational Service Agency No. 12, 1972.

Somerton, M. E., & Turner, K. D. *Pennsylvania training model individual assessment guide.* Harrisburg, Pa.: Pennsylvania Department of Education, 1975.

Sontag, E., Burke, P., & York, R. Considerations for serving the severely handicapped in the public schools. *Education and Training of the Mentally Retarded,* 1973, *8* (2), 20–26.

Spivack, G., & Spotts, J. *Devereaux child behavior rating scale.* Devon, Pa.: Devereaux Foundation, 1966.

Stillman, R. (Ed.). *The Callier-Azusa scale.* Dallas: Callier Center for Communication Disorders, 1974.

Tarjan, G., Wright, S. W., Eyman, R. K., & Keeran, D. V. Natural history of mental retardation: Some aspects of epidemiology. *American Journal of Mental Deficiency,* 1973, *77,* 369–379.

Terman, L. M. *The measurement of intelligence.* Boston: Houghton Mifflin, 1916.

Terman, L. M., & Merrill, M. A. *Measuring intelligence.* Boston: Houghton Mifflin, 1937.

Thompson, P. R. Wednesday morning keynote address (Untitled). In J. Moore & V. Engleman (Eds.), *The severely, multiply handicapped: What are the issues?* Proceedings from the Regional, Topical Conference, University of Utah, Salt Lake City, Utah, March 6–8, 1974, pp. 70–76.

Tilton, J., Liska, D., & Bourland, J. (Eds.). *Guide to early developmental training.* Boston: Allyn and Bacon, 1972.

Tredgold, A. F. *Mental deficiency* (6th ed.). Baltimore: William Wood & Co., 1937.

Wechsler, D. *Wechsler intelligence scale for children.* New York: Psychological Corp., 1949.

Wechsler, D. *Wechsler adult intelligence scale.* New York: Psychological Corp., 1955.

Wechsler, D. *Wechsler preschool and primary scale of intelligence.* New York: Psychological Corp., 1967.

Wechsler, D. *Wechsler intelligence scale for children (Revised).* New York: Psychological Corp., 1974.

Werner, E. E., Honzik, M. P., & Smith, R. S. Prediction of intelligence and achievement at ten years from twenty months pediatric and psychologic examinations. *Child Development,* 1968, *39,* 1063–1075.

Williams, W., Brown, L., & Certo, N. *Components of instructional programs for severely handicapped students.* Paper presented at the Conference on Education of Severely and Profoundly Retarded Students, New Orleans, April 1975.

Williams, W. & Gotts, E. A. Selected considerations on developing curriculum for severely handicapped students. In E. Sontag, J. Smith, & N. Certo (Eds.), *Educational programming for the severely and profoundly handicapped.* Reston, Va.: Council for Exceptional Children, 1977.

Notes

1. Down, J. L. H. Observations on the ethnic classification of idiots. *London Hospital Clinical Lecture Reports,* 1866, *3,* 229–262.
2. Hart, V., & DuBose, R. *A manual for the development of self-help in multiply handicapped children.* Unpublished manuscript, George Peabody College for Teachers, 1971.
3. *Student progress record.* State of Oregon Mental Health Division, Programs for Mental Retardation and Development Disabilities, 1973.
4. Walker, J., Tucker, J. A., Lucro, C., & Mirro, M. *Individualized programming for the severely multiply handicapped.* (Tech. Rep. No. 1). Austin, Tex.: Regional Resource Center, June 1975.
5. Brown, L., Scheuerman, N., Cartwright, S., & York, R. *The design and implementation of an empirically based instructional program for young severely handicapped students: Toward the rejection of the exclusion principle* (Vol. III). Unpublished manuscript, University of Wisconson, Madison Public Schools, 1973.
6. Brown, L., Williams, W., & Crowner, T. *A collection of papers and programs related to public school services for severely and handicapped studients,* (Vol. IV). Unpublished manuscript, University of Wisconsin, Madision Public Schools, 1974.
7. Brown, L., Crowner, T., Williams, W., & York, R. *Madison's alternative for zero exclusion: A book of readings* (Vol. V). Unpublished manuscript, University of Wisconsin, Madison Public Schools, 1975.

Introduction to Chapters 2 and 3

In the next two chapters Debbie Smith and I will try to help you address those ever-constant classroom needs (1) of observing and measuring the varied behaviors of your students, (2) of analyzing learning tasks into ordered, small steps, (3) of identifying and reporting on relevant long- and short-term goals, and (4) of applying with facility and finesse all the basic instructional procedures necessary to adjust the behavioral excesses and/or deficiencies most of your students exhibit. Without these skills it would be impossible to write or to carry out a relevant Individualized Educational Program for one of your students, let alone an entire class.

For many of you these pages will serve as reminders of familiar concepts, for others this content will be new. Yet the basic elements of instruction which we cover represent an essential volume of information you cannot successfully survive without. All the colorfully packaged materials, commercial teaching kits, curriculum guides, test manuals, and fancy media sets cannot begin to substitute for the readily available mastery of these teaching techniques. However, the task of translating these principles and weaving them into their appropriate classroom applications is a task far more complex than the ability to define a list of key terms or to score a high grade on a written test covering "classroom management and instruction of the severely handicapped." What I am saying is something that you as teachers are probably already well aware of—that understanding the elements of effective teaching is only the beginning of a teacher's job.

2

Classroom Management
and Instructional Planning

*This chapter was written by **Deborah D. Smith**,
George Peabody College for Teachers and **Martha
E. Snell**, University of Virginia.*

In this chapter, the reader will find information about
the use of applied behavior analysis techniques in
the classroom, data collection procedures and
measurement systems, behavioral assessment of
student performance, and task analysis. In Chapter
3, the influence and appropriate application of various intervention strategies are discussed. The intent was that these two chapters would serve as a
foundation for the remainder of the book; general
content is provided about verified educational procedures and strategies used in classrooms for the
moderately, severely, and profoundly handicapped.
In addition, definitions and examples of fundamental terms and concepts are provided.

Applied Behavior Analysis

Brief history

Probably the first and certainly the first well-documented account of the use of what we now call
behavior modification or applied behavior analysis
was the famous report of Itard's work with Victor in

the early 1800s (Itard, 1926). Itard, through the
systematic use of shaping, task analysis, systematic instructions, time out, and various reinforcement techniques, modified his young charge's
aberrant and infantile behavior so that he was
manageable and could adapt rather successfully
in a sheltered and structured environment.

Applied behavior analysis measurement techniques and research methodology grew out of well-
documented early experiments with laboratory
animals. Except for Watson's research in the early
1920s, possibly the first experimental analysis of
behavior study with a human subject was conducted
by Fuller (1949). Fuller demonstrated that an institutionalized, severely retarded adult would respond to
systematic shaping procedures and primary reinforcement. His pioneering laboratory research
bridged the gap from animal to human applications.

Azrin and Lindsley's (1956) classic study on cooperation between children was probably the first of
its kind. These laboratory researchers found that
the children's cooperative behavior could be controlled by environmental factors manipulated by the
experimenters. Bijou (1958) and Bijou and Orlando
(1961) also worked with children in their studies on
the influence of different kinds of reinforcement
schedules originally used in animal laboratory research. They found that as they could predict with
animals, they equally could predict with children.

Their successful application of experimental analysis of behavior procedures encouraged other researchers to apply and refine these procedures to further clinical and remediation research. A fine compilation of this early work can be found in two edited volumes (Krasner & Ullman, 1965; Ullman & Krasner, 1965); more recently published landmark studies can be found in Leitenberg (1976).

Encouraged by the results of their laboratory research, experimental behavior analysts began to work in applied settings. The type of work and subjects of their research were predicated by where they could gain admittance, of course, and initially these pioneer researchers found few settings ready for their experimentation. Most were limited to work in institutions with severely emotionally disturbed and severely retarded people—patients others had given up on long ago.

Extensive research demonstrated that applied behavior analysis designs, procedures, and methodology are effective in natural settings with individuals as well as small groups. Zimmerman and Zimmerman (1962) used reinforcement and extinction procedures to improve spelling and eliminate tantrums in two children. Homme and his team of researchers (Homme, de Baca, Devine, Steinhorst, & Rickert, 1963) were probably the first to systematically apply the Premack's Principle, scheduling high probability behaviors following low probability behaviors, to control disruptive classroom behavior. In 1964, Spradlin (Note 1) found that a young institutionalized girl could be taught to feed herself within a relatively short period of time through the use of the Premack's Principle and shaping procedures.

Wolf, Risley, and Mees (1964) eliminated many autistic and self-destructive behaviors in one young boy. Dicky, a youngster most probably bound for a lifetime of institutional care, became the bearer of hope for others wishing to remediate aberrant behavior in children. Nedelman and Sulzbacher (1972) in a follow-up study of Dicky found that the hopes of these early workers were borne out by the progress and success of this boy. Thirteen years after the first published work about Dicky, they found this youngster attending regular public school and succeeding both there and at home.

One of the first direct applications of applied behavior analysis procedures to general academic achievement was conducted by Birnbrauer, Wolf, Kidder, and Tague (1956) at Rainier State School in Washington. Soon, heralded by the success of these procedures in a narrow, although nonlaboratory setting, behavior analysts found themselves in more applied settings: classrooms for exceptional children.

A surge of research which used disruptive classroom behavior as the dependent variable then appeared in the literature. Time and time again, research indicated that talking out (Becker, Madsen, Arnold, & Thomas, 1967; O'Leary, Kaufman, Kass, & Drabman, 1970) and being out-of-seat (Osborne, 1969) could be modified in the classroom. Almost concurrently, researchers began to study "attending" to classroom assignments (Hall, Lund, & Jackson, 1968). These were some of the first attempts using this methodology to study classroom behavior of children. Although their dependent variable, attending, was an indirect measure of academic performance, it brought researchers closer to the direct study of children's acquisition of new skills.

Since then, most direct behaviors—the acquisition of language (Bricker & Bricker, 1970; Hester & Hendrickson, in press; Sailor, Guess, & Baer, 1973), self-help skills (Azrin, Bugle, & O'Brien, 1971; Edgar, Maser, Smith, & Haring, 1977; Horner & Keilitz, 1975; Nelson, Cone, & Hanson, 1975; O'Brien & Azrin, 1972), vocational and prevocational skills (Crosson, 1969; Gold, 1972), and daily living skills (Leff, 1975; Perske & Marquiss, 1973) —have come to be the target of both researchers and practitioners.

Application of applied behavior analysis

In a series of articles on analysis of behavior as applied to the classroom, Lovitt (1968, 1970, 1975, 1976, 1977) presented five different characteristics of this approach: *direct measurement, daily measurement, replicable teaching procedures, individual analysis,* and *experimental control.* First, the behavior under consideration is measured directly. In dressing, for example, the measure is the number of times the student wears each piece of apparel appropriately, rather than scores on an infrequently given assessment device for self-help skills. Second, the behavior is measured on a daily basis. The exact target response or set of responses is identified carefully and assessed as a problem for the student. If, for example, only one component of the dressing sequence is in error, that will become the target of instruction. The pupil is given the opportunity to execute the task on a daily basis before, during, and after an intervention is applied. Third, teaching procedures are applied systematically. All procedures are described fully to teachers and others who work with the student; frequently, the student is also informed of the operating procedures. Thus, if a specific kind of instructional tactic proves to be effective in teaching students to tie their shoes, those exact procedures can be related so that teachers wishing to improve their students' abilities to tie shoes can replicate the procedures. The fourth characteristic of the behavior analysis methodology is the presentation of individual student data rather than averages or groups of data. This ideographic presentation allows others to study the individual behavior patterns of their subjects. Fifth, the researcber or clinician demonstrates that experimental control was obtained and that, in fact, a functional relationship was established between the dependent and independent variables—that is, that it was the intervention itself (e.g., instruction) which produced the effect (e.g., correctly tied shoes) rather than some unknown variable (e.g., maturation).

A final characteristic of the analysis of behavior research approach is that, except for the collection of daily measures, the typical classroom routine usually is not disrupted. The characteristics of applied analysis of behavior encompass those tactics teachers often referred to as "good instruction." The key is that tactics are systematically applied in a consistent manner and are continually evaluated as the student's performance is monitored daily.

Research designs

Basically, there are three categories of research designs available to applied behavior analysts (Baer, Wolf, & Risley, 1968; Craighead, Kazdin, & Mahoney; 1975, Hersen & Barlow, 1976; Kazdin, 1975: (1) reversal or "*ABAB*" designs; (2) multiple baseline designs, of which there are three; and (3) cross-over procedures.

Reversal

This design (see Figure 2.1), sometimes referred to as *ABA* or *ABAB,* consists of a baseline phase *(A)* during which behavior is recorded until a stable trend is established; a treatment phase *(B)* during which the experimental condition is introduced; withdrawal of treatment phase (A_2); and finally, the reinstitution of the experimental condition (B_2). If the behavior altered during the *B* phase returns to its near baseline rate during the A_2 phase, a strong case can be made that a functional relationship was established between the independent (experimental variable) and the behavior in question.

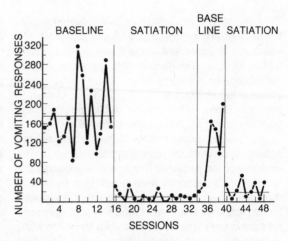

FIGURE 2.1   *An example of the reversal of "ABAB" design*

The number of vomiting responses in a 29-year-old, profoundly retarded, institutionalized adult occurring during observations one hour in length following each of three meals per day. Fifteen baseline observations, averaging 178 responses/hour (or 3/minute), were followed by the satiation treatment during which the subject was allowed to eat all the food he could consume at every meal with milk shakes offered after each observation to maintain the satiation effect. The first satiation treatment decreased vomiting responses to a mean level of approximately 15 per hour for 18 sessions. This was followed by a 6-session reversal to baseline conditions (no satiation treatment) which resulted in an increase in vomiting (about 100 response/hour); finally the treatment was reinstituted, resulting in a decline to about 20 responses/hour.

Source: G. M. Jackson, C. R. Johnson, G. S. Ackron, & R. Crowley. Food satiation as a procedure to decelerate vomiting. *American Journal of Mental Deficiency*, 1975, *80*, p. 224.

Often this design cannot be used because the target behavior will not or should not be reversed to the baseline level of performance. This situation occurs most frequently for academic tasks. For example, if a child demonstrates that he cannot compute specific kinds of arithmetic problems correctly during baseline and during the intervention condition achieves mastery, the hope is for the learned behavior to remain at the high level of accuracy achieved during the intervention period even when the instructional tactic is withdrawn. When this situation occurs, the return to baseline condition is called the maintenance phase. If the learner maintains the high, desired level of performance for a period of time, a posttest situation is then arranged on an intermittent basis, possibly weekly.

Since this situation does not verify experimental control of the dependent variable, it is necessary for the researcher to replicate his experiment. Sidman

(1960) refers to this as direct replication. Simply, the experiment is repeated again and again, both across subjects and/or across behaviors. If the results of these replications are consistent, experimental control is obtained. An example of this situation is displayed in Figure 2.2.

Multiple Baseline

As already described, there are instances in which learned behavior may prove either irreversible or undesirable to reverse. In addition, sometimes di-

rect replications are not convenient. In such cases, the multiple baseline design (see Figure 2.3) is appropriate. This alternative approach provides data across several behaviors of the same individual, data for the same individual across a variety of situations (e.g., math class and reading period), or data from a number of students in the same situation exhibiting the same class of behavior. In each case, several baselines are developed. Using the multiple baseline across behaviors as an example, a behavior modification procedure is applied to one of the

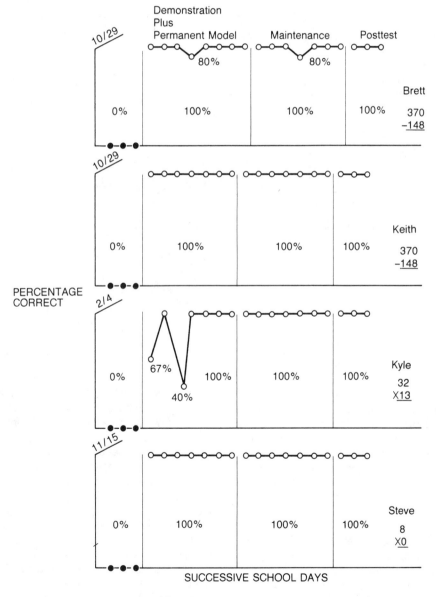

FIGURE 2.2   *An example of the modified reversal design with direct replications*

Source: Data shown were reported in Smith & Lovitt, 1975

48613

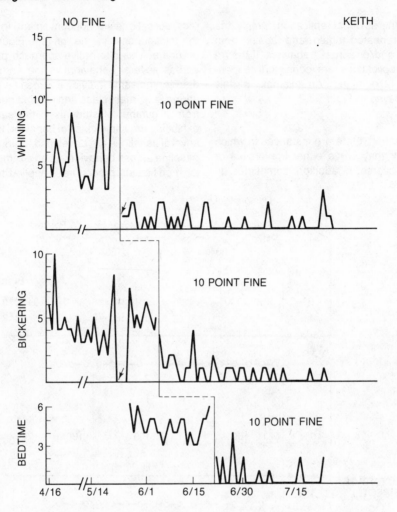

FIGURE 2.3   *An example of the multiple baseline design*

Source: E. R. Christopherson, C. M. Arnold, D. W. Hill, & H. R. Quilitch. The home point system. *Journal of Applied Behavior Analysis*, 1972, *4*, p. 492.

behaviors until that target behavior exhibits change. "Then, the same procedure is applied to a second behavior, later to a third, and so forth" (Hall, Cristler, Cranston, & Tucker, 1970, p. 247). It if is found that in each instance the target behavior alters upon introduction of the treatment, a functional relationship between the experimental treatment variable and the dependent behavior is demonstrated.

Cross-over

The cross-over research design (see Figure 2.4) is used primarily to compare within-subject multiple treatment interventions and to control for possible "order effects" stemming from the treatment series. It is designed to determine whether time rather than

the influence or power of the intervention affected the changes in behavior. To find out, the same behavior of two or more individuals of comparable entry levels is measured. "During baseline, no intervention is scheduled; during the next phase intervention A is associated with one pupil, intervention B with the other. A return to baseline conditions is then arranged, followed by another phase where the interventions are altered" (Lovitt, Note 2, p. 15). By alternatively associating each intervention with each subject in turn, any possible order effect of multiple intervention can be eliminated and a functional relationship of treatment to behavior can be demonstrated.

In summary, each of the three designs reviewed

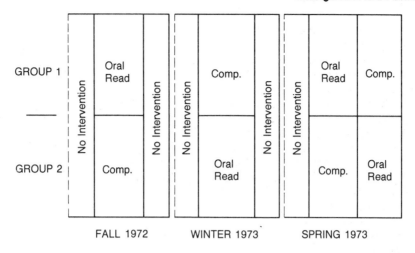

| | FALL 1972 | WINTER 1973 | SPRING 1973 |

FIGURE 2.4   *A representation of the cross-over design*
Source: C. L. Hansen & T. C. Lovitt. *The Journal of Special Education*, 1976, *10*, p. 54.

have certain common characteristics critical to curriculum research: direct measurement of behavior, continuous daily measurement, individual analysis, and experimental control. Together, these features enable the curriculum researcher to demonstrate that the intervention itself served to improve the learned behavior of the student.

Future Designs

The intent of this section is to inform the reader about those alternative research designs which might be appropriate for behavior analysts, and to emphasize that researchers are searching for and employing additional designs and methods for analyzing data. For example, time series, trend analysis, and other statistical techniques (see Campbell & Stanley, 1963; Hersen & Barlow, 1976; Kerlinger, 1964) are used by some experimenters who conduct research utilizing continuous data.

Typically, the kinds of research questions asked by behavior analysts are micro-organismic by nature. "The usual approach to the study of ongoing social interactive behavior is confined to a single aspect of an interaction, in which observation and measurement can be restricted to relatively few behavior measures" (Bobbitt, Gourevitch, Miller, & Jensen, 1969, p. 110). When researchers study the influence of a single intervention strategy on a small number of responses, the kinds of designs described earlier are most appropriate. However, as researchers begin to ask broader questions or attempt to generate hypotheses, theories, and constructs, these designs tend to be limiting.

In the past, many behavior analysts concerned themselves with monitoring and modifying individuals' behaviors by response classes. Wolf, Risley, and Mees (1964), for example, modified individual classes of Dicky's behavior: tantrums, wearing of glasses, autisms, etc. In the early Achievement Place studies (Bailey, Wolf, & Phillips, 1970; Fixsen, Phillips, & Wolf, 1972; Phillips, 1968; Phillips, Phillips, Fixsen, & Wolf, 1971), aggressive statements, bathroom cleanliness, doing homework, rule violations, promptness, room cleaning, and other behaviors were modified. In these cases, the hope was for individual modifications to lead eventually to remediation of larger problems for the individuals such as delinquency or severe behavioral disorders.

Even after many individual modifications, questions about relationships of treatment programs and constructs of behavior for groups basically are still unanswered. Several important questions must be addressed. For example, does the modification of individual skills lead to the remediation of a larger problem? To what extent can a mass of ideographic data be generalized to the larger population? Recently, Baer (1975) proposed a new design for researchers to study the influence of comprehensive treatment programs aimed at altering those indirect behaviors which form social problems (such as delinquency) or categories of behavior (such as language age). This design, a combination of the traditional pre- and posttest research techniques with the single-subject approach (see Figure 2.5), requires that two groups receive a pretest; multiple baseline designs are then employed across many behaviors for the individuals comprising the first group. The control group does not receive the treatment program, but behavior measurements as in an extended baseline are conducted. Once the treatment program is completed for the first group, both the experimental and control groups are "posttested." The treatment program is then instituted for the control group and behavior is monitored for the original experimental group. The strengths of this design, then, lie with the multiple baseline strategem—the smaller (individual) multiple baseline designs conducted within each group of subjects and the larger multiple baseline design conducted across the two groups—and the use of the traditional pre- and posttest research design and statistical analysis of the data.

To use language age as an illustrative example, one would conduct a traditional pretest using a standardized indirect measure of language age on two groups of youngsters. One group serves as the experimental (treatment) group and the other as the control (no treatment) group. The experimental group, represented by the top half of Figure 2.5, receives the pilot language remediation program and is treated individually through a series of multiple baseline design techniques. Both groups are tested on the standardized indirect measure of language abilities at the conclusion of the first group's treatment program. Then the control group, represented in the bottom half of Figure 2.5, becomes the experimental group, and the treatment is replicated. Concurrently, data are gathered on the first experimental group to test for maintenance. Once the program is concluded, both groups are tested again. Probably, although not included in Baer's sketch of this design, a maintenance period should also be assessed for the second experimental group.

This design, while intriguing, is appropriate only for researchers. The expense of collecting this kind of thorough data is inordinate and most likely will require grant support for the provision of the necessary funds. The most important implication of this example is the indication that researchers are continuing to explore new design strategies to study the relationship between treatment program and human behavior.

Reliability

Reliability is a keystone of the behavior analysis approach and gives a measure as to whether or not the planned intervention strategy actually caused behavior change. Regardless of the research design utilized, it is imperative that reliability measures

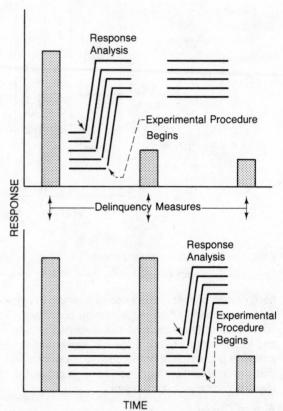

FIGURE 2.5   *An example of a combination research design aimed at investigating the influence of treatment programs*

Source: D. M. Baer. In the beginning, there was a response. In E. Ramp & G. Semb (Eds.). *Behavior analysis: Areas of research and application,* © 1975, p. 29. Reprinted by permission of Prentice-Hall, Inc., Englewood Cliffs, New Jersey.

be taken consistently across conditions. Baer, Wolf, and Risley (1968) clearly expressed the importance of measuring behavior change reliably. In order to insure reliability, data collection and analysis must be carried out so that other researchers may come to the same conclusions about the influence of the applied tactic and the magnitude of its effects.

Johnson and Bolstad (1973) also expressed the importance of reliability measures in analysis of behavior research. They made an important distinction between the traditional meaning of reliability—consistency of a measurement instrument over time—and the concept of reliability as "observer agreement and observer accuracy." In addition, if careful attention is not paid to reliable collection, analysis, and interpretation of the data, the results of the research are not useful for teachers and others implementing instructional programs.

Three types of reliability measures are available to researchers. If timings of student performance are used, it is important that accurate timings are made. If correct and error rates are used as the measure, for example, it is vital that the session time is obtained accurately. This is so because correct and error rates are calculated by taking the number of correct or error responses and dividing by session time; i.e.,

$$\frac{\text{number of correct responses}}{\text{session time}} = \text{correct rate.}$$

The second kind of reliability measure necessary is the accurate scoring of the responses. This may be obtained for nonpermanent products (e.g., social behavior) by determining the consistency of observations or by determining whether the permanent product (e.g., arithmetic papers) was scored accurately. Specific formulae for the calculation of reliability scores are provided later in this chapter.

The third type of reliability measure concerns procedures. Rarely is any mention of procedure reliability (the systematic application of the same procedures through an experimental condition) found in research reports. Without this information, the implication of the research findings as to the effect of the procedures is questionable. It is possible that in many cases the experimenter, during the course of his treatment period, altered or added to the planned intervention. If this occurs, the replicability of the research is negated. Although this information is difficult to obtain, it is important that researchers begin to address this issue clearly.

ABC analysis

As an expansion of Skinner's (1938, 1953) original description of operant conditioning, Lindsley (1964) was one of the first special educators who stressed that behavior be viewed within an operant framework. This framework emphasized the causal relationships between the stimulus *events* preceding or antecedent (E^A) to the *behavior (B)* (response or movement) and *events* following or *consequential* (E^C) to it. The particular *arrangement (A)* or contingency by which consequential events are made available to the behaving individual is directly related to the strength and frequency of the behavior. This process has been stated as: $E^A \rightarrow B \rightarrow A \rightarrow E^C$. For example, a teacher presents a common object (e.g., spoon, ball, etc.) with the request,

"What is this?" (E^A) followed by a child's verbal label for the object *(B)*. When the contingency or arrangement *(A)* is one-to-one, every correct label spoken by the child is followed by the teacher's praise and smiles (E^C).

Antecedent events include commands, instructions, teaching materials and setting, prompting, and behavior modeling; consequential events may be reinforcing (food, praise, tokens, activities), punishing (angry look and words, removal of toys, etc.), or neutral to the individual. Both antecendent and consequential events are often a result of staff (teacher, aide), parental, or peer behavior.

More recently (Worell & Nelson, 1974), the term "ABC Analysis" has been coined to refer to a descriptive analysis of behavior—"that operation of listing all environmental events subsequent and antecedent to or during a recurring behavioral event or the general setting in which that behavior occurs, with the purpose of attempting to identify possible discriminative and reinforcing stimuli" (White, 1971, p. 7). Kanfer and Grimm (1977) propose a model for organizing the symptoms of an individual's behavior difficulties which leads to systematic selection of target behaviors. This model, a more detailed variation of *ABC* analysis, would be useful for teachers interviewing parents, caregivers, or other teachers during the initial stage of behavior problem solving. Because behaviors are controlled by their antecedents and consequences, the *ABC* analysis is an important first step in the systematic teaching or changing of behavior.

How is an *ABC* analysis of a classroom problem carried out? First, let us isolate the typical teaching problems posed for the teacher and parent of the handicapped. These are threefold:

1. Teaching the individuals to do what they can do for themselves;
2. Teaching them to stop inappropriate behavior;
3. Teaching them to maintain what they have learned (Kauffman & Snell, 1977).

One may note that these teaching problems are similar to those for normal individuals, with the general exceptions that learning proceeds more slowly and by smaller steps and must be directed toward very functional goals. Therefore, instructional time becomes important and less margin is allowed for teaching errors. Although the questions a teacher must answer about the target behavior during an ABC analysis differ slightly depending upon which teaching problem exists, the following questions are of general concern:

1. *Antecedent Conditions*
   A. In what situation(s) does the target behavior occur (e.g., setting, time of day or night, peers or adults present, etc.)?
   B. What adult or peer behaviors occur just prior to the targeted behavior (e.g., teacher requests, presentation or removal of certain toys, change in schedule, etc.)?
2. *Behavior*
   A. How often does the individual independently perform the target behavior and how much of the target behavior can the individual currently perform without assistance (i.e., baseline level of target behavior)?
3. *Consequential Conditions*
   A. What types of comments are made or actions taken by staff and peers as the behavior is occurring or during the moments following the behavior?
   B. Approximately how often do these particular consequences occur in relation to the behavior (i.e., arrangement or contingency of the consequences)?

The remainder of this chapter is centered around the measurement of behavior, task analysis and setting goals and instructional objectives. Chapter 3 builds upon these basic concepts by focusing on the planning of instructional arrangements, events, and the use of operant conditioning or behavior modification rules which control the elements of Lindsley's framework: Antecedent Events → Behavior→Arrangement→Consequential Events *(ABC)*.

Data collection procedures

Behavior measurement is arduous, and data-based analyses are complex. For example, one may examine: (1) direction of change (increase, decrease, no change), (2) rate of change, (3) stability of change, and (4) amount of change in a behavior. Since the performance of many school-aged individuals, handicapped or not, never seems to occur long enough for counting or timing, how can behavior measurement be accomplished? Skinner (1953) recognized the arduousness of precise behavioral measurement:

Behavior is a difficult subject matter, not because it is inaccessible, but because it is extremely complex. Since it is a process, rather than a thing, it cannot easily be held still for observation. It is changing, fluid, and evanescent, and for this reason it makes great technical demands upon the

ingenuity and energy of the scientist. But there is nothing essentially insoluble about the problems which arise from this fact. (p. 15)

In recent years effective procedures have been developed which facilitate the measurement of the behavior of young children and adults in applied settings. These procedures can be classified as either: (1) direct observation of behavior, of which five types will be described, or (2) measurement of permanent products.[1] To apply these behavior measurement procedures, the observer must proceed meticulously through the following sequence:

1. Clearly describe the target behavior in observable terms.
2. Identify the characteristics of the target behavior (i.e., its duration, frequency, etc.), and select the appropriate measurement procedure.
3. Select a clinical design which adequately tests the effect of the intervention on the behavior.
4. Specify the conditions for observation which will yield an accurate measurement (e.g., when, where, and for how long the behavior will be observed).
5. Construct a data recording form or specify the way data will be recorded.
6. Collect the data through observation.
7. Estimate the reliability of the measurement procedure.
8. Display the data graphically.

Clearly Describe the Behavior

Once a behavior is defined precisely, it may be measured. All observable behaviors can be quantified in some way by counting, timing, or some combined quantification method. When defining a behavior, the wording should be phrased so that the observable characteristics are specified. If defined precisely, two or more observers can agree on the occurrence or nonoccurrence of the behavior. Behavior is defined independently of a specific person. What constitutes an instance of the behavior for one child must constitute an instance for another child. In addition, a behavior may be present or absent regardless of when a person is observed. "The behavior or event being recorded should be described so specifically that *any* time *any* child displays the behavior, it can be easily determined

---

1. For further expansion of behavior measurement techniques, the reader is referred to Cooper (1974), Hall (1971), Hall, Hawkins, and Axelrod (1975), Hersen and Barlow (1976), and Kazdin (1975).

whether or not the behavior has occurred" (Cartwright & Cartwright, 1974, p. 52).

Behavioral definitions that are imprecise or nonobservable generally arise from the observer's interpretation of vague descriptors, nonfactual terms, or inner "causes." These definitions are not comprehensive enough to designate clearly an instance of the behavior. Often, when imprecise definitions are used, nonobservable human emotions (e.g., happily, fearful, likes) or values (e.g., honesty, creativity, industriousness, understanding) are the referents. Instead, specification of the outward behaviors—facial and postural muscles, vocalizations, etc.—which may be equated with the expression of emotions or values should be measured. Sometimes definitions do not refer to inner "causes," but are stated too generally or arbitrarily for an observer to judge accurately the occurrence or nonoccurrence of a behavior. For example, "creativity," "sharing," "hyperactive," and "off-task" without further specification are too vague to count or time. Goetz and Baer (1973) and Baer, Rowbury, and Goetz (1976), however, constructed a behavioral definition of "creative block building" which allowed both the objective measurement and the environmental manipulation of "creativity." Creativity was equated with the child's original block-building performance so that whenever a *novel* block arrangement (one not occuring in prior session) was built by a child, its *first* occurrence in a session (but no subsequent occurrences in that session) was regarded as a new block form. In this case, the arbitrariness of "creativity" was replaced by precise specification of an individual's movement and the resultant effect on the environment.

If education and psychology are to function as sciences, behavioral data must conform to certain rigorous constraints. As Bijou, Peterson, and Ault (1968) stated, "the primary data are the observable interactions between a biological organism and environmental events, past and present. These interrelationships constitute the material to be recorded" (p. 176). Definitional terms are functional guides for measurement only when they specify: (1) the observable action, activity, or movement which constitutes the behavior, and (2) the behavior's onset or beginning and its offset or ending. Additionally, the behavior identified for change must be discrete enough so it is repeatable, but not so discrete as to obviate measurement. The behavior "toilet trained" is too "large," and is better stated as specific portions of the chain of behaviors involved in toileting (e.g., approaches toilet, removes pants,

urinates in toilet, or wets pants). Conversely, targeting a set of behavior such as "says words" for a highly verbal individual will make measurement quite difficult. One may limit an expressive target to specific response classes such as pronouns or the use of appropriate greetings depending upon the individual's expressive skills and deficiencies. Table 2.1 provides further examples of precise definitions of target behaviors.

Identify the Behavioral Characteristics and the Measurement Procedure

If a teacher is able to identify the relevant aspects of the behavior under concern, selecting the method of observation is simplified. The six observation procedures summarized in Table 2.2 are expanded and detailed in the following sections.

Measurement of lasting products. Frequently, if the target behavior is academic or vocational, student performance results in a product (e.g., correctly set table place, objects matched to pictures, number of plastic dinnerware and napkin combinations properly packaged, etc.). This tangible evidence of performance may be measured more conveniently after the student has completed the task—an advantage over behavior observation techniques. Since teachers frequently measure lasting products such as worksheets as part of normal classroom routine, this method fits naturally into everyday procedure. However, the specific product or bit of tangible evidence still must be identified clearly. For example, when teaching the home-living skills of ironing, a piece-rate measurement—number of articles correctly ironed per unit of time—could serve as the measurement procedure. Daily piece-rate data would be essential to evaluate the instructional program for an individual who has acquired the skill of ironing, but is so meticulously slow that the skill is not functional. If worksheets are used to assess performance daily on a single skill such as addition facts or coin/value matching, items may be arranged conveniently on a page to facilitate scoring. As in Figure 2.6, there are an even number of responses per line, spaces at the top for totaling correct and incorrect rate scores, and, for longer worksheets, spaces could be added at the end of each row for partial scoring.

White and Haring (1976) suggest that a time limit be set for a worksheet probe. The individual should be allotted enough time to complete ten responses: the smallest sample of data worth collecting. The

TABLE 2.1   *A comparison of definitions of target behaviors*

Nonobservable Descriptions	Observable Descriptions
1. A rarely verbal child *speaks spontaneously*	1. "Incidences of speech were recorded whenever she uttered a word or words which were not preceded by a question or a prompt by a peer or a teacher." (Bijou, Peterson, & Ault, 1968, p. 180)
2. The child *jumps*	2. "The child jumps forward a distance of at least one foot, from a standing position, and lands on both feet without falling over." (Cartwright & Cartwright, 1974, p. 53)
3. The child *shares*	3. "If the child is playing with a toy and another child approaches and asks to use the toy, the child gives the toy to the other child without any negative verbal statements." (Cartwright & Cartwright, 1974, p. 53)
4. The child *attends*	4. "The child sits in a chair at a desk and looks in the direction of the teacher and/or in the direction of the educational activity." (Cooper, 1974, p. 50)
5. *Talking out*	5. "Talking out is defined as a vocalization, comment or vocal noise initiated by the student. It cannot be in response to the teacher or another peer. Each occurrence is tallied as one talk-out if it is separated from another by a breath, time interval or a change of topic." (Cooper, 1974, p. 27)
6. *Noisy* classroom behavior	6. Noisy is defined by the level of sound in a classroom which exceeds 70dB as measured by a hanging microphone located in the middle of the classroom eight feet from the floor. The microphone is attached to a voice-operated relay system, calibrated for accuracy by a sound-level meter, which in turn will activate a recording system to tabulate the frequency and duration of 'noisiness.' (Wilson & Hopkins, 1973)

student must always be given more problems than can be completed in the time period. The worksheet products would be measured in rate—number of correct and incorrect responses per minute. Another alternative, although sometimes more cumbersome for the teacher, is to assign a constant number of responses and let time vary. Correct and error rate measures still can be calculated although the division process may be less automatic.

One other advantage of permanent records is that error analyses are possible. A teacher can examine the products for patterns of errors to determine which teaching procedures should be selected.

Numerous behaviors result in lasting environmental changes. They may be measured as estimates of the behavior change: correctly labeled *Language Master* (1974) picture cards, pieces of litter, weight of dirty diapers per day, number of children with clean teeth, number of windows cleaned, desk cleaned, beads strung, or puzzles completed.

Measurement of direct behavior observations. Unfortunately, many behaviors do not result in tangible products and, therefore, are most difficult to measure. Off-task, on-task, out-of-seat, talking out, hitting, and verbalizing are examples of transitory behaviors which must be measured as they occur. Hall, Hawkins, and Axelrod (1975) also listed those critical variables which determine how one selects the method of behavior measurement: (1) the duration of the behavior, (2) its visibility, (3) the number of other behaviors being recorded simultaneously, (4) the level of measurement precision required, and (5) the time and attention available for measurement.

Continuous recording or anecdotal records require the observer to quickly and objectively write down everything as it occurs rather than focusing attention on a specific behavior. Although various methods for continuous recording exist (see, e.g., Bijou, Peterson, & Ault, 1968; Cartwright & Cartwright, 1974; Wright, 1960), Cooper (1974) lists four

TABLE 2.2 *A summary of various classroom evaluation measurement procedures*

Procedures for the Measurement of Behavior	Advantages	Disadvantages	Analysis of Behaviors Measured
I. Direct measurement of lasting products	1. Measurement is taken after behavior has occurred 2. Specification of a tangible behavior is easier 3. More easily used by students 4. Such measurement often part of regular classroom routine	1. Behavior must have a tangible result 2. Inaccurate measurement may occur for individual counts when others are producing similar products during period before measurement	Number of puzzles completed Number of places set correctly at a dinner table Number of buttons ripped from clothing
II. Observational recording a. Continuous	1. When interobserver agreement is high, measurement is the most accurate 2. Useful in obtaining a broad view of interactive behaviors 3. May be used to examine antecedent and consequent variables surrounding a target behavior	1. Necessitates continuous attention over long periods of time 2. Without careful delineation of behaviors, accuracy is threatened	Child's interactive play during a school day Adolescents aggressive responses towards others and the antecedents and consequences that exist during recess
b. Event or frequency	1. Useful with a wide variety of discrete classroom behaviors 2. Often part of the regular classroom routine 3. Often only paper and pencil are needed	1. Necessitates continuous attention during observation period 2. Yields less accurate results with very high rate behaviors and/or behaviors taking varying amounts of time 3. Inappropriate for long-duration behaviors	Talk-outs; hits; correct or incorrect responses; attendance; tattling; accurate ball throws; obscene gestures; hand raising
c. Duration	1. Yields precise record of a behavior's length of occurrence 2. May be used to record total duration of each incident of behavior as well as response latency	1. Necessitates continuous attention during observation period 2. For best accuracy requires a stop watch 3. Inappropriate for high-rate behaviors of short duration	Attending; completion of tasks (eating, dressing, cleaning); work production; sporting event

TABLE 2.2   *(Continued)*

Procedures for the Measurement of Behavior	Advantages	Disadvantages	Analysis of Behaviors Measured
d. Interval	1. Requires less effort than continuous event or duration procedures 2. Yields sufficiently precise duration *and* frequency data 3. Accuracy is facilitated by timers 4. Does not require definition of a precise unit of behavior 5. Applicable to a wide variety of behaviors	1. Difficult to use with less visible behaviors 2. Low-frequency behavior must be measured frequently or records are deceptive 3. Size of interval must be appropriate to behavior frequency	Any of the behaviors in I or II, b and c above
e. Time sampling	Same as advantages for interval measurement above and, in addition, the time intervals need not be constant	Same as disadvantages for interval measurement above	Any of the behaviors in I or II, b and c above

components generally included in all continuous recording methods. First, the time sequence for the observation is reported, whether it be in short units of time (e.g., 4:00–4:02, 4:05–4:07, etc.) or longer continuous time blocks (e.g., 4:00–5:00). Second, since specific behaviors to be modified later are usually unidentified at this point, the potential of this observation method to select problem behaviors is increased. The observer is dealing with a wide range of unexpected, spontaneous behaviors. Some will emerge as target behaviors. Third, continuous observation produces narrative data which should describe objectively (i.e., without the use of vague, judgmental terms) a chronological sequence of events. This sequence includes those environmental events which precede the student's response(s) and those events which follow the student's responses. Those which come before are termed antecedent; those which follow, consequences. Finally, the narrative observations must be easily read. Wright (1960) offers more detail on these and other directives of observation recording, their reliability, and specific applications in child studies.

If specific behaviors can be identified in advance, continuous observation procedures are generally inappropriate and another direct observational method will be more efficient. Continuous observation is advantageous when the relationship between antecedent and consequential variables is being studied to identify "possible environmental conditions that set the occasion for student responses" and "possible consequent events that maintain behaviors" (Cooper, 1974, p. 32).

Continuous observation schemes which analyze the ongoing behavior interactions as antecedent and consequential events allow the observer to appraise the extent to which certain environmental factors are eliciting and maintaining or not affecting various behaviors. The Antecedent-Behavior-Consequence (*ABC*) analysis, described earlier, is similar to these methods of continuous observation and is often cited as a necessary step to formulate a successful intervention strategy. However, the intensive, time-consuming quality of continuous observation procedures makes them less useful for teachers, unless classroom aides or parent volun-

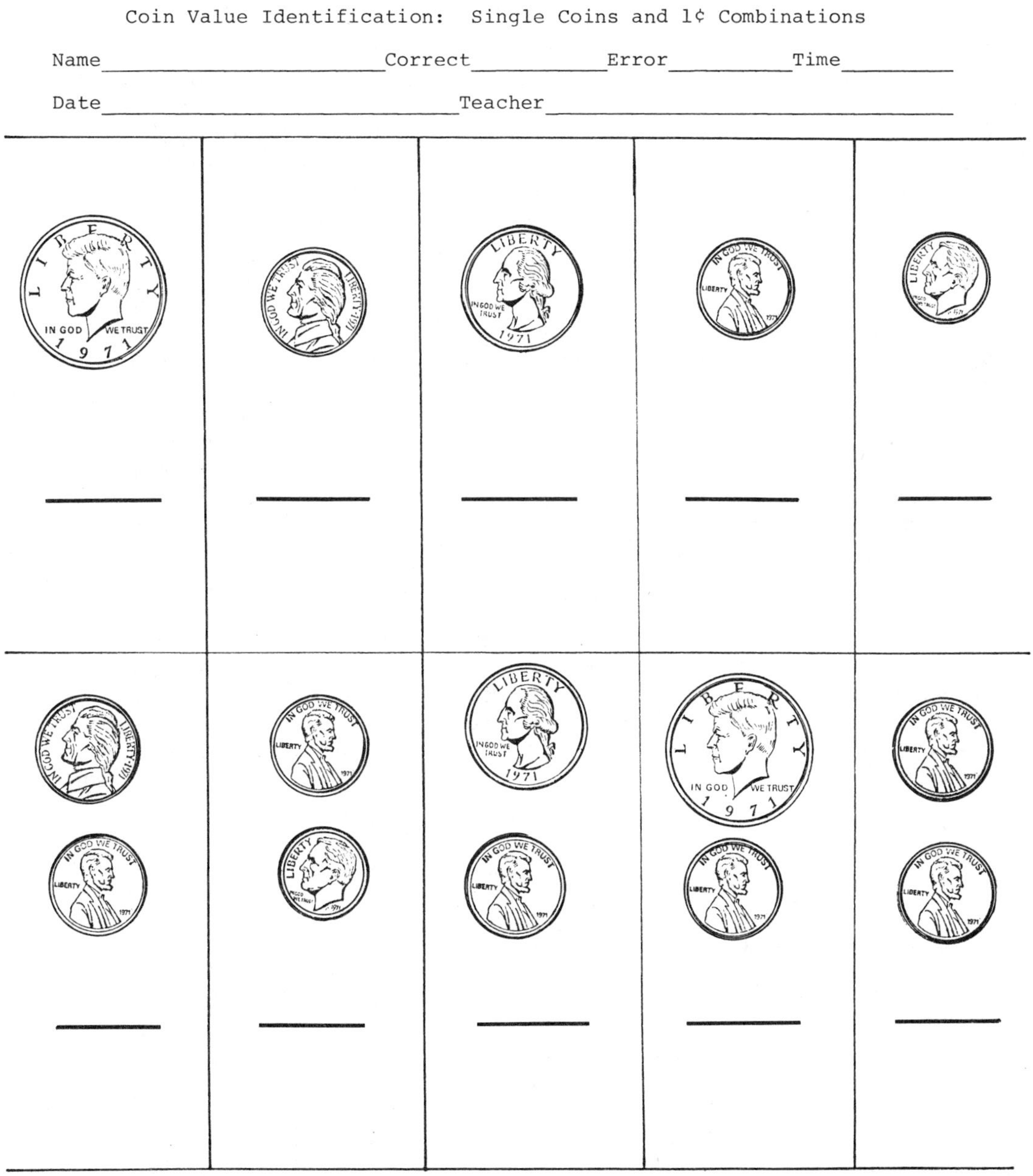

Coin Value Identification: Single Coins and 1¢ Combinations

Name_____Correct_____Error_____Time_____

Date_____Teacher_____

FIGURE 2.6   *Coin value worksheet*

teers are instructed to make objective observations during instructional periods or the teacher observes during recess, free play, or lunch time.

Event or frequency records allow a teacher to count, for a specified, constant period of time, the number of times a particular behavior occurs. Behaviors measured in this way must be those that can be readily divided into countable, discrete units and whose beginning and termination are not only easily visible but also uniform in length. Such behaviors may be described as inappropriate and occurring too often: talks during class discussion, pinches, hits, kicks, swears, uses color labels incorrectly, makes wrong responses in a picture recognition task, makes errors in a math fact flash-card game, is absent for an excessive number of days, etc.

Some behaviors may be appropriate but too infrequent and in need of acceleration: hand raising prior to speaking, incidents of toy sharing, quantities correctly counted, animals correctly identified, responses to "come here" commands, correct motor imitations, days present in school, etc. Since frequency provides a direct measure of the amount of behavior occurring, it is sensitive to changes produced by intervention programs.

When a behavior occurs at a very high rate or is ongoing and lasts for an extended period of time, a frequency recording procedure is generally inappropriate. In the first case, the probability of error is increased due to the difficulties in counting. However, if one substitutes the typical paper and pencil tally counts with the use of hand-held counters or wrist-worn golf counters (Lindsley, 1968), more accurate counting of these rapidly occurring behaviors is facilitated. For recording the frequency of multiple classes of behavior, multiple channel manual counters are useful (Cooper, 1974). Also with behaviors emitted at a high rate (self-stimulatory behaviors such as rocking, hand waving, and eye blinks are good examples) an easier recording procedure is one which totals duration or samples rate across time. These procedures—duration, interval, and time sampling recordings—are discussed in the following section.

When behaviors of long duration (e.g., out of seat for entire class periods) are measured by a frequency procedure, the numerical result is deceiving. These data, reported as frequency or as rate (number of behaviors per minute), will be in such small amounts that changes in the behavior will not be detected by the data. In such cases, duration is a more descriptive attribute of a behavior than rate or frequency.

If the opportunity for the behavior occurs only a fixed number of times per observation (e.g., the opportunity to brush one's teeth is made available only two times per day at school; the total number of correct sight words possible in a test list of 25 words is 25), then the frequency recording may be expressed as the percentage of behaviors observed out of the total possible (as illustrated in Figure 2.7) or as rate (number of behaviors per minute, hour, etc.). When the number of behaviors emitted is the variable (i.e., the observer is not able to predict the frequency ceiling or the maximum behaviors possible per unit of time), event records are reported by simple frequency (e.g., the total number of behaviors observed each day or 15-minute teaching session) or by rate of behaviors (number of behaviors per minute or hour). If simple frequency is used, however, time must be held constant. Strong argument (White & Haring, 1976) can be made for uni-

Date _APRIL 10-14, 1978_   Week 1 2 ③ 4 5 6 7 8

	hangs coat up	brushes teeth	recognize name-picture in circle	washes hands before lunch	cleans up after snack & lunch	completes job	total percentage completed
Anne	✓✓✓	✓ ✓	✓	✓	✓	✓	100
Bobby	✓	✓ ✓	✓	✓	✓	✓	70
Brenda	✓	✓ ✓	✓	✓	✓	✓	70
Joan	✓✓✓	✓ ✓	✓		✓	✓	90
Larry	✓✓	✓		✓	✓	✓	60
Lou	✓✓✓	✓ ✓	✓	✓	✓	✓	100
Mike	✓✓	✓ ✓		✓	✓	✓	90
Mary	✓✓✓	✓ ✓	✓	✓	✓	✓	100
Nancy	✓✓✓	✓	✓	✓	✓	✓	90
Ralph	✓✓	✓		✓		✓	50
Rosie	✓✓✓	✓		✓	✓	✓	80
Sally	✓✓✓	✓ ✓	✓	✓	✓	✓	100

FIGURE 2.7   *A sample record of behaviors with fixed frequency ceiling occurring during a single day without teacher reminder or physical assistance*

form charting of rate by the minute whether the resultant rate be a whole (5 min.) or a fractional number (0.5/min.—one every two minutes).

At times a teacher may need to record more than one behavior at a time. To do this the data-recording

Duration recording may be used by an observer interested in the length of time a particular behavior is performed by a student or a group of students. Response latency—the time taken for an individual to begin a response once the controlling stimuli are

	Free Play (20 min.)	Morning Recess (15 min.)	Afternoon Recess (30 min.)	Totals
Hitting	~~11111~~ 1	111	~~11111~~	14
Pushing	~~11111~~	~~11111~~ 11	~~11111~~ ~~11111~~	22
Pinching		11	11	4
Biting	11			2
Hair pulling			1	1

procedure is modified to allow separate, simultaneous tallying of each behavior. For instance, a teacher interested in the frequency of various aggressive behaviors by a child during recess and free play might use a form such as shown below.
For ease of recording, the higher frequency behaviors should be listed together.

Frequency measures must be taken for equal units of time which are long enough to obtain a representative sample of the behavior. If the observation time cannot be uniform, then frequency counts cannot be used to evaluate performance as they would not be comparable (e.g., the number of opportunities to perform in a one-minute period is not equatable with a 30-minute period). In these cases frequency must be converted into rate per standard unit of time. For example, if a child were observed to vocalize 15 times during a 10-minute observation and 60 times during a 30-minute observation, the vocalization rate per minute is calculated by simple division: number of behaviors observed/number of minutes observed. The resultant respective rates are 1.5 and 2 vocalizations per minute. However, with the severely handicapped, attention span and fatigue variables may make this "equation" practice unwise when the observation periods are widely discrepant (White & Haring, 1976).[2] Therefore, whenever possible observation periods should be of equal length.

---

2. The reader is referred to Cohen, Gentry, Hulten, and Martin (1972), White and Haring (1975), and White and Liberty (1976) for in-depth discussions of the use of rate recording and charting procedures with exceptional students.

presented—is also measured by duration. Duration measures have been used to measure length of time spent engaged in classroom assignments (Surratt, Ulrich, & Hawkins, 1969), cooperative play (Redd, 1969), thumbsucking (Kauffman & Scranton, 1974; Skiba, Pettigrew, & Alden, 1971), and social responses (Whitman, Mercurio, & Caponigri, 1970).

Duration is recorded by accumulating the number of seconds or minutes of behavior observed. For example, whenever a child initiates off-task behavior during a language lesson (i.e., looking away from teacher, teaching materials, or seatwork, or making inappropriate verbalizations unrelated to the task), a teacher could start an unobtrusively held stopwatch. As soon as the child re-establishes on-task behavior, the watch would be stopped, though not returned to zero. At each successive occurrence of off-task behavior the stopwatch would again be started and at each termination it would be stopped. At the end of the reading group session, the total time accumulated on the stopwatch would represent the total duration of off-task behavior during a single observation. However simple duration recording may sound, accuracy rests upon precise delineation of what constitutes the behavior's onset and its termination.

Duration of a behavior may be reported in terms of the total number of minutes or the percentage of time a behavior was engaged in during each observation. Percentage reporting is especially useful if the observation sessions vary in length, since the resulting percentages are roughly comparable to one another. The percentage of time a behavior occurs during a given observation is calculated by a simple percentage formula. If A equals the total

$$\frac{A}{B} \times 100 = X$$

amount of time a behavior occurs, and B equals the total length of observation, then X is the percentage of time behavior occurred during observation.

Duration records also may be kept when a teacher is interested in the amount of time a student takes to begin (response latency) or to complete a specific task for which no minimum or maximum time criterion has been set. For example, meal eating may range from five minutes to more than an hour, yet there still may be no time limitation set. A slow-eating child's baseline duration over 5 lunches, measured in minutes, could consist of the following lengths: 75 min., 50 min., 67 min., 43 min., 70 min. Behaviors for which no time criteria are set are reported in time units (seconds, minutes, etc.) since percentages are not meaningful without a maximum or minimum criterion.

Duration recording, as with event recording, requires the *complete* attention of the observer during each unit of observation. Duration records are most appropriate for behaviors which either have a high

or even rate or simply may be variable in their length from onset to end, making the frequency count a less meaningful measure. Time out-of-seat, for example, may vary in length from a few seconds to long periods of time. Although stopwatches facilitate more accurate duration measurements, wall clocks or wristwatches with second hands may be used as long as the observer is free to write down the duration of each occurrence of behavior. These separate occurrences are later totaled to yield a single duration for each unit of observation. Since interval measures are more adaptable to a variety of behaviors and are also time-based, they are often used in place of duration measures.

In *interval recording,* the observer divides the observation unit (2 minutes, 10 minutes, etc.) into equal time periods (5 seconds, 10 seconds, etc.) and notes for each smaller time period whether or not the behavior(s) under observation occurred. Regardless of the number of times a target behavior occurs during any single interval of time, only one tally is recorded for that observation unit. Interval recording allows the observer to capture both a measurement of the behavior's duration and of its frequency. As illustrated in Figure 2.8, more than

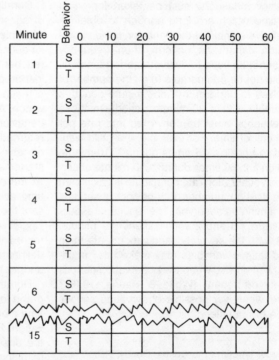

Out of Seat: Child's bottom is not in contact with the seat of the chair (S)

Talk-outs: Child does one or more of the following: (1) talking without raising hand, (2) making audible noises (such as animal calls) irrelevant to task, (3) talking or whispering to peers (T)

✓ : Behavior occurred at least once in an interval; if behavior does not occur the interval is left empty

FIGURE 2.8   *Interval recording form used to observe out-of-seat and talking out over 10-second intervals for 15 minutes*

one behavior may be observed simultaneously by adding additional rows of interval blocks. As with frequency and duration recording, the teacher's total attention must be directed toward the behavior during the entire observation period. In addition, the observer must have some method of timing each interval so as to move from one interval to the next at the appropriate time. Generally a watch or clock with a second hand is used to time the intervals. If available, a portable tape recorder with prerecorded interval counts and an ear plug attachment is less obtrusive although a timer with a light or sound flashing at regular intervals may also be used. For longer intervals (3 to 5 minutes) in both interval recording and time sampling, inexpensive egg timers, kitchen timers (with cotton taped around the bell to muffle the sound), and Memo-Timers (Foxx & Martin, 1971) have been used effectively.

According to Hall et al. (1975), an additional advantage of interval recording is that the observer need not "define or detect a precise unit of behavior" (p. 207).

If a teacher were interested in getting a withdrawn child to talk with peers, (s)he might wish to measure the amount of talking behavior without attending to the exact number of spoken words (or other response units). Anyone attempting such measurement in a child who interacts normally with peers can quickly appreciate the difficulties of detecting one response unit. Similarly, a teacher wishing to strengthen cooperative play (Hart, Reynolds, Baer, Brawley, & Harris, 1968) would find it difficult to define what constitutes one play response. Interval recording allows the observer to limit recording to simplify the presence of any amount of the behavior during the interval. (p. 207)

Interval recording may be applied to many behaviors—discrete, continuous, or sporadic—as long as the behavior can be classified as observed or not observed during any interval.

How long should an interval be? The answer to this depends on (1) the behavior being observed (its average length and frequency) and (2) the observer's ability to record and attend. In the first case, the more frequent the behaviors the smaller the interval for observation should be, so the observation may be an accurate measure of behavior frequency. For example, if the "talking out" of a disruptive child were measured in 30-minute intervals, a "+" tally in one interval would not begin to

reflect the behavior's density (i.e., did 35 talk-outs occur or did 3?). However, with infrequently occurring behavior, longer intervals are practical for classroom use but remain inadequate for experimental purposes. Also, the more obvious the behavior, the easier it is to record; behaviors that can be heard and seen (e.g., "talking out" versus attending to work) are more easily detectable. The reliability of classroom interval measurements is increased when the teacher has assistance, has good behavior management, observes during independent work periods, and/or observes more obvious behaviors, employs an unobtrusive interval timer, and selects smaller intervals (5 to 15 seconds).

A recent study (Repp, Roberts, Slack, Repp, & Berkler, 1976) compared the accuracy of observations taken by various interval procedures to frequency measures of the same behavior for the same time period. Low and medium rates of responding are accurately measured with 10-second intervals, but high-rate response patterns, either of a continuously high rate or with bursts of high rates, are grossly underestimated by interval measurements. They recommend that intervals less than 10 seconds or frequency procedures be used to measure behaviors exhibiting high response rates.

Behaviors may be defined in either a positive or a negative manner, depending on teacher preference (e.g., in-seat behavior, out-of-seat behavior). But, as noted by Hall et al. (1975), the results of measuring both positive and negative definitions are not the same:

Sometimes a teacher can ease the recording task by reversing the definition. For example, if a child is attentive to task 50 percent of the time and the teacher wishes to increase the attentiveness to 90 percent or more, the teacher would probably be wise to record the occurrence of inattentiveness. Thus, if the child looked away from his work at any time, the teacher would record the symbol for "yes, the behavior did occur." If the teacher were recording attentiveness, (s)he would have to record a "yes" in nearly every interval as the child successfully reached the goal. Of course, the results of using the two different definitions are not the same in interval recording. Whichever response constitutes a "yes" is inflated because even the briefest occurrence of the behavior causes a whole interval to be scored "yes." This procedure can give interval recording a certain practical (though not scientific) advantage over duration recording in that interval data can be more sensitive to changes in the behavior. A child who sucks his thumb for only 10 percent of the time may still have the behavior recorded in, say, 40 percent of the intervals, if he usually sucks his thumb for brief periods. A 50 percent reduction in the total duration of the behavior will show exactly that reduction if duration recording is used; if interval recording is used, a larger reduction will be evidenced by the data. The discrepancy results from the fact that interval data are affected by both duration and frequency of behavior. (p. 208)

When deciding whether to define behaviors in positive or negative terms for interval recording, the teacher is advised to measure the behavior which is or will become least frequent but to remain aware that changes in the interval data may be inflated over actual change due to the double effect of the behavior's duration and frequency upon interval measurement.

Momentary time sampling, another type of interval measurement, has many of the advantages of time interval recording plus an additional convenience feature with little or no reduction in accuracy (Hall et al., 1975). As in interval recording, the observer divides the observation unit into equal intervals, but the behavior is observed and recorded only at the *end* of each interval rather than continuously.

For recording purposes, it does not matter what the child does a few seconds before or after the samples; only the momentary state of the behavior at the predetermined time of the sample is measured. The procedure is analogous to taking a snapshot of the subject, that is, to capturing the subject's behavior at a given moment in time. As a result, the observer need watch the subject only at particular moments, an important advantage if the teacher is the observer. (Hall et al., 1975, p. 210)

Time samples need not be taken at regular intervals. Hall et al. (1975) suggest that after determining the number of samples to be taken during each observation session, a teacher may set a timer randomly, record the student's behavior immediately upon hearing the timer, reset the timer, and repeat this process during the observation for the predetermined number of times.

An alternate type of time sampling is reported by Quilitch and Risley (1973) in which a teacher could assess participation of an entire class in an activity. Placheck (Planned Activity Check) requires that the teacher carry out a series of three steps:

1. Define the planned activity or behaviors (e.g., on-task during math period, engaged in aggressive behavior, etc.) the teacher wants to measure in a group;
2. At given intervals (e.g., 5 minutes, 10 minutes, etc.), the teacher counts and records how many students are engaged in the activity;
3. Then the teacher immediately counts and records the total number of students present in the area of the activity.

The total number engaged in the planned activity is divided by the total number present and multiplied by 100 which yields the percentage of the group engaging in the defined behavior during the sampled interval. When used with longer activities, it is best to sample once in the middle or at equally spaced points (beginning, middle, and end of activity). If attending or on-task behavior is observed, the latter procedure will provide a rough indication of a group's length of interest for a particular activity.

For classroom data collection, momentary time sampling is generally an efficient observation procedure although not so accurate as continuous interval observation or frequency observations. Because it does not require continuous observation, time sampling is more easily used by a teacher than interval or duration recording. One difficulty arises when using time sampling to measure low-frequency or short-duration behavior—the results of an observation may indicate that the behavior never occurred only because the observation samples were too infrequent. With both low-frequency and short-duration behavior, the intervals must be sufficient to guarantee enough observation samples so an adequate measure of the behavior is obtained.

Continuous interval and time-sampling interval records have a number of advantageous features in common. Besides being appropriate to observe a wide variety of behaviors in individuals (discrete, continuous, or separate), interval measures may be employed to observe one or multiple behaviors across a group of individuals. This is done very effectively by sequentially rotating the brief interval observation across each member of the group until all have been observed, and repeating this sequence until the observation period is completed (Thomson, Holmberg, & Baer, 1974). The simple recording illustrated in Figure 2.9 may be adapted to fit differing numbers of individuals, intervals, and behaviors. For example, when recording data for a group of students, the observer records from the top to the bottom of the page observing each sub-

FIVE-SECOND INTERVALS

				✓	✓							
Robby 2✓ 50%	⊕–	⊕–	+⊖	+⊖	+⊖	+⊖	+⊖	+⊖	⊕–	⊕–	⊕–	⊕–
Jack 2✓ 0%	+⊖	+⊖✓	+⊖	+⊖	+⊖	+⊖✓	+⊖	+⊖	+⊖	+⊖	+⊖	+⊖
Diana 3✓ 25%	+⊖	⊕–	⊕–✓	+⊖	+⊖	+⊖✓	+⊖✓	+⊖	+⊖	⊕–	+⊖	+⊖
Andy 3✓ 33%	⊕–✓	+⊖	+⊖	+⊖	+⊖	+⊖	+⊖	+⊖✓	+⊖	+⊖	⊕–	+⊖✓

FIGURE 2.9   *Interval data recording form*

Each child was observed for one 5-second interval beginning with child 1 and moving to child 2, 3, and 4 every 5 seconds for a total observation of one minute each. Observations were made during a 15-minute language instructional period which focused upon the expression of agent-action and action-object phrases. Two behaviors were observed during each interval:

1. Inattention: occurred when child was not looking at the teacher, a responding peer in the group, or any instructional materials; if the child was out of seat, she/he also had to be engaged in one of the above "looking away" behaviors.
2. Approximate or correct responses (errors and no responses were not recorded).

If *inattention* was observed, a "plus" was circled; a circle around the minus indicated the child did not engage in any inattentive behavior during that 5-second interval. If the child made a correct or approximate response to a request or question asked by the teacher during an observed interval, a check mark ($\sqrt{}$) was made in that interval. For example, Robby was observed to engage in inattentive behavior 50% of the intervals and made 2 correct or approximate responses. Note that his attentiveness, represented by an absence of inattentive behavior (⊖), increased during and immediately after being called on. The teacher was attempting to use her attention to reinforce child attentiveness.

ject for the first interval, then uses the second column of intervals, and so on. The appropriate symbol is recorded in each interval depending upon whether the behavior occurred (1) anytime during the interval (for regular interval recording) or (2) during the end of the interval (for time sampling interval recording). Multiple coded symbols may appear in each interval box to represent different behaviors.

An additional advantage of both interval methods concerns the convenient conversion of interval data into percentages prior to graphing. Interval percentages are calculated simply by dividing the total number of intervals observed and multiplying by 100. When data are reported as "the percentage of intervals an individual engaged in a particular behavior," they are easier to understand.

Teaching designs

Once the type of measurement system is selected, the design must be determined. A brief discussion of the various kinds of designs available to researchers was provided earlier in this chapter. Although there is similarity between the designs used by researchers and those recommended for use by teachers or clinicians, there are some critical differences because of the inherent divergence in roles of practitioners and researchers.

Researchers must determine the functional relationship between specific behaviors and intervention strategies. This is an important function, for it is only through researchers' careful and meticulous efforts that practitioners will have the basic knowledge necessary to select the most efficient and effective teaching strategies for their students. For researchers to provide this information to teachers and clinicians with any certainty, they must control the environment carefully and systematically and consistently apply the procedure(s); insure the reliability of measurement; and determine the functional relationship of the treatment and behavior in question. Such stringent attention to details is not the role of the practitioner.

The role of the practitioner is to teach individuals new skills and help them maintain proficient levels of performance of skills already mastered. Their responsibility is to schedule interventions in accord with their students' performance and to evaluate the effectiveness of their teaching strategies. They need not, however, employ methods in the same rigorous manner as the researcher. Several "teaching" designs are available which facilitate the evaluation of consistent instructional techniques. They are all variations of and have their origins in the research designs already discussed.

Modified reversal design. One teaching design which is particularly effective and useful was displayed in Figure 2.2. Here, after a baseline or assessment period, an intervention strategy is implemented. If the target behavior changes in the desired direction and criterion is met, the intervention should be withdrawn to determine if the learner can perform the task without the aid of the intervention. This is the maintenance period. If the learner again demonstrates mastery of the task, daily sessions may be terminated, but the target behavior should still be monitored periodically in a posttest situation to insure that mastery is retained across time. Since experimental control is not obtained in this situation and the validation of the influence of a specific instructional tactic cannot be achieved, this design is not fruitful for researchers unless the direct replication feature is added. For teachers, however, the modified reversal design (without direct replication) is functional because it monitors student performance across the assessment, learning, maintenance, and posttest situations.

Often the first intervention strategy selected does not change the target behavior in the desired direction or does not produce a sufficient magnitude of change. In this case, another intervention strategy should be added to or substituted for the first. Our recommendation is to predetermine criteria for changing from one condition to the next. When using either the modified reversal or multiple baseline designs (described next), our experience indicates that only one or two days is not long enough to determine the influence of an intervention. However, it is not advisable to allow a student to remain in an intervention condition beyond what is efficient or effective. We feel that this decision can be made after collecting data on the behavior for five to seven days. Nevertheless, it is beneficial to have some idea of when an intervention shall be discontinued and another scheduled.

Regardless of the teaching design employed, it is also helpful to have some preconception of what scores need to be made by the learner for mastery to be achieved. This will help the teacher determine when to change conditions: either to schedule another intervention or to discontinue instruction. Many teachers believe that three consecutive days of 100% performance should be noted before a student moves to a maintenance phase. This, however, is too stringent for some learners on certain tasks and efficient teaching can not occur because the teacher is waiting too long for mastery before moving on to another skill. Once again, it is for the teacher to determine when enough is enough.

Multiple baseline designs. An example of a multiple baseline design was provided in Figure 2.3. This design is the one which is most applicable to both the teaching and research situation. Measurement across phases is conducted in one of three ways: one person's performance on one behavior in several settings; one person's performance on several types of behaviors or response classes; several peoples' performance on the same task or behavior. The major characteristic of this design is that the baseline or assessment phases are initiated concurrently (on the same day), but the intervention is scheduled at different times staggered across several days or even weeks.

Changing criterion design. This design originally described by Wolf et al. (1964) and discussed in some detail by Kazdin (1975) and Hartmann and Hall (1976) is comprised of three general phases: baseline, changing-criterion, and follow-up. After a traditional baseline or assessment period, an intervention (usually a contingency) is scheduled. In the beginning of the intervention condition, a minimal amount of behavior change is required. Gradually, however, during the course of this condition, closer and closer approximations of the target behavior or attainment of the aim score is demanded of the subject. This design (see Figure 2.10) is particularly appropriate when shaping procedures are used during the intervention period.

Behavioral chaining design. The data obtained using another kind of teaching design is displayed in Figure 2.11. This teaching design is necessitated when the material presented to the learner is programmed or is part of a larger sequence. For example, when teaching shoe tying, many discrete skills need to be mastered. It is not efficient to institute a maintenance condition for each skill in the sequence, because repeated practice of that skill occurs as the rest of the steps of the larger task are taught. In these cases, a mastery checklist is suitable to monitor a student's progress through a predetermined instructional sequence.

Generalization design. This design is used only in teaching situations; therefore, no published example is available. (A fabricated example is provided in Figure 2.12.) When several skills are subskills or subsets of a larger skill, this design might be appropriate. During the baseline condition, performance on the large or major skill is assessed. During succeeding conditions, isolated component skills are taught and mastered. In computational arithmetic,

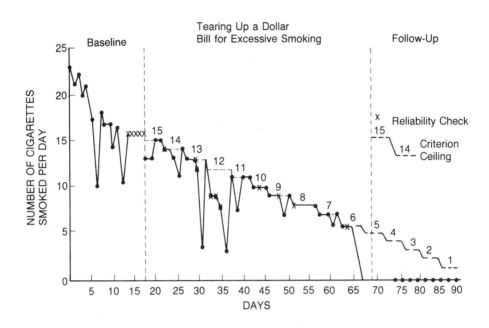

FIGURE 2.10   *An example of the changing-criterion design*

Source: S. Axelrod, R. V. Hall, L. Weis, & S. Rohrer. Use of self-imposed contingencies to reduce the frequency of smoking behavior. In M. J. Mahoney & C. E. Thoresen (Eds.). *Self-control: Power to the Person*. Copyright © 1974 by Wadsworth Publishing Company, Inc. Reprinted by permission of the publisher, Brooks/Cole Publishing Company, Monterey, California.

for example, the last skill in an operation would be assessed first during baseline, then the first subskill in the sequence is taught. Once that component skill is mastered, the final skill is probed. If generalization to the target skill did not occur, the next subskill in the sequence is taught. This process is continued until mastery of the target skill is achieved. If, for instance, the large or major skill to be taught is borrowing or regrouping in subtraction, problems requiring the borrowing process in three columns might be presented to the student during baseline. During the first intervention condition, only problems requiring borrowing in the units column are taught. After mastery is noted for these problems, the remaining response classes are presented in isolation, progressively.

Recommendations. Regardless of the type of clinical design employed, there are several recommendations which we would like to make. First, data collection procedures need to be simple so that many data collectors can be used: teachers, aides, volunteers, or students. Secondly, a period of baseline assessment must be scheduled before the intervention is scheduled. In this way, the teacher may determine whether the student needs direct

instruction on the target task and may begin to identify which type of strategy is the best for the first attempts. Third, an intervention procedure should be selected and consistently applied on a daily basis. Performance must be evaluated after a period of time to determine whether mastery will be achieved soon or another kind of intervention will be required. After this, the student's behavior should be monitored periodically to check for retention of mastery.

Reliability checks in teaching

Probably the most obvious difference between research and teaching designs lies with the issue of reliability. As stated earlier, reliability is a required component for research projects. Typically, this necessitates extra personnel trained in data collection and analysis. Usually such personnel are not available to clinicians or teachers, whose energies need to be directed entirely to remediation activities. Therefore, although desirable for all projects, the frequency of reliability checks by teachers certainly can be reduced; in many instances, they might even be eliminated. But, because it is still important for the clinician to be assured that student behavior is

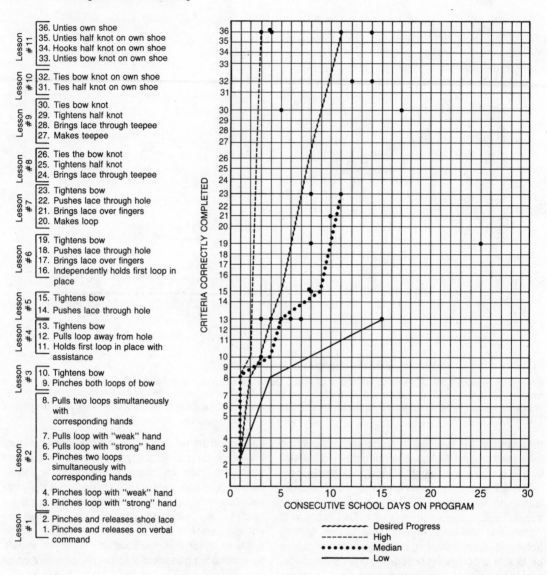

Lesson #11	36. Unties own shoe
	35. Unties half knot on own shoe
	34. Hooks half knot on own shoe
	33. Unties bow knot on own shoe

| Lesson #10 | 32. Ties bow knot on own shoe |
| | 31. Ties half knot on own shoe |

Lesson #9	30. Ties bow knot
	29. Tightens half knot
	28. Brings lace through teepee
	27. Makes teepee

Lesson #8	26. Ties the bow knot
	25. Tightens half knot
	24. Brings lace through teepee

Lesson #7	23. Tightens bow
	22. Pushes lace through hole
	21. Brings lace over fingers
	20. Makes loop

Lesson #6	19. Tightens bow
	18. Pushes lace through hole
	17. Brings lace over fingers
	16. Independently holds first loop in place

| Lesson #5 | 15. Tightens bow |
| | 14. Pushes lace through hole |

Lesson #4	13. Tightens bow
	12. Pulls loop away from hole
	11. Holds first loop in place with assistance

| Lesson #3 | 10. Tightens bow |
| | 9. Pinches both loops of bow |

| | 8. Pulls two loops simultaneously with corresponding hands |

Lesson #2	7. Pulls loop with "weak" hand
	6. Pulls loop with "strong" hand
	5. Pinches two loops simultaneously with corresponding hands

| | 4. Pinches loop with "weak" hand |
| | 3. Pinches loop with "strong" hand |

| Lesson #1 | 2. Pinches and releases shoe lace |
| | 1. Pinches and releases on verbal command |

Desired Progress
High
Median
Low

FIGURE 2.11   *An example of the graph used to record mastery of those steps which comprise the skill of shoe tying*

Source: E. Edgar, J. Maser, D. D. Smith, & N. G. Haring. Educational materials. *Education and training of the mentally retarded*, 1977, *12*, Feb. 1977.

being measured accurately, some reliability checks are recommended.

When reliability measures are taken, it is important that the "outside observer" not be an active participant in the project. One important reason for teachers to obtain reliability statements is to insure that behavior changes noted actually occurred. Often, when working daily with students, one becomes accustomed to unusual behavior patterns and the data recorded do not reflect the actual occurrence and topography of the target behavior. In addition, others working with such students may also experience this change in behavior expectancy. Therefore, another teacher or aide (rather than the usual classroom personnel) might well be the best reliability checker to select. An experience of one of the authors might serve as an example in point. Upon arrival of a new student, all of the classroom personnel noted the severe articulation difficulties this youngster presented. In fact, none of us could understand anything this child said to us. After a month or so in our class, we all commented on how much this child's language improved and were delighted by his progress. Soon after, a visitor came to our class to observe. The first comment made was in regard to one of our student's poor language abilities and his unintelligibility. It was at that point that we realized that it was our behavior (auditory reception) that was modified—not the child's.

One method for determining reliability of measurement is to obtain the percentage of agreement for two observers. In this case a fraction is made by using the smaller frequency of observations as the numerator and the larger score as the denominator. A percentage of agreement is then obtained by multiplying by 100. Basically, the following is the formula used to arrive at this reliability statement:

$$\frac{\text{smaller frequency}}{\text{larger frequency}} \times 100 = \frac{\text{percentage}}{\text{of agreement}}$$

If duration data are taken, merely dividing the larger duration score into the smaller and multiplying by 100 suffices. Reliability scores obtained in this manner must, however, be viewed with some caution, for only total frequency scores of two observers are considered and not the specific instances of the occurrence of the target behavior. As was noted by Kazdin (1975), a "percentage of agreement" of 90% between two observers:

. . . indicates that observers agree on the total frequency of the behavior with a 10% (100% minus 90%) margin of error. It does not mean that the observers agree 90% of the time. Although one observer recorded 18 responses and the other recorded 20 responses, there is no way of knowing whether they recorded the same responses. For example, if both observers each recorded 18 responses, the percent of agreement would be 100%. Yet one observer may have seen 18 responses that were different from the 18 responses seen by the other observer. Although this is unlikely, it is possible that at least some of the responses recorded may not have been for the same behaviors. Thus, reliability reflects agreement on the total number of responses rather than agreement in any specific instance. A potential disadvantage in using a frequency measure is that when the behavior is not carefully defined, a high percentage of agreement for frequency data may still conceal a substantial amount of disagreement. (p. 80)

When interval recordings are used, a different formula for reliability is required. If A equals the number of intervals of agreement, and B equals the number of intervals of agreements and disagreements, then X is the percentage of agreement.

$$\frac{A}{B} \times 100 = X$$

In this instance, the number of intervals in which both observers noted the occurrence of a behavior is used as the numerator and that number plus all those instances in which only one person recorded the behavior (disagreements) serve as the denominator. However, if the behavior occurred but neither observer recorded it, it is not indicated as an error in data collection.

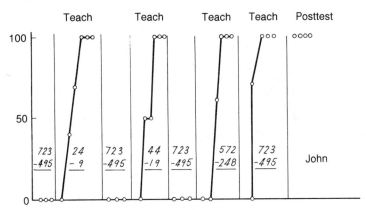

FIGURE 2.12   *A fabricated example of the generalization design*

This example shows one child's performance on a series of related arithmetic problems.

At what point should data be considered unreliable? There is not a standard answer to this question. In part, the type of measurement and kind of target behavior must be considered. Data obtained from permanent products should be 100% accurate; when agreement for counting permanent products is less than 100%, the products simply may be recounted and the data changed to represent accurate scoring. If data are gathered from observations, 100% agreement is rarely achieved. Lower percentage of agreement scores indicate a need to increase the number of reliability checks. Usually 80% is considered the minimal amount of reliability acceptable (Kazdin, 1975). In clinical settings, however, the purpose of the data collection should be considered when establishing what reliability score must be achieved.

Specify the Conditions for Observation

In addition to selecting the appropriate measurement procedure, the teacher must identify when and where measurement will be conducted. Generally, the time and place of measurement is determined by two factors: when inappropriate behavior is disruptive, and where it occurs. Whenever target behavior is observed prior to and during the implementation of intervention, the time and location for observing remain constant. Only when such consistency occurs can a teacher draw conclusions about the influence of the intervention procedure.

Some low-frequency behaviors occur only during specific activities (e.g., sloppy eating during snack at a classroom table and during lunch time in the cafeteria). Observation and modification strategies need to be implemented only at the times and in the settings where the behavior occurs. If observation is easier at one time than another, a teacher may decide to limit baseline and intervention to that setting. Multiple baselines, described earlier in this chapter, are particularly useful for those behaviors which occur in several settings because they allow the teacher to measure the effectiveness of an intervention systematically across settings.

For behaviors occurring frequently throughout the day, a teacher should select times and places for observation which meet a combination of requirements:

1. When and where the behavior or its absence is most troublesome;
2. When and where the teacher or aide is able to observe and record the behavior;
3. When and where it will be possible to implement intervention procedures.

The first consideration may be best decided after observing the behavior over several periods scattered across the whole day and determining whether performance varies during the day. Whenever possible, observations should be made at various times during the day so the data more accurately reflect the behavior.

Next, the teacher must examine two related questions: "How frequently should data be collected and how long should each observation period extend?" As a general guideline, behaviors should be observed as often as possible: daily or every other day. The length of each observation must be determined by the behavior's frequency and topography. To obtain an adequate representation of low-frequency behaviors, longer observation periods are required (e.g., one hour), while shorter periods (10–15 minutes) are sufficient for higher frequency behaviors.

Baseline or pre-intervention observations must be sufficient in number to represent an accurate picture of the behavior. For example, since a child's aggressiveness may fluctuate after weekends or vacations, the baseline measurement of behavior should extend beyond these atypical days. Cooper (1974) suggests that at least five measurement sessions occur before intervention is implemented. (Baseline stability and its effect upon the decision to intervene is discussed in the section concerning data display and analysis.) If the data collected are relatively stable and the individual scores are not discrepant, then baseline measurement may stop and intervention procedures begin. The data may show either a descending or ascending tendency and be considered stable. Stability is achieved when the scores are predictable. When an unstable baseline trend occurs which is in the same direction as the aim of the intervention (e.g., a disruptive behavior begins to decrease), it is best to withhold the intervention until stability is achieved (Hall, 1971). Without relative baseline stability, it is difficult to evaluate the actual effect of the intervention procedures. Hall (1971) described two variations in this general rule: intervention procedures may be initiated if the baseline of a *desirable* behavior is *descending* or if the baseline of an *undesirable* behavior is *ascending*. If the behavior under consideration is dangerously self-destructive or destructive to others, the period of baseline observation must be shortened considerably. This may be done by taking a series of measurements over a single morning and afternoon.

Construct a Data Recording Form

Data recording forms must be constructed to conform to the constraints set by:

1. The measurement procedure selected (e.g., permanent products, interval, frequency, etc.);
2. The number of individuals observed: sufficient space should be allowed so data for each individual are clearly separated and identifiable as in Figure 2.9;

3. The number of behaviors observed: intervals or observation periods (as with frequency and duration) need to be subdivided and coded so tallies or times recorded are identified with the behavior they measure as illustrated in Figure 2.10 and on page 43;

4. The length of each observation period: when frequency measures are used, enough space must be allowed for slash marks—more space for the

	DATE	RATE		TIME	NUMBER		%
	D M Y	Cor.	Error		Cor.	Error	CORRECT
M							
T							
W							
T							
F							
M							
T							
W							
T							
F							
M							
T							
W							
T							
F							
M							
T							
W							
T							
F							
M							
T							
W							
T							
F							
M							
T							
W							
T							
F							

(student / behavior / class / page)

FIGURE 2.13   *A sample data sheet used to compile and summarize one child's scores on a classroom activity*

more frequent behavior; when worksheets are the permanent product records as on the coin worksheet shown in Figure 2.6, or whenever a set number of tasks are supplied for the individual to perform, there must be *more* opportunities to perform than time allowed in the observation period so performance rate can show growth.

It is recommended that a rough draft of the data collection form be field tested, modified, and converted to a ditto master for easy reproduction since its repeated use will be necessary before, during, and following the intervention. Data forms may be constructed so several days' observation can be recorded on one form. This is particularly useful when measuring duration or permanent products. For example, when the permanent products are an individual's responses on worksheets testing a single skill, it is more convenient to record the daily data (correct and error rates) on a summary record sheet. In this way, a semester's worth of raw data can be summarized efficiently and a semester of worksheets need not be retained.

Every data form, regardless of the measurement procedure used, should include space for basic information: name of individual(s) observed; observer's name, date, time, and place of observation; length of each observation period; behavior(s) observed (with brief definition); room for data totals and/or percentages; and perhaps space for comment. A sample data sheet is shown in Figure 2.13.

Collect the Data

Accurate data are collected when the observer is both unobtrusive and consistent. The observer should be familiar with the situation and the individual being observed—otherwise, the individual's performance pattern may change merely as a result of the observation. The purpose of data collection is to measure the influence of an intervention strategy on a behavior. The observer must be careful not to confound the results by the measurement process. Occasionally, prebaseline observations are recommended. They serve two purposes: to "desensitize" the individual to the observation procedure and to familiarize the observer with the measurement methods (Balthazar, 1971).

Sometimes the observer can both collect data and interact with the individual who is the target of the remediation program. At other times, however, the observer should be a passive bystander. Regardless of the type of situation, the place, time,

teaching materials, and basic teaching methods must be held constant during any given phase of the program (i.e., baseline, intervention, changes in the intervention—intervention 1, 2, etc.; follow-up; reversal; etc.).

Display and Analyze the Data

Changes in a behavior's duration, frequency, and rate becomes much more visible when recorded as a graph. This is true for most individuals using the data: teachers, administrators, aides, parents, and even students whose behavior is being graphed. Basic behavior charts are simple, equal interval graphs on which days of the week or session number are plotted along the horizontal line or the *abscissa*. The scores or behavior measurement totals stated in percentage, duration, rate per minute, or frequency are plotted in equal intervals along the vertical line or the *ordinate*.

As illustrated in Figure 2.1, both the horizontal and the vertical axes are labeled before the data are plotted. Along the horizontal axis, it is valuable to label the days consecutively and include weekends and holidays rather than only allowing space for observation sessions (White and Haring, 1976). Although this procedure lengthens the graph, it allows for more accurate interpretation of changes which may occur because of lapses in the instructional program. In this way student performance which deteriorates after weekends or holidays will become apparent. The vertical axis must be divided into units which allow measurement of the entire range of behaviors possible, from zero (frequency, rate, duration, or percentage) to the highest possible score (e.g., 100%). This range extends from the behavior's baseline level or below to somewhat beyond the targeted level. Space should be allowed for extreme variability in the data. Depending on whether the behavior needs to be increased or decreased, the targeted level in the first case will be *above* and in the second case *below* the baseline level.

Data points for each phase of a program are connected by straight lines. However, plots are not connected *across* phase changes (baseline, intervention 1, intervention 2, etc.), weekends, or days absent within each program phase. Each phase is identified concisely across the top of the graph (e.g., instructions, modeling, feedback, praise, etc.), and vertical lines are drawn to separate the different treatment or program phases. If more than one behavior (or if the same behavior, in more than one individual) is being measured simultaneously in the same units (percentages, seconds, etc.), these may be plotted on a single graph. Color-coded lines or different-shaped data points may be drawn to indicate the various behaviors or individuals. For example, correct and error rates are usually plotted on the same graph.

When measurements of behavior are graphed in the manner just described, some general rules of data interpretation may be stated:[3]

1. An upward slope indicates an increase or an acceleration in the behavior.
2. A downward slope indicates a decrease or a deceleration in the behavior.
3. A flat or horizontal line indicates no measurable change but a maintenance of the behavior at the same level as the measurements just preceding.
4. The degree of the slope (upward or downward) is an indication of the speed with which the behavior is changing.

If the data collected are relatively stable and the individual scores are not discrepant, then baseline measurement may stop and intervention procedures begin. The data may show either a descending or ascending trend and be considered stable. Stability is achieved when the scores are predictable. When a baseline trend occurs which is in the same direction as the aim of the intervention (e.g., a disruptive behavior begins to decrease), it is best to withhold the intervention until an opposite trend or a leveling of data is recorded (Hall, 1971). Without relative baseline stability, it is difficult to evaluate the actual effect of the intervention procedures. Hall (1971) describes an exception to this:

> *Experimental procedures can sometimes be started when a baseline is ascending, if the intent is to* decrease *the strength of the behavior, or conversely, to begin experimental procedures when a baseline is descending, if the intent is to* increase *the strength of the behavior. This is often done in cases where it is desirable to reverse the trend of the behavior—for example, when a child is hitting his peers at an obviously increasing rate and the desire is to decrease the hitting behavior as quickly as possible. (p. 14) If the behavior under consideration is dangerously self-destructive or destructive to others, the period of*

baseline observation must be shortened considerably. This may be done by taking a series of measurements over a single morning and afternoon.

The data shown in Figure 2.14 are graphed cumulatively; that is, the value of each behavior measurement is added to the sum of the data points preceding that entry. With cumulative graphs, slope is interpreted somewhat differently. Increases in behavior are still represented by upward slopes but decreases in behavior are shown by a reduction in the upward slope or a "flattening" of the curve. Horizontal lines represent no change. Again, response rate is read as the slope of the line. Often this type of record is made automatically by the use of electro-mechanical equipment. Because cumulative graphs are difficult for the naive user to interpret readily, they are not used commonly for classroom data.

Another type of graph, the ratio chart or standardized semilogarithmic grid, is pictured in Figure 2.15. It is used to present daily rate data stated in movements or behaviors per minute. Although ratio charts may appear somewhat confusing, they are quickly mastered and possess numerous advantages over the interval charts already described in this section (White & Haring, 1976). Ratio charts tend to offer greater precision and flexibility in recording the rate changes of a wide range of behaviors from very slow (0.01 behaviors per minute) to very fast (1000 behaviors per minute).

A behavior chaining or task analysis graph is pictured in Figure 2.11. This is an interval graph on which the teaching steps are listed in sequence from the bottom to to the top of the axis. A frequency measurement procedure is used to collect data. As each step in the chain is performed independently, data points are entered at various heights on the graphs on the appropriate dayline. Such a graph allows specific interpretation of an individual's gains and losses and provides teachers with feedback on the adequacy of their task analysis.

Good instruction occurs when the target behavior is identified precisely, intervention strategies are matched to the target behavior and its entry level, and the influence of the intervention technique is evaluated by means of daily measurement procedures. Teaching plans must be developed from knowledge about the target behavior and the learner so efficient learning will result. Often, although specifiable, the target behavior is too

---

3. For more detail on this and related graphing procedures, the reader is encouraged to pursue Cooper (1974), Hall (1971), and White and Haring (1976).

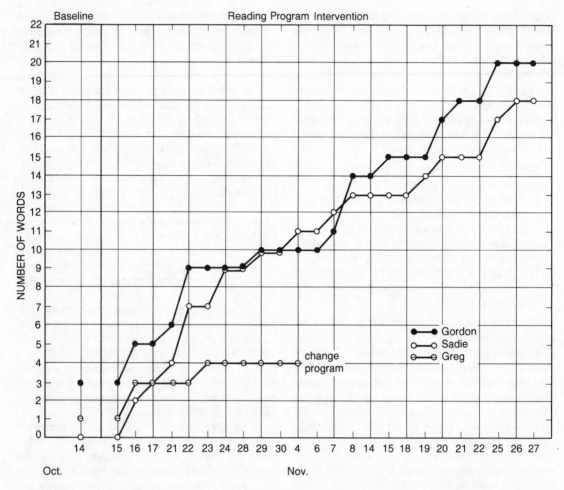

FIGURE 2.14   *Cumulative record of correct responses to "protective" words by three moderately re-*
tarded adults

Daily word tests were given each student before every instructional session.

"large" (as in the example provided in Figure 2.17). In these instances, the target must be submitted to further analysis of the type discussed in the next section.

Task Analyses

Teachers of moderately and severely handicapped youngsters are charged with the responsibility of teaching their students how to perform very specific tasks. Unfortunately, because of the low prevalence of those with severe learning disorders, commercially prepared materials and instructional sequences are not sufficiently available to facilitate the accomplishment of the vast number of skills

which need to be taught (Bender & Valletutti, 1976; Bender, Valletutti, & Bender, 1976a, 1976b; Brown & York, 1974). The more severely handicapped the student, the fewer appropriate instructional programs available. This situation necessitates that teachers of moderately and severely handicapped learners possess more skills in the area of instructional programming than their general education counterparts.

Typically, teachers of the handicapped must systematically teach their students skills which other children learn incidentally or in the home situation. For example, most children come to school possessing many self-help skills like dressing and toileting. This often is not the case for the more handicapped learner. Also, many children learn to

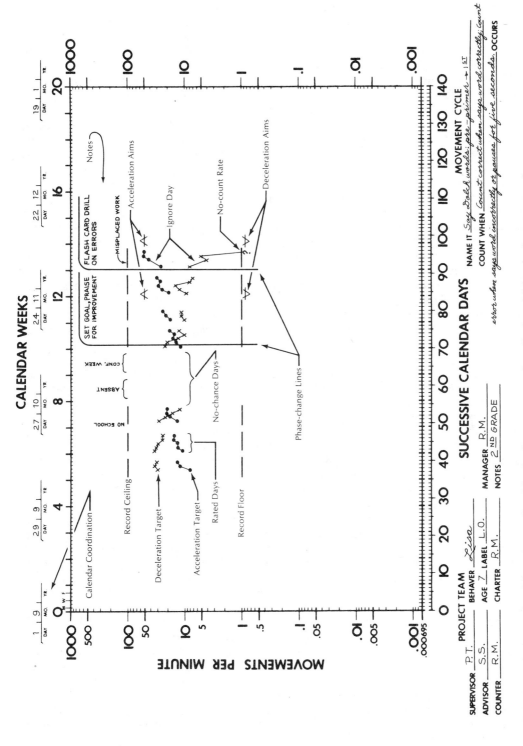

FIGURE 2.15   An example of 6-cycle, semilogrithmic chart paper used to display children's classroom performance

Source: White & Haring, 1976.

tell time and make change without direct instruction at school. Since these skills are not taught in the regular curriculum as discrete entities but rather as units in arithmetic texts, commercial materials which could be modified and adapted are not even available. Since many specific skills need to be mastered and unsystematic instruction seldom leads to successful learning for this population, the classroom teachers are themselves handicapped because of the dearth of verified instructional sequences designed for their pupils.

One teacher skill which should alleviate this desperate situation is task analysis. It is imperative that those academic and social skills which need to be taught be prioritized and ordered carefully. One way to insure that irrelevant tasks are not taught and relevant tasks are taught efficiently is to identify each curriculum goal and objective and judge the importance of each for the youngster. Through the task analysis process, goals and objectives are identified precisely and can be evaluated more easily. For example, Horner and Keilitz (1975) used a task analysis of toothbrushing to structure their teaching procedures. This facilitated the teaching of this skill and aided institutionalized, mentally retarded adolescents in acquiring this important self-help skill.

In recent years, much discussion has centered on goals, objectives, and their ordering. Mager (1962) and McAshan (1970), for example, clearly specified how instructional objectives are written and justified the expenditure of time spent in their preparation. Popham and Baker (1970a) showed how these objectives can be ordered into goals (terminal objectives) and small objectives (enroute behaviors). In their book entitled, *Planning an Instructional Sequence* (1970b), Popham and Baker discuss sequencing objectives for the arrangement of instructional activities designed to help children master specific educational tasks. They did not, however, propose a formalized way to sequence objectives.

Others, however, have provided examples of different methods for conducting the analysis of specific tasks. Gold (Note 3), for example, through his task analysis system, successfully facilitated the acquisition of fairly complex skills in a population of severely handicapped learners. Gold's view of task analysis is considerably more inclusive than the systems proposed by Williams and his associates (Williams, Coyne, Johnson, Scheuerman, Swetlik, & York, 1977) or by us, both of which are described later. Gold refers to task analysis as the entire pro-

cess by which specific strategies and procedures are employed to guarantee successful acquisition of a skill by the learner. Once the task to be taught is identified, the method used to execute the skill is determined. This "how-to" phase is important, because often there are many ways to complete a task. For the handicapped learner, consistency of presentation is vital for efficient learning. Once the method of task completion is determined, the content analysis phase of Gold's scheme is initiated. At this point, the task is broken into teachable components or steps. During this third phase, the format for presentation of each step is decided upon, e.g., backward or forward chaining, fading, or match-to-sample. In addition, criteria levels to indicate when mastery occurs for each step are determined. This information serves as a gauge against which to judge the success of the program and the mastery of the learner. Gold believes that his system yielded successful results in teaching complex tasks to severely handicapped individuals because of the systematic interaction between performance and procedures (Gold and Pomerantz expand this brief review of content-method-process task analysis in Chapter 13.)

Williams et al. (1977) believe that task analysis is the process of identifying the sequence through which a student proceeds to achieve mastery of an objective. Gold views the product of task analysis as student mastery of a specific skill. For Williams and his colleagues, however, the product of task analysis is a skill sequence: the delineation of those objectives and those behaviors prerequisite to successful mastery. They believe that efficiency of instruction will result from using a skill sequence, the product of task analysis. For instance, only skills or parts of skills which need to be acquired are taught. Essential components are presented to the learner and not omitted inadvertently from instruction. The skill sequence should facilitate the teacher's job of monitoring student progress.

Resnick and her colleagues (Resnick, Wang, & Kaplan, 1973) described a complex and comprehensive system of task analysis. Through their system, learning hierarchies are developed to match the natural sequence of children's acquisition of mathematics. The product of Resnick's system is not only an orderly presentation of objectives, but also a description of the stimulus situation presented to the child and the desired response emitted by the learner. Resnick's system is comprehensive and thorough in design, and the instructional sequences developed through this procedure should be reliable and useful to the classroom teacher. This system, however, is too rigorous for teachers to conduct for each skill needing to be taught to their students. Resnick's system is appropriate for curriculum developers to use: those whose full-time responsibility is the development of verified instructional sequences. Until sufficient numbers of skill sequences are available in the detailed manner which Resnick's group provides, teachers will need to use a simpler scheme of task analysis. One such system available to the teacher is the lattice.

The lattice is not an instructional sequence; it does not outline those teaching tactics used in the educational sequence: it only displays the components and sequence of skills in a standardized format. The lattice was originated by Myron Woolman (Note 4) to put structure in the ordering of educational activities. He felt that by sequencing a task before instruction begins, the teacher could see the relationship and integration of concepts to be taught.

Since Woolman initially proposed the format, others have adopted and modified his procedures. Budde and Menolascino (1971) showed how the lattice system can be applied to vocational habilitation. Bricker (1972) used a lattice format to display the sequence of language acquisition. Smith and Smith (Note 5) and Smith, Smith, and Edgar (1976) employed a modified lattice system before they developed structured, instructional programs for self-help and life skills.

Lattices can be very sophisticated or very simplistic. They can be constructed to show the relationship of one skill to another. They can become three-dimensional to indicate difficulty level as well as sequence. Complex systems, however, often are confusing. For the purpose of organizing educational activities or analyzing instructional skills, complexity may not be necessary or desirable.

For most teachers' purposes, a lattice should state simply the analysis of a task. Simplified formats allow for ease in communication. Another advantage of using a simple lattice is speed of construction. To meet the many educational needs of their students, teachers need to be able to analyze specific skills quickly.

Lattice construction

Since a lattice is a graphic display of an analyzed skill, there are specific procedures and a sequence of events which are followed in construction. The Procedural Lattice for Lattice Development was used to display this process (see Figures 2.16 and 2.17).

Prerequisite Knowledge

Teachers need to possess specific skills before they can analyze tasks, identify the sequence of the components, and diagram that analysis in lattice format. They must kmow what a lattice is and how to use one. Part of the procedural lattice summarizes the prerequisite knowledge a teacher should have.

Lattice system. A lattice provides a sequenced list of the major component parts (enroute objectives and subgoals) of a skill to be taught. After the skill is analyzed and put into the appropriate format, it is referred to as teaching is planned. The format used, therefore, must be consistently followed so interpretation of the analysis is identical to the sequence intended originally. For this to occur, some rules and conventions are followed when lattices are constructed.

This consistency also facilitates communication. If, for example, other teachers analyze skills in the same manner, lattices can be shared with colleagues. Skill analysis and sequences need not be created time and time again by teachers in contact with one another.

Subject matter. Understanding of the subject matter is imperative. The teacher should have adequate knowledge of the information to be analyzed. Neither an academic task nor a social skill can be analyzed by someone not thoroughly familiar with the material.

Task Analysis

After the teacher gains competence with the latticing procedures and is proficient at performing the target skill, the analysis phase is initiated.

Identify the skill. First, the skill to be analyzed is determined precisely and specifically. If an individual needs to learn how to set a table, for example, it is that task which is analyzed. One might also not know how to clear a table, but that is a different task and should be considered separately.

Determine entry behaviors. After the task is identified, the prerequisite skills need to be specified. If,

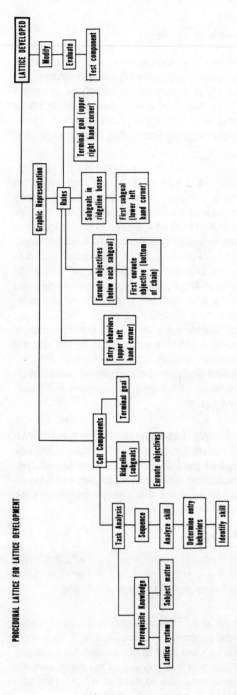

FIGURE 2.16   *The procedural lattice to use as a guide to developing new lattices*

Source: Smith, Smith & Edgar, 1976.

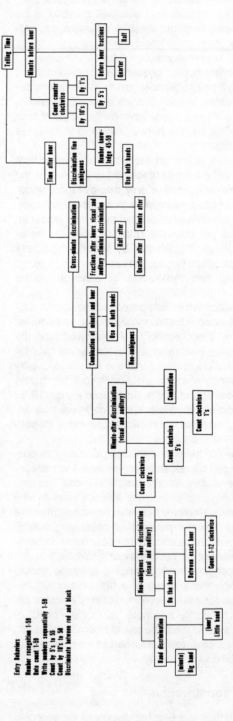

FIGURE 2.17   *A lattice for the skill of time telling*

Source: Smith & Smith, Note 5.

for example, the teacher plans to include telling time in the curriculum and a lattice is to be developed for that objective, a decision needs to be made regarding which skills must be mastered first. For example, number recognition is an important part of telling time. The teacher must decide whether competence in number recognition will be expected *before* the students begin to learn how to tell time or whether number recognition will be taught concurrently.

Our experience indicates that more efficient instruction occurs when prerequisite skills are mastered first. In many cases, entry behaviors are determined in an arbitrary fashion. Different teachers expect different entry levels from their students. Regardless, entry levels should be specified and expected of the student during the instructional sequence.

Analyze skill. One way to analyze a skill is to perform the task yourself and observe others execute the skill over time. In this way, the major components of the skill become apparent. As the task is repeated, actions should be scrutinized so as to identify each step.

Sequence. Once all of the component parts of the skill are identified, they are put into a sequence. Often, the sequence comes directly from the skill. In many motor and dressing skills, for example, a natural order is followed to complete the task. Some skills are sequenced according to curriculum tradition; others are sequenced in order of importance to the learner.

As the sequence is identified, a hierarchy of skills is determined. Some parts of the objective are major components or subgoals; others are subordinate steps or enroute objectives leading to the completion of the major components. The enroute objectives which comprise each subgoal are placed under the subgoal box to represent the hierarchy of the steps in the task.

When we analyze a skill, each part of the skill may be written on an index card. Then, the sequence of the components parts can be easily ordered and reordered.

All of these steps (identification of the skill, determination of entry behaviors, analysis of the skill, and sequencing of the steps used to complete the task) comprise the major elements of the task-analysis process.

Cell Components

Lattices are composed of a series of interlocking boxes or cells. Each cell must be placed in a position that represents both the sequence and the analysis as determined in the task-analysis phase. The terminal behavior or goal, subgoals, and enroute objectives are stated concisely (in two or three words, if possible) and marked for the graphic representation.

Enroute objectives. Those behaviors which lead to the completion of the subgoals are called enroute objectives and are placed below the subgoal boxes or ridgeline.

Ridgeline. The lattice ridgeline is comprised of the subgoals of a task. These are connected in a stepladder fashion and lead upward to the terminal behavior.

Terminal goal. Each lattice has a terminal goal or behavior. Depending on the complexity of the lattice, the terminal goal could be as concrete as "shoes tied" or as abstract as "time concepts." Regardless of the nature of the skill analyzed, all the subgoals and their enroute objectives lead directly to the completion of the *one,* concisely stated, terminal goal on each lattice.

Graphic Representation

For lattices to be interpreted and to retain consistent meaning, conventions need to be followed as the lattice is constructed. The lattice is a blueprint or master plan of the instructional sequence of a specific task; therefore, the graphic display of the analysis must be easily interpretable.

Rules. Rules about lines connecting cells and descriptions of cell placement are used to facilitate the consistent interpretation of a graphic display of the task analysis.

A stepladder format is used to display the sequence of the subgoals. The ridgeline boxes are connected by lines which form right angles and are read from left to right.

Whenever possible, enroute objectives are connected to each subgoal cell with straight lines. If several enroute objectives are not necessarily sequential or prerequisite to one another, each may be placed immediately under the subgoal cell and on the same horizontal plane with one another by using both straight and right-angled lines.

If one enroute objective must be completed before another is initiated, the cells are put together in a chain with the first objective in the sequence at the bottom. All of the ensuing enroute objectives lead up to the subgoal.

Sometimes, for broad curriculum planning, it is desirable to have an overall lattice which shows how various skills relate. The lattice system can be adapted easily for the purpose of displaying the progression of skills taught in one academic year for particular skill areas. One overall lattice might be created for all dressing skills to be taught over a period of several years. In this example, there might be entire lattices for each cell shown on the larger lattice.

First subgoal. The first subgoal in the sequence, the first ridgeline cell, is placed toward the bottom, left-hand corner of the page. The enroute objectives which pertain to the completion of this subgoal are positioned below this first ridgeline box.

Subgoals. The remaining subgoals are positioned in stepladder format (from left to right and bottom to top of the page) leading to the terminal behavior. These comprise the ridgeline.

Terminal goal. The terminal goal always appears in the upper, right-hand corner. It is stated concisely and is positioned to indicate clearly that it is the end-goal of the sequence.

Lattice Developed

This is the terminal goal of the task-analysis process. Before a lattice is truly completed, however, final testing and evaluation needs to be conducted.

Test component. The teacher should perform the latticed task again, using the newly developed lattice as a guide. Each component of the task should be scrutinized to be certain that the words that appear in each cell adequately and concisely describe the behavior. In addition, the sequence must be rechecked to guarantee accuracy.

Evaluate. The entire process needs to be evaluated. If the teacher finds that the lattice does not display the sequence or the analysis properly, this should be noted. If wording is misleading, those terms must be clarified.

Modify. If errors in the lattice are identified, they must be corrected. If entry behaviors were omitted,

they must be included. If the ordering of the subgoals was incorrect, they need to be adjusted. Once all of these final checks are completed, the task is analyzed and displayed so that instructional activities can be organized. These activities should aim at bringing the learner to mastery of each enroute objective and its subgoals. Mastery of these component parts of the lattice should lead the learner to mastery of the terminal behavior.

Sample lattices

A procedural lattice, such as the one described here and shown in Figure 2.16, does not depict the analysis of an academic or social skill. Most lattices which teachers construct, however, pertain to educational activities. Several lattices (see Figures 2.17, 2.18, and 2.19) were selected as illustrative examples of skill lattices. Also, lattices can display the analysis and sequence of complex, conceptual skills.

The lattice approach is only one way to conduct and represent a task analysis. It was selected because we felt it would be helpful to teachers as they plan their short- and long-term curriculum activities. The system allows teachers to specify skills their students need to master and to display the analysis of these skills in a simple format so that mastery of enroute objectives can be monitored easily.

The lattice system described here is an adaptation of Woolman's original system. It was modified for the academic-instructional situation. This adaptation attempts, in simple terms and format, to provide a model of a complex task or concept. It does not include every detail of the analyzed task. If it were so inclusive, it would not be a blueprint but rather an instructional program. The lattice system allows the teacher to assess students' abilities and to carefully plan educational activities designed to help students acquire new skills.

Behavior and Skill Assessment

Each school year, before direct instruction is initiated, the teacher should assess every student's behavioral repertoire across skill areas. In this way, she or he may determine which skills each student has mastered and therefore needs no further instruction in; those skills which are not yet mastered but which are in the student's repertoire, and those skills which are not within the parameters of the individual's capabilities at the present time. Only through careful and systematic behavioral and skill

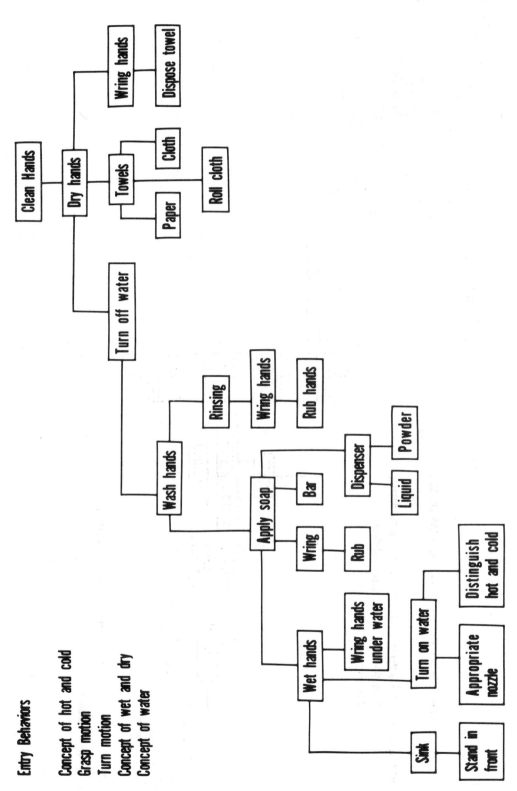

FIGURE 2.18   A lattice for the skill of hand washing

Source: Smith & Smith, Note 5.

Lattice to teach children to set and clear a table for a two course meal.

Entry behavior Know difference between main course and dessert.
Know difference between clean and dirty.
Rote count from 1-15.

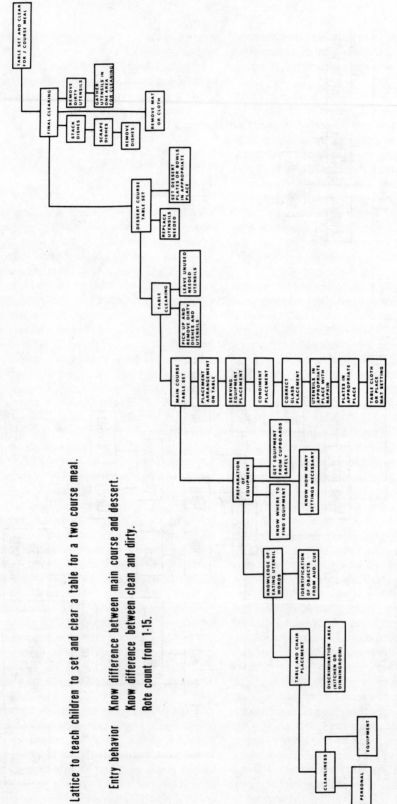

FIGURE 2.19   A lattice for the skill of table setting

Source: Smith & Smith, Note 5.

56

assessment can curriculum priorities be established for each learner. The ultimate goal of assessment is a skill profile from which instructional planning may stem.

Although general assessment is an important process for all teachers, it is even more critical for teachers of moderately and severely handicapped students. Because learning for these students is often a tedious venture, major skills and the minute, splinter skills of which they are comprised frequently become goals and objectives covering a substantial part of the school year. This situation often encourages the teacher of the seriously handicapped to become microscopic in viewing teaching. Typically, great excitement and much fanfare occurs when a student masters even one small, enroute objective. It is easy to lose sight of the larger curriculum picture. Periodic general assessments cause the teacher to take an objective overview of a student's performance. This provides a *gestalt* of the student's skills and the larger targets of curriculum planning. For this reason, it is suggested that general assessments be conducted three times a year: at the beginning, middle, and end.

General assessment needs to be comprehensive and inclusive of all areas relevant to the goal of maintaining oneself in the least restrictive environment. For severely handicapped learners, many and diverse skill areas become instructional targets, some of which are seldom included in the regular educational curriculum. For example, basic self-help skills are major curriculum targets for this population of learners. Assessment must be conducted in areas such as toileting, eating, dressing, grooming, housekeeping, etc., because instruction frequently must be planned for these activities. Many numerical skills are important for independent and semi-independent living. One-to-one correspondence, counting, time telling, measuring, keeping a checkbook, and even using a calculator are skills which can facilitate an individual's existence in society. Because of their ultimate importance and practicality, assessments of individuals' performance in these life-skill areas must be made periodically so that adequate instruction can be planned.

In addition to independent living skills, many social skills must be programmed for those who are handicapped. Cooperative play and work, selection of leisure time activities, independent work skills, question asking, and various interpersonal, interaction skills usually need to be programmed directly if these learners are to achieve independence or semi-independence in an environment as unrestrictive as possible.

In order to begin the task of identifying those behaviors which will become the instructional targets for each learner, the teacher must generally assess the learner's performance across a broad range of behaviors.

General Behavior and Skill Observation

The first stage in identifying curriculum targets for students is to create situations in which they can demonstrate their skills or lack of them. The student should be provided with opportunities to perform various skills, many of which are mastered. It is important to avoid undue frustration; students should not be scheduled for complete failure situations. In addition, this allows the teacher to be certain that skills mastered during the past academic year or indicated as mastered on an individual's record are still in the student's repertoire at a satisfactory level. The use of a behavior checklist should help the teacher gather most of this general skill assessment information.

Various checklists and other behavioral assessment devices are available. Although most are only guides, they should facilitate overall general planning of objectives and goals for severely and moderately handicapped learners. For example, Foster (1974) identified 399 target behaviors and grouped them into 40 behavioral classes and 10 behavioral domains. In his *Camelot Behavioral Checklist,* Foster provides detailed information for each domain: self-help, physical development, home duties, vocational behaviors, economic behavior, independent travel, numerical skills, communication skills, social behaviors and responsibility. This checklist is completed by all those who are knowledgeable about each aspect of an individual's behavior repertoire and provides a good indication of general areas of competencies and deficits of the learner. This system should provide the teacher with an overall framework from which program planning might start.

Project MORE (Note 6) developed general lists of critical training needs for each level of retardation: profound, severe, moderate, mild, and borderline. These were the only such lists located by us which identify target skills according to the learner's capability level. For each level, the same ten general areas are used: independent functioning; physical development; economic activity; language development; number, time, and dimension; occupation, domestic; occupation, general; self-direction; responsibility; and socialization. Under each of these general areas, specific skills are stated which are appropriate for each level of retardation. Although not standardized for handicapped learners, these general targets provide a useful guide for general curriculum planning activities.

Sailor and Mix (1975) developed a behavioral inventory specifically for moderately and severely handicapped children. The *TARC* inventory provides scores in the areas of self-help, motor, communication, and social skills. There are several advantages to the *TARC* system. The scoring system allows for within- and across-student comparisons: a reference for instructional evaluation which should be helpful to an instructional team. It requires that information be gathered on the learner over a period of time, rather than from a single observation, before evaluation is made. Also, it is easy to use. TARC should indicate to the teacher which specific behaviors are in need of remediation and provide a standard against which to judge an individual's general progress over time.

The *Massachusetts Educational Evaluation and Planning Package*, Vol. 1 (McCormack, Hamlet, Dunaway, & Vorderer, 1976), provides an extensive and thorough breakdown of skills in the areas of daily living, motor development, and early language development. A screening assessment device is provided for each general area. In addition, very detailed and specific behaviors are identified and arranged in such a way that further finite assessment can be conducted and information regarding quality of student performance may be obtained. Further, task analyses of these skills and their splinter skills are provided and make excellent guides for instructional planning. Although not an instructional program, this comprehensive guide should be most useful for both assessment and instructional purposes.

Project MEMPHIS (Quick, Little, & Campbell, 1974) provides an instrument for individual evaluation. This assessment device evaluates handicapped preschoolers' abilities in five areas: personal-social skills, gross motor skills, fine motor skills, language skills, and perceptual-cognitive skills. This instrument was developed for teachers to use in generally assessing preschool children's skills for the purpose of school programming. The results are translated into developmental age which allows the teacher to judge the amount of growth in each student's skills across the school year. In addition, Quick and Campbell (1976) developed 260 lesson plans which coincide with their assessment device. These products from Project MEMPHIS should be useful to those working with youngsters functioning below the developmental age of five.

Another detailed checklist and curriculum guide was developed by Bender and Valletutti (1976) and Bender, Valletutti and Bender (1976a, 1976b). Whereas Project MEMPHIS was designed for preschoolers, Bender and Valletutti's work is appropriate for the young as well as the developmentally disabled adult. This comprehensive work has many excellent features. They provide general and specific objectives in the areas of: behavior, self-care, gross and fine motor, communication, functional academics, socialization, leisure time, and safety skills. In addition to the objectives, the authors provide an excellent list of activities and instructional techniques which should facilitate the acquisition of these skills and criteria for judging mastery. Another excellent feature of this work is its outstanding reference lists for each general objective area.

Only a few of the many checklists and behavioral inventories available are reviewed here. Such skill inventories can be very helpful to the teacher while planning for at least one year of instruction for each student. A word of caution, however, must be stated regarding their use. For the more severely handicapped individual, the steps between each inventory item are frequently too great. Often, months of instruction are spent on splinter skills between items on the checklists. In other cases, the conditions under which the learner should be assessed are not specified. For example, a child who can tie his shoes in the classroom might not be able to do so at gym time or at home. Although behavioral checklists are exceedingly helpful and it is our strong recommendation that they be used, unfortunately, for some learners, the lists are not so specific or so detailed as necessary for comprehensive, general assessment.

Informal assessment devices made by teachers

Researchers (Bender & Valletutti, 1976; Brown & York, 1974) and practitioners agree, no matter which checklist assessment device or instructional program selected, teachers will uncover additional life skills, splinter skills, and social skills which must be assessed and programmed for in the absence of commercially available teaching materials. Possibly, sometime in the future, the perfect comprehensive curriculum will be available. Until that time, teachers must be able to design and conduct their own informal assessments.

Social Behavior

In addition to assessing each student's behavioral skills through the use of a checklist or more sophisticated assessment device, it is imperative that the teacher monitor her student's social skills in various settings: group and individual, structured and free, and school and home. Earlier in this chapter, a description of the ABC analysis and data-collection procedures was provided. By using these data-collection procedures across settings, the learner's strengths and weaknesses in interpersonal and social skills should become apparent.

Typically, aberrant behavior in need of modification can be classified as being either in excess or deficit. The type of intervention selected varies depending on the aim of the strategy and the nature of the behavior needing modification. For example, the rate of excessive, random verbalizations might be decelerated by an adult's ignoring each occurrence, whereas isolationism might be discouraged by a combination of praise and attention.

Moderately to severely handicapped people exhibit some excessive behaviors which are frequent targets for interventions aimed at remediation and, as such, are studied by researchers. For example, self-injurious behavior was eliminated by the use of time-out (Hamilton, Stephans, & Allen, 1967; Williams, 1959; Wolf et al., 1964), extinction or ignoring (Bucher & Lovaas, 1968; Lovaas & Simmons, 1969), reinforcement of incompatible behavior (Allen & Harris, 1966; Peterson, 1968), and shock (Bucher & Lovaas, 1968; Lovaas, Schaeffer, & Simmons, 1965; Lovaas & Simmons, 1969; Tate & Baroff, 1966). Excessive behaviors such as tantrums (Birnbrauer, Bijou, Wolf, & Kidder, 1965; Wolf, Risley, Johnson, Harris, & Allen, 1967; Zimmerman & Zimmerman, 1964), autisms or stereotypic behaviors (Flavell, 1973), and aggressive actions toward others (Bostow & Bailey, 1969; Roberts & Smith, Note 7) also have been the targets of applied research. Other behaviors, typically in excess, have not received adequate attention from researchers but must be handled by teachers if students are to achieve their maximal potential in social situations. One general area, and a frequent problem for our target population, concerns inappropriate repetition of certain social behaviors such as greetings, conversation, and laughter. Because it is difficult to read non-verbal social cues correctly, members of the moderately and severely handicapped population often do not know when to initiate or terminate conversations or to change from one activity to another. This typical behavior pattern only serves to accentuate an individual's handicap and must be modified if normalization is to be successful.

Behaviors which could be considered as deficits in a student's repertoire often are modified through the use of shaping procedures. Color naming (Larsen & Bricker, 1968), cooperative play (Strain, Shores, & Kerr, 1976), and eating (Spradlin, Note 1), for example, have been modified through the use of various kinds of shaping procedures. Other deficit behaviors such as child-child interactions during free play settings have been increased through restructured teacher interactions (Shores, Hester, & Strain, 1976) and the introduction of peer confederates (Strain, Shores, & Timm, 1977). Social language skills are frequently in deficit. The correct usage of socially appropriate expressions such as "excuse me," "thank you," "you're welcome," can be difficult to master even for those individuals with relatively good language skills. Many moderately and severely handicapped people have general difficulties in areas which, although apparent to parents and teachers, have not received scrutiny in the research arena as yet. For example, some individuals have deficit behavioral repertoires in the areas of flexibility (moving with ease from one activity to another), selection of appropriate-age leisure time activities, or verbal and manual cooperation and sharing—all of which need to be possessed by each learner.

Skill Assessment

Although the best efforts of individuals and teams of experts have been put into the development of comprehensive curriculum guides, serious gaps exist in the currently available ones. And, as Brown and York (1974) point out, "... rarely do curriculum guides contain the precision in content delineation mandatory for instructing severely handicapped students" (p. 6). Teachers will have to use their own skills to fill in the curriculum gaps and provide the precision necessary for overall curriculum planning. Perhaps more serious and more difficult for the teacher of the severely handicapped is the dearth and inappropriateness of the instructional materials available. Unfortunately, even when instructional sequences are found for particular curriculum targets, often they are not designed in a practical manner that presents concepts within the context of life experiences. Many times, examples and practice exercises are not consistent with the objective to be mastered. If, for example, the end-goal of instruction is for the student to be able to balance a checkbook using a calculator, then practice exercises should require the use of that skill in real situations. If an already prepared instructional sequence is found, but lacks this practical element, it must be adapted. Since overlearning can be achieved only through repetition and redundancy (practice of a skill under different conditions) and moderately and severely handicapped learners must have the opportunity for repeated practice through all stages of instruction if overlearning is to occur, the teacher must also insure sufficient redundancy in programs that are selected or planned. Brown and York (1974) believe that " . . . commercially available sequenced materials are not sufficiently concrete, precise, redundant, or relevant for use with most severely handicapped students. Thus, the teacher is forced to rely on his or her ingenuity to generate new or adapt existing materials" (p. 9). Teachers need more than ingenuity, however; they must be able to carefully assess and plan for the skill deficits of their students.

As time goes on, more instructional programs designed and field tested with moderately and severely handicapped populations will become available. Many good programs are now available. However, when separate instructional programs are used to facilitate mastery of individual skills, optimal continuity cannot occur without careful assessment and programming for each individual student. To do this, assessment of student skill levels must be conducted to determine where instruction is required.

To conduct informal skill assessments, the student must be given the opportunity to perform the target skill. Our experience indicates that the student should be encouraged to complete the target task in two situations: free and structured. We found that some students can adequately execute a task when the teacher is in control and has established a school-like situation but do not generalize their learning to the normal, free situation. Since situational, appropriate task completion is the aim of all instructional programming, skill assessment must be conducted in free as well as controlled situations.

If the learner demonstrates mastery of a task, further assessment of more difficult skills must be made to determine at which point instruction should be initiated. Once a student demonstrates nonmastery of a task, the component skills of that task must be assessed. It is at this point that task analysis is vital because of all the subskills and their sequences need to be delineated and available for reference. If the lattice system is used as the teacher's format for task analysis, each behavior specified in the ridgeline boxes should be assessed to determine the exact place at which to begin instruction.

Stage of Learning Assessment

Most assessment systems indicate only whether the student has or has not mastered a skill (Foster, 1974; Quick et al., 1974). Some (Bender & Valletutti, 1976; McCormick, Hamlet, Dunaway, & Vorderer, 1976) allow for an indication of student progression toward mastery. This, however, is not sufficient for complete program planning. The work of some researchers (Ayllon & Azrin, 1964; Hopkins, 1968; Smith, 1973; Smith & Lovitt, 1976; White & Liberty, 1976; Smith & Fleming, Note 8) indicates that there is more than one stage of learning and that the influence of intervention strategies is dependent on stage. Since one tactic might be influential in one learning stage but not another, it is important for the teacher to determine which learning stage an individual is in before interventions are scheduled.

There are at least three distinctly different stages of learning: acquisition, proficiency, and maintenance. During the acquisition period, the learner cannot execute the skill accurately. Initially, his correct percentage scores are zero, indicating that he needs to acquire competency in the target skill. Once the learner can perform the task correctly, he enters the proficiency stage. Here, the teacher must program the learner for proficient performance. In addition to concern for accuracy, speed of performance (proficiency) is the aim. Once the learner demonstrates that he can accurately perform the task at a rate fast enough to indicate proficiency, the student's performance level must be maintained.

Often, only accuracy is the target in instructional programming. Through the following example, one can see why this is not sufficient. In a vocational-training program, several moderately handicapped students were learning to work as busboys. They needed to learn to set a table correctly before they could receive on-the-job training. The teacher conducted a task analysis of the target skill. She assessed each student's abilities to set a table by a pretest developed from her task analysis. She then initiated her instructional program, carefully measured their daily performance, and kept daily records. She determined that three consecutive 100% days would be her indication of mastery. Great celebration soon occurred. All of her students reached this goal and were ready to enter their job-training situation; or were they? After the first day on the job, all but one of her students were returned with indication that their skills were not sufficient for on-the-job programs. What would cause this sad state of affairs? Simply that the teacher had not completed her instruction. Two very important phases were omitted. First, apparently all but one of her students were not proficient at the target task. In a work situation speed of performance as well as accuracy is vital. Our teacher should have asked the potential employer how quickly he expected his employees to set tables. This time quotient should have been added to the criteria for mastery. For some students, even more instruction will be required. Some students demonstrate skill proficiency in a classroom setting, but require further instruction to transfer or generalize that skill to a different setting. So, in addition, our teacher should have probed her students' newly acquired, proficient table-setting skills at the job site as well.

Clearly, there are two important reasons for attending to the stage of learning. First, moderately and severely handicapped persons will not be able to succeed in least restrictive environments unless they maintain proficient levels of performance across skill areas. Secondly, tactics selected for instructional purposes should match the stage of learning.

Several studies indicate that some intervention strategies are not appropriate in all situations. Hopkins (1968), for example, found that initial reinforcement contingencies were unsuccessful and did not facilitate the increase of a young institutionalized boy's smiling, because the target behavior was not within the youngster's abilities at that time. He then used instruction to bring the behavior to a level at which it could be reinforced. He found that instruction was necessary in the acquisition phase and reinforcement contingencies were influential in the proficiency phase. Ayllon and Azrin (1964) had comparable results. In their study, picking up the necessary cutlery to eat a meal in a socially appropriate manner was the target for institutionalized, severely disturbed women. Again, instructions had to be scheduled before the reinforcement was influential. Smith and Lovitt (1976) also found that reinforcement contingencies have various results

depending on the stages of learning. In purely acquisitional situations in computational arithmetic, reinforcement was not influential; but modeling techniques did produce the desired increase in percentage scores: 0% to 100%. Reinforcement, however, then caused the desired changes in correct *rates,* indicating the appropriate scheduling of this tactic in proficiency situations. It appears, therefore, that the assessment of the student's learning stage is also an important component of the preinstruction period.

The diagnostic components described in this section provide the teacher with the information necessary to make educational decisions about each student. Without a clear indication of each student's capabilities and a thorough profile of his performance patterns across diverse skills, it is not possible to develop appropriate goals, objectives, and instructional plans for the learner.

Setting Instructional Objectives

Many teachers have relied upon behavioral objectives to plan individualized curricula for their students since Mager (1962) popularized the notion in the early sixties. Behavioral objectives provide clear and precise goal statements and are worded in such a way that agreement on the description of the behavior—its topography and occurrence—is necessitated. The key element of behavioral objectives is that they must be stated in reliable and observable terms: the behavior specified can be demonstrated to the observer.

It is a relatively easy task to translate behaviors identified in the task analysis process into a series of behavioral objectives. Since reliably observable behaviors are stated precisely in all task analyses, the mere expansion of them into behavior statements or sentences produces at least simplified behavioral objectives. For example, part of the lattice for "Set Table" depicted in Figure 2.19 could be translated into a series of behavioral objectives as was done in Table 2.3.

The monitoring of students' achievement of skills specified in a series of behavioral objectives may serve as a checklist and record of their progress. If, however, sequenced behavioral objectives are used to provide indication of student progress, more information is required. For this purpose objective statements must include exact descriptions of the criteria for mastery as well as descriptions of the environmental conditions: the setting, time, and ma-

TABLE 2.3   *A comparison of formats of objective statements with criteria included*

Lattice Format	Traditional Objective Format	Criteria
	To set one place:	
Main Course Table Set	2.01–a The student is able to place a table cloth on a table in such a way that the overhang is even on opposite sides of the table.	2.01–a with 100% accuracy within 2 minutes
	2.01–b The student is able to put a placement on a table in such a way that the bottom edge rests along the edge of the table.	2.01–b with 100% accuracy within 15 seconds
	2.02–a The student is able to place a plate on the table so that the edge of the plate is approximately two inches from the edge of the table.	2.02 (a & b) with 100% accuracy 15 seconds
Correct Glass Placement	2.02–b The student is able to place a plate on a placemat centered across the horizontal plane in such a way that the lower edge of the plate is approximately two inches from the lower edge of the placemat.	
Utensils In Appropriate Place With Napkin	2.03 The student is able to place the appropriate eating utensils on the table in the proper relation to the plate.	2.03 with 100% accuracy (.01–.04) within 1 minute
	2.03.01 The student is able to place the dinner fork along side and approximately two inches from the left side of the plate.	
Plates In Appropriate Place	2.03.02 The student is able to place the salad fork along side and approximately one-half inch to the left of the dinner fork.	
	2.03.03 The student is able to place the knife, blade facing the plate, along side and approximately two inches to the right of the plate.	
Table Cloth Or Place Mat Setting	2.03.04 The student is able to place the spoon along side and approximately one-half inch to the right of the knife.	
	2.04 The student is able to place the drinking glass, upright, above and slightly to the right of the spoon.	2.04 with 100% accuracy within 15 seconds

Source: Smith & Smith, Note 5.

terials. The criteria for mastery must include an indication of aim scores: quantifiers (i.e., percentage scores, correct and error rates, frequency count) with which to determine and judge the acceptability of performance, such as 100% within a specific time period. In addition, the teacher needs to indicate where and when the behavior is expected to occur. If, for example, Johnny's objective is to "say his name and address upon command," the teacher expects that, after instruction, each time Johnny is asked by anyone what his name and address are, he will respond correctly within an appropriate length of time. Therefore, the refinement of the original objective should be: Whenever asked the question, "What is your name and address?" Johnny shall say, "My name is Johnny Jones. I live at 101 South Fifth Avenue, in Columbia, California" within 10 seconds of hearing the question, 100% of the time.

By having objectives which indicate the parameters of the desired response, the teacher may refer to them during all phases of instruction: diagnosis, direct teaching, and posttesting. If objectives indicate what will be considered proficient performance, they may also serve as indicators of mastery during acquisition and maintenance periods. The teachers, then, will know when to terminate direct instruction and enter into maintenance or posttest situations. A notion of when to shift from one situation to another facilitates efficient teaching. Table 2.3 provides examples of behavioral statements inclusive of aim scores from the skill latticed earlier.

Selecting appropriate goals

Although all people are individuals and should receive instruction tailor-made for their needs, interests, and abilities, the necessity of individualized instruction is most obvious and requisite for the moderately and severely handicapped population. With this group, individual differences are most apparent because there probably is no group of learners more heterogeneous. Within this group, there exists a wide range of abilities. The number and kinds of behavioral excesses and deficits are enormous. The degree of specific teaching varies because of discrepancies in individuals' abilities to generalize learning. Delayed intellectual functioning often is not the only predominant disability. In addition, many members of this group possess multiple and overlapping handicaps. Often, one or more sensory channels are damaged seriously enough to hinder instruction, and these conditions affect the selection of specific intervention strategies. Therefore, individualizing instruction and setting goals and objectives are especially necessary for this group of learners.

Specific objectives must be selected carefully. They must match each individual's needs in accordance with his specific behavioral characteristics. After a full and thorough diagnosis, instructional objectives must be selected which reflect the total profile of the individual's performance. The exact entry levels and performance capabilities must be considered. Performance deficits must be identified and weighed in the light of the ultimate goal of all objectives: the maintenance of each individual in the least restrictive environment possible.

Every time an objective is considered for an individual, the teacher should assess its value to the person's eventual ultimate functioning. Objectives must also be evaluated against one another to determine a hierarchy of objectives. This is always done by determining the usefulness of a target skill for the individual. In many cases, a compensatory device could be selected to facilitate mastery of a specific objective. For example, many moderately and severely handicapped youngsters can be taught computational arithmetic. In most cases, however, the amount of time and energy needed to achieve mastery of each computational process—addition, subtraction, multiplication, and division—is not warranted; instead, mastery in the use of pocket calculators would be a more efficient use of instructional time. It is impossible to overemphasize the importance of selecting objectives which are relevant to daily living, pragmatic, functional, and attainable.

It is important to remember that the selection of goals and objectives determines the instructional program and curriculum for each learner. Goals and objectives lock both the student and the teacher into a series of structured activities which may extend over a long period of time. Years can be spent mastering the many minor and major objectives which comprise one goal. If that goal is inappropriate for the learner, the time spent is wasted.

Selecting Pragmatic Long-Term Goals

The ultimate long-term goal for each individual is to become a functioning member of society and to live as independently as possible. If this goal is used as a standard against which all other long-term goals are evaluated, seriously handicapped persons will attain greater degrees of functioning and independence. Certain skill areas are vital for independence; if they are not mastered, independent or even semi-independent living is not possible. Most all of the self-help skills fall into this category and, therefore, must be emphasized in the curriculum. Mastery in areas such as grooming, dressing, toileting, and eating is imperative for independent living. For some individuals, however, these skills can never be mastered in the usual way because of certain specific handicaps. In these cases, compensatory skills should be taught whenever possible. To be able to dress oneself totally is a fine long-term objective for most moderately and many severely handicapped people. This goal is comprised of many subgoals. To be entirely competent in dressing skills, one must be able to button, zipper, snap, tie, select color combinations, and, in a standard sequence, put on and take off a variety of different kinds of apparel which varies seasonally. Some severely handicapped people may never achieve complete mastery of all the component dressing skills. Some will achieve this aim only through compensatory behaviors. For example, some individuals who do not have functioning hands and arms learn to use their feet and legs as substitutes and can dress themselves independently. Some individuals are able to dress themselves only if certain skills are avoided. For instance, some people, because of serious physical limitations, do not possess the necessary fine motor coordination to tie bows, hook, or button. If these skills are avoided, however, the individual will be able to dress himself independently. The teacher must teach not only the attainable dressing skills but also teach students how to select clothing which allows them to dress within the perimeters of their capabilities.

Comparable objective selection and adaptation must occur across all general areas vital to independent living. Long-term objectives should be determined not only in the self-help category but also for life and vocational skills. The number of different skills which need to be included in the long-term curricula for moderately and severely handicapped individuals is truly staggering. Many objectives, however, disappear when the scrutiny of the pragmatic teacher prevails. If every activity conducted within the classroom setting were analyzed carefully, many could be curtailed. How many times has instructional time been wasted because irrelevant activities were scheduled? How many times have

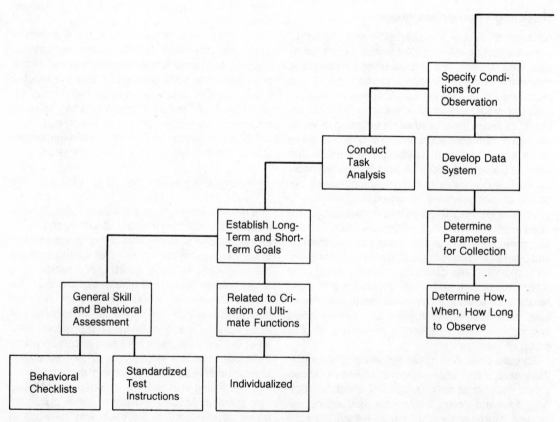

FIGURE 2.20   *A lattice for systematic assessment and instruction*

youngsters been asked to string beads merely to fill time? How many adolescents are still being drilled in simple addition? If long-term objectives which relate to independent living are first established, the smaller objectives become apparent.

There are many ways to establish pragmatic long-term objectives for severely and moderately handicapped learners. The best way is to talk with people who work with handicapped adults and visit community programs and job placement sites for handicapped people. If, for example, the hope is that Pete will be able to live in a group home after he graduates from school, that should be a long-term goal for him. The next important question which stems from this goal is "what skills does one need to successfully live in a group home setting?" The best way to find out is to visit a group home; systematically observe the environment and study the expected be-

havior patterns required; and question the house parents to determine which skills they feel are the most important to them and other residents. Subsequently, relevant objectives can be drafted. This same procedure should be initiated when vocational objectives and goals are considered. Visits to work activity centers, sheltered workshops, and other employment sites should be made. Many handicapped persons do not succeed in the job situation because appropriate goals were not part of their school curricula. Such goals need to be included if school is to be relevant and useful.

Selection of Short-Term Goals

Short-term goals must be developed from long-term goals. If one long-term goal relates to successful maintenance in a group-home living situation, another long-term goal must be maintaining a bed-

(continued on p. 66)

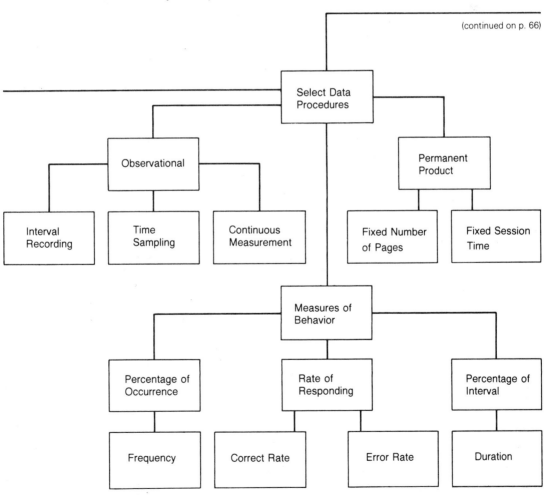

FIGURE 2.20   *Continued*

room: one must be able to dust, sweep, wash windows, put away articles of clothing in closets and dressers, make a bed, etc. One short-term goal from this set of long-term goals could be concerned with making a bed. There are two major goals in "making a bed"; each uses different sets of skills. One refers to daily bed making; the other to weekly bed changing. For the first skill, one needs merely to readjust the linen and blanket and perhaps put on a bedspread. The second skill, however, is substantially more difficult—sheets, blankets, and pillowcases need to be removed and replaced in an appropriate sequence and manner. The teacher de-

cides to work on the daily bedmaking skills first. This now becomes a short-term goal: the end-goal is "bed made." After conducting a task analysis of the target skill and assessing the student's ability at each step in the sequence, objectives are set and instruction begins. The teacher, however, must have some notion regarding the criteria for mastery; otherwise, the proper time for instruction to terminate will not be apparent. The teacher might have both long- and short-term mastery criteria. If the behavior was initially in the acquisition stage of learning (0%), at first only accuracy may be of concern and the first mastery statement might be 100%

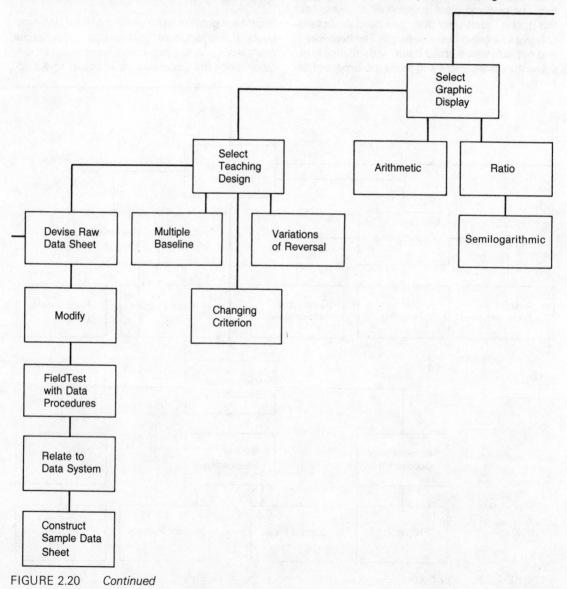

FIGURE 2.20   *Continued*

accuracy. As discussed earlier in this chapter, this is not sufficient. Soon rate or time required to complete a task must be considered. One way to determine this rate score is to observe the requirements for successful task completion in the natural environment. A trip or phone call to a group home could determine how long one is allowed to spend on making a bed each morning. This, then, will become the ultimate mastery criterion, and instruction should not be terminated until this rate is attained and maintained.

Lattice for Systematic Assessment and Instruction

A general lattice for implementing systematic instruction is displayed in Figure 2.20. Here, the general steps used in instructional situations are

outlined. Detailed descriptions of specific educational procedures are found throughout this book, with specific discussions about methodology in this chapter and about intervention strategies in the next chapter.

Briefly, the lattice for systematic instruction indicates the general sequence used in "good" educational programs. Clearly, this sequence is not meant to be overly structured or inflexible. In many instances, adaptations must be made and deviations must occur for instruction to be relevant and efficient for the learner. The following summarizes, in narrative form, both the general content of Chapters 2 and 3 and the lattice shown in Figure 2.20.

Initially, teachers and instructional personnel must assess their students' potential and current abilities. This can be accomplished through the combined use of standardized assessment instru-

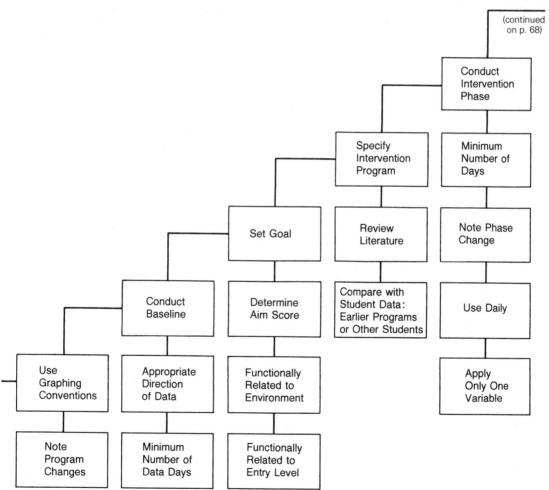

(continued on p. 68)

FIGURE 2.20   *Continued*

ments and behavioral checklists. The outcome of the assessment phase must be the determination of the students' current functioning levels (entry levels) across a number of skill categories and should result in the establishment of pragmatic long-term and short-term instructional objectives which are designed specifically for the learner, based on those strengths and weaknesses revealed through the assessment process.

Once the student's instructional objectives are determined, an educational program must either be found or constructed. In many cases, materials are not available commercially and instructional sequences must be designed for the individual student. When this situation occurs, the task to be taught must be carefully identified (pinpointed) and broken into teachable units. It is at this stage that the task analysis process is initiated, the product of which is a sequence of behaviors placed in a learning hierarchy.

Measurement of student progress is an integral part of systematic teaching and should occur across all stages of learning. The selection of the appropriate measurement system depends in a large part on the type of behavior under consideration. If, for example, tantrums are the target, the teacher might select duration as the type of measurement. If, however, oral reading is the target, correct and error rates would be the best measurement system to apply. Various types of measurement systems and related data collection procedures are available. The selection of the type of approach to utilize depends on each learning situation and the kind of information desired by the teacher. Once the data collection procedure is established, the accumulation of the data is facilitated by the development of a raw data form which serves to summarize the information gathered during teaching.

Various teaching designs are available to school personnel. Whether one selects a multiple baseline,

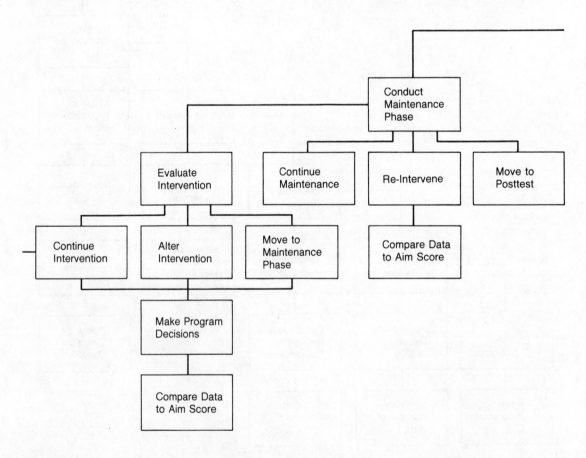

FIGURE 2.20   *Continued*

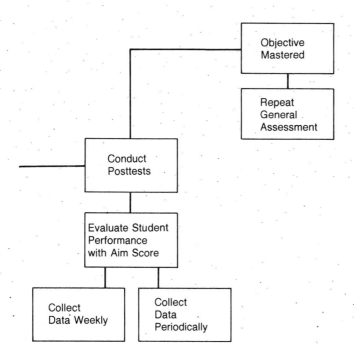

FIGURE 2.20   *Continued*

changing criterion, generalization, or reversal design depends on the kind of behavior (social or academic) being measured. If, for example, the influence of praise on a young child's social interaction is of concern, a reversal design would be appropriate; but if correct articulation of the "r" sound in clinic, classroom, and home is the target, a multiple baseline design is most applicable.

Data gathered during a teaching project are not only entered on raw data sheets but also plotted on a graph for visual display and quick analysis. Most often, arithmetic graphing procedures are selected for rate, duration, frequency, and percentage information that can be so displayed. Regardless of the type of graph paper, standard graphing conventions are used to insure consistent interpretation of the graph. The most obvious advantage of converting children's behavior to a statistical form and graphically presenting it centers on educational evaluation and decision-making. By visually summarizing each child's classroom performance, the influence of the scheduled intervention strategies can be judged against both the child's initial performance level (baseline) and his aim score (long-term or short-term goal). Also, the influence of specific intervention procedures can be compared to results of the same strategy reported in the literature and other situations (for other children or for the same child for other behaviors).

If it becomes apparent that the intervention is either not successful or not efficient, procedures must be altered. Another tactic could be added or substituted for the unsuccessful approach. In all cases, a learner's performance must be evaluated against the aim, and efficient growth toward that goal is the target.

Once the aim has been achieved, the maintenance period is initiated. The purpose of monitoring behavior during this time is to see whether the learner can retain his performance level from the last intervention period. If not, intervention strategies must be re-instituted. If retention is achieved, one can be certain through periodic posttests that the aim was totally obtained and mastery has occurred. Only through systematic assessment and instruction such as the procedures outlined here can teachers be confident that they have achieved the goal of their profession: a demonstration of significant growth in their pupils' ability to participate in society.

References

Allen, K. E., & Harris, F. R. Elimination of a child's excessive scratching by training the mother in reinforcement procedures. *Behavior Research and Therapy*, 1966, *4*, 79–84.

Axelrod, S., Hall, R. V., Weis, L., & Rohrer, S. Use of self-imposed contingencies to reduce the frequency of smoking behavior. In M. J. Mahoney & C. E. Thoresen (Eds.), *Self-control: Power to the person*. Monterey, Calif.: Brooks/Cole, 1974.

Ayllon, T., & Azrin, N. H. Reinforcement and instructions with mental patients. *Journal of Experimental Analysis of behavior*, 1964, *7*, 327–331.

Azrin, N. H., Bugle, C., & O'Brien, F. Behavioral engineering: Two apparatuses for toilet training retarded children. *Journal of Applied Behavior Analysis*, 1971, *4*, 249–253.

Azrin, N. H., & Lindsley, O. R. The reinforcement of cooperation between children. *Journal of Abnormal and Social Psychology*, 1956, *52*, 100–102.

Baer, D. M. In the beginning, there was a response. In E. Ramp & G. Semb (Eds.), *Behavior analysis: Areas of research and application*. Englewood Cliffs, N.J.: Prentice-Hall, Inc., 1975.

Baer, D. M., Rowbury, R. G., & Goetz, E. M. Behavioral traps in the preschool: A proposal for research. *Minnesota Symposia on Child Development*, 1976, *10*, 3–27.

Baer, D. M., Wolf, M. M., & Risley, T. R. Some current dimensions of applied behavior analysis. *Journal of Applied Behavior Analysis*, 1968, *1*, 91–97.

Bailey, J. S., Wolf, M. M., Phillips, E. L. Home-based reinforcement and the modification of the pre-delinquents' classroom behavior. *Journal of Applied Behavior Analysis*, 1970, *3*, 223–233.

Balthazar, E. E. *Balthazar scales of adaptive behavior for the profoundly and severely mentally retarded* (Section 1). Champaign, Ill.: Research Press, 1971.

Becker, W. C., Madsen, C. H., Arnold, C. R., & Thomas, D. R. The contingent use of teacher attention and praise in reducing classroom behavior problems. *Journal of Special Education*, 1967, *1*, 287–307.

Bender, M., & Valletutti, P. J. *Teaching the moderately and severely handicapped* (Vol. 1). Baltimore, Md.: University Park Press, 1976.

Bender, M., Valletutti, P. J., & Bender, R. *Teaching the moderately and severely handicapped: Curriculum objectives, strategies, and activities* (Vol. 2). Baltimore: University Park Press, 1976. (a)

Bender, M., Valletutti, P. J., & Bender, R. *Teaching the moderately and severely handicapped: Curriculum objectives, strategies, and activities* (Vol. 3). Baltimore: University Park Press, 1976. (b)

Bijou, S. W. Operant extinction after fixed-interval schedules with young children. *Journal of the Experimental Analysis of Behavior*, 1958, *1*, 25–29.

Bijou, S. W., Peterson, R. F., & Ault, M. H. A method to integrate descriptive and experimental field studies at the level of data and empirical concepts. *Journal of Applied Behavior Analysis*, 1968, *1*, 175–191.

Birnbrauer, J. S., Bijou, S. W., Wolf, M. N., & Kidder, N. D. Programmed instruction in the classroom. In L. Ullmann & L. Krasner (Eds.), *Case studies in behavior modification*. New York: Holt, Rinehart, & Winston, 1965.

Birnbrauer, J. S., Wolf, M. M., Kidder, J. D., & Tague, C. E. Classroom behavior of retarded pupils with token reinforcement. *Journal of Experimental Child Psychology*, 1965, *2*, 219–235.

Bobbitt, R. A., Gourevitch, V. P., Miller, L. E., & Jensen, G. D. Dynamics of social interactive behavior: A computerized procedure for analyzing trends, patterns and sequences. *Psychology Bulletin*, 1969, *71*, 110–121.

Bricker, W. A. A systematic approach to language training. In R. L. Schiefelbusch (Ed.), *Language of the mentally retarded*. Baltimore: Md.: University Park Press, 1972.

Bricker, W. A., & Bricker, D. D. A program of language training for the severely handicapped child. *Exceptional Children*, 1970, *37*, 101–111.

Brown, L., & York, R. Developing programs for severely handicapped students: Teacher training and classroom instruction. *Focus on Exceptional Children*, 1974, *6*, 1–11.

Bucher, B., & Lovaas, O. I. Use of aversive stimulation in behavior modification. In M. R. Jones (Ed.), *Miami symposium on the prediction of behavior: Aversive stimulation*. Coral Gables, Fla.: University of Miami Press, 1968.

Budde, J. F., & Menolascino, F. J. Systems technology and retardation: Application to vocational habilitation. *Mental Retardation*, 1971, *9*, 11–16.

Campbell, D. T., & Stanley, J. C. *Experimental and quasi-experimental designs for research*. Chicago: Rand McNally, 1963.

Cartwright, C. A., & Cartwright, G. P. *Developing observational skills*. New York: McGraw-Hill, 1974.

Christopherson, E. R., Arnold, C. M., Hill, D. W., & Quilitch, H. R. The home point system: Token reinforcement procedures for application by parents of children with behavior problems. *Journal of Applied Behavior Analysis*, 1972, *5*, 485–497.

Cohen, M. A., Gentry, N. D., Hulten, W. J., & Martin, G. L. Measures of classroom performance. In N. G. Haring & A. H. Hayden (Eds.), *The improvement of instruction*. Seattle: Special Child Publishers, 1972.

Cooper, J. O. *Measurement and analysis of behavior techniques*. Columbus, Ohio.: Charles E. Merrill, 1974.

Craighead, W. E., Kazdin, A. E., & Mahoney, M. J. *Behavior modification: Principles, issues, and applications*. Boston: Houghton Mifflin, 1976.

Crosson, J. E. A technique for programming sheltered workshop environments for training severely retarded workers. *American Journal of Mental Deficiency*, 1969, *73*, 814–818.

Edgar, E., Maser, J., Smith, D. D., & Haring, N. G. Developing an instructional sequence for teaching a self-help skill. *Education and Training of the Mentally Retarded*, 1977, *12*(1), 42–50.

Fixsen, D. L., Phillips, E. L., & Wolf, M. M. Achievement place: The reliability of self-reporting and peer-reporting and their effect on behavior. *Journal of Applied Behavior Analysis*, 1972, *5*, 19–30.

Flavell, J. E. Reduction of stereotypes by reinforcement of toy play. *Mental Retardation*, 1973, *11*(4), 21–23.

Foster, R. W. *Camelot behavioral checklist manual.* Parsons, Kans.: Camelot Behavioral Systems, 1974.

Foxx, R. M., & Martin, P. L. A useful portable timer. *Journal of Applied Behavior Analysis*, 1971, *4*, 60.

Fuller, P. Operant conditioning of a vegetative human organism. *American Journal of Psychology*, 1949, *62*, 587–590.

Goetz, E. M., & Baer, D. M. Social control of form diversity and the emergence of new forms in children's block-building. *Journal of Applied Behavior Analysis*, 1973, *6*, 209–217.

Gold, M. W. Stimulus factors in skill training of the retarded on a complex assembly task: Acquisition, transfer and retention. *American Journal of Mental Deficiency*, 1972, *76*, 517–526.

Hall, R. V. *Managing behavior. Part I—Behavior modification: The measurement of behavior.* Lawrence, Kans.: H & H Enterprises, 1971.

Hall, R. V., Cristler, C., Cranston, S. S., & Tucker, B. Teachers and parents as researchers using multiple baseline designs. *Journal of Applied Behavior Analysis*, 1970, *3*, 247–255.

Hall, R. V., Hawkins, R. P., & Axelrod, S. Measuring and recording student behavior: A behavior analysis approach. In R. A. Weinberg, & F. H. Wood (Eds.), *Observation of pupils and teachers in mainstream and special education settings: Alternate strategies.* Minneapolis, Minn.: Leadership Training Institute, University of Minnesota, 1975.

Hall, R. V., Lund, D., & Jackson, D. Effects of teacher attention on study behavior. *Journal of Applied Behavior Analysis*, 1968, *1*, 1–12.

Hamilton, J., Stephens, L., & Allen, P. Controlling aggressive and destructive behavior in severely retarded institutionalized residents. *American Journal of Mental Deficiency*, 1967, *7*, 852–956.

Hansen, C. L., & Lovitt, T. C. The relationships between question type and mode of reading on the ability to comprehend. *The Journal of Special Education*, 1976, *10*, 53–60.

Hart, B. M., Reynolds, W. J., Baer, D. M., Brawley, E. R., & Harris, F. R. Effect of contingent and noncontingent social reinforcement on the cooperative play of a preschool child. *Journal of Applied Behavior Analysis*, 1968, *1*, 73–76.

Hartmann, D.P., & Hall, R. V. The changing criterion design. *Journal of Applied Behavior Analysis*, 1976, *9*, 527–532.

Hersen, M., & Barlow, D. H. *Single case experimental designs: Strategies for studying behavior change.* New York: Pergamon Press, 1976.

Hester, P., & Hendrickson, J. Training functional expressive language: The acquisition and generalization of five-element syntactic responses. *Journal of Applied Behavior Analysis*, in press.

Homme, L. E., deBaca, P. C., Devine, J. V., Steinhorst, R., & Rickert, E. J. Use of the Premack principle in controlling the behavior of nursery school children. *Journal of the Experimental Analysis of Behavior*, 1963, *6*, 544.

Hopkins, B. L. Effects of candy and social reinforcement, instructions and reinforcement schedule learnings on the modification and maintenance of smiling. *Journal of Applied Behavior Analysis*, 1968, *1*, 121–129.

Horner, R. D., & Keilitz, I. Training mentally retarded adolescents to brush their teeth. *Journal of Applied Behavior Analysis*, 1975, *8*, 301–309.

Itard, J. M. G. [*The wild boy of Aveyron.*] (G. Humphrey & M. Humphrey, Eds. and trans.). New York: Appleton-Century-Crofts (Prentice-Hall), 1932, 1962. (Originally published in Paris by Gouyon, 1801.)

Jackson, G. M., Johnson, C. R., Ackron, G. S., & Crowley, R. Food satiation as a procedure to decelerate vomiting. *American Journal of Mental Deficiency*, 1975, *80*, 223–227.

Johnson, S. M., & Bolstad, O. D. Methodological issues in naturalistic observations: Some problems and solutions for field research. In L. A. Hamerlynck, L. C. Handy, & E. J. Mash (Eds.), *Behavior change: Methodological concepts and practice.* Champaign, Ill.: Research Press, 1973.

Kanfer, F. H., & Grimm, L. G. Behavioral analysis: Selecting target behaviors in the interview. *Behavior Modification*, 1977, *1*, 7–28.

Kauffman, J. M., & Scranton, T. R. Parent control of thumb-sucking in the home. *Child Study Journal*, 1974, *7*, 1–10.

Kauffman, J. M., & Snell, M. E. Managing the behavior of severely handicapped persons. In E. Sontag, J. Smith, & N. Certo (Eds.), *Educational programming for the severely and profoundly handicapped.* Reston, Va.: Council for Exceptional Children, 1977.

Kazdin, A. E. *Behavior modification in applied settings.* Homewood, Ill.: Dorsey Press, 1975.

Kerlinger, F. N. *Foundations of behavioral research.* New York: Holt, Rinehart & Winston, 1964.

Krasner, L., & Ullman, L. P. (Eds.) *Research in behavior modification: New developments and implications.* New York: Holt, Rinehart & Winston, 1965.

Larsen, L., & Bricker, W. A manual for parents and teachers of severely and moderately retarded children. *IMRID Papers & Reports*, 1968, *5*(22), Nashville: George Peabody College for Teachers.

Leff, R. D. Teaching TMR children and adults to dial the telephone. *Mental Retardation*, 1975, *13*(3), 9–11.

Leitenberg, H. (Ed.). *Handbook of behavior modification and behavior therapy.* Englewood Cliffs, N.J.: Prentice-Hall, 1976.

Lindsley, O. R. Direct measurement and prosthesis of retarded behavior. *Journal of Education*, 1964, *147*, 62–81.

Lindsley, O. R. A reliable wrist counter for recording behavioral rates. *Journal of Applied Behavior Analysis*, 1968, *1*, 77.

Lovaas, O. I., Schaeffer, B., & Simmons, J. Q. Building social behavior in autistic children by use of electric shock. *Journal of Experimental Research in Personality*, 1965, *1*, 99–109.

Lovaas, O. I., & Simmons, J. Q. Manipulation of self-destruction in three retarded children. *Journal of Applied Behavior Analysis*, 1969, *2*, 143–159.

Lovitt, T. C. Operant conditioning techniques for children with learning disabilities. *Journal of Special Education*, 1968, *2*, 283–289.

Lovitt, T. C. Behavior modification: The current scene. *Exceptional Children*, 1970, *37*, 85–91.

Lovitt, T. C. Applied behavior analysis and learning disabilities. Part I—Characteristics of ABA, general recommendations and methodological limitations. *Journal of Learning Disabilities*, 1975, *8*(7), 432–443.

Lovitt, T. C. Applied behavior analysis techniques and curriculum research: Implications for instruction. In N. G. Haring & R. L. Schiefelbusch (Eds.), *Teaching special children*. New York: McGraw-Hill, 1976.

Lovitt, T. C. *In spite of my resistance: I've learned from children*. Columbus, Ohio: Charles E. Merrill, 1977.

Madsen, C. H., Becker, W. V., & Thomas, D. R. Rules, praise and ignoring: Elements of elementary classroom control. *Journal of Applied Behavior Analysis*, 1968, *1*, 139–150.

Mager, R. *Preparing instructional objectives*. Palo Alto, Calif.: Fearon Publishers, 1962.

McAshan, H. H. *Writing behavioral objectives: A new approach*. New York: Harper & Row, 1970.

McCormack, J. E., Hamlet, C. C., Dunaway, J., & Vorderer, L. E. *Educational evaluation and planning package* (Vol. 1). Medford, Mass.: Massachusetts Center for Program Development and Evaluation, 1976.

Nedelman, D., & Sulzbacher, S. I. Dickey at 13 years of age: A long term success following early application of operant conditioning procedures. In G. Semb (Ed.), *Behavior analysis and education*. Lawrence, Kans.: University of Kansas Press, 1972.

Nelson, G. L., Cone, J. D., & Hanson, C. R. Training correct utensil use in retarded children: Modeling versus physical guidance. *American Journal of Mental Deficiency*, 1975, *80*, 114–122.

O'Brien, F., & Azrin, N. H. Developing proper mealtime behavior of the institutionalized retarded. *Journal of Applied Behavior Analysis*, 1972, *5*, 389–399.

O'Leary, K. D., Kaufman, K. F., Kass, R. E., & Drabman, R. S. The effects of loud and soft reprimands on the behavior of disruptive students. *Exceptional Children*, 1970, *37*, 145–155.

Osborne, J. G. Free time as a reinforcer in the management of classroom behavior. *Journal of Applied Behavior Analysis*, 1969, *2*, 113–118.

Perske, R., & Marquiss, J. Learning to live in an apartment. *Mental Retardation*, 1973, *11*(3), 18–19.

Peterson, R. F. Some experiments on the organization of a class of imitative behaviors. *Journal of Applied Behavior Analysis*, 1968, *1*, 225–235.

Phillips, E. L. Achievement place: Token reinforcement procedures in home-style rehabilitation setting for "pre-delinquent" boys. *Journal of Applied Behavior Analysis*, 1968, *1*, 213–223.

Phillips, E. L., Phillips, E. A., Fixsen, D. L., & Wolf, M. M. Achievement place: Modification of the behaviors of pre-delinquent boys within a token economy. *Journal of Applied Behavior Analysis*, 1971, *4*, 45–59.

Popham, W. J., & Baker, E. L. *Systematic instruction*. Englewood Cliffs, N.J.: Prentice-Hall, 1970.(a)

Popham, W. J., & Baker, E. L. *Planning an instructional sequence*. Englewood Cliffs, N.J.: Prentice-Hall, 1970.(b)

Quick, A. D., & Campbell, A. A. *Project MEMPHIS: Lesson plans for enhancing preschool developmental progress*. Dubuque, Iowa: Kendall/Hunt, 1976.

Quick, A. D., Little, T. L., & Campbell, A. A. *Project MEMPHIS: Enhancing development progress in preschool exceptional children*. Belmont, Calif.: Fearon Publishers, 1974.

Quilitch, R. H., & Risley, T. R. The effects of play materials on social play. *Journal of Applied Behavior Analysis*, 1973, *6*, 573–578.

Redd, W. H. Effects of mixed reinforcement contingencies on adults' control of children's behavior. *Journal of Applied Behavior Analysis*, 1969, *2*, 249–254.

Repp, A. C., Roberts, D. M., Slack, D. J., Repp, C. F., & Berkler, M. S. A comparison of frequency, interval, and time-sampling methods of data collection. *Journal of Applied Behavior Analysis*, 1976, *9*, 501–508.

Resnick, L. B., Wang, M. C., & Kaplan, J. Task analysis in curriculum design: A hierarchically sequenced introductory mathematics curriculum. *Journal of Applied Behavior Analysis*, 1973, *6*, 679–710.

Sailor, W., Guess, D., & Baer, D. M. Functional language for verbally deficient children: An experimental program. *Mental Retardation*, 1973, *11*(3), 27–35.

Sailor, W., & Mix, B. J. *The TARC assessment system*. Lawrence, Kans.: H & H Enterprises, 1975.

Shores, R. E., Hester, P., & Strain, P. S. The effects of amount and type of teacher-child interaction on child-child interaction during free play. *Psychology in the Schools*, 1976, *13*, 171–175.

Sidman, M. *Tactics of scientific research: Evaluating experimental data in psychology*. New York: Basic Books, 1960.

Skiba, E. A., Pettigrew, L. E., & Alden, S. E. A behavioral approach to the control of thumbsucking in the classroom. *Journal of Applied Behavior Analysis*, 1971, *4*, 121–125.

Skinner, B. F. *The behavior of organisms*. New York: Appleton, Century Crofts, 1938.

Skinner, B. F. *Science and human behavior*. New York: Macmillan, 1953.

Smith, D. D. *The influence of instructions, feedback and reinforcement contingencies on children's abilities to acquire and become proficient at computational arithmetic skills*. Unpublished doctoral dissertation, University of Washington, 1973.

Smith, D. D., & Lovitt, T. C. The use of modeling techniques to influence the acquisition of computational arithmetic skills in learning disabled children. In E. Ramp & G. Semb (Eds.), *Behavior analysis: Areas of research and application.* Englewood Cliffs, N.J.: Prentice-Hall, 1975.

Smith, D. D., & Lovitt, T. C. The differential effects of reinforcement contingencies on arithmetic performance. *Journal of Learning Disabilities,* 1976, *1,* 32–40.

Smith, D. D., Smith, J. O., & Edgar, E. B. Prototypic model for the development of instructional materials. In N. G. Haring & L. J. Brown (Eds.), *Teaching the severely handicapped* (Vol. 1). New York: Grune & Stratton, 1976.

Strain, P. S., Shores, R. E., & Kerr, M. M. An experimental analysis of "spillover" effects on the social intervention of behaviorally handicapped preschool children. *Journal of Applied Behavior Analysis,* 1976, *9,* 31–40.

Strain, P. S., Shores, R. E., & Timm, M. A. Effects of peer social initiations on the behavior of withdrawn preschool children. *Journal of Applied Behavior Analysis,* 1977, *10,* 289–298.

Surratt, P. R., Ulrich, R. E., & Hawkins, R. P. An elementary student as a behavioral engineer. *Journal of Applied Behavior Analysis,* 1969, *2,* 85–92.

Tate, B. G., & Baroff, G. S. Aversive control of self-injurious behavior in a psychotic boy. *Behavior Research and Therapy,* 1966, *4,* 231–287.

Thomson, C., Holmberg, M., & Baer, D. M. A brief report on a comparison of time-sampling procedures. *Journal of Applied Behavior Analysis,* 1974, *7,* 623–626.

Ullman, L. P., & Krasner, L. (Eds.). *Case studies in behavior modification.* New York: Holt, Rinehart & Winston, 1965.

White, O. R. *A glossary of behavioral terminology.* Champaign, Ill.: Research Press, 1971.

White, O.R., & Haring, N.G. *Exceptional teaching.* Columbus, Ohio: Charles E. Merrill, 1976.

White, O. R., & Liberty, K. A. Behavioral assessment and precise educational measurement. In N. G. Haring & R. L. Schiefelbusch (Eds.), *Teaching Special Children.* New York: McGraw-Hill, 1976.

Whitman, T. L., Mercurio, S. R., & Caponigri, V. Development of social responses in two severely retarded children. *Journal of Applied Behavior Analysis,* 1970, *3,* 133–138.

Williams, C. D. The elimination of tantrum behavior by extinction procedures. *Journal of Abnormal and Social Psychology,* 1959, *59,* 269.

Williams, W., Coyne, P., Johnson, F., Scheuerman, N., Swetlik, B., & York, R. Skill sequences and curriculum development: Application of a rudimentary development math sequence in the instruction and evaluation of severely handicapped students. In N. G. Haring & L. J. Brown (Eds.), *Teaching the severely handicapped* (Vol. 2), New York: Grune & Stratton, 1977.

Wilson, C. W. & Hopkins, B. L. The effects of contingent music on the intensity of noise in junior high home economics classes. *Journal of Applied Behavior Analysis,* 1973, *6,* 269–275.

Wolf, M. M., Risley, T., Johnson, M., Harris, F., & Allen, E. Application of operant conditioning procedures to the behavior problems of an autistic child: A follow-up and extension. *Behavior Research and Therapy,* 1967, *5,* 103–111.

Wolf, M. M., Risley, T., & Mees, H. Application of operant conditioning procedures to the behavior problems of an autistic child. *Behavior Research and Therapy,* 1964, *1,* 305–312.

Worell, J., & Nelson, C. M. *Managing instructional problems: A case study workbook.* New York: McGraw-Hill, 1974.

Wright, H. F. Observational child study. In P. H. Mussen (Ed.), *Handbook of research methods in child development.* New York: Wiley, 1960.

Zimmerman, E. H., & Zimmerman, J. The alteration of behavior in a special classroom situation. *Journal of the Experimental Analysis of Behavior,* 1962, *5,* 59–60.

Notes

1. Spradlin, J. E. *The Premack hypothesis and self-feeding by profoundly retarded children: A case report* (Parsons Research Project, Working Paper 79). Unpublished manuscript, Kansas University and Kansas Bureau of Child Research, 1964.
2. Lovitt, T. C. *Applied behavior analysis techniques and curriculum research: Implications for instruction* (National Institute of Education, Grant No. 0703916). Seattle: University of Washington, 1974.
3. Gold, M. W. *Task analysis: A statement and an example using acquisition and production of a complex assembly task by the retarded blind* (National Institute of Child Health and Human Development Program, Project Grant No. HD05951). Unpublished manuscript, University of Illinois, Institute for Child Behavior and Development.
4. Woolman, M. *The concept of the program lattice.* Unpublished manuscript, Washington, D.C.: Institute of Educational Research, Inc., 1962.
5. Smith, J. O., & Smith, D. D. Research and application of instructional material development. In N. G. Haring (Ed.), *Annual report: A program project for the investigation and application of procedures of analysis and modification of behavior of handicapped children.* Washington, D.C.: National Institute of Education, (NIE Grant OEG-0-70-3916, 607), 1974.
6. Project MORE. *Critical training list for basic skills.* Unpublished manuscript, Nashville, Tenn.: George Peabody College for Teachers, 1975.
7. Roberts, M. B., & Smith, D. D. *The influence of contingent instructions on reducing inappropriate behavior of preschool children.* Unpublished manuscript, Nashville, Tenn.: George Peabody College for Teachers, 1974.
8. Smith, D. D., & Fleming, E. C. *A comparison of individual and group modeling techniques aimed at altering children's computational abilities.* Unpublished manuscript, Nashville, Tenn.: George Peabody College for Teachers, 1975.

3

Intervention Strategies

This chapter was written by **Martha E. Snell,** *University of Virginia, and* **Deborah D. Smith,** *University of New Mexico.*

In the last twenty years a powerful teaching technology has been developed. This technology rests upon a functional analysis of the controlling relationship between a given behavior and the environmental factors surrounding that behavior. Although the roots of this technology are embedded in techniques applied years ago with the handicapped by teachers such as Jean Itard (Lane, 1976), Édouard Seguin, and Maria Montessori, it is only in more recent years that reliable observational procedures, experimental design features, and the methods of applied behavior analysis have become widely used and respected intervention approaches. Unfortunately, many moderately and severely handicapped persons have not reaped the benefits of this technology and some have been subjects of its abuse.

Once behaviors in need of change have been selected, specified, measured, and criterion levels targeted, a teacher is ready to identify intervention strategies and describe the means by which such strategies will be programmed to teach these behaviors. While this part of teaching is enormously complex, an admirable intervention plan is only admirable if the behaviors selected for intervention are currently relevant for the particular student. The intervention strategies described in this chapter are powerful and their results are predictable when the user understands their workings. However, the technology from which these strategies develop does not dictate behavioral goals, it only describes how goals might be achieved. It is also true that this technology is value-free—it does not have built-in rules governing its application (Skinner, 1971). When teaching goals are carelessly selected or merely reflect the fickle whims of a teacher, researcher, or parent, the intervention strategies, if correctly applied, may lead to perverse patterns of behavior.

On the other hand, careful selection of behavioral targets appropriate for a handicapped student and skilled delineation of an intervention plan does not guarantee that these targets will be realized. When the teacher does not understand *how* to apply intervention strategies or is neglectful of consistency in their application, a student may become confused, learn nothing, or learn maladaptive forms of behavior as a consequence.

The purpose of this chapter is to review information basic to the understanding and use of behavioral strategies with the moderately and severely handicapped. However an author cannot monitor the application of a book's contents—this always shall be the responsibility of the reader. (In-depth descriptions of behavior modification and its application to the handicapped learner should be sought elsewhere.)[1]

Positive reinforcement, central to behavior modification, is by far the most essential and powerful strategy a teacher may employ. As such, it is worthy of a lengthy discussion devoted to the variables inherent in its operation. To introduce the discussion, brief definitions of reinforcement, both positive and negative, are given. The concepts of punishment and extinction are dealt with as methods to decrease undesirable behavior; both methods are discussed more fully later in this chapter.

Intervention Strategies Aimed at Increasing Behavior

When the occurrence of a behavior is increased because specific consequences (reinforcers) consistently follow all or most instances of that behavior and are not available in the absence of that behavior, a reinforcement *contingency* is in operation. It is this interdependent or contingent arrangement between behaviors and consequences which enables a teacher to change behaviors purposefully and this is commonly called *contingency management.* As illustrated in Figure 3.1, two classes of contingent reinforcement exist: positive and negative. *Positive reinforcement* occurs when the presentation of rewarding consequences (called positive reinforcers), made contingent upon a behavior, leads to an *increase* in the performance of that behavior. Negative reinforcement operates in a different manner but with the same resultant effect —an increase in the reinforced behavior. *Negative reinforcement* occurs when the removal of aversive events (called negative reinforcers) immediately following the performance of a behavior results in an increase in the frequency of that behavior. Therefore, to reinforce behavior means to strengthen behavior—increase its frequency, its duration, or its intensity.

The moderately to profoundly handicapped require instruction across a diverse range of skills: social interaction, self-care, motor, cognition, and

language. When initial levels of such skills are mastered, instruction in the following advanced areas will be appropriate for many: functional use of academic skills, daily living skills, and vocational skills. Intervention strategies described in the following sections should serve as methodological guides for systematic teaching of these and related skills.

Positive reinforcement

Selection of Positive Reinforcers

A false notion, held by many, is that certain items or events in and of themselves serve as positive reinforcers for all individuals. Common examples of these assumed "reinforcers" include words of praise, smiles, and certain sweets (such as the ubiquitous candy-coated, chocolate bits). We already stated that reinforcers are defined by their effect upon an individual's behavior—the "acid test" is whether the object or event when made contingent upon a behavior causes an increase in that behavior. If this is not the outcome, a positive reinforcer has not been selected. What is reinforcing to one individual may not be to others because of past experiences or personal preference. For example, many youngsters initially do not like carbonated beverages; with repeated tastes, however, they learn to like them. Some children learn to fear water, although most learn to enjoy it. The reinforcing value of some events depends partially upon an individual's mental abilities. This can be illustrated by an adult's verbal praise and cash rewards which are reinforcing only if the individual has respectively some basic understanding of the language and the currency system involved.

The determination of reinforcers should not be a product of guessing. This information can be gained precisely by using four general techniques. To select an individual's reinforcer list or "menu," one can:

1. Question the individual directly about his or her likes and dislikes.
2. Ask others familiar with the individual's likes and dislikes for a list of potential reinforcers.
3. Observe the individual over a period of days in his natural setting and formulate a list of observed reinforcing events.
4. Structure the individual's environment so a period of reinforcement can be observed.

The direct questioning procedure, while often effective with the verbal individual, is nonfunctional

---

1. The reader interested in more detailed information on behavior modification and applications with mentally retarded and emotionally disturbed individuals should consult Birnbrauer, 1977; Browning & Stover, 1971; Gardner, 1971; Gelfand & Hartmann, 1975; Kazdin, 1975; MacMillan, 1973; Madsen & Madsen, 1974.

TYPE OF EVENT

	Presented	Positive Reinforcement Effect: frequency of positively reinforced behavior *increases*	Punishment Effect: frequency of punished behavior *decreases;* other side effects may occur
OPERATION PERFORMED AFTER A RESPONSE	Removed, Withdrawn	Punishment Effect: frequency of punished behavior *decreases;* other side effects may occur	Negative Reinforcement Effect: frequency of negatively reinforced behavior *increases*
	Withheld, Not Presented	Extinction Effect: frequency of behavior placed on extinction *decreases*	

FIGURE 3.1   *An illustration of the influence principles of operant conditioning based upon the presentation, removal, or withholding of various events in consequence to the performance of a response*

Source: Adapted with permission from A. E. Kazdin. *Behavior modification in applied settings.* Homewood, Ill.: Dorsey Press, 1975 ©, p. 25.

with many severely handicapped individuals because of its reliance upon receptive and expressive language. For the individual lacking only expressive skills, a teacher may first teach the child to communicate by a manual signing system (Snell, 1974), by simply gesturing "yes" or "no," or by looking at pictures of potential reinforcers (e.g., pictures of foods, activities, and toys) and pointing to those preferred.

When asking other teachers, parents, siblings, or relatives to identify reinforcers for an individual, it is especially important to verify their responses with one of the other three methods. While both questioning methods may seem to be the most efficient, they are likely to yield inaccurate or useless information, for often what is reinforcing in one setting is impractical, ineffective, or unavailable for use in another.

If carried out systematically for a representative period of time, direct observation of an individual's preferences for foods, beverages, toys, songs, people, classroom and playground activities, clothes,

etc., probably yields the most accurate list of reinforcers. A teacher may employ any of the measurement procedures described in Chapter 2 to record these preferences (e.g., duration of time spent in various activities, frequency of selecting various toys).

The use of a structured observation, as opposed to a natural observation during the course of a regular day, enables a teacher to observe an individual's reaction to potential reinforcers which are normally unavailable. A variation of this procedure called "reinforcer sampling" was effectively used with institutionalized psychotic adults (Ayllon & Azrin, 1968). They allowed a limited "free" exposure to novel activities such as participation in social evenings, religious services, and musical activities as a method to teach the adults the reinforcing value of an event before making that event contingent upon certain behaviors. In a structured observation, an individual first is allowed to sample briefly a small group of similar items (foods, beverages, toys) or events (listening to a music box, rocking on a toy horse, being pushed in a wagon). Then the individual is provided with the entire group of potential reinforcers and the frequency or duration of choices is recorded. After a group of possible reinforcers is sampled and the free-choice observation is recorded, other groups may be observed similarly. When an individual's response to food groups is observed, the best time is just prior to a meal. As with natural observations, structured observations do not depend upon the individual's language skills —an advantage with many severely handicapped individuals.

Primary and secondary reinforcers. Although reinforcers have unlimited range and vary from tangible items and activities to abstract thoughts of self-approval, all reinforcers are of two general types: *primary* (unlearned or unconditioned) or *secondary* (learned or conditioned). The first category includes the "universal" or automatic reinforcers to which everyone responds (although not continuously) without any prior instruction. Primary reinforcers for one in a state of hunger, thirst, or uncomfortable chill include food, drink, and warmth.

Secondary reinforcers are those events which have obtained a reinforcing value to an individual through conditioning. For example, with varying amounts of experience and mental ability, a child may come to value the activities of playing with toys, riding a bike, listening to music, receiving pay for work, receiving praise, and accomplishing a goal. Secondary reinforcers begin as neutral stimuli and acquire their value through repeated pairings with already existing reinforcers (primary or other secondary). Eventually these events take on reinforcing value in and of themselves. For example, Miller and Drennen (1970) established social praise ("good") as a secondary reinforcer for institutionalized and severely disturbed individuals by intermittantly pairing praise with primary reinforcers such as candy and brownies. In comparison to social reinforcement alone and no reinforcement, social praise with intermittent primary reinforcers was most effective in modifying the residents' verbal behavior.

Generalized reinforcers are highly effective secondary reinforcers which acquire their reinforcing power by association with many other reinforcers (primary and secondary). Money, affection, attention, and approval by others are all examples of generalized reinforcers because each necessitates learning and each is associated with many additional reinforcers (e.g., money purchases food, various activities, clothes, toys, etc.).

Generalized reinforcers commonly used in educational settings include attention, approval, and *tokens.* Token systems or economies are analogous to a currency-payment system except the value of a token is limited to the immediate setting and is controlled by the teacher, parent, or psychologist who implements the system. Tokens come in an assortment of forms—washers, poker chips, checkers, slips of specially marked paper—and may even take the less tangible form of checkmarks placed on an "official" checksheet. As with other reinforcers, tokens are made available contingent upon target behaviors and, in turn, are exchangeable for the "purchase" of *back-up* primary and secondary reinforcers. Tokens possess advantages over many other reinforcers because they may be distributed in classrooms conveniently and, because of their exchange power, are durable in their reinforcing quality. Unlike money, tokens possess no value outside the behavior modification program, but the token exchange value within the program may be easily and quickly adjusted by the teacher. Tokens have been used in combination with praise as the reinforcers to modify a wide variety of behaviors in the moderately and severely handicapped (Kazdin & Bootzin, 1972) —math skills (Baker, Stanish, & Fraser, 1972; Dalton, Rubino, & Hislop, 1973), language skills (Baer & Guess, 1973; Baker et al., 1972), and the increase of attention and the decrease of inappropriate behavior (Hislop, Moore, & Stanish, 1973).

Most token economies, such as those just cited, have a specific and additive exchange value. Some use a variety of tokens each with their own specific value, much like our own currency system. Although counting may be taught via a token system, many severely handicapped individuals may be unprepared to learn counting and the concept of purchasing. In these cases, tokens cannot be established as generalized reinforcers. A modified token economy, based on varying rather than specific values, may be employed with these individuals (Kent, 1974). With varying value systems, tokens are awarded contingent upon specific behavior(s) but are exchanged for back-up reinforcers singly or, more commonly, in varying amounts whenever the teacher deems a more tangible reinforcer is necessary to maintain the generalized reinforcing value of the tokens. Also, the individual is "token trained" prior to implementing such a system. The series of steps listed next comprise token training and act to establish for the student an association between tokens and their back-up reinforcers.

1. A behavior or class of behaviors, easily performed by the individual, is selected (e.g., imitation of movements, following simple commands —"Show me the *baby*," "Comb your hair," "Look at me").
2. A choice of known back-up reinforcers (arranged on a tray or cupcake pan), a token container (one-pound coffee can), and a uniform set of at least 30 tokens (poker chips, washers, checkers, etc.) are readied at a training table.
3. The individual is requested to perform the behavior and:
   A. is reinforced immediately following the behavior with a single token placed into the individual's hand and with enthusiastic praise.
   B. is prompted if the behavior is not forthcoming, and then is reinforced with a token and praise immediately following the behavior.
4. Immediately the trainer holds out a hand to collect the token (with prompting if necessary) and presents the reinforcer tray from which the individual is prompted to select one reinforcer.
5. This cycle—request for the behavior, praise and token reinforcement, and immediate exchange —is repeated until the individual, without any prompts, shows evidence of making an association between tokens and token exchange. For example, an individual may reach for the tokens after a response as an attempt to "speed up" the exchange process. Then the exchange schedule is increased gradually from one token to an accumulation of four or five tokens before exchange.
6. While remaining at four or five tokens the token container is introduced to facilitate the collection and exchange process. Tokens are then dropped into the can by the teacher and the individual is shown how to lift and empty the contents during exchange time.
7. The exchange ratio is increased gradually over the remainder of the token training session, which should not last beyond 15 to 20 minutes.
8. At this point, tokens may be used during actual teaching sessions as the method of reinforcement. Initially, a brief review (a few immediate or low ratio exchanges) may be necessary to remind the individual of the tokens' exchange value.

This type of token system has been effective with many nonverbal, profoundly handicapped individu-

als (Rowland, 1973). After the initial token training, praise and tokens served as reinforcers for correct responses during daily 20-minute language training sessions. Token exchanges were scheduled for some only at the end of each session; for others, exchanges were scheduled at both the middle and the end of the training sessions.

Although token economies have been useful with many handicapped individuals, a teacher must be aware of the complexities involved in implementing a token economy (e.g., purchase of back-up reinforcers, delivering tokens, making token exchanges, tabulating accumulated tokens) in comparison to contingent, individualized application of praise and privileges (Kazdin, 1975; Kazdin & Bootzin, 1972). However, token economies are more manageable when they are not used all day for all students. Token systems have proven influential for small groups or individuals during specific training periods when other behavior modification strategies were ineffective.[2]

Reinforcer Schedules and Durability

Schedules of reinforcement indicate how many and which responses are reinforced, and, thereby, they affect the resultant response pattern. Reinforcement schedule is the "*A*" or "arrangement" element in Lindsley's (1964) operant framework: $E^A \rightarrow B \rightarrow A \rightarrow E^C$. Reinforcement may be made available to individuals according to the number of responses performed (*ratio* schedules) or the passage of time in relation to the performance (*interval* schedules). Both types of schedules may be based either upon absolute amounts of responses or time (referred to as *fixed* schedules) or upon averaged amounts of responses or time (*variable* schedules). For example, when one reinforcer is presented for every occurrence of the target behavior, a fixed ratio schedule of one (*FR:*1) is in operation—commonly referred to as *continuous reinforcement.* (All other schedules may be generally labeled *intermittent reinforcement* schedules.) An *FR:*5 would be a fixed pattern of reinforcement for every fifth response; in a *VR:*5 schedule, reinforcement would be variable rather than regularly applied to an average of every fifth response. This *VR:*5 pattern might consist of: three occurrences of a tar-

---

2. The reader interested in more detailed readings on token systems should consult Allyon & Azrin (1968) and Stainback, Payne, Stainback, & Payne (1973).

get behavior, reinforcement, seven occurrences of the same target behavior, reinforcement, two occurrences of the target behavior, reinforcement, eight occurrences of the target behaviors, etc. In interval schedules the first target response occurring *after* a regular time period of so many seconds or minutes (fixed interval or *FI*) or an averaged period (variable interval or *VI*) is reinforced.

In many regular classrooms, reinforcement schedules are time-based (at the end of a class period) and teacher-dispensed social reinforcers may be as meager as one per minute. In a classroom of 30, this converts to a schedule of one reinforcement every half-hour—a rather sparse schedule (Hotchkiss, 1966; Patterson, Cobb, & Ray, 1972). Also most classroom schedules are more often variable rather than fixed; that is, teachers provide reinforcement when they judge enough "work" has been done or sufficient time has passed. "Sufficient" and "enough" tend to vary from one day to the next, resulting in variable schedules. If the teacher is unaware of the reinforcement schedule, the child probably will not learn in ways as predictable as if schedules were planned. For example, increasing a child's speed or proficiency in counting money is facilitated by the use of fixed ratio schedules which the teacher adjusts as the child improves (e.g., initially one reinforcement per correct counting, later one reinforcement every other counting, then one reinforcement every correct third, fifth, and so on). Differential reinforcement of high rates of behavior (*DRH*) is a useful reinforcement schedule also requiring the teacher to conscientiously identify a target rate of performance which may be achieved gradually over a period of instruction. *DRL* or differential reinforcement of low rates of behavior is another ratio reinforcement schedule which is the complement of *DRH: DRL* is employed to reduce undesirably frequent misbehaviors.

In general, fixed schedules, especially fixed interval schedules, are not easily found in school settings. While rewarding a child at the end of a time period (class, day, grading period) may appear to be a *FI* schedule, it often is not. That is, after the interval has passed, the target behavior must occur, after which reinforcement is given rather than merely reinforcing at the end of a time period (MacMillan, 1973).

Satiation, the overuse of a reinforcer, can affect the durability of a reinforcer over time. It is quite possible to "satiate" or tire of an event so that it is no longer reinforcing. This may happen if the reinforcer, although still contingent upon a behavior, is supplied too frequently or is given less often but in large amounts. The satiation process is closely related to reinforcement scheduling as well as to the quantity of reinforcer provided. For instance, if too much of an edible reinforcer is given or if food is offered too frequently, the reinforcing effect is lost or satiated.

Satiation may be used to advantage. As described in Figure 2.1, food satiation was used by Jackson, Johnson, Ackron, and Crowley (1975) as the means to decrease vomiting and rumination in two severely retarded adults. The more satiated with food the individuals were after meals, the less likely they were to regurgitate. The food satiation treatment caused regurgitation to lose its reinforcing effects.

However, satiation is often an unwelcomed consequence. After extensive involvement with certain toys or activities, the novelty lessens and the desired behavior is no longer effectively reinforced. This same outcome occurs when reinforcers are given freely or non-contingently—the individual has unlimited access to certain events which devalues their contingent effect on the target behavior. Because of satiation effects, a teacher must take measures to preserve the "special" quality of objects or activities selected as reinforcers.

Because of the powerful influence which reinforcement schedules have upon behavior, some related considerations concerning the scheduling of reinforcement should be understood by the teacher in arranging the learning conditions for instruction. Briefly, some of these considerations include:

1. Reinforcers should be available only when they are made contingent upon the performance of appropriate behavior or a realistic approximation of that behavior.

2. During the beginning or acquisition stage of learning, every instance of behavior should be encouraged by the continuous provision of smaller amounts of contingent reinforcement (e.g., small bits of food, a few seconds of music, etc.) rather than larger amounts less often. Continuous reinforcement yields a high rate of performance.

3. After a higher rate of behavior has been established (i.e., proficiency or maintenance stage of learning), reinforcers should be provided on an intermittent schedule; that is, the reinforcement schedule should be thinned slowly so that more behavior is required for each reinforcement. This will "strengthen" the behavior in that the individ-

ual will learn to tolerate periods of nonreinforcement rather than to abruptly "give up" and stop
responding when reinforcement is not forthcoming.

4. Intermittent reinforcement also acts to avoid
satiation because of the efficient use of fewer
reinforcers for more behavior while less training
time is occupied in the administration of reinforcers.

5. Variable schedules generally produce more
even patterns of behavior than fixed schedules
because the individual cannot learn to predict
the occasions for reinforcement.

6. To avoid satiation, a variety of reinforcers is preferred over a single reinforcer, and, whenever
feasible, it is best to let the student select the
reinforcer.

7. Reinforcers should be arranged in a comparative order from the most preferred/powerful to
the least preferred/less powerful. This arrangement allows a teacher to match reinforcers with
the effort required by the individual to perform a
particular behavior and to reserve the most powerful reinforcers for use during the more "difficult" teaching programs (e.g., behaviors which
after a lot of instruction have shown minimal
progress toward the aim).

Reinforcer Hierarchy

Besides arranging an individual's reinforcers from
most to least preferred, reinforcers may be viewed
along a continuum from immature (unlearned, primary) to mature (conditioned, secondary, and generalized). An individual capable of more mature
levels of reinforcement also has learned to expect
less immediate and less frequent reinforcement.
The following hierarchy illustrates an arrangement
from primary reinforcers to secondary and generalized reinforcers:

1. Food
2. Toys and entertainment activities
3. Tokens with backup reinforcers from categories
1 and 2
4. Letter grades which indicate progress
5. Parental, peer, or teacher approval
6. Self-praise for accomplishment of a goal

Two variables are related to this concept of *reinforcement hierarchy* (MacMillan, 1973): mental age
and social age (or appropriateness to the individual's level of adaptive behavior). With regard to the

first variable, mental age, as the degree of retardation increases, the general effectiveness of less
tangible or secondary reinforcers (e.g., social approval) is noticeably less (Byck, 1968; Locke, 1969).
Although this inverse relationship is due primarily to
the dependence of the more mature reinforcers
upon learning, it does not mean that lower functioning individuals cannot be guided to more complex
levels of reinforcement. The success of carefully
implemented token economies in the modification
of the severely handicapped illustrates this point
well.

Within the level of reinforcement preferred by an
individual, a teacher needs to select actual reinforcers which are appropriate to the individual's
chronological and social age range. For example, if
the reinforcers for a severely handicapped adolescent boy included food and toy play, the teacher
probably would want: to reinforce with food less
often or not at all; to select toys which could be used
instructionally (geared to his mental age) and yet
are appealing (e.g., category picture cards of transportation vehicles, animals, community helpers,
etc.); to reinforce with understandable praise prior
to every instance of tangible reinforcement while
gradually reducing reinforcement with tangibles;
and to develop new nontangible or activity reinforcers (e.g., passing out milk at lunch, listening to
music, etc.) which could replace the tangibles. The
teacher and parent are responsible for reducing the
excessive use of reinforcers, eliminating inappropriate reinforcers, and encouraging individuals to function at more complex levels of reinforcement.

Premack's Principle

This principle (Premack, 1959), referred to by some
as "Grandma's Law," follows the common childhood dictum, "First you eat your vegetables, then
you can have your dessert." In other words, if the
opportunity to perform a high probability behavior
(*HPB*) is made contingent upon the performance of
a low probability behavior (*LPB*), the frequency of
the *LPB* will increase as a result of positive reinforcement. *HPB*s are simply activities found to be
reinforcing to an individual (e.g., riding bikes, recess, listening to music on earphones, even being
allowed to run and yell for three minutes) which may
be parceled out in controlled amounts following the
completion of less popular activities (e.g., sorting
400 bolts of varying sizes, completion of a page of
money addition problems, finishing a specific clean-
up task).

*HPB*s have an advantage over tangible reinforcers in that they tend to be readily available, generally free of cost, and naturally occurring as opposed to artificially applied—a feature important in the maintenance of learned behaviors. However, some difficulties arise with *HPB* reinforcers, for they tend to be time-consuming, interruptive, and not easily "turned on and off." Each of these disadvantages can result in a delay of reinforcement which, in turn, may mean accidental reinforcement of intervening behaviors. To counteract these potentially disastrous side-effects, a teacher may reinforce the target behavior immediately with tokens or activity "pictures/tickets" which can be exchanged at a more convenient time. Both procedures serve to remind the individiual of the appropriate behavior and the delayed reinforcement, thus helping to bridge the delay between behavior and reinforcement with a *HPB*. Kitchen timers may facilitate an individual's understanding and cooperation, for they structure the beginning and end of a *HPB*. Finally, it is not ethical to identify an individual's essential activities or use basic possessions as *HPB*. Of course, the ethical issues surrounding the application and withdrawal of all intervention strategies must always be considered. As emphasized by Kazdin (1975):

> *The ideology of presenting activities and other potentially reinforcing events (e.g., meals and sleeping quarters) non-contingently was developed to ensure that individuals would not be deprived of basic human rights. Institutionalized clients are usually deprived of many amenities of living simply by virture of their institutionalization. Withholding or depriving individuals of the already limited number of available reinforcers is viewed as unethical. (p. 122)*

The solution lies in the introduction of a variety of novel, optional events which may serve as *HPB*s (e.g., special snack, use of a new bed spread, extra leisure time, etc.).

Although Premack's Principle sounds logical and has led to many practical reinforcement contingencies, the theoretical basis for this "principle," or more accurately for this hypothesis, has not been confirmed in applied research with humans (Knapp, 1976). The teacher is recommended to take particular care therefore in reinforcer (*HPB*) and punisher (*LPB*) identification as well as in observation of the contingent effect of *HPB*s and *LPB*s upon a target behavior.

Immediacy of Reinforcement

Positive reinforcement is hardly a simple process. As already discusssed, its effectiveness is influenced by the schedule of reinforcement and the quality or intensity of the reinforcers. A third inter-related factor which acts to control the degree of behavior change concerns reinforcing timing. The relationship is direct—the more immediately the reinforcers are presented following the behavior, the greater their effect. Immediacy promotes an association of reinforcement with performance of the target behavior—an understanding of the contingency placed in operation by the teacher. Immediacy is especially important for children and adults with limited language skills who are less able to learn contingencies from verbal contracts (e.g., "after you perform a certain behavior, you may do or have a particular reinforcer"). Immediacy also decreases the chance that intervening behaviors, not targeted for positive reinforcement, will be reinforced accidentally.

Two additional points regarding reinforcement timing must be expressed. First, immediacy is more essential during the acquisition of a target behavior than during the later stages of learning (proficiency and maintenance), when the behavior is performed more reliably. Secondly, after a behavior is in the proficiency state ("speeding up" the acquired behavior to acceptable rates) or the maintenance stage of learning (reviewing a learned behavior so it will not be forgotten), the individual should be taught to tolerate delays as well as a reduction in reinforcement, thereby lessening the dependency on reinforcement.

Shaping

Two major reinforcement strategies are available to build new behavior repertoires and to improve or expand present behavior. These strategies are shaping and chaining. Both operations concern the selective provision of reinforcing consequences for certain improvements in behavior or for specific amounts of behavior. In other words, the teacher must focus careful attention on the learner's responses so that instant judgments may be made concerning the quality of any particular response in comparison to: (1) earlier occurrences and (2) the targeted criterion level.

Shaping consists of the reinforcement of successive approximations or better and better "attempts" of the target response. Every behavior or response actually exists within a larger response class—slight variations of the same basic movement. For example, one does not always sit in exactly the same manner; however, we may think of each variation of "resting primarily upon the buttocks or haunches" as being within the sitting response class. When a response such as sitting is *not* in the individual's repertoire of behaviors, shaping must be preceded by identification of prerequisite response classes— earlier approximations which lead to the target response. To teach sitting to delayed children, these prerequisites could include (1) lifting one's head while lying in a prone position, and (2) briefly holding up one's head and trunk with the arms and hands while in a prone position. Knowing which response classes represent earlier approximations to a target behavior is part of the skill of shaping.

A closer examination of the shaping process reveals that extinction (the withholding of positive reinforcement) plays a role complementary to reinforcement. As each successively closer approximation of the desired response class is reinforced, the earlier, less precise approximations are no longer reinforced and, thereby, placed on extinction. Extinction (described in more detail in a later section) acts to decrease the frequency of the earlier approximations since these approximations no longer lead to reinforcement and to encourage more variation in the newly learned response. This latter occurrence often produces the next improvement in the direction of the target behavior which is then reinforced and increases in frequency. Shaping leads to the development of new behaviors which often do not resemble earlier approximations.

Response Chaining

At times referred to as forward and backward shaping, response chaining is somewhat different from shaping. While shaping is used to develop new behaviors, chaining is usually employed to sequence together a series of functionally related responses already in the individual's repertoire. Most skills actually consist of a chain of smaller component responses. For example, self-care behaviors (toileting, face washing, and eating), daily living skills (vacuuming a room, grocery shopping), and vocational tasks (parts assembly, "punching in" at work) provide many illustrations of response chains relevant to the severely handicapped.

To teach these chains, the response is first divided into an ordered list of separate "teachable" behaviors. Task analysis often facilitates this step.

Since chaining may proceed in a forward or backward direction across the sequence of behaviors, it is necessary to select the order in which the skill components will be taught. An examination of both chaining orders will clarify some guidelines for this choice. In Figure 3.2, face washing is analyzed into steps which are arranged in a backward order from the bottom of the graph to the top. Face washing could be divided into 10 steps or 40 steps depending upon how finely the chain is separated. The number of responses any given chain is divided into, although somewhat arbitrary, will vary for different levels of beginning skills and must meet the following general criteria:

1. Each step must be observable and easily measured.
2. The chain must be divided finely enough so that the addition of each successive teaching step does not result in an excess of errors.
3. There must not be too many steps or instruction becomes inefficient.

If chaining proceeds *forward,* the individual is taught initially to perform the first unmastered step in the chain, as identified during baseline observation. If, however, baseline performance is inconsistent and only some nonsequential steps are mastered, instruction should start with the first step. It may be necessary to shape this first behavior until no errors occur or to assist the individual with one of the prompting methods described in the next section. Reinforcement is given for successive approximations until the individual can adequately perform the first teaching step without assistance. Then the individual is taught to perform the next step by shaping or prompting methods, yet is expected to continue the correct completion of the preceding step already mastered. Reinforcement is given only after completion of the teaching step. The individual may or may not be assisted through all the remaining steps in the chain but is not expected to perform them independently until each successive step in the sequence is mastered. If, for example, the skill of shoe tying is to be taught through forward chaining, the first skill in the sequence to be mastered is the half-knot. Afterwards, the bow loop and then the remaining steps in the chain are taught.

In *backward chaining,* teaching generally begins with the last step and progresses toward the beginning of the chain. Sometimes baseline performance will indicate that the learner has mastered one or more steps at the end of the chain. For example, in

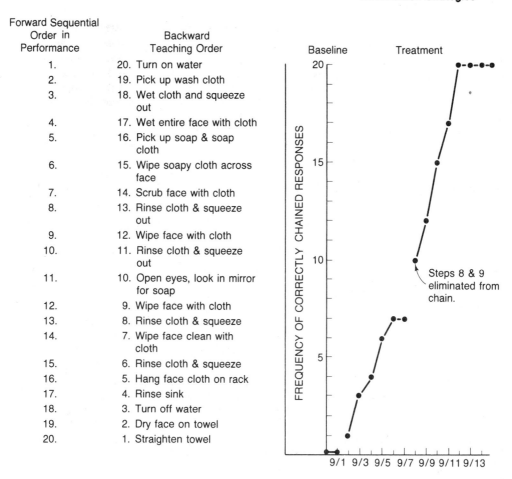

Forward Sequential Order in Performance	Backward Teaching Order
1.	20. Turn on water
2.	19. Pick up wash cloth
3.	18. Wet cloth and squeeze out
4.	17. Wet entire face with cloth
5.	16. Pick up soap & soap cloth
6.	15. Wipe soapy cloth across face
7.	14. Scrub face with cloth
8.	13. Rinse cloth & squeeze out
9.	12. Wipe face with cloth
10.	11. Rinse cloth & squeeze out
11.	10. Open eyes, look in mirror for soap
12.	9. Wipe face with cloth
13.	8. Rinse cloth & squeeze
14.	7. Wipe face clean with cloth
15.	6. Rinse cloth & squeeze
16.	5. Hang face cloth on rack
17.	4. Rinse sink
18.	3. Turn off water
19.	2. Dry face on towel
20.	1. Straighten towel

FIGURE 3.2 *A type of graph especially useful in recording frequency of correctly chained responses in forward and backward chaining instruction*

In this figure an individual's performance in face-washing skills, taught by backward chaining, is graphed. Note that steps 8 and 9 proved unnecessary for this individual during later performances and were omitted from the chain.

Figure 3.2 the student was able to straighten the towel during baseline testing. Teaching therefore would begin with the nineteenth step—drying face —but the learner would be expected to continue unprompted performance of the last step of straightening the towel. With some behaviors (e.g., eating, toileting, dressing) the individual actually may be guided through the preceding steps in the chain until the teaching step is reached. At other times, the individual may simply be started at the teaching step. Then, by means of shaping or prompting, this unmastered step is taught. Reinforcement is given only after the last step in the chain is completed. When teaching steps preceding the last step, the individual may be prompted to perform the target step but is expected to perform all the remaining steps in the chain without assis-

tance and then receives reinforcement. Eventually, as the remaining steps are learned and added to the behavior chain in a backward order, the entire chain is performed and the individual is reinforced at its completion.

It is quite likely that forward and backward chaining will be used in combination when teaching certain skills or particular students. This is true with students whose baseline performance demonstrates scattered success across the behavior chain (i.e., ability to perform more than a single step or a single group of steps). Both chaining procedures may also be combined when a skill's primary behavior occurs in the middle of a longer chain rather than at its completion. In the basic self-care skills of eating with a spoon and elimination on the toilet, both the eating and elimination responses are preceded and followed by preparatory or related behaviors. The first step in teaching spoon usage probably would be removal of the food from the spoon after a filled spoon is guided to the student's lips. Teaching could proceed both backward and then forward from this step.

Discriminative Stimulus

In both types of chaining the learner begins to associate the stimuli just preceding reinforcement (e.g., various teaching commands, materials involved in the chained responses, the response step just prior to reinforcement) with reinforcement itself. Since these antecedent stimuli signal or set the occasion for reinforcement, they also become reinforcing (secondary reinforcers) through a conditioning process. Such stimuli are often referred to as *discriminative stimuli* and each stimulus is referred to as an S^D. They play an important role in bonding the chained response together. For example, in the face-washing chain (Figure 3.2) perhaps a token and teacher praise are provided whenever the individual completes the chain. The stimuli in the first teaching step, straighten towel, include the towel and the straightening response itself. After learning this response, seeing the towel as well as the straightening movement both serve as discriminative stimuli in that they signal the occasion for reinforcement. Also the constant pairing of "straightening towel" with reinforcement at the end of the chain leads to its becoming a secondary reinforcer for the response just preceding (dry face on towel). As learner moves backward toward the beginning of the chain, each learned response becomes a S^D for the next response in the chain and a secondary reinforcer for the response just preceding it in the chain. Therefore, when teaching Steps 16 and 17 have been mastered (17: wets face with cloth; 16: picks up soap and soaps cloth), the completion of "wetting face" acts to signal the eventual reinforcement as well as the performance of "soaping cloth"; while Step 16, when performed, reinforces the previous response in Step 17.

Response Priming

The discussion, thus far, has been concerned with the arrangement of positively reinforcing consequences to increase behavior. Since behavior must occur before it can be shaped, the teacher must strengthen behavior that either does not occur naturally or occurs infrequently, for it is inefficient merely to wait for an accidental occurrence. This relates to the thwarted teaching situation which Skinner

(1968) refers to as "the problem of the first instance of behavior" (p. 206). The solution lies in the application of various types of assistance *antecedent* to the response which act to increase the likelihood that the desired behavior or a better approximation will be performed by the learner. This assistance, in the form of directions, models, cues, or physical prompts, primes the desired behavior—hence, the term "response priming."

Lent and his Project MORE colleagues (Lent & McLean, 1976) have employed a prompt hierarchy in which a teacher advances to increasing levels of instructional assistance depending upon the learner's ability to respond in a task (Figure 3.3). These response primes serve only as temporary means to obtain behavior during the acquisition period of learning. Eventually, this guidance must be eliminated so that stimulus control is transferred from the priming stimuli to the appropriate discriminative stimuli (S^Ds) or antecedent events which operate naturally in the environment—those stimuli in the presence of which the target behavior is appropriate and results in reinforcement. Let us illustrate such a problem. If a pupil is always reminded that five pennies equal a nickel by a nod of the teacher's head, then that individual will not acquire an understanding of a nickel's value. The teacher must fade her support gradually so the individual may practice independence in performance and thus gain mastery. Knowing when and how much to help a student perform and when and how much to withhold help constitute a large portion of the art of effective teaching.

Rowbury, Baer, and Baer (1976) demonstrated the multifaceted power of teacher guidance in combination with a token-mediated contingency upon the completion of preacademic tasks by moderately handicapped preschoolers. They used a "teacher guidance package" which consisted of instructions, physical assistance, modeling, and praise for correct responses. This combination of techniques was an essential element in the acquisition of the tasks (e.g., use of form box, picture dominoes, geometric inserts, word matching). The authors found that it was not possible to analyze the single effect of each teacher guidance behavior because of the overlap between them.

A given teacher event could serve as an instruction and/or praise and/or prompt, if an appropriate physical cue was added. An example is the comment, "Good, you are finding all of the red ones." This statement could serve as praise, or

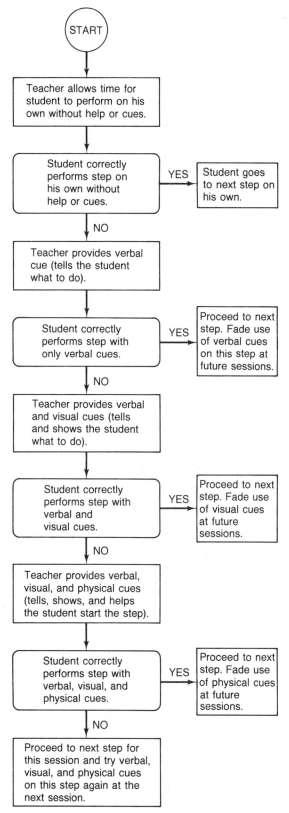

as an instruction to find more red objects, or as a prompt to stay with red. (pp. 101–102)

Cuing and reinforcement procedures affect developing behavior from the initial acquisition of isolated responses to combinations and extensions of chained responses and to gains in proficiency or response rate.

Verbal directions offered before and during the performance of a behavior often serve as guides for responding. For example, when a teacher asks a student to select seven red checkers from a group of mixed checkers by saying, "Count out a pile of seven red checkers," many different behaviors are requested of the child. The discriminative stimuli, which come to control the individual's behavior, demand action, number selection, and color discrimination. Initially, the adult may need to assist with additional directions which serve to prompt the correct behavior. If the student begins to count out black checkers, the teacher might repeat the word "red." If the student miscounts, the teacher might say the numerical sequence for the student or, if he hesitates, the teacher could prompt the child to "count faster." The most important thing to remember when using verbal directions to prompt a behavior is that the directions must be understood by the student. Sometimes the teacher must speak slowly and use simple word combinations and vocabulary, and even use accompanying gestures or cues to facilitate understanding.

Instructions provided for moderately and severely handicapped individuals may be given in a variety of modalities and formats: verbally, verbally with gestures, verbally with models or demonstrations, by means of a single picture or a sequentially arranged set of pictures, pictures and text, and text alone. Pictures and text promote independence from the teacher as well as creating opportunities to practice the more cognitively demanding skills of picture and word comprehension. Of course the learner must demonstrate a variety of prerequisite skills (picture-object association and word-object association) before illustrated and written instructions will be appropriate. Chapter 11, on Daily Living Skills, which provides a realistic extension of the picture

FIGURE 3.3   *Project MORE teaching strategy— increasing levels of assistance provided to the learner*

Source: Project MORE, University of Kansas Bureau of Child Research, Parsons State Hospital and Training School, 1973. Reprinted in Lent & McLean, 1976, p. 226.

instruction format, also emphasizes that such instructions serve as available references or only as temporary reminders of complex multi-stepped behaviors like cooking simple foods or mopping a floor.

Whatever way the teacher selects to provide instructions, certain qualitative aspects of the instructions must be matched to the language abilities of the learner (Berman, 1973). These include the number of specific instructions given simultaneously, the duration of instruction, the complexity of language comprising the instructions, and whether gestures and demonstrations accompany them. Additionally the prior relationship between the instructor and the student will affect the learner's attention and resultant tendency to benefit from or carry out the instructions.

Modeling consists of demonstrating part or all of the desired behavior in the presence of the learner and having the learner imitate or repeat the action immediately. The modeled response may be performed by the teacher or by the learner's peers, or the modeled response may be represented more permanently through illustrations (e.g., copying a teacher's colored block arrangement or a printed name card). Modeling has been used to prompt responses in the self-care chains of toileting (Azrin & Foxx, 1971; Mahoney, Van Wagenen, & Meyerson, 1971), toothbrushing (Horner & Keilitz, 1975), and correct utensil usage (Nelson, Cone, & Hanson, 1975). Since the learner must view the demonstration in order to imitate, visual attending skills are important and imitative skills are essential. The effectiveness of modeling as a prompt with severely handicapped individuals is increased when:

1. The individual's attention is gained prior to presenting the model.
   A. If the individual attends part of the time, physical prompts may be used in conjunction with shaping to improve attending behavior.
   B. If the individual does not attend to a model's demonstration despite verbal requests or attends only infrequently, it is best to teach attending behaviors first. This training would include increasing eye contact with the presence of the instruction (S^D), "Look at me," and increasing directed looking with the instruction (S^D), "Look at this" (point to an object). (Refer to the Chapter 5 on Language Skills, and to Bricker, Dennison, & Bricker, 1975; Kent, 1974; Simmons & Williams, 1976; Striefel, 1974.)

2. The individual readily imitates movements and sounds and this imitative behavior is under the stimulus control of simple commands such as, "Do this."
   A. If the individual imitates part of the time, physical prompts may be used after the model is presented in conjunction with shaping to encourage better imitations.
   B. If the individual does not imitate or does so only infrequently, imitation skills must be taught before using modeling as a method to prompt behavior. Imitation training relies upon shaping and prompting techniques and begins with mutual imitation or the matching of the *child's* responses by the teacher (Bricker et al., 1976; Parton, 1976; Uzgiris & Hunt, 1975), then proceeds to the presentation of models which are familiar to the child and visible as they are performed (Baer, Peterson, & Sherman, 1965; Bricker et al., 1976; Parton, 1976; Striefel, 1974; Striefel & Phelan, 1972). (The reader is referred to Chapter 5 on Language Skills for a detailed description of imitation training.)

3. When directionality of the response is important, models are presented so that the orientation of the viewed model is similar to the behavior as it is being performed by the individual (Parton, 1976). This means that an individual will not have to reverse the direction of what is modeled because it originally was performed along side rather than across from the learner (e.g., eating and dressing movements, hand-writing strokes) or in front of the learner with the model's back to the individual's front (e.g., walking, dancing, ball throwing).

4. Initially the length or complexity of the modeled response or the chain of responses should be short and simple. Extensions are added to the modeled response as successful imitations occur. When errors occur in an individual's imitations, the modeled response may need to be repeated in segments.

5. Models are preceded typically by an antecedent event (S^D) which eventually should trigger the desired response so that when the model and the imitative command are faded, stimulus control transfers more readily to the appropriate cue. A verbal command (e.g., "Brush your teeth") or situational stimuli (e.g., objects such as a toothbrush and toothpaste, times of the day such as the period following a meal, and places such as the bathroom area), or a combination of com-

mand and situational stimuli are events which eventually should stimulate a response (toothbrushing). Even verbal directions should be faded since the continued use of directional prompts will not lead to independence.

Cuing a behavior, at times similar to modeling, is different from manual guidance in that cuing acts to direct the learner's attention to the teaching materials without physically contacting the learner. For example, in a multiple-choice object location task, an individual is taught to associate a label ("ball") with a particular object (small, green ball) in the presence of the instruction (S^D), "Show me the *ball*," while ignoring other objects also visible (toy, car, spoon, shoe). The correct choice may be cued in a variety of ways.

1. Movement cues: pointing to, touching, or tapping beside the correct choice.
2. Position cues: placing the correct choice closest to the student.
3. Redundancy cues: pairing one or more dimensions of color, shape, size, or position (as in position cues) with the correct choice (e.g., *color:* a white piece of paper is always placed under the correct choice while other choices all have red paper or perhaps no paper; *size:* the correct choice is always physically larger than the other choices as with some coins; *shape:* the correct choice, for example in color discrimination, is represented in a square shape while all incorrect choices are round).

In an effort to learn more about cuing, Gold (1972) compared the effectiveness of color redundancy cuing with form cuing for severely handicapped individuals learning to assemble bicycle brakes in a sheltered workshop. Color cues were placed on one side of every part so that when assembled correctly the colored part faced the worker. The presence of color cues led to significantly faster acquisition and longer retention of the task than did cues provided only by the form or shape of the individual brake parts.

A fourth type of cuing, match-to-sample, is similar to modeling. When prompting by means of match-to-sample, the teacher simply gives the instruction (S^D), "Find the nickel," and cues the correct response by showing the learner a sample of the correct choice. The learner merely must select a matching object from a group of choices. While movement cues only rely upon attending and imita-

tion skills to successfully prompt a response, redundancy and match-to-sample cues depend upon a person's ability to visually discriminate between different dimensions such as color, size, and shape. In addition, the ability to use match-to-sample cues requires that similarities between stimuli can be distinguished. If an individual has difficulty discriminating between different samples of a single dimension (e. g., different shapes of the same color and size), additional redundant cues will tend to facilitate the discrimination (Zeaman & House, 1963; Fisher & Zeaman, 1973). That is, an individual will learn to select the circular shape more quickly when it is represented as a large, red circle shown with a plain, small square. The differences between the choices is made more obvious as additional redundant stimuli are added. Likewise difficulties in matching skills may be overcome when fewer choices are offered from which to select the match and, more importantly, when all the nonmatching choices differ widely from the stimulus object to be matched (Gold & Scott, 1971).

Manual guidance, sometimes referred to as molding a behavior or physical prompting, consists of various degrees of "putting the learner through" the response. The difference between "putting through" as contrasted with "doing for" is subtle but important. For example, the provision of complete manual guidance during dressing may mean standing behind an individual, taking the back of his hands and moving his fingers to grasp the top of his pants, and applying an upward pull to complete the behavior of pulling up his pants. The child's pants are not simply pulled up for him. If backward chaining was the teaching method selected for this task, the pants-up prompt would be provided up to the training step. Then, only as needed by the learner, instructions, modeling, cues, and partial guidance would be offered in that order of increasing assistance.

As with other types of response primes, when manual guidance is in the stages of being faded, it may consist simply of a small portion of the actual response—such as touching the back of a learner's elbow to begin an arm moving forward or touching the bottom lip of a child rather than molding the lips to prompt an "m" sound. Additionally, at this fading stage, the stimulus control is being transferred from a manual guidance S^D to more natural stimuli, often in the form of verbal commands or situational stimuli. In other words, a learner is mandated to attend to stimuli which have more relevance to the behavior than did the artifically applied prompting stimuli. This fading process is illustrated in Figure 3.4.

With a group of institutionalized severely handicapped adults Nelson et al. (1975) compared the effectiveness of modeling to manual guidance for priming correct use of eating utensils (e.g., eating with spoons and forks, cutting and spreading with a knife). Individuals given manual guidance with praise demonstrated significant improvements, while modeling, which relies upon the ability to imitate, yielded very small gains by comparison. The authors suggested a number of reasons for this finding. First, manual guidance does not require that the individual have imitative ability. Secondly, it provides tactile, kinesthetic, and proprioceptive cues in addition to the visual and auditory cues provided by modeling. And, when manual guidance is given, it is necessary that the trainer have acquired secondary reinforcing power and be physically close to the learner.

Fading Response Primes

If response primes are arranged in an order of complexity and by their reliance upon prerequisite skills, manual guidance would be considered the least complex—relying as it does primarily on cooperation and minimal amounts of attention. Manual guidance would be followed in an increasing order of difficulty by cuing (movement cues, position cues, redundancy cues, and match-to-sample cues), modeling, and verbal direction (oral, then written). Also, at each level of complexity, an individual prompt may range from complete—serving to evoke the complete response—to partial assistance—serving to evoke less than the complete response. Complete and partial manual guidance prompts were illustrated in Figure 3.4 at the beginning and middle stages of learning.

Fading refers to the gradual changing of the stimulus, "controlling an organism's performance to another stimulus, reinforcer or contingency usually with the intent of maintaining the performance without loss or alteration, but under new conditions" (White, 1971, p. 63). In order to achieve this maintenance of performance, fading must be a gradual process, moving from complete prompts to partial prompts. Fading may also include a reduction in the number of prompts provided (e.g., demonstration and instructions faded to just instructions) and the substitution of less complex prompts with more complex prompts as long as the individual possesses the skills necessary to benefit from the type of prompt used (see Figure 3.3). For example, when teaching severely retarded individuals to brush their

Stage of Behavior Acquisition	ANTECEDENT STIMULI		Behaviors	Consequence
	Instructions	Manual Guidance		
Beginning	"Look at me."	Turns head with both hands	Child's head is manually turned to face teacher and held until the eyes approximate contact	Praise, 5 seconds music (continuous schedule)
Middle	"Look at me."	Touches cheek and applies gentle turning pressure	Child turns head toward teacher after touch on cheek and looks at teacher	Praise, 5 seconds music (continuous schedule)
Final	"Look at me."		Child turns and looks at teacher	Praise, 5 seconds music (Music faded to intermittent schedule after criterion of 10 consecutive correct responses is met.)

FIGURE 3.4   *Stages in the acquisition of eye contact behavior from a completely guided response to total fading of the prompt*

teeth, Horner and Keilitz (1975) employed a sequence of three decreasing levels of assistance: (1) toothbrushing equipment present, manual guidance, and verbal instruction; (2) equipment, demonstration, and verbal instruction; (3) equipment and verbal instruction. Depending upon the individual's baseline level of performance, *increasing* amounts of prompts were provided until the behavior was performed correctly. Then prompts were completely faded in the reverse direction (i.e., from 1 to 3) so that eventually stimulus control was changed to level 4: equipment present.

Another means of gradually fading prompts includes the use of progressive *delay procedures* (Touchette, 1971). That is, whatever prompt or prompts are employed to reduce errors and facilitate occurrence of the correct behavior are delayed by gradually increasing increments, thereby allowing the learner time to anticipate the correct response without assistance. For example, in matching tasks (object to object, object to picture, numeral to numeral, etc.) and comprehension instruction (pointing to objects or body parts on command, performing actions, etc.) the learner is given a request and a choice of stimuli to select from. Prompts often include redundancy cues (correct choice placed on red square), teacher pointing to answer, or moving the child's hand to the correct selection. Delay procedure would require that the prompt be given after longer and longer intervals (e.g., increases of one second for each correct trial) following the request. Touchette (1971) used delay procedure successfully to teach severely retarded individuals visual discriminations with little or no error occurring during learning.

Although fading must be planned and orderly, it should be done as rapidly as possible without causing undue loss of the behavior. Two pieces of information aid the teacher in these decisions. First, the record of daily performance allows one to evaluate the stability of performance and progress toward criterion. When the goal is to increase a behavior, prompts should be faded when the graphed response shows increases or begins to plateau but not when the frequency declines. Secondly, a teacher may observe the individual's performance during *probes* or during teaching trials when all prompts (or some prompts) are withheld. If performance during probes is improved, maintained, or does not decline noticeably, prompts may be withdrawn. However, if performance is greatly suppressed, fading must be more gradual and at a rate delineated by daily performance records.

Negative reinforcement

Although very different in nature from the intervention strategies just discussed, negative reinforcement is similar in the sense that it serves to increase the frequency of behavior. Scheduling, immediacy, and durability of negative reinforcement function as in positive reinforcement. Also, the identification of negative reinforcers or "aversives" can be accomplished in the same manner described earlier for positive reinforcers. It is important to remember that a negative reinforcer is functionally related to an individual's behavior: an event is only a reinforcer when the behavior it is made contingent upon increases. Negative reinforcers may also be primary or unlearned (e.g., shock or fear) as well as secondary (e.g., "No!" or disapproving looks).

As shown in Figure 3.1, the operation of negative reinforcement requires the existence of a punishing or aversive situation antecedent to the response behavior. The behavior is often an attempt by the individual to eliminate or escape the aversive event. The quick *buckling* of a buzzing seatbelt, *covering* one's ears in the midst of excruciating noise, and *picking up* a loudly crying child who instantly becomes quiet—all illustrate negatively reinforced behaviors because each is followed by a reduction of the unpleasant aversive event. Learning to avoid an aversive event is negatively reinforcing also, although the process, a combination of operant and classical learning, is a bit more confusing. For example, viewing the seatbelt (conditioned stimulus) reminds one of the buzzer (unconditioned stimulus) and comes to elicit (classical conditioning) the same buckling response which is then reinforced by the avoidance of noise (operant conditioning).

The concept of negative reinforcement is important to understand both because of its natural occurrence and predictable effect upon behavior in escape and avoidance learning situations and because of its inadvertant occurrence in many demanding teacher-child or parent-child interactions. In these latter situations, the child or adult *creates* an aversive situation, often in the form of a demand upon the other (e.g., nagging requests to work, threat of punishment, insistance upon extra privileges, etc.). This situation may amplify undesirable behavior because both positive and negative reinforcement are operating.

1. The behavior which ends the aversive situation is negatively reinforced—
   A. *Aversive Antecedent Event:* Child begs and whines for an extra 10 minutes of recess

B. *Behavior:* Teacher grants child's request
C. *Negatively Reinforcing Consequences:* Child begs and whines stop (for at least 10 minutes!)

2. However, the behavior of the individual creating the aversive situation is positively reinforced by the compliant behavior of the other—
   A. *Aversive Antecedent Event:* Not identifiable
   B. *Behavior:* Child begs and whines for an extra 10 minutes of recess
   C. *Positively Reinforcing Consequences:* Teacher grants child's request

Apart from some therapeutic applications with severely handicapped individuals, such as the increase of social interactive behavior by the contingent termination of shock (e.g.,Lovaas, Schaeffer & Simmons, 1965), negative reinforcement is not a widely employed behavior-building strategy because it requires the creation of aversive situations (Kazdin, 1975). Negative reinforcement comprises techniques less useful than those which positively reinforce behavior building. Negative reinforcement should not be confused with punishment, for it involves the removal of the aversive stimulus and increases the target behavior. In punishment the aversive stimulus is applied and decreases the target behavior. Either strategy should be employed only after positive events have been scheduled unsuccessfully.

Intervention Strategies Aimed at Decreasing Behavior

The "fair pair"

Although there are more desirable behaviors which need strengthening or shaping in the handicapped than there are undesirable behaviors which need reduction, teachers often are more concerned with the reduction of behaviors which have an upsetting effect on the classroom routine. The "fair pair" rule (White & Haring, 1976) emphasizes the significance of balancing behavior modification programs. When it is necessary to decrease an undesirable behavior, one should select a desirable behavior to increase at the same time. This procedure results in a repertoire of appropriate behaviors, thereby providing the student with alternative responses rather than merely eliminating behavior. For the teacher more opportunities are created to positively reinforce students.

At times, the desirable half of the "fair pair" of behaviors will be simply the behavior opposite from that to be eliminated (out-of-seat and in-seat; incorrect labels and correct labels). However, when this practice produces the absence of behavior (e.g., excessive crying and no crying), it is better teaching strategy to select a behavior which can be accelerated and does not occur at the same time as the behavior to be eliminated. Depending upon the abilities of the individual, the positive half of "excessive crying" could be "requests items by name" while "handwaving and staring" could be paired with "eye contact with teacher and objects presented by the teacher."

Intervention programs directed toward the reduction or elimination of undesirable behavior should always include a program component which improves or builds a replacement or a counteracting, desirable behavior. This practice may entail the reinforcement of behaviors that are *incompatible* with the behavior placed on extinction (e.g., eating finger food appropriately versus playing with food). It also may provide the individual with an alternative means of achieving some hypothetical goal (adult attention, peer approval, etc.) that is being sought by performance of the misbehavior. In this latter situation, a teacher may hypothesize that the misbehavior frequently is followed by her attention. Therefore, she may decide to model and reinforce hand raising and appropriate requests to show classwork while ignoring shouting-out behavior.

The withholding of reinforcement (extinction), the presentation of aversives (punishment), and the removal of reinforcers (punishment) are three different classes of consequences which may be provided contingent upon a behavior as a strategy to reduce or eliminate that behavior. Additionally, for many severely handicapped students, the antecedent application of classroom rules may prevent undesirable behavior from occurring in the first place. If extinction, punishment, or classroom rules are to result in predictable outcomes, a teacher needs to understand clearly how their operation acts to modify behavior.

Extinction

As illustrated in Figure 3.1, extinction refers to the intentional withholding of positive reinforcement by the teacher (parent or peer) as a consequence to an individual's response. Reinforcement is *not* withdrawn, which would constitute punishment, rather it simply is not presented. To ignore a behavior, which formerly was attended to, every time it was performed, constitutes the placement of that behavior on extinction. The resultant effect is a decrease in the frequency of the behavior.

During extinction the rate of decrease in a behavior's frequency is related directly to the behavior's reinforcement history—its earlier schedule(s) of reinforcement. For example, if a behavior was always on a continuous schedule of reinforcement, the change to extinction would be abrupt and highly noticeable to the individual and the behavior would extinguish more rapidly. In such cases as few as one or two nonreinforced instances of a behavior may lead to total cessation of the behavior. One could say that for this behavior, the individual had little resistance to extinction because he was not exposed to instances of nonreinforcement. However, the individual for whom behavior initially was developed on a continuous schedule of reinforcement, but was shifted to an intermittent schedule (e.g., reinforcement of every tenth response) has learned to perform nine consecutive times without reinforcement. During extinction, this person will tend to continue with these bursts of performance prior to an eventual decline in frequency. Histories of gradually developed, variable, lean schedules (many responses occur before each reinforcement) lead to the strongest responses and are most resistant to extinction.

Some additional factors act in combination with reinforcement history to influence a behavior's resistance during extinction.

1. The *amount of reinforcement* presented during the learning or acquisition of the behavior acts to affect the speed of extinction, such that the larger the amount of reinforcement for each behavior provided prior to extinction, the greater the resistance.
2. The *length of the learning period* before extinction is initiated acts to affect the speed of extinction, such that longer periods of reinforcement yield more extinction-resistant behaviors.
3. The *number of times* a behavior is placed on a lengthy extinction schedule affects the speed of extinction, such that the more exposures to extinction the faster the behavior will extinguish during each successive schedule. ("Lengthy periods of extinction" do *not* mean ignoring a few behaviors, then applying reinforcement again.)

Although extinction is a useful procedure to reduce a large range of undesirable behaviors displayed by the severely retarded, there are some situations and some classes of behavior for which extinction is *not* the recommended strategy. First, extinction is not effective unless the reinforcers which are maintaining an individual's undesirable behavior are known and their availability is controlled by the teacher. In classroom settings, the task of controlling peer reinforcement is difficult and makes extinction an ineffective strategy for reducing mildly annoying behaviors such as swearing, burping, "showing-off," etc. Also when the mere performance of the behavior produces the reinforcement, such as with self-stimulatory behavior (i.e., rocking, arm movements, hand waving), the teacher is unable to control reinforcement and therefore cannot contingently withhold the reinforcers.

Secondly, because extinction is a slow process, it is not recommended for use with destructive behaviors—behaviors which result in the destruction of materials, are self-aggressive and/or harmful to others. For some severely retarded individuals in whom self-stimulatory (e.g., regurgitation and hand waving) and destructive behavior (e.g., hitting self, tearing pages) are the primary concern, extinction will be a less useful strategy. To illustrate this further, Bucher and Lovass (1968), as an alternative to punishment, removed the arm restraints from a self-aggressive severely retarded child during brief, daily extinction periods. After eight days, the behavior finally decreased to near zero levels. However, the extinction process was painful in that it entailed ignoring more than 10,000 self-directed blows. So, although extinction eventually acts to decrease the frequency of self-aggressive behavior, it may endanger the individual before the behavior is eliminated.

Because most seriously undesirable behaviors tend to have a long, varied reinforcement history, the rate of extinction may be very slow. And, since consistency in the application of extinction is an essential element for its effectiveness, the teacher must determine his or her ability to tolerate the presence of the behavior. If the behavior is a frequently occurring one, the need for consistency becomes more taxing. In addition, if the behavior is particularly disruptive and annoying to others in the classroom, even if it is not destructive, then the use of extinction as the deceleration strategy is more demanding upon the teacher and the entire class. The requirement for consistency in providing extinction conditions contingent upon every occurrence of the behavior is strongly threatened in these situations.

In general, extinction is applied easily and effectively as a contingent consequence to less frequently occurring misbehaviors when performance will not endanger the individual or others and is not self-reinforcing. Extinction must be applied contingently and consistently to be effective. In addition, the effects of extinction are magnified greatly when positive reinforcement is made available for one or more desirable behaviors.

When extinction first is applied as the consequence for a behavior, the behavior may become worse before it gets better. That is, before the frequency of the behavior declines it may increase. This effect, referred to as "extinction burst," appears to be due simply to the individual's prior learning that the behavior previously was followed by reinforcement. Unknown to some parents, temper tantrums and whining behavior are shaped when parents "give in" to the increased demands (the extinction burst) of a child placed on extinction. Reinforcement of behavior during extinction bursts will cause the effects of extinction to take longer and may even render it an ineffective strategy for that behavior.

Classroom rules

When reinforcement for misbehavior cannot be controlled because it is distributed by the individual's peers, classroom rules become a more effective means of behavior management than extinction. Inevitably there are *rules* to guide the effective use of rules in the classroom. First and most essential, the rules must describe behavior in ways understandable to the members of the class. In many situations, pictures and simple wording yield comprehensible rules; with other classrooms, role playing will result in more complete understanding. Invariably, however, it is the consistent enforcement of the rules which will lead to this comprehension. In classrooms where comprehension skills are only in beginning stages, the use of simply stated rules is still justifiable for two reasons. First, even in early stages of language development, the child learns to associate an adult's facial expressions, tone of speech, and some words such as "No!" or "Good!" with punishing or reinforcing consequences. Secondly, the presence of rules may serve to increase a teacher's consistency in the application of various contingent consequences to behavior.

In addition to the verbal statement of rules in comprehensible terms, we recommend (1) that rules be stated positively whenever possible so that appropriate behavior, within the capability of the class, is described, (2) that the number of rules be limited so enforcement may be guaranteed, and (3) that the teacher review new classroom rules daily until infractions of these rules decrease. Rules will need periodic revision in order that they remain relevant to the specific school situation, the classroom curriculum (i.e., what has been taught to the students), and individuals within that class. Whenever possible, class members should be encouraged to assist in the formulation of new rules or the revision of old rules.

If a rule is stated positively (e.g., "We eat with a spoon"), the teacher should attempt to reinforce those who follow the rule, restating the rule as they are praised (e.g., "Good eating with a spoon"). If positively stated rules are broken, the teacher may choose *either* to punish the behavior ("No, use the spoon," removal of food for three minutes) *or* to ignore it. If a rule is stated negatively (e.g., "NO swearing in class"), then infractions cannot be ignored but must be punished in some way or the rule becomes meaningless. However, with both types of rules, whenever the individual is punished for an infraction, it is important to ask the child to restate the rule prior to punishment. Prompts should be offered if the individual cannot state the rule. This verbal rehearsal of rules prior to punishment will act to facilitate an understanding of the contingency. The eventual self-rehearsal of rules is a critical strategy in self-control. Finally, if punishment is used, it is essential that the teacher determine in advance what punishing consequences will be employed and when they will be applied in relation to rule infractions. That is, whether a single warning will be given before punishment is applied or whether punishment will be applied following the first infraction of the rule. The discussion of punishment which follows should aid in formulating answers to these questions.

Punishment

An often misunderstood term, punishment as a formal operation is related functionally to behavior and is defined by its effect—i.e., a decrease of behavior. Figure 3.1 identified two different punishing operations which yield this effect: the presentation of an aversive event (e.g., slap, reprimand) and the removal of positive reinforcers (e.g., loss of privileges, removal of tokens, isolation from an enjoyable situation) immediately following a behavior. The first type of punishment includes aversive conditioning, overcorrection, and firm verbal statements; the second includes response cost and time out. Both types of punishing consequences act to decrease the frequency of a behavior. If the behavior is not decreased, the operation of punishment has not occurred—the "aversives" which were presented actually were not aversive to that individual or the events or objects removed were not reinforcing to the individual in the first place.

Along with this predictable reduction in the punished behavior, other, less desirable, effects are apt to occur with punishment. These may include a suppression of unpunished behaviors (desirable or undesirable); emotional reactions by the punished individual such as counteraggressive behavior, avoidance or escape, and anxiety in the punishment situation or in the presence of the punisher; a future reoccurrence of the punished behavior; and/or failure to suppress the behavior completely. Because of these potential side effects and because some forms of punishment are unacceptable strategies to reduce behavior, it is essential that teachers know and follow guidelines when seeking to achieve behavior deceleration.

As with reinforcers, punishers range along a hierarchy from primary to secondary and must be identified individually because they differ across persons. Aversives need to be selected in terms of the functional maturity of the individual and their effect upon the behavior. In addition to the selection of the punisher, MacMillan, Forness, and Trumbull (1973) identified seven variables which alter the effects of punishment: timing, consistency, intensity, alternative behaviors, adaptation (satiation), prior relationships, and cognitive ability.

Timing

When a punisher is applied as a consequence to a misbehavior, its timing is very important. To maximize its effect, the punisher should be delivered immediately after the misbehavior is apparent. The longer the delay or latency between the initiation of the undesirable act and the delivery of punishment, the less effective the punishment in inhibiting the behavior. Therefore, if a child has completed the behavior and punishment is delayed for some reason, it may be best to wait for the next instance of the behavior rather than risk punishing the wrong behavior or a desirable behavior.

Consistency

Punishment must be consistently applied in the same manner for every instance of the behavior and by all persons involved with the child. Consistency includes the carrying out of threats. The contingency of punishment for a behavior will be learned most quickly if the same degree of punishing consequences is applied every time the misbehavior occurs, at a point early in its performance or immediately after its termination.

Intensity

Initial administration of the punishment should be at full intensity rather than escalating the intensity with each successive occurrence of the behavior. First the teacher must determine the level of intensity which constitutes punishment for an individual and then always apply that level of punishment. For example, if the removal of dessert was shown to be insufficiently aversive to control behavior (e.g., food stealing), then perhaps the entire meal must be removed. When using verbal aversives, intensity must not be interpreted as loudness but rather as firmness. In fact, soft, firm reprimands directed toward the appropriate individual are more effective in a classroom than loud reprimands and avoid "spillover effect"—the suppression of behavior in others located near the punished individual. In order to implement the intensity rule, one must be careful not to overpunish and to remember to seek alternatives to punishment.

Alternatives to the Behavior

Whenever punishment is employed to reduce a behavior's frequency, one should provide alternatives to the punished behavior (see "fair pair"). This can be done by reinforcing behavior which competes with the punished behavior (e.g., reinforce eating with a spoon, punish eating with hands). When these competing behaviors are not in the repertoire of the individual, various prompts and shaping procedures should be applied so that alternative behaviors may be learned and thus compete with undesirable or inappropriate behaviors.

Adaptation or satiation lessens the effects of a punisher upon a behavior and is interrelated with both consistency and intensity. Escalating the intensity of a punisher often allows the child to adapt—become accustomed—to each degree of punishment. The use of the same specific punishers to the exclusion of others can lead to satiation. Varying aversive consequences of the same degree of intensity tends to increase awareness of the contingency.

Prior Relationship

The more positive the prior relationship of the one who punishes with the individual being punished, the more immediate the effects. When teachers who are "liked" by the students apply punishment (either present an aversive or withdraw reinforcement), they also automatically withdraw the reinforcing consequences of their attention and affection. This increases the effectiveness of the punishment.

Cognitive Variables

Lastly, cognitive variables are of utmost importance in influencing the effects of punishment upon the severely handicapped. Since the goal of punishment is to decrease a behavior by teaching the recipient to associate aversive consequences with the behavior, learning is facilitated if the child understands which behavior is being punished. Either the teacher should use simple terms to identify the behavior being punished at the time punishment is applied or the child should be asked to state the classroom rule which was broken. Furthermore, if punishment must be delayed, these simple verbal explanations become essential.

The use of aversive conditioning which employs strong primary aversives (such as electric shock and slapping) to eliminate behavior may be defensible in two general instances: when the behavior is so dangerous or self-destructive that positive reinforcement and extinction are not viable methods of modification, or when the behavior totally interferes with other learning and positive means of behavior change are unsuccessful (e.g., these behaviors could be repetitive, self-stimulatory movements). Numerous studies have used contingent shock with severely retarded and/or disabled individuals to control self-destructive behavior (Bucher & Lovass, 1968; Frankel & Simmons, 1976; Lovaas & Simmons, 1969), engaging in dangerous activities such as climbing (Risley, 1968), play with hazardous equipment (Bucher & King, 1971), and self-stimulation and persistent vomiting (Jackson et al., 1975; Kohlenberg, 1970). It is beyond the scope of this chapter to specify guidelines for the use of contingent shock. However, milder forms of punishment employed to control behaviors less prone to change by other methods are discussed next.

Overcorrection

This is a punishment procedure in which the punished individual must either correct the consequences of a misbehavior by restoring the disrupted situation to a "better-than-normal" state (restitutional overcorrection) or practice an exaggerated form of the behavior as a consequence to each performance of the misbehavior (positive practice). Restitutional overcorrection was used to eliminate the stealing of food among institutionalized severely handicapped individuals. In their study, Azrin and Wesolowski (1974) required that the thief not only return the stolen food to his victim but also give the victim a second identical item of food. Azrin & Foxx (1971) employed positive practice techniques during a toilet-training program as one means to punish toileting accidents. Repeated practice of correct toilet-approach responses were made contingent upon every instance of wet pants. Self-stimulatory behaviors such as rocking, head weaving, and hand staring were eliminated by requiring the individual to maintain, without resistance, a reversed form of the stereotyped posture for 30 seconds (Azrin, Kaplan, & Foxx, 1973). While Azrin and Foxx and their coworkers have obtained successful results in eliminating many undesirable behaviors in the severely handicapped (stripping, pica, biting, screaming, object throwing, noncompliant behavior, etc.) by the contingent application of overcorrection techniques, more research is needed to clarify these operations, to provide replicative support, and to specify guidelines for its use in classroom settings (e.g., length of overcorrection, size and strength of student in comparison to teacher administering overcorrection, activities selected as the overcorrection procedure, etc.). For example, a recent study (Rollings, Baumeister, & Baumeister, 1977) employed overcorrection contingent upon stereotypic behaviors such as head weaving and nodding, self-hitting, finger movements, and body rocking in two severely retarded adults. Some interesting findings were obtained.

. . . (a) overcorrection procedures, applied contingently on the occurrence of stereotyped behavior, may produce deceleration in rate of that behavior, but the magnitude of the effect varies considerably between subjects; (b) punishment and nonpunishment conditions are well discriminated by the subject, partly on the basis of trainer proximity; (c) increased collateral stereotypic and emotional responding may accompany deceleration of target behaviors; (d) no spontaneous generalization of suppression is observed from training to living areas; and (e) suppression effects obtained under the procedures employed here are not durable. In general, we may conclude that the overcorrection procedure is actually a very complex package of contingencies and that the effects on behavior may also be complex. (pp. 42–43)

The authors suggested the use of overcorrection procedures of shorter duration (2–3 minutes), training sessions with a variety of teachers and settings to facilitate generalization of the suppressed behavior, and a strong plan to promote an increase in rates of desirable behaviors.

Firm Verbal Statements

A common punishment procedure consists simply of firm verbal statements presented as soon as the misbehavior is initiated with or without restraint. Verbal punishment alone or in the form of repetitive threats is often overused, ineffective, and may even be reinforcing. However, when combined with restraint, overcorrection, response cost, or time out (described later), firm verbal statements serve as effective immediate aversives to stop a misbehavior and increase the individual's awareness of the relationship between the misbehavior and the punishment.

Generally statements are short negative imperatives (e.g., "No!" "Stop!") or brief restatements of the infracted rule (e.g., "No hitting!" "Stop eating with your hands!"). In addition the teacher may firmly, but nonpainfully, grasp the child's shoulders to force his attention to the statement and stop or restrain the behavior. Verbal statements and restraint of the misbehavior have been applied effectively to reduce inappropriate behavior in severely handicapped individuals. As the punishment for object banging and string twirling, Pendergrass (1972) combined verbal aversives ("No, don't bang!") with two-minute time outs which eliminated the behaviors. In a program to teach proper meal-time behavior, O'Brien and Azrin (1972) decreased incorrect responses such as touching food with hands, taking oversized bites, stealing, and drooling by use of an "interruption-extinction" procedure. This procedure consisted of the trainer saying "No!" while returning the food to the plate and wiping the individual's hand or mouth. After acquisition training, a time-out procedure, which consisted of food removal for 30

seconds, was combined with verbal punishment and the interruption of the response. As a method to prevent crawling in children who had learned to walk, O'Brien, Azrin, and Bugle (1972) punished crawling behavior through restraint periods in which the child was held for five seconds then placed on his feet.

While verbal punishment needs to be firm rather than loud to be effective, the teacher must be careful to prevent peers in close proximity from mistaking the punishment as applying to their own behavior. Statements should be brief but fit the individual's level of verbal comprehension and should be accompanied by a frown or other nonverbal signs of disapproval. For some individuals, verbal punishment and restraint are sufficiently aversive to maintain low rates of a misbehavior. As stated earlier, however, the teacher must select a sufficiently powerful punisher so the intensity of the punishment need not be escalated with each successive infraction. Thus, verbal statements may be employed primarily to stop and identify a misbehavior but might also accompany an additional punishing consequence.

Response Cost

This procedure employs the contingent removal of reinforcers already in the possession of the individual. In essence, a fine or penalty for the misbehavior is invoked. Fines may include the removal of money, tokens, points, stars, food, free time, or privileges. Contingent upon a misbehavior, the removal of colored slips of paper on which the individual's name had been written constituted an effective punisher for emotionally disturbed boys (Hall, Axelrod, Foundopulos, Shellman, Campbell, & Cranston, 1971). In order for response cost to be used as a decelerating strategy, the punished individual must already possess a valued commodity which may be removed. Response cost is easily employed as a part of a primarily positive intervention program in which the individual earns reinforcers, such as in a token economy. As with other forms of punishment, the effectiveness of response cost is increased when careful attention is given to the seven variables described earlier.

Time Out from Positive Reinforcement

Time out achieves its punishing effects by the removal of positive reinforcers, generally in the form of teacher and peer attention. Applied contingent upon misbehavior, time out eliminates social interaction and opportunities to obtain positive reinforcement. As a method to reduce inappropriate behaviors in the severely handicapped, time out was applied successfully to self-destructive behavior (Lucero, Frieman, Spoering, & Fehrenbacher, 1976), aggressiveness (Bostow & Bailey, 1969; Clark, Rowbury, Baer, & Baer, 1973; Vukelich & Hake, 1971; White, Nielsen & Johnson, 1972) and disruption during mealtime (Barton, Guess, Garcia, & Baer, 1970).

Time out ranges from informal to more formal forms. In its simplest form, the teacher merely turns away from the misbehaving child and refuses to interact or present instructional stimuli for a brief period of time. As a more complex punishing consequence, the misbehaving individual is removed from a reinforcing situation and taken or sent to a neutral place where he remains for a period of time with return to the reinforcing situation being contingent upon an absence of misbehavior. *Neutral places* include something as simple as a chair facing the wall or a screened corner of a room. However, for individuals unlikely to remain in a chair, a small, empty room with adequate lighting and ventilation may be necessary. Although the ultimate effectivenss of time out as a deceleration strategy is dependent upon the consistency and immediacy of application, the user will benefit from heeding the following specific guidelines:

1. Use a neutral time-out area which is neither reinforcing nor punishing. Generally this means that no books, windows, toys, or peers are available but that the space is comfortable, well-lighted, and ventilated.
2. When the individual is sent or accompanied to the time-out area, the teacher should refrain both from using angry words and giving positively reinforcing attention. Interaction should be limited to a simple restatement of the broken rule or the reason for time out (e.g., "No hitting").
3. To facilitate immediacy of punishment, the time-out area should be close to but visually isolated from the teaching areas.
4. The length of time out may vary. With moderately and severely retarded individuals, White et al. (1972) found that short time outs (1 minute) were as effective as longer time outs (15 to 30 minutes). However, if a teacher first used 1-minute time outs and then switched to longer time outs, reapplication of 1-minute time outs resulted in a lessening of their punishing effect. Therefore, it is best to select shorter time outs (e.g., 1 minute, 3 minutes) and, with the assistance of a kitchen timer, apply them consistently so that a greater proportion of time is allowed for instruction and the opportunity to obtain positve reinforcement.
5. After the time out has ended, the individual is returned to the reinforcing situation *only* if he is *not* engaging in disruptive behavior. If tantrums or other inappropriate behavior are contiguous with the end of the time-out period, the teacher should wait until the first quiet moment to remove the individual from time out.
6. When a time-out booth or room is being used with a resistive individual and an outside lock is necessary to maintain time-out conditions for the specific period, it is especially important to measure the duration of time out. Also, one must keep exact records of the occurrence of the target behavior to insure that the punishment is not abused or inconsistently applied.
7. For time out to be successful, there must be an ongoing program of positive reinforcement from which the individual can be removed. Although this last point is obvious, it cannot be overstated since time out relies upon the individual's perception of the contrast between the neutral conditions of time out and the reinforcing conditions that precede and follow it.

In summary, there are a number of variations of punishment, all of which center on the decrement of the frequency of undesirable behavior. These strategies should be implemented only if positive tactics such as instruction or the reinforcement of incompatible behaviors alone was not successful. Even in these cases, a positive program to increase appropriate behaviors should be placed in operation concurrently with the use of punishment to decrease undesirable behaviors. While parental participation in program planning is especially important, it is critical that parents be consulted and grant their permission when an instructional program makes use of any form of punishment.

Summary

This chapter has reviewed basic intervention strategies to increase and decrease behavior and provided, whenever possible, research-based guidelines for their classroom application to the moderately and severely handicapped. Positive reinforcement was described and its parameters outlined—reinforcer selection, types of reinforcers, scheduling, and reinforcement procedures (Premack's Principle, shaping, and chaining). Methods available to begin behaviors which do not readily occur were explained as were the means by which these response primes may be ultimately faded to promote independence in skill performance. Extinction, classroom rules, and punishment were delineated as strategies to decrease inappropriate behavior. Specific methods of punishment—overcorrection, time out, response cost, and firm verbal statements—were described. Cautions to be heeded in the application of all three deceleration strategies were emphasized while guidelines for their use were provided.

References

Ayllon, T., & Azrin, N. H. Reinforcer sampling: A technique for increasing the behavior of mental patients. *Journal of Applied Behavior Analysis,* 1968, *1,* 13–20.

Azrin, N. H., & Foxx, R. M. A rapid method of toilet training the institutionalized retarded. *Journal of Applied Behavior Analysis,* 1971, *4,* 89–99.

Azrin, N. H., Kaplan, S. J., & Foxx, R. M. Autism reversal: Eliminating stereotyped self-stimulation of retarded individuals. *American Journal of Mental Deficiency,* 1973, *78,* 241–248.

Azrin, N. H., & Wesolowski, M. D. Theft reversal: An overcorrection procedure for eliminating stealing by retarded persons. *Journal of Applied Behavior Analysis,* 1974, *7,* 577–581.

Baer, D. M., & Guess, D. Teaching productive noun suffixes to severely retarded children. *American Journal of Mental Deficiency,* 1973, *77,* 498–505.

Baer, D. M., Peterson, R. F., & Sherman, J. A. *Building an imitative repertoire by programming similarity between child and model as discriminative for reinforcement.* Paper presented at the biennial meeting of the Society for Research in Child Development, Minneapolis, Minnesota, March, 1965.

Baker, J. G., Stanish, B., & Fraser, B. Comparative effects of a token economy in nursery school. *Mental Retardation,* 1972, *10*(4), 16–19.

Barton, E. S., Guess, D., Garcia, E., & Baer, D. M. Improvement of retardates' mealtime behaviors by timeout procedures using multiple baseline techniques. *Journal of Applied Behavior Analysis,* 1970, *3,* 77–84.

Berman, M. L. Instructions and behavior change: A taxonomy. *Exceptional Children,* 1973, *39,* 644–650.

Birnbrauer, J. S. Mental retardation. In H. Leitenberg (Ed.), *Handbook of behavior modification.* New York: Appleton-Century-Crofts, 1977.

Boston, D. E., & Bailey, J. B. Modification of severe disruptive and aggressive behavior using brief timeout and

reinforcement procedures. *Journal of Applied Behavior Analysis,* 1969, *2,* 31–37.

Bricker, D. D., Dennison, L., & Bricker, W. A. *A language intervention program for developmentally young children.* Miami, Fla.: University of Miami, Mailman Center for Child Development, Monograph No. 1, 1976.

Browning, R. M., & Stover, D. O. *Behavior modification in child treatment.* Chicago: Aldine/Atherton, 1971.

Bucher, B., & King, L. Q. Generalization of punishment effects in the deviant behavior of a psychotic child. *Behavior Therapy,* 1971, *2,* 68–77.

Bucher, B., & Lovaas, O. I. Use of aversive stimulation in behavior modification. In M. R. Jones (Ed.), *Miami symposium on the prediction of behavior: Aversive stimulation.* Coral Gables, Fla.: University of Miami Press, 1968.

Byck, M. Cognitive differences among diagnostic groups of retardates. *American Journal of Mental Deficiency,* 1968, *73,* 97–101.

Clark, H. B., Rowbury, T., Baer, A. M., & Baer, D. M. Time-out as a punishing stimulus in continuous and intermittent schedules. *Journal of Applied Behavior Analysis,* 1973, *6,* 443–455.

Dalton, A. J., Rubino, C. A., & Hislop, M. W. Some effects of token rewards on school achievement of children with Down's syndrome. *Journal of Applied Behavior Analysis,* 1973, *6,* 251–259.

Fisher, M. A., & Zeaman, D. An attention-retention theory of retardate discrimination learning. In N. R. Ellis (Ed.), *The international review of research in mental retardation* (Vol. 6). New York: Academic Press, 1973.

Frankel, F., & Simmons, J. Q. Self-injurious behavior in schizophrenic and retarded children. *American Journal of Mental Deficiency,* 1976, *80,* 512–522.

Gardner, W. I. *Behavior modification in mental retardation.* Chicago: Aldine/Atherton, 1971.

Gelfand, D. M. & Hartmann, D. P. *Child behavior: Analysis and therapy.* New York: Pergamon Press, 1975.

Gold, M. W. Stimulus factors in skill training of the retarded on a complex assembly task: Acquistion, transfer and retention. *American Journal of Mental Deficiency,* 1972, *76,* 517–526.

Gold, M. W., & Scott, K. G. Discrimination learning. In W. B. Stephens (Ed.), *Training the developmentally young.* New York: John Day, 1971.

Hall, R. V., Axelrod, S., Foundopulos, M., Shellman, J., Campbell, R. A., & Cranston, S. S. The effective use of punishment to modify behavior in the classroom. *Educational Technology,* 1971, *11* (4), 24–26.

Hislop, M. W., Moore, C., & Stanish, B. Remedial classroom programming: Long-term transfer effects from a token economy system. *Mental Retardation,* 1973, *11* (2), 18–20.

Horner, R. D., & Keilitz, I. Training mentally retarded adolescents to brush their teeth. *Journal of Applied Behavior Analysis,* 1975, *8,* 301–309.

Hotchkiss, J. M. *The modification of maladaptive behavior*

of a class of educationally handicapped children by operant conditioning techniques. Unpublished doctoral dissertation, University of Southern California, 1966.

Jackson, G. M., Johnson, C. R., Ackron, G. S., & Crowley, R. Food satiation as a procedure to decelerate vomiting. *American Journal of Mental Deficiency*, 1975, *80*, 223–227.

Kazdin, A. E. *Behavior modification in applied settings.* Homewood, Ill.: Dorsey Press, 1975.

Kazdin, A. E., & Bootzin, R. R. The token economy: An evaluative review. *Journal of Applied Behavior Analysis*, 1972, *5*, 343–372.

Kent, L. R. *Language acquisition program for the severely retarded.* Champaign, Ill.: Research Press, 1974.

Knapp, T. J. The Premack principle in human experimental and applied settings. *Behaviour Research and Therapy*, 1976, *14*, 133–147.

Kohlenberg, R. J. The punishment of persistent vomiting: A case study. *Journal of Applied Behavior Analysis*, 1970, *3*, 241–245.

Lane, H. *The wild boy of Aveyron.* Cambridge, Mass.: Harvard University Press, 1976.

Lent, J. R., & McLean, B. M. The trainable retarded: The technology of teaching. In N. G. Haring & R. L. Schiefelbusch (Eds.). *Teaching special children.* New York, McGraw-Hill, 1976.

Lindsley, O. R. Direct measurement and prosthesis of retarded behavior. *Journal of Education*, 1964, *147*, 62–81.

Locke, B. Verbal conditioning with retarded subjects: Establishment or reinstatement of effective, reinforcing consequences. *American Journal of Mental Deficiency*, 1969, *73*, 621–626.

Lovaas, O. I., Schaeffer, B., & Simmons, J. Q. Building social behavior in autistic children by use of electric shock. *Journal of Experimental Research in Personality*, 1965, *1*, 99–109.

Lovaas, O. I., & Simmons, J. Q. Manipulation of self-destruction in three retarded children. *Journal of Applied Behavior Analysis*, 1969, *2*, 143–159.

Lucero, W. J., Frieman, J., Spoering, K., & Fehrenbacker, J. Comparison of three procedures in reducing self-injurious behavior. *American Journal of Mental Deficiency*, 1976, *80*, 548–554.

MacMillan, D. L. *Behavior modification in education.* New York: Macmillan, 1973.

MacMillan, D. L., Forness, S. R., & Trumbull, B. M. The role of punishment in the classroom. *Exceptional Children*, 1973, *40*, 85–96.

Madsen, C. H., Jr., & Madsen, C. K. *Teaching/discipline, a positive approach for educational development.* Boston: Allyn and Bacon, 1974.

Mahoney, K., VanWagenen, R. K., & Meyerson, L. Toilet training of normal and retarded children. *Journal of Applied Behavior Analysis*, 1971, *4*, 173–181.

Miller, P. M., & Drennen, W. T. Establishment of social reinforcement as an effective modifier of verbal behavior in chronic psychiatric patients. *Journal of Abnormal Psychology*, 1970, *76*, 392–395.

Nelson, G. L., Cone, J. D., & Hanson, C. R. Training correct utensil use in retarded children: Modeling versus physical guidance. *American Journal of Mental Deficiency*, 1975, *80*, 114–122.

O'Brien, F., & Azrin, N. H. Developing proper meal time behavior of the institutionalized retarded. *Journal of Applied Behavior Analysis*, 1972, *5*, 389–399.

O'Brien, F., Azrin, N. H., & Bugle, C. Training profoundly retarded children to stop crawling. *Journal of Applied Behavior Analysis*, 1972, *5*, 131–137.

Parton, D. A. Learning to imitate in infancy. *Child Development*, 1976, *47*, 14–31.

Patterson, G.R., Cobb, J.A., & Ray, R.S. Direct intervention in the classroom: A set of procedures for the aggressive child. In F.W. Clark, D.R. Evans, & L.A. Hamerlynck (Eds.), *Implementing behavioral programs for school and clinics.* Champaign, Ill.: Research Press, 1972.

Pendergrass, V. E. Timeout from positive reinforcement following persistent, high-rate behavior in retardates. *Journal of Applied Behavior Analysis*, 1972, *5*, 85–91.

Premack, O. Toward empirical behavioral laws: I. Positive reinforcement. *Psychological Review*, 1959, *66*, 219–233.

Risley, T. R. The effects and side effects of punishing the autistic behaviors of a deviant child. *Journal of Applied Behavior Analysis*, 1968, *1*, 21–34.

Rollings, J. P., Baumeister, A. A., & Baumeister, A. A. The use of overcorrection procedures to eliminate the stereotyped behaviors of retarded individuals. *Behavior Modification*, 1977, *1* (1), 29–46.

Rowbury, T. G., Baer, A. M., & Baer, D. M. Interactions between teacher guidance and contingent access to play in developing preacademic skills of deviant preschool children. *Journal of Applied Behavior Analysis*, 1976, *9*, 85–104.

Rowland, M. E. S. A study of the use of higher functioning retardates as language acquisition trainers of lower functioning retardates in attendant supervised training sessions on institutional wards (Doctoral dissertation, Michigan State University, 1973). *Dissertation Abstracts International*, 1974, *34*, 7613A-761A. (University Microfilms, No. 74-13, 694.)

Simmons, V., & Williams, I. *Steps up to language for the learning impaired* (Vol. 1). Tuscon, Ariz.: Communication Skill Builders, 1976.

Skinner, B. F. *The technology of teaching.* Englewood Cliffs, N. J.: Prentice-Hall, 1968.

Skinner, B. F. *Beyond freedom and dignity.* New York: Alfred A. Knopf, 1971.

Snell, M. E. Sign language and total communication. In L. R. Kent (Ed.), *Language acquisition program for the severely retarded.* Champaign, Ill.: Research Press, 1974.

Stainback, W. C., Payne, J. S., Stainback, S. B., & Payne, R. A. *Establishing a token economy in the classroom.* Columbus, Ohio: Charles E. Merrill, 1973.

Streifel, J. A., & Phelan, J. G. Use of reinforcement of behavioral similarity to establish imitative behavior in young mentally retarded children. *American Journal of Mental Deficiency,* 1972, *77,* 239–241.

Striefel, S. *Behavior modification: Teaching a child to imitate.* Lawrence, Kans.: H & H Enterprises, 1974.

Touchette, P. E. Transfer of stimulus control: Measuring the moment of transfer. *Journal of the Experimental Analysis of Behavior,* 1971, *15,* 347–354.

Uzgiris, I. C., & Hunt, J. McV. *Assessment in infancy: Ordinal scales of psychological development.* Urbana, Ill.: University of Chicago Press, 1975.

Vukelich, R., & Hake, D. F. Reduction of dangerously aggressive behavior in a severely retarded resident through a combination of positive reinforcement procedures. *Journal of Applied Behavior Analysis,* 1971, *4,* 215–225.

White, G. D., Nielsen, G., & Johnson, S. M. Timeout duration and the suppression of deviant behavior in children. *Journal of Applied Behavior Analysis,* 1972, *5,* 111–120.

White, O. R. *A glossary of behavioral terminology.* Champaign, Ill.: Research Press, 1971.

White, O. R., & Haring, N. G. *Exceptional teaching.* Columbus, Ohio: Charles E. Merrill, 1976.

Zeaman, D. & House, B. J. The role of attention in retardate discrimination learning. In N. R. Ellis (Ed.), *Handbook of mental deficiency.* New York: McGraw-Hill, 1963.

Introduction to Chapter 4

In the next chapter, the authors undertake an enormous task in describing a model for teaching cognitive skills to the severely handicapped based upon Piaget's original formulations with Uzgiris and Hunt's (1975) more recent additions. In order that the model be understood it has been necessary that they define the conceptual framework in which Piaget views learning. Because of the senior author's rich experiences with multiply handicapped infants and children at the Meyer Children's Rehabilitation Center at the University of Nebraska, the training procedures detailed in this chapter are a product of extensive field-testing. Photographic illustrations attest to this empirical base.

Corry and Jacques Robinson have emphasized the elements of cognitive development that occur during the normal child's first 2 years of life—the sensorimotor stage. Because a large fraction of our students presently function and will continue to function with cognitive abilities characteristic of this period, the stage of sensorimotor functioning is of critical interest to us. It is clear that this stage of cognitive development underlies all other facets of development. During the sensorimotor stage the foundations for receptive and expressive language, purposeful physical movement, problem solving and reasoning are laid. Later when you read about language prerequisites in Chapter 5, you will note an important cross-referencing of skills stemming from the critical interdependence of language and cognitive development. Language is perceived as being dependent upon the prior acquisition of cognitive skills. The same phenomenon of skill overlap will reoccur when you read the early portions of Chapter 6 that depict the beginnings of gross and fine motor skills. These beginnings include the young child's watching his own hands, visually directed grasping, visual tracking of objects as they move in and out of view, putting objects into containers and emptying them out again, and navigating around barriers to reach a desired goal.

Historically we have attempted to classify information to facilitate more logical organization of what we know about child development. However the practice of viewing development as consisting of 4 or more emerging sequences of separate and distinct skills (e.g., motor, cognitive or adaptive, language, personal-social) is so simplistic it is apt to be misleading. A more accurate view of skill development for normal as well as severely handicapped individuals is one that recognizes a multitude of skills emerging from a common center with much interdependency and combination. This center may be regarded as the early cognitive functions described in the following chapter.

Reference

Uzgiris, I. C., & Hunt, J. McV. *Assessment in infancy.* Urbana, Ill.: University of Illinois Press, 1975.

4

Sensorimotor Functions and Cognitive Development

*This chapter was written by **Cordelia C. Robinson,** Meyer Children's Rehabilitation Institute, University of Nebraska Medical Center, and **Jacques H. Robinson,** Special Education Department, Kent State University.*

Part I: Sensorimotor Functions and Cognitive Development

The purpose of this chapter is to describe a model of systematic instruction designed to foster the development, in the handicapped, of the sort of sensorimotor and cognitive processes which undergird the behavior of the normal child during the first 2 years of life. Of course, in the case of the severely and profoundly handicapped, the individual may or may not mature beyond the performance levels of a 2-year-old child. But we cannot know this unless we try. The fact that an individual does not display the usual sort of autonomous development must not be taken as evidence that such growth cannot be stimulated. Sometimes, often, we must redefine what "success" in a learning task is. But we cannot permit these adjustments in our instructional targets to form the basis for the self-validating premise that the severely handicapped cannot respond to systematic instruction or that efforts to enhance more normal development are not worthwhile.

The general approach to be taken will be to examine the implications of two psychological schools of thought, or traditions, associated with the works of B. F. Skinner and Jean Piaget. Neither of these men has been concerned directly with the handicapped. However, their work, and that of their coworkers and students, is of profound import to those of us who do work with the developmentally disabled. We will examine this work within a frame of reference supplied by (1) our basic task, the systematic instruction of the handicapped, and (2) some fundamental ideas and observations about the development of the human infant.

The early parts of this chapter stress the work of Piaget and particularly his views on early human development. Applied behavior analysis, which follows from the Skinnerian tradition, and its implications for the systematic instruction of the disabled will not be developed so fully. This imbalance is not an implicit statement of relative importance. Rather, it is assumed that the reader has prior knowledge about applied behavior analysis and systematic instruction. (For a review of these topics the reader is referred to Chapters 2 and 3.)

Education involves a dynamic interplay between curriculum decisions and instructional decisions. Curriculum decisions relate to the *ends,* the goals, of education and are directed to answering the question "what to teach." Instructional decisions relate to the *means* of education and are concerned with answering the question "how to teach." In this context, Piaget's work is extremely useful in determining what to teach the child. The concepts and principles of applied behavior analysis are particularly relevant to problems centered around how to teach the child.

It is useful, for conceptual and expository purposes, to separate and contrast *instruction* (means) and *curriculum* (ends). In the real world, however, means and ends cannot be separated in other than a very arbitrary and abstract sense. Rather, "real world" educational processes reflect emphases, temporary and dynamic balances or imbalances between means and ends. For example, in the course of a practice teaching experience, the focus is generally upon how, not what, to teach. However, the systematic use of these procedures is determined by, and derives its significance from, the goals of teacher training. Conversely, a committee of teachers redesigning a high-school English course is apt to agree on what to teach and to allow for, even encourage, different ways of teaching it. In setting goals, however, the committee cannot operate without a consideration of means. Resources and predominant teaching behaviors are relevant to goals. While temporary emphases, or imbalances, are quite appropriate, it is clear that an attempt to act as if means and ends are independent would be an error. Over the long haul, equilibrium is essential if education is to be organized to meet the adaptive needs of the learner.

In line with the above, it is an oversimplification to say that Piaget offers an answer as to "what to teach" and behavior analysis an answer as to "how to teach it." More precisely, Piaget's explanation and synthesis of the scope and sequence of early human development is a fundamental basis for the *curriculum* decision, the "what to teach" question. On the other hand, his observations of the concrete behavior of children, particularly his own, is a rich source of help in determining instruction, how to foster development.

Applied behavior analysis offers a powerful model to modify behavior and is most useful when the behavior is available, observable, and at a reasonable operant rate or when precursor or substitute behaviors can be shaped into the desired behavior. Thus, the concepts and strategies of applied behavior analysis also are relevant to the structuring and modification of short-term and intermediate goals

and the confirmation of readiness states (both motivational and cognitive). Such concerns, of course, relate to instruction as well as to curriculum.

In summary, Piaget offers us useful advice on long-term curricular goals and sequences as well as immediate instructional strategies. Applied behavior analysis is a major source of a generalized instructional technology and strategies related to modification of behavior, but is also relevant to the definition of readiness states and the structuring and modification of short-term goals.

A frame of reference: Human values and human development

The purpose of this section is to establish a frame of reference, based upon the early development of the normal human infant, within which to view instructional programming for the handicapped in general and the role of applied behavior analysis and Piaget in particular. The first issue has to be: "Why this normative frame of reference?" Why can we not accept the handicapped person as an individual, at face value, without fracturing our image of him through the prism of "normal development"?

Several points are relevant. In the first place, terms such as "handicapped" (severe or otherwise), "abnormal," "deviant," etc. have no meaning except in oppositional or complementary contrast to "normal" development or adaptive life processes. Yet, in the absence of such terms, one assumes such normalcy. This assumption is not a value judgment. It does not imply that normal is better; even if this is a value position frequently espoused in our culture and by many special educators. Further, to characterize an individual as either "normal" or "handicapped" is *not* to deny that person's individuality.

But why label at all? When it is so easy for some to depersonalize and devalue the disabled, why provide the target that a label offers? The immediate response to this question is to affirm that (1) labeling cannot be prevented, or (2) labeling can also be a means of marshaling unusual resources to meet the needs of the handicapped. Such responses are not apt to be positively reinforced. They seem too pat and simpleminded. And yet, who can say these things are not true?

The present authors' stress on "normal" human development should not be taken to imply that normal is *good* and abnormal is *bad.* The more salient distinction is between "deviance" and "incompetence." Both of these terms are defined in contrast to "normality." However, "incompetence" connotes the absence of a potential for choice to be normal or abnormal.

As teachers, we must accept responsibility for all the unnecessary incompetencies displayed by our students. Likewise, as professionals, we must accept responsibility for complete, appropriate curricula directed toward a reversal of incompetencies observed in our students. Piaget offers a model of the development of human competence as a biological process. This model offers a goal structure which reflects the value posture of the authors. The investment is in "competence" as a criterion, not in "normality" per se—in "normalization" of the child's behavior, or his environment, as a means to individual fulfillment and competence and not an end unto itself.

Early human development: Fundamental features

Certain features of early human behavior and development are outstanding and any account of human development must deal with them. Among these features are:

1. The striking dependency of the human neonate relative to other species.
2. The autonomous character of human development.
3. The accelerating acquisition of systems of behavior that are highly organized, flexible, and adaptable.
4. The startling capacity of the child to develop symbolic processes and abstract thought.
5. The dynamic interplay between maturation and learning in human development.
6. The vast range of individual differences in human behavior.

The writings of Hebb (1949) and Hunt (1961) are particularly illuminating in validating and defining these features with respect to the normal child's development. Further discussion is beyond the scope of this chapter. However, these features supply a basic context in which to view our present concerns. It is in this context, first, that the lack of normal development has such import and, second, that the diagnosis of severe handicap and its associated prognosis has such a devastating impact. Thus, it is in the context of normal human development that the instruction of the handicapped must find its meaning.

A number of theories have been offered to account for different aspects of cognitive development. A common characteristic of these models is their focus upon the development of *concepts* or classifications of environmental events and the development of *strategies* for responding to those events.

There are some differences in the various definitions of the term "concept." Most involve the idea that a concept is the basis for responding to environmental stimuli as "the same" even if the stimuli are quite different in some ways. For example, a child learns to say "cup" when she sees one. Maybe the cup is her own, which might be short, wide, white, and plastic. When she can verbally identify that cup, she has acquired a response. But not until she can label a cup she has never seen before, maybe a yellow china cup, do we say that the child has acquired the concept of cup. The concept, of course, is an idea, not a cup and not a label, and cannot be seen or heard. The "existence" of the concept must be inferred from the child's *generalized response.* The child also may *overgeneralize* and say that glasses and jars are cups too. On the other hand, she may omit all blue cups from the class of cups by attending to an irrelevant dimension (color) and cue (blueness). Thus, it is not enough that the child identify the cups she has seen before. She must discriminate or identify new cups, and only new cups, before we can say that she "has the concept." These features, of course, hold for the child's response to most of the objects and events in her world. However, there are radical differences in the complexity and degrees of abstraction involved between concepts. Having a cup is not the same as having a cup of milk or a cup of water, nor the same as drinking milk, interacting with mother, having an apple or an orange, having an orange cup or a plastic cup, etc.

Let us assume that a mother wishes her child to develop a generalized response of labeling all cups (and only cups) as "cups." Some basic principles of applied behavior analysis are relevant to any attempt to instruct the child systematically. In this situation the discriminative factor which will become the stimulus to evoke the child's behavior is known. As soon as it is clear that there is a stable relationship between a specific training stimulus (say, the child's cup) and the appropriate response, it is possible to start generalization training. The procedure is to introduce many other cups, of different sizes, shapes, and colors as stimuli and model the response "cups." It is also appropriate to contrast the cups with stimuli which serve as exemplars of "not-cups" to inhibit overgeneralization. It might, or it might not, be necessary to reinforce the child's imitation of mother's modeling with tangible reinforcement. Generally it is not.

Another fundamental idea used to describe and explain the organization and adaptability that characterizes the young child's behavior is the notion of *strategy*. A strategy is much more than a concept although concept learning is involved. Strategies may be addressed to either the attainment or the utilization of concepts at various levels of complexity and abstraction. Strategy implies intent and planning and is generally manifest in the child's behaviors. But strategies generally are rather complex and difficult to interpret.

The example of the cup may serve to highlight the problems in inference. If, after generalization has begun, the child seeks out a new cup, brings it to mother, and says, "Cup?", this is a strategy. In fact, it is an exemplar of several strategies. One strategy relates directly to the display of concept or label generalization. Another involves a request for confirmation of the generalization—the child is seeking feedback on her behavior. Still another strategy might be to obtain a smile, a hug, or even a drink from mother.

After strategies are well practiced, they may become *routines*. They become so well integrated as ends in themselves that they may be emitted in the service of still higher-order strategies. In such a case, they become *subroutines*. For instance, the child may have used a "climb-up-on-the-chair-and-get-it-because-it's-high" subroutine in getting the cup to show to mother.

One of the problems with strategies is that they may, through unanticipated generalizations, be displayed at times or directed at goals that mother may not be inclined to reinforce in a positive manner. Let us suppose that the cup the child gets is a valuable, irreplaceable, fragile family heirloom. And suppose that mother, all too humanly, responds negatively and reinforces by screaming, "No! No! That's a NO-NO!" What are apt to be the consequences of this? First, the child might drop, or even throw, the cup. But what might she learn? That it is not a cup? That mother punishes confirmation behavior or punishes concept generalization? Or, that it is one of those days to avoid mother? Or that my cup is the only cup? Or my cup is the only cup I can touch? Or I can't touch any cup anymore? It is difficult to say.

Only careful observation can validate the appropriate inferences.

Following the precepts of applied behavior analysis, mother would be advised not to introduce any verbal punishment at all. The first move might be to get the cup. The delay in reinforcement associated with this maneuver might well be appropriate. Then it might be best to respond to the generalization/ confirmation strategies and confirm that it is indeed a cup. One could then switch to modeling a new discrimination, "MY cup, not your cup."

The bulk of the preschool curriculum consists of learning specific and basic content (e.g., recognition and identification of colors, shapes, numerals) and applying strategies to that content (classification by color and shape, matching numerals to quantities). While the use of strategies enhances knowledge of the content, this use also reinforces generalization of the strategy to other classes of objects on some dimension of similarity (function, size, etc.). These strategies become increasingly important as the child gets older and as what she can do, and is expected to do, becomes more complex. Thus, it is important to systematically develop such strategies as well as content skills in order to enhance later learning.

Piaget's theory of human development

It is not the purpose of this chapter to provide the reader with a detailed discussion of Piaget's approach to studying development. Such material is available in Furth (1969), Hunt (1961), and Flavell (1963). Piaget (1954, 1963) and Uzgiris and Hunt (1966, 1975) provide more detail on the descriptions of the tasks that form the basis of the activities included here.

Piaget uses the terms "mental structure" and "schema," or the plural "schemata," to refer, in a global sense, to what are called "concepts" and "strategies" above. Concepts and strategies or mental structures represent two sides of the same coin, the organizational and adaptive patterns of the child's developing cognition. Piaget organizes this development into an ordinal sequence of cognitive stages. Each stage may be characterized in terms of a complex of recurrent observable behaviors which reflect a system, a mental structure, or a pattern of concepts and strategies. These structures serve as a synthesis of prior learnings and as a basis for development yet to occur. This will lead to a new, qualitatively different pattern or stage in development. For example, relatively early, in the sensorimotor period, the child displays systematic search behaviors directed toward the recovery of partly or completely hidden objects. This search behavior serves as a basis for the inference that the child has developed "object permanence." At 5 or 6 years of age, the child displays "the conservation of mass" which presupposes object permanence and which is characterized in behavioral terms as the ability to adequately explain how it is that one of two clay balls, if transformed into a sausage shape, without any removal or addition of clay, is still equal in mass to the other ball.

The present authors use the terms "concept" and "strategy" to emphasize the relevance shaping and learning have to the sensorimotor (SM) stage. However, as will be established later, *intention* or purposeful use of a strategy is a result of SM development. Further, Piaget sees SM development as being preconceptual, occurring before the development of cognition. The issue is one of definition and convention. In any event, it must be understood that SM functions (1) are qualitatively different from cognitive functioning in later periods and (2) appear to be absolutely essential to subsequent cognitive development.

Each of the stages within Piaget's theory are characterized by the acquisition of specific content. Environmental experiences provide the material for learning. Development takes place as a function of the complementary processes of *assimilation* and *accommodation*. The function of assimilation is the integration of new information or experience into the organism's existing behavioral repertoire.

During assimilation the input is changed by the child's existing way of thinking; during accommodation the child changes thinking processes to align more closely with the input. Therefore the function of accommodation is to modify and elaborate existing thinking processes (schemes, concepts, and strategies) so that they will acquire greater applicability. Accommodation leads to the emergence of a more advanced level of thinking processes.

In his writing Piaget uses many concepts from biology, one of which is *equilibration*. For Piaget, development reflects the dynamic processes of assimilation and accommodation. Each fluctuates in dominance. When one process predominates, a state of disequilibrium is said to exist. The course of these two processes coming back into more equal balance is equilibration and the state is one of equilibrium.

When the child has adjusted (accommodated) to the newness of the situation and integrated (assimilated) the new information to existing schemata, there usually follows a period of repetition of the newly formed scheme which acts to incorporate more completely the new form of behavior into the child's repertoire. In a sense, the child "practices" the new behavior; this practice is not characterized by boredom but rather appears to be self-reinforcing.

Piaget's descriptions of stage and sequences in the development of specific concepts can be used in the construction of instructional sequences for handicapped individuals as well as for normal children. Stephens (1971, 1977) has developed an excellent overall summary of Piaget's developmental stages (Table 4.1).

This chapter focuses upon development during the sensorimotor (SM) period—a period from birth to about 2 years in children of average development. During the SM stage, practical or motoric intelligence develops rapidly. Much of the child's accumulation of "mental structures" during this period comes about through active physical exploration and manipulation of the environment. It is only toward the very end of this period that the child can utilize language to guide her behavior. Among the early developments of this period are the recognition of the permanence of objects, the use of objects as tools to solve problems, the functional use of objects, and increasing competency in motor imitation. While each of these skills are separable, their emergence is characterized by hierarchical interdependency as illustrated by the flow chart in Figure 4.1. All these developments occur, for the typical child, as a function of her daily interactions during the first 2 years of life. For the severely handicapped this development will be much more gradual, its rate being a product of teachers, parents, and the learner herself.

As can be seen in Table 4.2, Piaget divides the sensorimotor period into 6 substages involving increasingly complex applications of the sensorimotor schemata. These areas of application, which go through progressive differentiation during the SM period, involve the development of object permanence means-ends relationships, and causality and spatial organization. Table 4.2 contains a matrix of the sensorimotor concept areas and the level of the concept corresponding to each of the substages. An effort has been made to describe each of the substages in operational terms. These brief descriptions are expanded next.

TABLE 4.1   *Piaget's stages of intellectual development*

Stage and Approximate Age	Characteristic Behavior
I. Sensory-motor operations	
A. Reflexive (0–1 month)	Simple reflex activity; example: kicking.
B. Primary circular reactions (1–4.5 months)	Reflexive behavior becomes elaborated and coordinated; example: eye follows hand movements.
C. Secondary circular reactions (4.5–9 months)	Repeats chance actions to reproduce an interesting change or effect; example: kicks crib, doll shakes, so kicks crib again.
D. Coordination of secondary schema (9–12 months)	Acts become clearly intentional; example: reaches behind cushion for ball.
E. Tertiary circular reactions (12–18 months)	Discovers new ways to obtain desired goal; example: pulls pillow nearer in order to get toy resting on it.
F. Invention of new means through mental combinations (18–24 months)	Invents new ways and means; example: uses stick to reach desired object.
II. Pre-operational	
A. Preconceptual (2–4 years)	Capable of verbal expression, but speech is repetitious; frequent egocentric monologues.
B. Intuitive (4–7 years)	Speech becomes socialized; reasoning is egocentric; "to the right" has one meaning—to his right.
III. Concrete operations (7–11 years)	Mobile and systematic thought organizes and classifies information; is capable of concrete problem-solving.
IV. Formal operations (11 years upward)	Can think abstractly, formulate hypotheses, engage in deductive reasoning, and check solutions.

Source: B. Stephens, The appraisal of cognitive development. In B. Stephens (Ed.), *Training the Developmentally Young.* New York: John Day, 1971, p. 48.

Functional adaptation of observation and instruction to the needs of the handicapped

Before describing the SM instructional program, it seems advisable to discuss some questions and problems associated with systematic instruction for severely disabled individuals who are functioning at the SM level. Of particular importance are concerns to the observation and measurement of SM behavior and accommodating instructional goals and methods to the child's disabilities.

The reader will find the content of Chapter 5 of immediate relevance to the observation and recording of SM behavior and the shaping of task atten-

tion, imitation (motoric and vocal), action patterns, and the discriminative use of objects. Because the focus in Chapter 5 is on shaping early language behavior, a skill area that dovetails with SM behavior, there is little point in describing these prelanguage skills here.

The focus in this section is on accommodating to the handicap. In implementing a program to induce more normal development, certain basic questions must be addressed. Among these concerns are: What reinforces the child? Are the response criteria appropriate for a given child? Are the instructional objectives appropriate for a given child? Are the instructional methods appropriate for a given child? Are the procedures to evaluate learning appropriate

TABLE 4.2   *Sensorimotor stages and accomplishments*

Sensorimotor Stage	Object Permanence	Means-End	Causality	Spatial
I. *Reflexes* Slight modifications of initial reflexes (sucking, grasping, arm/leg movements)	No differentiation of developments in these areas. Behavior is at the level of exercising reflexes.			
II. *Primary Circular Reactions* Reflexes undergo adaptations to environmental experience; coordinations between responses beginning (e.g., looking at grasped object)	There are no special adaptations as yet to the vanished object. Related developments during this period include visual pursuit of a slowly moving object by (1) following through arc of 180°; (2) reacting to disappearance of a slowly moving object by maintaining gaze at point of disappearance	Differentiation between means-end and causality is not possible at this stage. The following are prerequisites for both: (1) visual examination of hand, (2) visually directed grasp, (3) repetition of movements which produce environmental effect, (4) refinements in reach and grasp		Child: (1) switches gaze from one visual stimulus to another, (2) turns to localize a noise made outside of visual field, (3) looks to other end of opaque screen when object disappears at one end
III. *Secondary Circular Reactions* Schemata are repeated. This systematically produces a change in, and effect on, the environment	Child: (1) moves to look after a fallen object, (2) searches for a partly hidden object, (3) returns gaze to starting point when a slowly moving object disappears, (4) searches for object under single screen	Child: (1) moves to object out of reach, (2) pulls a support to obtain a toy attached to the support	Child responds to cessation of a spectacle (that she cannot reproduce) by touching the adult or the toy	Child: (1) follows movement of rapidly moving object, (2) rotates trunk to retrieve object moved behind her, (3) examines objects by turning them over
IV. *Coordination of Secondary Circular Reactions* Schemata are used together for intentional results	Child finds an object hidden under one of two screens by searching directly under the correct screen, up to three screens	Child: (1) does not pull support if object is held above it, (2) expands pulling scheme to other tools such as strings both horizontal and vertical (vertical use requires object permanence as object is not in view)	Child responds to cessation of a spectacle by handing the toy to the adult, but may first try to reproduce the spectacle by direct action on the toy	Child: (1) brings functionally related objects together, i.e., cup and spoon, (2) begins container play by taking an object out of container then placing one in at a time, building to larger numbers

TABLE 4.2 *(Continued)*

Sensorimotor Stage	Object Permanence	Mean-End	Causality	Spatial
V. *Tertiary Circular Reactions* Child, through trial and error procedures, discovers new means to obtain desired goals. Requires combination of previous schemata	Child: (1) finds an object after a single invisible displacement, (2) follows objects through a series of visible displacements and searches in correct location, (3) finds an object hidden from view and taken through successive displacements	Child uses an unattached tool such as a rake to get an object	Child: (1) lets a toy continue activity without intervention, (2) attempts to activate a toy after demonstration	Child: (1) empties container by dumping, (2) moves around barriers to obtain objects, (3) builds a tower of blocks
VI. *Invention of New Means through Mental Combinations* Child is assumed to solve problems representationally and then applies a solution to the problem situation	Child searches along path in a complex problem when object is left in first location and the examiner's hand moves through the entire path. The child searches systematically until the object is found	Child solves problem through "foresight"; for example, does not attempt to stack a solid ring on a pole	Child displays spontaneous attempt to activate a toy	Child recognizes absence of familiar persons

109

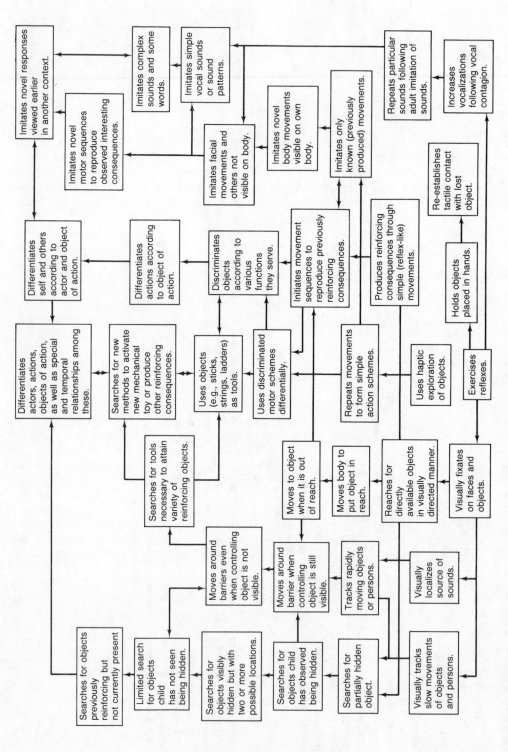

FIGURE 4.1   A hierarchy of skill sequences occuring during the sensorimotor stage

Source: Adapted from J. W. Filler, C. C. Robinson, R. A. Smith, L. J. Vincent-Smith, D. D. Bricker, and W. A. Bricker, Mental retardation. In N. Hobbs (Ed.), *Issues in the Classification of Children* (Volume 1), p. 219. San Francisco: Jossey-Bass, 1975. Copyright 1975 by Jossey-Bass. Reproduced by permission.

for a given child? Each of these questions will be considered in turn.

What Reinforces the Child?

In the sensorimotor activities described in this chapter the functional definition of a reinforcer is assumed, that is, a positive reinforcer is a stimulus, the presentation of which results in an increase in a particular response. When confronted with a child who does not demonstrate the desired behavior, one must determine whether the consequences of the behavior lack reinforcement value for the child by observing the effect of other stimuli as reinforcers. The intrinsic functional value of the behavior is particularly important during the sensorimotor period when the child is dependent upon a physical or spatial connection between two events in order to relate them. For example, the reinforcer for uncovering an object is getting that object and the reinforcer for pulling on a string attached to a toy is the access to the toy. It has been our experience that to superimpose a primary reinforcer, in the form of an edible, upon these tasks is not functional. Primary reinforcers can be effectively used within the tasks themselves, as the hidden object or the goal object in the means-end problem.

Are the Response Criteria Appropriate for a Given Child?

Various developmental researchers have identified particular tasks as criteria for assessing whether a given child has grasped certain concepts. From the Piagetian descriptions of sensorimotor intelligence we have identified concepts that are part of the young child's accomplishments during the first years of life. These conventional tasks also make demands upon the child's physical abilities. There tends to be close correspondence between the child's increasing physical abilities and his problem-solving abilities. When working with severely handicapped children we inevitably encounter individuals with multiple handicaps, both physical and sensory in nature. Thus, it often happens that the conventional behavioral criteria which serve to validate an inference about the individual's stage of cognitive development are inappropriate in light of some handicapping conditions.

One of the advantages of the Piagetian approach to cognitive development is that it provides us with a sequence of concepts rather than simply an empirical arrangement of tasks. Thus, we have conventional tasks to use as operational definitions of the sensorimotor concepts of object permanence, means-end, and causality. However, by identifying specific concepts we can then operationally define them in ways that involve accommodation of a task to a particular individual's response capabilities if the conventional criterion cannot be used.

Object permanence, for example, typically has been operationally defined as uncovering and obtaining an object that has been covered. This operation cannot be demonstrated by many severely handicapped students because the prerequisite skills of visually directed reach, grasp, and visual tracking are not possible for them. These responses may be impossible due to visual defect or abnormal persistence of certain early reflex patterns such as the asymmetric tonic neck reflex (i.e., abnormal muscle tone in neck and trunk) that prevent coordination of reach and grasp or visual tracking. If we were to persist with only one operational definition of the concept of object permanence for these individuals, we still would be working on the prerequisite behaviors for that operation. But let us return to the concept of object permanence. It involves the recognition, in the absence of sensory contact with an object, that the object still exists. There must be some alternate responses in the individual's repertoire from which we may infer that the individual recognizes the existence of the object despite a loss of sensory contact with the object (object permanence). The behavior from which we infer object permanence does not have to be visually directed reach, uncover, and grasp of the object. The child who is unable to reach and uncover and grasp could tell someone else "it is under the cup over here." However, if in addition to physical limitations, the individual lacks speech, the recurrent response of looking in the direction of the desired object may be substituted.

This strategy of adapting a response to the person's physical abilities can be applied to any content area. It is possible to carry out this adaptation more readily when the curriculum is organized around the teaching of concepts. Working through a behavioral checklist of skills arranged in an empirically determined hierarchy such as the items involved in standardized infant assessments presents problems. While infant assessments can be adapted, the concept the item is measuring must be analyzed first in order to select an alternate response.

Are the Instructional Objectives Appropriate for a Given Child?

The primary question to be considered when identifying instructional objectives for any child concerns the functional utility of a particular form of behavior for the child. Before including any objective and the activities for meeting that objective in a child's educational plan, one must ask whether this objective will increase this child's competence in daily interactions with home, school, and play environments. At one level we might say that all of the typical preschool activities increase a child's competence. However, if pressed for specifics regarding the manner in which puzzles, bead stringing, and color sorting relate to activities that come later in a child's curriculum, we are frequently unable to provide them.

Time spent teaching behaviors which may not be physically possible for a child and that are questionable prerequisites to later tasks is wasted. Selection of instructional activities should be based upon an affirmative answer to one or both of the following questions: Does the behavior being taught lead toward a skill that enables the child to have additional control over her *physical* environment? Does the behavior being taught lead toward a skill that enables the child to have additional control over her *social* environment? If it is not possible to answer affirmatively either of these questions, then there is reason to exclude the activity from the child's program.

The rationale for the emphasis upon increasing the child's control over her environment stems from a growing body of literature on the topic of "learned helplessness" (Seligman, 1975). This term refers to behaviors that provide no opportunity to control one's environment, typically an aversive situation. After 5 years of work with moderately to severely handicapped infants and toddlers, we are finding that this description frequently applies to situations in which we place these children. In some cases their limited mobility, sensory capabilities, motivation (or combination of the three) results in a child who has few opportunities to act upon her environment in a systematic manner even if the act is something as simple as swatting at a musical hanging toy. With such individuals the overall rate of movement is low and the number of repetitions necessary to bring a response under discriminative control is often great. Therefore every possible opportunity for learning a response should be taken. For example, when a child displays no ability to

voluntarily repeat a response (arm wave, foot kick, or head turn) which results in a visually interesting or sound-producing event, our first major goal is to teach some form of this behavior. The specific stimulus or response is not important. What is critical is that there be a relationship established between a behavior on the child's part and some predictable occurrence in the child's environment. While it may be related to only a very minute aspect of the environment initially, the child will have some opportunity to exercise control. This basic relationship can be then extended by planning other activities over which the child can exercise control. It has been our experience that before long the child will be inventing opportunities for generalizing this strategy. The response strategy can then be extended over an increasing number of daily events. This provides the child with a series of very predictable occurrences throughout the day. It is in the context of these predictable events, which require specific action from the child, that the concepts of object permanence, means-ends activities, causality, specific actions on objects, and spatial relationships can then be taught.

The second criterion for the inclusion of objectives and activities relates to the child's social environment. Although similar to the development of control over the physical environment, the two types of events are separated to place additional emphasis upon the need for both types of control. During the initial development of our curriculum activities at the Meyer Children's Rehabilitation Institute, more emphasis was placed upon the manipulation of the physical environment than upon social interaction. After many hours observing and working with children, we have begun to recognize this as a problem and now are trying to correct previous mistakes. Specifically, we see communication as a basic strategy that develops and takes a number of forms (gesture, vocal, communication board). By not restricting communication to one specific mode, we immediately create more opportunities to require a child's use of a mode of communication to act upon the environment.

There are opportunities for communication in every interaction that occurs with the child. Consider the young child who enjoys moving up and down in a bouncy seat. This activity is provided, the activity stops, and the child continues to bounce a little. A parent interprets the child's bouncing as "make it happen again," and they do make it happen again. This subtle sequence can be the beginnings of a communication strategy. After going through this sequence many times, the child starts to bounce as soon as she is put in the seat. Once that occurs the parent may require the bounce first from the child before they make the seat "go." In general terms, this routine involves interpretation of the child's use of a procedure for reproducing an interesting event as a request for the event to happen again. This routine can be applied to any event during the child's day. It is a very primitive form of communication. It requires much shaping and interpretation on our part. But it is the material from which a formal communication system will be developed.

It is important to insure that instructional objectives focus upon behavior relevant to the child's control over her environment. In addition, however, objectives also must be adapted to the child's specific handicaps, her potential for development in a given area, and the physical requirements of the task. Often the prediction of a child's future performance will be difficult and "educated guesses" must be extrapolated from the child's performance data with the assistance of program therapists.

To use the example of object permanence again, if a given child seems to have some difficulty in hand use but the eventual development of functional reach and grasp is feasible, the teacher may assess object permanence with the conventional task. The child must reach, uncover, and grasp the hidden objects. The task provides a natural consequence for use of reach and grasp. It is, therefore, a good teaching situation for two objectives—refinement of reach and grasp and object permanence. If, however, reach and grasp are so difficult for the child that efforts to reach with accuracy result in a distraction from the object permanence task, it will be best to use an alternative response during assessment and training, such as a directed gaze. The question of the best response system for a given child needs to be determined according to the characteristics of the individual child. The decision is based upon current child data but may be revised as more information becomes available.

A task analysis of skills involved in any one objective will often provide guidelines for adapting tasks to a given child's physical capabilities and sensory capabilities. Sometimes the child shows delay in a particular area of prerequisite skills. In such cases, the task may be modified to substitute an alternate skill for the one in which the child is delayed and keep the skills which he can do as part of the task. For example, if visual tracking is poor but reach and grasp are adequate, the teacher may wish to construct the object permanence task in such a way that the child can use a strategy of alternate glancing or tactile following of the movement of an object in the sequential search tasks. Alternate strategies for the development of communication, which include communication boards or signing systems, provide excellent examples of adapting tasks to a particular child's conceptual and motoric capabilities.

Are the Instructional Methods Appropriate for a Given Child?

The sensorimotor period has been referred to as the period of practical intelligence because the tasks learned during this period are based upon direct sensory and motor experience. The term "practical intelligence" reminds us that the tasks are most likely to be accomplished by the child at her current level of functioning and during the course of naturally occurring events. "Naturally occurring" does not mean that the teacher should function as an ecological psychologist and wait for events to occur to record the child's response. Rather, instructional events must be arranged using the daily routine and the problems which the child encounters during daily activities as the instructional method.

We are generally accustomed to dividing our instructional time into segments according to content areas (e.g., language time, arithmetic skills, art time, and gross motor activities). This scheduling, however, is not appropriate for the child who is functioning at the sensorimotor level. If you try to require a child to search for different objects for 5 trials and then switch to 5 trials of tool use and then 5 trials of putting objects into a container, you typically encounter a very exasperated child. This is probably because you are constantly taking objects away from him. An approach that is more successful is to intersperse the activities so that after the child finds an object or uses a tool to get an object, you allow time for her to examine it. During this time you may record the schemata with that object. Then you might demonstrate a new scheme and try to get her to imitate you. Go on to another object only after interest in the first seems exhausted for a time.

Instruction in causality objectives generally requires some form of gesture. This need not be a formal sign but a movement that has been associated with a particular consequence. Development of this early gesture system is best accomplished by making daily events center around routines such as eating, dressing, toileting; these and other favored events would be made contingent upon the designated "gesture." For example, the child is not picked up unless she moves her hands up. She does not get another bite of food unless she touches the hand of the person feeding her. She doesn't get rocked in the rocking chair unless she taps the arm of the chair. These gestures, which are the beginnings of communication, indicate an understanding of causality.

In order to stimulate ambulation, the child might be expected to walk (roll, scoot, or crawl) to her favorite activities which may include snack or music time. This exemplifies the Premack Principle (Premack, 1962). This principle involves the use of a more highly preferred activity to reinforce the occurrence of a less probable form of behavior. It is critical that the arrangement of activities for the child involve many very brief opportunities to respond rather than lengthy periods directed toward instruction in isolated content areas. The necessity of making very close temporal arrangements among the antecedent events, the response, and the consequential events is characteristic of the sensorimotor period.

Are the Procedures to Evaluate Learning Appropriate for a Given Child?

Procedures for evaluating cognitive learning are essentially the same as those for any other content area. Generally, there are two measurement levels to consider. The first is simply the presence or absence of the skill. The assessment sequences from Uzgiris and Hunt's work (1966, 1975) on sensorimotor development are included later in this chapter to provide an example of this type of evaluation. In order to set goals for any child we must begin with an assessment of the child's performance on a series of tasks. The child is presented with tasks in an increasing order of difficulty until the point of initial failure. Both the child's responses to that task and the task itself are analyzed to determine whether the child's failure may be the physical or the cognitive requirements of the task. If the particular response modality has contributed to the child's failing performance, then the task is modified to meet the child's response capabilities. If the child is still unable to correctly respond in another modality, the task is presented using different antecedent conditions (cues and prompts) in an effort to find some condition under which the child demonstrates the response. Teaching activities are initiated using the antecedent conditions which resulted in the initial correct performance. The usual goal is to teach

the student to perform under standard task conditions.

Initial assessments are meant to determine the presence or absence of a behavior. Eventually, however, we must engage in a second level of assessment and examine the proficiency with which the child demonstrates a particular form of behavior. Proficiency can refer to the generalizability of the response across a variety of stimuli as well as to the rate at which the response can be performed.

In the area of cognitive development we are particularly concerned with the former aspect of proficiency—the generalizability of the response across stimuli. In fact, generalization of a response to new stimuli constitutes the operational definition of a concept and the underpinnings of cognitive development. The eventual goal in working on all the sensorimotor areas is to develop the concept involved, not simply the isolated behaviors of searching under cups or pulling on strings. We want the child to learn the general principles that objects still exist when we cannot see them and that objects and events can be used as tools to solve problems encountered in the environment. How a generalized response, with respect to the sensorimotor schemata, will be accomplished must be answered individually for each child. One of the characteristics we can expect in the severely retarded is that of difficulty in skill generalization. Research has demonstrated that retarded individuals need many, many examples from one class of antecedent events before the response is spontaneously generalized to a new example of that same class of stimuli. Deficiencies in skill generalization have been particularly evident in training motor imitation and learning set in the severely retarded (Bricker, 1970). Indeed, some have suggested that the amount of training required to achieve a generalized response is a better means of identifying retardation than is the sum of a person's accumulated knowledge.

When working with a child on a particular activity such as the simple object permanence problem, we begin with several different objects for hiding and perhaps two different screens with which to hide objects. We start with variety in order to facilitate generalization. If we find a very low rate of searching, we reduce to one screen but still use whatever variety we can in terms of the hidden object. Once the child searches under one screen, we introduce a second, third, fourth, and fifth screen. This goes on until we see correct responding within several trials of the first introduction of a new screen. Generally we find that a change in the form of the screen (towel, cup, box) is more likely to result in a breakdown in behavior than a change in a screen characteristic such as color.

The physical location or task setting is another important factor to consider in response generalization. For example, one child we worked with would search diligently for a completely covered object placed in front of her. However, if the object was moved partly out of sight to the side, she would not pursue the search, suggesting that adequate generalization training had not been provided for physical location.

Since, for any one task, it may not be possible to test adequately for generalization, problems at the next level of difficulty in the sequence may help to identify gaps in generalization training. The best test for skill generalization includes placing a child in a natural situation where the newly learned concept is required to solve an immediate problem. It is with successful performance under such conditions that we have confidence in the adequacy of the response as a generalized strategy.

Part II: Instructional Sequences

1. Sensory organization responses

The sensory organization responses are organized somewhat arbitrarily into the following tasks: (1) visual fixation, (2) visual tracking, (3) sound localization, (4) development of maintenance of grasp on an object (grasp maintenance), and (5) visually directed reach and grasp.

Each of these 5 sensory organization tasks, in turn, is described as an instructional sequence for the purpose of providing information necessary for teaching. Therefore comments, organized in a standardized format, are directed to terminal objective, rationale, and conditions and task sequence. Included under the latter heading are the following subheads under which further teaching suggestions are provided for each task: child characteristics, positioning, materials, subsequent task, test for generalization, and general comments.

Later sections of this part of the chapter outline, in a similar format, sets of tasks and instructional sequences leading to *object permanence, means for achieving environmental events,* and the development of *spatial relations.*

Task 1: Visual Fixation

Terminal objective. Visual fixation is defined as regard of a stimulus which is held in a fixed position. Reflection of the stimulus in the child's pupil(s) serves as an indication of visual fixation. The teacher should continue work on visual fixation until the child is able to look at objects within 1 to 10 seconds of their presentation and maintain gaze for 10 to 15 seconds at a time (see probe sheet in Figure 4.2).

Rationale. Visual fixation is a prerequisite skill to all other visual sensory organization responses. It

OBJECTIVE: Child maintains gaze on brightly colored object for 3 seconds on 4 out of 5 presentations. Maximum latency allowed until child fixes gaze is 10 seconds.

ADMINISTRATION: Child is in supine tilt position with head centered; present bright colored patterned stimuli for maximum of 15 seconds. If child fixates, present until no longer looking at stimulus.

RESPONSE CRITERION: Child maintains gaze for 3 seconds on 4 of 5 presentations on 5 consecutive days.

Date	Stimulus	Latency of 1st Fixation (Seconds)	Duration of Each Fixation (Seconds)	Frequency of Fixation Per Trial	Type of Fixation (R, L, Both Eyes)	Comment
2/10	orange ball	6	2 3	3	1. Right 2. Bilateral	
2/10	mother's face	5	1 2	4	1. Bilateral 2. Right eye	
2/10	"Lite Brite"	2	5 5	6	1. Bilateral 2. Bilateral	

FIGURE 4.2   *Visual tracking probe record*

forms the basis for development of visual tracking or alternate glancing behaviors which in turn serve as building blocks for the development of object concepts.

Conditions and task sequence.

Child characteristics. Visual fixation is one of the primary behaviors we expect from children. There are no observable prerequisite behaviors or conditions for working on visual fixation. Visual fixation occurs during the reflexive state, and therefore it is extremely rare for a child not to show some visual fixation behavior unless there is no optic structure at all.

Positioning of child. In working for visual fixation it is important to position the child so that she has sufficient support for her head to be stable and centered at the midline. In this position conjugate gaze (both eyes focused on the same point) is most likely to occur with the gaze directed straight ahead. Some children may have deviations of gaze coincidental with persistence of abnormal reflex patterns. This may make visual fixation unlikely without special positioning arrangements such as the head centering cushion depicted in Figure 4.3. For some children the need for this type of prothestic may be only temporary. For others, whose neuromotor involvement is severe, the need may be permanent. A discussion of some types of deviations of gaze and strategies for positioning may be found in Fieber and Robinson (Note 1).

Materials. Two important factors to be considered when working on visual fixation are the stimulus characteristics and the distance of the stimulus from the child. There is a well-documented developmental sequence for the types of stimuli that infants prefer to look at when they are given a choice (Fantz & Nevis, 1967). Knowledge of this sequence can be helpful in selecting stimuli. Initially the child tends to respond to light sources and brightly colored objects. Before long the child prefers patterned stimuli, especially faces.

Some types of stimuli that are useful in working on visual fixation include light sources, such as the "Lite Brite" toy, which is especially nice because the pattern may be varied, and flashlights, which can be used directly if muted with some colored cellophane or used indirectly by reflecting light onto other objects. Other useful stimuli include brightly colored objects, patterned objects and cards such as checkerboard contact paper, faces (people or dolls) or facial representation with pictures or schematic drawings, objects that may or may not make noise. However, the most important consideration is the child's interest in the stimulus. Without this, visual fixation becomes difficult to shape.

Frequently it is necessary to present stimuli at different distances from the child's face to find the ideal distance for presentation.

Subsequent task. The next task is likely to be horizontal visual tracking. Alternate glancing between 2 objects is appropriate if visual tracking is not possible for a given child.

Test for generalization. Generalized visual fixation is accomplished when the child is observed to look at objects in her immediate visual environment. This is what one might call visual inspection of surroundings (Bayley, 1969). The teacher would want

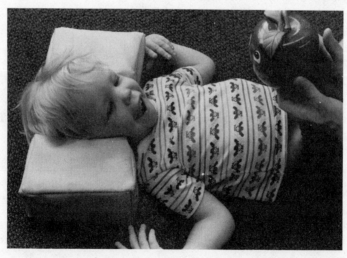

FIGURE 4.3   *This child's head is placed on a centering cushion; cushion is used to assist visual fixation*

TABLE 4.3   *Task Summary 1: Visual Fixation*

Task Description	Response Description	Criteria/Specific Commentary
Check reinforcement value of the stimuli. Visual fixation is one of the child behaviors from which we infer the reinforcement value of an object or event. Therefore, when working on visual fixation the teacher must be prepared to present a variety of different objects until something is found which the child regards.		*Behavior on a single trial:* Teacher presents, for example, an orange ball for 15 seconds and records the child's performance as follows: (1) Latency (in seconds) between object presentation and fixation. (2) Duration of fixation (in seconds). (3) Frequency of fixations during the trial and whether the fixation was right, left, or bilateral.
Teacher positions the child for most functional use of vision (head centered, etc.). Teacher records child's response with respect to the information required on the visual fixation probe sheet in Figure 4.2. After the child has looked at the object, the teacher may let the child feel the object by bringing it to the child's hand(s), or hear the object if it makes noise as well. It is also appropriate to praise the child for visual fixation.	Child looks at object. If child's gaze seems to be at a point behind the object, move the object farther away from the child's face. (The child may be far-sighted and consequently sees things farther away more readily.) If the child does not seem to be aware of object, try moving it closer to her face. (The child may be near-sighted and thus only sees objects held very close to her face.) If child does not respond, try a different object.	*Criterion for intermediate level of fixation:* Child maintains gaze for 3 seconds on 4 of 5 presentations for a variety of objects on 5 consecutive days.

to observe a child looking at a variety of different objects and people. The child should be able to maintain gaze for increasing periods of time.

General comments. It is by now apparent that there are a number of antecedent conditions that must be considered with respect to this seemingly rather simple response. As with all instructional routines, one also must consider the consequences of the response. With the sensory organization responses and indeed, with the sensorimotor activities in general, we are assuming, along with Piaget, that the motivation for reproducing a cognitive scheme is intrinsic to the scheme or structure itself (Flavell, 1963; Piaget, 1963).

Therefore we do not use edibles as a reinforcement for visual fixation, tracking, and sound localization. Instead, we use praise accompanied by positive inflection and tactile stimulation such as tickling or patting and contact with the stimulus object itself.

Task 2:   Visual Tracking

Terminal objective. The criterion level of skill in visual tracking is for the child to follow the movement of a slowly moving object through a horizontal, vertical, or circular trajectory of 180 degrees. This trajectory requires the child to be able to maintain gaze and follow the objects across the midline point with respect to his body and up to the speed of a person walking across the room.

Rationale. It is the ability to follow the movement of objects that forms the experiential basis for the child to later learn that objects are permanent and constant (i.e., that they still exist in the same form despite movements through space).

Conditions and task sequence.

Child characteristics. The development of visual tracking of slowly moving objects begins during the sensorimotor substage of reflexive behavior and is shaped into the terminal behavior during the substage of primary circular reactions (see Table 4.2).

Before demonstrating visual tracking, the child will visually fixate. However, the child may exhibit the earliest form of visual tracking, visual pursuit of a moving object through a trajectory of a few degrees, well before she has accomplished generalized visual fixation. Thus, while tracking follows visual fixation in developmental sequence, the earliest level of visual tracking begins before the most well-developed visual fixation is accomplished. The teacher often works on objectives in each area concurrently. Observe the child for any evidence of visual tracking whenever the first evidence of visual fixation is observed, so as not to underteach the child.

Positioning of child. The eventual criterion response for visual tracking is that the child demonstrates oculocephalic pursuit (OCP). That is, both eyes and head turn in pursuit of moving object when the child is placed in an upright, minimally supported position such as sitting on mother's lap with trunk support provided at the child's waist. There will be many intermediate steps before the individual child has this level of visual tracking and trunk control. One intermediate behavior is ocular pursuit (OP) which involves only eye tracking rather than both eye and head following. For some, visual tracking

without extensive trunk support may not be accomplished for years, if ever. The important aspect of visual tracking is the visual pursuit of an object through the greatest distance. Whatever positional support required for that pursuit should be provided for as long as necessary.

Materials. Those materials the child regarded in the visual fixation work should be utilized for visual tracking. If the child only looked at lighted objects during visual fixation, then it will probably be necessary to use lighted sources during visual tracking.

Subsequent task. After development of visual tracking through a trajectory of 90 degrees, we would expect the child to follow movement through a wider trajectory. From 90 degrees to one side and a return to midline, eventually the child would follow for 180 degrees beginning at far right (or left) crossing midline to far left (or right). The child should also be able to track vertically and in various slanted directions between the horizontal and vertical axis in a frontal plane.

Following development of this level of visual tracking, we see the child use visual tracking to follow objects to the point at which they disappear (perhaps roll off the table) and maintain gaze at the point of disappearance.

Criterion of generalization. The child can be said to have a generalized level of visual tracking when

TABLE 4.4   *Task Summary 2: Visual Tracking*

Task Description	Response Description	Criteria/Specific Commentary
Check reinforcement value of the stimuli.	*Response progression:* (1) Child focuses on object.	Teacher records child's response according to information required on the visual tracking record of probes (Figure 4.3) as follows: (1) Ocular fixation on stimulus (right, left, bilateral). (2) Ocular pursuit (OP) or oculocephalic pursuit (OCP). (3) Direction of pursuit (right, left). (4) Range of tracking (in degrees).
An object that the child has looked at is presented in front of the child's face at the distance that the child has been observed to focus best (looks at longest).	(2) Child fixes and follows with both eyes focused on object.	
	(3) Child turns eyes and head in pursuit of object.	
Teacher moves the object through a horizontal trajectory to the child's right, returns to midline, and moves object to child's left.	(4) Child follows movement to right side.	
	(5) Child follows movement of object through 90° to the right but does not follow during object's return to midline position.	*Criterion for Single Trial:* Child follows movement of object 90° to right or left on an individual trial.
Teacher provides the child the opportunity to touch and/or hear the object she has followed visually.		*Criterion for Task 2:* Child follows movement of objects 90° on 4 of 5 trials to both left and right sides on 5 occasions.

OBJECTIVE: Child visually follows movement of object 90° from midline to right and/or midline to left with an eye-head pursuit (OCP).

ADMINISTRATION: Child is in supine tilt position; objects are held about 5–6 inches from her face. Lighted stimuli are used in darkened room.

CRITERION: Child follows movement of object 90° on 4 of 5 trials to both left and right sides for 5 sessions.

RANGE OF TRACKING

Date	Stimulus	Trials R, L, B	OP/OCP	Direction	A Few Degrees	Less Than 90°	90°	Greater Than 90°	90° and Return	180°	Descriptive Comments
2/10	"Lite Brite"	Bilateral	Oculocephalus pursuit (eye-head, OCP)	Right			X				
2/10	Flashlight on orange ball	Bilateral	OCP	Left		X					
2/10	Checker board card	Right eye only	Ocular pursuit (eye only, OP)	Right	X						
2/10	"Lite Brite"	Bilateral	OCP	Left			X				
2/10	Orange ball	Right	OP	Left	X						Appears to need lighted stimuli but will check this out more thoroughly.

FIGURE 4.4   Visual tracking probe record

119

she is observed to follow the movement of a variety of objects such as mother, father, bottle, a spoon in mother's hand, and the family pet, as each moves or is moved around the room. At this level we know that visual tracking is an available skill that keeps the child in sensory contact with important people and objects in her environment. This, of course, is the ultimate function of visual tracking.

General comments. Some children with severe neuromotor handicaps may not develop smooth oculocephalic pursuit of the moving object. They simply are not capable of the motoric response. An alternative response, which will provide them with similar information and will advance them toward object permanence problems, is *shift of gaze.* Shift of gaze involves visual fixation at one point, release of gaze, and visual fixation at another point in space. This is seen initially back and forth between two objects or points but could eventually be elicited to a series of points on a horizontal or vertical trajectory.

Task 3: Sound Localization

Terminal objective. Sound localization at the advanced level involves a head turn accompanied by visual fixation upon the object used to produce the sound. This is done regardless of the position of the object in relation to the child (i.e. to his side, in the same plane as his ear, below his head, above his head, etc.).

Rationale. Visual localization of sounds in the environment is one of the infant's primary skills observed within the first several months of life. The combined auditory and visual sensory information provides the basis for organizing schemata of people and events in the environment and the development of object permanence, means-end strategies, and understanding of spatial relationships.

Conditions and task sequence.
Child characteristics. The developmental sequence leading to the terminal objective for sound localization begins during the reflexive stage. The child indicates her awareness of sounds by an alerting response. The child becomes quiet, there may be eye movement, but she does not actually turn to localize the sound. This response is refined throughout the sensorimotor substages of reflexive, primary, and secondary circular reactions. Consequently, it is an objective which may be part of a child's individual program for a considerable period of time.

The developmental sequences for sound localization consists of an identifiable progression of skill acquisition (Murphy, 1969) (see Table 4.5).

The individual child will typically acquire objectives in this progression concurrently with increasingly complex objectives in visual tracking. This leads to the sensory organization skills necessary for the development of the sensorimotor concepts of object permanence, means-end, and spatial relationships.

Materials. Stimuli used should include a variety of sound-producing objects and voices. Sounds should be selected to represent a full range of frequencies from very high frequency sounds such as bells, metal chimes, squeak toys, to low frequency sounds such as rattles, drums, deep voices. Sounds also should vary from loud to relatively quiet.

Subsequent task. The child who has attained localization has a skill available which can be used to obtain information about the correlation of sensory experiences, particularly visual and auditory, in her environment. Later the child is able to use volume information to locate sources of sounds she cannot immediately locate visually.

Test for generalization. The child has a generalized level of sound localization when she can visually locate a variety of sounds in different locations. The ability to localize is no longer dependent upon having just seen or touched as well as having heard the object.

Comments. The effect of a single variable upon assessment of a child's level of functioning was illustrated at the Rehabilitation Center by a child whom we had been preparing for audiometric assessment. In this case the important condition was the location of the stimulus with respect to the child. This child had become quite reliable at localizing sounds made out of sight but in a plane several inches or more from the child's ear and in a direct line with his ear. The results of audiometric testing, however, indicated no systematic sound localization. However, the task involved in the audiometric assessment was that of localizing sounds coming from speakers above and at an acute angle from the child's head. This is a developmentally more difficult response. The sequence outlined above provides a guide to the analysis of conflicting results regarding a child's sound localization abilities.

Task 4: Development of Maintenance of Grasp on an Object

Terminal objective. The child maintains grasp on an object for 30 seconds working against gravity,

TABLE 4.5   *Steps in the development of sound localization*

Stimulus	Response	Approximate Age
1. Sound is made outside of child's visual field to side of child's head in same plane as child's ear (child is lying down).	A. Child becomes alert, quiets (stops what she is doing, but does not turn head to side).	As new born
	B. Child searches with eyes for source of sound.	0–1 month
	C. Child turns head in direction of sound and searches with eyes for source of sound.	1–2 months
2. Stimulus is same as in Step 1 except child is in sitting position with support at waist.	A. Child turns head to source of sound but does not necessarily visually locate source of sound.	Attained at 4 months of age.
3. Sound is made outside child's visual field in a horizontal plane below the child's head.	A. Child turns head to side and then gaze is directed down to visually localize source of sound.	Starts at 5 months. Is well established by 6 months.
	B. Child turns head laterally and begins downward gaze in a sweeping motion and localizes source of sound.	Starts at 6 months. Is well established by 7–8 months.
	C. Child turns head and directs gaze downward simultaneously making a direct diagonal visual localization of sound.	Starts at 7 months. Is well established by 9–10 months.

Source: Adapted by C. C. Robinson from K. Murphy, Differential diagnosis of hearing impaired children. *Developmental Medicine and Child Neurology*, 1969, *11*, 561–568.

TABLE 4.6   *Task Summary 3: Sound Localization*

Task Description	Response Description	Criteria/Specific Commentary
Check reinforcement value of the stimuli.		Teacher records sound used and child's response: (1) alternating, (2) eye search, (3) eye-head turn, (4) eye-head turn with visual localization of object.
Teacher shows child object to be sounded; allows child to touch object.	Child looks at and touches object (may be assisted with latter).	
Teacher presents sound from side (alternates between right and left randomly) in a position alongside child's ear.	*Response progression:* (1) Child quiets, as if she has heard sound.	Inconsistencies in sound localization may be due to hearing loss in a specific frequency range. Such an observation on the teacher's part will be helpful to the audiologist evaluating the child.
Teacher does this in such a way that her hand does not serve as a cue for the location. If the teacher is in front of the child, one hand is placed on either side of the child's head. If the person activating the sound is behind the child, this precaution may not be necessary.	(2) Child's eyes move as though searching for sound. (3) Child turns eyes and head in direction of sound. (4) Child turns head and visually localizes source of sound.	Child demonstrates level of sound localization, i.e., turns and visually localizes source of sound on 4 of 5 trials to each side on 5 occasions.
Teacher gives the object to the child and assists her in manipulating the object if necessary.	(5) Child touches the object; turns it over in her hands.	

that is, not merely with her hand around an object and resting on a surface such as a table or in her lap.

Rationale. The ability to maintain grasp on an object and move one's arm without losing grasp is an essential skill for any object manipulation. Maintenance of grasp and simple manipulation of objects forms the beginning of actual tool use. The hand is the child's primary tool. This may be considered as a first step toward intentional goal-directed behavior.

Conditions and task sequence.

Child characteristics. The development of grasp leads to visually directed reach and grasp. It begins, as do the other sensory organization responses, during the reflexive period. The initial accommodations of grasp to objects of different shapes is evidence of primary circular reactions.

Simple placement of an object in the child's hand may cause the child to maintain grasp on the object (possibly with hand in a supported position). This is an initial skill with no observable prerequisites. It is an experience that should be provided immediately with any child who does not demonstrate this form of behavior.

This task starts with the development of maintenance of grasp on an object placed in the child's hand. Experience should then be provided to facilitate progression through the sequence in the development of visually guided reach and grasp as outlined in Table 4.7.

TABLE 4.7   *Sequence of child behavior in the development of visually guided reach and grasp*

1–1½ months	Child is in asymmetric tonic neck reflex (ATNR) position but does not regard her hand(s). Grasping, looking, sucking, are all schemata that the child has, but each is done in isolation. Hands are generally fisted.
1–2 months	Child tends to be in ATNR position and gaze is occasionally fixed on hand facing eyes (head is turned to one side and child regards hand on same side for period up to 5–10 seconds).
2–2½ months	Child is able to keep head closer to midline position; eyes converge and focus on stimulus at 5″. Swipes or bats at stimulus to side with near hand (beginning eye-arm coordination). Hand is fisted and child makes no attempt to grasp object. If object is placed in hand, child brings grasped object to mouth and may suck object.
1½–3 months	Child's head is often in midline and limbs are symmetrical in their position. Child regards hand for sustained periods. Converges and focuses on stimulus at 3″. Visual accommodation is increasing. Child swipes at objects with alternate looking between object at which she swipes and her hand.
3–3½ months	Child's head is mostly in midline. The hands are predominately open. Child continues hand regard and also plays with hands at midline. Occasionally she looks at hands while playing. The child moves hands to grasp at object she is sucking. The child is beginning to look at object she is holding. When an object is presented in front of child, a bilateral or one-handed reach up is elicited.
3½–4 months	Head is in midline with little or no asymmetric tonic neck reflex observed. Child looks at own hand play. Stimulus object presented to child's midline evokes a bilateral grasp. When the child is reaching, she also orients torso toward object,
4–4½ months	When an object is presented within reach at midline, the child reaches up with both hands or one while the other hand remains at midline. Grasp results when hand and object are both in view. Child raises hand slowly with alternate glancing at hands and object, grasping on contact is awkward.
4½–5 months	The criterion level reaching involves the child rapidly lifting her hand from out of view to an object which is in view. Hand opens in anticipation. Increased looking at grasped object.

Source: Adapted from an unpublished table prepared by Nany Fieber (1975, Meyer Children's Rehabilitation Institute), based upon research of White, Castle, and Held (1964) and White, Held, and Castle (1967).

Positioning of child. Since the eventual objective is the coordination of vision with grasping, positions in which a child has to do a lesser amount of work against gravity in order to see her hands frequently facilitate the initial development of this coordination. The side-lying position (see Figure 4.5) encourages some children to visually and tactually explore their hands. A beneficial position, if a child tends to keep shoulders and arms pulled back, is the supine tilt. In this position the child's shoulders are kept rounded and slightly forward but not so far forward that head control becomes a problem. This is accomplished with pillows or a tilted seat such as an infant chair.

Materials. Look for cylindrical objects that do not require very much accommodation of the reflexive grasp position. The objects should also make noise fairly easily. Such a toy is the "Single Jingle Bell" (offered in *Child Craft* catalogues), an easily grasped object, ideal in both shape and ease of sound production.

Subsequent task. After the development of grasp maintenance accompanied by arm waving and movement of hand and object to mouth, the child typically begins to reach for an object. This is followed by coordination of vision and reaching.

Generalization task. The child may be said to have a generalized grasp scheme (1) when she maintains a grasp for 30 seconds or more on a variety of different (but still cylindrical) objects and (2) when she attempts to carry objects to her mouth or engage in other simple motor schemata with an object in hand.

Task 5: Visually Directed Reach and Grasp

Terminal objective. The final objective in this sequence requires that the child lift her hand when it is out of the visual field and grasp an object that is in the visual field. Optimally the child anticipates the shape of the object to be grasped.

Rationale. This task is an important component motoric skill of many of the later sensorimotor concepts. There is, apparently, a concept of hand as a "tool object" which is learned during the development of reach and grasp. In this sense, it is a prerequisite skill to subsequent use of other objects as tools.

Conditions and task sequence.

Child characteristics. The development of reach and grasp begins during the reflexive subperiod of development. However, development of the final objective involves refinements during the primary and secondary circular reaction subperiods of sensorimotor development. For the child who does not have specific neuromotor problems or visual deficits the development of reach and grasp is very likely to follow the sequence outlined in Table 4.7. The child with neuromotor problems may have difficulty with voluntary control of arm and hand movements. For example, a child that exhibits abnormal persistence of the asymmetric tonic neck reflex (ATNR) may begin reaching by looking at the object but will lose visual contact with the object as she

FIGURE 4.5
Physically handicapped child exhibiting the effect of asymmetric tonic neck reflex (ATNR)

TABLE 4.8   *Task Summary 4: Maintenance of Grasp on an Object*

Task Description	Response Description	Criteria/Specific Commentary
Check reinforcement value of the stimuli.		
Teacher places cylindrical, small object in the child's hand.	Child maintains grasp on object for 30 seconds.	Child maintains grasp on object for 30 seconds for 4 out of 5 trials with each hand on 5 occasions.
If child does not move arm and hand, teacher prompts arm movement.	Child maintains grasp when arm is moved and continues movement without prompting.	Child maintains grasp on object in either hand through at least 3 self-initiated arm waves or carries object to mouth on 5 occasions.
If child's hand opens when arm is moved and the release seems to be involuntary, teacher may place her hand over the child's fisted hand and guide arm-waving movement.	Child's fisted hand and arm are guided through movements to shake the grasped object.	The amount of assistance given in guided movement should gradually be decreased.
Teacher may tie object into child's hand with a piece of yarn so that the object stays attached to the child's hand when she opens hand. Thus it is available for grasping when she closes her hand.	Child opens and closes hand on object tied into hand.	The procedure of tying objects into the child's hand should only be done for 5–10 minutes at a time.
		It is likely that both procedures (tying and manual prompt) will be used at different points during the day to maximize opportunities to experience using the hand as a tool.

extends her arm. This occurs because the ATNR reflex dominates her movement. This pattern is illustrated in Figure 4.6. The side position (as illustrated in Figure 4.5) facilitates visually directed reach and grasp for such a child. When physical handicaps are encountered, consultation is recommended with a physical or occupational therapist in order to select the most appropriate conditions for working on reach and grasp.

Difficulties in learning to reach and grasp are further complicated when the child is visually impaired and lacks opportunity to coordinate visual and tactual input. This coordination seems to provide the experiential basis for learning to use the hand as a tool.

Materials. The materials needed for working on reach and grasp objectives include items that are easily grasped. However, during the period when the child's reach takes the form of swatting at an object, any visually interesting object is a good stimulus. During this period brightly colored patterned cloth, chimes, and brightly colored roly-poly toys often work well as stimuli.

2.   Object permanence

The final goal of object permanence is for the child to demonstrate systematic search behavior for an object when the exact location is unknown. There are, however, many steps in the development of this goal that can be defined and utilized as individual objectives. It is convenient to classify these objectives into 3 task sequences: (6) prerequisite object permanence skills, (7) simple object permanence

FIGURE 4.6   *This child is in a sidelying position, which is used to facilitate hand use*

problems, and (8) complex object permanence problems. Each task is discussed separately in the format employed in the instructional sequences already described.

Task 6:   Prerequisite Object Permanence Skills

Terminal objective. The final step in the development of skills prerequisite to object permanence involves search for a partly covered object. In this situation, the child is shown (and perhaps allowed to hold an object) which is then *partly* covered (with a cloth, cup, paper, box, etc.). The child may either take the cover off the object and pick it up or obtain the object by pulling the object from under the screen.

Rationale. The objectives in this task sequence provide opportunities for further development of the visual tracking skills. These skills are important to the solution of later object permanence problems.

Conditions and task sequence.
    Child characteristics. The prerequisite sequence begins with visual tracking at the primary circular reaction stage and continues into the substage of secondary circular reactions. The child typically develops increasing trunk control during this period. This makes it possible to pursue objects visually through greater distances. Another development during this period is visually directed reach and

grasp which are prerequisite skills for the conventional object permanence task.

Positioning of child. The basic position for the prerequisite tasks is "supported sitting." For the activities in Part A of Task 6, as much support is provided as is necessary for the child to have maximum head control. For Part B (partly covered objects), support is given so that the child has maximum use of her hands.

For the child with special neuromotor problems, adaptations of the task to side-lying or supported sitting positions may be necessary.

Materials. Use a variety of objects in which the child has shown interest by visually tracking and/or reaching for them. Yarn or string will be needed for suspending the object when the task involves anticipation of a trajectory.

Subsequent task. After achieving criterion performance on the task of the partly hidden object, the child will be ready for the problem of the completely hidden object described in Task 7.

Generalization test. The child picks up a variety of different objects partly covered with a variety of different screens. She should also be playing peek-a-boo by pulling the cover off a person's face or peeking around the edge of the screen the person is behind. There should also be an attempt to initiate peek-a-boo by pulling a piece of clothing up to her face.

Other related tasks can be found in the spatial development sequence. These include turning the head to look toward a falling object.

TABLE 4.9   *Task Summary 5: Visually Directed Reach and Grasp*

Task Description	Response Description	Criteria/Specific Commentary
Level A Swiping at objects. Check reinforcement value of the stimuli.		
Teacher observes child.	Child engages in hand watching play in ATNR position. That is, when lying down with head turned to side, child watches hand on that side.	This behavior indicates a good time to place a visually interesting object close to that hand.
Teacher places visually interesting object several inches from child's head with the child lying on her back.	Child looks at and swipes or bats at object, but does not attempt to grasp object.	Child needs many opportunities on this activity with each hand. After the batting response is learned, she begins more direct reaching for object suspended over head. Objects do not need to be graspable. Patterned cloth, chimes, etc., are useful at this stage.
Teacher presents visually interesting object at a point closer to child's midline.	Child swipes at objects, looking alternately at hand and at object.	As child becomes more proficient, an object is presented closer to and finally at midline. Gradual movement toward midline should take place alternately from both sides to the middle. Child may progress toward middle more quickly from one side than the other.
Teacher observes child's response.	(1) Child plays with her hand in midline position, occasionally she is also looking at her hands while playing with them. (2) Child moves hand to grasp at object she is sucking.	This is a behavior that systematically precedes the direct visually guided reach. Side-lying position may facilitate the occurrence of this behavior for some children.
Level B Reach and grasp without accommodation for object shape.		
Teacher physically guides child's arm to assist bringing a held object into visual range.	Child looks at the object in her hand. On subsequent occasions she brings hand and object into view spontaneously.	This behavior may also be facilitated with side-lying for some children. The child should be bringing almost all grasped objects into view.
Teacher presents an object in front of the child in such a way that both the object and the child's hands are in her visual field.	Child reaches out with one or both hands to object but does not accommodate hand(s) to shape of object before touching object.	The child should demonstrate this behavior with a variety of objects.
	Child engages in midline play with hands while also looking at her hands.	This coordination of visual and tactile schemata typically precedes the next development in reach and grasp.

TABLE 4.9   *(Continued)*

Task Description	Response Description	Criteria/Specific Commentary
Teacher presents an interesting object to child with both object and child's hand in her visual field.	Child grasps object with both hands and also orients toward object if it is not presented at midline.	Child should be doing this with a variety of objects. Objects should be presented for grasping rather than being put in her hands at this stage.
Teacher presents object to child but at a greater distance from child.	Child raises hand slowly, glancing alternately between her hand and the object. When she grasps the object, her accommodation to its shape is often awkward.	Child should have many opportunities for this activity. Include times when objects are suspended in easy reach over the child as she is lying down or sitting in a chair.
Level C Reach and grasp with hand accommodation anticipated		
Teacher presents object to child at a distance which requires reaching for it.	Child lifts a hand which is out of her visual field directly to object. She accommodates the position of her hand to the object's shape.	Child should be able to do this with a variety of objects. Following this accomplishment, she will be able to reach for and grasp objects on a surface in the same manner.

*Task 7: Simple Object
        Permanence Problems*

Terminal objective. The most difficult problem among the simple object permanence problems requires that the child (1) visually track the movement of an object moved through 3 locations and then (2) search for and recover the object in the last location. The teacher selects an object in which the child is interested, then moves the object under the first 2 screens (allowing the child to see it between each location). Then the object is left in the last location. If the child searches in either of the first two locations, her response is considered incorrect. This problem is not ambiguous with respect to the location of the object if the child visually tracks the movement of the object. She should reach directly to the last location and recover the object.

Rationale. The problems in this sequence are considered "simple" because the exact location of the hidden object is not ambiguous if the child uses her visual tracking strategy. This series of simple object permanence problems provides the child with the experiential basis of searching for, and recovering, hidden objects. This prepares her for the more complex problems in which the exact location of the object is unknown. Thus, the child must engage in systematic search behavior to recover the object.

Conditions and task sequence.

Child characteristics. The child is able to solve the first simple object permanence problem toward the end of the substage of secondary circular reactions. The remainder of the tasks are accomplished during the substage of coordination of secondary circular reactions. In order to learn even the simple object permanence problems, the child will need to master three prerequisite skills: (1) visually directed reach and grasp for objects on a surface, (2) recovery of partly covered objects, and (3) smooth visual tracking of objects through interrupted trajectories.

Positioning of child. These activities will typically be worked on with the child in a sitting position. She should be offered as much support as is necessary for optimal use of her hands. That is, she should not have to use her hands for balance as this makes it less probable that she will be able to reach and grasp well.

Materials. The goal object on a given trial can be anything in which the child shows an interest. A child of this developmental age usually indicates interest by (1) reaching for an object that is within reach or (2) prolonged looking at an object that is out of reach. Edibles may be used as the goal object if the child initially is not interested in very many other objects. If edibles are used, they should be faded as quickly as possible. In addition to changing goal objects, a variety of covers are needed—cups,

TABLE 4.10 *Task Summary 6: Prerequisite Object Permanence Skills*

Task Description	Response Description	Criteria/Specific Commentary
Level A Check reinforcement value of the stimuli. Tracking and anticipation.		
Visual tracking: Teacher selects an object in which the child has demonstrated interest and moves it in a trajectory from one side of the child's head to the other.	Child smoothly and completely tracks movement of an object through a horizontal 180° trajectory.	Child tracks a variety of objects through at least a 180° trajectory on 4 out of 5 opportunities on 5 occasions. A variety of objects should be used for this activity.
Anticipation of trajectory of a slowly moving object: Teacher presents an object suspended from a string in front of the child and moves it out of view to one side of the child's head and continues movement in back of child's head, bringing object back in front of the child, slightly above the child's eyes.	2 levels of responding indicating different levels of development may be noted: (1) Child's gaze lingers at point where the object disappears. (2) After several presentations, child turns gaze to point of reappearance before object reappears.	The first is a transition response which should be replaced by a second level response after some experience with the task. Child turns in anticipation of reappearance of the object when presented to each side on 4 of 5 trials on 5 occasions.
If child does not turn in anticipation of appearance of the object, teacher may present a sound cue to bring the child's attention to the object.	Child turns and visually localizes object by sound cue.	Presentation for only one direction should be continued until the sound cue can be faded. A variety of objects should be used for this activity.
Level B Reach and grasp. Check reinforcement value of the stimuli.		
Movement to maintain object in visual field: Teacher presents an object to the child and moves the object (that the child is tracking visually) out of view.	Child has to rotate the torso as well as the head in order to maintain gaze on object moved out of view to side.	Child moves to keep object in view when it is moved to either side on 4 of 5 trials on 5 occasions. A variety of objects should be used in this activity.
Search for partly covered object: Teacher presents an object to the child.	Child reaches for or picks up the object.	By doing this the teacher has confirmed the probable reinforcement value of the object.
Teacher retrieves the object from the child and partially covers the object.	Child removes cover and picks up object or reaches under cover and picks up object. The child who can reach and grasp must pick up the object to be credited as correct.	Child retrieves partly covered object on 4 of 5 opportunities on 5 occasions. A variety of different objects and covers should be used for this activity. Child at this level will also begin to enjoy peek-a-boo with the game being covering and uncovering of the child by the adult, and then the child can uncover herself when covered.

TABLE 4.11   *Task Summary 7: Simple Object Permanence Problems*

Task Description	Response Description	Criteria/Specific Commentary
Level A Check the reinforcement value of the stimuli.		
The teacher should place an object presumed to be interesting to the child before her and observe whether the child tries to pick it up.	Child shows interest in the object by reaching for it, looking at it, and smiling or behaves in some way that indicates interest in the object.	Child searches for an object on 4 of 5 opportunities on 5 occasions. Trials should include a variety of objects under at least 3 different covers.
Finding an object which is completely covered: The teacher may then hide that object under a screen (cloth, cup, box, chair cushion, etc.) in such a way that the object is not showing. The object should be moved under the screen as opposed to setting the object down and placing the screen over the object.	Child uncovers and picks up hidden object. Alternate responses: (1) Child grabs both screens. (2) Child does not pick up object.	Teacher allows child to play with object. Strategies: (1) Teacher moves screens farther apart so child has to choose one or other. (2) Use another object.
Level B Finding a completely covered object which is hidden alternately between 2 places: Teacher selects an interesting object and hides it under screen on one side of the work surface. Teacher then hides object under screen on opposite side of work surface.	Correct response: Child uncovers and obtains object. Alternate response: Child pulls correct screen but does not pick up object.	Teacher allows child to play with object. Teacher encourages child to pick up object; count trial as prompted.
Level C Finding an object after 2 sequential visible displacements: Teacher selects an "interesting" object. The object is visible in the teacher's hand as she moves the object under one screen and out the other side and under the second screen, leaving the object under the second screen and bringing her empty hand out to show to the child.	Correct response: Child goes directly to location where the object was left, uncovers it, and picks up the object. Incorrect responses: (1) Child grabs both screens. (2) Child does not visually track movement and child searches under first screen. (3) Child uncovers correctly but does not pick up object.	The child should search for a variety of objects under a variety of screens on 4 of 5 opportunities on 5 occasions. Trials should involve random variation between 2 locations. Strategies: (1) Teacher places screens farther apart. (2) Teacher calls child's attention to reappearance of object after passing under one screen. (3) Teacher tries a new object since child's interest in first probably has waned. Objects may be varied from trial to trial as necessary to maintain the child's interest.

TABLE 4.11   *(Continued)*

Task Description	Response Description	Criteria/Specific Commentary
Level D Finding an object after 3 sequential visible displacements: Teacher does the same as in the 2 screen displacement problem, merely adding a third location with the object left under third screen.	Correct response: Child searches directly under third screen and picks up object.	The child should search for a variety of objects under a variety of screens for 4 of 5 opportunities on 5 different occasions. Once the child searches correctly several times in this problem, the direction used (right to left or left to right) can be varied from trial to trial. Child is expected to achieve same criterion as in the 2-screen problem. This problem merely requires an increased level of skill in visual tracking and makes greater demands on the child's memory.

boxes, cloth, cushions, etc. Anything that can be used to hide another object will do.

Subsequent task. Once the child meets criterion performance on the series of simple object permanence problems, she is ready to begin looking for objects in more complex problem situations (Task 8).

Generalization test. As the child meets criterion on each of the problem situations, sufficient variability in goal objects and screens has been introduced so that she has a generalized search strategy for a specific situation. The ultimate generalization criterion is accomplished when the child uses her search strategy in daily play situations as objects go out of sight.

General comments. When the child first is responding to the single screen problem, there may be a number of limitations on her search behavior. For example, the child may uncover and retrieve the object only if she was already reaching for it as it was covered. Searching for an object that is covered while sitting on a surface is simpler than searching for an object that is moved across the surface and then placed under a cover. Sometimes the child only searches for objects she has had an opportunity to hold just before they were hidden. All of these conditions may affect performance at the first introduction of the completely covered object problem.

It appears that the dimension of difficulty involves the length of time between the moment that the object is removed from sight and the point when the child can physically begin to search for the object. Mastery of the simple object permanence problem implies that search behavior should be reliable under all the situations described. That is, the child will search whether or not she has just held the object, whether it is placed on the surface and covered or is moved under the cover. We expect the child to be able to seek out and retrieve any object in which she demonstrates interest (1) in a variety of hiding situations and (2) up to about 5 seconds between the time the object is removed from sight and the child starts to uncover and retrieve the object.

Some of the cues that were originally thought by researchers to facilitate searching for the completely hidden objects, such as making a sound with the object or leaving a lump under the screen, are ineffective as cues at this level of development. In order for a lump or a noise to serve as a cue, each must represent the hidden object for the child. Children at this stage of cognitive development are not capable of such representation (Piaget, 1954).

Task 8: Complex Object Permanence Problems

Terminal objective. The terminal objective in this task sequence is that the child persist in searching for an object when its precise location is ambiguous. This situation involves showing a child an object, then hiding it in one's hand, passing one's hand through 3 hiding locations, and leaving it under one of the screens. The child is then expected to continue looking in those locations until she uncovers the object.

Rationale. The ability to search systematically for a missing object is a culminating feature of sensorimotor development. It requires that the child be able to remember the successive displacements of an object and, in essence, reproduce the displacements by looking in several locations. Some degree of object permanence has been consistently observed in young children before they begin to develop functional use of objects or object-name associations (Bayley, 1969). This is not to suggest that a necessary and sufficient relationship of object permanence to receptive language has been established. Rather, object permanence skills consistently appear to precede the development of receptive understanding of object and action names.

Conditions and task sequence.

Child characteristics. The ability to solve this sequence of more complex problems begins during the subperiod of tertiary circular reactions. The child begins with trial and error procedures to discover new solutions. Development extends into the sixth subperiod—invention of new means through mental combinations. At that time the child is assumed to solve problems through representational thought.

Typically, before the child is able to solve the first problem in this complex problem sequence, she will have solved the means-end problem of attached tool use and also will engage in simple container play. This is the usual situation assuming the typical kinds of infant and toddler age-appropriate experiences. However, one is likely to find considerable variability in this pattern as the child's development and experience deviate from the typical.

Positioning and materials. The positioning of the child and materials used as stimuli are essentially the same as in the simple problem sequence, with the exception that the child does not require as much physical support in sitting.

Subsequent task. Accomplishment of the representational search problem marks the final point of sensorimotor development within the object permanence sequence. Object permanence is now a generalized concept available in combination with other concepts and strategies for solutions of preoperational problems—the next stage of cognitive development.

Modifications of Object Permanence Tasks for the Physically Handicapped Child

Severely and profoundly handicapped persons often have limitations on their physical abilities. Attempts to apply our typical sensorimotor activities to these children may fail because they are physically incapable of many of the tasks. Thus, the problem becomes one of separating the concepts from the physical requirements of tasks typically used to assess the concepts. Are the skills of visual tracking, visually directed reach and grasp, uncovering, and picking up an object necessary in order to say that a child has object permanence? Is some alternative response possible? A response such as directed gaze at the location of the object in a situation involving choices among 2 or more locations may do, or pointing toward the correct location also is acceptable. Once the child learns to play the game of "look-at" or "point-to" the correct location, the same response can be used throughout the object permanence sequences of simple and complex problems.

Again, it is extremely important for the child to have an opportunity to experience the object. This can be accomplished by demonstrating its use to the child if she cannot manipulate the object herself.

3. Development of means for achieving environmental events and operational causality

The steps in this sequence are described as means-end developments. The child learns successively more complex ways of acting upon her environment to cause desired environmental events. From the Piagetian point of view, this sequence involves the development of intentionality. Others would describe this sequence as the development of operant responding. From either perspective this development marks an extremely important refinement in the child's behavioral repertoire.

The means-ends sequences are organized into the following tasks: (9) repetition of early schemata for environmental effect (systematic repetition), (10) development of attached tool use, (11) use of separated object as a tool, and (12) development of operational causality

Background

The first step in the sequence involves the child's repeating an early motor movement scheme (hitting or shaking) and systematically keeping an object,

TABLE 4.12   *Task Summary 8: Complex Object Permanence Problems*

Task Description	Response Description	Criteria/Specific Commentary
Check the reinforcement value of the stimuli.		
Level A Invisible displacement of object with 1 screen: Teacher shows the child an interesting object and then hides the object in her hand. Next she moves her hand under a screen leaving the object under that screen.	The child uncovers the object and picks it up. The child may check the teacher's hand to look for the object there first.	The child is allowed to play with the object.
Invisible displacement of object with 2 screens: Teacher shows child an interesting object and then hides the object in her hand. Next she moves her hand under 1 of 2 screens, leaving the object under 1 of the screens.	The child searches only under the correct screen and uncovers the object and picks it up. The child may check the teacher's hand first.	The child is allowed to play with the object. The child searches correctly on 4 of 5 opportunities on 5 occasions. Trials should be alternated randomly between the 2 locations. A variety of objects and screens should be used.
Sequential invisible displacement with 2 screens: Teacher shows child an interesting object and then hides the object in her hand and moves her hand under 1 screen and out the other side and then under a second screen, leaving the object under the second screen.	Alternative correct responses: (1) Child picks up second screen and recovers object. (2) Child picks up first screen, the object is not there; she then picks up second screen and recovers the object. Incorrect response: Child stops searching after not finding it under first screen.	Child is allowed to play with object. Child searches correctly using either pattern on 4 of 5 opportunities on 5 occasions. Again a variety of objects and screens are used. Show her where it is and cover it again, encouraging her to continue to search.
Level B Sequential invisible displacement with 3 screens: Teacher does same as in 2-screen problem with the only change being that a third screen is present and the object is left under the third screen.	Alternate correct responses: (1) Child picks up third screen and recovers object. (2) Child picks up first and second screen, not finding the object. Child picks up third screen and recovers the object.	Child is allowed to play with object. Same criterion. If the child searched from the first to last screen during the preceding activity, this activity is not necessary. However, it is unlikely that a child would persist with that strategy once she found the object in the last location several times.
Representation of sequential invisible displacement: Teacher shows child an interesting object and hides object in her hand. Then moves hand through the 3 locations, reappearing after each screen. But the object is left in the first location.	Child searches systematically from the last screen to the first in the order of last, middle, first, and picks up object.	Child is allowed to play with object. Same criterion as other responses. If the child has difficulty with the 3 screen problem, it can be simplified by going back to 2 screens first. The goal is to teach systematic search behavior. After she accomplishes the 3-screen problem, she can be presented with 4- and 5-screen problems.

FIGURE 4.7   *This child is using the alternate response strategy of directing his gaze at the correct location in an object permanence problem*

such as a bell, rattle, wind chime, or rolling musical toy, active. Piaget's description (1963) of his children between 2 and 4 months of age provides an excellent example of this period of development. He suspended a toy above his child's crib and tied a string from the toy to the child's wrist. Since a child of that age usually plays by moving her arms and legs, it was not long before the child's movement resulted in a movement of the toy animal. Then the child quieted and looked at the animal. After a brief period, the animal stopped swinging and the child started to fuss and in doing so moved again. The animal was in turn activated, the child quieted and watched, and then the animal stopped again. This cycle continued for some time and the child's behavior changed from flailing of arms and legs to systematic movement of one arm with gaze directed at the object. Once this response was firmly established, Piaget switched the string from the child's right wrist to his left. The child would continue to move his right wrist but the animal did not move. After a period of time the child again became fussy and returned to his flailing movements of both arms. After a period of time he again isolated his movement to one arm, this time the left arm. This isolation of the response to the second limb typically occurred in less time than the isolation to the first limb when the activity was started. This increase and differentiation of responding characterizes learning in the means-end sequence. This type of learning is not restricted to arm movement responding. The response can be of any form as long as it can be described and reliably counted. Therefore, foot

kicks, head turns, vocalizations, open or shut mouth, or movement of one finger may qualify. Once the response is selected, it is necessary to arrange some environmental event so that its occurrence is contingent upon the child's response.

In addition to Piaget's work, there is a growing body of literature suggesting the importance that contingent stimulation has upon learning in infants. Some of this work includes that of Watson and Ramey (1972) and Watson (1971) who studied the learning rates of 3 groups of 8-week-old infants when exposed to a mobile in their own homes. One group experienced mobile turns contingent upon a head-turning response. The second group saw a nonmovable hanging stimulus, a "stabile" (the same visual stimulus as the mobile, but it did not turn). The third group experienced noncontingent mobile turns. The contingent group was the only group that showed a reliable change in head-turning behavior. Six weeks later all 3 groups were exposed to a different mobile that turned contingently for all 3 groups. The original contingent and stabile groups demonstrated reliable responding. Thus, they controlled the movements of a new mobile in the laboratory situation. The original noncontingent group did not show this same change in their rate of responding. The authors suggest that a positive learning effect results from a contingent experience, whereas a maladaptive effect results from experience with random responsiveness of environmental events.

More recently, Finkelstein and Ramey (Note 3) demonstrated that infants who had learned a lever-pressing response to control stimulation in the treatment phase of a study later learned to vocalize so as to control the presentation of the stimulation slides used in the previous contingent situation. Infants in a noncontingent group who were presented with the same amount of visual stimulation, but who did not have to emit a specific response for the stimulation to occur, did *not* demonstrate the vocalization response on the posttest. Thus, it may be that experience with contingent stimulation is more than simply learning a single response. Rather, infants who receive contingent stimulation may become, in general, more competent and efficient learners (Finkelstein & Ramey, Note 3). These results suggest that contingent experience produces a "learning-to-learn" phenomenon.

Another line of research suggests that noncontingent stimulation may have equally potent negative effects. Seligman (1975) labels these effects "learned helplessness." Seligman emphasizes the importance of experiencing predictability in, and control over, environmental events. When one has no control over positive or negative events, this lack of control or "helplessness" often leads to nonresponsiveness in situations where access to positive reinforcers or avoidance of noxious stimuli is controllable. Seligman specifically cites as an example the baby's first opportunity to control contingent stimulation from her caregivers. Helplessness can be prevented or, in some cases, overcome with careful arrangement of contingent experiences.

In his work with retarded children and young adults, Cromwell (1963) posited a lower expectancy for success on the part of individuals who are retarded, particularly when they are confronted with failure experiences. There are many parallels between Cromwell's work, Seligman's work on learned helplessness, and Watson's research on contingency awareness and the negative effects of noncontingent stimulation. All warrant much more investigation. Further research may provide information regarding the optimal characteristics of learning environments for the severely handicapped.

The greater the number of daily events contingent upon the individual's responses, the more adequate will be that individual's educational experience. The limitations on arranging contingent experiences are practical ones. These may be overcome by examining a child's response potentials and daily activities and then arranging these events to maximize contingent experiences. For example, if the child is dependent during eating or dressing

activities, a teacher may choose to make every bite of food contingent upon a response from the child. This response may be as simple as touching the hand of the person feeding her. The same type of response sequence may be established in dressing activities. When the learner is shown a sock, the child moves her foot. When she is shown a shirt, she lifts her arms to whatever extent possible. For the severely physically involved child, the objective may not be an approximation of the feeding or dressing skill movements. Rather, a very simple response (either vocal or motor) becomes a signal that the child anticipates the next event that will happen. In a sense, she is requesting the occurrence of the next event in a learned sequence.

Task 9: Repetition of Early Schemata for Environmental Effect

Terminal Objective. The terminal objective for the initial means-end level of responding requires the child to display a variety of different responses, each specific to producing a particular environmental effect.

Rationale. The ability to differentially respond to stimuli (such as wind chimes, shaking a bell or rattle, or kicking to get the teacher to activate a bouncing seat) serves as the basis for providing the child with strategies for acting on the environment. Uzgiris and Hunt (1966; 1975) refer to this as a learning set of "If I act, I can make interesting things happen and can find interesting things to do" (p. 40). This learning set results in a variety of operant responses and provides behaviors which then can be shaped into more elaborate responses.

Conditions and task sequence.

Child characteristics. Repetition of responding is observed in the typical baby during the second to fourth month. In fact, infant researchers requiring less elaborate motor responses have begun to document evidence of primary circular reactions during the neonatal period (Bower, 1977). Consequently, we recommend arranging some type of response-contingent experience as soon as possible for the child who does not already have an "if I act" response. There are no observable prerequisite responses for beginning this activity except that the child must have some voluntary response. It can be any response, an arm wave, a foot kick, any vocalization, etc. By the time the child achieves the differentiated responding described in the terminal objective statement, she will have progressed to (1) the level of secondary circular reactions (Piagetian terminology) and (2) discriminated operant responding (terminology of applied behavior analysis).

Position of child. In order to work on the level of initial means-end development, the child must display some response. First, the response that is to be increased is selected. Then the position in which the child displays that response most frequently is the position in which to place the child.

Materials. There is not a particular set of materials to use for these activities. Any object in which the child shows interest and to which she can apply a response that produces an effect will do. Materials such as wind chimes, mobiles, toys that turn when batted, bells, and rattles are especially good. In addition, some brightly colored yarn may be used to construct a mobile (see Figure 4-8).

General comments. There are several important points to consider when working on the early means-end objective with a child. For the child to learn the concept "If-I-act-I-can-make-interesting-things-happen," it is important to identify a consequence for the selected response that is an effective reinforcer. It may take a number of trials with different sound, visual, or tactile events before a reinforcer is found. Once a reinforcing event is determined, it is not possible to assume that that event will remain a reinforcer indefinitely. After mastering a particular event the child may become bored with it. Such boredom is inferred from a decrease in responding. Therefore, it is necessary to vary the consequence and, perhaps, even the response. Because of this satiation, it is essential that particular environmental events be arranged for only selected periods during the day. Further, the child's behavior should be observed to detect any evidence of decrease in responding. If a decrease is observed, potential explanations such as satiation, seizure activity, and physical discomfort can be considered and modifications made accordingly. If the child has had a seizure or is physically uncomfortable, we might not change the task or consequence. However, if the child is satiated with the activity, we would change the consequence. If an increase in activity is still not observed, perhaps the response should be changed.

In the case of this objective, the particular response or reinforcing event used is irrelevant. The objective is not that the child move an arm or leg or turn her head or vocalize but that the child have a variety of responses to produce corresponding responses in the environment. As a generalized response, the child should utilize these behaviors by testing them in new situations until a behavior is found that produces a spectacle. Very often teachers stop working on an activity when the child masters one response in one specific setting. One response in one setting is not a sufficient level of competence on this objective.

Generalization training and subsequent tasks. The development of generalized responding involves showing different movements appropriate to different situations. At the level of repetition of an early scheme, the child is likely to begin demonstrating movement to an object that is out of reach, the next task to be described.

Locomotion as a means-end response. Once a child demonstrates a generalized means-end repertoire (the repetition of responses which produce environmental events), the next step in the means-end sequence involves the use of some means of locomotion to obtain an object that is out of reach. Again, the important aspect of this response is not

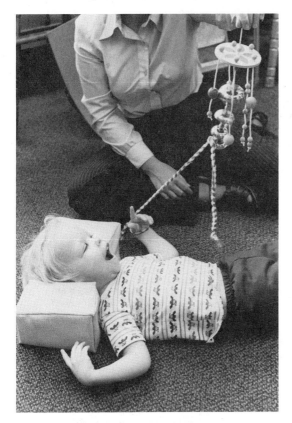

FIGURE 4.8 *Child demonstrates beginning level of means-end behavior*

TABLE 4.13 *Task Summary 9: Repetition of Early Schemata for Environmental Effect (Systematic Repetition)*

Task Description	Response Description	Criteria/Specific Commentary
Check reinforcement value of stimuli.		
Teacher takes data on movements occurring in the absence of stimuli.		
Without presenting any toys or objects, teacher observes child in a variety of positions, recording movements such as arm waves, foot kicks, head turns, etc. This observation should be done for 3–5-minute periods on several occasions. The top row of Figure 4.9 provides a means for the collection of such data.	Possible responses: (1) Child moves arms at a fairly high rate (more than 10 per minute). Follow procedure under Level B.	Child is lying on floor with firm pillow under head and shoulders. This keeps the child's shoulders somewhat rounded, making it easier for her to move. (1) This rate is sufficiently high so that simply presenting a stimulus such as a wind chime will be possible. Refer to Figure 4.11 which presents an example of data over a 4-week period. On Dec. 12, child demonstrates rate of 23 bilateral arm movements per minute.
	(2) Child moves arms at a low rate (less than 10 per minute). Follow procedure under Level A; after rate has increased, follow Level B procedure.	(2) If child's rate is low and amplitude of movement is slight (lifts arm only a slight amount), teacher may decide to "rig" environment to facilitate movement (see Figure 4.8).
Level A Low-baseline arm movement rate.		
Teacher ties piece of yarn, one end to child's wrist and other end to wind chimes suspended over child.	Child moves arm slightly, wind chimes are activated, child quiets and looks at chimes, chimes stop; child moves again and cycle is repeated.	Child shows an increase in the rate of arm movements over baseline rate. Example of repetition of early scheme behavior (arm movement) at advanced level.
Teacher shows child the toy and activates it, then presents toy successively to each of the child's limbs. Toy may be wind chime, roly-poly ball, mobile, etc.	Child moves all limbs and gradually isolates movement to limb where toy is placed.	The child demonstrates a generalized primary circular reaction means-end strategy when she isolates the movement to each limb appropriately.
Level B High-baseline arm movement task.		
Teacher presents wind chimes in a position close to child's arm which she moved most frequently during baseline and records child's arm movements.	Child waves arm and most arm movements come into contact with chimes. The child alternates between moving arm and quieting and looking at chimes. This is an early phase, however, so hitting and looking do not occur together.	Initially the child may move both arms during no stimulus and stimulus conditions. After several weeks (Jan. 3 in Figure 4.11) the child's overall rate of movement is less. But she moves the arm closest to the chimes more frequently. She has become more efficient in controlling the chimes. After another 2 weeks (Jan. 17 in Figure 4.10) her rate is closer to her initial rate of responding in stimulus condition but is predominately unilateral movement (indicating greater efficiency of responding).

the form of the specific motor locomotion. Rather, the question is, will the child use any available method of locomotion to secure an object? For the child who is developing typically, the mode of locomotion is likely to be crawling. With the handicapped child, it may vary from rolling to walking. In the case of the severely physically involved child, we do not want to confuse the motoric ability to locomote with the concept that the body can be used as a tool to obtain objects that are out of reach. For some, locomotion as a means-end response may begin with only a turn from back to side in order to obtain the object. Then the distance that the child must travel in order to retrieve the object (or to have physical contact with a person) is gradually increased. The ability to persist over a great distance is correlated with increasing competence in visual pursuit of a disappearing object and search for the partly covered object.

Task 10: Development of Attached Tool Use

Background. The development of tool use occurs in two steps. Initially, for the child to use one object (the means) to obtain another object (the end), the means and end must be physically connected. Examples might be a string attached to a toy or an object resting on a piece of cloth. This ability comes about as part of the subperiod of secondary circular reactions and becomes a generalized skill through coordination of various secondary circular reactions. The second step in the means-end developmental sequence involves the ability to use an object that is *not* connected to the goal object. An example would be the use of a stick to pull a box off a shelf. This type of problem-solving ability begins during the fifth sensorimotor subperiod (that of tertiary circular reactions) and becomes a generalized strategy during the subperiod of invention of new means through mental combinations.

Terminal objective. The terminal objective for the solution of attached tool problems requires that the child be able to use a variety of objects (string, pillows, pieces of cloth, box tops, etc.) as tools for bringing desired objects into reach. The child should be able to differentiate when a tool is functional or not functional. Such evidence of differentiation could be the child who does not pull on strings that are not attached to a goal object or does not pull on a cloth that does not have a goal object sitting on it.

Name: _____   Date _____

Condition	Right Arm	Left Arm	Bilateral Arm Movement
No stimulus present.			
Total minutes observed ____	Rate/min ____	Rate/min ____	Rate/min ____
Stimulus held within child's reach above *right* arm.			
Total minutes observed ____	Rate/min ____	Rate/min ____	Rate/min ____
Stimulus held within child's reach above *left* arm.			
Total minutes observed ____	Rate/min ____	Rate/min ____	Rate/min ____
Stimulus held within child's reach but at midline.			
Total minutes observed ____	Rate/min ____	Rate/min ____	Rate/min ____

FIGURE 4.9   *Means-end data sheet for recording the child's arm movements under various conditions.*
Arm movement frequency is observed and recorded as hash marks in the appropriate space on the sheet. When a stimulus is present, arm movement is defined as contact with the hanging object. Record should include notation as to the object used, whether it was suspended over the child, tied in hand, etc., and any unusual events, such as seizures.

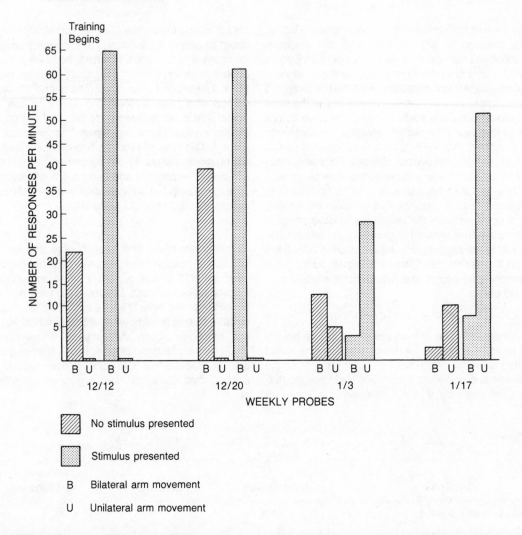

FIGURE 4.10   *Arm movement (with one arm or both arms) with and without stimulus*
Arm movements in the stimulus condition progressed from primarily bilateral and less accurately aimed at swiping the toy and thereby activating it, to primarily unilateral and directed toward activating the wind chimes, an example of systematic repetition of an environmental effect. In addition, the child exhibits less arm movement when the wind chimes are not present, thereby discriminating presence and absence.

Rationale. The use of tools attached to objects serves as an intermediate step between using the hand as a tool and the final step, locating and using an unattached tool to obtain a desired object.

Conditions and task sequence.
Child characteristics. This sequence of tool use begins during the subperiod of secondary circular reactions. Children typically show some evidence of search for the partly covered object at least before they begin to use supports or strings as tools. Also, the typical tool-use situation requires good visually

directed reach and grasp. It is important, again, to separate the motoric requirements of the task from the problem itself. The use of some type of intermediary to obtain an object which is out of reach is the goal and the problem to be solved. Sometimes a very simple modification, such as tying a wooden bead to the end of a string or attaching some similar type of handle to a cloth, can make the tool more feasible for a physically handicapped child with poor grasp.
Materials. Materials for this type of activity are objects in which the child has demonstrated some

TABLE 4.14   *Task Summary 10: Development of Attached Tool Use*

Task Description	Response Description	Criteria/Specific Commentary
Check reinforcement value of the stimuli.		
Level A Use of support as tool.		
Teacher presents an object to the child.	Child reaches for the object.	Teacher feels confident that object is interesting.
Teacher moves the object out of reach and sets it on a support which is within reach. Possible supports include a towel, pillow, box top, string, etc.	Possible responses: (1) Child begins to pull forward onto table surface, falls back, but object is now within reach.	Child is likely to become gradually more direct and efficient in her response.
	(2) Child does not pull support but may request help.	Child should begin to pull spontaneously on new trials after several demonstrations.
If child does not pull support, teacher demonstrates.	(3) Child pulls support after demonstration.	
	(4) Child has pulled in past but does not now.	Teacher probably needs to change goal object.
	(5) Child pulls support directly and obtains object.	
Test for understanding of the "unattached" tool problem (object held above support making support useless as tool).		
This test is given only after child successfully uses the support as a tool to obtain an object resting upon it.		
Teacher allows child to play with object, then takes it out of reach and holds it a few inches above the "tool" support the child has just used.	Possible responses: (1) Child pulls pillows and looks surprised.	Teacher moves pillows back, sets object on pillow, and encourages child to reach for object.
	(2) Child pulls pillow, stops, and then immediately reaches up for the object.	Teacher gives child the object if it is likely that she will soon start reaching directly. This problem should then be presented with other tool situation.
	(3) Child reaches up for object and does not touch pillow support.	
Level B Use of string as tool on surface (vertical string problem).		
Teacher presents an object to the child.	Child reaches for the object.	Teacher feels confident that object is interesting.
Teacher moves the object out of sight over edge of table but leaves string tied to the object within reach. Teacher makes point of showing child where object has gone.	Possible responses: (1) Child plays with string and, while playing, object comes within reach; then child picks up the object.	Child is likely to become more efficient on repeated trials.

TABLE 4.14   *(Continued)*

Task Description	Response Description	Criteria/Specific Commentary
	(2) Child does not pull string but requests help.	Child should begin to pull spontaneously on new trials after demonstration. Teacher should change goal object.
	(3) Child pulls string after demonstration.	Child should begin to pull spontaneously on new trials.
	(4) Child has pulled string in past but does not now.	Teacher needs to try new goal object.
	(5) Child pulls on string directly and obtains the object, either with hand-over-hand motion or a quick jerking motion.	This is the level of response desired. Child should demonstrate this behavior on at least 5 different occasions.

interest. Pieces of yarn, cloth, paper, or any other object may serve as the attached tool.

Subsequent task. Once the child has demonstrated generalized use of attached tools (including the vertical use of the string) and is able to alter her own behavior according to whether a given tool is functional, she is ready for problems requiring use of an unattached tool.

Generalization test. A child should be able to use a variety of tools to obtain a number of goal objects at this level. In addition, she should spontaneously employ (without demonstration) a tool not previously used on the first presentation of that new tool.

Task 11:   Use of Unattached Object as a Tool

Terminal objective. By the end of the sensorimotor period, the child should be using objects within reach (rakes, sticks, chairs, etc.) in order to obtain objects which are out of reach (toys, cookie jars on counters, etc.).

Rationale. It is the novel combination of means to ends that marks the child's increasing readiness for representational problem solving. Experience with situations in which the child has to use tools to obtain desired ends (rather than simply having goal objects brought to her) is the final elaboration of the means-end skill. That is, the child must act in increasingly complex ways in order to make interesting things happen.

Conditions and task sequence.

Child characteristics. Before the child solves this type of problem, she is likely to have demonstrated some systematic search behavior for the object that has just been hidden. She will engage in sequential container play—putting a series of objects into a container—as well as attempt to activate some mechanical toys.

Position of child. It is very important to construct the situation so that there is not an alternative means of obtaining an object. For example, we find that children are unlikely to use the unattached tool if they are seated on the floor or even at a table where they can readily reach the object by stretching. They seem more likely to use a tool when an object is out of reach on a higher place. At any rate, it is important that there be a functional necessity for use of the tool rather than the whim of the teacher. This is a form of problem solving best observed when the child is moving around her environment rather than in a structured situation.

Materials. Again, this type of tool-use problem requires some fine motor skills which the physically handicapped child may not have. In a successful effort to modify this task for a physically handicapped child, one teacher attached a magnet to the end of a stick.

Subsequent task. Use of an unattached tool is the highest skill in the tool-use realm of means-end cognitive development. Uzgiris and Hunt (1975) describe an extension of the means-end problem-solving tasks which require more foresight by the learner. The problem situations include (1) placing a long string of beads in a tall, narrow container and (2) the problem of the solid ring (pp. 173–175). In the first situation, the child will be unsuccessful because of the container's unsteadiness unless she invents a means to stabilize the container (e.g., holding the glass and dangling the necklace over it, rolling up the necklace first, etc.). In the second problem, the child is provided with a set of rings and a rod for mounting them, however one ring is made solid by taping over the hole. The foresightful youngster will not attempt to stack the solid ring but instead will set it aside.

Generalization test. Once the child demonstrates the following: (1) using a new tool spontaneously, (2) subsequently using other tools in situations where she may have to move a short distance to obtain the tool, (3) returning to the problem and using the tool to obtain the goal, she has accomplished criterion for invention of a means to obtain desired ends.

Task 12: Operational Causality

Background. The development of causality involves the ability to separate actions from the results which they produce. This separation occurs in a developmental sequence which begins similarly to the means-end sequence. In the first steps the child examines her hands, next she is observed to repeat actions which produce an interesting result. The next activity in this sequence involves showing the child an interesting spectacle such as a toy top, a wind-up toy, or any event which she cannot reproduce by direct action on the object. We can then observe the child and record her level of response. Does she make some kind of gesture that suggests she wants to experience the spectacle again (e.g., hitting her hand on the table or bouncing up and down)? Does she use a more formal type of gesture such as pushing the object toward you or bringing your hand toward the object? Does she try to recreate the spectacle by manipulating the toy manually such as by sliding a friction toy back and forth with-

out removing her hand from the toy? Finally, does she explore various means to reproduce the spectacle such as turning the key on a wind-up toy? There is not a correct or an incorrect response on this sequence. Rather, different skill levels correlate with different stages in the child's development of causality. The level of searching for a means to reproducing the spectacle, such as winding the key on a mechanical toy, is the terminal objective described for the sensorimotor period.

Rationale. The first step in this series of skill levels is a very opportune point to begin establishing a basis for communication. This is accomplished by reinforcing the rudiments of a gesture system. Think of the 7- or 8-month-old baby being bounced on her father's lap. When the bouncing stops, the baby is likely to continue the bouncing and do some additional wiggling. Dad is likely to interpret this movement as "Oh, you want more." Dad then resumes the bouncing. This continuing movement on the child's part was not initially a response to make Dad bounce her some more. However, this interpretation on the father's part typically results in the development of a more explicit gesture by which the child indicates that she wants more. Thus, in this example, we have the roots for a communication system with the child. This type of situation offers a number of opportunities throughout the day to require the child to use a rudimentary gesture system.

An example of the process was illustrated by one of our teachers and a student who liked to bounce on the teacher's lap. The teacher used this event as a reinforcing activity with this child after the child engaged in less preferred activities. In addition the

TABLE 4.15　*Task Summary 11: Development of Unattached Tool Use*

Task Description	Response Description	Criteria/Specific Commentary
Check reinforcement value of stimuli.		
Teacher arranges a situation in which an object the child has requested (through word or gesture) is out of reach, but a tool (rake, chair, stool, etc.) is available to obtain the object.	Possible responses: (1) Child uses tool to obtain the object only after demonstration. (2) Child uses the tool to obtain the object spontaneously.	Once the child (1) uses a new tool spontaneously, (2) subsequently uses other tools in situations where she may have to move a short distance to get the tool, and (3) returns and obtains the goal, she has accomplished the generalized criterion for invention of a new means to obtain desired ends.

teacher worked toward rudimentary communication by requiring that the child request the bouncing. After initially bouncing the child on his lap, the teacher stopped and asked the child whether he wanted more. The response that had been selected for this child to indicate that he wanted "more" is an "ah" sound. In a period of 4 days, the number of times the teacher had to ask a child if he would like more before the child responded appropriately decreased from a mean of 3.2 to 1 on individual trials. The next step in this objective might be to require the "ah" sound before the first bounce in response to the question, "Do you want to bounce?" The teacher is working toward the point when the child not yet on the teacher's lap responds positively (and by now the response may be a head nod for "yes") to the question, "Do you want to bounce?", before he is even allowed on the teacher's lap. The progression in this sequence is to gradually move to situations where the child must employ gestures or sounds in the presence of fewer and fewer contextual cues. This shapes the child's progress closer to that expected in situations which require communication in a representational context.

Conditions and task sequence.

Child characteristics. The intial step in the causality sequence is differentiated from the means-end sequence in that it requires the child to repeat a gesture (hitting hand on surface, kicking, vocalizing, etc.) when a spectacle, such as a moving toy, stops. This level of responding typically begins during the subperiod of primary circular reactions. Prerequisite behavior is the repetition of motor schemata that produce an interesting effect.

Subsequent task. The remaining steps in the development of a generalized concept of causality represent refinements in the type of action required to produce particular consequent events. This results from experience with a variety of mechanisms, wind-up toys, tops, light switches, strings to pull, and keys to insert. In many cases, the means for activating the spectacle may be physically impossible for a particular person. This should not limit opportunities to experience this type of control over one's environment. Observe a person's response to an interesting event such as a wind-up toy. Then select some component of that response (e.g., reaches toward the key when it stops) and require that response in subsequent situations before reproducing the event.

General comments. Again, specific examples have been given to illustrate operational causality. The context, the response, and the reinforcer for each level of causality, however, are each examples of entire classes of situations, responses, and reinforcers. This is not an objective that one works on for 15 minutes out of the day. Rather, it is a principle —that of requiring some form of communication from the child before every event that occurs during the day. The limitations in applying this principle are, as has been previously emphasized, of our own making. It is our responsibility to organize the child's daily activities to create a match between her response capabilities and environmental demands.

To utilize this principle, begin with only a few situations during the school day. Gradually introduce new sequences of context (antecedent events), required responses, and reinforcing consequences as the child masters the previous sequences. If meals are generally positive for a child, the training should begin in that context. Perhaps initially the child is expected to open her mouth when she sees the spoon. Or perhaps she has to touch one's hand before she receives another bite. Whatever the response, the essential characteristic of the situation is that the child must do something consistently in order for a specific environmental event to occur.

In the examples used so far, the child has been asked to respond to contextual cues (e.g., being on the teacher's lap or the filled spoon) as the discriminative stimulus for a "gesture." With some children, tactile prompts are necessary during beginning work. For example, a touch on the child's chin to get her mouth open or a tap on the shoulder to cue sitting down may work. Additional information about the use of tactile cues for the beginnings of communication work may be sought when failure to develop this means-end communication persists (Fieber, Note 1).

Once the child begins to use these primitive gestures spontaneously, a tremendous step in the development of communication has been accomplished. The child now uses her responses as a means to control events which she cannot directly manipulate. This separation of action and consequent events is the essence of operational causality.

4. Spatial relations

"Localization of objects in space" is the phrase Uzgiris and Hunt (1975) use for a collection of skills typically observed in the toddler's repertoire. These skills include items that we feel may be divided into

TABLE 4.16   *Task Summary 12: Operational Causality*

Task Description	Response Description	Criteria/Specific Commentary
Check reinforcement value of stimuli. *Level A* Actions to prolong interesting events. Teacher performs a spectacle such as swinging a toy, spinning a top, or rocking the child, playing peek-a-boo or pat-a-cake.	Levels of responding: (1) Child responds in some way when the spectacle stops; it may be a foot kick, hitting, hand on table, or vocalizing.	Teacher selects most useful future behavior for the child and requires that behavior from the child before she reproduces a desired spectacle. Once the child uses the gesture upon seeing the object used in the spectacle or the person who produced the spectacle, she has developed expressive communicative response. At this level it is likely to be limited to perhaps one or two events.
Teacher initiates a familiar spectacle or game as described above and stops abruptly.	(2) Child attempts to restart the activity with an action that is part of the game.	While this type of responding initially occurs in only one or two situations, with repeated contingent experience it will become a generalized strategy for acting in the environment.
Level B Actions to reinstate interesting spectacles. Teacher presents some type of mechanical toy (wind-up toy, jack-in-the-box, etc.) but initially does not permit the child to see the means by which it is activated.	Levels of responding: (1) Child touches the object or the teacher's hand as a gesture to the teacher to make the event happen again. (Teacher should do so this time, showing the child how it was activated.)	There is not a correct or incorrect response in this series, rather different responses indicate different levels of understanding on the part of the child. (1) Subperiod of secondary circular reactions.
	(2) Child makes the mechanical toy perform its activity manually. (Child should be allowed to do so.) (3) Child hands object back to the teacher and waits.	(2) Subperiod of coordination of secondary circular reactions.
	(4) Child explores for a way to activate the toy. (5) Child attempts to imitate means for activating the toy.	(3) Subperiod of tertiary circular reactions. (4) The child does not have to succeed but merely try, since many toys are very difficult to activate. The most difficult type of toy is one which requires combining events such as inserting a key into the toy and then turning it. This solution does not come about until the sixth subperiod.

three task sequences: (13) localization of objects in space, (14) examining and relating to objects, and (15) container play.

Task 13:   Localization of Objects in Space

Terminal objective. The terminal objective for this task requires that the child follow the path through which an object is moved to a point some distance away before it is removed from view. The child must then move around any barriers to that object and retrieve it.

Rationale. This series of behaviors develops in parallel with object permanence skills. It represents a coordination of the concepts of object permanence and understanding of the consistency with which objects move in space. The steps in this sequence represent a generalization of the object permanence concept as the child must pursue hidden objects over greater distances and, consequently, over longer periods of time.

Conditions and task sequence.

Child characteristics. This series of items begins during the subperiod of primary circular reaction. The learned behaviors include alternating gaze, localization of sounds, and anticipation of horizontal trajectories. Development proceeds into the subperiod of secondary circular reactions when the child learns to follow rapidly falling objects and to rotate his body to retrieve objects. Pursuit of objects around barriers (first transparent, then opaque barriers) is accomplished during the later subperiod of tertiary circular reactions.

The initial behavior in this series, alternate glancing, typically follows the development of visual fixation and visual tracking. For the physically involved child, however, this actually may be more feasible than visual tracking. Anticipating the direction of a horizontal trajectory is an accomplishment that comes about concomitant with the activities prerequisite to object permanence (e.g., anticipation of the trajectory behind the child's head). Trunk rotation to pursue objects and localization of a fallen object lag slightly behind the ability to search for objects in the single screen situation. Finally, pursuit of objects around barriers follows, in developmental sequence, the accomplishment of the complex object permanence problems.

Any one of these tasks might be too motorically complex for the physically handicapped child. For example, recall what happens when you try to pur-

sue an object moved behind you without using your hand for support as you turn. Modifications, both in the response and the consequences, may be necessary. With the barrier problems, locomotion may be difficult for a child whose mode of ambulation is rolling without much directional control. If the child cannot ambulate, you may have to act out the situation with a doll. This involves asking the child to indicate whether the doll or puppet is going the "right way" to get the object. If it is necessary to go to this type of "pretend" situation, the concepts involved will be more difficult. Considerable initial teaching centered on the object of the game will be required before one can feel confident that the child has the concept.

Materials. Materials used in these activities are, most importantly, objects in which the child has shown some interest. Barriers may be simply pieces of furniture placed in the room.

Subsequent task. Following the accomplishment of object pursuit around barriers in immediate situations, the child should be able to learn to search systematically for objects played with and left alone as much as an hour earlier (and, eventually, several hours earlier). This degree of memory indicates that the child is using object names to mediate her actions in time. She may not be able to tell you what she is looking for. Once she finds it, however, she knows she has accomplished what she set out to do. Such behavior is the culmination of the sensorimotor stage and serves as a transition to the initial phases of the preoperational level of intellectual functioning.

Task 14:   Examining and Relating Objects[1]

Terminal objective. This category of spatial relationship activities involves two accomplishments: (1) examining objects in such a way as to note different parts and (2) bringing together functionally related objects in a manner which indicates understanding of the conventional functional relationships.

Rationale. Accomplishment of these two behaviors may be monitored by observing a child's schemata (her movements and actions with objects) in relation to objects. These schemata are typically observed before the child displays understanding of

---

1. For additional training suggestions for the functional use of objects, see Chapter 5.

TABLE 4.17   *Task Summary 13: Localization of Objects in Space*

Task Description	Response Description	Criteria/Specific Commentary
Check the reinforcement value of the stimuli.		
Level A		
Alternate glancing between objects.		
Teacher presents two interesting visual stimuli in front of the child, holding them about 12 inches apart.	Child switches gaze from one visual stimulus to another 4–5 times in 10 seconds.	This achievement typically follows in sequence the development of visual tracking. Its occurrence denotes a significant development in sensory organization skills—that of voluntary control over visual attention. The younger infant has difficulty selecting what stimuli to look at and can frequently shift her attention only by closing out stimuli altogether.
Localization of an object by its sound:		
Teacher presents auditory stimulus outside of the child's visual field.	Child turns and focuses gaze on object.	This objective was discussed in more detail in the sensory organization sequence.
Anticipation of trajectory of an object moved behind a screen:		
Teacher: (1) selects an object that the child has tracked visually, (2) shows the child the object, (3) begins moving it in a horizontal plane behind an opaque screen, and (4) then moves the object out from behind the screen on the other side. The teacher should begin the trajectory of the object at least 8–10 inches from the first side of the screen and keep an even pace of movement throughout the manuever. This should always be done from the same direction (i.e., right to left) until the child is responding correctly.	Child tracks the object to the point of disappearance and then immediately shifts gaze to the other side of screen. The child may not do this on the first trial but begins to after several presentations.	The child has reached criterion level of responding when she anticipates the trajectory on at least 4 of 5 opportunities on 5 occasions for each direction used.
If child does not shift gaze immediately, a sound cue may be used to draw her attention to the other side of the screen.	Child shifts gaze when sound cue is provided.	Continue activity until child shifts gaze to other end of screen without a sound cue. Once child is shifting gaze correctly without a sound cue, the same task can be presented with trajectories that follow other directions—left to right etc.

TABLE 4.17   *(Continued)*

Task Description	Response Description	Criteria/Specific Commentary
Level B Following trajectory of a rapidly falling object. Teacher selects an object in which the child has shown interest. Teacher holds the object above the child's head and calls the child's attention to the object.	Child looks up at the object.	
Teacher drops object in such a way that it makes very little noise when dropped. (This may be because it is a "quiet" object such as a ball or paper or aluminum foil or because it falls on a padded surface.)	Child follows the trajectory of the object to the point where it disappears, such as below the table surface and then moves to look for it. The child may locate it visually or with a pointing response, or behave in some consistent manner from opportunity to opportunity so that the teacher is confident that the child is trying to locate the object.	This behavior is most likely to be seen as the child plays with objects and drops them. While we would establish an arbitrary criterion of demonstrating the behavior on 4 of 5 trials on 5 occasions, when we see the child use the strategy of visually pursuing and then using that information to locate a fallen object, we are confident that the child has reached an appropriate level of generalization of the response.
Level C Motoric pursuit of a moving object. Level 1 Teacher takes an object with which the child has been playing and moves it behind the child. The teacher moves the object in such a way that the child visually follows the object for a portion of the trajectory. Level 2	Child searches with her hand behind herself and retrieves the object or rotates her trunk about 45° in the direction of the object and retrieves the object.	Criterion performance means the child retrieves the object when it is moved to either side on 2 of 3 opportunities (for each side) on 5 occasions. This problem is at about the same level of complexity as the object permanence problem with one screen.
Teacher takes an object with which the child has been playing and moves it behind the child in such a way that she cannot visually pursue the object during the movement.	The child is correct if she rotates her trunk or actually turns around and retrieves the object. She may turn in either direction.	Criterion performance means the child retrieves the object on 2 of 3 opportunities when it is moved to each side on 5 occasions. This problem is at about the same level of complexity as the object permanence problem with two screens.
Level D Pursuit of objects around barriers. Level 1: Transparent barriers. Teacher takes an object child has been playing with and moves it behind a transparent barrier (such as a plexiglass screen) situated behind a chair, that the child can see under but cannot crawl under.	Child moves (creeps or walks) around barrier and retrieves the object within 10–15 seconds. (For a child whose movement is very slow, a longer period may be allowed but the teacher should feel confident that the child is pursuing the object all along.)	Criterion performance means the child moves around a variety of barriers to obtain an object on 4 of 5 opportunities on 5 occasions. Some of these opportunities may be observed incidently during the course of play.

TABLE 4.17   *(Continued)*

Task Description	Response Description	Criteria/Specific Commentary
Level 2: Opaque barriers. Teacher takes an object that the child has been playing with and moves it behind an opaque barrier such as a door or table or chair that the child cannot see under.	Child moves (creeps or walks, etc) around barrier and retrieves the object within 10–15 seconds.	Criterion is same as that for Level D1.

TABLE 4.18   *Task Summary 14: Examining and Relating Objects*

Task Description	Response Description	Criteria/Specific Commentary
Check reinforcement value of stimuli.		
Recognition of reverse side of objects. Teacher positions a desired object in an upside-down orientation and observes for appropriate child behavior.	Child grasps an object which has a definite front and back, or top and bottom (i.e. doll, baby, bottle, cup) and turns it to the "right side" or examines the object by turning it over several times.	This behavior should be observed with at least 10 different objects before one is confident that the child has this scheme well established. The 10 occasions may be counted for over a period of time.
Relate functionally related objects. Teacher presents 2 functionally related objects such as cup and spoon, drum and drumstick, close to each other.	Child relates the 2 objects in an appropriate manner, stirring in the cup, hitting the drum, feeding a doll a bottle, etc.	Criterion level of responding would be for the child to relate appropriately 10 different pairs of objects in a functionally appropriate manner. The 10 occasions may be accumulated over a period of time.

action and object names. Demonstration and training in functional use of objects forms one of the bridges between sensorimotor "cognitive" and language developments.

Conditions and task sequence.

Child characteristics. Examination of objects typically begins during the subperiod of secondary circular reactions. This coincides with the solution of single-screen object permanence problems and the use of attached tools in the means-end sequence. Conventional, functional object use typically begins during the coordination of secondary circular reactions subperiod. Functional use is then generalized across more complex combinations of objects through the remaining subperiod. The beginning of functional use typically follows the ability to search in the 2-screen situations and more complex tool use (use of the vertical string).

Subsequent tasks. The "appropriate" functional use of objects—such as using a cup to drink from or stirring with a spoon in a cup—systematically precedes evidence of the understanding of the object's name. One should not be unduly constrained, however, by the term "appropriate." In a given context, for example when playing with hats, a cup or bowl might make an appropriate hat. At the culmination of this objective, we hope to observe the child engaged in "pretend" play with a variety of objects in a variety of situations. The "pretend" play at this point generally will be a single action. The child may do a series of things but they may not relate to one another functionally.

Comments. In the "relating objects" task sequence, we begin by observing the child to see if she examines objects by turning them over, poking fingers in holes, or feeling individual parts. When children at this point in the development of schemata do not examine objects, we find that modeling such behavior produces little change in the child's behavior. Imitation skills have not been developed adequately. A better method to teach examining behavior and other complex motor schemata is simply to provide the child with many different objects. These might include different containers, different kinds of paper or cloth, balls, pieces of yarn, and small toys which have movable but firmly attached parts. As the child shows evidence of trying out new schemata with objects, the teacher can begin to use the familiar schemata to initiate motor imitation activities. Then, slight variations on these familiar movements are introduced for the purpose of expanding the child's repertoire to include relating 2 objects (a stick and a xylophone, a cup and spoon, a crayon and paper, and sliding a car with wheels on a surface, for example).

In Figure 4.11, Uzgiris and Hunt (1975) depict the developmental hierarchy of schemata for relating to objects. Functional use of objects corresponds to socially instigated actions (item *h* in Figure 4.11). If a child is deficient in those earlier, more basic behaviors for manipulating objects, she will not be successful in learning to use objects functionally. See Chapter 5 for additional training suggestions to facilitate this type of performance.

Task 15:   Container Play

Terminal objective. The terminal objective for container play (at the sensorimotor level of development) is that the child continue placing objects into a container or place nested containers together until the play sequence is completed (i.e., all beads in a cup; all cups properly nested).

Rationale. Container play is an activity that the young child frequently engages in spontaneously. Often mothers of toddlers describe their children as getting into cupboards and playing with pots and pans for long periods of time. The gradual increase in the number of objects the child will place into containers relates to the child's ability to work with more materials (greater levels of distraction) without losing sight of the initial task. The development of dumping out filled containers represents the child's functional understanding of gravity. This concept forms the basis for much active experimenting at the sensorimotor and preoperational levels.

Conditions and task sequence.

Child characteristics. This sequence of container play typically begins during the subperiod of coordination of secondary circular reactions. The child consistently searches for hidden objects before she shows reliable interest in container play. Progression to the point of placing large numbers of objects into containers is not accomplished until the end of the sensorimotor period. When working on container play objectives, the teacher should remember that the first step is that of *taking objects out of a container one at a time.* We have no simple explanation to offer for this, it is simply an observation. At this point, try to give the child manipulation experience with a variety of containers: cups, boxes, pots, bowls, measuring cups, boxes with holes in the sides, or cellophane windows. Demonstrate placing objects into various containers and allow the child to take the objects out. Expect imitation of putting *in* only after numerous demonstrations of putting an object into a container. In the development of container play, the severely handicapped child is likely to remain for several months at the level of putting only 1 or 2 objects in a container (even if numerous objects are available) and then taking them out again, one at a time. Usually after several months, the child begins to place all of the available objects in the container, with 12 being the approximate limit. Up to this point, the child typically places objects in and takes them out of a container one at a time. After an experience with putting a series of objects into a container one by one, the child will group several objects together and then pick them up and put them into a container. Next the child learns to dump the contents rather than taking objects out one at a time.

This gradual skill building also occurs with putting pegs in a pegboard and pieces into a formboard. However, it is often ignored when teachers try to teach container and form concepts. When the objective includes using a covered container, another frequently ignored prerequisite is object permanence. We often meet resistance from a child when she is asked to place objects in a container she cannot see into. If the child is without object perma-

Name:
Birthdate:
Date of Examination:

		Objects Presented to Infant					
		1	2	3	4	...	15
				Plastic			
Schemes Shown	For Example:	Rattle	Doll	Fish	Foil		
a. Holding		___	___	___	___	...	___
b. Mouthing		___	___	___	___	...	___
c. Visual inspection		___	___	___	___	...	___
d. Simple motor schemes:							
1. Hits or pats with hand		___	___	___	___	...	___
2. Hits surface with object		___	___	___	___	...	___
3. Hits two together		___	___	___	___	...	___
4. Shakes		___	___	___	___	...	___
5. Waves		___	___	___	___	...	___
Other:		___	___	___	___	...	___
e. Examining		___	___	___	___	...	___
f. Complex motor schemes:							
1. Slides		___	___	___	___	...	___
2. Crumples		___	___	___	___	...	___
3. Swings		___	___	___	___	...	___
4. Tears or stretches		___	___	___	___	...	___
5. Rubs or pats		___	___	___	___	...	___
Other:		___	___	___	___	...	___
g. "Letting go" actions:							
1. Drops		___	___	___	___	...	___
2. Throws		___	___	___	___	...	___
Other:		___	___	___	___	...	___
h. Socially instigated actions:							
1. Drinks		___	___	___	___	...	___
2. Wears		___	___	___	___	...	___
3. Drives		___	___	___	___	...	___
4. Builds		___	___	___	___	...	___
5. Hugs		___	___	___	___	...	___
6. Dresses		___	___	___	___	...	___
7. Sniffs		___	___	___	___	...	___
8. Making "walk"		___	___	___	___	...	___
Other:		___	___	___	___	...	___
i. Showing		___	___	___	___	...	___
j. Naming		___	___	___	___	...	___
(List name used by infant)							

FIGURE 4.11 *Developmental hierarchy of schemata for relating to objects.*

Source: I. Uzgiris and J. McV. Hunt, *Assessment in Infancy: Ordinal Scales of Psychological Development.* Urbana, Ill.: University of Illinois Press, 1975, p. 220.

nence, objects cease to exist once she no longer sees or touches them.

Materials. Again, the primary characteristics to consider when selecting objects to go into containers (and the containers themselves) is that the child be interested in them. Experience with a variety of containers and materials should be provided.

Subsequent task. Culmination of the container play sequence means that the child is prepared for more difficult tasks involving (1) matching objects according to specific physical characteristics and (2), at a later time, sorting. This takes us into the preoperational period.

Comments. For the child with moderate to severe physical involvement of the upper extremities, container play does not make a good deal of sense as an educational activity. The physical constraints make it unlikely that the child will do the activity with any degree of facility. The time involved does not seem worthwhile. It is possible, however, to demonstrate filling and dumping to the child and give her the opportunity to indicate through a signal system when there are still objects to go into a container or when it is filled and perhaps even tip it over herself. Again the task difficulty is slightly increased by this modification.

With formboard activities, one may adapt the task by putting handles on the form pieces or having the child indicate their placement and then helping her place the form. It is not necessary to physically place something in order to know its correct location. For the child who cannot physically manage indicating the location for an object, we can match the form to different locations and ask her to use a yes/no system for indicating whether the match is correct or incorrect.

A note of caution is in order here. You may find that a child, responding correctly to the task, begins to say "yes" to incorrect locations and "no" to correct locations on very familiar items. The child usually giggles after her "error" and the teacher has the impression that the child is teasing. While this behavior can be annoying, it is important to recognize the achievement that it heralds. The child is now sure of the correct response and can make intentional errors for their effect on the teacher or parents. Before becoming annoyed, consider the importance of this development for a child who has few opportunities to engage in the usual forms of teasing available to preschoolers. This form of teasing may occur in any of the task situations described thus far. It is likely to occur as the child advances to

more complex cognitive and language concepts, and it is probably a good indication that she is ready for concepts at the preoperational level. However, so as not to encourage the child it is best to say, "No," and correct her response in a matter-of-fact manner.

Imitation and Schemata for Relating to Objects

In their sensorimotor assessment series, Uzgiris and Hunt (1975) include identification of schemata in relation to objects and verbal and gestural imitation among the skill sequences. These sequences represent two extremely important developments during the sensorimotor period. In this book, these two developments are discussed and strategies for training them are described in Chapter 5. The exclusion of these two skill sequences from this chapter should *not* be inferred as a minimization of their importance. They are extremely important prerequisites to later cognitive and language development.

Summary

In summary, by the end of the sensorimotor period of intelligence (as conceptualized by Piaget), we see a child who has accomplished a number of very important steps in cognitive growth. As Piaget puts it: "The elaboration of the universe by sensorimotor intelligence constitutes the transition from a state in which objects are centered about a self which believes it directs them, although completely unaware of itself as subject, to a state in which self is placed, at least practically, in a stable world conceived as independent of personal activity" (Piaget, 1954, p. 395).

For the child, the culmination of stage six in the sensorimotor period has the following results. In the area of *object permanence* the child now sees objects as things separate from herself, subject to movement in space independent of herself. She still has not learned all there is to know about the invariant properties of objects. Such refinements come during the preoperational and concrete operational periods. But the foundation for concepts such as conservation lies in the sensorimotor concept of object permanence (Flavell, 1963).

Stage six sensorimotor behavior with respect to *causality* results in two new achievements: (1) "the

TABLE 4.19   *Task Summary 15: Container Play*

Task Description	Response Description	Criteria/Specific Commentary
Check reinforcement value of stimuli.		
Level A Stacking blocks Teacher provides some blocks and demonstrates stacking them.	Levels of responding: (1) Child combines blocks in air. (2) Child stacks 2 blocks. (3) Child stacks 3 blocks. (4) Child stacks 4 or more blocks.	Step (1) usually precedes putting objects into a container and usually comes after child has started putting 1–3 blocks into a container. This step usually follows child putting a series of 3 or more objects into a container.
Sequence of steps in putting objects into a container and removing them. Teacher presents objects and a container into which the object may be placed and demonstrates putting objects in and taking them out.	Levels of responding: (1) Child takes 1 or 2 objects out of container 1 at a time. (2) Child places 1 or 2 objects into the container singly and takes them out singly. (3) Child places a series of 3 objects into container and then takes out singly. (4) Child places a series of 4 or more objects into a container 1 at a time and opens the container to try to remove the objects.	Children typically spend a great deal of time at each of these levels. The teacher will find the best teaching strategy is to provide opportunities for playing with appropriate materials and demonstrate responding at a step just ahead of child's current level.
	(5) Child picks up a couple of objects at a time and places them into container and will place as many as a dozen objects into the container. Removes the objects by dumping the container if she physically can or up-ending the container if it is too big for dumping.	This is the most advanced level of container play and is typically accomplished before the child is ready for formboards or form boxes.
Level B Arrangement of nested objects in a series. Teacher presents a series of 4 nested containers (round containers initially).	Child places smaller container inside larger for 3 insertions. However, she does not necessarily get the 2 closest in size together. If she tried to nest all 4 and made an incorrect insertion, she cannot correct it by removing only the incorrect piece; she must take all pieces apart, start again, and is likely to make the same error over.	By the end of the sensorimotor period the child may have started using a systematic strategy for placing 3–4 pieces together but working successfully with more than 4 at one time is an indication that the child has started the transition to the preoperational period.

child can, through representation, infer a cause, given only its effect; and (2) foresee an effect, given its cause" (Flavell, 1963).

Imitation is also influenced by the stage six development of representation. The child begins to imitate objects as well as persons. This includes combinations of behaviors she cannot see herself perform. Also in the culmination of the sensorimotor period, the child begins to demonstrate what Piaget calls "deferred *imitation:* the child reproduces an absent model through memory" (Flavell, 1963, p. 126).

Spatial concepts for the child in stage six mean "he is able to keep a running tab on his own movements in space, internally representing his own previous displacements relative to those of other bodies. And . . . he is able to represent the invisible displacement of external objects" (Flavell, 1963, p. 141).

Thus, the accomplishments of the sensorimotor period result in a child who can, not only through trial and error but also through representation, solve problems involving differentiation of cause and effect and who has begun to construct an external reality through the beginnings of the concepts of object, space, and time permanence.

The next phase in development, in Piaget's conceptualization, is the subperiod of preoperational thought. This subperiod extends from 1.5–2 years (the sensorimotor period) to 6–7 years (the beginnings of concrete operations). The primary accomplishment of this period is the child's growing independence of the need for the physical presence of objects and events in order to act. During the preoperational period the child becomes capable of symbolic functioning whereby she can assign "a signifier (a word, an image, etc.) to objects and events which symbolizes a perceptually absent event" (Flavell, 1963, p. 151) and thus act upon them in their absence. In the sensorimotor period the child behaved in such a way as to acknowledge the permanence of objects. In the preoperational period the child can extend that concept to more active manipulations of her environment.

References

Bayley, N. *Manual for the Bayley scales of infant development.* New York: Psychological Corporation, 1969.

Bayley, N. Development of mental abilities. In B. Mussen (Ed.), *Carmichael's manual of child psychology* (3rd ed.). New York: John Wiley, 1970.

Bower, T. G. R. *A primer of infant development.* San Francisco: W. H. Freeman, 1977.

Bricker, W. A. Identifying and modifying behavioral deficits. *American Journal of Mental Deficiency,* 1970, *75,* 16–21.

Cromwell, R. L. A social learning approach to mental retardation. In N. R. Ellis (Ed.), *Handbook of mental deficiency.* New York: McGraw-Hill, 1963.

Fantz, R. L., & Nevis, S. The predictive value of changes in visual preferences in early infancy. In J. Hellmuth (Ed.), *Exceptional infant: The normal infant.* New York: Brunner/Mazel, 1967.

Filler, J. W., Robinson, C. C., Smith, R. A., Vincent-Smith, L. J., Bricker, D. D., & Bricker, W. A. Mental retardation. In N. Hobbs (Ed.), *Issues in the classification of children* (Vol. 1), San Francisco: Jossey-Bass, 1975.

Flavell, J. H. *The developmental psychology of Jean Piaget.* Princeton, N.J.: Von Nostrand, 1963.

Furth, H. G. *Piaget and knowledge: Theoretical foundations.* Englewood Cliffs, N.J.: Prentice-Hall, Inc., 1969.

Hebb, D. O. *The organization of behavior.* New York: John Wiley, 1949.

Hunt, J. McV. *Intelligence and experience.* New York: Ronald Press, 1961.

Langer, J. *Theories of development.* New York: Holt, Rinehart, and Winston, 1969.

Murphy, K. Differential diagnosis of learning impaired children. *Developmental Medicine and Child Neurology,* 1969, *11,* 561–568.

Piaget, J. *The construction of reality in the child.* New York: Ballantine, 1954.

Piaget, J. *The origins of intelligence in children.* New York: W. W. Norton, 1963.

Premack, D. Reversibility of the reinforcement relation. *Science,* 1962, *136,* 255–257.

Seligman, M. E. P. *Helplessness: On depression, death, and development.* San Francisco: W. H. Freeman, 1975.

Stephens, B. The appraisal of cognitive development. In B. Stephens (Ed.), *Training the developmentally young.* New York: John Day, 1971.

Stephens, B. A Piagetian approach to curriculum development for the severely, profoundly and multiply handicapped. In E. Sontag (Ed.), *Educational programming for the severely and profoundly handicapped.* Reston, Va.: Council for Exceptional Children, 1977.

Uzgiris, I., & Hunt, J. McV. *Instrument for assessing infant psychological development.* Urbana, Ill.: University of Illinois, 1966.

Uzgiris, I., & Hunt, J. McV. *Assessment in infancy: Ordinal scales of psychological development.* Urbana, Ill.: University of Illinois Press, 1975.

Watson, J. S. Cognitive-perceptual development in infancy: Settings for the seventies. *Merrill-Palmer Quarterly,* 1971, *17,* 139–152.

Watson, J. S., & Ramey, C. T. Reactions to response contingent stimulation early in infancy. *Merrill-Palmer Quarterly,* 1972, *18,* 219–227.

White, B. L., Castle, P., & Held, R. Observations on the development of visually directed reaching. *Child Development,* 1964, *35,* 349–364.

White, B. L., Held, R., & Castle, P. Experience in early human development. Part I. Observations on the development of visually directed reaching. In J. Hellmuth (Ed.), *Exceptional infant, Vol. I: The normal infant.* New York: Brunner/Mazel, 1967.

Notes

1. Fieber, N. M., & Robinson, C. C. *Some relations of oculomotor coordination to postural control and interventions in cerebral palsied and multihandicapped children.* Paper presented at American Academy of Cerebral Palsy, Denver, Colorado, November 1974.
2. Fieber, N. M. *Movement in communication and language development of deaf-blind children.* Paper presented at National Deaf-Blind Workshop of Physical, Occupational and Recreational Therapists, Dallas, Texas, August 1975.
3. Finkelstein, N. W., & Ramey, C. T. *Learning to control the environment in infancy.* Chapel Hill, N.C.: University of North Carolina, 1976. (Unpublished)

Introduction to Chapter 5

In classrooms for the severely handicapped one often finds a language period in which the teacher is the only one who speaks in sentences or even uses words. Many of you are familiar with this phenomenon. Yet, even though the development of language progresses slowly, our goal is to teach all handicapped individuals to communicate, if not by voice, then by manual language (Stremel-Campbell, Cantrell, & Halle, 1977) or through the use of communication boards, symbol systems, and yes-no motions (Harris-Vanderheiden & Vanderheiden, 1977). Some of our students will learn to read—their sight vocabulary will include words commonly found on street signs and in grocery stores.

But let me return to the basic system of communication—language and its precursors—attending, imitation, functional use of objects, and word recognition. When faced with students severely deficient even in the prerequisites for communication, what can be done? How would you facilitate the emergence of functional speech in a young child who appears lethargic, takes no interest in toys or people, and who seldom makes noises except to cry? If allowed, this child will spend most of the day rocking or waving his hands in repetitive meaningless motions. How do you teach the adolescent who speaks in phrases but primarily in imitation of others and only rarely demonstrates comprehension of simple requests? In this next chapter Diane Bricker and Laura Dennison describe a sequence of steps for training the prerequisites to verbal behavior. This sequence is not simply a conglomeration of other language programs nor is it an untested review of the literature. Instead the training steps reflect years of application and revision on populations of moderately and severely handicapped children, first at the J. F. Kennedy Experimental School at George Peabody College and at present in the Debbie School at the Mailman Center for Child Development of the University of Miami. Their chapter traces the sequence of skills leading to language and outlines a series of observation and measurement procedures a teacher may use to determine which prerequisite language skills are deficient. The order of instruction is dictated by the interdependence of skills inherent in the sequence. Instructional methods and materials specific to each skill are clearly portrayed.

This chapter gives a striking impression of the complexity of prelanguage skills as contrasted with the common view that these skills are simple, easily developed, and necessarily present in all children. For example, the process of acquiring imitation is still unclear as noted by Parton (1976):

> The fundamental and largely unanswered question regarding imitation is how the organism achieves the capacity to exhibit the response which is identical to an observed behavior. . . . Since imitation involves the recognition of similarities and differences among multidimensional stimuli and the production of responses which match aspects of such stimuli, imitation is possibly the most complex cognitive performance exhibited during the first year of human life. (p. 28)

The language-training procedures presented in this chapter center upon prerequisite skills. Some of the children and older students you teach may be well beyond these beginning skills and you may seek references to other training programs whose emphasis is upon one, two, and three-word expressive combinations. Bricker, Dennison, and Bricker (1976) and Bricker, Ruder, and Vincent-Smith (1976) expand the upper end of the present program to include comprehension and production of three-word constructions involving agent, action, and object elements—"Boy open window," "Sally drink milk."

A second, two-part program by Guess, Sailor, and

Baer (1976a, 1976b) describes a validated, 29-step training sequence focusing upon receptive and expressive abilities. These two references detail testing, recording, and teaching procedures beginning with the ability to name simple objects and to understand object labels and extending to asking and answering questions about actions taken upon objects. [e.g., Teacher: "What do you want?" Student: "I want wagon." Teacher: "What are you doing?" Student: "I push(ing) wagon."] Additional parts in the program are presently being developed; these will include the communication of possession and more advanced forms of syntax.

Over the last 15 years our understanding of how language emerges in normal and language delayed children has advanced more quickly than our ability to update classroom teaching procedures. The technology for measuring and instructing language and its precursive behavior is becoming available to teachers in usable program form. Unfortunately there remain many unknowns; most research on early communication examines small fragments of this technology and reveals more questions than answers. As teachers of the moderately and severely handicapped, you may rely upon this current technology to guide your efforts in the instruction of functional communication systems; however, you must be ready to incorporate programmatic changes as research untangles the many remaining issues of language acquisition and generalization.

References

Bricker, D., Dennison, L., & Bricker, W. A. A language intervention program for developmentally young children. *Mailman Center for Child Development Monograph Series, 1976, No. 1,* Miami, Fla.: University of Miami.

Bricker, D., Ruder, K., & Vincent-Smith, L. An intervention strategy for language deficient children. In N. Haring & R. Schiefelbusch (Eds.), *Teaching special children.* New York: McGraw-Hill, 1976.

Guess, D., Sailor, W., & Baer, D. M. *Functional speech and language training for the severely handicapped, Part I.* Lawrence, Kan.: H & H Enterprises, 1976. (a)

Guess, D., Sailor, W., & Baer, D. M. *Functional speech and language training for severely handicapped, Part II.* Lawrence, Kan.: H & H Enterprises, 1976. (b)

Harris-Vanderheiden, D., & Vanderheiden, G. C. Basic considerations in the development of communicative and interactive skills for nonvocal severely handicapped children. In E. Sontag, J. Smith, & N. Certo (Eds.), *Educational programming for the severely and profoundly handicapped.* Reston, Va.: Council for Exceptional Children, 1977.

Parton, D. A. Learning to imitate in infancy. *Child Development, 1976, 47,* 14–31.

Stremel-Campbell, K., Cantrell, D., & Halle, J. Manual signing as a language system and as a speech initiator for the non-verbal severely handicapped student. In E. Sontag, J. Smith, & N. Certo (Eds.), *Educational programming for the severely and profoundly handicapped.* Reston, Va.: Council for Exceptional Children, 1977.

Training Prerequisites to Verbal Behavior

*This chapter was written by **Diane Bricker** and **Laura Dennison,** of the Mailman Center for Child Development, University of Miami. Support for this chapter comes in part from Grant No. OE G0075 021220 to the University of Miami from the Department of HEW, USOE, Bureau for the Education of the Handicapped; Contract No. 300–75–0306 with the University of Miami from the Department of HEW, USOE, Bureau for the Education of the Handicapped; and the Mailman Foundation.*

*Portions of this chapter were taken from **Bricker, D., Dennison, L. & Bricker, W. A.** A language intervention program for developmentally young children. Mailman Center for Child Development Monograph Series, 1976, No. 1, Miami, Fla.: University of Miami.*

This chapter has been written for a target audience of direct interventionists. The term "teacher" has not been used because traditionally this label has excluded from its professional domain parents, daycare workers, and others who do not have a specific form of certification. This chapter is directed to any professional, paraprofessional, parent, or student who is involved in the direct application of a language program to the developmentally young. The developmentally young refers to two specific populations: young children who are significantly delayed in acquiring early forms of behavior necessary for the acquisition of language and older severely/profoundly handicapped children who have multiple problems that hinder their acquisition of necessary sensorimotor prerequisites for language.

Although the major emphasis of this chapter is on the application of the suggested training approach, introductory sections have been included which discuss the rationale for our approach. The focus of the sections on the acquisition of sensorimotor and early language behavior and on the developmental approach which underlies this training program have remained pragmatic and, therefore, do not include a discussion of the arguments and controversies surrounding the advancement of any theory or position which lacks complete empirical support. For those readers interested in pursuing more theoretical discussions of psycholinguistic theory and child development, we recommend the following sources: Piaget (1952), Hunt (1961), Reese and Lipsett (1970), Skinner (1957), Edmonds (1976), Dale (1976), Bowerman (1973), Chomsky (1975), Brown (1973), and Slobin (1971).

Language deficits or disorders appear to be one of the major handicapping conditions associated with mental retardation (Bricker & Bricker, 1974; Schiefelbusch, Copeland, & Smith, 1967). One would undoubtedly have difficulty finding a child or adult who has been labeled severely mentally retarded who does not provide overt evidence of a language problem. We agree with the position that severe mental retardation can be described in terms of language difficulties; however, we would expand this position to suggest the basic deficit may be in the underlying cognitive structures. In our opinion, basic cognitive structures or sensorimotor intelligence forms the foundation for the development of a generative language system. For the severly impaired child, language dysfunctions do not begin at age 18 to 24 months when most children develop expressive language but rather we believe that language problems arise because the child has failed to develop the prerequisite sensorimotor behavior. If this assumption is accurate, language training for the severely/profoundly handicapped child should be preceded by insuring the development of basic sensorimotor skills.

From the writings of Piaget (1952), Bricker and Bricker (1974), and psycholinguists such as Bloom and Lahey (1976), we believe the development and use of a symbolic system such as language is predicated on the acquisition of an entire array of prerequisite behaviors which develop during the sensorimotor period. For this reason the focus of this chapter will be on the description of a training program for developing those skills thought to be prerequisites for the comprehension and production of a formal language system.

Acquisition of Sensorimotor and Early Language Behavior

Over the years, our exposure to the direct interventionists working with handicapped children has suggested that information about normal growth patterns and skill acquisition is incomplete and often inaccurate. For this reason, we have included a section outlining the development of behavior during the early sensorimotor period and the "normal" pattern of language acquisition.

Sensorimotor development

Most babies arrive in the world with reflexive behavior that allows them to emit a variety of simple motor movements, such as sucking, startling, crying, and breathing. In the normal infant, certain environmental events appear to produce relatively consistent forms of reflexive behavior. For example, a loud noise or sudden bright light often produces a startle reflex, stimulation of the lips produces a rooting or

sucking response. As the infant exercises specific reflexes in response to certain general categories of antecedent events, this activity often produces other interesting or comforting environmental events. For example, stimulation of the lips produces the sucking reflex, which, in turn, may result in the attainment of nutriment, usually a very pleasureable event. If the bottle or breast or stimulus which produced the sucking is removed, the newborn infant will cease sucking. The event which elicited the behavior, lip stimulation, is no longer present. As the infant interacts with the environment, reflexive behaviors apparently begin to change form. For example, if a child has frequent experience with bright lights and loud noises, the startle reflex diminishes. The sucking reflex, however, undergoes topographical changes as the child has the opportunity to practice sucking. At first the infant learns to adapt the sucking response to different nipples and later nonnutritive sucking and mouthing develop as a means to explore objects rather than to ingest food.

During the first month of life, the infant begins to "learn" that continuation of an activity which was initially elicited by some stimulus will often reinstate the event. For example, continuing to suck or actively searching for the nipple following removal of the breast or bottle (the eliciting stimulus) often produces the pleasurable event again. Piaget has called this stage of development, which stems from reflexive behavior, primary circular reactions. During this stage, the child is learning to repeat actions which brought about or produced interesting or desirable consequences; his activity is no longer necessarily preceded by the stimulus, which at one time elicited the reflexive behavior. In the normally developing infant, primary circular reactions generally begin between the first and fourth month.

As the infant gains more experience with the environment, more control is gradually acquired over movements. For example, if the child accidentally swats a mobile and the motion of the mobile is interesting, he will attempt to repeat the action to reproduce the interesting event. At first this repeated activity may be quite imprecise, but with practice the child's movement becomes more directed and leads to the development of secondary circular reactions—an amalgamation of earlier development movement patterns which are self-reinforcing and therefore tend to be repeated over and over by the child. During this stage of development, the child is learning to discriminate between objects and events. The infant learns that a particular object (the mobile) will produce a consequence (movement) in response to a particular behavior (swatting). The infant is also beginning to anticipate events in the environment. For instance, the sight of an object arouses the child to activity.

As the infant develops a number of secondary circular reactions, he begins to coordinate these responses. This coordination of secondary circular reactions begins in a normally developing infant at about ten months. Now, instead of *accidentally discovering* an interesting event, the child *actively initiates* behavior at the sight of the object. Using the mobility which most children have learned by this age, a child will coordinate crawling behavior with grasping behavior when a visible desired object is out of reach. That is, the child will creep across the room in order to acquire the desired toy. Such coordination of action schemes is an important milestone because the child is beginning to initiate "purposeful" activity. Activities are no longer constrained by single responses; now a series of moves is coordinated to act differentially on the environment. The child learns to combine activities not previously combined, such as swatting at the mobile and then pulling on it as well as trying out "old" activities, such as swatting with objects never swatted before, such as a ball or a string of beads. Consequences of actions lead the child to prefer specific actions with certain objects; for example, the child learns that the event which occurs after he pushes a ball (i.e., the ball rolls) is much more interesting than the event which occurs after he pushes a string of beads (i.e., the beads don't roll). However, another activity such as shaking produces more interesting consequences with the beads than with the ball.

Consistently using specific action schemes with certain objects is one of the first indications that an infant is learning to classify objects, events, and people—an essential prerequisite to language. The child is also learning that the intensity of actions produces differing intensities of events. Shaking the beads vigorously may make a louder noise than when they are shaken with less vigor. As the child discovers relationships between actions and results, he begins to search for "novelty." He will interact with objects in an "experimental" fashion, using new and different actions with a variety of objects and people. For example, the child may throw the beads and watch where they land, then retrieve them, only to drop them slowly, bead by bead, to the floor. Piaget (1952) describes these behaviors as tertiary circular reactions, and they be-

gin to occur in the normally developing infant at about the twelfth month. During this period most children are satiated by known events and actively search for novelty in order to test and expand their existing repertoires.

The final stage of the sensorimotor period Piaget has termed the "intervention of new means through mental combinations." In this stage, the child is apparently beginning to engage in internal manipulation of environmental events rather than having to physically manipulate his environment to produce the effect. In other words, he can anticipate the effect of his actions without having to actually perform the activity. At this stage of development, the child has developed an astonishing repertoire of movements and discriminated relationships which allow him to solve new problems, search for lost objects, anticipate events, and seek interesting activity in his environment. This stage is viewed as a natural outgrowth of the previous five stages and provides the basis for the development of a representational system such as language.

In summary, Piaget has described six stages of development in the first two years of life; These stages do not follow static, rigid, developmental formats; the child's repertoire changes through a gradual acquisition of more complex behaviors which the child constructs through further interaction of simpler response forms with the environment. Early sensorimotor behavior provides the basis for understanding the physical environment and forms the underlying structure for the acquisition of language.

Language development

During the first few months of an infant's life, the vocal behavior produced is not like speech but is composed primarily of vowel-like sounds (Oller, Note 1, 1975). The infant seems to be learning to operate his sound production mechanism, and at this stage can often produce noises and sounds that an adult has difficulty imitating. Early sound production indicates that the infant has learned quickly to differentiate vocal activity into "pleasurable" (i.e., cooing) and "distressful" (i.e., crying) vocalizations. At this early age, the infant has also learned to differentiate some environmental sounds. For example, an adult talking to an infant using adult-like speech patterns will rarely elicit any vocal activity from the infant; however, when the adult imitates the child's vocalizations, by cooing and engaging in infant-like speech patterns, the infant will often smile, engage in eye contact, and increase his own mouth movements (Uzgiris & Hunt, 1975).

Other behaviors which appear to be necessary for later language acquisition begin to develop at this early age. The infant learns to attend to objects in his environment and will gaze at them for long periods of time. He learns to shift his gaze from one object to another and will even turn his head to bring an object into view. Around the fourth month of life, the infant begins to vocalize when he hears sounds which are similar to those he is producing. Although this is not imitation, as generally defined, such responses indicate the child is differentiating among environmental sounds. The infant is also learning to localize sound sources at this stage and will turn his head and look in the direction of the sound. Another indication that the child is becoming aware of particular aspects of his environment is the tendency to engage in a body movement similar to the adult's. Although not technically imitation because of the gross and seemingly uncoordinated movements of the infant, the regularity of each activity suggests initial attempts by the infant at reproducing the adult's activity. For example, if an adult waves or moves an arm, the infant, if watching, will often move his arm (Uzgiris & Hunt, 1975).

At this stage, the child uses fairly predictable action schemes to interact with objects. He will mouth, wave, and bang objects. He soon learns to prefer some activities with certain objects. Such activity indicates that a child is learning to discriminate among objects, a task which is necessary for the later naming of objects. The child also begins to examine objects closely, turning them over in his hands, feeling their surface, and manipulating wheels, levers, and projections on the object.

At 7–10 months, most babies becomes adept at vocalizing the same sounds repeatedly. This frequent form of elementary vocal behavior has been termed reduplicated, canonical babbling (Oller, Note 1, 1975). Reduplicated babbling consists of producing similar speech-like sound sequences such as "ba-ba-ba," "ma-ma-ma," or "pa-pa-pa."

Although the relevancy of babbling to formal linguistic behavior remains disputed, Bricker, Ruder, and Vincent-Smith (1976) have pointed out:

Babbling provides the opportunity for most children to acquire several skills. First, the child learns to develop more precise control over his articulators. Second, the environment generally responds favorably to the child's babbling. If babbling occurs at the appropriate stage of de-

velopment, the child is encouraged to continue to produce sounds which more closely approximate those sounds most often used in his language or those which produce the greatest effect in his social environment. For example, "mama" is one of the first consistent sounds emitted by many babies. In most cases it originates in the early babbling behavior of the infant. That particular sound is more apt to get the mother's attention than other sound combinations. The responsiveness of a mother to "mama" leads to more frequent and consistent use. This transaction is an example of the initial stages of the child using verbal behavior to manipulate his social environment. Babbling serves an important function in the language-acquisition process and should be viewed as a behavior to be encouraged. (pp. 304–305)

By the ninth month, the child has learned to differentiate these babbling sounds as evidenced by his ability to imitate an adult with the accurate sequence when the adult provides a model within the child's repertoire.

The child is also developing more of an "object sense" at this stage and is able to look for an object which someone hides from his view. Such behavior indicates that the child recognizes the object's existence even though it is not visible. In other words, he has an internal image to "represent" the object. As mentioned above, language is a representational system, which is noted here to point out the importance of acquiring necessary prerequisite skills such as object constancy.

At about the seventh month, a child learns to imitate accurately a gesture which is already in his repertoire, and by the ninth month he will attempt to imitate a new movement which an adult may model. Also, at about the ninth month, the child begins to show evidence of beginning receptive language. Dale (1976) reports a study by Greenfield in which a child looked at the father when the experimenter used the sound sequence "dada." In the absence of the father, the child would look at the mother. Dale explains that the characteristic feature of "dada" seemed to be "caretaker." A few weeks later, the child would look at the mother when "mama" was spoken and at the father when "dada" was uttered.

By about the tenth or eleventh month, the child's babbling has acquired many aspects of adult inflection. The force, quality, and pitch characteristics of vocal behavior are called prosodic features, and acquisition of early forms of prosodic features coincides developmentally with the acquisition of speech sounds (Reese & Lipsitt, 1970). In a general sense, prosodic features can be described as the "melody" of language, while the content of words are the "lyrics." Ruder and Smith (1974) suggest that the production of prosodic features seem to be such a basic behavior that children, beginning with the acquisition of their first words to the time they are producing adult-like sentences, utilize subtle features of inflection as part of their communicative behavior.

By the tenth and eleventh months, most children have become facile imitators. They imitate gestures which are novel if they can view the activity while doing it. For example, a child may be able to imitate touching his index fingers together but might have difficulty imitating pulling on his earlobe or touching his index finger to his forehead. Vocally, he will repeat and sound already within his repertoire, but he still cannot usually imitate a novel sound, nor attempt to approximate that sound.

The child's receptive language skills become more demonstrable immediately prior to the first year. He will stop and turn when his name is called, will cease activity when an adult says "no," and will often produce simple gestures when an adult makes a familiar request, such as "Wave bye-bye," or "Do you want to play patty-cake?" His "object sense" has improved and he has learned to search systematically for an object which he has lost from view. The child is beginning to discover the social meaning which his culture attaches to objects. For example, he will pick up a toy telephone (and sometimes a real one!) and babble into the receiver. He has learned to hug a doll, push a toy car, and bang happily with a toy hammer. This sophisticated interaction with objects indicates that he is becoming an active participant in the social network which surrounds him and that he is actively attending to the behavior of others in his environment.

Although most children have been producing a variety of sounds during their first year of life, it is not until the second year that the first real words are generally acquired. Between 12 and 15 months most babies begin producing consistent sound patterns (words) to indicate objects, persons, and/or animals. The study of first-word acquisition suggests that toddlers use their earliest labels or names to refer to objects in environmental contexts (Nelson, 1974). That is, the name appears to include events or functions related to the object rather than only the specific object. For example, the young child may have had many different interactions and associations with the family pet such as romping, being licked, watching the dog eat and sleep, or poking its eyes. Many or all of these activities or functions may be included in the child's developing concept underlying the word, "Fido." Objects or, in this case, animals appear to be conceptualized in the context of familiar environmental happenings and therefore, for the child, the label may refer as well to all those associated activities. The child may say "Fido" while pointing to the dog drinking out of his water bowl or when seeing the dog sleep. It is not that the child cannot discriminate the dog from his bowl or the bowl from the dog's bed, it is rather that all of these activities and objects are included in the child's concept of "Fido." It is our view as well as that of others (Nelson, 1974) that words are mapped on underlying concepts and therefore the development of such early concepts are prerequisites to first-word production.

By 20 to 40 months most young children have developed an impressive receptive vocabulary and have acquired the names for many objects, individuals, and activities. At about this time most children begin combining words. Producing two-word utterances is generally considered to be the initial stage of grammatical or syntactic development. Consistent sequencing of words implies that the child has developed a rudimentary organizational system that functions by using rules. These rules enable a child to convey his intentions in such a way as to be understood by members of his language community. Bellugi (1972) and others have argued convincingly that young children do produce sentences on the basis of generative rules. That is, children learn that classes of words are sequenced following some systematic patterns rather than randomly strung together.

Most initial two-word combinations produced by young children can be classified as representing a variety of semantic relations such as recurrence, nonexistence, location, possession, agent-action, action-object, or agent-object (Brown, 1973). "Doggie sit," for instance, represents the semantic relation of an agent (doggie) and an action (sit) whereas the two-word sequence "eat banana" suggests an action-object relationship. The child may also use two-word strings to communicate the more complex semantic relation of agent-action-object but such relationships can only be inferred from the context in which the verbalization occurs. For example, after throwing a ball a child may utter either "throw ball" or "me throw." The first verbalization is clearly an action-object statement, but he may understand the semantic relation between the agent (himself), the action (throw), and the object (ball) even though he did not express the agent. In the second example, he did not express the semantic relation between the agent-action and the object, although he may have understood this relationship. Thus, in two-word utterances the child utilizes structures which reflect the underlying semantic relations of an agent, an action, and an object (relationships among three discrete semantic/grammatical functions) while still limited to productions of no more than two words in length. Bloom (1972), Bowerman (1973), and Brown (1973) have described these early two-word strings as also expressing such underlying semantic relations as possession ("my dog"), re-occurrence ("more milk"), location ("ball here"), and negation ("no drink"). When the child begins producing three-word constructions, the functions previously expressed in two-word strings, such as the "play boat" example, now appear in three-word strings such as "boy play boat."

A child's linguistic competence appears to grow by the inclusion of new elements or the modification of the basic kernel phase structure (Bricker, Ruder, & Vincent-Smith, 1976). These new elements include prepositions, modifiers, and articles which serve to enrich and give further precision to the child's communication functions. The acquisition of basic language structures is accomplished in an amazingly short time by most children. Such a feat tends to produce great respect for the capacity of the "normal" human organism. Viewed from this perspective, the challenge of assisting children who do not develop language can leave one doubting our ability to produce an artificial training sequence that must account for the developing of an awesome array of skills. However, *not* trying relegates a significant number of children to growing up in a world where communication is absent.

General Training Procedures

Target population

The target population for this training program is the developmentally young individual, which includes two distinct groups: the infant or young child who gives evidence of significant developmental problems early in life and the older child whose impairments have severely restricted the acquisition of even primitive responses. The format and structure of this program should be appropriate for both

groups. However, the specific training activities may need modification based on the child's experiential background, handicapping conditions, and motivational system.

Target behavior

The goal of a language curriculum should be the development of a generative language system, which means that the communicative system is not restricted to the specific language behaviors which have been trained but rather is generalized to new and different environments based on the acquisition of a set of rules. The focus of this program, however, is on the development of behaviors which are necessary prerequisites to the development of formal language. We have chosen to present this aspect of language training because it is too often ignored in many classroom language curricula being used with the developmentally young. The following goals established for this program should be viewed as initial steps in the movement toward the production and comprehension of meaningful, grammatical sentences. The four major objectives of this program are as follows:

1. On-task behavior
   Definition: Child can consistently focus attention on selected tasks for a reasonable, predetermined time period.
2. Imitation
   Definition: Child can reproduce vocal sounds and gestures produced by a model.
3. Discriminative use of objects
   Definition: Child can carry out activities with objects generally considered relevant to the characteristics of an object (e.g., pound with a hammer, eat with a spoon).
4. Word recognition
   Definition: Child can associate meaningful auditory signals with appropriate events.

To reach each of the above four objectives a sequence of training steps has been developed. These steps and the suggested training sequence are contained in Figure 5.1. This program can be initiated using one of three strategies depending upon the child's repertoire prior to the initiation of training. For older children who present control problems, we recommend beginning by training the child to sit in a chair. With older children who are able to work on tasks, we suggest beginning by training imitation. Finally, with the developmentally young child or infant, begin with strategies to increase vocalization. Read through the entire pro-

ON-TASK
BEHAVIOR

IMITATION

DISCRIMINATIVE
USE OF OBJECTS

WORD
RECOGNITION

FORMAL
LANGUAGE

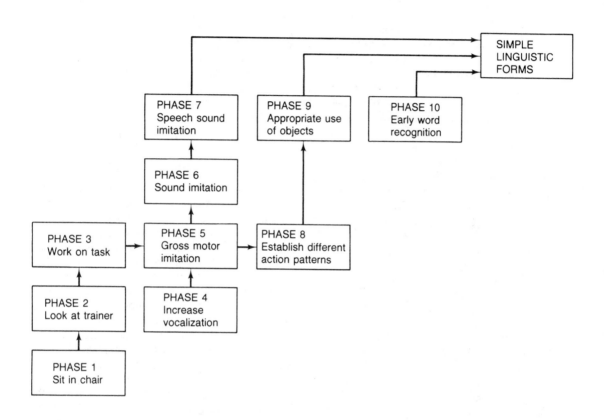

FIGURE 5.1   *Sequence of training steps*

gram and examine the child's entry skills before establishing that sequence which would be appropriate for the child or children to be trained.

If training is begun by teaching the child to sit in a chair, the next step or target is to look at the interventionist on command. Once this is accomplished, increasing the duration of working on task becomes the focus of training. For many children gross motor imitation can be used as the selected training task; for others, simple manipulation of an object may be more appropriate. When the child can consistently imitate simple gross motor movements, training shifts to vocal imitation, although with some children vocal imitation can be trained simultaneously with motor imitation. While working on vocal imitation, the child can also be exposed to training procedures to establish different action patterns with objects. The final phases of the program include early word recognition, appropriate use of objects, and speech sound imitation. A child who reaches criterion on these skills is ready to begin training on formal linguistic skills and is referred on to a training program such as the one described by Bricker, Ruder, and Vincent-Smith (1976) and Bricker, Dennison, and Bricker (1976).

General programmatic procedures

Several important points should be remembered and used throughout this training program. First, the child's general functioning level must be determined before beginning training. Observations of the child in the classroom or at home as well as the use of adaptive or behavioral measures will assist in ascertaining this form of general evaluation. Second, once you have established the child's general level of functioning, you need to assess specific behaviors in order to determine precisely where to begin training. A suggested assessment format is specified for each training step in this program. The use of such assessments before training and periodically throughout training helps to establish the child's level of functioning before and during intervention. If a child's repertoire is unknown in a specific area, evaluation of developmental progress as a result of training is impossible. Third, the behaviors which are assessed and targeted for training must be carefully selected and defined. For example, in assessing the amount of a child's vocalizing, define precisely those responses to be counted. Do you mean crying? Does whining count as a vocalization? The more specifically defined a behavior, the more accurate the assessment is likely to be. Fourth, specify the length of the training sessions and the number of trials to be presented each session. The number of trials per session should be relatively constant across time. The time of the day in which the assessment is given may also be important. A child's behavior may vary widely over the day; therefore, indication of when an assessment was done may be useful. Assessments which are given on a periodic basis throughout training are called "probes." Each probe should be given individually without the use of cues, prompts, or assistance (unless carefully specified) in order to determine more objectively the child's progress. Fifth, always consider the importance of generalizing the skills the child has learned in a specified training situation to a broad range of objects, environments, and people. For example, if a child learns to use a particular cup appropriately, this functional activity should occur with all types of cups the child may encounter from time to time. Finally, whenever possible, we suggest training children in small groups. Group training allows children to provide stimulation for one another, generally fosters more efficient use of a direct interventionist's time, and approximates natural learning environments more closely (Brown, Nietupski, & Hamre-Nietupski, 1976).

Training throughout this program is based on a developmental approach which means that more difficult skills are built upon the attainment of simpler skills. Most behavior is acquired in a developmental pattern in which simple basic skills are modified into more complex response forms. For example, it appears that a child must learn to vocalize before producing words or to produce single words before producing word strings or sentences. Consequently, we believe that it is essential for a child to master the necessary prerequisite processes before training on a more difficult skill. Fol-

lowing the developmental sequence outlined in this program should result in the child's systematically acquiring an increasingly complex repertoire.

This training program is designed to encourage a flexible and generative environment for language training. It is important to read and understand the development of sensorimotor and language behavior outlined earlier in this chapter and in Chapter 4 in order to develop the necessary flexibility in setting criterion performance levels, establishing training environments, and selecting training stimuli.

Training Program

Section 1:   On task behavior

In this program "on-task behavior" refers to any behavior or constellation of behaviors that will facilitate the acquisition of a new response or modification of an existing response. For example, if an interventionist is attempting to teach motor imitation, it is essential that the child sit quietly and look at the trainer. An attempt to teach any response to a child who is running around the room and refusing to focus on the teacher or training materials is a difficult educational situation at best. Many older handicapped children who do not have motor impairments have learned that disruptive behaviors such as throwing training materials or closing their eyes will quickly end the training situation. This section of the program is geared primarily to this population of children. The articulation of such procedures have been included here because we believe that every direct interventionist has the responsibility to develop on-task behavior if it is not in the child's repertoire when training is begun.

The procedures described in this section are designed to enable the child to attend to the interventionist and to engage in behaviors which will facilitate the process of learning language. These responses include: (A) sitting quietly for a reasonable period of time, (B) looking at the interventionist when appropriate, and (C) working on a specific task.

As stated earlier, before establishing specific training criteria, the developmental level of the child must be considered. Expecting a child who is very young developmentally to sit in a chair and attend to a task for 10 minutes is unrealistic; however, such responses are appropriate for a child who is more sophisticated cognitively and physically. Therefore, the length of time established for criterion behavior will vary with respect to the child's general developmental level. The training location may also vary as a function of the child's entry behavior. A child who is quite young developmentally might begin training cradled in your lap. A mobile, active child may begin training seated on the floor if that position is more appropriate initially.

Once you have established appropriate training targets, take a baseline measure on these responses. A baseline measure means that a consistent rate of the behavior is recorded. The child who remains seated for 10 minutes in a 10-minute training period on day 1, 59 seconds on day 2, and 4 minutes on day 3 is not presenting a stable rate of behavior. Collection of baseline data *should* be continued until a stable rate of activity is recorded. However, this rule, like most rules, has exceptions. If the child's rate of behavior does not stabilize but the general trend indicates the need for training in a specific area, the interventionist is probably advised to begin intervention.

As you read through the following sections, formulate your objectives for the child based on your knowledge of his developmental level and the particular training situation which would be most appropriate. Establish your criterion behavior by specifying the task, the time period, and the location.

Phase 1: Sit in Chair

Teaching a child to sit quietly in a chair can be approached in several different ways; however, we have found the procedure outlined below generally to be effective. Locate an appropriate table, chair, and a few toys you feel certain the child enjoys manipulating. Show the child the toy on the table and then seat him so he can reach the toy. Conduct

several sessions so the child becomes accustomed to playing at the table while sitting in a chair. During these sessions, collect baseline data by noting on a form similar to the one found in Table 5.1 the length of time the child remains seated and any other information you feel is relevant. Once you have a consistent estimate of the child's behavior in this situation, begin to intervene if the child does not remain seated for the time period you have targeted as the criterion level.

Seat the child in a chair and begin an activity which requires some response the child is capable of emitting and seems to enjoy. When he has engaged in this activity for a short period of time, allow him to play with a favorite toy. With each session gradually increase the length of time that you interact with the child while he is sitting in the chair but end the session by letting him play with a toy. Start out with just one- or two-minute sessions. There are many games you can play to encourage sitting. For example, you can play "point to your tummy, point to your toes" which is much easier to do while sitting in the chair. You can play pushing a truck or car across a table and through a box with holes cut in either side. Whatever games you chose, it is important to be certain the child is interested.

Some children may be extremely resistant to sitting in a chair. With difficult-to-control children, you may have to use some mild physical restraint. If you decide restraint is in order, we suggest the following procedure. Pick a moment when the child is being cooperative. Try to be positive by taking him to a table and chair and playing with him while he is sitting. If he attempts to get up, remove the toys from the table, and gently restrain him from leaving.

TABLE 5.1 *Sample recording form for phases 1, 3, and 4*

Total Time	Seconds of Desired Response Produced by Child	Comments
1.		
2.		
3.		
4.		
5.		
6.		
7.		
8.		

As his activity subsides, tell the child he is sitting nicely and gradually withdraw your restraint. Return the toys to the table and let the child play with them while seated in the chair. It may happen that you and the child get into a "chair battle." If this occurs, remember that the major aim of this phase is to get the child seated so that language training is facilitated. Therefore, you might shift language training to the floor if the child will sit quietly there and train chair sitting at a later date.

After a specific number of training sessions, administer a probe on the number of seconds the child remains in the chair and compare it with the data from the baseline period. If the data show the child is consistently sitting for the time period you have established as criterion (e.g., 5 to 10 minutes depending upon the individual's developmental level), move to the next training step. If the information indicates the child still is not remaining seated for the established time period, examine modifications in training that might prove more successful. For example, try some different toys or perhaps a glass of juice.

Phase 2: Look at Trainer

Now that the child is able to remain seated in the chair, the next step is to teach him to look at you on command. This is an important prerequisite skill for later in the program when gross motor imitation and vocal imitation are to be trained.

First obtain some objective evidence about the child's ability to look at you when asked. Seat the child and say, "Look at me." Do this for a predetermined number of times, recording the child's response each time on a form similar to the one found in Table 5.2. If the child does not look at you when asked in at least 75% of the instances, begin intervention training.

Take the child's face between your hands and direct his face toward yours. If the child gives you even the most fleeting glance, reward him. Gradually lessen the prompts and reward the child for longer and longer gazes. Talk to the child while you are looking at each other.

If the child does not look at you following your verbal command or physical prompting, another method of attracting his attention should be used. For example, hold a toy which interests the child close to your eyes while saying, "Look at me." If he looks at the toy or your face, reinforce this by giving him the toy. Continue this procedure, varying the toys, until the child will look at your face immediately upon request. Gradually decrease the number of times the toy is used to establish facial contact.

TABLE 5.2   *Sample recording form for phases 2, 5, 6, 7, 8, and 9*

Training Target or Model	Child's Response		
	Appropriate	Inappropriate	Approximation
1.			
2.			
3.			
4.			
5.			
6.			
7.			
8.			
9.			
10.			
11.			
12.			
13.			

After a specific number of training sessions, test the child's ability to look at you on command and compare the results with his baseline performance. If the child is able to look at you following your request at least 75% of the time, move on to the next phase.

Phase 3: Work on Task

Before assessment, determine how many minutes or seconds in a set period of time you will consider an acceptable demonstration of on-task behavior; next, choose the task. Training imitation of simple motor actions such as ringing a bell is one class of responses we suggest for shaping "on-task" behavior. You may wish to choose a different motor action for imitation or a different task entirely, such as water play. Use a form like that found in Table 5.1 to describe objectively how many minutes or seconds the child engages in on-task behavior before any intervention is initiated. If the child does not meet the criterion level established prior to assessment, begin training. If you are using motor imitation as the activity, take the child to his seat, tell him to look at you, then do some action which is fun and easy, such as ringing a bell while saying, "Do this." If the child does not imitate, physically prompt his bell-ringing. Repeat this process, gradually diminishing your prompts and always praising the child when he rings the bell. Remember that your goal is *not* imitation but working on a task for a predetermined period of time. This phase is more demanding than Phase 1 in that the child must be attending to the task. In the earlier phase, the child was required only to remain seated. This phase can be difficult to document for the interventionist, in that there must be a specific definition of what is meant by "on-task" and "off-task" behavior. For example, if a child looks away from the task when someone enters the room, is this off-task behavior? Realistically it should probably not be counted as off-task behavior. To resolve this dilemma you may want to count both off-task and on-task behavior. In this manner, the child would not be penalized for appropriately looking away from the task occasionally.

Changing the activity frequently helps some children to stay on task. For others, changing from one activity to the next can cause disruption. You know the child best, place him in the most optimal situation initially, and gradually increase the difficulty of the task.

After a predetermined number of training sessions, re-administer a probe. If the child is able to perform at the criterion level, go on to Section 2.

Section 2:   Imitation

Imitation refers to the child's ability to copy or reproduce the actions or sounds of a model. Specifically, "verbal imitation" means the child is able to imitate a vocal sound produced by another source. Verbal imitation can range from the imitation of a single sound such as /a/ to imitation of a sequence of words. Table 5.3 contains a list of the major sounds used in English which fall into three major categories: consonants, vowels, and diphthongs.

TABLE 5.3   *Major phonemes in English*

Categories	Phonemes					
Consonants	/b/	by	/ʰ/	ball	/t/	to
	/d/	do	/m/	me	/tʃ/	chew
	/f/	fine	/n/	no	/θ/	thin
	/g/	go	/ŋ/	sing	/ð/	they
	/h/	he	/p/	pie	/v/	vine
	/j/	yes	/r/	rip	/w/	we
	/k/	key	/s/	sip	/ʍ/	which
	/l/	lip	/ʃ/	she	/z/	zip
			/j/	yes	/ʒ/	measure
Vowels	/ɝ/	burnt	/a/	ask	/o/	oval
	/ə/	sofa	/ɑ/	calm	/U/	cook
	/ɛ/	bet	/æ/	bat	/u/	cool
	/I/	bit	/e/	vacate	/ʌ/	cut
	/i/	beet	/ɚ/	mother	/ə/	jaw
Diphthongs	/eI/	late	/aU/	how	/ju/	you
	/aI/	dine	/ɔI/	boil	/oU/	soap

The major thrust of this program is on training consonants or consonant-vowel combinations. Table 5.4 presents the difficulty levels for imitating the different English consonants.

For the language-handicapped child, imitation, both gestural and verbal, is an important training tool and, once acquired, will be used extensively as a means of evoking and improving the target behaviors throughout this training program. The tasks to be imitated in the earlier training phases are simpler responses than the tasks to be imitated in the later training phases. For children who already imitate, you need not be concerned with this portion of the program and can move on to training in the discriminative use of objects and early word recognition.

Phase 4:   Increase Vocalization

Initially an infant or child who does not talk may make only a small variety of sounds. He may cry, whimper, cough, or make little noises with his throat and mouth. He is learning to exercise the muscles he later will use for talking. Therefore, in this phase the primary objective is to get the oral muscle complex working by increasing the number of vocalizations in general and the throat and mouth noises in particular.

Taking a baseline on the number of times a child vocalizes during a certain period of the day is necessary before attempting to increase the number of vocalizations. First, identify the time of day during which the child seems to vocalize most often. Some children seem to vocalize more in the mornings, others are more vocal in the afternoon. Second, specify exactly what you will be counting as a vocalization. For example, with some children you may be counting grunts and whines; other children may have vowel sounds targeted for measurement. Third, schedule a block of time and count the number of vocalizations which occur during this period. Record your information on a probe sheet similar to the one found in Table 5.1. Do this until a consistent pattern emerges. This procedure will give a rough estimate of the average number of vocalizations that occur during the given time period. Fourth, set your criterion level or goal for the child in terms of the number of vocalizations per minute or hour.

Now you can begin your intervention. Start by attending to any appropriate vocalizations which the child produces. Do this by imitating the child's vocalizations or by coming to him when he vocalizes; however, it is not necessary to drop what you are doing and rush over to the child when you hear him make noises. You can simply answer his vocaliza-

TABLE 5.4   *Consonantal imitation in order of increasing difficulty*

Level	Consonant	Representative Word
1	b	boy
	w	way
	m	man
	t	toy
	d	dog
2	h	hut
	n	no
	k	cut
	p	pipe
3	g	go
	s	see
	f	fat
	dʒ	judge
4	ʃ	shoe
	r	run
	l	lump
	tʃ	church
	z	zoo
5	ʒ	measure
	ð	that
	θ	thin
	v	vest
	j	yellow
	ŋ	sing

According to Bricker, 1967.
Source: Bricker, 1967.

tions by imitating him from wherever you happen to be.

Try to increase the child's opportunity to vocalize. Schedule special training periods in which concentrated efforts are made to evoke vocal responses from the child. Make the situation as pleasant as possible for the child since making noises and sounds should be an enjoyable experience. Good times for these training periods are those that are part of the child's normal routine, such as mealtime, diaper-changing time, and just before or after naptime. Physical stimulation seems to be an important aspect of increasing vocalizations. By increasing the child's activity levels through physical stimulation, the number of vocalizations seems to increase. By "physical stimulation," we mean "rough housing," rolling on the bed or floor, tossing the child in the air, swinging, tickling, and other activities which involve a lot of action.

While you are engaged in these activities, make cooing or babbling sounds. These vocalizations may stimulate the child to make "happy" vocalizations, such as laughing and cooing. His vocalizations can then be rewarded with more tickling, touching, or rough housing. Repeat the sounds the child makes, as sometimes this will stimulate him to make the sound again. Occasionally he will become quiet and just watch you making the noises. The establishment of eye contact here is important for later verbal imitation training.

Additional training sessions can be arranged in which you sit with the child on your lap. Physical stimulation such as rocking or swinging will often evoke vocalizations from the child which can be reinforced by repetition of his sounds and additional rocking or swinging. You might place the child near a record player or radio which may prompt the child to make sounds. Some children seem to vocalize more when they hear music or other speech sounds. You can use other times during the day to talk to the child and to reinforce all vocalizations that occur spontaneously. Always keep in mind that during this part of the program, or any other part, the activities suggested as possible rewards or reinforcers may not be appropriate for a particular child. An activity or object is only a reinforcer if it produces an acceleration or increase in a form of behavior. What "turns one child on" simply may not appeal to another. Also keep in mind that if a bright red ball produces good results on Monday, it might have no effect on Tuesday. Do not persist with training materials or presumed rewards that have no interest for the child. Be watchful for changes in the child's motivational state and shift the activities and materials as necessary.

In this phase, as in all other phases, you should schedule regular probe periods. Compare the number of vocalizations produced during this new baseline or probe period with your criterion level which you established after the first baseline period. If the child performs at this level, move on to the next phase of training. If the child's number of vocalizations does not meet criterion levels, continue training on this phase. Don't get discouraged, but continue to evaluate what you are doing. Vary the stimuli you have been using: for example, a new mobile, a squeak toy, or a music box might provide some variation. Spending two or three days noting the number of vocalizations that occur within half-hour time blocks and the activity in which the child was engaged during vocalization. Identify those periods in which the most vocal activity occurred and note the other aspects of the environment or the activity of the child. Try to recreate these situations to increase vocalization.

When the child's vocalizations have increased to criterion level, go on to the next phase. Because the training activities for increasing vocalization seem to be important interactions in the communicative process, continue them while working on the next training phases.

Phase 5a: Gross Motor Imitation (Familiar Actions)

The child begins his imitative behaviors by attempting to copy the actions and sounds of the people around him, but he generally does this only when they are like the actions and sounds he can already make. For example, if a young child waves his arms and fists in the air and then watches an adult repeat his actions, often he will begin again to wave his arms and fists. Perhaps these repetitions are to keep the action and noise going. He may not realize that someone else is making some of the actions and sounds and he is making others because he may not have learned to differentiate his activity from other aspects of his environment. These exchanges of actions and sounds between an adult and the child are chains of events which Piaget (1962) calls "mutual imitation" and we are calling "imitation chains," specifically movement chains and vocal chains.

In the early stages of imitation, the child will respond only if he initiates the interaction and only if the gesture or sound is familiar. Later, you will be able to initiate an imitation chain, and the child will often immediately imitate you. Much later, the child will learn to imitate new activities. The first objective of this training step is to teach the child the game of movement chains. He will make a gross body movement which you imitate, and then he will make the body movement again. The movement he makes following your imitation does not have to be exactly like his first movement or your imitation. He only has to grossly approximate either one of the actions.

In order to determine whether the child needs this type of training, it will be necessary to take baseline information. Using a form similar to Table 5.2, record the child's action and his response to your imitation of those actions. Unless you have a large floor-length mirror, limit your baseline to only those actions which the child can see himself do, for example, waving hands or clapping.

Before establishing the baseline, observe the child and identify which activities you are going to imitate. Then decide what responses you will accept as appropriate, inappropriate, and approximations; and what percentage or rate of imitation you will accept as criterion performance.

To begin recording, sit or stand where the child can see you. When he demonstrates an action (which is readily observable to himself and which you have targeted for imitation), repeat his action. If he responds by performing an action which is similar to your imitation, score the response in the appropriate category. Repeat this procedure several times throughout the day or over a predetermined period of several days. If the child is feeling ill or fussy, do not administer the baseline test but wait until he is more cooperative and playful. When you have imitated the child's behavior at least 15 times, you should have a clearer picture of his ability to subsequently copy your actions. If he is capable of imitating you under these conditions about two-thirds of the time (12 out of 15 times), repeat the baseline-training sequence with you initiating the interaction using only familiar, observable actions.

Training consists of giving the child many opportunities to watch you copy his actions. When he is being fairly active, sit or stand where he can see you and repeat his actions. The child may attempt to move again, he may just watch you or he may ignore you. If you have been training for several sessions and the child does not continue his activity after your imitation, begin to prompt the action. For example, if he pats the table with his hand, imitate his activity and then take his hand and help him to pat the table again. If he resists this intervention, you may want to imitate the child as soon as he begins an activity and while he watches you. Gradually, he will learn to continue his activity so the two of you are responding simultaneously (Kauffman, Snell, & Hallahan, 1976).

You can place toys in front of a mirror to stimulate activity and then repeat the child's actions when they occur. Hanging toys or mobiles from the ceiling in front of the mirror will often encourage the child to swat at them. Place toys that roll between you and the child and help him push them, then push them back to him. Throughout training continue to assess the child's progress on a regular basis. Compare the results of your probe with the established criterion level.

When the child demonstrates criterion performance, repeat the baseline-training sequence with the trainer, rather than the child, initiating the re-

sponses. The modeled responses should be observable, familiar actions. Again keep consistent records on the child's progress toward imitation of the model-initiated familiar actions. For some children it may be appropriate to begin simultaneous training in imitation of sounds (Phase 6).

Phase 5b: Gross Motor Imitation (Unfamiliar Actions)

In this portion of the program, the child should learn to imitate actions which you may not have seen him do before but which are relatively easy to perform. Before taking a baseline of the child's ability to imitate relatively unfamiliar actions, observe him while he performs readily and frequently. Target four or five of these actions as well as three or four items from Table 5.5, which is a list of gross motor activities that can be used for imitation training. Before establishing the baseline, decide what determines a correct response for all of the items to be probed and what your criterion level will be for this assessment. On a form similar to Table 5.5, list each activity you have selected for training. Sit down with the child, demonstrate the activities one at a time, and record the child's response to each item. Discontinue the probe before the child becomes tired. Repeat this procedure over a period of 1 or 2 days until the child has had several opportunities to imitate each action. If he is not able to imitate your actions at the level set as criterion performance, begin training. If he is clearly capable of imitating your model, go on to sound imitation training.

Intervention consists of training the child to imitate your movements when you model them, even if he has never imitated these particular movements previously. Begin teaching the child some very easy movements and gradually make them more difficult. Choose a quiet area of the room for training so the child will not become distracted. Select a gross motor action which you are fairly certain the child can do, for example, clapping hands is usually fun and easy. Say to the child, "Do this," and clap your hands, then wait a few seconds to observe his response. If he gives no indication of imitating consistently over a period of time, go back to the earlier motor imitation phase. Gradually increase the difficulty of your unfamiliar models and gradually withdraw your prompts.

Encourage imitation in less-structured situations also. For example, if you ride on an elevator, have the child imitate your pushing the button. Additionally, gross motor imitation is a good group activity. The children can watch and imitate one another.

TABLE 5.5   *List of suggested gross motor activities for imitation training*

Activity	Definition of Appropriate Response
1. Ring bell	Child picks up a bell off the table or floor and shakes it so that sound is produced.
2. Beat drum	Child holds a drumstick in hand and strikes the upper surface of a drum, producing a sound.
3. Squeak toy	Child applies pressure to a small squeak toy with his hand, producing a squeaking sound.
4. Pat board	Child strikes the surface of a small smooth board with the palm of his hand, producing a thumping sound.
5. Roll ball	Child rolls a ball across a surface in such a manner that the ball maintains contact with the surface while traveling a distance of at least a foot.
6. Hands on head	Child places one or both hands on top of his head (above the ears at least).
7. Pat knees	Child hits both knees with palms of hands, striking knees at least twice.
8. Clap hands	Child strikes palms of hands together at least twice.
9. Wiggle fingers	Child holds both hands up in front of him and wiggles the fingers of his hands simultaneously.
10. Rub tummy	Child places one hand on his stomach and moves it around.
11. Blow feather	Child blows air from mouth so that feather can be observed to move while teacher holds feather for child.
12. Arms waving	Child extends both arms so that hands are over his head and moves arms back and forth.

Administer probes periodically and compare the behavior with your original criterion. When the child is able to imitate at this level, go on to the next phase which trains sound imitation and begin working simultaneously on Section 3 (appropriate use of objects).

Phase 6a: Sound Imitation (Self-Initiated)

A child appears to begin his imitative vocal behavior by attempting to copy the sounds of the people around him, but he generally does this only when they are like sounds he can already make. As the child babbles and coos, his voice begins to develop the musical and rhythmic qualities of intonation. These sounds will sometimes be quite unlike the sounds of everyday speech. This does not matter because he is learning to experiment with the different vocalizations he can make, and he is learning to distinguish the differences between the sounds he can hear. Children will often try to repeat sounds you make. These exchanges of sounds between you and the child are chains of events which we call

"vocal chains." In the early stages of imitation the child may respond only if he initiates the vocal interaction. Later you will be able to initiate a vocal chain and he should immediately imitate you. The primary objective of this phase is to teach the child the game of vocal chaining. He will produce a sound, you imitate that sound, and then he will make the sound again. The sound he makes following your imitation does not have to be exactly like his first sound or your imitation. He only has to make a second sound following your imitation.

Before you begin training, listen to the sounds the child makes and select those which occur regularly to be used during the baseline period. At this time you should also determine what you will consider an appropriate response and how many trials will constitute the baseline session.

Collect the baseline information over a period of at least 2 days. When you notice the child is vocalizing, stand or sit where the child can see and touch you. Wait until the child vocalizes and then imitate his sound. You can use a form like the one found in

Table 5.2 to record whether he vocalizes within 5 seconds after your imitation. Repeat the baseline session many times over the 2-day period. When you have finished with your baseline period, look at your data. Did the child vocalize at criterion level (around 75%) following your model, for example, 15 of the 20 times you imitated him? If so, he is probably ready for the next phase. If not, begin training.

Intervention activities are designed to increase the number of times the child vocalizes spontaneously and to give him the opportunity to vocalize immediately following a model's imitation of his sounds. Repeat all the sounds the child makes, even the gurgles and clicking sounds. This may stimulate him to repeat the sound. Be especially alert when the child makes a new sound. Repeat his new sound to him and give him a chance to imitate you. By hearing you repeat the sound, he may have a better chance of remembering his newly invented sound.

Probes should be given on a regular basis. The interval between probes will depend on the rapidity with which the child appears to be developing the target responses; but for each child, intervals between probes should be consistent. When you notice that the child is vocalizing, stand or sit where the child can see you. Wait until the child vocalizes and then imitate his sound. Record whether or not he vocalizes within 5 seconds after your imitation. Each probe session should have a consistent number of opportunities or trials. When the child meets criterion performance, he is probably ready for the next stage of training.

Phase 6b: Sound Imitation (Model Initiated)

The child is now able to imitate many of the sounds and movements a model makes provided those sounds and movements are ones which he can already produce spontaneously and which he has initiated. Training now shifts to the model initiating the imitation chain. You will remember that in Phase 6a the child was the initiator. The primary objective of Phase 6b is to teach the child to imitate the sounds produced by a model. These sounds should be ones the model has heard the child produce spontaneously.

The first task is to get a good idea of the sounds the child makes most frequently. You should have this information from the baseline data of the previous phase. It is also useful to note the child's intonational patterns while he is vocalizing. Target 5 or 6 sounds which the child makes most frequently, decide what constitutes an appropriate response, set

your criterion level of performance, and begin the baseline period.

Over a period of at least 2 days, choose moments when the child is alert and making some vocalizations. Stand or sit where the child can see you. Wait until he has been quiet and then present him with one of the target sounds using an intonational pattern similar to his own. Record whether the child attempts to imitate you. If he does imitate you, reinforce him with a hug (or whatever he likes); if he does not, play with him for awhile. Be sure not to just get up and leave him. Present him with a predetermined number of opportunities to imitate over the 2-day period. If the child imitates you three-fourths of the time, or whatever appropriate criterion level you have selected, he is ready to go on to the next phase. If the child does not imitate you at the established criterion level, you should initiate training.

Training focuses on providing the child with many opportunities to imitate. In the beginning, he may only engage in a vocal chain which he has started. Gradually, you can begin to increase the length of time between his spontaneous vocalization and your imitation. Set up many opportunities to engage in a vocal chain which the child has initiated. Instead of immediately repeating his sound, pause a second or two (the time it takes to smile) and then imitate. Systematically increase the time between his vocalization and your imitation. Gradually the child should begin to imitate you when you initiate the vocal chain.

Phase 7: Speech Sound Imitation

As the child moves along in the program, he should begin to produce closer approximations to English sounds, for example, "mama" and "dada." He may also begin using intonations which sound very much like yours. During this stage, you are interested in teaching the child to imitate sounds which make up the phonemic components of English. At first the child's attempts to imitate your new sounds will be clumsy and may not sound at all like your productions. The child may not even attempt to imitate your new sound and will only move his lips. Gradually the child's imitations should sound more like your vocalizations. In his spontaneous speech the child may be making many sounds when he is babbling and cooing and some may already sound like words. He will try to imitate the sound patterns or phrases you use with him all the time, for example, "go bye-bye," "time to eat," "time to go night-night," and "play ball."

The primary objective of this phase is to teach the

child to imitate simple English speech sounds. Before beginning to collect baseline information for this phase, read ahead through Section 3 on the appropriate use of objects. You can work on Phases 7 and 8 simultaneously.

In order to establish what items should be used for the baseline, it is important to know what English sounds are the easiest for the child to imitate. Consult Table 5.4 for consonants which are easier to imitate and select five consonant-vowel combinations for initial training. Enter this information on a form similar to Table 5.2. Decide the number of trials which will constitute your probe, set your criterion, and begin your baseline sessions. Over a period of a few days when you notice the child is alert and vocalizing, stand or sit where the child can see and touch your face. Wait until the child has been silent for a few seconds and then present him with one of the five items you have chosen. Record whether he imitates you. If his imitation is similar to your model, count this as an appropriate imitation. If he vocalizes, but the vocalization does not sound at all like your model, count this as an approximation. If he does not try to imitate you vocally, count this response as inappropriate. Present the items a consistent number of times over a period of a few days and record the child's responses. If he imitates you correctly three-fourths of the time, or whatever criterion you selected, he does not need to work on this phase and you are ready to move to the next training section. If the child does not imitate you at criterion level, begin training.

Training consists of teaching the child to imitate new sounds. At first, begin by working only with sounds he can already say. Gradually introduce new sounds one at a time. Use training activities that have been described in earlier phases. Remember to work on vocal imitation during care-taking activities, such as diapering, bathing, and feeding. These are times when many children tend to vocalize more and playing the imitation game during these activities can make efficient use of time. You can often improve the game by working on motor as well as verbal imitation during these times or any other periods you may find more appropriate for your child. Specifically, encourage your child to imitate the speech sounds which correspond to action patterns he has mastered. For example, while he is pounding a hammer, encourage him to imitate "pa" each time he bangs the toy.

As with the other phases, administer probes on a regular basis. The decision to continue training or to move to the next section should be based on an objective evaluation of the child's performance. If the child appears motivated and has been working on some specific sounds without reaching criterion for several days, it may be wise to re-examine the sounds you selected for training and/or the training procedures being employed.

Section 3: Discriminative use of objects

Children learn through systematic interaction with their environment. Environmental interaction produces the ability to differentiate objects and events. Initially a child's interactions with his environment are simple, he may only bang, wave, or mouth objects, or he may engage in one activity or action pattern with most objects he is capable of manipulating. As the child engages in an activity with a variety of objects, he learns that some objects, because of their various properties, are better to bang and wave, such as a rattle (which makes noise), and others are better to mouth, such as a spoon (which is ideal for putting in the mouth). He differentiates his activity based on the properties of the object.

As the child develops more experience with his environment, he begins to engage in more complex activities or action patterns based on the object's unique characteristics. For example, he may drop a string of beads into a bowl, swirl them around inside the bowl, pluck the beads from the bowl, bang them on the high chair, and then throw them on the floor. The child is learning many things about an object when he plays with it in this way. He is learning about the weight, texture, contour, and reactions various objects have. He is learning about distance in relation to weight and size: some things throw better and go further than others. He is learning about other physical properties such as size and appearance: some things can fit in his mouth and other things cannot, some things have handles to grab or to stick in his mouth and others have no handle. By combining several action patterns in this way with the same object and with different objects, the child learns the different characteristics of objects and how to differentiate among objects. The ability to differentiate among objects and among other events is a critical prerequisite to the development of a formal language system.

Phase 8: Establish Different Action Patterns

The primary objective of this stage is to teach the child a variety of action patterns to be used with different objects. Before taking a baseline prior to intervention, do some structured observation to determine if intervention is necessary. Select several objects around the house or classroom which are unbreakable and too large to fit in the child's mouth (e.g., a plastic bowl, a pan with a lid, a box with a top, some spoons, beads, a drum and stick, some aluminum foil, keys, a toy car or truck, some small blocks, a pull toy). Place a few of the items in front of the child and record his responses. Do this several times over a period of a few days until you have a good idea about his usual interaction with these items.

Intervention is necessary only if the child engages in the same activities with all or many of the objects. For example, does the child only mouth each item? Does he only wave and bang objects? If so, then intervention is appropriate. If he engages in different activities with many of the objects (for example, shaking the keys, banging the blocks together, and tearing the aluminum foil), then go to Phase 9 on the appropriate use of objects and Phase 10 on early word recognition.

To initiate training select 5 or 6 items which seem to be interesting to the child and determine one or two appropriate activities for each item. Decide the criterion performance for each item and the criterion for exit from this phase. Now you are ready to establish a baseline with these items.

Using a form similar to Table 5.2, record the child's activity with each item as you present it in the categories of appropriate, inappropriate, or approximation. Over a period of a day, present and score each item the same number of times. If the child does not meet criterion, begin training. Intervention can be informal and may consist of playing with selected objects with the child. Place a few of the items in front of the child and demonstrate an activity with the object. For example, if you place a truck in front of the child, give the truck a push and say "go truck" or "push truck." Then give the child the truck and observe his response. If he imitates you, this can be turned into a game of imitation. If the child does not imitate you, observe his response. Is it the same type of activity he performed during baseline? If so, gently prompt a different, yet easy, activity. If the activity is new, encourage his novel interaction even if it is not the same as your demonstration. The actions which you demonstrate for the child, and those which he may do spontaneously, need not be restricted to a training activity only. A white styrofoam cup is interesting to drink from, to put on one's head, to cover one's eyes with, and to roll in a circle. While you are playing with the cup, talk about what you are doing. For example, you

might talk about drinking milk from the cup (even if it is "pretend milk"), or making the cup into a hat by putting it on your head. A string of beads becomes a train when it is pulled across a table; when you wiggle it, it becomes a snake. This type of play, using different action patterns with many objects, coupled with simple verbalizations describing the events may be important events for later generative language. While playing with the child, encourage him to use the objects in many different ways and model new interactions for him. This exploratory play can involve using all the senses. Making sounds into an old milk carton will alter slightly the nature of the sounds, and this can be an interesting event. Looking down through the base of an empty clear plastic glass distorts vision in an interesting manner. Encourage the child to manipulate the objects so he will learn about them through his actions.

The child is ready to move on in the program when he either meets criterion by demonstrating the new activities you have trained or by engaging in novel activities which he has constructed by himself. Remember the goal is to use different action patterns with objects. If he meets criterion by demonstrating untrained actions, this is acceptable. Also, the child may perform some of the same actions with several objects. As long as he engages in some activities which are unique to the properties of the object, this should satisfy criterion. When the child exits from this phase, go on to Phases 9 and 10.

Phase 9: *Appropriate Use of Objects*

As mentioned before, children learn about objects and their characteristics through the development of action patterns which are unique to particular objects, people, and events. Following this differentiation of objects, the child begins to demonstrate activity which reflects the child's culture and people-object interactions which he has observed. The goal of Phase 9 is to train the child to interact or play appropriately with objects. Table 5.6 provides a list of the different settings and object combinations which are suggested for training. Initially, we suggest using objects from the kitchen area; however, choose any location that may be more suitable to your child or setting. The objects we have chosen are cup, spoon, and pan, but any other safe, common kitchen item can be used. We have included a doll so the children can model feeding, drinking, and other care-taking activities they commonly experience. We have chosen the kitchen as the first setting because it is an area which is familiar to most

TABLE 5.6   *Suggested settings and objects for phase 9*

Setting	Objects
Kitchen area	cup, spoon, pan, doll, plastic tumbler, teapot, plate, table, chair
Bedroom area	shoe, hat, comb, soap, bed, dress, shirt, doll, pillow, chair
Outdoor area	truck, car, shovel, pail, toy dog, doll, boat

children. Many of their first words are objects or events that can be found in the kitchen, such as cup, cookie, drink, or bottle.

To begin, select four training items. Determine what response you will accept as a demonstration of appropriate use. Table 5.7 presents descriptions of some appropriate and inappropriate responses for the suggested items. For example, stirring with the spoon on the table may be fun and appropriate for some situations, but in this case it would not be acceptable. Following selection of the objects, define the appropriate response(s) for each item and

administer a probe individually to each child. Use a recording form similar to the one found in Table 5.2. If a child can use each object in two appropriate ways or has at least one appropriate use of each object which he demonstrates at least twice within a predetermined time, he probably does not need training in this phase.

During training, have one set of objects for the teacher and for each child in the group. The number of children in the group can vary depending on the ability of the children as well as their manageability. Take the child or children into the kitchen or kitchen area of the classroom and have them sit around a small table. Place the items to be trained in front of each child. Show the children one appropriate use of an item and then have the children copy you. For example, if the item to be trained is a cup, take a drink from your cup and prompt or encourage the children to imitate you by drinking from their cups. If any child does not respond, physically prompt him to respond correctly. If the children imitate you, or attempt to imitate you, praise them, hug them, or do something to reinforce their appropriate activity. Once they are imitating your actions reasonably well, move on to other uses of the item you have selected. Also, be alert to self-initiated appropriate activities the child might perform with the object and be sure to reinforce these responses.

TABLE 5.7   *Description of appropriate and inappropriate use of suggested objects for phase 9*

Object	Sample Appropriate Response	Sample Inappropriate Response
Cup	drink from cup dip liquid with cup give baby drink stir with spoon in cup pour from cup into another container	bang cup put cup on head throw
Spoon	spoon objects into a container stir with spoon in a container feed self feed baby	beat table or other surface with spoon throw sit on spoon
Pan	place lid on pan stir in pan drink from pan pour from pan into another container	throw spin pan bang
Baby	hug or kiss baby rock baby feed baby make baby hold spoon or cup give baby a drink	chew on baby's hand throw bang

At this point, begin to incorporate other items so that the children learn to combine two objects into a single action pattern, for example, holding the cup with one hand and stirring in the cup with a spoon with the other hand. Introduce only a few new actions at a time. Gradually teach the children the appropriate use of each of the items. As the children are able to produce the action without your immediate model, begin to encourage variation in the use so the children will learn to use the items appropriately in several different ways. Although the children are not required to understand or verbalize the names of the objects in this phase, name the objects frequently and talk about what you are doing in simple, short sentences.

Children need to practice new responses outside the training situation; therefore, when possible, take the children to a different location to practice their new skills. Use different examples of the items you are training once you feel confident that the children are able to imitate you. For example, when you are playing with the child, you could use several different types of cups and let him drink from each one.

Administer probes on a regular basis. When the child is able to demonstrate criterion performance, move on to Phase 10 if you have not already done so.

Section 4:   Word recognition

In order for the child to associate sounds in his environment with objects and actions, it is important that he hears the names of the objects, people, and events while he is interacting with them. In other words, it is important to talk about the things the child sees and does in simple, consistent language. In order for language to be meaningful to the child, it must be relevant and directly related to his on-going experience.

Prior to the association of language and the environment, the child learns to associate certain events with certain other events. For example, Daddy's shoes are associated with Daddy, keys are associated with going for a ride in a car, and warm clothing is associated with going outside. We know that children begin to make these associations by their demonstrated anticipatory behavior. The sight of car keys will often bring about excited bouncing and arm waving in the small child and the sight of dinner preparation will often result in similar anticipatory behavior.

When the child is demonstrating this association of one event with another, it is important that he hear language which is appropriate and relevant to the occasion. In this way he begins to associate sounds (words and phrases) with their referents. The goal of this phase is to teach the child to respond appropriately to simple words and phrases when they occur in relevant situations.

Phase 10:   Early Word Recognition

To begin, choose five appropriate items (such as those listed in Table 5.8). The items should have labels which most children hear often. Enter each of these items several times on a sheet similar to Table 5.2. Predetermine appropriate, inappropriate, and approximate responses for each of the items and decide four criterion performance for mastery of this phase.

Collect your baseline data over a period of at least 2 days. Say these words and phrases to the children in the appropriate setting and at appropriate times and record his responses. If the child indicates that he has understood you by completing an appropriate task or action, record his response as appropriate. If he engages in an incorrect activity but indicates he is attempting to do something for you, record this as an approximation. If the child does not respond, score this as inappropriate. Each item should be presented a predetermined number of times over the 2-day period. If the child performs at criterion level, he has completed this prelanguage training program and you should begin to train him to engage in formal language activities (Bricker, Ruder, & Vincent-Smith, 1976). If the child does not meet criterion, begin training on this phase.

Training consists of teaching the child to respond appropriately to several words and commands. For example, if you are training the appropriate response to the word "up," prompt him to raise his arms when you say "Do you want up?" (Don't forget to pick him up! Language must be meaningful.) As Table 5.8 shows, each of our suggested items is accompanied by a definition of a suggested acceptable response. If you do not feel that the response is appropriate, use another response which you feel will be more useful for the child and the situation. Remember that the primary objective of this phase is not imitation, it is comprehension or word recognition; therefore, do not expect the child to repeat the words or sounds, but encourage any form of expression should it occur.

Administer probes regularly. When the child has met criterion by indicating appropriate activities in response to your words and commands in context, he has completed this training program.

TABLE 5.8   *Suggested comprehension items for phase 10: early word recognition*

Comprehension Items	Suggested Response
Hi	Wave or smile
Bye-bye	Wave hands
Night-night	Wave or indicate going to bed
See the———(familiar object such as dog or person. Be careful not to point.)	Child looks in direction, searches for object, e.g., dog, or looks at a closely related item, e.g., water dish
Up or down	Child indicates anticipation of being picked up or put down
Ride the horsie	Child indicates anticipation of bouncing up and down on your knee
I'm gonna tickle you	Child smiles, laughs, or indicates the tickle game is about to follow
Do you want some———(favorite food)?	Child looks or points in direction of food, cupboard, refrigerator, etc.

Once the child has reached the targets established in this training program, he/she is ready to build his formal linguistic comprehension and production skills. For such training programs the reader is referred to Bricker, Dennison, and Bricker (1976), Guess, Sailor, Keogh, and Baer (1976), Kent (1974), Miller and Yoder (1974), and Stremel and Waryas (1974).

Summary

Each individual should be entitled to necessary assistance in acquiring fundamental skills that provide independence from environmental constraints. The ability to communicate is surely a vital skill; and for children growing up in our culture, verbal language is the primary form of communication. Assisting the severely impaired child in developing language has been clearly documented as a difficult task. The enormity of the undertaking is probably responsible for the traditional unwillingness of the speech pathologists, educators, and psychologists to involve themselves in such a "doomed" venture. Humane reasons being insufficient, recent legal agreements and legislative enactments have mandated changes in the expenditure of resources for the education of all children.

The purpose of this chapter has been to describe an intervention program to aid the developmentally young child in acquiring the responses we believe to be prerequisite to the subsequent production and comprehension of verbal language. The primary training strategy of this program is to shape simple, primitive responses through systematic environmental interaction into successively more complex response forms. The training content is derived from cognitive and linguistic theories of development. If this program has a unique aspect, it is its focus on the development of knowledge of the concrete, physical environment (sensorimotor intelligence) before training a representational system such as language.

The training program has targeted four training areas: (1) on-task behavior, (2) imitation, (3) discriminative use of objects, and (4) word recognition. The training sequence, with attention to the individual needs of the child, should result in movement toward the development of skills which are prerequisite to the acquisition of verbal language.

References

Bellugi, U. Development of language in the normal child. In J. E. McLean, D. E. Yoder, & R. L. Schiefelbusch (Eds.), *Language intervention with the retarded.* Baltimore: University Park Press, 1972.

Bloom, L. Semantic features in language acquisition. In R. L. Schiefelbusch (Ed.), *Language of the mentally retarded.* Baltimore: University Park Press, 1972.

Bloom, L., & Lahey, M. *Language development and language disorders.* New York: Wiley, 1976.

Bowerman, M. F. *Learning to talk: A cross-linguistic comparison of early syntactic developments, with special reference to Finnish.* London: Cambridge University Press, 1973.

Bricker, D., Dennison, L., & Bricker, W. A. A language intervention program for developmentally young children. *Mailman Center for Child Development Monograph Series, 1976, No. 1,* Miami, Fla.: University of Miami.

Bricker, D., Ruder, K., & Vincent-Smith, L. An intervention strategy for language deficient children. In N. Haring & R. Schiefelbusch (Eds.), *Teaching special children.* New York: McGraw-Hill, 1976.

Bricker, W. A. Errors in the echoic behavior of preschool children. *Journal of Speech and Hearing Research,* 1967, *10,* 67–76.

Bricker, W. A., & Bricker, D. D. An early language training strategy. In R. L. Schiefelbusch & L. Lloyd (Eds.), *Language perspectives: Acquisition, retardation, and intervention.* Baltimore: University Park Press, 1974.

Brown, L., Nietupski, J., & Hamre-Nietupski, S. Criterion of ultimate functioning. In *Hey, don't forget about me! Education's investment in the severely, profoundly, and multiply handicapped.* Reston, Va.: Council for Exceptional Children, 1976.

Brown, R. *A first language.* Cambridge, Mass.: Harvard University Press, 1973.

Chomsky, N. *Reflections on language.* New York: Pantheon, 1975.

Dale, P. S. *Language development: Structure and function* (2nd ed.). New York: Holt, Rinehart & Winston, 1976.

Edmonds, M. H. New directions in theories of language acquisition. *Harvard Education Review,* 1976, *46,* 175–198.

Guess, D., Sailor, W., Keogh, B., & Baer, D. Language development programs for severely handicapped children. In N. Haring & L. Brown (Eds.), *Teaching the severely handicapped.* New York: Grune & Stratton, 1976.

Hunt, J. McV. *Intelligence and experience.* New York: Ronald Press, 1961.

Kauffman, J. M., Snell, M. E., & Hallahan, D. P. Imitating children during imitation training: Two experimental paradigms. *Education and Training of the Mentally Retarded,* 1976, *11,* 324–332.

Kent, L. *Language acquisition program for the severely retarded.* Champaign, Ill.: Research Press, 1974.

Miller, J., & Yoder, D. An onotogenetic language teaching strategy for retarded children. In R. Schielfelbusch & L. Lloyd (Eds.), *Language perspectives: Acquisition, retardation, and intervention.* Baltimore, Md.: University Park Press, 1974.

Nelson, K. Concept, word and sentence: Interrelations in acquisition and development. *Psychological Review,* 1974, *81,* 267–285.

Piaget, J. *The origins of intelligence in children.* New York: Norton, 1952.

Piaget, J. *Play, dreams, and imitation in childhood.* New York: Norton, 1962.

Reese, H. W., & Lipsett, L. P. *Experimental child psychology.* New York: Academic Press, 1970.

Ruder, K., & Smith, M. *Issues in language training.* In R. L. Schiefelbusch & L. Lloyd (Eds.), Language perspectives: Acquisition, retardation, and intervention. Baltimore: University Park Press, 1974.

Schiefelbusch, R., Copeland, R., & Smith, J. O. (Eds.). *Language and mental retardation: Empirical and conceptual considerations.* New York: Holt, Rinehart & Winston, 1967.

Skinner, B. F. *Verbal behavior.* New York: Appleton-Century-Crofts, 1957.

Slobin, D. I. *Psycholinguistics.* Glenview, Ill.: Scott, Foresman, 1971.

Stremel, K. & Waryas, C. A behavioral-psycholinguistic approach to language training. In L. McReynolds (Ed.), *Developing systematic procedures for training children's language.* American Speech and Hearing Association Monograph, 1974, *18,* 96–124.

Uzgiris, I., & Hunt, J. McV. *Assessment in infancy.* Chicago: University of Illinois Press, 1975.

Note

1. Oller, D. K. *The emergence of the linguistic sound system in Down's Syndrome infants.* Paper presented at the meeting of the American Speech and Hearing Association, Washington, D.C., October, 1975.

Introduction to Chapter 6

Underlying all skills is movement, whether it is actual or simply viewed. In this next chapter Linda Bunker tackles the chore of charting how body management is encouraged and shaped into the fundamental large and small muscle movements and later into personal, vocational, and leisure-time applications. The relevance of motor learning is continuous throughout every moderately and severely handicapped learner's existence. To assume that the motor development of your students will progress evenly and without encouragement is a serious mistake. Also it is true that gross and fine motor skill assessment and instruction is not so easily managed as some of the preacademic skills.

As you progress through this chapter, you may be surprised to discover the complexity of balance and endurance, of crawling, walking, and ball-throwing, to name only a few. Although this chapter covers both gross and fine motor development, an extensive discussion of physical disabilities would be beyond the capacity of this book. The reader is referred to the self-care chapter for brief discussions of handling and positioning the cerebral palsied learner as well as to the more extensive works of Bigge (1976), Bricker, Davis, Wahlin, and Evans (1977), Copeland, Ford and Solon (1976), Cruickshank (1976), and Finnie (1975), and to the brief but functional chapters on adaptive equipment by Campbell, Green, and Carlson (1977); on occupational and physical therapy services by Sternat, Messina, Nietupski, Lyon, and Brown (1977); and on positioning, handling, and feeding the physically disabled learner by Utley, Holvoet, and Barnes (1977).

References

Bigge, J. L. *Teaching individuals with physical and multiple disabilities.* Columbus, Ohio: Charles E. Merrill, 1976.

Bricker, D., Davis, J., Wahlin, L., & Evans, J. A motor training program for the developmentally young. *Mailman Center for Child Development Monograph* No. 2, 1977.

Campbell, P. H., Green, K. M., & Carlson, L. M. Approximating the norm through environmental and child-centered prosthetics and adaptive equipment. In E. Sontag (Ed.), *Educational programming for the severely and profoundly handicapped,* Reston, Va.: Division on Mental Retardation, Council for Exceptional Children, 1977.

Copeland, M., Ford, L., & Solon, N. *Occupational therapy for mentally retarded children.* Baltimore: University Park Press, 1976.

Cruickshank, W. (Ed.). *Cerebral palsy: A developmental disability.* Syracuse, N.Y.: Syracuse University, 1976.

Finnie, N. R. *Handling the young cerebral palsied child at home.* (2nd ed). New York: E. P. Dutton, 1975.

Sternat, J., Messina, R., Nietupski, J., Lyon, S., & Brown, L. Occupational and physical therapy services for severely handicapped students: Toward a naturalized public school service delivery model. In E. Sontag (Ed.), *Educational programming for the severely and profoundly handicapped.* Reston, Va.: Division on Mental Retardation, Council for Exceptional Children, 1977.

Utley, B., Holvoet, J., & Barnes, K. Handling, positioning, and feeding the physically handicapped. In Sontag, E. (Ed.), *Educational programming for the severely and profoundly handicapped.* Reston, Va.: Division on Mental Retardation, Council for Exceptional Children, 1977.

6

Motor Skills

*This chapter was written by **Linda K. Bunker,** Motor Learning Laboratory, University of Virginia.*

Human movement provides the basic psychomotor framework for development, for through movement all children discover critical elements about their bodies, their environment, and their social interactions. All young children must "move to learn and learn to move," and as they move, reach, touch, and explore, they begin to develop a concept of their body. Infants learn that their arms, hands, legs, and body provide a way to integrate information from the sensory systems with that from the world outside. The development of movement skills and the acquisition of an accurate body image are therefore critical in the developmental process of all children, but particularly for the mentally retarded child.

Children use the information acquired about their bodies to form a reference point around which all information is organized. The child's body provides a "measuring stick" for judging the size, shape, texture, and distance of all other objects and persons. For this reason it is essential that the "measuring stick" have experiences in many different positions, environments, and movements. Children should be encouraged to move around independently in order to obtain information about the outside world

through visual, auditory, and tactile sensory receptors and about the child's own body through internal kinesthetic and proprioceptive stimuli.

The movement behavior of children and adults must be built upon the acquisition of a foundation of body management abilities. These abilities form the building blocks upon which fundamental movement skills are built and, in turn, provide for the development of more complex personal, vocational, and leisure-time movement skills.

Body management abilities are focused primarily on the child's ability to deal with his/her own body and its relationships to the environment. This level of functioning is concerned with (1) the development of body awareness and an accurate body percept, (2) experiences involving the various rhythms and qualities of movement, (3) the understanding of the relationship between movement and external objects and people, and (4) the acquisition of concepts of space. These body awareness skills are then coupled with the development and maintenance of basic levels of physical fitness to provide functional body management abilities. Physical fitness is a particularly critical component since it not only affects the later development of motor skills but also may influence social development as well.

Fundamental movement skills are dependent upon a functional level of body management abilities; without these fundamental abilities, skill development would be impossible (see Fig. 6.1). The basic movement skills discussed in this chapter may be considered in terms of fine motor skills which involve only isolated body parts or gross motor skills which require the integrated use of the entire body. Gross motor skills may be further differentiated as locomotor skills involving movement through space and as manipulative skills which involve an interaction with an external object.

Motor Skill Development in Retarded and Normal Individuals

The typical sequence of motor development is highly predictable, yet the number of individual variations may be quite large. The age norms provided in this chapter simply refer to the average age of demonstration of a particular skill among normal children and do not adequately reflect the age *range* at which the skill may be developed. For example, in terms of locomotor skills, some children may show a rather precocious ability to crawl, sit, or stand, and yet the development of walking or skipping may be on-age or even somewhat delayed.

Mentally retarded children often lag behind in functional motor skills in one or more areas of body management or fundamental skills. Problems in body management skills may include general body awareness, mobility, the development of spatial concepts, an awareness of body postures and control of body actions, body image, and self-help skills (as discussed in Chapter 7). In addition to these basic skills, these children may also have difficulty with efficient locomotor patterns, such as skipping, hopping, and jumping, and with both gross and fine motor manipulative skills such as writing, drawing, throwing, striking, kicking, and catching. These basic skill deficiencies may also be compounded by the lack of participation in vigorous activities which may require the utilization of these skills. Consequently these children do not participate in activities necessary for the development of physical fitness components such as strength, endurance, agility, and balance.

Delays in motor development may be the result of many factors. Among the most prevalent are environmental limitations which may restrict the types of experiences available to the child (i.e. confinement to playpens, homes without stairs, slippery shoes or floors). In addition to these conditions which physically limit a child's motor development, parents and peer groups often aid in the limiting process by being overly protective and cautious. Such developmental lags are often, but not necessarily, overcome when children are placed in stimulating, appropriate, and secure environments.

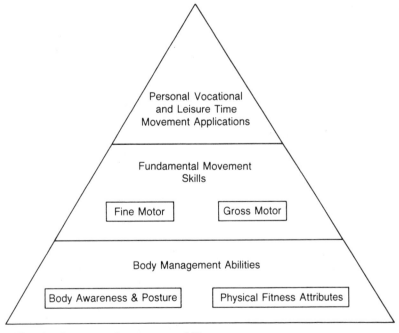

FIGURE 6.1   *The development of movement skills*

The motor problems of the mentally retarded child may be directly related to the degree of damage to, or lack of development of, the central nervous system. However, these children are also subject to the same environmental variables which may delay the motor development of normal children: the omission or interruption of motor experiences, illness, accidents, sex biases in experiences and expectations, sympathetic but overprotective parents, awkward and unsure performance, lack of self-confidence necessary to seek new and challenging situations, or late physical and/or neurological maturation.

The more serious developmental irregularities may be caused by various physiological conditions. For some children physical maturation may simply be delayed, as with lower rates of myelination of the spinal cord and lack of strength, all of which will normally improve with time. Problems of muscular imbalance, i.e. excessive muscle tone, as in cerebral palsy, may also cause severe delays in motor development, in which case the underlying problem must be medically treated.

The perceptual problems of deafness and/or blindness can also result in some motor delay. The reduction or absence of visual or auditory input have a marked effect on the exploration of a child's environment and will therefore affect the nature of motor variations in a child's repertoire. For blind children, movement is not visually stimulated and, coupled with the lack of a steering mechanism, the development of motor skills will necessarily be dependent upon adult guidance and encouragement in exploring the unseen environment (Adelson & Frailberg, 1974).

Orthopedic handicaps such as spina bifida, polio myelitis, talipes, Osgood-Schlatter disease, and others may have a direct effect upon the development of motor skills. The onset of various motor skills may be delayed or absent, and, in addition, these children may require specific modifications of movement experiences in order to compensate for these conditions.

Variability in motor performance

There are extreme individual differences among severely and profoundly retarded individuals. For example, retarded children are much more variable than normal children in terms of both physical growth and motor performance, with 25–50% more variability in such measures as weight, muscular power, muscular endurance, balance activities, and test of fine motor coordination (Clausen, 1966; Rarick, Dobbins, & Broadhead, 1976).

The degree of motor deficiency in the moderately and severely handicapped may be quite dramatic, with 60–80% of the severely handicapped children performing below their "normal" counterparts. It is also important to note that in almost all motor skills this deficit is more marked in retarded girls than boys (Rarick et al., 1976). Some of this observed deficit may be the result of "real" neurological causes, but much of it may stem from the lack of well-designed learning experiences. These differences become even more marked as the level of retardation becomes more severe, because secondary physical handicaps become more frequent and may often be accompanied by social-emotional problems. A detailed discussion of the secondary orthopedic and physical handicaps is beyond the scope of this chapter. The reader is referred to references which provide in-depth descriptions based on the nature of the secondary handicap, such as Bobath (1969), Bobath and Bobath (1962, 1964), Copeland, Ford, and Solon (1976), Farber (1975), Finnie (1975), Holser-Buehler (1966), Macey (1974), Mysak (1963), Robinault (1973), and Semans (1967).

Children who are moderately to profoundly retarded may demonstrate problems in the area of total motor development. In terms of general gross motor skills, their movements may appear somewhat uncoordinated, and they are often characterized as being "clumsy." For example, walking is often flat-footed, with arms held at the side rather than contributing to the movement. In addition, some motor skills will lack effective control, even though the actual skill may be present (i.e. the child can run rapidly, but cannot control stopping or changing directions). Fine motor skills may also appear to be awkward or inept, as the child has difficulty with such tasks as buttoning buttons and manipulating zippers.

Body management skills

Mentally retarded children have been found to acquire body management skills at a slower rate than normal children. The basic body awareness skills which deal strictly with movement appear to be less affected by retardation than the allied skills such as identification of body parts and the development of concepts of spatial relations and laterality, which may be associated with more cognitively oriented skills.

The development of body management skills follows the same basic pattern of neurological maturation in retarded children as it does in normal children, with the activities progressing from simple to complex and from gross to fine, or large to small movements. If a child is able to perform easily the early developmental activities, she/he should be encouraged to progress to more complex activities. If, however, a child is unable to perform any activity in a typical developmental sequence, special emphasis should be placed on the building of the ability through the repetition of the necessary prerequisite behaviors as well as the behavior at hand.

The physical fitness abilities of retarded children may also reflect a differential development. For example, retarded children have been found to possess only 50% as much strength and flexibility, fatigue 30% more quickly, and carry 35% more fat than nonretarded children of the same age (Hayden, 1964; Rarick et al., 1976). These basic deficits in physical fitness components are often most obvious in the weight and postural problems of the retarded populations. It should, however, be pointed out that with proper attention and movement experiences, these physical fitness and postural problems are generally correctable or can be completely avoided.

The lack of fundamental skills and movement experiences also seems to add to the general, unrealistic self-concept possessed by many retarded individuals (Elrod, 1972; Fine & Caldwell, 1967; Gardner & Barnard, 1969; Guthrie, Gorlow, & Butler, 1967; Piers & Harris, 1964). It has, however, been found that engaging in physical activity enhances self-concept (Johnson, Fritz, & Johnson, 1968) and that increased skill development may facilitate social interactions.

Fundamental Movement Skills

Research has indicated that the moderately retarded child may be from 2 to 4 years behind the normal child in the development of fundamental movement skills (Cratty, 1974; Francis & Rarick, 1959; Howe, 1959; Keogh, 1968; Lillie, 1968). In addition, this motor performance remains relatively fixed with age, thus causing the retarded child to fall farther and farther behind the normally developing child of the same age. As a child grows older, it becomes increasingly more difficult to improve motor performance, therefore the importance of early motor experiences is emphasized.

In terms of specific fundamental skills, retarded children are much poorer in such activities as the overarm throw for distance, the 50-yard dash, the standing broad jump, and railwalk (Rarick et al., 1976). These differences are more marked in females than in males and become progressively worse with increased age.

Several general trends in motor performance differentials should be highlighted. For example, while retarded children have poorer levels of both muscular endurance and power, the difference is much less on the power measures. This may be due to a general lack of endurance on the part of retarded children, or it may be that these children do not tolerate the discomfort associated with most endurance tasks.

The extent of performance deficits for mentally retarded children in fine motor skills is generally greater than in gross motor skills. These motor impairments are most obvious in the more precise manual and finger dexterity tasks and become less marked in tasks requiring visual-motor tracking (Rarick et al., 1976). Motor deficits are also more marked in retarded girls than in boys, a finding which is opposite the "normal" superiority of girls in fine motor tasks and gross motor skills involving balance, grace, and agility (Espenschade & Eckert, 1967).

A second major characteristic of fundamental motor skill development in retarded children concerns the lack of selective utilization of skills. That is, a movement may be used inappropriately from task to task, or a learned movement may not transfer from one situation to another (i.e., a child can zip a jacket, but cannot use this same skill to zip boots). Similarly, these children often persevere with the same movement when the task requires a modification of that movement, as in maintaining an even-beat run when the music changes to an uneven rhythm for a skipping pattern. In addition to a basic lag in motor skill development, it has been found that as either age or the complexity of the skill increases (i.e., standing broad jump and squat thrust), this discrepancy increased (Francis & Rarick, 1960; Rarick, Widdop, & Broadhead, 1967).

Retarded children need to be taught many of the basic skills which normal children seem to learn informally. These basic skills provide the foundation for the retarded child to reach functional performance level and yield experiences which encourage social interaction with a variety of family members and peers.

The Development of Body Management Skills

Every child's individual motor performance is affected by the fundamental level of perceptual functioning and the physiological capabilities of the body. Many underlying physical and anatomical factors help to determine a child's ability to perform perceptual-motor tasks. For example, the skill of bicycle riding depends on a series of factors, including the utilization of force, maintenance of speed as determined by the amount of force produced, sufficient balance to remain in an upright position, an understanding of space and speed, and the complex interaction of the visual-motor system for steering. Similarly, sewing a button on a coat requires sufficient finger dexterity to hold the button, flexibility and agility to manipulate the needle, strength to pull the needle through the cloth, and rather sophisticated visual integration to guide the needle through the holes in the button. Each of these skills develops as a result of sound body management abilities, including accurate body awareness and functional physical fitness attributes.

Body awareness

Body management skills provide the most fundamental level of motor capabilities, including the means for acquiring a basic body awareness and understanding the capabilities of the body in motion. In addition, body management skills help the child acquire a sound awareness of body postures and control over body movements.

Body awareness provides the key to all fundamental motor learnings as it allows for the establishment of a sound body image around which most other movement behaviors are developed. An accurate body image provides the focal point for the development of an awareness of space and spatial relations. Children begin to locate objects in space in relation to their bodies as their bodies acquire a stable right and left side (laterality). Later, laterality becomes critical in spatial perception as it facilities the recognition of shapes and sizes. Thus many of the more cognitive, perceptual skills have their foundation built on body awareness which provides for the perception of external relationships.

Movement permits the child to explore the capabilities of her body, including the identification of body parts and their functions in both locomotor and nonlocomotor movement. These body management skills furnish a means for children to understand and discover the movement capabilities of their bodies in such situations as bending, stretching, twisting, turning, supporting, balancing, and falling.

In addition to this fundamental level of self-development, the concept of body awareness also includes the relationship of the body to other objects and people. As body awareness improves, children also should be given experiences to facilitate the development of the concepts of space-time relationships and the social interactions of working with others in either cooperative or competitive situations. This social interaction is particularly important in the case of retarded children and will be greatly enhanced by a strong basic level of body awareness and physical fitness abilities.

Basic physical abilities

Each child's motor performance is based in part on the development of body awareness skills and on the ability to cultivate and utilize the basic physical abilities which underlie each action. These basic physical abilities, sometimes labeled physical fitness abilities, provide the fundamental factors necessary for all skill development and include five basic components: *strength, flexibility, agility, balance,* and *endurance;* and three combination abilities: *power, speed,* and *coordination.*

1. *Strength* may be defined as the amount of force which can be exerted by a single muscle or a group of muscles in one maximum effort. This ability to exert force can apply to specific muscle groups, as in gripping, or to the strength production of the entire body as in weight-lifting or running. It is a critical component in almost every perceptual-motor act, from the first attempts at lifting one's own head, to sitting, crawling, block-building, standing, climbing, writing, jumping, throwing, and kicking.

Strength is fundamental to all movement, for it is the capacity to exert variable and appropriate amounts of force to resolve particular performance requirements. There have been three basic types of strength identified: *static, dynamic,* and *ballistic.* Static strength may be thought of as the ability to exert force (pounds of pressure) against an immovable object. Dynamic strength refers to force applied through a range of motion, in a controlled manner, such as pushing a large box across the floor, and ballistic or explosive strength is the ability to propel a relatively heavy object by using a rapid, powerful movement followed by a continuous, momentum-produced movement, such as is required to throw a basketball.

2. *Flexibility* may be defined as the range of motion present at a given joint, and refers to the ability to move the body and its parts through a maximum range of motion without undue strain on the articulations and muscle attachments. Typically, flexibility is measured in degrees of motion, in either flexion (where the angle of the body and its articulations are decreased through movement, as in bending the elbow) or extension (where the angle is increased, as in straightening the arm). Various aspects of flexibility are obvious in such things as bending and stretching and may be easily observed in children's play as twisting, turning, leaning, squatting, weaving between the bars of the jungle gym, doing back bends or toe touches, turning on the parallel bars, or just sitting on the floor.

The maximum utilization of each child's body depends on the harmonious use of the limbs, a situation which requires a balance of strength and flexibility. During childhood, both strength and flexibility increase simultaneously; however, near the onset of puberty, flexibility tends to decline while strength continues to improve (Leighton, 1964). It should be noted that even though flexibility seems to diminish as strength increases, it is not necessarily limited by strength, nor is it directly related to the length of body parts (Matthews, Shaw, & Woods, 1959). Flexibility, like strength, is specific to various body parts and, because of this specificity, it is *not* possible to use the flexibility measured at one location as a valid prediction of the range of motion in other body parts (Clarke, 1975).

3. The ability to rapidly change body position and/or direction is referred to as *agility*. Agility is particularly important in such activities as tag games, running obstacle courses, stunts and tumbling skills, or folkdancing. The term "agility" is often confused with flexibility and/or speed because it involves the ability to make rapid, successive movements in different directions. The concept of agility emphasizes that the directional shifting of the body is completely under the control of the individual. Agility may also be displayed in fine motor skills such as writing, typing, drawing, or playing the piano.

4. *Balance* can be defined as the ability to maintain equilibrium relative to gravity. There are three primary ways in which young children manifest this ability: static balance, dynamic balance, and object balance. Static balance refers to the maintenance of equilibrium in a stationary position and presents a major task for the young child who is just learning to sit or stand or for the older child who attempts to balance on one foot with eyes closed. Dynamic balance provides an even more difficult task because it involves locomotion, and may vary from walking and running to skipping on the flat top of a wall, riding a bicycle, walking on the hands or on a balance beam. The third classification of balance provides a slightly different approach to the nature of equilibrium in that it refers to one's ability to balance an external object such as a pencil on a finger, a book on the head, or an armful of dishes.

All types of balance depend on the interaction of various components which influence equilibrium. The degree of stability of an object or person depends primarily upon the equal distribution of weight on each side of the vertical axis and is most often affected by altering the location of the center of gravity relative to the base of support. This interaction thus involves the relative positions of three components: the center of gravity, the line of gravity, and the base of support. The center of gravity refers to that point about which the body weight is equally distributed; the line of gravity is a vertical line passing through that point. Objects are generally said to be in balance when their center of gravity and line of gravity are squarely over the base of support (i.e., all parts in contact with the supporting surface). As the center of gravity and line of gravity move from the center of the base of support, the object loses equilibrium.

The attainment of good balance is essential to the development of most motor and perceptual skills in childhood, for the balanced body provides the primary internal reference system for geometric vertical and horizontal orientations. The maintenance of a position of equilibrium depends upon the integration of the information from the vestibular (labyrinthian) mechanisms of the inner ear, the muscular feedback from the postural muscles, and information from the visual system. The basic physiological development of the muscular and visual systems is relatively mature in the young child, but it takes a great deal of experience for the child to be able to "utilize" this available information to orient the body in space.

Balance is not a constant factor but an ever-changing component of total body movement. The ability to balance is extremely important to all children since it underlies almost all complex motor skills. It is necessary for the efficient execution of the various motor patterns and also for the safety of the child. Children must be able to "automatically" balance their bodies before they can undertake learning (1) gross motor skills such as walking on a curb or batting a ball and (2) fine motor skills, such as writing, tying shoes, and hammering.

5. *Endurance* is defined as the ability to sustain activity over a relatively long period of time. In general, the endurance of children increases with age (as do most other physical abilities) and can refer to the sustained activity of the muscular system or of the cardiorespiratory system. Two distinct types of endurance are therefore considered: muscular endurance and cardiorespiratory endurance.

Muscular endurance refers to the ability of a muscle to repeat identical movements or pressures or to maintain a certain degree of tension over a period of time. In general, muscular endurance manifests itself in such situations as doing continuous sit-ups, push-ups, squat thrusts, hops, some forms of assembly line work, or in the ability to maintain a particular position or exertion over time—such as a flexed arm hang.

Lack of muscular endurance does not appear to be a very dramatic limitation in physiologically normal children unless they are forced to continue activity beyond their psychological and physical limits. Historically there has been some essentially unfounded concern about the safety of children who seem to lack endurance. The "Child's Heart Myth" began as early as 1879 when Beneke warned of the dangers of repetitive work on the child's heart and muscular system due to the "natural disharmony" between the development of the size of the heart muscle and the size of the large blood vessels (Corbin, 1973). On the other hand, Karpovich (1937), Astrand (1956), and others have shown that although the size of the aorta is smaller in proportion to the heart in young children than in older children, the blood carrying capacity is still proportionate to heart development. Corbin (1973) is even more emphatic and specifies that "a healthy child cannot physically injure his heart by physical exercise."

The second type of endurance, *cardiorespiratory,* refers to the combined ability of the human organism to supply oxygen to the working muscles and the ability of the muscles to utilize this oxygen to support work. This type of endurance is enhanced by placing a stress on muscle groups for an extended period of time through such activities as running, swimming, and cycling. The circulatory and respiratory systems must be taxed to a point where they are required to supply greater quantities of oxygen to the muscles for continued work.

The development of endurance in the child is re-flected in the gradual decline with age of the resting pulse rate and breathing rate and the increase in ability to sustain activity. By 9 years of age the pulse rate is rarely above 90 beats per minute and respiration is approximately 20 per minute. All children around this age are characteristically easily fatigued but recover rapidly. As children continue to develop (usually by age 12), their heart rates generally reduce to 80–90 beats per minute and respiration rate declines to 15–20 while at rest.

In addition to the five physical abilities discussed above—strength, flexibility, agility, balance, and endurance—three other fundamental physical abilities are found in the more complex motor skills: power, speed, and coordination. These more complex physical characteristics may be considered as combinations of the five fundamental physical abilities. A powerful child is therefore one who can combine the basic abilities of strength plus speed in an effort to produce an explosive movement. The production of *power* is critical to many forms of perceptual-motor performance and is reflected in such activities as the high jump, broad jump, 100-yard dash, or the football kick.

Similarly, the concept of *speed* involves the rapidity of muscular contraction as is required to move from one place to another very quickly and may demand the use of other abilities such as strength, flexibility, and power. Often the utilization of speed also requires that a child respond to some specific environmental stimulus (i.e., starting gun) and then execute a prescribed movement sequence (i.e., run 100 yards). This relatively simple-sounding sequence actually requires the complex use of two independently defined concepts, reaction time and movement time. These are described as the ability to perceive a stimulus and to react to that stimulus by beginning and then completing a movement. Speed is therefore a component of many skills and is implicit in such movements as running, swimming, and throwing.

Perhaps the key to efficient motor behavior is the child's ability to coordinate the individual physical capacities in a meaningful way. The development of *coordination* results in rhythmic, synchronous movement of the entire body. It is ultimately reflected in the smooth, balanced, flowing movements of the professional athlete and in the principles of opposition (i.e., hand and foot opposition in walking), rotation, and sequential joint action of many of the perceptual-motor skills. The concepts of opposition and symmetry are critical to human movement because of the use of both sides of the body. That is to say, each movement pattern of the child follows a sequence of development from the relatively undifferentiated "raw" skill to the highly organized efficient movement which demonstrates a high level of coordination involving the arms, legs, and total body.

Posture

One of the most meaningful manifestations of the development of body management abilities in children has to do with the integration of body awareness and physical fitness attributes to produce a pleasing, fundamental posture. Posture refers to the manner in which one stands, sits, moves, and performs daily activities. It is generally judged by the relationship of various body parts to one another, and may be affected by the relative strength and flexibility of various muscle groups and by the child's visual and proprioceptive perception of verticality.

Body posture is one of the key factors in all motor skills, for it provides the basic starting position from which all movement occurs. Good body alignment is important not only for proper functioning of internal organs but also because it can reflect a child's general health and psychological well-being (self-image). Body posture is important because of its contribution not only to static, nonlocomotor behavior but also to dynamic, moving activities, which contribute to all aspects of daily living, including pushing, pulling, holding, carrying, sitting, and climbing stairs.

The functional posture of children may be considered with respect to the relationship between the base of support and the five main weight centers of the body: head, chest and shoulders, pelvis, knees, and feet. If these weight centers are considered as five independent blocks of wood, it is easy to see the effect of a well-balanced column representing the body's standing posture (see Figure 6.2). It is also easy to describe the typical postural problems in childhood as misalignment of the various weight centers.

If one were to hold a plumb line adjacent to a child, a good standing posture would result in the plumb passing slightly behind the ear, through the shoulder, through the hip, behind the knee, and in front of the ankle (see Figure 6.2). Two of the most common postural problems in children, and particularly retarded children, are illustrated in Figure 6.2: kyphosis and lordosis. The term "kyphosis" refers to a postural problem generally characterized by rounded shoulders and a somewhat forward head.

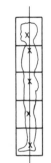

Good Segmental Alignment

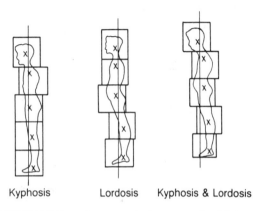

Kyphosis   Lordosis   Kyphosis & Lordosis

FIGURE 6.2   *Segmental alignments in children*

This change in thoracic curvature of the spine may be due to an imbalance of the musculature, with the anterior chest muscles being too tight and the posterior (upper back muscles) too loose (lacking muscular tonus). To aid a child with this problem, it would be important to strengthen the muscles of the upper back and stretch the muscles on the chest side.

Lordosis is a very common problem in children (and particularly teenage and adult females) in which there is an increased forward curvature of the lumbar spine, often referred to as a "hollow back" or "protruding tummy." As is the case with kyphosis, this condition may be alleviated (in nonpathological cases) by a conscious effort at strengthening certain muscles and relaxing or stretching others. In the child with lordosis, this would involve strengthening the abdominal muscles and stretching or relaxing the muscles of the lower back through flexibility exercises.

Conditions such as lordosis and kyphosis are often combined to produce a kind of zig-zag alignment which places certain muscles and ligaments in stretched positions while others must work constantly to maintain a balanced position. In addition, these misalignments may also place undue stress on joint structures such as the hips and knees. For example, many retarded children stand with their toes pointed outward and their knees "locked" in order to maintain a counterbalanced position.

The development of basic body management skills, including body awareness, physical fitness attributes, and postural characteristics, makes it possible to acquire more sophisticated skills, such as locomotor and manipulative skills.

The Development of Fundamental Locomotor Skills

The development of larger, gross movement skills involves two primary classifications of movement: locomotor and manipulative. Locomotor skills involve the coordination of perceptual-motor abilities such as walking and running which are primarily designed to transport the body through space. These locomotor skills allow for an interaction *with* the environment, whereas manipulative skills provide for action *on* the environment. These manipulative or purposeful skills are primarily designed to have an effect on some external object, such as throwing, catching, or bouncing a ball.

Locomotor skills develop in a consistent sequence from crawling and creeping to the more complex upright locomotor skills such as walking, running, jumping, and skipping. Many of these skills are discussed in terms of the chronological or mean age of occurrence. These age levels provide a guide for the normal *sequence* of development for various motor skills, and it is this sequence which is important. For example, in mildly retarded children, both the sequence of development and the actual age of developmental manifestation should be the same as for normal children. However, as the degree of retardation becomes more severe, it may effect the ontogenetic or developmental age but probably not the sequence of development (unless there are other handicapping conditions present). Therefore, the remaining sections of this chapter emphasize the sequence of development for various motor skills, with age levels cited only as a frame of reference.

The most fundamental locomotor skills develop with the young child's ability to navigate in a prone position by crawling and creeping. After these early prone locomotor movements have developed, the assumption of an erect posture becomes the key to the eventual achievement of a wide variety of upright locomotor skills. The initial attainment of an upright posture, however, must be accompanied by three basic abilities: (A) the ability to maintain the body in balance while in an upright moving position, (B) sufficient strength and flexibility to propel the body by alternate movements of the legs and arms, and (C) the coordination of the arms and legs in a synchronized fashion. Well-developed, upright locomotor movements, then, are efficient, balanced, and effectively timed functions of the entire body resulting in symmetrically coordinated use of both sides of the body. This symmetry is displayed in mature walking or running where the limbs move alternately in an oppositional pattern, that is, the right arm and left leg move forward simultaneously, followed by the left arm and right leg.

Crawling and creeping

The rudiments of locomotor behavior can be observed in reflex form during prenatal and neonatal crawling movements. These early manifestations of reflexive locomotor patterns lend support to the concept that the basic movements necessary for locomotion are innate and that they are developed through normal maturational processes. The first manifestation of volitional locomotor movement occurs as the child begins to crawl, generally between 6 and 8 months. Often the first movements are accidental as the prone child attempts to reach for a distant object. If the object is out of reach, the child's chest will return to the floor causing a forward slide as she attempts to pull forward with both arms. This early crawling behavior is characterized by the exclusive use of the upper extremities. The child usually attains a prone arm support position, releases the arm support as the head and chest drop, extends the arms forward, and pulls forward to re-establish arm support position—thus accomplishing a forward movement. At this developmental stage the pelvis and lower extremities provide little propulsive force.

As the child progressively involves both upper and lower extremities, two forms of quadripedal locomotion will generally develop. The crawling pattern may manifest a well-coordinated movement involving the simultaneous action of the right arm and left leg in an oppositional fashion. At approximately the same point in development, the child will also demonstrate a hand-knee position and the characteristic knee rock may be seen. In this position the child is supported by the palms and knees and rocks back and forth in a steady forward-backward sway. The hand-knee position represents a definite attempt at maintaining a creeping posture, even though there is no actual locomotion.

Once the child has mastered this hand-knee position, locomotion is almost inevitable. The early creeping movements are characterized by high intraindividual variation as well as interindividual variation; arm and leg coordination is quite erratic, with unilateral, bilateral, and crosslateral movements randomly interspersed. These three arm and leg movements may be defined as follows:

Unilateral—arm and leg on the same side of the body move simultaneously (i.e., right arm and right leg move together, and then left arm and left leg).

Crosslateral—arms and leg on opposite sides of the body move simultaneously (i.e., right arm and left leg move together, and then left arm and right leg).

Bilateral—the same two appendages move together (i.e., both arms move together, and then both legs)

At this point some children may demonstrate a somewhat systematic exploration of the coordination of arms and legs while others persist in the use of one set of extremities (i.e., two-leg push) or only one appendage at a time (i.e., right arm followed by left knee, followed by left arm and then right knee). Approximately 20% of the children demonstrate a unilateral pattern of movement (i.e., right arm and right knee, then left arm and left knee) (Cratty, 1970). It is also quite common to see children using three appendages with the fourth atop a moveable toy, as seen in Figure 6.3. Finally, in mature creeping, the arms and legs move smoothly and crosslaterally (i.e., in opposition, with right arm and left knee moving forward simultaneously) to provide for balance as well as efficient locomotion (McGraw, 1945).

This early creeping behavior provides a very important set of experiences for the systematic organization of the two sides of the body. The oppositional limb pattern of this early quadriped locomotion will become a key factor in many other skills. For this reason some researchers have suggested that it is essential that all children learn to crawl and then to creep effectively. Recent evidence, however, suggests that this is not so critical as the later establishment of well-coordinated locomotion and consistent lateral dominance (Corbin, 1973; Cratty, 1970).

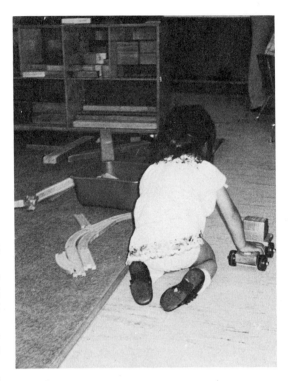

FIGURE 6.3   *Demonstration of early creeping with the aid of a push toy*

Walking

The child's first locomotor patterns are generally that of crawling and creeping, although some children do bypass these patterns in favor of seat sliding or scooting or begin to move directly from an upright posture. The attainment of a standing position is in itself a task worth noting because it is dependent upon a rather complex combination of more basic physical abilities, including balance, strength, and flexibility. In order to gain a standing position most children roll from their front and then rise to a stand. The child first learns to sit and later to be pulled to a stand by either being pulled up by some other person or pulling themselves up on a stable object. Once in an upright position, the child may proceed to walk, provided some relatively stable object (such as a chair or an adult's hand) is present to provide support.

In general, the child's first locomotion is restricted to the area of hand holds (e.g., chairs, tables, parents), which furnish the limits of exploration and "freedom" in an upright position (Figure 6.4). It is therefore essential that a child's early environment encourages locomotion by providing supporting

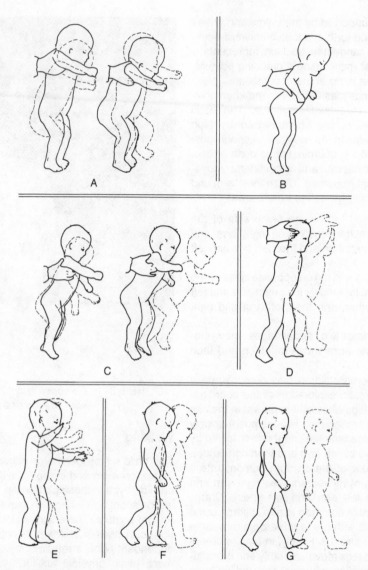

FIGURE 6.4   *The development of erect locomotion*

Source: M. B. McGraw, *The Neuromuscular Maturation of the Human Infant*. New York: Columbia University Press, 1945. By permission of the publisher.

stimuli. The child's first attempts at independence are a major milestone, both physically and socially, and the reinforcement given at this stage is of major importance in the continued rapid development of independent walking.

The development of truly independent stepping occurs after the attainment of both an upright posture and initial bipedal locomotion requiring hand support. The first independent steps are hesitant, irregular in length and rate, and quite unstable. The young child generally exhibits a wide stance with

knees flexed. The toes are usually turned out in an attempt to increase the base of support. The initial steps are often quite irregular and sometimes appear to consist of a few running steps with arms upheld. After the child attains some confidence in this early walking pattern, the rate of walking tends to stabilize at approximately 170 steps per minute between the ages of 18 months and 2 years (Espenschade & Eckert, 1967). This is a rather rapid rate, considering that a briskly walking adult with a longer stride moves at 140–145 steps per minute. The child's rate of walking tends to remain at a relatively constant rate, although the stride length continues to increase during the first two years.

The arm pattern in walking also progresses through a series of developmental changes, with the initial outstretched arm position being a rather noncontributing one, probably utilized as an antigravity mechanism. During the intermediate stages of walking, the arms may swing with the legs in a unilateral fashion (i.e., right arm and right leg swing forward together), whereas in the mature walk the arms swing in opposition to the legs to help counterbalance the hip rotation.

The well-integrated, mature walk is characterized by a narrower and more rhythmic gait, with feet pointed straight ahead and a heel-toe progression of weight bearing. The foot motion is as if the inner borders of each foot were placed along opposite sides of a line rather than directly in front of each other, as in the "model's walk." Obvious arm-leg opposition and decreasing up-down motion should also be observed as the walk matures at approximately 50 months (Gutteridge, 1939).

Once this initial walking pattern is attained, walking up and down stairs requires only a modification of the fundamental pattern of walking, for it demands the integration of sufficient strength, control, and balance to support the body weight on one foot while moving forward and either downward or upward. The first independent attempts at stair climbing are characterized by a "marking time" movement in which one foot advances a step, the trailing foot comes to rest on that step, and then the lead foot again advances one step. In general, children are able to walk upstairs with help by the average age of 16.1 months and to independently mark time upstairs by about 25.1 months but do not attain the downward skill until approximately 25.8 months (Bayley, 1969).

During the time when this developmental process for negotiating stairs is occurring, it is common to have children climb the stairs and then cry for help because they are unable to descend them. Other intermediate solutions for descending stairs are utilized by children who have not mastered climbing down, such as either walking or crawling backward down the stairs or sitting down and scooting down the steps. These intermediate skills will generally drop out with experience, and by 30 months the child will be able to walk up the steps using alternate steps and, by 48 months, be able to descend the stairs successfully, thus providing one very visible

measure for adults to evaluate subjectively the perceptual-motor development of young children.

In general, the studies which have investigated stair-climbing abilities and associated developmental sequences have all found that climbing up stairs develops before climbing down stairs, that shorter flights of stairs are negotiated before longer flights, and that stairs with lower risers are mastered before higher and deeper stairs (Bayley, 1935; Gesell & Thompson, 1929; Shirley, 1933; Wellman, 1937). Some variations have been reported across these studies but the basic sequence has remained consistent, suggesting that stairs should be scaled to meet the child's body size and physical abilities (Espenschade & Eckert, 1967).

Other climbing skills reflect similar developmental patterns. For example, ladder climbing is also characterized by a sequence in which the child "marks time" while leading with the same foot initially, stepping on each rung, and then progresses to the use of leading with either foot. The size and height of the rungs of the ladder obviously affect the child's performance, as does the angle of inclination. Many other activities of the young child require either the use of the basic walking pattern or its modification. It is therefore particularly important that children be provided with a wide range of environmental stimuli. Schools and homes should have stairs, ladders, lofts, bridges, and so on to climb.

A wide variety of upright locomotor skills develops from this basic walking pattern and they can be grouped by characteristic movement patterns and by the rhythmic quality of the movement. There are eight, basic, upright locomotor movements, each of which can be identified by a specific sequence of foot movements and by the underlying rhythm of movement. Of these eight, there are five even locomotor patterns (2/4 or 4/4 time) which are basic modifications of the walk and are briefly defined below:

Walk—the transfer of weight from one foot to the other while moving forward or backward. One foot must always be in contact with the floor.
Run—the transfer of weight from one foot to the other (as in the walk) but with a momentary loss of contact with the floor, providing a period of flight when neither foot is in contact with the ground.
Leap—the transfer of weight from one foot to the other foot as in the run, but with a more sustained period of flight and the attainment of greater height and distance. In the mature form of the

leap, the toe of one foot is the last to leave the floor and the toe on the opposite foot is the first to land.

Hop—the transfer of weight from *one* foot to the same foot, with the opposite foot never touching the surface. In the mature form, the toe is the last to leave the floor and the first to contact again on the downward flight.

Jump—the transfer of weight from *one* or *both* feet, with a landing on *both* feet.

These five even locomotor patterns are combined with three uneven locomotor patterns (sometimes called two-part or long-short rhythms) (see Figure 6.5) and may be differentiated as follows:

Gallop—moving in a forward direction with the *same* foot in front, in a step-close sequence.

Slide—moving in a sideward direction *with* the same foot always leading. The weight is sequentially transferred from the lead foot to the closing foot and back to the same lead foot.

Skip—moving forward with a combination of long step-hop patterns during which the lead foot is alternated.

Running

The first major locomotor pattern, *running,* is primarily an adaptation and extension of the basic walking movements. As previously mentioned, the well-integrated walk is characterized by a narrow, rhythmic gait with feet pointed forward and heel-to-toe transfer of weight over each foot. The basic walking pattern is modified to produce a run in which

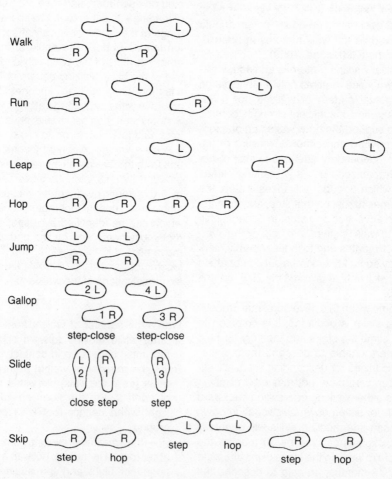

DIRECTION OF MOVEMENT ⟶

FIGURE 6.5   *Foot patterns for the eight fundamental locomotor skills*

there is a nonsupport or flight phase, in contrast to the walk in which one foot is always touching the ground. Little adjustment in limb pattern is required as the child moves from a walk to a run, provided that the neuromuscular system is capable of dealing with the increased tempo and with alterations in the balance and strength requirements necessary for incorporation of a period of nonsupport or flight. Arm and leg opposition are critical both to the well-balanced and efficient walk and to the run.

As the running pattern of the child matures, several developmental changes occur, each contributing to a progressive increase in speed. Perhaps the most obvious changes occur as a consequence of replacing the straight-legged swing with intermediate flexion of the knee. This permits the length of stride to increase and the legs to swing through more quickly (Clouse, 1959). The increase in duration of flight is also recognized as an early developmental sign and indicates greater propulsive force from the driving foot (Dittmer, 1962). These changes in leg action also cause an alteration in the movement of the entire body. In the early running patterns, the child exhibits a great deal of up-and-down motion, so that if the movement of the center of gravity of the child were plotted it would move up-and-down in a sharply peaked fashion: /\/\/\/\/\/\ . In the mature run, the up-down motion is subdued: ⌇⌇⌇⌇ (Beck, 1966; Wickstrom, 1970).

Another highly significant maturational step occurs in the running pattern as the child begins to move the arms in opposition to the legs. In the early run, arms and legs often move unilaterally (i.e., right arm and right leg forward simultaneously), causing a great deal of upper body rotation. During this stage the arms are generally extended and swing through a very short arc, in a pattern similar to the leg action. As the knee and leg actions increase, the arm swing also becomes more rapid and flexed, often cutting across the midline of the body in front and then looping outward on its backward swing (Wickstrom, 1970). Finally, in the mature run, the arms are flexed to approximately 90 degrees at the elbow and swing through a large arc in the vertical plane, remaining synchronized in opposition to the legs.

The developmental changes occurring in the mature running pattern have been described by many authors, particularly Espenschade and Eckert (1967), Okamoto and Kumamoro (1972), and Wickstrom (1970), and may be summarized as a gradual increase in speed, characterized by the following:

1. Increased length of the running stride
2. Increased time in flight
3. Less up-down movement of the center of gravity
4. Increased extension of the propulsive leg to drive the body forward and increased leg flexion, height of the knee and heel, and speed of swing of the free leg in its forward swing
5. Increased rate of swing and flexion of arms, which move in opposition to the legs and in a vertical plane
6. Maintenance of the forward lean of the trunk throughout the pattern, accomplished by a forward shift of the line of gravity of the body to directly over the point of contact of the forward foot.

Leap

The *leap* is probably the most obvious modification of the fundamental running pattern. It is characterized by a take-off from one foot and a landing on the opposite foot. The arms are held in opposition to the legs as in the run. The major distinction then is that in the leap the period of flight is greatly extended and the distance covered during the flight phase is proportionally increased, therefore requiring a greater propulsive thrust of the take-off leg. The attainment and maintenance of this increased nonsupport phase is greatly influenced by the maturation of the complex systems of balance and neuromuscular coordination and is not often observed in children until between 4–5 years. The leap is a complex skill in that it is dependent upon three component parts: (A) the strength required for the initial thrust, (B) the balance and coordination required for the inflight phase, and (C) the strength and balance required for a controlled landing.

Figure 6.6 illustrates a child engaged in a spontaneous leap over a playground tire. Notice the somewhat immature arm pattern with the left arm and left leg forward and the right arm raised for balance. As the leaping pattern matures, the arm and leg action will be in opposition as in the run. It may also be noted that in the advanced leap the toe of one foot is the last to leave the floor and the toe of the other foot is the first to land.

Jumping

Modification of the walking and running patterns to accomplish *jumping* requires the ability both to maintain the body in balance while suspended off the ground and to generate sufficient strength to propel the body into that suspended position.

FIGURE 6.6   *A spontaneous leap over an embedded playground tire* (Notice the early homolateral arm and leg action.)

The mature jump is further complicated by the necessity of coordinating a take-off from *one or both* feet, a flight phase, and a landing on *both* feet.

The jumping pattern of early childhood progresses through a gradual increase in the height of a "step-down" jump from a stair or box, to a two-footed jump-down technique, and finally to a two-footed take-off and landing. The two-footed landing develops rather early, but the two-footed take-off is the final stage to develop because it requires a complex coordination effort involving simultaneous double limb propulsion (Espenschade & Eckert, 1967). Typically the first "step-down" jump from 18 inches will be observed by about 27 months, an independent one-foot version by 31 months, and a two-footed jump by 37 months (Wellman, 1937).

The first jumps are done in a rather rigid and jarring manner, with the legs remaining stiff. The arms are generally held out to the side and tend to produce only moderate counterbalancing. As the child continues to progress, the leg action involves more flexion and propulsion with the legs and arms tending to lift forward and upward to aid in the propulsive phase (Wickstrom, 1970).

Two basic jumping patterns emerge during motor development: a vertical jump and a horizontal or broad jump. Both of these jumps develop from the same common "jump-down" sequence and require relative sophistication of arm-leg coordination (Hellebrandt, et al., 1961). The developmental sequence of both of these patterns follow similar courses during early childhood, with the only sex-linked differences occurring after puberty when boys become much stronger.

An analysis of the vertical jump (jump for height) reveals several developmental changes. The early jump is characterized by little contribution of the arms, which often swing backward or are held out to the side (see Figure 6.7). During this same stage, the leg action involves great flexion at the knees, causing the trunk to tip forward in a noncontributing fashion. A downward visual focus is also predominant at this stage, causing the head to be flexed forward. In comparison, the mature vertical jumping

pattern can be divided into six primary movements (Wickstrom, 1970):

1. Flexion at the hips, knees and ankles during the preparatory crouch
2. Vigorous forward-upward thrust of the arms to begin propulsion
3. The addition of a forceful extension of the hips, knees, and ankles
4. Continued extension of the body until the feet retouch the surface
5. Elective downward thrust of one arm in opposition to the reaching arm
6. Absorption of force upon recontact, by flexion of the hips, knees, and ankles.

Several modifications of the basic vertical jump are necessary to accomplish an effective horizontal jump. Of primary importance in modifying the basic jumping pattern is an increase in the depth of the preliminary crouch and a decrease in the take-off angle (Hellebrandt et al., 1961). In order to accomplish these, the arm swing must emphasize a forward-outward movement rather than an upward thrust. This sequential arm action is perhaps the most difficult aspect because the child's first use of the arms is essentially for a breaking movement and then for counterbalance (Wickstrom, 1970).

Hopping

The development of *hopping* skills requires a rather sophisticated ability to maintain dynamic balance. Because of the balance and strength problems,

FIGURE 6.7 *An early illustration of the vertical jump pattern* (Notice the use of the arms and the uneven take off from the two feet.)

FIGURE 6.8 *The sliding pattern of early childhood is quite difficult because it requires looking in one direction and moving in another.*

many children are able to execute a series of irregular jumps in which both feet are used in landing well before they are able to hop on only one foot. For many children the ability to balance on one foot is a major accomplishment and is only partially achieved at approximately 29 months of age (Bayley, 1969; Gesell, 1940). Yet it is not until approximately 50 months that the average child will be able to hop 2 meters in a free fashion (Bayley, 1935), and by about five years of age, most children will be able to hop over longer distances at greater speeds (50 feet in 10.5 seconds) (Cratty, 1970).

The addition of more complex facets such as changes in direction, speed, rhythm, or alternating feet add varying degrees of difficulty to the fundamental hopping pattern. These variations also generate some differences in performance, with relatively straight-forward hops of varying distances being mastered well before shorter and more asymmetrical hops which involve changes in direction or foot sequence (Keogh, Note 1, 1965).

Galloping

The development of the child's ability to *gallop* marks the first sign of an *uneven* or two-part locomotor movement. This step-close pattern with the same foot leading at all times combines the basic patterns of the even locomotor movements into an uneven rhythmic pattern and apparently emerges as a direct response to an uneven musical rhythm. It is this rhythmic requirement which greatly increases the degree of difficulty of the gallop as compared to the even-rhythmed skills of the walk, run, leap, hop, and jump. A greater degree of sophistication in the basic balance mechanisms is also required in order to control the forward momentum generated in this step-close pattern.

The first true galloping pattern may occur as early as 36 months and is often characterized initially by stiff legs and a jarring appearance (Gutteridge, 1939), sometimes associated with a child's imitation of the stamping done by horses. In this early pattern the body weight appears to be thrown forward over the leading leg and then rocks back onto the closing foot. As the pattern matures, the forward leg demonstrates greater flexion at the hip and knee, with the body weight staying forward throughout the pattern. Most 5-year-olds can demonstrate a recognizable pattern, however it is not until 6½ years of age that most children are considered skillful at galloping (Breckenridge & Vincent, 1956; Gesell, 1946). Children who demonstrate some problems with gal-

loping can often be assisted by placing a "broomstick" horse between their legs so that if the child alternates the lead foot the broomstick will drop out.

Sliding

Sliding may be considered the same movement pattern as galloping—a step-close with the same foot leading. The major distinction between the gallop and the slide is in the direction of the movement. In the gallop, the body faces and moves forward, whereas in the slide, the body faces forward and moves sideward. There is, in addition, a qualitative difference in the uneven rhythm of the gallop and the slide. The gallop is generally performed in a rather staccato or sharp rhythm; the slide is often characterized as a smooth, flowing movement. This qualitative difference is not, however, the primary reason that the gallop is mastered earlier than the slide.

Modification of a basic locomotor pattern to provide for sideward movement without direct visual guidance creates a substantial problem in the development of sliding. The visual problem is illustrated by the fact that the basic foot pattern required for sliding is established with the development of the gallop, between 24–36 months, yet the mature slide does not appear until much later in the developmental process, at approximately 48 months (Sinclair, 1973). Figure 6.8 illustrates some of the variations observed during the initial attempts at sliding.

Skipping

The *skipping* movement of early childhood can be defined as a sequential step-hop pattern in which the lead foot alternates with each phase. Because of this complex sequence of alternating body movements, skipping is generally the last of the locomotor skills to develop, although some children begin to exhibit a type of preliminary skip or shuffle step by as early as 38 months (Espenschade & Eckert, 1967). This initial shuffle step has few similarities to the skip and is more often considered a type of forward slide. The most frequently observed actual precursor to the skip is a type of one-legged skip in which one foot produces a step-hop sequence but the other foot merely steps forward—sometimes resembling a lame-legged skip.

The mature alternate-foot pattern skip is generally not achieved until much later (approximately 60 months) and for some children may require the as-

FIGURE 6.9   *The skipping pattern of early childhood*

sistance of a partner skipping on each side of the child to emphasize the alternation of the lead foot. This well-developed foot pattern is accompanied by oppositional movement of the arms in relation to the legs and a high degree of flexion in the hip and knee of the lead foot. For example, the child in Figure 6.9 has good leg action, but immature arm action. The difficulty of accomplishing this complex sequence can be noted by the fact that only 22% of the 5-year-olds can be classified as skipping well as compared to 90% of the 6-year-olds (Gutteridge, 1939).

Summary of locomotor skill development

Locomotor skill development will be most facilitated by a physical environment in which there are open spaces and obstacles to climb on and move around, through, over, and under. This environment should be made up of a variety of textures—carpeted areas, tiled floors, wood and plastic materials, and soft and hard surfaces. As children become more adept at locomotor movements, experiences of greater variety are essential. Playground environments should be naturalistic and include obstacle courses and apparatus for climbing, jumping, swinging, and balancing.

The development of play behaviors should be encouraged. A wide variety of games may be utilized to provide good experiences for children's play and simultaneously for the development of locomotor skills. For example, games such as Hide and Seek, Jack in the Box, Mulberry Bush, Do This—Do That, and Follow the Leader stimulate a child's curiosity and require locomotor skill practice at the same time. The games of childhood should include more and more sophisticated skills and challenges requiring the continued exploration and modification of locomotor patterns and the addition of greater degrees of precision of movement, strength, speed, and balance. In addition, these activities should be made available to all children in order to encourage equal opportunity at skill development. Several researchers have suggested some differences in performance based on sex, with boys being more proficient at tasks requiring strength and girls being superior at hopping tasks which require precision and accuracy (Cratty, 1970; Espenschade & Eckert, 1967; Keogh, Note 1, 1965). However, it should be noted that these differences may be due to experiential variables and not necessarily to sex-linked characteristics.

Several major studies have identified significant milestones in the sequence of locomotor pattern development. The data from these studies have been combined in Table 6.1 to provide a summary of locomotor development. This sequence serves as an ordered instructional guide for teachers of severely handicapped individuals whose locomotor development may be delayed and who often require monitoring and systematic instruction.

Table 6.1 demonstrates a rather stable sequence of developmental changes. This *sequence* remains essentially unaltered for the moderately handicapped, although the more complex skills may be somewhat delayed. For example, jumping and skipping may not be observed at all before 3 or 4 years of age in some handicapped children, or they may appear in a rudimentary form but not reach the normal level of integrated symmetry.

The Development of Fine Motor Skills

The fundamental skills of locomotion and manipulation are essential for all motor behavior. Daily living tasks, self-help skills, and many vocational skills are

TABLE 6.1 *Summary of locomotor skill development*

Movement Outcome	Average Chronological Age of Accomplishment
Sits alone	4 to 8 mos.
Crawling/creeping (Bayley, 1969)	5 mos. to 1 yr.
Stands with help (Shirley, 1933); stepping movements when held (Bayley, 1969); walks holding onto furniture (Frankenburg & Dodds, 1969)	6 mos. to 1 yr.
Walks sideward or backward (Bayley, 1969); walks well (Frankenburg & Dodds, 1967); walks upstairs with help (Bayley, 1969); shuffle run with stiff legs (*Lexington Developmental Scale*, 1973)	1 yr to 1½ yrs.
Walks upstairs, marking time (Bayley, 1969); jumps from bottom step (Bayley, 1969); runs well and can stop and start safely (*Lexington Developmental Scale*, 1973); jumps in place (Frankenburg & Dodds, 1967); distance jumps 4–14" (Bayley, 1969)	1½ to 2 yrs.
Walks on slightly elevated board, walks on tip toes (Bayley, 1969); gallops (Sinclair, 1973); jumps 4 or more times on bouncing board (Sinclair, 1973)	2 to 3 yrs.
Walks downstairs alternating feet (Bayley, 1969); "skips" on one foot (*Lexington Developmental Scale*, 1973); hops 1–10 times consecutively (Wellman, 1937); slides to preferred side (Sinclair, 1973); running broad jump 23–33" (Corbin, 1973)	3 to 4 yrs.
Skips alternating feet (*Lexington Developmental Scale*, 1973); hops more than 2 yards (Bayley, 1969); slides in either direction, gallops well (Espenschade & Eckert, 1967); walks full length of 4" board (Gesell, 1940)	4 to 5 yrs.

based on the stability and body control abilities initially acquired through general movements requiring body management and then specifically developed as fundamental skills. In addition, many of the specific tasks required for daily living and economic sufficiency are dependent on knowledge of fundamental skills. For example, a cafeteria worker or assembly-line worker is more efficient if the work is performed with competent locomotor skills, while custodial and housekeeping tasks necessitate competence in manipulative skills.

Fundamental skills also provide the basis for social and leisure-time activities. The ability to engage in socially interactive situations, such as individual or group play, is dependent upon a functional level of fundamental skills. For example, a child cannot participate in a simple game of catch, croquet, or hopscotch without some degree of locomotor and manipulative skill development.

The value of fundamental skills in the prevocational and vocational training of moderately and severely handicapped children cannot be overestimated. Of particular importance to adult life are the object-control skills which encourage indepen-

dence and self-expression and provide information about the external world. This information may come through fine motor skills which involve a complex integration of visual and fine motor skills. These skills are based in part on the development of *manual dexterity*, the ability to make skillful and controlled arm and hand movements, and *finger dexterity*, consisting of rapid and fine finger movements, and the combined utilization of these skills. For example, the child's ability to grasp and hold objects provides a means of exploring the world. A child needs experiences with handling different objects in order to learn to identify and discriminate among various objects in terms of size, shape, texture, weight, and firmness. These experiences also help the child to learn to match sensory input from various sense modalities, including visual, tactile, and kinesthetic data.

The fine motor skills involved in reaching, grasping, and manipulating objects develop in a sequential fashion, based upon a combination of the child's early experiences, chronological and physiological age, mental age, handicapping conditions, and the establishment of hand preference. The early experiences with grasping generally begin as part of the entire flexion pattern in which the child exhibits a tightly clinched fist. As the child grows and matures, the entire body begins to relax, and with this relaxation the child begins to explore his/her entire being, but particularly the fingers and hands. A great deal of hand-eye and hand-mouth exploration continues to provide new kinesthetic and tactile input to add to the visual data.

Manual Dexterity: Grasping

One of the most important fine motor skills to develop is the ability to grasp objects. The first real grasping behaviors occur as both arms reach for an object and then one entire hand clenches around the object. One hand reaching requires a much more sophisticated combination of visual skills and the ability to maintain equilibrium. Similarly, transferring objects from hand to hand and releasing them at will develop in a fairly sequential pattern. The early cognitive elements of the visually directed grasps are discussed in more detail in Chapter 4.

Five fundamental grasping patterns have been identified in all children: palmar, dagger, shovel, scissors, and pincer grasps (Halverson, 1931; Kamin, 1972) as seen in Figure 6.10. Each of these grasps is designed to accomplish specific goals and is therefore essential in specific types of tasks.

The most fundamental form of volitional grasping has been described as a *palmar grasp,* and involves an essentially flat-handed approach to objects. In this pattern, the fingers are generally spread and somewhat extended, much as one would grasp a hair brush. This type of grasp prevents accurate finger and wrist manipulation and requires most action to be generated by the entire arm.

The *dagger grasp* provides for more solid control as the fingers are flexed around the outside of the object. The most typical arm action utilized with this grasp involves wrist or elbow and shoulder action much like a jab or stab. The *shovel grasp* is a modification of the basic dagger grasp in which the useful action is toward the thumb (radial) side, rather than toward the little finger (ulnar). The thumb is a critical component of both of these grasps and may be used in several different ways: thumb wrapped around and enclosed by fingers, thumb over fingers, thumb used as lever, thumb used alongside fingers (Kamin, 1972). Both of these grasps are typically used in such actions as tooth brushing and hammering.

The *scissors grasp* is accomplished by placing

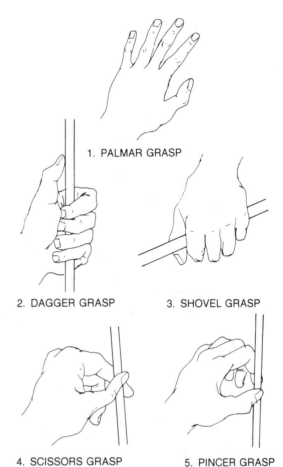

FIGURE 6.10   *Developmental stages of grasping*

Source: P. Kamin, Fine motor development and the grasp function. In J. S. Molloy (Ed.), *Trainable Children: Curriculum and Procedures.* Copyright 1972 by the John Day Co., New York. Reprinted by permission.

the thumb against the side of the index finger and is based primarily on the child's ability to separate the thumb movements from those of the other fingers. Both scissors and tongs can be effective implements to encourage the development of the visual fine-motor skills of opening and shutting the fingers. Scissors should be grasped with the thumb and middle finger inserted in the handles, with the first finger used to add leverage.

The *pincer grasp* is probably the most sophisticated grasp, and requires a great deal of precision motion. Objects held in a pincer grasp are manipulated by the thumb and tip of the index finger, as in holding a pen or paint brush, pulling a zipper, sewing with a needle.

An awareness of the child's ability to utilize various types of grasps will aid the teacher in establishing learning tasks which are appropriate to the child's readiness levels. For example, if a child is still handling a crayon with a dagger grasp, it will only generate frustration to attempt to encourage shoe tying. On the other hand, if the child can utilize a scissors grasp, many self-help and prewriting skills may be appropriate.

In addition to these basic, one-handed grasping skills, many other fine motor skills require the use of *two* hands. Two-handed movements which involve the same movement performed bilaterally, including such things as pushing oneself up from a prone position or clapping the hands, are somewhat more difficult to accomplish than one-handed skills. Two-handed activities which demand different movement on each side appear to be particularly difficult for the retarded child.

Manual and Finger Dexterity: Drawing

Children's drawing is another example of the demonstration of a skill requiring not only fine motor skills but also visual-motor integration. Drawing represents not only how the child sees the world but also how he/she feels about the world. An examination of a child's drawing skills may provide a great

deal of information about each of these areas of development and also about the child's fine motor skill development.

The following developmental sequence, modified from Lowenfeld and Brittain (1975), suggests some important considerations for the teacher. In the earliest forms of drawing, children are primarily involved with the creative act of making marks and are not at all interested in the final product. During this *random scribbling stage,* children generally hold the crayon or pencil in a palmar or dagger grasp and the drawing action is generated by moving the entire arm and shoulder (see Figure 6.11). Children at this stage have probably not yet acquired sufficient neuromotor skills to be ready to learn the fine motor coordination necessary for the self-help skills of independent buttoning or zippering, cutting with scissors, or gluing.

The children's drawings shown in Figure 6.11 also demonstrate two additional types of skills. The child at the right has her free hand on a series of lines which have been generated by an up-down or *push-pull* action; the child on the left has progressed to a *circular* motion which requires a greater degree of finger and wrist control.

Toward the end of the first scribbling stage, chil-

FIGURE 6.11   *The development of drawing and writing skills in the young child follows a fairly predictable pattern beginning with the scribbling stage. Here is the characteristic circular scribbling that occurs at approximately three years of age. These girls have not yet developed the writing/drawing grasp.*

dren begin to shift from random marks to *named scribbles* (Lowenfeld & Brittain, 1975). At this point, children begin to make purposeful lines and patterns as they attach meaning to their pictures. Fine motor skills are becoming more precise as exemplified by a form of modified scissors grasp which signals a new level of "readiness."

From this point, children enter a *preschematic* stage in which they represent their understanding of the world and their own being. Circular motions become tree tops or heads, longer lines become tree trunks, arms, or legs. During this preschematic and later *schematic* stage, children are beginning to develop the two primary requirements of handwriting skills: the recognition of shapes and sizes in their environment and the sophistication of visual and fine motor skills to allow for these shapes to be represented on paper.

Manual and Finger Dexterity: Handwriting and Dominance

One of the most meaningful skills related to both manual dexterity and finger dexterity is the acquisition of handwriting. The achievement of being able to write (print) one's own name is a tremendous personal accomplishment for a retarded child besides reflecting a rather sophisticated integration of visual and motor coordination. This integration is dependent on several underlying factors including a pre-established lateral dominance, a level of neuromuscular skill, and some measure of fundamental visual-motor skill. It therefore becomes important for the teacher to assess these three factors before undertaking a handwriting program.

Dominance. The determination and reinforcement of dominance is a key factor in both fine motor and gross motor skills and includes both eye dominance and foot dominance in addition to hand dominance. To ascertain the preferred side of a child, one could administer a standardized test, such as the *Test of Lateral Dominance* (Harris, 1958), and carefully observe the behavior of a child in everyday activities. For example, to determine the preferred eye, ask a child to look through a telescope or peek through a small hole in a piece of paper. If the child consistently uses one eye, that is the dominant eye. Foot preference is a somewhat more task-specific skill which emphasizes the importance of consistent preference rather than sidedness, since a child may consistently kick a ball with the right foot but choose to balance on the left foot.

The establishment of a dominant or preferred side is particularly significant as children begin to acquire fine motor skills. Research on the effect of mixed dominance is inconclusive; however, there is strong support for the need to establish consistent use of the same appendage for the same task (Flowers, 1975; Ingram, 1975; Palmer, 1963; Steingrueber, 1975). It is therefore essential, once it has been determined that a child is right- or left-handed, that handedness is encouraged. It is not advisable to attempt to change a left-handed child to a right-hander, but rather encourage and reinforce one dominant hand. If no preference is apparent, you should provide additional experiences for experimenting with each hand and encourage the development of a preference.

Handwriting. Children must also have some degree of neuromuscular coordination in order to undertake prewriting skills. For example, a child who still grasps a pencil with a dagger grasp will have a great deal of difficulty learning to control a pencil accurately, since in order to write effectively children must use either a scissor or pincer grasp. The relative level of tension in the grasping hand may also have an effect on the ultimate success of the writer and may indicate not only a neuromuscular but also a potential emotional problem which may require an extra degree of positive reinforcement and success-generating experiences (Holladay, 1966).

In terms of the visual-motor prerequisites of writing, children should be able to discriminate between various shapes (i.e., "b" versus "d") and also to make from memory copies of such simple shapes as a square, triangle, and circle. Training programs such as the Frostig workbooks can be helpful in establishing this skill (Frostig, 1973). It may also be helpful for the teacher to observe whether the child is in the scribble, push-pull, or circling stages of drawing. Once the child can perform these activities, copying skills will develop rapidly between the ages of 2½ and 5 and continue to mature for many years. This sequence of development will be the same for all children, although it may be somewhat *delayed* for handicapped children. For example, the average 5-year-old can copy a square and a triangle, but will not be able to copy a diamond until about 7 years of age. Biologically then, in terms of visual and fine motor skills, most children will be ready to begin prewriting by age 5 or 6.

There are many techniques available for teaching handwriting, although most teachers have found the more simplistic, straight-line systems to be most easily mastered. In terms of the actual alphabet, the straight-line letters are also the easiest for children to reproduce (A, E, F, H, I, K, L, M, N, V, W, X, Y, Z) and may therefore be used to form the building blocks of writing. The "ball-stick" letters (a, b, d, g, o, p, q) are also relatively easy to reproduce, but extremely difficult in terms of visual-motor discrimination because the only distinguishing feature is in the placement of the "ball" with respect to the "stick." In contrast the letters "e," "r," and "s" are perhaps the most difficult to produce but relatively easy to visually discriminate.

Advocates of printed manuscript writing emphasize that this form is simpler because its essential composition of lines, circles, and diagonals is generally more legible and has a higher degree of transfer to the acquisition of reading skills (Johnson & Mykleburst, 1969; Mecham, Berko, & Palmer, 1966; Slingerland, 1971). In contrast, some authors advocate the teaching of cursive writing because of the advantages of the rhythmic left to right progression and the fact that reversals seem to be more avoidable because of the continuous flowing motion and the more distinctive differences between such letters as "b," "d," "p," and "q" (Cruickshank, 1961; McGinnis, 1963). It is this author's opinion that for moderately and severely handicapped children it may be more advantageous to teach manuscript style because of its similarity to typed print. One would also probably teach each child to write her signature, but probably would *not* teach complete cursive skills.

Other Fine Motor Skills

Many other childhood skills require fine motor skills which must become progressively more precise and steady. For example, as children acquire the basic eye-hand coordinating movements, they engage in activities that require greater degrees of precision and steadiness. These skills in turn demand more sophisticated visual-motor integration and greater degrees of patience and perseverance. Because of these added elements, retarded children often appear to tire easily; as their patience wanes, so does the relative steadiness, thus creating a frustrating, failure-laden situation. However, many of these situations can be avoided by the careful planning of learning environments. The frustrating experiences can become the rewarding experience through the use of small, carefully sequenced steps (i.e. task analysis) and the gradual shaping of desired behaviors.

Activities which require fine motor skills including precision and steadiness can be found in most classroom settings. For example, children seek activities such as building with blocks, and their creations are often quite complex in terms of precision. The most simple block towers may be seen as early as one year, with children progressing from rows, to bridges, to enclosures, and to complex patterns (Johnson, 1974). Similarly moderately and severely handicapped children and young adults enjoy putting puzzles together, modeling with clay, and hammering nails, each of which requires a more complex integration of one or both hands in accomplishing a task (see Figure 6.12). The average assembly job in a sheltered workshop setting thoroughly taxes one's adeptness in steady, precise, eye-hand coordinating movements besides requiring long periods of perseverance. Prevocational preparation in simple but realistic assembly-disassembly tasks should become part of the day's curriculum for the severely handicapped adolescent. The speed and accuracy of an assembly as well as the duration of productive work combine with the specific fine motor movements of the task (e.g., twisting, grasping, squeezing, etc.) to create a complex instructional situation. More on the topic of vocational training is discussed in Chapter 13 and 14.

Summary of fine motor skill development

The developmental progression of fine motor skills begins very early in life as the child begins to manipulate objects in the environment, oftentimes by vigorously banging, shaking, and mouthing almost everything within reach. This manipulation may involve both hands simultaneously, a single hand, or two hands doing two different things.

As the child becomes more sophisticated in fine motor tasks, many other behaviors emerge, including block building, peg pounding, tooth brushing, coloring, tracing, and drawing. Table 6.2 represents a simplified survey for the development of fine motor skills. This sequence represents the progressive development of fine motor skills; although the time frame may be altered for the retarded child, the order is essentially the same.

It should also be recognized that the demands upon the fine-motor skills of retarded children are probably emphasized to a greater degree than any other skills. The young child is required to develop the precise hand-eye skills necessary for school-related tasks such as writing, drawing, cutting, and copying while the older child must accomplish these

FIGURE 6.12   *Fine motor skills are required to perform many leisure time, daily living, and vocational activities, including sewing, cutting, modeling clay, and working puzzles.*

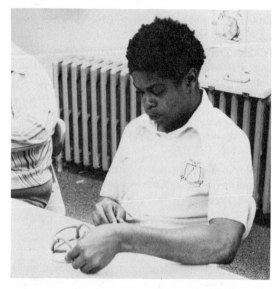

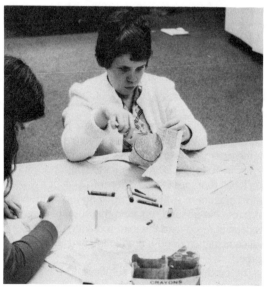

TABLE 6.2 *Summary of fine motor development*

Movement Outcome	Average Chronological Age of Accomplishment
Hands fisted at rest; finger play; manipulates red ring (Bayley, 1969)	0 to 4 mos.
Hand open or loosely fisted (Halverson, 1931); retains 2 cubes in hands (Bayley, 1969); grasps rattle, ring; palmar grasp (Kamin, 1972)	4½ to 8 mos.
Finger-thumb opposition (Cattell, 1960); accurate reading grasp (Gibson, 1970; scissors grasp of pellet (Cattell, 1960); grasp and release of cube (Bayley, 1969; Gesell, 1940); bangs 2 cubes together (Frankenburg & Dodds, 1967)	9 mos. to 1 yr.
Builds tower of 2 cubes (Bayley, 1969); scribbles spontaneously (Frankenburg & Dodds, 1967); forefinger grasp (Halverson, 1931); unwraps packages (Cattell, 1960); lifts and holds cup (*Lexington Developmental Scale*, 1973); neat pincer grasp (Gesell, 1940)	1 to 1½ yrs.
Imitates vertical or horizontal lines (Bayley, 1969); turns pages of book one at a time; strings 3 1-inch beads; builds bridge with cubes (Cattell, 1960); solves 2-piece puzzle (McCarthy, 1972)	1½ to 3 yrs.
Cuts with scissors; spreads butter with knife (Hurlock, 1964)	3 to 4 yrs.
Cuts with knife (Hurlock, 1964); laces shoes (*Lexington Developmental Scale*, 1973); shows preferred hand dominance (Flick, 1967); imitates drawing (McCarthy, 1972)	4 to 5 yrs.
Can brush and comb hair; prints first name (Ames & Ilg, 1951); enjoys cutting and pasting; cuts with scissors along lines and colors within lines (Terman & Merrill, 1960)	5 to 6 yrs.
Prints entire alphabet, with some reversals; carpentry and sewing skills (Gesell, 1946)	6 to 7 yrs.

tasks as well as many other prevocational skills such as sewing, hammering, cooking, object assembly, and packing. Emphasis should not be placed on the precision of these skills until the basic skill patterns have been acquired.

The Development of Gross Motor Manipulative Skills

Manipulative or purposive skills are primarily designed to allow the individual to have an effect on some external object and may involve both fine and gross motor skills. Throwing, catching, and bouncing a ball represent three different types of manipulative movements, the first requiring the production of force, the second requiring the absorption or reception of force, and the third requiring the sequential combination of both production and reception of force.

The production of force sufficient to have some effect on an external object or person is a primary accomplishment for children and often signals the first major goal-directed activity in which the child acts *on* the environment. The production of force to manipulate external objects requires, not only sufficient strength to overcome the specific resistance, but that this strength also is controlled in terms of the magnitude of the force and the duration or length of time of its application. Similarly, the absorption or reception of force, as in catching, includes the complex visual-motor interaction required for maintaining balance (equilibrium) while judging the position of an object and receiving the impetus or momentum of that moving object. This problem is often further complicated by the necessity to absorb the force without allowing the object to rebound from the body or to cause injury.

Many perceptual skills are involved in the execution of a manipulative skill which requires the ability to identify an object's size, weight, and speed. In addition, manipulative movements are dependent upon the attainment of varying degrees of visual-motor coordination. The eyes must focus on the object to be received or acted upon and the appropriate body parts must respond to the judgments made through the sensory systems. Throwing, catching, striking, and kicking a ball are propulsive skills which require the establishment of eye-hand or eye-foot coordination. In addition, coordinative problems may become magnified as the child begins to move through space while executing propulsive movements (i.e., running and kicking or catching a ball, pushing and pulling objects through space) or when an implement is added (i.e., baseball bat or croquet mallet) or when an implement is used to generate the movement (i.e., riding a tricycle).

Developmental sequences for gross motor manipulative skills have been fairly well established by such researchers as Wellman (1937), Wild (1938), McGraw (1945), Deach (1950), Wickstrom (1970), and Sinclair (1973). Developmental aspects of these patterns have been studied in terms of two types of changes: product (the force or distance and accuracy) and process (the aesthetic and mechanically efficient form). These types of pattern changes will be discussed in the following sections.

Throwing Patterns

Overarm throwing pattern. One of the first manipulative skills to develop in children is the overarm throwing pattern. A young child demonstrates the rudiments of this skill as objects are hurled from the playpen, as spoons are thrown down from the highchair. Even at this early developmental level, the pattern is characterized by arm action consisting of the forward movement of the elbow (ahead of the forearm), and then the full extension of the arm before the object is released.

A basic developmental sequence for the overarm throwing pattern was identified by Wild (1938) and has been verified and amplified by many other observers through cinemagraphic techniques (Bunker, 1975; Deach, 1950; Halverson & Roberton, 1966; Hanson, 1961; Jones, 1951; Wickstrom, 1970). The fundamental characteristics of the overhand throwing pattern, as identified by researchers, generally indicate a progression through four distinct phases of movement: monoplanar action, whole body rotation, unilateral action, and sequential, cross-lateral movement.

In the first or monoplanar stage, objects are thrown with almost all the force produced by the

extension of the arm at the elbow in an anterior-posterior plan of movement as seen in Figure 6.13. This arm action occurs with little or no trunk rotation or effective leverage as the feet remain side by side. In addition, the action is restricted to the anterior-posterior (forward-backward) plan of movement, hence the term "monoplanar."

In the second, or rotatory stage, the arm action is joined by trunk rotation occurring simultaneously with the action of the throwing arm. This addition of the rotational component involving the hips, spine, and shoulders adds to the force, but the total force is still somewhat limited by the square base of support and the simultaneous rotation of the body and extension of the arm. The addition of a forward step marks the advancement into the third or unilateral stage. During this phase, a forward step with the

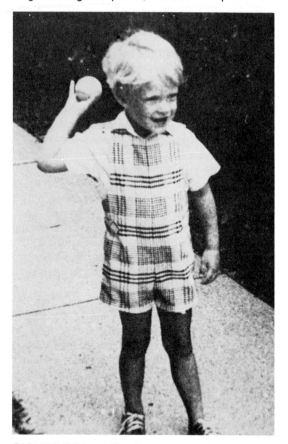

FIGURE 6.13   *The first or monoplanar stage of the overarm throw, in which most action involves simple anterior-posterior movement of the arm and little or no trunk movement.*

foot on the same side as the throwing arm is added to increase the force production. Unfortunately, however, the addition of this forward step may limit the amount of preliminary trunk rotation and therefore continues to restrict the range of movement, even though some additional hip flexion is observed.

In the mature, crosslateral pattern, the arms and trunk rotate backward in preparation for the throw, followed by a step forward with the leg opposite the throwing arm (cross-lateral). As the hips, trunk, and shoulders derotate, the elbow swings forward, the forearm extends, and the wrist snaps in releasing the ball. This sequence provides the key to a successful overarm throwing pattern and is generally made possible by assuming an oppositional stance (i.e., left foot forward for a right-handed thrower) and then, sequentially, rotation of the hips and the trunk and finally the arm action and natural follow-through.

The mature overarm throwing pattern does not consist of a specific, rigid skill but is rather a modifiable sequence of actions designed to be applied in many different situations. For example, the basic characteristics of an oppositional stance, hip and trunk rotation, and arm action are only slightly altered to accommodate the different skill requirements of a baseball throw, javelin throw, and football throw. In addition, this same underlying pattern can be further modified to produce effective movements which involve the striking of an object with the hand, such as an overarm volleyball serve, or the imparting of force through another implement, such as a tennis serve or hammering a nail. Thus the basic overarm pattern provides a very flexible sequence of movements which can be applied to a variety of skills.

Underarm throwing pattern. The developmental sequence for the underarm pattern is very similar to that demonstrated for the overarm pattern. During the early stages of this pattern, children generally throw with their entire body in a monoplanar fashion. The second phase is essentially a rotatory movement in which the sequential action of the entire body "slings" the arm in an oblique angle. The third stage adds a homolateral forward step to the pendular arm action.

In the mature, crosslateral underarm throw, the arms and trunk rotate backward in preparation for the throw, followed by the step forward with the opposite leg as the hips, trunk, and shoulders derotate and the arm swings through. The sequential

action of the various body parts contributes greatly to the force produced, as did the sequential joint action discussed in the overarm pattern. This underarm pattern is a very flexible movement sequence which can be modified to produce many types of movements, including bowling, underarm badminton and volleyball serves, and horseshoe pitching. A second form of underarm striking is perhaps better classified as an oblique downward pattern, as might be used to shovel snow or swing a golf club. The early golf-type swings reported by Wickstrom (1968) involve a type of modified sidearm pattern in which children seem to bend down and swipe at the object.

Sidearm throwing pattern. The sidearm pattern is not generally observed in its mature form during early childhood. Most young children prefer to utilize either the overarm or underarm patterns to execute a throwing motion. The preference is probably the result of both the changed visual orientation and the somewhat more difficult arm action. This sidearm pattern requires an arm swing which is parallel to the ground and a somewhat erratic whip-like action as the arm extends to execute the actual throw.

The development of a sidearm pattern (for either throwing or striking) requires a major adjustment in the integration of the visual-motor system because of the side stance rather than a forward position. In the early stages of striking, the overarm pattern will predominate, but gradually, without special assistance, this vertical swing moves downward through a series of increasing angles until it is essentially a horizontal, sidearm position. This early sidearm pattern is characterized by the initial action of the arm, which causes limited trunk rotation (Halverson & Roberton, 1966). The initial trunk rotation is therefore a result of the arm action rather than a source of increased force. The developmental sequence is similar to other throwing patterns in that gradually the child adds a forward weight shift followed by more joint actions, including hip-trunk rotation and eventually the arm action (Collins, 1960; Halverson and Roberton, 1966). This sequential pattern of force production, from feet through trunk to the arm, is characteristic of all throwing/striking patterns and emerges in a very predictable fashion.

The early stages of sidearm pattern development are often contaminated by the recurrence of overarm striking patterns. Wickstrom (1968) found that children younger than 30 months often revert to overarm actions rather than sidearm movements when striking. This may be because if simply requested to throw a tennis ball, very few will voluntarily select a sidearm throw. Yet, if a tennis ball is suspended at waist height, most children will select a sidearm striking pattern to hit the ball. This selection seems to depend on the task at hand since children will use the sidearm pattern when given a light plastic paddle (Halverson & Roberton, Note 3, 1966) or when simply asked to hit the ball with their hand (Bunker, Note 2, 1975), thus emphasizing the importance of carefully creating learning environments that will elicit the desired responses.

Striking Patterns

The developmental sequences for striking behaviors are similar in direction and rate to the progress of throwing skills. Part of this association is no doubt due to the similarity of the three movement patterns: overarm, sidearm, and underarm. In addition, striking skills are affected by the same variables which affect throwing skills, namely: the size of the object being struck, the speed of the object, the direction and trajectory of the object, the source of force for the object, anticipatory adjustments required (spatial and/or locomotor), and the weight of the object. In addition to these object-related considerations, several additional factors related to the implement and the performer must be considered. For example, the striking surface may be part of the body (hand, foot, head) or it may involve an external object (bat, racket, paddle, stick, etc.) whose weight, size, and shape must also be considered as factors. A third area of consideration concerns the interaction of the object and implement. There are two basic interactive combinations: (1) the object is at rest and the implement is moving (croquet), or (2) both the object and the implement are in motion, which requires a more complex visual-motor integration in order to accomplish the coincident timing task (batting, playing tennis, etc.). Any consideration of striking behaviors must therefore be concerned with not only the physical skill of striking but also the visual-motor integration necessary for successful contacts.

The observed striking behavior of children is a dramatic example of individual variability which can be influenced by environmental factors. For example, the effect of the weight and size of the striking implement has been observed to affect significantly the characteristics of the movement patterns. When children are given a heavy, large object, such as a wooden paddle, their movement patterns have been observed to regress from well-developed sidearm swings to a poking, overarm action pattern

(Seefeldt & Haubenstricker, Note 4, 1974); (Halverson & Roberton, Note 3, 1966).

This tendency toward regression of pattern utilization is also observed when the psychological or physiological task demands of a particular situation become too difficult. A child who is instructed to "hit the ball as hard as you can" will often demonstrate the whole body rotation pattern of an earlier stage rather than the sequential joint action of the more mature pattern. Changes in the visual-perceptual requirements of a particular task can also result in the regression of movement skills to meet the increased demands. For example, if a child has previously been striking at a suspended ball and then the ball is tossed or bounced to the child, the striking pattern may revert to a slapping, arm action pattern. This regression in the face of more difficult task requirements has great implications for teachers. A new skill must be well learned before being placed into situations which increase the difficulty of task performance. Similarly, the planning of small, sequential steps will facilitate the positive transfer of skills from one situation to another, whereas large steps may produce negative results.

The basic developmental sequence for striking is similar for all children and all three striking patterns: overarm, sidearm, and underarm. The mature patterns of each skill contain three essential components: (1) the body weight is shifted forward, usually onto the opposite foot; (2) the trunk is rotated rapidly to add to the sequential force production; and (3) the arm action follows at the moment of maximum speed of rotation or force. The difference in the striking patterns are quite obvious, but these three underlying similarities will be critical variables in each pattern.

Ball Bouncing

Ball bouncing is a somewhat unusual skill in that it requires the sequential combination of both the production and reception or redirection of force. The first manifestation of this skill probably occurs as an accidental dropping of a ball and then the later addition of a series of taps upon the ball until control is lost. The mature ability to control successive bounces of the ball requires a very accurate visual-motor integration, since the ball must be met by the hand during the upward portion of the bounce and then redirected downward.

The immature pattern often illustrates the difficulty a child has in coordinating the movement of the object with the movement of the hand. This inability can be seen as the child attempts to "catch up" with the ball when it is already on its downward phase. The mature ball bounce also seems to require that the ball and the child's hand are proportionate in size, so that some degree of directional control can be attained (Espenschade & Eckert, 1967).

Some children also attempt to utilize a two-handed bounce, often because the ball is too large to be accommodated by one hand. Unfortunately, the two-handed bounce may cause more difficult coordinative problems, as the hands may exert unequal force or compete for location on the ball and therefore cause problems of control. It is not surprising then, as Wellman (1937) pointed out, that young children (30–40 months) are able to use a one-handed bounce on a small ball much more successfully than a two-handed bounce on larger balls.

Kicking

The kick is a rather unique form of manipulative skill in that it is a propulsive movement pattern which requires a sophisticated interaction of the visual system with the lower appendages. Children have little past experience in using their feet to impart force. When kicking, they need to be able to stand on one foot. Thus kicking requires unusually difficult integrative skills between the visual and motor systems. Because of this added requirement of balance, it is generally thought that the young child must be able to run and balance effectively before being able to kick (Gesell, 1940).

In the early stages of "kicking," balance is a major problem, and the child seems merely to push the ball forward to avoid losing equilibrium. The first actual manifestation of kicking has been described as consisting of leg action in a forward direction only, as in pushing action (Deach, 1950). Children appear to be able to execute this rudimentary kick shortly after they are able to run effectively. The second stage merely adds some preliminary backward leg action in a pendular type of motion, to provide for a more powerful leg swing, and is later accompanied by a compensatory action of the opposite arm in the third state (see Figure 6.14). The mature kick is characterized by the addition of a sequence of preliminary hip extension and knee flexion, followed by forceful leg extension accompanied by a slight backward trunk lean and compensatory arm action (Dohrman, 1967; Wickstrom, 1970). This is often combined with a preparatory phase, including an approach to the ball via walking or running.

FIGURE 6.14
The kicking pattern of this young girl demonstrates the compensatory action of the arm opposite the kicking leg.

The balance problems implicit in the kick are illustrated by the fact that many young children alternate the balancing foot by almost random selection of the right or left foot for kicking. Part of this problem is due to experiential factors, as children who have great difficulties in balancing will choose their preferred foot to balance on while others will use their preferred foot to impart the force. As the kicking pattern continues to mature, the child becomes more proficient in selecting a preferred foot for kicking and in the accurate placement of the opposite supporting foot in relation to the object to be kicked. If the child lands too close to the object, some compensation must occur and the ball will likely be hit with the instep, whereas if the child plants the stabilizing foot too far behind the ball, there will be a tendency to contact the ball with the end of the toe.

Thus far we have discussed only the relatively simple task of kicking a stationary object. As we discuss the problems involved in kicking a moving object, the complex interaction of the visual-motor system becomes even more obvious. For example, if the object to be kicked is dropped as in a punt or rolled toward the child, she must not only be prepared to execute an appropriate kick but the difficulty of that skill is greatly increased because the kick must be timed to coincide with the arrival of the ball. This difficulty may be further magnified by combining a locomotor dimension with the performance and thereby adding another visual-motor variable (Figure 6.15). This coincident timing task requires a great deal of experience to coordinate the balance and force production problems of locomotion and kicking with the information received through the visual system.

The general developmental changes in punting skills have been identified by Halverson and Roberton (1966), and Wickstrom (1970) and include the basic addition of more body parts acting in a sequential order to produce maximum force. For example, as the pattern matures, the child achieves more momentum from the addition of a forward step and increased backward lean of the trunk to allow for the more forceful extension of the kicking leg. In addition, the mature pattern includes a vigorous extension of the leg coupled with an instantaneous pause of the thigh as the lower leg "slings" through to contact the object (Burdan, 1955; Glassow & Roberts, 1966–1968). At this stage the body also appears to move upward and forward beyond the point of contact as a result of the momentum generated in the force-producing phase (Bunker, Note 2, 1975).

FIGURE 6.15   *Punting is a rather difficult visual-motor skill for young children because it requires the simultaneous combination of dropping a ball and then kicking it. In the above illustration, the child threw the ball into the air, rather than merely dropping it, and then compensated for the location of the ball by leaning quite far backward. This backward lean is also frequently adopted for balance purposes.*

Catching

Catching and throwing skills are sometimes thought to be linked together as part of a single motor pattern. However, from the previous discussions, it is clear that this is *not* an accurate perception. Throwing and catching develop quite independently of each other, with throwing skills generally thought to precede catching by as much as 12–24 months (Gutteridge, 1939; Wickstrom, 1970).

Like throwing, catching can involve several different types of movements and can be affected by many external variables. Wickstrom (1970) and Ridenour (1974) have pointed out six major variables affecting both the performance and analysis of catching patterns: the size of the ball, the speed of the ball, the distance the ball travels before it is to be caught, the method of projecting the ball, the direction of the ball in relation to the catcher, and the arm action of the catcher. In addition to these variables, several other factors should also be considered: the shape of the ball, the trajectory of flight, and the position of the catcher (i.e., stationary or moving). Bruce (1966), Ridenour (1974), and Williams (1968) have proposed that the most important variables are ball velocity and direction. The actual skill of catching may be further divided into three separate aspects: the visual-perception of the moving object, the preparatory movements of the body, and the actual stopping and controlling of the moving object.

The child's first experiences with catching usually involve the very fundamental task of dealing with a rolling object. With this simple task, the first preparatory aspect of catching is generally eliminated by having the child sit on the ground with legs spread. Catching a rolled ball then involves primarily hand-eye coordination necessary for dealing with the speed, size, and direction of the object. From this stationary seated position, most children progress to the more complex visual-motor skills involved in catching an object while in a standing position.

Initial attempts at catching moving objects generally result in a variety of frustrations, usually met by chasing the ball after it has rebounded off the body. The actual sequence of catching behaviors is a much more complex phenomenon and has been subjected to some extensive investigations which are summarized in this section (Deach, 1950; Espenschade & Eckert, 1967; Gutteridge, 1939; Hanson, 1965; McCaskill & Wellman, 1938; Pedersen, 1973; Seefeldt, Note 5, 1972; Sinclair, 1973; Victors, 1961; Wickstrom, 1970).

The initial stages of catching may be characterized by a fear reaction in which the child senses a need for self-protection (Deach, 1950). This fear element is also observed in many children during later stages of skill development as they turn their head to the side and their trunk leans slightly backward in order to avoid being hit by the object. These manifestations of fear appear on occasion over many developmental stages, especially as the

speed of the object continues to increase and the size of the object decreases (Wickstrom, 1970).

The first real stage of catching is characterized by a scooping or nesting type of response in which the child's arms are extended in front of the body with the palms facing upward. This waiting position remains constant until the ball makes contact with the arms and then the elbows are flexed as the arms and hands attempt to secure or trap the ball against the chest. Gradually the child will begin to anticipate the moment of contact and begin to encircle the ball while pulling it into the chest as seen in Figure 6.16.

The second major change in catching behavior is marked by the child's attempts to catch the ball with the hands. Since this requires a rather sophisticated visual-motor process, it often results in the ball be-

FIGURE 6.16   *Catching a large rubber ball is often accomplished by clasping the ball between the hands and the chest. This early catching movement may also be accompanied by a turning of the head.*

ing cradled between the arms or secured to the chest where it is controlled by the flexed arms. In the next stage of the catching pattern, the ball is caught using the hands only, with flexion of the arms used to absorb the force. Ultimately, in the mature catch, the child may combine this upper body action with a change in the stationary base of support by placing one foot forward, in order to allow the total body to aid in the absorption of force. These characteristic catching behaviors undergo a particularly marked improvement in children between 7–9 years of age (Victors, 1961).

This basic developmental sequence for catching holds several implications for teachers. For example, in the first stages children are most likely to attempt to trap objects against their chests, thus indicating that large, soft objects are more likely to be successfully caught than small, hard objects. This size requirement is also significant in that it is probably the opposite of the smaller sizes desired for throwing. The size of the object to be caught can also affect the type of catching behavior. For example, a child of five may respond to catching by using an arm-trapping type of motion with a large ball, but the same child may execute a hand clasp catch when a small ball is tossed (Halverson & Roberton, Note 3). Similarly, during the initial attempts at catching, children should be encouraged to "make a nest for the ball, and hold it close to your chest"; during later stages children should be told to catch with the hands only. Also during the early stages children are much more successful at catching a ball which has been allowed to bounce first (Pedersen, 1973).

Other Manipulative Skills

Many other types of gross motor manipulative skills are observed in children, though few of these activities have been subjected to careful evaluation. Sinclair (1973) in an extensive study of children's motor patterns has considered pushing, pulling, and carrying as typical movements in early childhood. The developmental trends for each of these tasks includes the mobilization of the "total body assembly" in order to produce sufficient force to accomplish the task at hand. This utilization of the total body assembly is particularly important because of the effective use of the legs to help generate the force, with the back being used primarily for stability.

Other gross motor manipulative skills in early childhood include such things as riding a tricycle and eventually a bicycle. These skills are particularly complex in that they require the coordination of both arms and legs, while simultaneously integrating the changing visual environment. However, tricycle riding is one of the most self-rewarding and pleasurable experiences of childhood, and its development is particularly dependent upon having appropriate early experiences with tricycles of various sizes and shapes. Given the opportunity to experiment with tricycle riding, most children will master this skill by 3 years of age (Espenschade & Eckert, 1967). Similarly, bicycle riding is also dependent upon early experiences, but this visual-motor task is further complicated by the additional requirements of balancing on a two-wheeled object. For this reason, many children will benefit from the addition of training wheels attached to the rear axle of the bicycle to aid in balance. These learning aids may be used as a temporary assist but should either be removed or raised off the ground as soon as familiarity with the bicycle and basic skills have been attained. It has also been observed that most children will require some actual physical experience with a pusher, rather than training wheels, to learn to ride a bicycle (Ridenour, 1975). Because of this increased balance problem and the dramatic effects of early experiences, normative data on bicycle riding should be carefully evaluated and the observed average age of accomplishment—5 years, 5 months—should be tentatively used, especially with respect to the delayed overall motor development of handicapped children.

Summary of gross motor manipulative skill development

The successful accomplishment of a variety of manipulative skills requires a complex interaction between the child and the environment. These manipulative skills may take on several forms, including such purposive skills as throwing, catching, and striking, as well as skills such as pushing, pulling, carrying, and riding a tricycle or bicycle or roller skating.

It would be impossible to summarize each of these patterns adequately, but it is possible to identify a few generalizations about the developmental sequences of manipulative skills involving the production of force. For example, we have previously discussed the importance of three concepts:

1. The shift from unilateral to crosslateral action of arms and legs. This shift provides for better balance and force production.

2. The weight transfer in the direction of the force to be produced or received. In general, this is made possible by the oppositional stance, with the foot opposite the preferred hand being placed in front of the body and the body weight shifted either forward (to produce force) or backward (to absorb or receive force).
3. The increased distance over which force is produced (or absorbed) with more forceful results. This involves the sequential joint action made possible by increased rotation and the forward step and follow-through. This principle is also true for absorption of force (i.e., catching), where it involves meeting the force in front of the body and "giving" with it by shifting the body weight backward.

The manipulative skills discussed in this chapter have been analyzed in terms of the developmental changes which can be observed in each pattern. These sequential changes represent the various stages through which a skill generally progresses before it can be labeled a mature movement. Several landmarks of development have been identified to represent the average age of accomplishment for various manipulative skills (Table 6.3).

These average age ranges should however be interpreted with caution since in fact they indicate that approximately 50% of the "normal" children will accomplish the skill before the given age and 50% will not accomplish it until sometime later. With handicapped children these skills will generally be observed at later ages, and the amount of individual variability will be even greater than for "normal" children.

The Instructional Process

The broad range of individual difference in the motor behavior of retarded children provides compelling evidence for the use of many exploratory experiences to encourage a wide variety of responses and individualized forms of teaching based on careful evaluations of individual learners. The success of combining child-centered, movement exploration techniques with individualized instruction has been dramatically demonstrated in several experimental studies (Rarick et al., 1976). An individualized approach to learning motor skills has several implicit advantages, including the obvious specificity of task, the avoidance of socially embarrassing or

TABLE 6.3   *Development of manipulative skill*

Movement Behavior	Average Chronological Age of Accomplishment
Throws a ball in any fashion (Bayley, 1969)	6 mos. to 1½ yrs.
Throws ball overhand (Frankenburg & Dodds, 1967); kicks ball forward (Frankenburg & Dodds, 1967); kicks a ball without overbalancing (Gesell, 1940); pedals tricycle (Frankenburg & Dodds, 1967)	18 mos. to 2 yrs.
Bounces 9" ball 1–3 feet with one hand (Wellman, 1937); catches 2 of 3 well-tossed large balls (Sinclair, 1973); strikes ball off batting tee (Sinclair, 1973); catches large ball with arms straight (Wellman, 1937)	2 to 3 yrs.
Rides tricycle proficiently (Espenschade & Eckert, 1967); catches bounced ball (Frankenburg & Dodds, 1967)	3 to 4 yrs.
Operates two-wheeled scooter or wagon (Espenschade & Eckert, 1967); throws ball overhand 20 ft. (Sinclair, 1973)	4 to 5 yrs.
Roller skates (Espenschade & Eckert, 1967); catches large ball with elbows at side (Wellman, 1937); bounces large ball with 2 hands, 1–3' (Wellman, 1937)	5 to 6 yrs.
Kicks with good balance and arm-foot opposition (Halverson & Roberton, Note 3); hits hurled ball with bat 2 of 10 times (Johnson, 1962)	6 yrs.
Overarm throw with opposition and rotation (Wild, 1938)	6½ yrs.

competitive situations, and the increased availability of individual attention, reinforcement, and assistance. If this individualized approach is to be optimally effective, it must be built on a wide range of past experiences and based on an accurate assessment of each child's present motor functioning.

Assessment of motor behavior

The assessment of motor behavior is a very complex process. A child who is experiencing difficulty in even a superficially simple skill such as throwing a beanbag into a box in fact may be manifesting developmental problems in any one of several areas such as inadequate strength to throw the beanbag, inappropriate visual information about the target, an immature throwing pattern, a lack of comprehension regarding the task, or a complex combination of these problems. In addition, it is not sufficient to evaluate the end product only, for it is possible that a child will successfully hit the target but the motor behavior may still be immature or incomplete in terms of effective and efficient motor skills. Or the child will not be able to hit the target and the teacher can describe only the end-product deficit, not the underlying motor functioning problem. It is therefore essential that the entire process of motor behavior, from input through output, be evaluated.

In terms of practicality, however, practitioners and teachers need a simple, quick screening device which will give an overall estimate of the child's capabilities in specific tasks. It has been suggested that practitioners need access to the "what and when" of the products of motor performance as provided through various screening devices, but that the "how and why" of the process must be obtained through specific diagnostic tests (Newell, Note 6, 1975). It is essential then that the teacher and/or school determine which evaluation should come first, task observation or process assessment. In addition, Public Law 94-142 (1976) emphasizes that in individual, movement-education programs, both short-and long-term objectives need to be identified and appropriate assessments made.

Assessment instruments and screening devices are very useful for measuring the current status of children's motor performance and the level of attainment of various objectives. However, these tests may be difficult to administer and evaluate for retarded individuals because many have difficulty understanding verbal instructions or following a sequence of instructions. These children are often sensitive to new situations when they do not understand what is expected of them. In addition, some are also hyperactive with short attention spans or have physical handicaps which require medication or special environmental conditions. Each of these variables will affect the test performance and make it more difficult to obtain an accurate evaluation of the individual's abilities.

Many types of standardized assessment instruments are available to the teacher. When selecting an instrument it is important to know if the potential information will be an aid in establishing the specific motor characteristics of each child. This evaluation, therefore, is dependent upon the reliability and validity of the test and the evaluative criteria. Of particular importance in assessing the motor behavior of retarded children is the decision to utilize either criterion-referenced or norm-referenced measures. Criterion-referenced measures yield information which specifies the degree of competency attained by an individual child in relation to an absolute standard of performance. On the other hand, norm-referenced measures provide information which only derives meaning from the comparison of one individual's performance to the performance of others.

There are many standardized assessment instruments available for the determination of motor behavior. Most of these tests can be classified as either a rating scale, in which children are judged on a criterion-referenced scale, or a checklist, which uses a pass/fail basis. Two particularly encouraging research projects have recently provided some excellent diagnostic and prescriptive materials in the area of motor development for use with retarded children. *The Peabody Developmental Motor Scales* (1974) provide an index for gross and fine motor skills in children from 0–7 years of age as well as information about the motor skills of children and a program of activities designed to teach each skill included in the series.

The second set of materials, the I CAN curriculum (1976), is one example of a "canned" program. However, all programs which facilitate an individualized, diagnostic-prescriptive approach to physical education for severely handicapped individuals should include the following components (I CAN, 1976):

1. Criterion-referenced measures which may be used as diagnostic tools for assessing individual student strengths and needs.

2. Prescriptive teaching/learning activities which are coded according to the need assessment and include cues for environmental manipulation, physical manipulation, verbal cues, and modeling.
3. A teacher behavioral model which delineates the tasks for individualized instruction.
4. Associated materials to provide "active learning options" which integrate all major behavioral objectives germane to the physical activity and classroom learning. This makes it possible for "the activity to reinforce, and be reinforced by, each of the classroom subject areas, including art, music, math, science, language arts and health and daily living."
5. Progress reporting and record keeping which allow continuous evaluation of student outcomes.

The process of student evaluation and the provision for feedback are critical to any positive learning environment because they provide for both accurate assessment of student progress and for positive reinforcement leading to a motivated learning attitude. For example, a checklist evaluation instrument can be used to assess a child's ability to perform a specific skill. Figure 6.17 illustrates such a checklist (I CAN, 1976) which divides movement behavior into distinct developmental stages, each of which has several behavior components for evaluation on a pass/fail basis.

Body management and physical fitness assessments

The attainment of body management abilities is critical to the development of each child. There are numerous standardized assessment instruments available to determine the present functioning of motor behavior or the learning or change in motor behavior (through use of pre- and posttest administrations). A summary of selected body management and physical fitness tests is provided in Table 6.4.

Fundamental motor skill assessments

The assessment of fundamental motor skills must include an evaluation of both fine motor and gross motor skills. In addition, it is also often important to evaluate selected visual and tactile skills which interact with the motor skills to accomplish the fundamental skills. Although these assessment instruments often undertake a broad and somewhat superficial evaluation of perceptual-motor functioning, many of the specific items can be used to evalu-

ate well-defined motor skills. A summary of selected assessment instruments for fundamental motor skills is provided in Table 6.5.

Teacher-designed assessment instruments

As a rule, assessment measures should be both reliable and valid instruments. However, the typical classroom teacher should not be hesitant to employ a self-designed checklist or rating scale to aid in recognizing specific deficits or strengths. For example, the following items gleaned from various standardized instruments could form the basic skills to be observed; others may be added as the need arises.

1. Body Management Skills
   A. Identify 7 or more body parts
   B. Recognize and consistently use right and left appendages
   C. Walk a 4-inch walking board forward and then backward
   D. Stand on tiptoes
   E. Relax or tense body on command
   F. Climb a jungle gym without fear
2. Fine Motor Skills
   A. Pick up toothpicks and place in box
   B. Cut out simple geometric figures
   C. Trace over simple figures
   D. String beads
   E. Draw shapes and write name
   F. Turn pages in a book
3. Locomotor Skills
   A. Run an obstacle course
   B. Jump with two feet
   C. Hop five times
   D. Gallop with each foot leading
   E. Skip with good balance
   F. Slide with sideward facing
4. Manipulative Skills
   A. Catch a ball on the bounce
   B. Kick a stationary ball
   C. Throw a ball overhand at a target
   D. Bat a ball off a batting tree
   E. Bowl a ball accurately
   F. Bounce a basketball 5 times

Each of these skills should be defined in terms of specific behavioral objectives. For example, the first item in each category might read:

1. Be able to point accurately to the following body parts: knees, head, eyes, ankles, nose, ears, chin

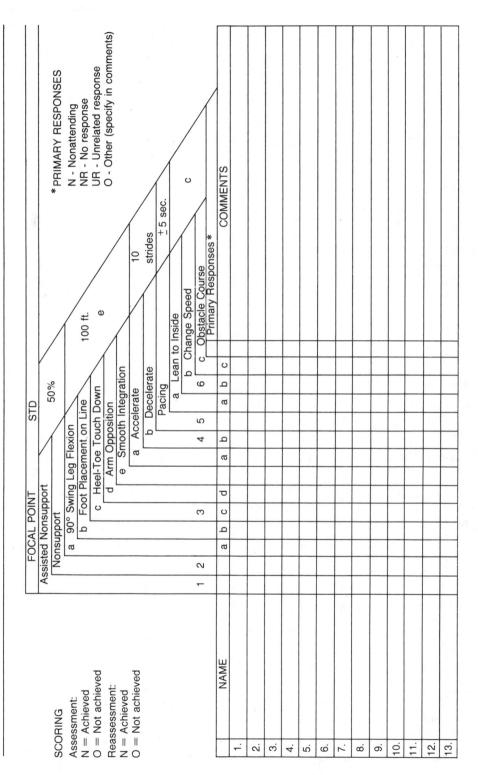

FIGURE 6.17   Rating scale from I CAN curriculum

215

TABLE 6.4 *Body management and physical ability tests*

	Cardiorespiratory Endurance	Agility	Flexibility	Balance	Muscular Endurance	Strength	Speed	Explosive Power	Coordination	Posture	Body Awareness
Basic Motor Abilities for Retardates (American Institute for Research, 1967)			X	X		X	X				
Basic Motor Fitness (Hilsendager, 1970)	X	X	X	X	X	X	X	X	X		
Centennial Athletic Programme Testing Program	X			X	X		X		X		
Fitness Screening Test (Croft Educational Service, 1972)		X	X			X					
Test of Lateral Dominance (Harris, 1958)				X		X					X
Kraus-Weber Test of Minimum Muscular Fitness (Kraus & Hirschland, 1955)			X		X	X					
Lincoln-Oseretsky Motor Development Scale (Sloan, 1954)				X		X	X	X	X		
Motor Fitness Test for the Moderately Mentally Retarded (AAHPER, 1976a)	X	X			X		X	X			
Move-Grow-Learn Movement Skills Survey (Orpet & Heustis, 1971)	X	X	X	X	X		X		X		
Peabody Test of Physical Fitness	X	X						X			
Physical Fitness for the Mentally Retarded (Note 7)	X		X		X		X	X			
Physical Fitness Test Battery for Mentally Retarded Children (Fait, 1972)	X	X		X	X		X				
Posture Checklist (Dauer, 1975)										X	X
Purdue Perceptual-Motor Survey (Kephart, 1966)			X	X	X						X
Special Fitness Test for the Moderately Mentally Retarded (AAHPER, 1976b)	X	X					X	X	X		
Teaching Research Motor Development Scale for Moderately and Severely Retarded Children (Fredericks, Baldwin, Doughtry, & Walter, 1972)	X			X	X		X				

Source: Adapted from AAHPER, *Testing for Impaired, Disabled and Handicapped Individuals,* 1975b.

TABLE 6.5 · *Assessment instruments for fundamental movement skills*

	Tactile Discrimination	Auditory	Visual Tracking	Visual Discrimination & Copying of Forms	Visual Discrimination & Copying of Rhythm Pat.	Fine Motor Coordination	Dynamic Balance	Static Balance	Spatial Body Perception	Agility	Fundamental Movements	Gross Motor Coordination, Eye-Foot	Gross Motor Coordination, Eye-Hand
Basic Motor Fitness (Hilsendager, 1970)			X		X		X	X			X	X	X
Denver Developmental Screening Test (Frankenburg & Dodds, 1967)		X	X	X	X	X	X	X	X		X	X	X
Developmental Test of Visual Perception (Frostig, 1973)			X	X					X				X
Evanston Early Identification Scale (1967)				X					X				
Evaluation Test for TMR Children (Note 8)			X	X	X	X	X	X	X		X	X	X
Florida State University Diagnostic Battery of Recreative Functioning for the Trainable Mentally Retarded (Mundy, Note 9)			X	X	X	X	X	X			X	X	X
Functional Neurological Evaluation (Note 10)	X	X	X	X	X	X	X				X	X	X
Motor Developmental Activities for the Mentally Retarded (Bowers, n.d.)			X				X	X		X	X	X	X
Move-Grow-Learn Movement Skills Survey (Orpet & Heustis, 1971)			X			X	X	X	X	X	X	X	X
MVPT Motor-Free Visual Perception Test (Calarusso & Hammill, 1972)			X	X					X				
Lincoln-Oseretsky Motor Development Scale (Sloan, 1954)			X			X		X			X	X	X
Peabody Developmental Motor Scales	X	X	X	X	X	X	X	X	X	X	X	X	X
Perceptual Motor Attributes of Mentally Retarded Children and Youth (Note 11)			X					X	X	X	X		X
A Psychoeducational Inventory of Basic Learning (Valett, 1968)	X	X	X	X	X	X	X	X	X	X	X	X	X
Purdue Perceptual Motor Survey (Kephart, 1966)			X	X	X		X		X		X		
Teaching Research Motor Development Scale for Moderately and Severely Retarded Children (Fredericks, et al., 1972)			X			X		X	X		X		X
T.M.R. Performance Profile (DiNola, Kaminisky, & Steinfeld, n.d.)		X								X	X		X

Source: AAHPER, *Testing for Impaired, Disabled and Handicapped Individuals*, 1975b.

2. Be able to individually pick up 20 toothpicks and place each in a box within 15 seconds
3. Be able to run a figure-8 course consisting of 3 cones placed 10 feet apart in less than 20 seconds
4. Be able to catch a 10-inch playground ball which was tossed 8 feet into the air and allowed to bounce once.

In addition, each of these skills could be evaluated on a simple pass/fail basis or by using a more complex scale in which points are awarded: 4 = performed well; 3 = performed satisfactorily; 2 = performed poorly; 1 = tried, but failed; 0 = did not try. It is particularly important in this system to differentiate between unsatisfactory performance and no performance at all, especially with retarded children; and the teacher may also wish to incorporate the level of assistance required (i.e., assisted with model) into the scoring system.

It may be difficult to generate test items and behaviors that can be specifically categorized in terms of a single motor or perceptual skill. For example, the task of catching a bounced ball depends upon having adequate strength and balance, accurate visual perception, and a high degree of eye-hand coordination. It is therefore extremely important in selecting test items or in evaluating standardized test batteries to choose tasks in which the majority of the performance requirements can be attributed to a single perceptual or motor factor.

Once a particular test battery or item has been administered, a teacher must evaluate the test results to ascertain the relative areas of motor performance strength and weakness. Specific motor activities should then be designed (prescribed) to enable children to work in the areas of weakest performance. Students then work on related and varied activities to strengthen their performance as measured on additional repetitions of the informal assessment.

Determination of instructional objectives and methods

The assessment of individual motor performance is essential to the development of an educational environment based on the needs of each individual and on the diagnostic-prescriptive approach. Several general objectives in the psychomotor, cognitive, and affective domains have been established for physical education experiences in general:

1. To improve physical condition and movement skills

2. To develop and maintain a healthy body
3. To provide experiences in success and increase pride and self-confidence
4. To provide opportunities to participate in play and leisure activities common to society
5. To develop positive attitudes and interactions with others.

In addition to these five fundamental objectives, one of the most prominent goals for handicapped individuals is to provide skills and develop interests to foster social acceptance through the enjoyment of leisure times. The need for companionship and for developing a sense of belonging can be met through physical activities. This is particularly important since many authors have suggested that retarded individuals are more often rejected by society because of antisocial behavior than because of a lack of intellectual skills (Johnson & Capobianco, 1969; Predmore, 1965).

Physical exertion can also provide a significant aid in lowering anxiety, particularly for the mentally retarded child. This may be because of several factors, including the fact that exertion is an active and assertive response which is incompatable with anxiety; it is a natural consumption of physiological arousal and tension; and/or it may exhaust or inhibit the capacity for further anxiety arousal (Driscoll, 1976).

Motivation for the mentally retarded can be a very real problem, for these children have generally been dominated by a sense of failure and frustration. Their attitudes toward new tasks may be of anticipated failure, and their general self-concept may be quite weak and/or negative. The development of a positive self-image in an active, success-oriented program can foster healthy growth and development—physical, mental, emotional, and social. Matching the instructional tasks with the cognitive, social, and motoric development of the child can provide each child with successful task completion experiences. Learning the skills necessary for controlling one's own body, developing stability and other physical fitness abilities, discovering oneself, relating and interacting with others, and learning about the physical world are important ingredients in each child's development.

The goals of a strong program of movement experiences are therefore quite varied, as they contribute to the overall development of each child. The specific goals and objectives will vary not only in terms of specific needs but also in relation to the age of the child. Table 6.6 summarizes the relative

TABLE 6.6   *Physical education goals for the severely handicapped aged 3–14*

Goal Areas	Percentage Allocation of Emphasis at Each Age Level			
	3–5 yrs.	6–8 yrs.	9–11 yrs.	12–14 yrs.
1. Competence in human movement				
A. Basic body management skills: body awareness, posture and control of body	20%	20%	10%	5%
B. Development of fundamental skills:				
Locomotor skills	15	15	15	10
Object control	15	15	15	15
Rhythmic abilities	20	15	15	15
C. Participation in leisure time activities				
Sport skills	—	5	10	10
Simple games	10	10	10	15
Sports	—	—	5	10
2. Development of physical fitness abilities*	—	—	—	—
3. Competence in selected social skills	10	10	10	10
4. Knowledge of selected cognitive concepts, relationships, movement vocabulary	10	10	10	10

*Physical fitness abilities, especially body management skills, should be developed through all activities, no specific percentages are allocated.

shift in importance of the various goals at each age range.

The contributions of a well-rounded, motor development program to the overall education of the severely handicapped are very diversified. Of major importance, however, are (1) the development of body management abilities and fundamental movement skills; (2) the development of desirable social skills and interaction progressing from independent, parallel, and dual play to group activities which may be either cooperative or semi-competitive and understanding interpersonal relationships; and (3) the learning and reinforcing of other "academic" information and verbal skills through physical activity. In addition to these primary goals for all of physical education, the moderately to severely and profoundly handicapped child may also benefit from the development of (4) optimal and controlled arousal or attention levels which allow for sufficient alertness and motivation; (5) increased independence, self-direction, and perseverance; and (6) creative fulfillment and joyful participation.

Instructional objectives

The adequate assessment of present student status, coupled with the general goals or objectives of movement experiences, provides the framework around which an instructional program may be shaped. Instructional objectives which maximize the results are sought through the instructional program. The development of these objectives is essential in the process of providing optimal learning environments and experiences.

Specific instructional objectives should be individually formulated, based on the needs of the child and the overall objectives of the program. These objectives should describe specific behaviors (1) which can be directly observed; (2) which lend themselves to specific teaching procedures and will facilitate the attainment of the objective; and (3) which can be directly evaluated through observation of actual performance.

Objectives incorporating these elements provide the key to instruction.

Guideline for the teaching process

Basic guidelines for the creation of learning environments for motor skills are not unlike those previously discussed in Chapters 2 and 3. The following will be listed here as they specifically relate to the development of motor skills in retarded individuals.

1. *Assessment of initial level of attention.* Each child comes to the learning environment with unique

past experiences and with certain predispositions. For example, the length of attention span varies greatly among retarded children, and it must be a major consideration in the teaching-learning environment. If a child is not able to remain attentive or to focus visual attention for a minute or two without specific reinforcement, it will be extremely difficult to provide an efficient learning experience. Similarly, if a retarded child is not able to control irrelevant responses, the teacher must begin with shaping a more appropriate attending behavior and then proceed to the learning tasks.

2. *Provision for successful experiences.* All children are motivated by successful experiences; in terms of motor skill development, this is particularly significant as a reinforcer of positive performance. For handicapped children, success not only augments their attention but also helps to build more positive self-concepts and attitudes toward learning.

3. *Sequential Learning Experiences.* In order for children to build upon their existing capabilities, the teacher must provide systematic progressions of learning experiences which begin at the child's present ability level. By concentrating on starting where the child is, each performer has an opportunity to be successful and to expand their movement repertoires simultaneously.

4. *Verbalization.* The vocabulary used in teaching should involve functional language rather than technical nomenclature. Children should be encouraged to verbalize about their movements both before and after performance so that they will be able to express their ideas and feelings about movement. A functional vocabulary of motor terms will make it possible to communicate about movement and to acquire new motor skills more efficiently. In addition, action-oriented words will help the performer recognize the important elements within a specific movement and may serve as effective verbal cues for the teacher. A suggested list of functional vocabulary words to provide for symbolic representation is given in Table 6.7. This list may need to be simplified for the more handicapped or younger learner.

5. *Modeling.* In combination with verbal direction or by themselves, models provide a useful means of transmitting information. Demonstrations are particularly helpful for simple tasks; but as skills become more complicated, they must be broken down into their component parts in order to be effectively demonstrated.

6. *Physical Manipulation.* In motor development, physical manipulation and tactile stimulation become important aids to the explanation-demonstration sequence. The amount of physical manipulation should be gradually reduced through fading and eventually eliminated completely.

7. *Repetition.* Verbal and motor repetition must be balanced with the problems associated with short attention spans, boredom, and low levels of comprehension. Therefore it is important to encourage participation in a variety of motor skills, including the more complex and difficult activities which compose the normal developmental sequence, but which may not be immediately masterable. Participation in these more complex undertakings provides an opportunity for the child to begin to integrate the skills and abilities learned at the lower levels of performance. In addition, these varied experiences encourage the development of flexible and modifiable skills rather than rigid and stereotyped ones.

Repetition of motor skills also provides a key to motivation. When a child has successfully accomplished a motor skill, it should be repeated and enjoyed several times. This provides an important experience for the development of self-confidence and mastery before moving onto a more complex skill. This repetition must be coupled with continued reinforcement as well as an opportunity to apply the skill in somewhat different situations.

8. *Part-whole learning.* Activities should be developed in small, discrete steps that build on or reinforce previously learned skills. Learning for the severely handicapped child will require a slower pace, greater redundancy, and greater time for practice and participation by each student. This concept of sequential building blocks of instruction coupled with a high level of repetition must be counterbalanced with the level of interest and motivation of the students. Thus the interest level often dictates the type of repetition, the sequence of learning, and the changes in activity.

9. *Multisensory motor experiences.* The learning environment should provide things for children to hear, see, and feel so that as many sensory systems may be brought into play as is possible. This multisensory approach may involve the simulta-

TABLE 6.7   *Action word vocabulary relevant to motor skill instruction*

accent	far	little	stand
after	fast	long	straddle
arms	feet	look	stretch
around	fingertips	lower	stride
ankles	fist		strike
away	floor	move	stoop
	flex	narrow	step
back	foot	nose	stop
balance	forward	near	stomach
base of support	front		straight
beat		out	support
behind	general space	over	sway
bend	gallop		swing
beside	go	palms	
between		personal space	take-off
big	hang	point	target
both	head	posture	tempo
bottom	hard	push	throw
bounce	hands	pull	toes
	heels		together
carry	high	ready	top
catch	hold	reach	toward
center	hop	right	touch
change		roll	tripod
change directions	imitate	rotation	trunk
chest	inside	run	tuck
chin	inverted		turn
circle		scale	twist
curved	jump	seat	
	knee	shape	under
direction	kick	shake	up
dismount	kick-up	short	
distance		shoulders	
down	land	side	waist
	large	skip	walls
elbow	lean	slide	walk
even	leap	slow	wide
extend	left	small	waist
eyes	level	space	
	leg	spotting	
facing	lift	sprint	
fall			

neous presence of a variety of stimuli or it may employ alternating stimuli and directed attention (e.g., how the tennis ball feels, what it looks like, how it sounds when it bounces, low versus high bounce, etc.).

10. *Careful use of competition.* Competition can be a very useful motivating device for the attainment of motor skills in regular physical education programs. However, in programs for the severely handicapped, a desire to compete for social approval

coupled with unsuccessful performance may result in disinterest, aggression, or withdrawal.

Games. A variety of minimally organized games can be used to facilitate the development of motor skills and allow for a low level of competition. For example, dodgeball, tag, and other simple games rely upon the use of a variety of motor skills, but also allow children intermittent success and temporary lack of success. These games, as well as innumerable other games and relays, provide an obvious aid in teaching the importance of successful skills in order to play the game.

Special Olympics. The Special Olympics, founded and supported by the Joseph P. Kennedy Foundation (AAHPER, 1972), has provided an opportunity for retarded individuals to learn a variety of sports, to participate in track and field competition, to compete with others of similar abilities, and to enlarge their social interactions with both retarded and nonretarded individuals. This program is particularly noteworthy because the level of competition is generally well controlled, with all children allowed to experience pleasure and self-reward for their participation and their increasing skill levels.

11. *Creating learning environments.* One of the most fundamental techniques for providing good learning experiences has to do with controlling the child's environment to stimulate a desired response. This can be accomplished by specific physical manipulation, as in the passive movement of a child's arm through an overhand throw, or the manipulation may be brought about by a particular environmental condition, such as placing footprints on the floor in a skipping pattern and asking the child to follow the pattern. These assisting techniques may involve either the arranging of antecedent conditions (i.e., the footprints) or direct intervention with the learner. Direct intervention techniques include physical manipulation of passive movements as well as the provision of verbal directions or models for imitation.

In summary, challenging and meaningful progressions of learning experiences can be created by first determining the instructional objectives based upon behavioral assessment and then establishing the desired movement outcomes. These outcomes can be facilitated by arranging antecedent conditions to encourage the appropriate responses and by selecting activities which stress the target movement pattern; provide high levels of initial success; and, through the application of direct intervention with the learner (verbal cues, models, and physical manipulation), assist successful performance during early learning.

Summary

The motor development of moderately and severely retarded children follows essentially the same sequence as normal children, although the rate of development for some individuals may be somewhat slower. The variability of motor skill performance among the handicapped is as great or greater than that among other populations. In addition, a variety of other generalizations can be made concerning the motor development of retarded children (AAHPER, 1975):

Motor abilities are organized similarly for all children.

Motor abilities follow similar developmental sequences for all children.

Retarded children can learn all the motor skills their nonretarded peers learn.

Learning environments should progress from simple to complex in order to facilitate optimal learning.

Multisensory stimuli should be utilized to stimulate learning.

Positive reinforcement and success are the keys to stimulating learning.

Transfer of skill does not occur automatically, there is a great deal of specificity in motor activity.

Motor skill level can be greatly improved through a program of well-stimulated learning experiences.

Well-rounded movement programs contribute to the development of desirable social skills as well as increased independence, self-direction, and perseverance.

Creative fulfillment and joyful participation should be a natural outcome of movement for all children.

References

AAHPER. *A guide for programs in recreation and physical education for the mentally retarded.* Washington, D.C.: American Alliance of Health, Physical Education, and Recreation, 1968.

AAHPER. *Motor fitness testing manual for the moderately mentally retarded. Manual.* Washington, D.C.: American Alliance of Health, Physical Education, and Recreation, 1976 (a), 1976. (b)

AAHPER. *Physical education and recreation for impaired, disabled and handicapped individuals . . . Past, present, and future.* Washington, D.C.: American Alliance of Health, Physical Education, and Recreation, 1975. (a)

AAHPER. *Special olympics instruction manual—From beginners to champions.* Washington, D.C.: American Alliance of Health, Physical Education, and Recreation, and the Joseph P. Kennedy Foundation, 1972.

AAHPER. *Testing for impaired, disabled and handicapped individuals.* Washington, D.C.: American Alliance of Health, Physical Education, and Recreation, 1975. (b)

Adelson, E., & Frailberg, S. Gross motor development in infants blind from birth. *Child Development,* 1974, *45,* 114–126.

American Institute for Research. *Basic motor abilities test for retardates.* Silver Spring, Md.: AIR-AOR Monograph 86-2/67-FR, 1967.

Ames, L. B., & Ilg, F. L. Developmental trends in writing behavior. *Journal of Genetic Psychology,* 1951, *79,* 28–46.

Astrand, P. O. Human physical fitness with special reference to sex and age. *Physiological Review,* 1956, *36,* 307–335.

Bayley, N. The development of motor abilities during the first three years. *Monographs of the Society for Research in Child Development,* 1935, No. 1. Washington, D.C.

Bayley, N. *The Bayley scales of infant development.* New York: Psychological Corporation, 1969.

Beck, M. *The path of the center of gravity during running in boys, grades one to six.* Unpublished doctoral dissertation, University of Wisconsin, 1966.

Bobath, B. The treatment of neuromuscular disorders by improving patterns of coordination. *Physiotherapy,* 1969, *55,* 18–22.

Bobath, K., & Bobath, B. An analysis of the development of standing and walking patterns in patients with cerebral palsy. *Physiotherapy,* 1962, *48,* 144–153.

Bobath, K., & Bobath, B. The facilitation of normal postural reactions and movements in the treatment of cerebral palsy. *Physiotherapy,* 1964, *50,* 246–262.

Bowers, L. *Motor developmental activities for the mentally retarded.* Tampa, Fla.: University of South Florida, no date.

Breckenridge, M., & Vincent, L. *Child development.* Philadelphia: W. B. Saunders, 1956.

Bruce, R. *The effects of variations in ball trajectory upon the catching performance of elementary school children.* Unpublished doctoral dissertation, University of Wisconsin, 1966.

Burdan, P. A. *Cinematographical analysis of three basic kicks used in soccer.* Unpublished master's thesis, Pennsylvania State University, 1955.

Calarusso, R. P., & Hammill, D. C. *MVPT motor-free visual*

perception test. San Rafael, Calif.: Academic Therapy Publications, 1972.

Cattell, P. *The measurement of intelligence of infants and young children.* New York: Psychological Corporation, 1960.

Centennial athletic programme testing program. Toronto, Canada: Canadian Association for Retarded Children, no date.

Clarke, H. H. Joint and body range of movement. *Physical Fitness Research Digest,* 1975, Series 5, No. 4.

Clausen, J. *Ability structure and subgroups in mental retardation.* London: Macmillan, 1966.

Clouse, F. *A kinematic analysis of the development of the running pattern of preschool boys.* Unpublished doctoral dissertation, University of Wisconsin, 1959.

Collins, P. A. *Body mechanics of the overarm and sidearm patterns.* Unpublished master's thesis, University of Wisconsin, 1960.

Copeland, M., Ford, L., & Solon, N. *Occupational therapy for mentally retarded children.* Baltimore: University Park Press, 1976.

Corbin, C. B. *A textbook of motor development.* Dubuque, Iowa: William C. Brown, 1973.

Cratty, B. J. *Perceptual and motor development in infants and children.* New York: Macmillan, 1970.

Cratty, B. J. *Motor activity and the education of retardates.* Philadelphia: Lea & Febiger, 1974.

Croft Educational Service, Inc. *Fitness screening tests.* New London, Conn.: Croft Teacher's Service, 1972.

Cruickshank, W. M., Bentzen, F. A., Ratzeburg, F. H., & Tanhauser, M. T. *A teaching method for brain-injured and hyperactive children.* Syracuse, N.Y.: Syracuse University Press, 1961.

Dauer, V. P. *Dynamic physical education for elementary school children.* Minneapolis: Burgess, 1975.

Deach, D. *Genetic development of motor skills in children two through six years of age.* Unpublished doctoral dissertation, University of Michigan, 1950.

DiNola, A. J., Kaminisky, B. P., & Steinfeld, A. E. *T.M.R. performance profile for the severely and profoundly retarded.* Ridgefield, N.J.: Reporting Service for Exceptional Children, no date.

Dittmer, J. *A kinematic analysis of the development of the running pattern of grade school girls and certain factors which distinguish good from poor performance at the observed ages.* Unpublished master's thesis, University of Wisconsin, 1962.

Dohrman, P. Throwing and kicking ability of eight year old boys and girls. *Research Quarterly,* 1967, *35,* 464–471.

Driscoll, R. Anxiety reduction using physical exertion and positive images. *Psychological Record,* 1976, *26,* 87–94.

Elrod, J. M. *The effects of perceptual-motor training and music on perceptual-motor development and behavior of educable mentally retarded children.* Unpublished doctoral dissertation, Louisiana State University, 1972.

Espenschade, A. S., & Eckert, H. M. *Motor development.* Columbus, Ohio: Charles E. Merrill, 1967.

Evanston early identification scale. Chicago, Ill.: Follett, 1967.

Fait, H. *Special physical education: Adaptive, corrective, developmental.* Philadelphia: W. B. Saunders, 1972.

Farber, S. *Sensorimotor evaluation and treatment procedures for allied health personnel.* Indiana University–Purdue University, Indianapolis Medical Center, Occupational Therapy Program, 1975.

Fine, M. J., & Caldwell, T. E. Self-evaluation of school-related behavior of educable mentally retarded children. A preliminary report. *Exceptional Children,* 1967, *33,* 324.

Finnie, N. R. *Handling the young cerebral palsied child at home.* New York: E. P. Dutton, 1975.

Flick, G. L. Sinistrality revisited: A perceptual motor approach. *Child Development,* 1967, *38,* 415.

Flowers, K. Handedness and controlled movement. *British Journal of Psychology,* 1975, *66* (1), 39–52.

Francis, R. J., & Rarick, G. L. Motor characteristics of the mentally retarded. *American Journal of Mental Deficiency,* 1959, *63,* 792–811.

Francis, R. J., & Rarick, G. L. *Motor characteristics of the mentally retarded.* Washington, D.C.: AAHPER, 1960.

Frankenburg, W. K., & Dodds, J. B. The Denver developmental screening test. *Journal of Pediatrics,* 1967, *71,* 181–191.

Fredericks, H. D., Baldwin, V. L., Doughtry, P., & Walter, L. J. *Teaching research motor development scale for moderately and severely retarded children.* Springfield, Ill.: Charles C Thomas, 1972.

Frostig, M. *Developmental test of visual perception.* Chicago: Follett, 1973.

Gardner, T. D., & Barnard, J. H. Intelligence and the factorial structure of person perception. *American Journal of Mental Deficiency,* 1969, *74,* 212–217.

Gesell, A. *The child from five to ten.* New York: Harper & Row, 1946.

Gesell, A. *The first five years of life.* New York: Harper & Row, 1940.

Gesell, A., & Thompson, H. Learning and growth in identical twin infants. *Genetic Psychology Monographs,* 1929, *6,* 1–24.

Gibson, J. The ontogeny of reading. *American Psychologist,* 1970, *25,* 136–143.

Glassow, R., & Roberts, E. Analysis of kicking. *DGWS speedball-soccer guide.* Washington, D.C.: American Alliance of Health, Physical Education, and Recreation, 1966–1968.

Guthrie, G. M., Gorlow, L., & Butler, A. J. The attitude of the retardate toward herself: A summary of research at Laurelton State School and Hospital. *Pennsylvania Psychological Quarterly,* 1967, *7,* 24–34.

Gutteridge, M. A study of motor achievements of young children. *Archives of Psychology,* 1939, *34,* 1–244.

Halverson, H. M. An experimental study of prehension with infants by means of systematic cinema records. *Genetic Psychology Monographs,* 1931, *10,* 107–286.

Halverson, L. E. Development of motor patterns in young children. *Quest,* 1966, *6,* 44–53.

Hanson, M. *Motor performance testing of elementary school age children.* Unpublished master's thesis, University of Wisconsin, 1965.

Hanson, S. K. *A comparison of the overhand throw performance of instructed and non-instructed kindergarten boys and girls.* Unpublished master's thesis, University of Wisconsin, 1961.

Harris, A. J. *Test of lateral dominance.* New York: Psychological Corporation, 1958.

Hayden, F. J. *Physical fitness for the mentally retarded.* Toronto, Canada: Metropolitan Toronto Association for Retarded Children, 1964.

Hellebrandt, F. A., Bauck, G. L., & Caine, M. D. Physiological analysis of basic motor skills. Growth and development of jumping. *American Journal of Physical Medicine,* 1961, *40,* 14–25.

Hilsendager, D. A. *Basic motor fitness.* Philadelphia, Pa.: Temple University Press, 1970.

Holladay, H. H. *An experimental and descriptive study of children's pre-representational drawings.* Unpublished doctoral dissertation, Cornell University, 1966.

Holser-Buehler, P. The Blanchard method of feeding the cerebral palsied. *American Journal of Occupational Therapy,* 1966, *20,* 31–34.

Howe, C. A. A comparison of motor skills of mentally retarded and normal children. *Exceptional Children,* 1959, *25,* 352–354.

Hurlock, E. B. *Child development.* New York: McGraw-Hill, 1964.

I CAN: Physical education program. Field Service Unit for Physical Education and Recreation for the Handicapped, Department of Health, Physical Education, and Recreation, Michigan State University. Northbrook, Ill.: Hubbard, 1976.

Ingram, D. Motor asymmetries in young children. *Neuropsychologia,* 1975, *13,* 95–102.

Johnson, D. L., & Myklebust, H. R. (Eds.). Disorders of written languages. *Learning disabilities: Educational principles and practices.* New York: Grune & Stratton, 1969.

Johnson, G. O., & Capobianco, R. J. Physical condition and its effect upon the learning in trainable mentally deficient children. *Exceptional Children,* 1969, *11,* 3–5.

Johnson, H. M. The act of block building. In E. S. Husch (Ed.), *The block book.* Washington, D.C.: National Association for Education of the Young Child, 1974, 9–24.

Johnson, R. D. Measurement of achievement in fundamental skills of elementary school children. *Research Quarterly,* 1962, *33,* 94–103.

Johnson, W. R., Fritz, B. R., & Johnson, J. A. Changes in self-concept during a physical development program. *Research Quarterly,* 1968, *39,* 560–565.

Jones, R. *A descriptive and mechanical analysis of throwing skills of children.* Unpublished master's thesis, University of Wisconsin, 1951.

Kamin, P. Fine motor development and the grasp function. In J. S. Malloy (Ed.), *Trainable children: Curriculum and practices.* New York: John Day, 1972.

Karpovich, P. Textbook fallacies regarding the development of the child's heart. *Research Quarterly,* 1937, *8,* 33.

Keogh, J. F. Incidence and severity of awkwardness among regular school boys and educationally subnormal boys. *Research Quarterly,* 1968, *38,* 806–808.

Kephart, N. C. *The Purdue perceptual-motor survey.* Columbus, Ohio: Charles E. Merrill, 1966.

Kephart, N. C. *The slow learner in the classroom.* Columbus, Ohio: Charles E. Merrill, 1960.

Kraus, H., & Hirschland, R. Minimum muscular fitness test in school children. *Research Quarterly,* 1955, *25,* 178–188.

Leighton, J. R. Flexibility characteristics of males 6–10 years of age. *Journal of the Association for Physical and Mental Rehabilitation,* 1964, *18,* 1–20.

Lexington developmental scale: An instrument of measurement. Lexington, Ky.: United Cerebral Palsy of the Blue Grass, Inc., 1973.

Lillie, D. L. Effects of motor development lessons on mentally retarded children. *American Journal of Mental Deficiency,* 1968, *72,* 803–808.

Lowenfeld, V., & Brittain, W. L. *Creative and mental growth.* New York: Macmillan, 1975.

Macey, P. G. *Mobilizing multiply handicapped children: A manual for the design and construction of modified wheelchairs.* Lawrence, Kans.: University of Kansas, Division of Continuing Education, 1974.

Matthews, D. K., Shaw, V., & Woods, J. W. Hip flexibility of elementary school boys as related to body segments. *Research Quarterly,* 1959, *30,* 297–302.

McCarthy, D. *McCarthy scales of children's abilities.* New York: Psychological Corporation, 1972.

McCaskill, D., & Wellman, B. A study of common motor achievements at the preschool years. *Child Development,* 1938, *9,* 141–150.

McGinnis, M. *Aphasic children.* Washington, D.C.: Alexander Graham Bell Association for the Deaf, Inc., 1963.

McGraw, M. *The neuromuscular maturation of the human infant.* New York: Hafner, 1945.

Mecham, M. J., Berko, F., & Palmer, M. *Communication training in childhood brain damage.* Springfield, Ill.: Charles C Thomas, 1966.

Molloy, J. S. *Trainable children: Curriculum and practices.* New York: John Day, 1972.

Mysak, E. D. *Principles of a reflex therapy approach to cerebral palsy.* New York: Teachers College, Columbia University, 1963.

Okamoto, T., & Kumamoro, M. Electromyographic study of the learning process of walking in infants. *Electromyography,* 1972, *12,* 149–158.

Orpet, R. E., & Heustis, T. L. *Move—grow—learn movement skills survey.* Chicago, Ill.: Follett, 1971.

Palmer, R. D. Hand differentiation and psychological functioning. *Journal of Personality,* 1963, *31,* 445—461.

Peabody developmental motor scales. Institute of Mental Retardation and Intellectual Development. Nashville, Tenn.: George Peabody College, 1974.

Peabody test of physical fitness. Institute on Mental Retardation and Intellectual Development. Behavioral Science Monograph, No. 75. Institute on School Learning and Individual Differences. Nashville, Tenn.: George Peabody College for Teachers, no date.

Pedersen, E. J. *A study of ball catching abilities of first, third, and fifth grade children on twelve selected ball catching tasks.* Unpublished doctoral dissertation, Indiana University, 1973.

Piers, E. V., & Harris, D. B. Age and other correlates of self-concept in children. *Journal of Educational Psychology,* 1964, *55,* 91–95.

Predmore, H. L. *The effects of a thirty-day physical education program on the intellectual, physical and social development of mentally retarded boys.* Unpublished master's thesis, Furman University, Greenville, S.C., 1965.

Rarick, G. L., Dobbins, D. A., & Broadhead, G. D. *The motor domain and its correlates in educationally handicapped children.* Englewood Cliffs, N. J.: Prentice-Hall, 1976.

Rarick, G. L., Widdop, J. J., & Broadhead, G. D. *The motor performance and physical fitness of educable mentally retarded children.* Madison, Wis.: University of Wisconsin, 1967.

Ridenour, M. D. Influence of object size, speed and direction on the perception of a moving object. *Research Quarterly,* 1974, *45,* 293–301.

Ridenour, M. D. Bicycles and tricycles for preschool children. *Physical Educator,* 1975, *32,* 71–73.

Robinault, I. P. *Functional aids for the multiply handicapped.* New York: Harper & Row, 1973.

Semans, S. The Bobath concept in treatment of neurological disorders. *American Journal of Physical Medicine,* 1967, *46,* 732–783.

Shirley, M. M. *The first two years: A study of twenty-five babies* (Vol. 2). Minneapolis: University of Minnesota Press, 1933.

Sinclair, C. B. *Movement of the young child, ages 2–6.* Columbus, Ohio: Charles E. Merrill, 1973.

Slingerland, B. H. *A multi-sensory approach to language arts for specific language disability children: A guide for primary teachers.* Cambridge, Mass.: Educators Publishing Service, 1971.

Sloan, W. *The Lincoln-Oseretsky motor development scale.* Chicago: C. H. Stoelting, 1954.

Stein, J. U. Motor function and physical fitness of the mentally retarded: a critical review. *Rehabilitation Literature,* 1963, *24,* 231.

Steingrueber, H. J. Handedness as a function of test complexity. *Perceptual and Motor Skills*, 1975, *40*, 263–266.

Terman, L. M., & Merrill, M. A. *Stanford-Binet intelligence scale*. Boston: Houghton-Mifflin, 1960.

Valett, R. E. *A psychoeducational inventory of basic learning*. Belmont, Calif.: Ferron, 1968.

Victors, E. A. *Cinematical analyses of catching behavior of a selected group of seven and nine year old boys*. Unpublished doctoral dissertation, University of Wisconsin, 1961.

Waite, K. B. *The educable mentally retarded child*. Springfield, Ill.: Charles C Thomas, 1971.

Wellman, B. L. Motor achievements of preschool children. *Childhood Education*, 1937, *13*, 311–316.

Wickstrom, R. L. *Developmental motor patterns in young children*. Unpublished film study, 1968.

Wickstrom, R. L. *Fundamental motor patterns*. Philadelphia: Lea & Febiger, 1970.

Wild, M. The behavior pattern of throwing and some observations concerning its course of development in children. *Research Quarterly*, 1938, *9* (3), 20–24.

Williams, H. G. *The effects of systematic variation of speed and direction of object flight and of skill and age classifications upon visual-perceptual judgments of moving objects in three dimensional space*. Unpublished doctoral dissertation, University of Wisconsin, 1968.

Notes

1. Keogh, J. F. *Motor performance of elementary school children*. (Tech. Rep. USPHS Grant MH 08319 and HO 01059). Department of Physical Education, University of California, Los Angeles, 1965.
2. Bunker, L. K. *Striking and throwing patterns in young children*. Unpublished research, University of Virginia, Motor Learning Laboratory, 1975.
3. Halverson, L. E., and Roberton, M. A. A study of motor pattern development in young children. Paper presented at American Alliance of Health, Physical Education and Recreation research conference (Chicago), (March) 1966.
4. Seefeldt, V., and Haubenstricker, J. *Developmental sequence of striking*. Unpublished material from Motor Development Conference, Michigan State University, July 1974.
5. Seefeldt, V. *Developmental sequence of catching skill*. Paper presented at the National Convention of the American Association of Health, Physical Education and Recreation, Houston, Texas, March 26, 1972.
6. Newell, K. On the assessment of motor impairment. Paper presented at a roundtable in Research on the Psychomotor Development of Young Handicapped Children. University of Wisconsin, Milwaukee, September, 1975.
7. *Physical Fitness for the Mentally Retarded*. Toronto, Ont. Metropolitan Toronto Association for Retarded Children, no date.
8. *Evaluation test for TMR children*. Greely, Co.: University of N. Carolina, Dept. of Special Education and the Rocky Mountain Special Education Instructional Materials Center, no date.
9. Mundy, J. *The Florida State University diagnostic battery of recreative functioning for the trainable mentally retarded*. Tallahassee, Fla.: Department of Recreation, Florida State University, no date.
10. *Functional neurological evaluation*. Dallas, Texas: Dallas Academy, no date.
11. *Perceptual motor attributes of mentally retarded children and youth*. Los Angeles, Calif.: Los Angeles County Department of Parks and Recreation, and the Special Education Branch, no date.

Introduction to Chapter 7

In this chapter you will be exposed to an extensive review of current research on basic self-care instruction. There has been much study of such instructional procedures, particularly with retarded populations. Undoubtedly some, if not all, of your students will demonstrate some deficiencies in either the basic skills of toileting, eating, and dressing or in more advanced self-help abilities such as grooming (hair and nail care, toothbrushing, bathing and showering, shaving, etc.), clothing care, and social eating skills (food passing, table manners, etc.).

Teaching the highest level of independence possible in basic self-care abilities is critical for the moderately and severely handicapped. Not only will their care be simplified and more pleasant for parents and teachers but, more importantly, to the extent a severely handicapped individual is capable of caring for his or her personal needs, exclusion from educational programs and services is far less probable.

The younger or the more handicapped the learner, the more useful you should find this chapter since basic skill instruction is pertinent for these individuals. To employ the content described in this chapter you will draw heavily from the observation and measurement techniques, the methods of task analysis, and the intervention strategies outlined in chapters 2 and 3.

7

Self-Care Skills

*This chapter was written by **Martha E. Snell**, University of Virginia.*

The development of self-care skills which begins early in the normal child's life represents a beginning of independence from parental care. For handicapped children and adults this independence is of equal significance although deficiencies in the individual's mental, physical, or behavioral repertoire as well as in environmental expectations may act to slow, limit, or indefinitely postpone development of these basic adaptive proficiencies. Feeding, dressing, and toileting are regarded as the most basic self-care areas. Early grooming skills supplement these basic abilities and include handwashing, face washing, toothbrushing, nasal hygiene, and later bathing and showering, hair combing and washing. Although most of these tasks are performed daily, all involve complex arrays of subskills that are learned in a highly organized sequence in concert with the acquisition of early cognitive, social, and motor abilities.

At the upper end of the self-care continuum are nail care, skin care, application of deodorants and simple cosmetics, shaving, and hair setting and styling, in addition to menstrual hygiene for females. Furthermore, facility in a multitude of daily living tasks and basic elements of safety directly influence

the quality of self-care an individual is able to provide himself. The following examples reveal this mushrooming interdependency of skill mastery: clothing purchase and care (simple repair, selection and coordination of colors and style, clothing size, cleaning, ironing, storage, etc.), dressing appropriately (weather, stylishness, age-suited, etc.), careful use of prescription and nonprescription drugs and medications, healthy eating habits (balanced diet, adequate amounts, food purchase and preparation, etc.), and concepts of sexuality and sexual behavior (awareness of sexual differences, respect for privacy, male-female social interaction, etc.). To view self-care instruction for the severely handicapped as a narrow curriculum relevant primarily in the early years and free of a dependency upon cognitive skills is erroneous. Just as expressive language has been shown (Edmonds, 1976) to have its roots in such prerequisite abilities as recognition of object permanence—"the awareness that an object has a separate, independent existence apart from the child, while existing and moving in a space common to both it and the child" (p. 185)—even the first elements of self-care skill development, other than reflexive eating behaviors, rely upon such cognitive prerequisites as visual tracking, visually directed grasping, gestural imitation, recognition of the reverse side of objects, and the presence of complex motor patterns such as sliding, crumpling, tearing, stretching, patting objects, placing objects into containers, and "letting go" actions (Uzgiris & Hunt, 1975). Skill training in one "area" (self-care, language, etc.) cannot be carried out efficiently if there is ignorance of the individual's performance in other dependent areas. Therefore, a teacher of the severely handicapped will find it essential to perform ongoing behavior observations for three purposes: to assess entry or baseline levels of skill in a wide range of overlapping areas of development, to monitor growth during instruction, and to detect behavior maintenance and application after instruction. The focus of this chapter is on the basic self-care areas—feeding, dressing, toileting, and early grooming skills—and how performance in these areas may be measured and taught.

Behaviors Influencing Self-Care Skill Learning

Although the severely handicapped individual frequently is delayed in the mastery of self-care skills, various causes beyond mental retardation may account for or contribute to this delay. For example, some of the fine motor skills which are prerequisites to self-care abilities may be inadequate, or physical handicaps (visual, motoric) may accompany the retardation or emotional disturbance. When manipulative motor abilities are weak, the individual's reaching, grasping, and eye-hand coordination need careful examination in comparison to the expected sequence of development (Chapter 6 provides direction for this assessment). Physical handicaps such as cerebral palsy (CP) require close guidance in assessment and training by a physical or occupational therapist so that realistic targets may be set rather than encouraging high levels of dependency. For example, the athetoid CP individual has problems of muscle control which are vastly different from the individual with severe spastic CP; these differences mandate procedural prescriptions for positioning, transporting, and specific movement requirements for eating, toileting, and dressing (Finnie, 1975).

If an individual is lacking in some of the preverbal and early cognitive skills—visual attention, motor imitation, comprehension of simple commands and phrases—the training techniques employed by a teacher will be quite different from those used with a verbal and attentive learner. For example, the use of verbal instructions ("Pick up your spoon") must be limited to the most relevant single word verb and

noun requests with more reliance upon gestures (Bensberg, Colwell, & Cassel, 1965). At times it will be more efficient to strengthen attending and imitation first before programming self-care instruction. However, much successful self-care research has been carried out with individuals initially demonstrating little or no comprehension of verbal directions or cues (Bensberg et al., 1965; Minge & Ball, 1967). Many of these studies document that gains in self-care skills were accompanied by increased comprehension of verbal requests to perform these skills. This same logic also may apply when the learner exhibits extensive disruptive behaviors which result in inattention (repetitious hand staring, rocking, etc.) or aggressive behavior (hitting self or others, throwing food, or destroying clothing). Therefore a teacher may elect to deal directly with the disruptive behaviors while reinforcing any improvements or even cooperation in self-care activities but not to teach new skills until self-control is more predictable. More often training in self-care and behavior management will proceed simultaneously and because of the differential reinforcement of self-help behaviors along with ignoring (extinction) or timing-out (punishment) of misbehaviors, the incidence of disruptive behavior will be reduced (Azrin & Armstrong, 1973; Christian, Hollomon, & Lanier, 1973; Minge & Ball, 1967; O'Brien & Azrin, 1972; Song & Gandhi, 1974).

An additional class of behavior—noncompliant behavior—may falsify assessment results and confuse teaching techniques. Noncompliance refers to the habitual tendency to refuse to engage in skills or portions of skills which actually are in the individual's repertoire. Such behavior is often inadvertently maintained by a teacher who provides help at the child's least refusal to perform or complete a task or who inconsistently requires that the learner perform self-care behaviors, alternating between firmness in task completion and "giving in" to extreme forms of refusals or to time constraints. For example, dressing training can be done at relevant times (preceding dismissal) but enough time must be available so refusals to perform can be ignored without necessitating dressing the child yourself.

The informal assessment period should not only allow measurement of self-care behavior but also must produce an estimate of those additional behaviors influencing self-care training: physical handicaps and their effect on self-care behavior, level of fine motor development, attending, motor imitation, comprehension of simple commands appropriate to self-care instruction (e.g., "Look here," "Eat with your spoon," "No," "Do this"), and disruptive or noncompliant behaviors which occur during meals, dressing periods, and toileting times. In some cases it is possible for a teacher to observe another teacher (parent or aide) working with a learner during self-care periods. Such observations enable one to observe the child's response to commands given, various prompts and reinforcement procedures, the learning situation, etc. and to make predictions about the success of changes in current antecedent or consequent events. Whenever possible, parental interviews or observations of the parents' interaction with their child during self-care times are recommended. Information needs to be gathered on the parents' expectations for performance, their understanding of analyzing tasks into small steps and reinforcing successive approximations, their consistency in approach, the use of imitative models, the appropriateness of the teaching materials (e.g., texture, flavor of food, level of toilet seat, size and complexity of clothing) and their feelings about the teaching program (Barnard & Powell, 1972). All of this information along with the self-care skill data will be valuable in creating and monitoring an individualized instructional program.

Normal Development of Self-Care Skills

The sequence of normal motor and self-care development may serve as a training guide to teachers of the severely handicapped because the developmental sequence tends to be the same for all populations although the rate and age of acquisition differs. In the logical order of skill development, complex skills emerge from the mastery, modification, and combination of necessary prerequisite behaviors. This mandates that teachers be familiar with characteristics of normal child growth. With this knowledge, curricula may be logically sequenced, the content of assessment checklists may be determined, and teachers may decide an individual's readiness for instruction in a particular skill. For example, the developmental information on dressing and undressing in Table 7.1 can be converted into an informal assessment device (Figure 7.1) by:

1. Grouping items into smaller specific skill sequences (e.g., undresses—shirts; dresses—pants; buttoning)
2. Adding additional prerequisite items from related skill sequences (e.g., picks up small object with pincer grasp; grasps object by handle)

3. Stating items in measurable terms
4. Arranging items for each specific skill in developmental order
5. Adding a column in which directions given by the teacher are stated
6. Specifying scoring criteria and symbols (e.g., +, correctly performed; +M, correctly performed with model)

An alternative to the informal developmental test involves a task analysis of the skill. The lattice method of task analysis, described in Chapter 2, was employed to reduce the skill of buttoning into its component parts (Figure 7.2). Of course, the teacher must be aware of related developmental information so that entry or prerequisite skills may be identified, as noted in the upper left corner of the lattice. Next, the task analysis may be converted into an assessment checklist by listing component behaviors in sequential order, adding necessary teacher directions and specifying scoring criteria (Figure 7.3).

If the results of the developmental checklist (Figure 7.1) reveal that an individual has all the entry skills for buttoning (i.e., items 1, 2, and 3) but demonstrates difficulty in buttoning, then the same individual should be observed more closely with the task analysis checklist (Figure 7.3). This observation will provide answers as to *why* the individual is unsuccessful at buttoning. Additionally, after the missing behavior(s) has been identified, the task analysis serves as a guide for lesson planning during instruction.

Developmental sequences for eating, toileting, and basic grooming skills will be provided in later sections of this chapter.

Summary of Self-care Instructional Decisions

Because Chapter 2 delineated the steps involved in systematic instruction, the following list shall serve only to remind the reader of the instructional decisions involved in the teaching of feeding, toileting, dressing, and basic grooming skills.

1. What foods, toys, activities, and types of social attention and praise are reinforcing to the learner, appropriate to his chronological and social age, and may be efficiently employed during teaching?

TABLE 7.1   *The sequence and expected age for the occurrence of dressing and undressing skills in the normally developing child*

Chronological Age for Normally Developing Child	Dressing/Undressing Skills
1 to 1½ years	A. Child will cooperate in dressing by extending arm or leg. B. Child will remove simple clothing such as socks, shoes (will not untie), hat, mittens. C. Child will attempt to put shoes on. D. Child may remove pants if assistance provided in first half of chain.
1½ to 2½ years	A. Child will undress self including removing shoes, if laces are untied, and unzipping zippers. B. Child will assist in dressing and is able to pull on simple garments. C. Child will attempt to unbutton.
2½ to 3 years	A. Child will undress rapidly including front and side buttons. B. Child will dress with lightweight garments but has difficulty with heavy outer clothes; may button 1 or 2 buttons but needs help with zipping up. C. Child apt to confuse front and back of garments.
3 to 4 years	A. Child will dress and undress with only minor assistance, especially if all clothing is selected and waiting; buttons 3 to 4 buttons. B. Child is able to discriminate front and back of clothing. C. Child intent on lacing shoes even though it is usually done incorrectly.
4 to 5 years	A. Child dresses and undresses carefully and rapidly without assistance except on belt buckles, back buttons, and shoe tying. B. Child learning to tie shoes but can lace shoes.
5 to 6 years	A. Ties single knot with shoe lace around pencil (with a model); later ties shoe lace.

Source: Cohen, Gross, and Haring (1976); Copeland, Ford, and Solon (1976); Gesell and Amatruda (1947).

2. What procedures or aversive events may be applied to control and reduce undesirable behaviors interfering with the performance of self-care skills?
3. What self-help training objectives will be set for the learner?
   A. What self-care behaviors are of most immediate importance to the individual, his home, or school setting?
   B. What is the individual's current or baseline performance in these identified self-care behaviors?
4. What instructional methods will be employed to achieve the set objectives?
   A. Teacher instructions and requests
   B. Effective prompts
   C. Training setting and instructional materials
   D. Teaching times and frequency
   E. Task analysis of behavior
   F. Specific teaching techniques (shaping, backward chaining, dry pants check, positive practice, etc.)
5. How will changes in the learner's performance be monitored?
6. How will gains in self-care behaviors be maintained?
7. How will gains in self-care behavior be generalized to other teachers, materials, and settings?

Toilet Training

Frequently, independent toileting skills have been an unattained goal for the more severely handicapped individual. This failure often leads to exclu-

Name: _____ Date(s): _____

Skill: Buttoning/Unbuttoning

	Score	Directions/Materials	Behavior (Normal Chronological Age)
1.	_____	Place 5 buttons of varying sizes on table one at a time; say "Get the button," while pointing to the button.	Picks up small objects with a precise pincer grasp (12 months)
2.	_____	Place 5 buttons one at a time beside a small spice bottle into which buttons will fit; gesture and say, "Put the button in the bottle."	Picks up and drops buttons into bottle with pincer grasp (18 months)
3.	_____	Place a front buttoning garment on child buttoned; point to an easily visible button and say "Take off your *shirt*," gesturing toward button.	Unbuttons one large button located in front of garment (30 months)
4.	_____	Same as above except do not button garment; say "Button your *shirt*."	Buttons one large button located in front of garment (31 months)
5.	_____	Same as #3.	Unbuttons 3 accessible buttons (as above) (33–36 months)
6.	_____	Same as #4.	Buttons 2 buttons (as above) (33 months)
7.	_____	Same as #4.	Buttons 4 buttons (as above) (60 months)

Score Key: + successful with single direction (100%)
                  V+ successful with additional verbal/gestural cues
                  M+ successful with one model
                  – attempts but incorrect
                  0 will not attempt

FIGURE 7.1   *Assessment device based on developmental sequence*

sion from social and recreational programs and public schooling, acts to reduce teaching time between parent or ward attendant and the "accident prone" individual, causes serious health hazards in the form of inadequate residential hygiene, dysentary, and intestinal infection, and results in an individual who is less pleasant to be around. The high prevalence of daytime incontinence in this population is surpassed by nighttime incontinence or enuresis. One researcher (Sugaya, 1967) estimated that 70% of the institutionalized severely retarded in Japan were incontinent at night—a fact confirmed by a bedwetting survey in similar U.S. institutions (Azrin, Sneed, & Foxx, 1973).

In a 5-year survey of the toileting skill changes occurring in a group of 3,427 institutionalized re-tarded individuals, Lohman, Eyman, and Lask (1967) discovered that 63% of the sample—those with the highest functioning capabilities (IQ 20)—were or became toilet trained during the 5 years rather easily by traditional methods without any special equipment or systematic operant techniques. However, 31% made no progress or regressed. This group tended to demonstrate one or more of the following characteristics: IQ$\leqslant$10, severely disturbed behavior, medically significant physical problems. The remaining 6.2% possessed an IQ between 10 and 20 and achieved or made progress during the 5 years toward daytime regulation (e.g., eliminated on toilet when taken but no self-initiation) when exposed to traditional methods of toilet training. The authors hypothesized that the unsuccess-

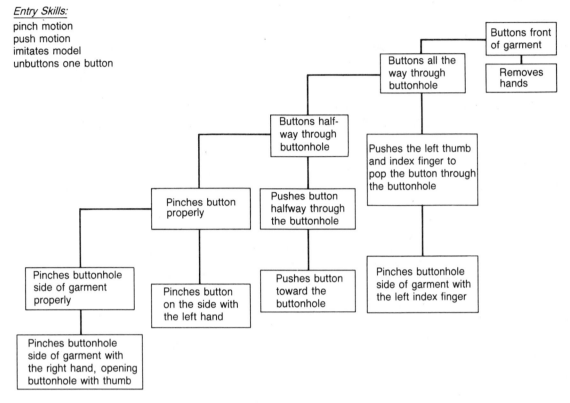

Entry Skills:
pinch motion
push motion
imitates model
unbuttons one button

Buttons front of garment

Removes hands

Buttons all the way through buttonhole

Buttons half-way through buttonhole

Pushes the left thumb and index finger to pop the button through the buttonhole

Pinches button properly

Pushes button halfway through the buttonhole

Pinches buttonhole side of garment properly

Pinches button on the side with the left hand

Pushes button toward the buttonhole

Pinches buttonhole side of garment with the left index finger

Pinches buttonhole side of garment with the right hand, opening buttonhole with thumb

FIGURE 7.2   *Lattice for buttoning*

Source: D. D. Smith and J. O. Smith, Research and application of a prototypic model for instructional material development. In N. G. Haring (Ed.), *A program project for the investigation and application of procedures of analysis and modification of behavior of handicapped children: Annual report.* National Institute of Education Grant OEG-0-70-3916 (607), Project No. 572247, 1974.

ful group demonstrating "complex custodial problems" would probably never achieve improvement, whereas the smaller group of 6.2% would respond to intensive operant training procedures.

Motivated by these statistics and their negative effect on further development of the handicapped, teachers and applied behavior analysts have in the last 15 years created, tested, and revised treatment procedures for incontinence. The intent of this section is to set forth the basic elements of successfully documented toilet-training procedures, drawing heavily upon recent research studies and curricular applications that exist in this area.

Entry skills for toilet training

As with other tasks, toileting is learned in a logical developmental sequence building upon certain prerequisite behaviors. The developmental sequence in Table 7.2 reveals a number of things important to a teaching program.

1. Daytime regulation and training precedes nightime training.
2. Bowel movements are regulated before urination but toileting independence in both is generally learned at the same time.
3. The additional skills of undressing, dressing, and wiping "slow down" total independence in the normal child.

Some of these entry behaviors are directly requisite to independent elimination, such as bladder and bowel regulation. However, the presence of other entry skills such as walking, vision, comprehension of simple verbal commands, though not mandatory, will facilitate learning greatly. These two classes of entry skills will be differentiated next and procedures to measure them described.

Essential Entry Criteria

There are probably three essential characteristics to indicate readiness for toilet training. All three are

Name: _____ Date(s): _____

Entry Skills: pinch, push, pull finger motions; can imitate a model; unbuttons 1 button.

Skill: Buttoning

Directions: Hand individual a loose, front-buttoning garment with 5 medium to large buttons (3/4"). Say, while gesturing appropriately, "Put on the shirt and button it all up, please." (Garment should have buttons on left panel for right-handed persons.)

	Score	Behavior
1.	_____	Pinches buttonhole side of garment with the right (dominant) hand opening hole with thumb.
2.	_____	Pinches button on the side with left (nondominant) hand.
3.		Buttons halfway through buttonhole:
	_____	A. pushes button toward the buttonhole
	_____	B. pushes button halfway through
4.		Buttons all the way through buttonhole:
	_____	A. pinches buttonhole side of garment with the left index finger
	_____	B. pushes the left thumb and index finger to pop the button through the buttonhole
5.	_____	Removes hands.

Score Key: + successful with no assistance
                 − attempts but incorrectly
                 0 not observed

Note: Enter scores for every trial on each step (e.g. #3a, + − − + +).

FIGURE 7.3   *Assessment checklist based on a task analysis of the skill*

interdependent and relate to physiological development—specifically the maturity of the central nervous system and the elimination sphincters.

1. The individual should demonstrate a rather stable pattern of elimination. This regularity means that urination and bowel responses occur within certain daily time periods (as illustrated in Figure 7.4) rather than "dribbling" throughout the day or having bowel movements at random times.

2. The individual should have daily stable periods of dryness—an ability to withhold eliminations which extends from 1 to 2 hours (as illustrated in Figure 7.4).

3. The chronological age (CA) of the moderately to profoundly retarded individual should be 2½ years or greater. For retarded individuals there appears to be a positive relationship between

progress in training and CA which relates to central nervous system (CNS) maturity; however, research results are somewhat inconsistent (Osarchuk, 1973). Hundziak, Maurer, and Watson (1965) noted that CA is a less important readiness criterion because of the indirect relationship between CA and the ability of the CNS to exert sphincter control. The relationship of mental age and success in toilet training is even less clear but recommendations reflect the rule: the greater the retardation, the longer one should wait before initiating training (Foxx & Azrin, 1974). The rationale for this rule concerns inadequate physiological readiness. For mildly retarded individuals little or no delay in the initiation of training appears necessary (Bensberg et al., 1965). Foxx and Azrin (1973a) recommended that moderately retarded individuals be at least 2½, while train-

TABLE 7.2   *Developmental sequence of toileting skills*

Chronological Age	Behavior
12 months	Bowel movements regulated (12–15 months). Usually dry following nap time. Indicates desire to be changed after a bowel movement by fussing.
15 months	Indicates when pants are wet.
18 to 21 months	Urination regulated. Bowel movement control attained.
2 years	Daytime urination control attained. May need reminders to use bathroom. Requires assistance with clothes and wiping.
2½ years	Informs an adult of need to use bathroom. Requires assistance with pulling pants up and fastening and wiping but able to pull pants down.
3 to 3½ years	Goes to bathroom alone. Independent at clothing manipulation if garments are simple. Requires assistance wiping.
4 to 5 years	Cares for self at toilet (clothing, setting, wiping, and flushing). Toilets independently.

Source: Barnard and Powell (1972); Copeland, Ford, and Solon (1976); Gesell and Amatruda (1947).

ing may proceed best if a CA of 5 is reached for the severely and profoundly retarded. However, if an individual meets the first two criteria listed above but is slightly less than 2½ and functions in the moderate range, or is less than 5 and functions in the severe range, training should probably be initiated anyway.

Additional Entry Skills

Although the following skills are *not* considered essential indicators of readiness, their presence will facilitate learning. Their absence, in part or total, will mean the teacher must make special additions to the instructional procedure (e.g., instruction in wheelchair mobility and transfer; modification in wheelchair design; instruction in attending and sitting, sign language, or simple gestures; mobility training; etc.). These additional entry skills include the following behaviors:

1. The individual is ambulatory and can walk to and from the bathroom independently.
2. The individual has adequate manipulative skills to learn the basic undressing and dressing tasks needed for independent toileting.
3. The individual indicates a need to eliminate by means of facial expression or posture.
4. The individual dislikes being wet or soiled and indicates by showing displeasure.
5. The individual will remain seated for at least five minutes.

6. The individual *understands* some simple commands (e.g., "Look at me," "Come here," "Sit," "Eat this," etc.).
7. The absence of behavior problems: aggressiveness, self-destructive behavior, withdrawal from social contact (Lohman, Eyman, & Lask, 1967).

Measurement of Entry Skills

Daytime regulation and dryness may be measured with the same elimination charting procedure. While many toilet-training programs for the handicapped exist and provide a range of recommendations about methods to record this baseline data, a number of consistencies emerge.

Data recording form. Using a data collection form similar to that pictured in Figure 7.4, check the individual at the beginning of every half hour from waking to bedtime and record whether he is wet (W or B) or dry (D or blank); if wet, is it due to bowel movement (B), urination or wetting (W), or both (W/B)? Furthermore, some record must be made of whether the elimination occurred off the toilet (Ⓦ Ⓑ Ⓦ/Ⓑ) or on the toilet (W, B, W/B). As shown in Figure 7.4, accidents are indicated by circling the appropriate symbol. Additional symbols may be developed to indicate whether the toileting behavior was child-initiated (W+). If the individual was placed on the toilet and no elimination occurred a X could be recorded, while self-initiated toileting

Name: _____   Date: _____

Time of Response	5/1	5/2	5/3	5/4	5/5	5/6	5/7	5/8	5/9	5/10	5/11	5/12	5/13	5/14
AM 7:00			W					W						
7:30	W			W		W					W		B	
8:00		W			W		W		W	W		W	W	W
8:30														
9:00	B		B		B		B		B		B			
9:30		B		B				B		B		B		B
10:00														
10:30														
11:00														
11:30						B								
PM 12:00														
12:30				W										
1:00	W	W	W		W		W	W		W		W		
1:30					W				W		W		W	W
2:00														
2:30														
3:00														
3:30		W				W		W		W				
4:00	W		W	W	W		W		W		W	W	W	W
4:30														
5:00														
5:30														
6:00												W		
6:30					W				W					W
7:00	W	W	W	W		W	W	W		W	W		W	
7:30														
8:00														
8:30		W							W					
9:00	W		W	W	W	W	W			W	W	W	W	W

Response Key:

(W) Accident Wet	W+ Child-Initiated Wet	W− Teacher-Assisted Wet
(B) Accident Bowel	B+ Child-Initiated Bowel	B− Teacher-Assisted Bowel

FIGURE 7.4 *Sample data collection chart for toileting*

Source: M. D. Linford, L. W. Hipsher, and R. G. Silikovitz, *Systematic instruction for retarded children: The Illinois program, Part III Self-help instruction*, Danville, Ill.: Interstate, 1972, p. 146.

which resulted in no elimination would be recorded as X+.

Depending upon the child and the method of training employed, Fredericks, Baldwin, Grove, and Moore (1975) suggest additional codes—a small dot in a half hour square would indicate liquids were given to the individual, M would be placed in those intervals where meals occurred, and naps would be marked on the chart with arrows extending from beginning to end. As long as the essential information is recorded in the appropriate time interval (wet or dry, type of elimination, accident or on-toilet elimination, and child-initiated or adult-initiated), any symbols may be used to record baseline data. If mechanical devices are going to be employed to teach toileting, then additional records may be employed during intervention.

During the collection of these data it is essential that the individual is changed into dry clothing immediately after each accident with neutral teacher-child interaction (neither punishing nor reinforcing) so that each additional accident will not be confused with earlier accidents. Clothing students in training pants rather than diapers will facilitate changing and detection of accidents.

Length of data collection. While some programs recommend a minimum of 3 (Foxx & Azrin, 1973b) to 7 days of baseline records (Copeland, Ford, & Solon, 1976), others employ at least 15 days with a possible extension to 30 days if necessary to establish whether reliable toileting patterns exist. (Fredericks et al., 1975; Giles & Wolf, 1966; Linford, Hipsher, & Silikovitz, 1972).[1]

---

1. The purposes of baseline charting vary depending upon the method of toilet training applied. While all programs may employ a 3- to 30-day baseline as a standard to evaluate the effectiveness of an intervention, some methods (referred to in this chapter as "the improved traditional methods") rely upon baseline records to determine the expected time of elimination for each student. These expected times for urination and bowel movement become the training periods. However, in methods which employ additional fluids and mechanical signaling devices (Azrin & Foxx, 1971; Foxx & Azrin, 1973b; Mahoney, Van-Wagenen, & Meyerson, 1971) pretraining accident and success records are kept to obtain "an objective means of evaluating the seriousness of the incontinence problem and the need for the program" (Foxx & Azrin, 1973b, p. 25). Longer baselines revealing more accurate elimination schedules are probably most important for use with the improved traditional methods.

Task Analysis of Toileting Skills

In 1963 Ellis proposed an analytical model of the stimuli and responses involved in toilet training which served as the first task analysis. Ellis reasoned that before toilet training, the elimination response (R_e) occurs in the presence of unpleasant bladder and rectal tension which act as the discriminative stimuli (S^D) for these initially reflexive responses. R_e results in immediate reduction of the unpleasant tension, a process of negative reinforcement; however, as the child matures, the unpleasant consequences of wet and soiled clothes and parental disapproval are added. Ellis represented this as:

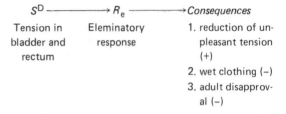

$$S^D \longrightarrow R_e \longrightarrow Consequences$$

Tension in bladder and rectum	Eleminatory response	1. reduction of unpleasant tension (+)
		2. wet clothing (−)
		3. adult disapproval (−)

During toilet training an individual is taught a variety of responses which precede elimination (R_A, approach to the toilet, preparation for toileting) and result in additional intermediate discriminative stimuli (S_A, cues generated by approach response; S_T, cues associated with toilet) in the presence of which the elimination response occurs.

This model not only stimulated toilet-training research with the institutionalized retarded population but also served as the first task analysis of elimination as a "conditionable" behavior.

A more detailed task analysis of the approach response and the behavior that immediately follow

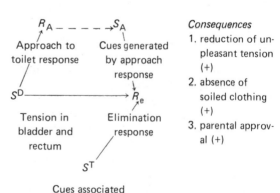

R_A – – – –→ S_A
Approach to   Cues generated
toilet response   by approach
response

S^D ——————→ R_e
Tension in   Elimination
bladder and   response
rectum

S^T

Cues associated
with toilet

Consequences
1. reduction of unpleasant tension (+)
2. absence of soiled clothing (+)
3. parental approval (+)

elimination (e.g., wiping, pants up and fastened, etc.) will identify the teachable steps and serve as a checklist assessment of baseline skill. Figure 7.5 provides a sequenced breakdown of the behavior chains occurring before and after elimination. As is true of all task analyses, the number and order of the behaviors will vary as well as the actual behaviors themselves if one teacher's task analysis is compared to another's. For example, with younger children a better method of teaching wiping requires that the child stand up first and then wipe rather than remain seated; if skirts or dresses are worn, the pants down and up sequence will change; some teachers will prefer to teach boys to stand and face the toilet bowl rather than sit during urination. Although this task analysis consists of eight behavior chains or components, some of which are further subdivided, the number of components and their subdivisions are dependent upon the method selected to perform the task and the amount of detail imposed upon this content.

Directions for use of this checklist suggest that multiple baseline observations be made to obtain more accurate measurement. Also the teacher is directed to use the verbal and gestural cues (in addition to the initial cue) only if the individual stops performing or omits one or more of the eight component chains of behavior. A teacher may wish to add additional scoring categories for varying levels of approximate responses as was illustrated on the buttoning checklist described earlier (Figure 7.1).

An assessment checklist, such as this, should be used prior to toilet training and readministered periodically during training, whereas the toileting behavior chart (Figure 7.4) should be used before and *throughout* training. The information obtained from these two measurements is needed to set training objectives and to evaluate progress during teaching.

General elements of toilet training

After determining the learner's readiness for training, baseline elimination schedule, and current skills in the toileting task analysis, the teacher must make instructional decisions regarding effective reinforcers and punishers as well as set instructional targets and specify methods to teach.

1. *What training objectives will be set?*
A. *Elimination.* Will bladder control *and* bowel control be taught together or separately? If separately, which will be taught first? Although teaching

may proceed either way, the learner must demonstrate a stable pattern of elimination (in urination or bowel movement) in the area or areas selected for training. If only one area is selected for training, accidents in the other area must *not* be punished, although success certainly would be treated with the same reinforcing consequences as the targeted behavior.

B. *Daytime or night training.* Only after the individual has mastered daytime toileting skills (e.g., eliminates on toilet most of the time when taken, and has little or no daytime accidents) should night training begin (Azrin & Foxx, 1974; Baller, 1975; Copeland et al., 1976; Finnie, 1975; Foxx & Azrin, 1973b; Linford et al., 1972). Fredericks et al. (1975) suggest that night training begin at this time regardless of whether the individual has begun to express a need to go to the toilet or to self-initiate toileting.

C. *Related toileting skills.* After a careful examination of the individual's performance in related toileting tasks, what deficiencies emerge as potential teaching targets? Does the learner require prodding to walk to the bathroom or restraining to remain seated on the toilet? Is the person unable to manipulate his belt, snaps, and zippers? Does the child perform four of the nine steps in handwashing but hesitate or fail on the remaining five? The selection of additional training targets beyond the elimination target relates partly to the teacher's time but primarily to the learner's deviation from performance expected at his age and with his mental and physical ability. Because elimination training requires performance of at least five additional chains of behavior (toilet approach, pants removal, sitting, pants replacement, and leaving the bathroom), a teacher should identify how much of these behaviors a learner is capable of and, at the very minimum, require that level of performance while reinforcing any improvements.

2. *What instructional methods will be selected?* As discussed in the next section, there are two major daytime training methods: improved traditional training and rapid training procedures involving intentionally increased elimination with or without the use of mechanical signaling equipment. Variations of both methods may be employed for night training as well. Because teaching procedures should complement an individual learner's entry skills and learning preferences, care should be taken to specify the following elements of the teaching program. Some of these instructional elements will be determined by the toilet-training method employed.

Individual: _____ Date(s): _____

Directions: Test the child at least 3 times over a period of 2 or 3 days. Try to select a time when bladder or bowel tension is most likely. Give the first cue, observe and score the performance; give successive cues only if child hesitates for more than 5 seconds or omits a behavior after completion of the entire preceding behavior. Place an asterisk by the first behavior in every chain which you must cue. Use a + if behavior is performed without help, a − if attempted but imperfect or incomplete, and a 0 if not tried. Place averaged score in small blank at far right.

Final Internal Cue (S^D) after Training	Intermediate Training Cues (S^D)	Behavior	Score
Bladder and/or Bowel Tension	1. "Go to the bathroom" (gesture)	1. Walks directly to bathroom without more than a 3-second delay in initiating the response	1. _____ ____
	2. "Pull your pants down" (gesture)	2a. Unfasten buttons, zippers.	2a. _____ ____
		b. Hooks thumbs into tops of underpants	b. _____ ____
		c. Removes under- and outerwear to at least mid-thigh	c. _____ ____
	3. "Sit on the toilet" (gesture)	3. Sits appropriately	3. _____ ____
	4. "Go *potty*"	4. Eliminates	4. _____ ____
	5. "Wipe yourself" (gesture)	5a. Reaches and grasps toilet paper	5a. _____ ____
		b. Pulls out and tears off an appropriate amount	b. _____ ____
		c. Bends and wipes self	c. _____ ____
		d. Drops paper into toilet	d. _____ ____
	6. "Flush the toilet" (gesture)	6a. Places hand on top of flusher	6a. _____ ____
		b. Pushes down until toilet flushes	b. _____ ____
	7. "Pull your pants up" (gesture)	7a. Grasps top band of underwear with both hands	7a. _____ ____
		b. Pulls underpants up and into place	b. _____ ____
		c. Grasps top band of outer pants with both hands	c. _____ ____
		d. Pulls pants up and into place	d. _____ ____
		e. Fastens buttons and zippers	e. _____ ____
	8. "Wash your hands" (gesture)	8a. Approaches sink	8a. _____ ____
		b. Turns water on	b. _____ ____
		c. Wets hands	c. _____ ____
		d. Picks up soap and rubs hands on and around soap	d. _____ ____
		e. Replaces soap	e. _____ ____
		f. Lathers hands	f. _____ ____
		g. Rinses hands	g. _____ ____
		h. Turns water off	h. _____ ____
		i. Reaches for towel and dries hands	i. _____ ____
		9. Leaves bathroom	9. _____ ____

FIGURE 7.5   *Toileting skill checklist*

A. *Instructions.* Verbal and gestural directions must be matched to the comprehension capabilities of the learner. Assessment of the individual's language skills will aid appropriate selection of meaningful instructions. For some individuals one-word commands accompanied by gestures are necessary whereas others may be able to follow more lengthy verbal instructions. With both extremes consistency is of utmost importance. Also instructions must be selected and standardized for each training objective.

B. *Effective prompts.* At times a teacher will simply reinforce improvements in the toileting performance (shaping); but more often the need arises to prompt a nonoccurring behavior. Prompts may range from additional verbal directions (e.g., "Flush the toilet"), to demonstrations (e.g., by a teacher or peer models), to pointing and various amounts of physical assistance. Good instruction means the provision of the *least* amount of assistance necessary to get the learner to perform. This practice allows the learner to perform more of the behavior and makes the eventual removal of the assistance easier.

C. *Training setting and materials.* When a child is beginning to learn toileting skills, one bathroom area as close to the classroom as possible should be used. If the bathroom is too far away and if some learners have difficulty walking, the teacher should consider moving portable toilets or potty chairs into one screened portion of the classroom. Some rapid methods involving signaling equipment (Azrin & Foxx, 1971; Foxx & Azrin, 1973a, 1973b) suggest moving the classroom into the bathroom. This will be explained in more detail later. Since there should be as many toilets or potty chairs as there are learners in a toileting program, the purchase of additional portable toilets may be necessary.

The type of toilet depends upon the learner. Those with weak muscle control such as cerebral palsied individuals need toilet seats that provide good support at the back and side. Finnie (1975) provides examples of commercially available and adapted toilets.[2] If the toilet is adult size and the learners are small, wooden steps and toilet seat insets should be obtained to allow independence in climbing up onto the toilet and reduce fear and balance problems involved in sitting on the seat. The learner's feet should be able to rest solidly on the

floor or a step while he is seated on the toilet. The sinks also may need steps to provide independent access.

Once an individual has learned to use one toilet and sink reliably, the training setting should be expanded to include other bathrooms. Although the need for adapted equipment may complicate this stage of teaching for some learners, it is essential that skill generalization be taught so that learning may occur in places other than the classroom.

Reinforcers must be individually determined and their effectiveness pretested before training begins. This determination may also include what *quantity* will be effective with different-sized individuals (Osarchuk, 1973).

D. *Teaching times and frequency.* If the improved traditional method is employed, toilet training will occur just before *every* normally expected time for urination and bowel movements (or one type of elimination, depending upon the teacher's objectives). With the rapid methods, additional fluids, milk of magnesia, or suppositories (Giles & Wolf, 1966) are given, thereby creating the need for more elimination and more training sessions. However, with both methods students may be taught to perform various aspects of the toileting chains (e.g., pants up and down, toilet approach, handwashing at times other than when bowel and bladder tension exist or are believed to exist). This extra training must only supplement that which is done in association with the internal bladder and bowel stimuli.

E. *Task analysis.* The task analysis provided earlier may be used during assessment and as a teaching guide. Many teachers will need to modify this task analysis to suit the particular needs and additional handicaps of their students (e.g., shorten, lengthen, employ entirely different behavior chains, etc.).

F. *Specific training techniques.* Although some techniques were developed as part of a larger toileting program, many techniques can be used in the original or in a modified form to create another toilet-training program. For example, the "dry pants inspection," a procedure first described by Azrin and Foxx (1971), was one of many techniques in their rapid toilet-training method. Bender and Valletutti (1976) and Linford et al. (1972) include a dry pants inspection although on a less frequent basis in their toileting programs. Generally these *new* toilet-training "packages" have not been experimentally tested; however, if a teacher clearly understands the learning outcome of a particular procedure, can adjust the elements of that procedure to

---

2. See also the list of commercial catalogues provided at the end of the chapter.

suit a specific individual, and employs a data system of program evaluation, then new combinations of techniques are justified.

Dry Pants Inspection

This technique (Azrin & Foxx, 1971; Foxx & Azrin, 1973b) consists of three steps:

1. Question the individual about his dryness using simple phrases and gestures (e.g., "Are you dry?").
2. Prompt the person to look at and feel the crotch area of his pants.
3. A. If the learner's pants are dry, reinforce him with praise for dryness (e.g., "Good, you have dry pants!") and an edible.
   B. If the learner's pants are wet, verbally chastise him and withhold the edible (e.g., "No, you have wet pants, no candy!").

In a rapid training program where extra fluids are given, dry pants inspections are carried out every five minutes unless an accident occurs to delay the next inspection (Foxx & Azrin, 1973b). If dry pants inspection is part of a more traditional program, then it would be less frequent.

Accident Treatment

Many accidents will be prevented by strict adherence to a toileting schedule, maintenance of a standardized eating and drinking pattern, and strong positive reinforcement for correct toileting behavior. However, not *all* accidents will be prevented and a regular procedure for responding to accidents should be determined. Consequences applied for inappropriate toileting responses may range from ignoring or extinction to punishment. Unless mandated by the toilet program, select an accident treatment that best suits the learner. If, under the traditional method, daytime accidents continue after two months, a more punishing accident consequence may be appropriate. Instead of this, the teacher may wish to systematically change some single element of the program at a time: reinforcers, toileting schedule, change to a more rapid method, addition of signaling equipment, etc.

1. *Extinction.* Without talking to the child, change his pants and clean him using lukewarm water. Be careful not to provide any reinforcing activity too soon after an accident.

2. *Mild punishment.* As soon as an accident is discovered, approach the individual, have him feel and look at his pants, and provide verbal dissapproval (e.g., "You wet your pants" or "No, you have wet pants"). The child may be left wet for a few minutes to experience the discomfort of wet pants. The teacher then changes the child using the extinction procedure or may apply one or more overcorrection procedures such as described by Azrin and Foxx (1971) and Foxx and Azrin (1973b). These include cleanliness training and positive practice which were developed for use with urine-signaling underpants.

A. *Cleanliness training.* As soon as the accident is signaled, the individual is grasped and told "No, you wet your pants!" Next he is told to undress and is given a tepid shower. Then the person is expected to dress in clean clothing, place his clothes in a sink, immerse them in water, wring out the water and spread them to dry, and clean the floor or chair where the accident occurred with a mop or cloth. Individuals resisting cleanliness training are physically assisted through every step. Additionally no reinforcers, social or edible, are made available for a 1-hour period following an accident. A shortened version of cleanliness training which excludes clothing change and washing is suggested for use during initial bladder training (Foxx & Azrin, 1973b), whereas the expanded version just described is used once the individual begins to toilet himself without a prompt (self-initiation stage). If the individual is verbal, this overcorrection procedure may be enhanced by requiring that the person verbalize the relationship between the overcorrection procedure and soiling with a statement such as "I am cleaning my pants because I soiled them and will have to do this each time it happens" (Doleys & Arnold, 1975, p. 16).

B. *Positive practice.* Immediately after cleanliness training for an accident, Foxx and Azrin (1973b, 1974) employ positive practice—the continuous repetition of movements related to toileting: toilet approach, pants down, sit for a few moments, rise, pants up, leave toilet area. Positive practice is continued, with prompting as needed, for the remaining portion of the half hour cycle used in the Azrin and Foxx (1971) rapid training procedure. If the shortened cleanliness training is used, the individual still has his wet pants on and a dry pants inspection follows at the end of every positive practice cycle. This means the individual feels his wet pants and is verbally chastised.

C. *Other punishment procedures.* Toileting accidents have been punished by spankings (Marshall, 1966), termination of meals, requirements that the child remain in soiled clothes, and use of a restraining jacket (Giles & Wolf, 1966).

If used for accidents, aversive consequences must be determined specifically for each learner, be applied immediately and consistently following each accident, and employed only in conjunction with a strong positive reinforcement program for appropriate toileting behavior. The immediacy problem—discovering accidents as soon as they occur—is best solved by urine signaling equipment but also may be decreased if dry pants inspections are done more frequently.

Instruction of Behaviors Related to Appropriate Elimination

Most toilet training involves early shaping of behaviors preceding and following toilet elimination—walking to the toilet, pulling pants down, sitting on the toilet, etc. Although this training would naturally be undertaken with every scheduled toileting, extra training also may be carried out so the individual masters these skills before elimination control.

Using forward chaining in combination with prompting, fading, and shaping, Mahoney, Van Wagenen, and Meyerson (1971) taught normal and retarded youngsters first to approach the toilet when they heard an auditory signaling device. Next, reinforcement was made contingent upon toilet approach and pulling pants down, *then* approach, pants down and sitting (or standing). At this point fluid intake was increased and the signaling device was modified so that each in-pants urination produced the auditory signal. Individuals who did not go to the toilet upon signaling were prompted by the experimenter— "No! Go potty!" If some urine was deposited in the toilet, reinforcement was forthcoming.

Giles and Wolf (1966) initially fed severely retarded individuals their meals contingent upon sitting on the toilet for the purpose of increasing toilet-sitting behavior. Next, after suppositories and milk of magnesia were given to increase the probability of bowel movements, the students were reinforced only for sitting and eliminating on the toilet. Similarly, Marshall (1966) shaped the behavior of an autistic young boy by reinforcing correct performance of each successive component of the toileting chain. Even in an institutional setting where the attendant-resident teaching ratio often was 1 to 10, this procedure of forward chaining to build the chain of responses related to elimination prior to and concurrent with toilet training was successful (Levine & Elliot, 1970).

The work of Azrin and Foxx also supports this practice of building behavior related to correct toileting. A recent application of their rapid training methods to normal children (Azrin & Foxx, 1974) employs an imitation play procedure whereby the child "teaches" a doll to potty herself. The child guides the doll through all the steps involved in the child's own training: giving the doll a drink, lowering the pants and placing on potty, reinforcing the doll for wetting (a wetting doll filled with water is used), emptying the potty, dry pants inspection, scolding for accidents, and positive practice. Although not tested with retarded individuals, the authors suggest that this procedure be employed if the individual appears to understand the meaning of the doll's actions, and they predict effectiveness of the doll-modeling procedure with some moderately and severely handicapped individuals.

Moisture Signaling Devices

Regardless of whether extra fluids are employed or moisture signaling pants are used in a training program, immediacy of reinforcement may be given more quickly if one knows the moment of sphincter relaxation and elimination. Because training consists primarily of associating reinforcing consequences with sphincter control leading to elimination that occurs on the toilet, urine-signaling devices for the toilet allow the teacher to provide reinforcement without delay. Listening or looking for the movement of urination or defecation (even with aluminum foil placed in the potty to magnify the sound) tend to be inaccurate and time consuming in comparison to moisture-detecting equipment.

Moisture-detecting devices may be built into a potty chair or into a plastic bowl which fits inside the regular toilet-bowl (Figure 7.6). One way to build such a device involves fastening two snap studs about ½-inch apart to the bottom center of the plastic bowl. Next, following the circuit schematic pictured in the upper half of Figure 7.7, detachable insulated wires are connected to the studs and run to a circuit box containing batteries. Urination as well as feces falling into the potty bowl act to complete a low voltage circuit between the two metal studs which in turn produces a sound from a small speaker located in the circuit box. Herreshoff (1973) describes two wiring plans for sensing devices which connect to a record player or a light. Also, sensing plates have been used in place of snap studs (Training Resource Center, Note 1). As soon as the signal sounds, the teacher reinforces the individual for a successful elimination and detaches the wires from the bottom of the bowl so that it may be emptied into the toilet, rinsed, dried, and reconnected in preparation for the next toileting.

Whereas a moisture-detecting potty chair signals the moment for positive reinforcement, moisture-detecting underpants (one design is pictured in Figure 7.8) may be employed to signal the moment an accident occurs. At this signal accident procedures may be implemented without delay. Wet pants are disconnected from the circuit box by unsnapping the wires. Dry pants are reconnected and placed back on the individual. If both moisture-detecting pants and potties are part of the toileting program, as in Azrin and Foxx (1971) and Foxx and Azrin (1973b), two different sounding signals need to be employed so that the associated responses (i.e., accidental eliminations and correct eliminations) will not be confused. The wiring schematic for underpants, pictured in the lower portion of Figure 7.7, involves a somewhat similar circuit plan to the potty signal but the alarm box is attached to the back of the pants or worn in a pocketed vest or chest harness.[3] Other designs (Van Wagenen & Murdock, 1966; Training Resource Center, Note 1) employ cloth-encapsulated parallel wires running along the crotch of the pants and up the back to a circuit-box connection.

Mahoney et al. (1971) used more elaborate auditory signaling devices in combination with urine-detecting pants (Van Wagenen & Murdock, 1966). The experimenter in the study operated an FM radio transmitter while the child being trained wore urine-detecting pants, an FM receiver, and an earphone. By pushing a button on the transmitter a signal was generated in the child's receiver and sound transmitted through the earphone. In addition, the same signal could be triggered by urination. Training involved forward chaining whereby each step in the toilet approach chain was shaped, using prompts as needed, in response to the signal triggered from the FM transmitter. Once this chain was learned, elimination training began. Children were given extra fluids, radio devices were removed from them, and urination alone produced the signal. The child was reinforced for quickly going to and sitting on the toilet as long as some urine was deposited in the toilet. Although Mahoney et al. (1971) did not em-

ploy toilet-signaling devices or punishment for inappropriate eliminations, as was done by Azrin and Foxx (1971) and Azrin, Bugle, and O'Brien (1971), they were successful in training severely and profoundly retarded individuals.

Improved traditional methods

A primary assumption of the more traditional methods of toilet training is that training proceeds best if one can accurately cue toileting performance at the times when bladder and bowel tension are greatest. Toileting records kept over a period of 15 or more days to identify these times, generally once daily for bowel movements and 3 to 5 times daily for urination. It is then that the learner is cued to sit on the toilet and praised for any successful elimination. In a recent review of toileting research with the severely retarded, Osarchuck (1973) stated that at best such records provide only "a very rough estimate of elimination probability" (p. 432). However, a number of toileting programs employed with the severely handicapped describe additional techniques which may be added to this traditional method to increase its success rate (e.g., Bensberg et al., 1965; Fredericks et al., 1975; Giles & Wolf, 1966; Hundziak et al., 1965; Levine & Elliot, 1970; Linford et al., 1972; Marshall, 1966). These techniques, which have been described, include: dry pants check; teaching related responses such as approach, sitting, pants down and up, etc., before teaching elimination control or on a more intensive schedule than simply preceding each elimination; use of urine-detection devices; specific accident procedures; consistent instructions and reinforcement for correct responses; and self-control training.

Linford et al. (1972) view toilet training as consisting of three stages: baseline (14 to 28 days), initial implementation of toilet training, and the development of self-control. During the second stage, after obtaining an accurate record of the child's eliminations, the trainer decides whether a consistent toileting pattern exists in urinations and/or bowel and selects the area(s) and times for instruction. Fredericks et al. (1975) recommend that the trainer choose only 2 times during the day during which to begin training. After the individual eliminates 75% of the time when taken at the 2 selected periods, another time period is added until the same 75% success rate is achieved. This practice continues until the entire day is covered. The rationale for the gradual expansion evolves around the time commitment

---

3. Urine-detecting training pants may be obtained commercially, already built or ready to assemble. Information on company, addresses, prices, and references is provided at the end of this chapter.

FIGURE 7.6   *The urine alert* (The plastic bowl fits into normal toilet bowl and rests on its top edge. The detachable wires connect the moisture-detecting snaps to the signal box which can rest on the floor or top of the toilet. The signal box sounds a tone when urine or feces touches the snaps.)

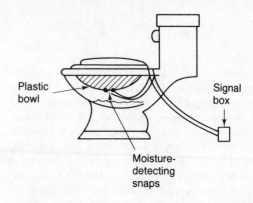

Source: Foxx and Azrin, 1973b, p. 30.

FIGURE 7.7   *Schematic of toilet-signal chair circuit (top) and wet-alarm pants circuit (bottom)*
Component identifications are as follows: R-1 and R-1a, 100 ohm, 1/8 watt resistor; R-2 and R-2a, 15,000 ohm, 1/8 watt resistor; R-3, 22,000 ohm, 1/8 watt resistor; C-1, 100 mfd capacitor, 15 volts; C-2, 22 mfd capacitor, 15 volt; T-1, T-1a, and T-3; transitor #GE-2; T-2, transitor #GE-7; S-1, "Bleep-tone" signal tone device available from C. A. Briggs Co., Glenside, Pa.; S-1a, speaker, 1.5 inch, 0.1 watt, 8 ohm; B-1 and B-1a battery, Eveready #216, 9 volt, or equivalent; snaps, Nu-Way, available from Burstein-Applebee Co., Kansas City, Mo. The A-snaps attach to matching snaps on the training pants; the B-snaps attach to matching studs on the toilet chair.

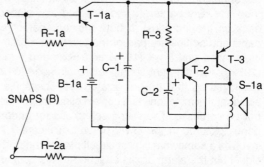

WET-ALARM PANTS CIRCUIT

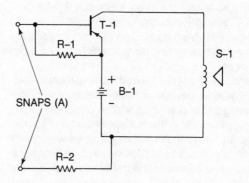

TOILET-SIGNAL CHAIR CIRCUIT

Source: N. H. Azrin, C. Bugle, and F. O'Brien, Behavioral engineering: Two apparatuses for toilet training retarded children, *Journal of Applied Behavior Analysis*, 1971, *4*, 251.

FIGURE 7.8   *The pants alarm*
The front view shows the moisture-detecting snaps fastened to the briefs. The back view shows the two flexible wires which lead from the snaps to the signal box. The snaps on the end of the wire are manually removable from the snaps on the clothing. The signal box is pinned to the back of the briefs (back view). A tone is sounded by the signal box when urine or feces moistens the area between the snaps.

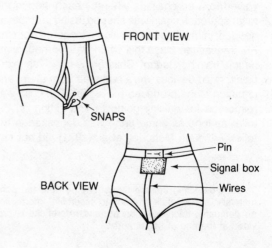

Source: Foxx and Azrin, 1973, p. 32.

involved in each toileting (approximately 20 minutes).

Actual training proceeds according to the following steps:

1. Approximately 10 minutes before an elimination typically will occur, the individual is requested in simple terms to go to the bathroom. (For example the child charted in Figure 7.4 would be taken at 7:30 a.m., 8:50 a.m., 12:15 p.m., 3:50 p.m., 6:15 p.m., and 8:50 p.m. if both bowel and urine control were being taught for the entire day.)
2. If the individual has not eliminated after sitting for 10 minutes, he may be asked to replace his clothes and continue his other activities for 5 minutes. This should be done without any criticism or praise. Next the individual is requested to go to the toilet; an interval of 5 minutes is allowed for elimination. If the learner is successful, he is immediately reinforced; if the learner is unsuccessful, he is neutrally requested to leave the bathroom and return to his activities.
3. All eliminations (accidents, correct urinations, and bowel movements) are recorded on a chart posted in the bathroom. Symbols may be used to record those times when no elimination occurred on the toilet.
4. Whenever the individual is taken to the toilet, the trainer should teach the related skills (approach, pants down, etc.) providing, only when necessary, a minimum of prompts beginning with verbal instructions and proceeding to demonstration, then physical assistance as needed.
5. Since all correct elimination and related toileting behaviors must be reinforced immediately the trainer needs to monitor the child's performance closely. Simple, specific praise throughout performance may be accompanied by activity or food reinforcers.
6. The routine is repeated for all the times selected for training.

An accident treatment procedure should be determined and placed into effect only during training periods. Simple extinction should be applied as a consequence for accidents occurring at other times. Dry pants checks may be added to the routine as may other techniques described earlier (extra practice on related toileting skills, moisture-sensing devices, etc.).

In the third stage of training the child is taught to develop self-control. To accomplish this goal, the teacher gradually fades out all prompts (physical assistance, demonstrations, and verbal instructions) employed during the second stage to teach related toileting skills and to take the individual to the toilet at the scheduled times. Linford et al. (1972) suggest that the teacher ask the child if he needs to go to the bathroom and prompt a headshake or a "yes" or "no" response. Additionally all spontaneous indications to self-toilet must be reinforced vigorously, while the trainer should decrease the amount of time spent in the bathroom.

Rapid toilet training methods

It is important to note that although Linford et al.'s (1972) and Frederick et al.'s (1975) toilet-training procedures have been used with moderately and severely handicapped individuals, no results have been reported by which to evaluate the effectiveness of these procedures. "Rapid" toilet-training methods which involve procedures to increase elimination (increased fluid intake, milk of magnesia, suppositories) do not rely upon baseline toileting schedules because the addition of extra fluids or suppositories changes the normal elimination pattern. Although these methods were originally developed for use with the mechanical signaling equipment described earlier (Azrin & Foxx, 1971; Mahoney et al., 1971), rapid methods may be employed with the handicapped in the absence of moisture-detecting devices (Azrin & Foxx, 1974; Bender & Valletutti, 1976; Copeland et al., 1976).[4]

Azrin and Foxx Procedure

Foxx and Azrin (1973b) describe four stages in their daytime rapid method: baseline, initial bladder training, self-initiation, and maintenance. After a three-day minimum baseline period, the trainer may begin initial bladder training which should extend a minimum of 4 consecutive hours per day. The teaching ratio may vary from one trainer per student to one to three, while the *average* learning time to achieve toileting independence for ambulatory, institutionalized, retarded individuals with this rapid method is 4 days (8 hours per day) with faster learning related to higher levels of intellectual functioning. All training during the initial bladder stage takes place in the

---

4. The reader interested in employing a rapid method is recommended to the original references for complete, detailed procedures (Azrin & Foxx, 1971, 1974; Foxx & Azrin, 1973b; Mahoney et al., 1971, Van Wagenen, Meyerson, & Kerr.1969).

bathroom. Two chairs and liquid and food reinforcers must be available. The resident should be wearing the urine-alert pants and the moisture-detecting toilet bowl insets must be in place. One hour before training, fluids are given to the learner so that urination might occur during the first half hour sequence. As described in Table 7.3 and illustrated in Figure 7.9, there is a sequence of 9 steps to follow during every half hour period. A prompting-fading procedure is used to guide the learner through the sequence but once the individual independently carries out part of the chain (approaches the toilet, pulls pants down, etc.) no additional prompts are provided. Trainer-student interaction is kept to a minimum until successful voiding occurs or until the student is off the toilet seat. Accidents, of course, are signaled by the pants alarm and after disconnecting the alarm are followed by the brief cleanliness training and positive practice. Clean pants are provided and reconnected to the alarm at the end of the next scheduled toilet-approach trial.

Self-initiation training begins once the learner tries to toilet himself totally unprompted. This stage of learning is characterized by the following instructional modifications:

1. Give fluids immediately following an elimination.
2. No further toilet-approach prompts.
3. Continue to provide guidance and prompts for dressing and undressing and for flushing the toilet, if necessary, but never at a level greater than that needed on previous toiletings.
4. Move resident's chair farther from toilet on each successful self-initiation.
5. Gradually lengthen the time between dry pants inspections.
6. Intermittently reward correct toileting.
7. When resident is self-initiating from the area where he spends most of his time, remove urine alert from the toilet bowl, pants alarm from resident's briefs, and the chair.
8. Require resident to show you that he can find the toilet from various areas on the ward.
9. Include resident on the maintenance program after 9 self-initiations (Foxx & Azrin, 1973b, p. 54).

Reinforcement for dry pants and correct elimination is faded onto an intermittent schedule, prompts are systematically faded, and the toilet approach distance is gradually increased, then varied to yield more generalized behavior. The brief cleanliness training consequence for accidents is replaced by the full cleanliness training, described earlier, and continues to be accompanied by a period of positive practice.

A maintenance program is begun once the learner achieves 9 self-initiated toiletings. In this stage of learning 6 dry pants inspections are provided daily—before every meal and snack, before

TABLE 7.3   *Sequence of steps in the bladder training procedure.* (Step one in the sequence is begun exactly on the half-hour)

---

1. Give as much fluid to the resident as he will drink while seated in his chair.
   A. Wait about 1 minute.

2. Direct resident to sit on toilet seat using the minimal possible prompt.

3. Direct resident to pull his pants down using the minimal possible prompt.
   A. When resident voids, give edibles and praise while seated, then direct him to stand.
   B. If resident does not void within 20 minutes after drinking the fluids, direct him to stand.

4. Direct resident to pull up his pants using the minimal possible prompt.
   A. If resident voided, direct him to flush the toilet using the minimal possible prompt.

5. Direct resident to his chair using the minimal possible prompt.

6. After resident has been sitting for 5 minutes, inspect him for dry pants.
   A. If pants are dry, give edible and praise.
   B. If pants are wet, only show him the edible and admonish him.

7. Check resident for dry pants every 5 minutes.

8. At the end of 30 minutes, begin the sequence of steps again.

Notes: If self-initiation occurs at any time, start the self-initiation procedure.
Continuously praise resident for being dry while he is seated in his chair.
Source R. M. Foxx and N. H. Azrin, *Toilet training the retarded*. Champaign, Ill.: Research Press, 1973b, p. 45.

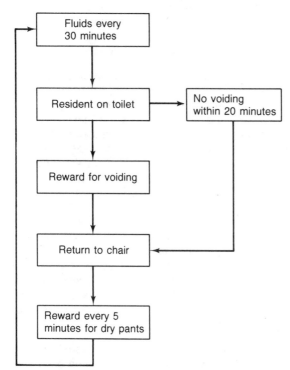

FIGURE 7.9   *Flow chart of the bladder-training sequence* (The specific steps involved in this flow chart are listed in Table 7.3.)

Source: R. M. Foxx and N. H. Azrin, *Toilet training the retarded*. Champaign, Ill.: Research Press, 1973b, p. 47.

going to bed, and spontaneously so that one occurs every 2 hours. While dry pants are praised, wet pants are followed by the full cleanliness procedure and positive practice; accidents detected before meals, snacks, and bedtime also result in a 1-hour delay of eating and sleeping. Maintenance training is terminated when no accidents have been recorded for 2 weeks.

Mahoney, VanWagenen, and Meyerson (1971) Procedure

This rapid procedure, also successful with severely and profoundly handicapped children, differs from Azrin and Foxx's procedure in a variety of ways. The toilet approach responses were taught before elimination training and in response to an auditory signal sounded by the trainer over an FM transmitter into an earphone worn by the subjects. A gradual prompting-fading process was employed to teach these first three prerequisite phases:

1. The individual learns to walk to the toilet in response to an auditory signal.
2. The individual learns to walk to the toilet and lower his pants in response to an auditory signal.
3. The individual learns to walk to the toilet, lower pants, and to take male stance or to sit on the toilet.

Next, extra fluids were provided and the moisture-detecting pants signal was connected for automatic triggering of the auditory signal. Students were both signaled by the experimenter for practice (sat on the toilet for 30 seconds) and by their own urinations. Whenever the latter situation occurred, the child who did not immediately go sit on the toilet was approached quickly by the trainer and told, "No, go potty," and assisted if necessary. In either case reinforcement was made contingent upon the presence of *some* urine in the toilet. No toilet signaling devices were employed nor were accidents followed by punishment.

At this phase in learning subjects were taught to pull up their pants after urinating or sitting on the toilet. By this time trainers recognized behaviors which preceded elimination (increase in movements, tugging at genitals, etc.) and at first signaled toilet approach with the transmitted signal when it was not self-initiated. Next all signaling equipment was removed and reinforcement was made contingent upon unsignaled correct elimination. In the last phase verbal subjects were taught to answer "potty" in response to the question "Where are you going?"

An informal comparision of the Mahoney et al. (1971) procedure to that of Azrin and Foxx (1971) reveals a similar speed of training with *perhaps* a slight success advantage attained by Azrin and Foxx. Success resulting from individual application of either method will vary depending upon the trainer's skills and the handicapping conditions of the learner.

Nighttime toilet training

After the learner has achieved reliable toileting during 75% or more of the day, training may be extended to develop nighttime bladder control. As with daytime training, various methods have been successful with enuretic children (those with a history of bedwetting after daytime control is attained) and others with the severely handicapped and retarded. These methods include traditional procedures, the use of bedwetting signaling equipment, and rapid methods.

Traditional Procedures

Linford et al. (1972) and Fredericks et al. (1975) describe variations in traditional procedures successful with the severely retarded but unfortunately do not report any outcome data to ascertain the degree of effectiveness. Specific accident treatment procedures described earlier and urine-signaling devices for the bed and toilet may be added to improve these traditional methods. The parent or ward attendant follows the general steps listed below, taking special care to continue the daytime schedule, *reduce* fluids prior to bedtime, and keep accurate accident and toileting records so that a schedule may be prepared to guide parent-initiated toiletings at night.

1. Decrease the amount of liquids in the evening and give none within 1½ to 2 hours of bedtime. (Extra fluids may be provided during the day.)
2. Request that the child toilet himself just prior to a fixed bedtime.
3. If the child has the potential for understanding, instruct the child in simple language (perhaps showing him the reward) that a dry bed in the morning will be rewarded (special toy, activity, etc.). Check his bed in the morning and reinforce him if it is dry but ignore wet beds.
4. About 1½ hours after the child has been in bed, awaken him and check for accidents or dryness, recording this on a nighttime chart.
   A. If dry, reinforce the child (dry pants inspection procedure may be used).
   B. If wet, either neutrally change the pants, pajamas, and sheets (extinction procedure for accidents) or request his assistance in this process. (A variation of the cleanliness training procedure may be used alone or accompanied by positive practice trips from the wet bed to the bathroom.)
5. Depending upon the parents' or ward attendant's time, check the child as often as possible (every hour) so that a night schedule may be obtained. Most parents will find this convenient only during their waking hours.
6. Awaken the child prior to his usual accident time and direct him to go to the toilet using procedures described earlier. Require that the child sit on the toilet without sleeping for five minutes or less if a urination occurs. Praise and chart successes; in a neutral manner return the unsuccessful learner to bed, charting his failure to eliminate.

7. If the child is wet when awakened, it is important to chart the accident and awaken the child earlier the following night. Fredericks et al. (1975) provide an example to clarify this step.

Take the case of Jane, who went through the procedure of being told about a reinforcer, reduced her fluid intake, was awakened before the parents' bedtime, but was still wetting during the night. The parents usually retired at 11:00; Jane usually wakened in the morning at 7:00; thus there was an eight hour period of sleep. The parents divided the night in half (four hours), set their alarm at 3:00 and woke Jane at that time. Jane was wet for the first five nights that they awoke her. The parents then decided to awaken Jane at 1:00; half way between 11:00 and 3:00. Awaking her at that time, they found that Jane was dry. If she had been wet, they would have awakened her at 12:00. However, since she was dry they had her go to the bathroom and eliminate. This procedure succeeded in keeping her dry for the entire evening (p. 13).

8. Once the wake-up time has been identified which allows the child to be toileted once and remain dry, it is important to strengthen the child's ability to withhold urine for longer periods each night. This is done by gradually moving back the wake-up time in intervals of 10 minutes with continued charting to monitor accident rate. Jane, for example, would be awakened at 12:50, then 12:40, then 12:30, etc.
9. Powerful reinforcers should continue to be provided in the morning for dry beds while social praise at the least should be given during the night for correct elimination or dry bed checks.

Bed-Wetting Signaling Equipment

A number of signaling apparatuses have been developed to treat enuretic individuals with or without the additional handicaps of deafness, blindness, mental, or emotional deficiencies (Coote, 1965; Lovibond, 1963; 1964; Mowrer & Mowrer, 1938; Seiger, 1952). Two general designs exist.[5] The "sandwich" pad employs two pieces of screen or foil separated by fabric which when wet results in contact between the positive and negative layers completing an electric circuit. In a manner similar to

---

5. Commercially available bed-wetting signal devices are listed at the end of this chapter.

the signaling underpants already described, this sounds a buzzer alarm and an optional light to wake the bedwetter. More expensive designs employ a one-piece pad which can be wiped dry after accidents, eliminating the need to replace the wet separating fabric in the above model.

The treatment procedure, which does not involve a reduction of fluid intake, tends to take several weeks or months to establish initial control but does so in about 80–90% of enuretics, although relapse is common (Jones, 1960; Lovibond, 1964; Yates, 1970). Although the exact training procedures varies, a few similarities may be outlined (Baller, 1975). First, the child and parent or ward trainers should thoroughly understand the functioning of the equipment; "dry run" demonstrations, especially important for the handicapped individual, will aid this process. This familiarization includes correct placement on the bed, turning off the signal once activated, and the steps followed by the parent and child once an instance of urination is signaled (turn off alarm, go to the bathroom to complete or practice voiding, change sheets and pajamas, and reconnect signaling wires). A positive attitude should accompany the treatment with social praise and perhaps more powerful reinforcers for dry beds. Records should be kept for accidents and successful urinations including the date, time, and perhaps size of the wet spot. Finally Baller states that criterion for dryness before discontinuation of the equipment is 10–14 dry nights with apparatus reinstatement contingent upon later accidents.

During an 11-week treatment period in an institutional ward, Sloop and Kennedy (1973) reported successful results with 52% of those moderately and severely retarded residents that were trained using bed-wetting signaling equipment. However, a relapse rate of 36% indicated a need for modification in the procedure—perhaps of the type tested by Azrin et al. (1973) with profoundly retarded institutionalized residents which will be summarized next.

Rapid Bedtime Training Procedure

Using methods similar to their rapid daytime bladder training program, Azrin et al. (1973) were able to reduce nighttime accidents in 12 profoundly retarded individuals by 85% during the first week following a single night of intensive training and then to 95% by the fifth week. Unlike other nighttime procedures there was no relapse during a 3-month follow-up.

Because the procedure outlined in Table 7.4 was developed for institutional use, trainers were readily available on the midnight shift. Use of this rapid procedure by parents in a home setting would necessitate some modification as described in a later study (Azrin et al., 1974) with normal enuretic children. With further modifications, Bollard and Woodroffe (1977) found that parents could apply Azrin's et al. (1974) steps and obtained more success with their bed-wetting children when signaling equipment was used.

Eating Skills

Independence in self-feeding comes gradually over a 5-year period in the normal child (Table 7.5). Eating represents perhaps the ideal skill for training because food ingestion is the final step in the eating chain, making additional primary reinforcement unnecessary. Related to this "built-in" feature is the natural punishment for inappropriate eating—the removal, interruption, or postponement of eating (O'Brien, Bugle, & Azrin, 1972).

With moderately and severely handicapped individuals, learning to self-feed may be uncomplicated and without delay or only slightly delayed when there are no behavioral, physical, or environmental inadequacies. However, the presence of motoric or neurological handicaps (cerebral palsy, arm and hand deformities, uncontrolled seizure activity, etc.), structural abnormalities in the oral cavity and musculature, attentional problems, extreme disruptive behaviors, special dietary needs, sensory deficiencies (deafness, blindness), or inadequate learning environments (overprotective or uninterested parents, uninformed teachers, poor teacher-child ratio) may lead to delayed, incomplete, or abnormal development of eating skills. To promote independence in eating and related table skills, the teacher will seek answers to the instructional decisions listed earlier, individualizing these answers to suit the specific needs of each learner. Often assistance must be sought from physicians and physical and occupational therapists during observation and assessment, selection of adapted eating equipment, program development, and implementation.

This provides basic assessment and teaching techniques which have been successful with the severely handicapped. Although some discussion is devoted to complications resulting from physical handicaps, curricular details must be sought in the references provided.

TABLE 7.4 *Dry-bed procedure*

I. *Intensive Training*
   A. Before bedtime
      1. Bedwetter drinks fluids
      2. Urine alarm placed on the bed
      3. Potty-alert placed in toilet bowl
   B. Hourly awakenings
      1. Minimal prompt given for awakening the resident
      2. Resident instructed or guided to the toilet
      3. Resident seated on toilet bowl
         a. If urination does not occur within 5 minutes
           (i) return resident to bed
           (ii) at bedside give resident fluids and praise as reinforcers
         b. If urination does occur within 5 minutes
           (i) give resident praise, snacks and fluids as reinforcers
           (ii) return resident to bed
      4. Praise resident for having dry bed (require resident to touch the dry sheets)
      5. Resident returns to sleep
   C. When accident occurs—45 min of cleanliness training and positive practice
      1. Disconnect the sound of the urine-alarm
      2. Awaken resident
      3. Reprimand resident for wetting and direct him to the toilet to finish urination
      4. Cleanliness training
         a. Bedwetter changes wet linen
         b. Attendant reactivates urine-alarm
      5. Positive practice in toileting
         a. Bedwetter lies down in bed for 3 minutes
         b. Bedwetter awakened with minimal prompt after 3 minutes
         c. Bedwetter directed to toilet
         d. Repeat steps a, b, c about 9 times
      6. Bedwetter returns to sleep when 45 minutes have elapsed since accident was detected

II. *Monitored post-training phase*
   A. Initiation of monitored post-training
      1. When resident has no more than 1 accident during a training night
      2. When the resident correctly toilets on at least 50% of all opportunities during a training night.
   B. Procedure
      1. Urine-alarm on bed
      2. Whenever accident occurs, reprimand, cleanliness training and positive practice follow for 45 minutes
      3. No fluids, no hourly awakenings, no reinforcers
   C. Termination of monitored post-training
      1. Terminated 7 nights after last accident

III. *Normal procedure*
   A. Initiated after resident goes 7 nights without accident
   B. No urine-alarm, no reinforcers, no positive practice, etc.
   C. Bed inspected each morning
      1. If bed wet, resident remakes and cleans bed (cleanliness training)
      2. If 2 accidents occur within a given week, the monitored phase is reinstated

Source: N. H. Azrin, T. J. Sneed, R. M. Foxx, Dry-bed: A rapid method of eliminating bedwetting (enuresis) of the re-tarded, *Behaviour Research and Therapy* 1973, *11*, 430.

TABLE 7.5   *Developmental sequence of eating skills*

Chronological Age	Behavior
1 to 3 months	Sucking and rooting reflex present. Able to swallow pureed foods; takes cereal from spoon. Sucking, swallowing, and breathing are coordinated.
4 to 6 months	Tongue thrust more common with cup than spoon feeding. Uses tongue to move food inside mouth. Holds cup using both hands in an overhand grasp; messy! Begins chewing motions using gums.
7 to 8 months	Feeds self soft finger foods (banana) and later most finger foods; messy! Uses pincer grasp to pick up food. Gums and mouths solid foods. Holds own bottle.
9 to 12 months	Drinks from glass and/or cup with little assistance. Holds spoon but unable to use without help.
13 to 18 months	Spoon often inverted before insertion. Drinks from cup unassisted using digital grasp or handle. Better control of spoon.
1½ to 2½ years	Handles cup well and uses small glass without much spill. Some spilling from spoon but spoon inserting done without inverting.
2½ to 4 years	Only a minimum of spilling from spoon. Spears food with fork, eats with fork; spills. Interest in table setting. Pours liquids from pitcher. Serves self at table. Spreads butter with knife.
4 to 5 years	Eats well with fork and spoon. Cuts with knife.

Source: Barnard and Powell (1972); Cohen, Gross, and Haring (1976); Copeland, Ford, and Solon (1976); Gesell and Amatruda (1947).

Assessment of eating skills

In addition to the construction of assessment devices based on task analysis and developmental information, a variety of techniques exist[6] to observe and directly measure an individual's baseline eating skills. As with toileting skills, if the assessment procedure allows one to measure performance of skills through the observation of finely analyzed steps comprising these skills, then selection of appropriate teaching targets and daily monitoring of learning will be more precise and accurate. A few commercially available assessment procedures will be described to illustrate those available. Frequently teacher-constructed or -modified assessment devices are more useful.

The *Balthazar Scales of Functional Independence* (1971) allows for the measurement of eating abilities from a level of dependent feeding to finger

6. Balthazar (1971); Barton, Guess, Garcia, and Baer (1970); Behavioral Characteristics Progression (1973); Bender and Valletutti (1976); Copeland et al. (1976); Ferneti, Lent, and Stevens (1974); Nelson, Cone, and Hanson (1975); O'Brien and Azrin (1972); etc.

foods, spoon and fork usage, and drinking (Figure 7.10). The examiner unobtrusively observes the individual eating during a number of meals while assigning scores on a proportionate basis (0 to 10) depending upon the frequency of behavior occurrence. On the score sheet, behaviors within each skill class are arranged developmentally by increasing complexity. Indented behaviors represent those of greater complexity compared to items from which they are indented. Therefore, in scoring indented items, it is not possible to achieve higher scores (better performance) on subscale items than the score awarded to the preceding simpler items. For example, in the finger food class, "When a subject eats approximately half of his finger foods, he receives a score of '5' on item 1, 'Eats finger foods.' Consequently, the highest score he can receive on the indented item 2, 'Holds finger foods,' is a '5' also" (p. 16). An eating checklist, scored simply as "present," "not present," or "no opportunity to perform," allows the rough measurement of before, during and after the meal activities.

For some individuals it will be useful to time eating duration if work appears necessary in adjusting the speed of eating (slowing down or speeding up). Ad-

EATING SCALES   Meal: _____   Date: _____

ITEM SCORING SHEET

CLASS I – DEPENDENT FEEDING

1___Mouth is open,
  2___voluntarily,
    3___without physical stimulation.
    4___Removes food with mouth,
      5___with lips.
      6___Allows spoon removal.
7___Retains food,
  8___in upright position.
Subtotal   9___Manipulates food in mouth.

CLASS II – FINGER FOODS

1___Eats finger foods.
  2___Holds finger foods.
    3___Hand to mouth movement.
    4___Reaches for finger food.
    5___Separates finger foods,
      6___with mouth.
        7___Does not stuff mouth with separated foods.
        8___Bites off appropriate sizes.
Subtotal   9___Does not stuff mouth with appropriate sizes.

CLASS III – SPOON USAGE

1___Eats tray foods.
  2___with spoon,
    3___held in finger position,
      4___palm up.
    5___Fills spoon independently.
      6___Attends to filling.
      7___Manipulates with precision.
      8___Fills appropriate amount.
  9___Directs spoon independently.
    10___Moves arm toward mouth.
    11___Directs spoon accurately.
    12___Does NOT spill from spoon.
Subtotal   13___Does NOT stuff mouth.

CLASS IV – FORK USAGE

1___Eats tray foods,
  2___with fork,
    3___held in finger position,
      4___palm up.
    5___Fills fork independently.
      6___Attends to filling.
      7___Manipulates with precision.
      8___Fills appropriate amount.
  9___Directs fork independently.
    10___Moves arm toward mouth.
    11___Directs fork accurately.
    12___Does NOT spill from fork.
Subtotal   13___Does NOT stuff mouth.

CLASS V –DRINKING

1___Takes liquids,
  2___from cup.
    3___Swallows liquids.
    4___Retains liquids,
      5___in upright position.
6___Contact with cup.
  7___Drinks from cup independently.
  8___Lifts cup off table with two hands.
    9___Does NOT spill while lifting.
    10___Does NOT spill while drinking.
    11___Lifts cup off table with one hand.
      12___Does NOT spill while lifting with one hand.
Subtotal   13___Does NOT spill while drinking with one hand.

FULL SCALE SCORE: _____

EATING CHECKLIST

A: Self Service

1___Pours own drink.
2___Gets own tray.
3___Selects own tray.
4___Carries own tray.
5___Serves self food.
6___Uses napkin.
7___Takes back dirty dishes.
8___Cleans off dirty dishes.
9___Proper dispensing of dirty dishes.

B: Assistive Devices

10___for drinking.
11___for eating.
12___eats with hand restraint.

C: Type of Food

13___Fed by gavage.
14___Drinks full liquids.
15___Blender-strained.
16___Blender foods.
17___Child bite-size.
18___Adult bite-size.

D: Positioning

19___Lying down.
20___Reclined position.
21___Upright with body restraint.
22___Upright alone.

E: Rate of Eating

23___Eats too fast.
24___Eats too slowly.

F: Advanced Utensil Usage

25___Uses spoon for correct foods.
26___Uses fork for correct foods.
27___Spreads with knife.
28___Cuts with knife.

G: Supervision

29___Eats without supervision.
30___Responds to supervision.
31___Maintains corrected behavior.
32___Does NOT respond to supervision.
  a. Eating skills.
  b. Stealing food.
  c. Behavior problem.
  d. Self induced emesis.
  e. Other_____

FIGURE 7.10   *The Balthazar scales of functional independence: Eating-drinking scales.*

Source: E. E. Balthazar, *Balthazar Scales of Adaptive Behavior for the Profoundly and Severely Mentally Retarded, Section 1.* Champaign, Ill.: Research Press, 1971.

ditionally, as described by Balthazar (1971), the size of the bite, the amount placed in the mouth, and the extent of spilling are not easily measured but exemplify typical problems which should be measured.

The Project MORE eating program (Ferneti, Lent, & Stevens, 1974) employs a simpler measurement procedure for eating skills. Also, step-by-step teaching procedures are provided for each of the 16 behaviors assessed. More advanced abilities are included in this assessment, pictured in Figure 7.11, such as discriminating when to begin eating, passing and serving food, and rotating eating rather than eating all of one food at a time. Therefore less attention is directed toward assessing the acquisition of spoon usage, finger food eating, and drinking from a cup. This emphasis makes the MORE program in

eating more useful for individuals who have already mastered the basic elements of these three self-feeding skills.

As in other areas of self-help ability, it may be useful to pinpoint and measure behaviors in addition to eating which appear to influence self-feeding skills. These may include fine motor hand movements and object manipulation, sitting at the table, visual attending during utensil and cup usage, comprehension of simple eating instructions and the words for training materials (spoon, cup, dessert, etc.), as well as disruptive mealtime behaviors (stealing or throwing food or utensils, aggressive behavior toward others at table, regurgitation of food, etc.).

In order to plan effective instruction a teacher

EATING SKILLS FOR DAILY LIVING PROGRAM

Student Names
1 JoAnn Mead
2 Hank Ford
3 Bill Boyer
4 Joseph Conray
5 Tammy True

SESSION RECORD SHEET
Session Number ___8___
Date ___7/16/73___
Teacher ___Mrs. Dodge___

Write each student's name in one of the boxes below.

Section	Step	1 JoAnn	2 Hank	3 Bill	4 Joe	5 Tammy
1	1. Beginning to set the table	✓	✓	✓	✓	✓
	2. Putting place settings on the table	✓	✓	✓		✓
	3. Setting the table completely	✓	✓	✓	✓	✓
	4. Sitting down at the table	✓	✓	✓	✓	✓
	5. Waiting for others to begin eating		✓	✓	✓	✓
	6. Using a napkin	✓	✓	✓		✓
2	7. Picking up food			✓		✓
	8. Passing and serving food					✓
	9. Using condiments		✓	✓	✓	✓
3	10. Using a spoon					
	11. Using a fork					
	12. Using a knife					
	13. Rotating eating					
4	14. Taking second portions					
	15. Leaving the table					
5	16. Buttering bread					
	TOTAL NUMBER OF STEPS PERFORMED CORRECTLY	5	7	8	5	9

FIGURE 7.11   *Eating skills for daily living programs: sample session record sheet*

Source: C. L. Ferneti, J. R. Lent, and C. J. Stevens, *Project MORE: Eating.* Bellevue, Wash.: Edmark Associates, 1974, p. 11.

needs to know which types of prompts will work with a given student. Will verbal instructions be comprehended? Does the student imitate demonstrations or respond to pointing gestures made by a teacher? Performance data collected on the prompt categories as well as skill assessment data will enable the teacher to select initial teaching targets, monitor performance changes during training, and adjust instructional objectives as learning occurs.

Selection of teaching targets

Eating skills develop in a general order beginning with various aspects of dependent feeding (anticipates spoon, uses lips to remove food, etc.) to finger foods, to spoon and cup usage, followed by fork usage, then knife spreading and cutting, food serving, condiment usage, rotation eating, and table manners. Multiple targets may be selected from assessment data but these objectives tend to center around a given range on this developmental continuum. For example, it is likely that a child may be taught to bite from finger foods rather than tear into pieces first while also learning to use a palm-up spoon grasp rather than a finger or fist grasp and to drink with less spilling. At the same time, instruction may occur with such related eating skills as handwashing, appropriate table behavior, indicating desire for more food, and assisting in plate clearing. As described in the chapter on motor skills, concurrent objectives and training may occur for fine motor behaviors (grasp, object manipulation, etc.) which will directly effect improvements in utensil and food manipulation.

General elements of instruction

Teaching Times and Place

Depending upon the particular objectives, most instruction should occur before, during, and after eating in the school or home dining area. Azrin and Armstrong (1973) increased the number of daily training sessions by dividing meals into smaller portions or "mini-meals" which were served hourly during the day. This allowed more intensive instruction for the profoundly retarded learners and resulted in appropriate, independent eating after an average of 12 days of instruction.

If related targets have been identified for fine motor skills, it is likely that instruction also will occur at times when the child is not eating. For example, the child may be scheduled to string large beads and put together form boards—activities which develop manipulative and eye-hand coordination skills (Copeland et al., 1976; Utley, Holvoet, & Barnes, 1977).

Because the MORE eating program teaches a variety of advanced skills not necessarily requiring that the learner ingest food, Ferneti et al. (1974) suggest that training sessions use real as well as artificial food (e.g. half-inch-thick styrofoam squares for bread, dried peas for peas, artificial fruit, etc.) to teach all skills except spreading butter. Use of food substitutes allows classroom teachers to provide more teaching sessions and opportunities to teach passing, condiment usage, second helpings, etc., when no school lunch program exists. Because individuals participating in the MORE program will have mastered some of the basic elements of utensil usage during actual meals, skill generalization from artificial food to real should be simpler than it would be for individuals in earlier stages of acquisition; however, it is critical that the final stages of training and assessment employ actual eating situations.

For students who have received most of their instruction in classroom or home settings, generalization training should be added as an additional goal. Figure 7.12 shows a child learning to go through a school cafeteria line. Such instruction will necessitate prior task analysis and the creation of assessment checklists based upon the analysis for a particular school lunchroom, cafeteria line, restaurant, or eating area. Most programs focusing on basic self-feeding reduce mealtime distractions by including only the learners and the teachers in the training area, employing smaller dining rooms, and/or using regular dining areas at times other than regular scheduled mealtimes (Azrin & Armstrong, 1973; Barton et al., 1970; Groves & Carroccio, 1971; O'Brien et al., 1972; Song & Gandhi, 1974).

Teaching Materials

The food, utensils, and related eating materials are directly determined by an individual's particular instructional objectives and the entry skills. For example, special considerations, individually prescribed, are necessary when feeding the cerebral palsied individual and again when implementing the first steps toward self-feeding. The major feeding problems of a cerebral palsied individual include: the "lack of mouth, head and trunk control, lack of sitting balance and inability to bend his hips sufficiently to enable him to stretch his arms forward to grasp and to maintain that grasp irrespective of the position of his arms; finally his inability to bring his

FIGURE 7.12   *Moderately handicapped young students are learning to negotiate the school cafeteria line independently, to pour milk from a thermos without spilling, and to spread butter on a slice of bread.*

hands to his mouth and his lack of eye-hand coordination" (Meuller, 1975, pp. 114–115). To overcome these problems when an individual is in a stage of learning which requires feeding by an adult, some antecedent considerations will include selection of the appropriate sitting or semireclining position, type of bottle or glass, adaptations in the spoon (metal or plastic-coated metal with a deep bowl, etc.), method of jaw control, as well as consistency of food (Figure 7.13). The complexity of making these educational decisions mandates that consultation be sought from additional reference materials[7] and certainly from physical or occupational therapists. Again, when teaching the physically handicapped child to self-feed, recommendations may be made to employ a nonslip mat under the place-setting, a bowl with steep sides for scooping food against rather than a plate, or temporary use of adaptive equipment such as spoons with built-up or curved handles, holding straps, or swivel bowls, and drinking cup holders or weighted cups with enlarged handles. As is generally the case with the CP person, seating positions which facilitate head and trunk control are of central importance during self-feeding instruction, as illustrated in Figure 7.14.

A preceding evaluation will help the teacher specify the physically handicapped learner's entry skills and limitations in order that teaching equipment and methods be matched appropriately. Seriously handicapped children often must be taught to suck, swallow, chew, remove food from a spoon, and sip from a cup because they may not automatically acquire these basic eating skills (Finnie, 1975; Stainback et al., 1976).

Utley et al. (1977) list baseline information that needs to be sought through assessment conducted by a physical therapist, an occupational therapist, and/or a speech therapist with the teacher's assistance.

1. What is the student's muscular status (hypotomia, hypertomia, involuntary muscle actions, etc.)?
2. What pathological or primary reflexes are present (symmetrical tonic neck reflex, rooting reflex, etc.)?
3. What degree of head control does the student demonstrate?
4. Can the student grasp and release objects?
5. Does the child have hand-to-mouth movements?
6. Does the child's sitting balance require the use of his arms?
7. What particular mouth functions does the individual demonstrate?
   A. Tongue movements
   B. Sucking reflex
   C. Bite reflex
   D. Gag reflex
   E. Swallowing
   F. Drooling and lip closure
   G. Oral hypersensitivity

The more physically impaired the learner, the more important it is that self-help instructional programs be formulated and evaluated by an interdisciplinary staff. The reader is referred to the references listed earlier for specific detail on techniques to teach rudimentary eating skills.

When the handicapped learner is not cerebral palsied or otherwise disabled in body control, coordination, or balance, adaptive eating equipment and therapeutic positioning do not present complex issues. However, the teacher must make some decisions concerning instructional materials. For example, the chair and table height should match the learner's size and allow his feet to rest firmly on the floor or a foot block; utensil and cup size should fit the child, the food must be appealing to the learner, nourishing, and suited to the teaching goals (finger foods if this skill is targeted; slightly sticky foods when spoon instruction begins, etc.). For many beginning learners, placing wet washcloths, suction cups, or rubber mats beneath plates and bowls will prevent slipping and allow easier spoon filling. After basic eating skills are mastered, additional teaching materials will be needed in order to expand eating skills. Those may include: forks and knives, paper napkins, salt and pepper shakers, serving bowls and spoons, milk cartons, cafeteria trays, straws, and specific types of food (e.g., thin soup, butter to spread, gravy to dip or pour, thermoses to pour from, spaghetti to eat, meat to cut, etc.). Finally, to facilitate skill generalization, a variety of materials and eating settings should be programmed for mealtime instruction. If a child has learned to use paper napkins, will he balk at the use

---

7. For detailed information on positioning, feeding techniques, and nutritional considerations for cerebral palsied learners, the reader is referred to Ball, Hendricksen, and Clayton (1974); Campbell, Green, and Carlson, 1977; Copeland et al. (1976); Finnie (1975); Holser-Buehler (1966); Lemke and Mitchell (1972); Macey (1974); Meuller (1972, 1975); Pipes (in press); Schmidt (1976); Stainback, Healy, Stainback, and Healy (1976); Utley et al. (1977).

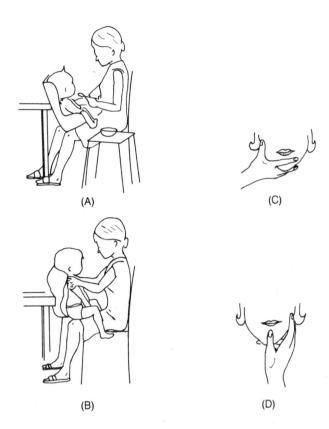

FIGURE 7.13   *Techniques for feeding the cerebral palsied child*
(A) Half-sitting position for the child with some sitting balance. Remember to put the food in front of him. If the child still needs support, an "Infant Seat" can be used resting against the table edge (Mueller, 1975, p. 117).
(B) When sitting balance improves, sit the baby up straight with his legs abducted and his hips well flexed. You may still have to control him from the shoulders (Mueller, 1975, p. 117).
(C) Jaw control as applied when the child is on your right side with your arm around his head; thumb on his jaw joint, index finger between chin and lower lip, middle finger behind chin applying constant firm pressure (Mueller, 1975, p. 119).
(D) Jaw control as applied from the front; thumb between chin and lower lip, index finger on jaw joint, middle finger applied firmly just behind the chin (Mueller, 1975, p. 119).

Source: H. Meuller, 1975. From *Handling the Young Cerebral Palsied Child at Home*, Second Edition, by Nancie Finnie. Copyright © 1974 by Nancie Finnie, F.C.S.P.; additions for U.S. edition, Copyright © 1975. New York: E. P. Dutton, and reprinted with their permission.

of a cloth napkin? If a young man performs very well in the small school cafeteria where there are no food choices, how will he fare in the average cafeteria restaurant that provides many menu choices? This instructional concern relates to the performance criterion beyond the mere learning of a skill (i.e. napkin usage); the generalization criterion deals with the successful use of the skill in realistic situations where that skill will be of ultimate use (Gold, 1976).

Basic methods to teach self-feeding

The primary procedures to teach basic eating skills and self-feeding include prompting of targeted behaviors with resultant fading or delay of prompts

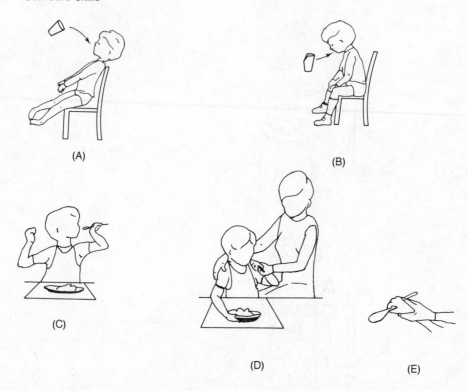

FIGURE 7.14   *Teaching self-feeding to cerebral palsied individuals*
(A) Wrong. The cup is presented from above and the child is tilted back (Mueller, 1975, p. 123).
(B) Right. The child is in a sitting position for drinking, with the trunk and head well forward, the beaker is presented from the front (Mueller, 1975, p. 123).
(C) Wrong. Self-feeding without control in hyperextension and in an asymmetrical pattern (Mueller, 1975, p. 127).
(D) Right. Self-feeding at the table, with control at the shoulder and supination of the hand holding the spoon (Mueller, 1975, p. 127).
(E) Adding supination to the hand by turning it out lightly from the root of the thumb.

and shaping. Since many of the terminal goals actually involve chains of behavior (such as utensil usage and going through a cafeteria line), the teacher will employ both forward and backward chaining separately and in combination to "string together" the learned portions of these lengthly targeted skills. The reader should refer to Chapter 3 for clarification of these procedures.

Finger Foods

Referring to developmental sequence in Table 7.5, the first sign of independence in self-feeding is the predictably messy stage of eating finger foods. At this early stage, a child practices his pincer grasp to pick up food and refines his hand-to-mouth move-

ments (which already have received extended use to explore objects by mouthing) in combination with the sucking, gumming, chewing, and swallowing of many soft foods such as bananas and saliva-softened toast. Finger feeding provides an essential opportunity to improve the movements necessary for learning utensil usage at a later time.

If baseline assessment of the handicapped individual reveals deficiencies in utensil use as well as poor coordination of grasp, lift, and placement of finger foods into the mouth, then finger food instruction should have first priority. The teacher must specify the particular portion(s) of the finger food chain which are missing or weak: food location, grasp, lift from table to mouth, opening of mouth at appropriate time, putting food into open mouth, leaving food in mouth (releasing grasp or biting off a portion), chewing food, or swallowing food. In addition, the child's ability to deal with large pieces of food should be noted: does she tear food into smaller pieces or does she gum or bite off smaller pieces from what is held to the mouth (the more advanced method). Finally, if sloppiness or mouth stuffing is the primary problem, then its cause should be determined and targeted for instruction. For example, sloppiness may be caused by child's placing too much food in his mouth. However, if other difficulties exist besides stuffing, spilling, and sloppiness, then these areas should be reserved for later work because early approximations of self-feeding inevitably will be messy. That is, beginners should not be punished for sloppiness until the motor coordination necessary for neatness has been developed.

It is recommended that finger food self-feeding be taught at the beginning of the meal when the child is the hungriest. Food consistency should be adjusted depending upon the presence or absence of teeth and the amount of ability the child already has; for example, bananas and breads will be more easily placed in the mouth, chewed, and swallowed than will partially cooked vegetable pieces and hot dog bits or raw vegetables. Guided assistance may be the most useful type of prompt since demonstrations require good attending and imitation skills (Nelson et al., 1975). However, this physical prompting must be provided from behind while sitting beside the child so that the teacher's movements follow the natural pattern. The use of simple, consistent instructions ("Open;" "Chew, chew, chew") may be helpful if paired with teacher modeling and gestures during the early stages of learning. Later, after prompts are faded, the simple instructions could be used as needed to remind the learner. Above all, the teacher should not communicate anger about the messiness that will be present during early stages of learning.

Drinking from a Cup or Glass

Initially children will assist the parent or teacher in holding the cup or glass and lifting it to the mouth. At this early stage and when an individual first drinks from a cup independently, both hands will be used for holding. Straw drinking is not targeted until a child can drink from a cup. Also, as with finger feeding and utensil usage, the learning process will be messy. As with all the self-care skills, a task analysis of drinking will facilitate obtaining an accurate assessment of the beginning performance and needs.

For children with limited self-drinking abilities, manual guidance through the entire chain will be necessary, with fading proceeding backwards and forwards from points of successful performance in the chain. Often, it is easiest to begin fading assistance at the point in the chain after the glass is rested on the lower lip and before any liquid is tipped into the mouth. Especially if the child is thirsty and likes the liquid, success with this small step will be immediately reinforced. Assistance may be reapplied to complete the chain. Fading of manual guidance would proceed gradually backward first and then forward to the last step in the chain (glass is placed back onto table).

Utley et al. (1977) and Stainback et al. (1976) recommended some techniques for assisting the dependent drinker into gradual independence. First, use a small (8 ounce), soft plastic or paper cup which is translucent so that the liquid is visible and positioning may be controlled more easily by the teacher. If, as in Figure 7.14, a semicircle is cut in the rim of the glass, the child will be able to get liquid without having to tilt his head and will "fight" cup drinking less. At this stage of learning, when the teacher provides a lot of assistance, the glass should be fairly full so the child will not need to tilt his head. Avoid the use of spouted or nipple cups which stimulate abnormal sucking (Meuller, 1975). Because sweet liquids stimulate drooling and milk thickens the saliva, other fluids such as unsweetened orange juice or cool to warm broth make better initial training liquids. Stainback suggests a slightly thickened liquid to stimulate swallowing and decrease spilling. So as not to encourage the learner to bite the edge of the cup, place the rim of the cup against the lower lip, not between the teeth. If it is necessary to aid the child in opening her mouth, position the hand as in Figure 7.13 with the index finger on the child's chin, the third finger under the chin, and the thumb on the cheek or upper lip. The cup is tilted until liquid touches the upper lip and tongue, thereby encouraging the child to perform part of the task. The cup is held in this position by the teacher and child until a few swallows (with rests in between) have been taken. As the teacher allows the child to perform more of the task alone, smaller amounts of liquid should be used to lessen spilling.

Only after the individual learns to drink holding the handled cup or small glass with both hands will the teacher begin to emphasize a reduction of spilling. Spilling will occur while drinking but may also happen as the glass is grasped, lifted, or replaced on the table. Handled or adapted cups may be more easily held, depending upon the child. Glasses with smaller circumferences and filled with lesser amounts are also helpful modifications. Eventually, as drinking and other self-feeding skills improve, the learner should be reminded to lift his glass only with the dominant hand.

Eating with a Spoon

Spoon usage is the simplest of the utensil skills, followed in difficulty by eating with a fork, transferring spreads with a knife, spreading with a knife, cutting finger-grasped bread with a knife, and cutting meat with a fork and knife. When a child has learned to grasp objects and demonstrates some success in manipulating finger foods, an assessment should be made of his ability to pick up and eat with a spoon.

Barnard and Powell's (1972) task analysis of spoon usage consists of 18 steps which could be used as a guide for assessing and training this skill.

1. Orients to food by looking at it.
2. Looks at spoon.
3. Reaches for spoon.
4. Touches spoon.
5. Grasps spoon.
6. Lifts spoon.
7. Delivers spoon to bowl.
8. Lowers spoon into food.
9. Scoops food onto spoon.
10. Lifts spoon.
11. Delivers spoon to mouth.
12. Opens mouth.
13. Inserts spoon into mouth.
14. Moves tongue and mouth to receive food.
15. Closes lips, removes spoon.
16. Chews food.
17. Swallows food.
18. Returns spoon to bowl. (p. 97–98)

After field-testing a task analysis, modifications may need to be made by simplifying the more difficult steps; for example, food scooping (Step 9) has been identified by some as the most difficult step to teach severely retarded individuals (Song & Gandhi, 1974). In addition, it is important to note how often the spoon is abandoned in favor of the fingers, how much spilling occurs and why (e.g., on the way to the mouth due to poor wrist rotation), and how the spoon is grasped. Younger children with immature grasps will hold the spoon in a palm-down, finger or

fist position, while the more mature palm-up position will be learned only after the child makes gains in fine motor development.

The beginning point and order of instructions will be determined by the child's eating skills and the expected developmental sequence. However, it is best to teach the first 3 to 4 steps first (orientation to and reaching for the spoon) while the child is still in the dependent feeding stage—being spoon-fed by the parent or teacher. To do this the teacher calls the child's name and, when he looks, places the spoon on the table within reach. The spoon may be gently tapped to cue the child's attention. The food is presented as a consequence for looking at the spoon. Later the child will be expected to reach toward the spoon. Other guidelines for encouraging more active participation during dependent feeding (Mueller, 1975; Stainback et al., 1976) include the following:

1. A short and shallow-bowled spoon with a rounded end will avoid stimulation of the gag reflex.
2. If the learner has a strong bite reflex and tends to bite the spoon, two procedures may be helpful. Present the filled spoon from the side of the mouth, moving it slowly toward a normal midline presentation as the child is successful. Also, if the bite reflex is activated when the spoon is removed, it should not be wrenched from between the teeth; if pressure is applied under the child's chin near the base of the tongue, the bite often will be released.
3. Initially place food near the front of the spoon to facilitate its removal.
4. As the spoon is removed from the child, use manual assistance if necessary to close his lips. This allows the tongue to move the food in rather than out of the mouth.
5. If the teacher scrapes the spoon against the lips or upper teeth as it is removed, two maladaptive consequences are apt to occur—tongue thrust may be stimulated and the child is not expected to actively participate in food removal.

Progressing from dependent feeding to initial stages of teaching spoon usage will be gradual, occurring after the child demonstrates some skill in eating finger foods, reaches for and holds the spoon, and is able to drink from a cup but not without spilling. Once baseline performance has been measured and an intervention plan initiated, instructional time should fill at least the initial part of most meals (if not the whole meal) when the child is hungry and progress to the entire mealtime. That is, a teacher may choose to feed the child during the latter third of a meal only after working on self-feeding. Eventually all dependent feeding should be replaced by instruction in self-feeding.

At least two shaping and prompt-fade methods have been described to teach spoon usage to severely and profoundly retarded individuals. O'Brien et al. (1972) divided spoon usage into 6 steps and manually guided the child's hand through all the steps, fading the guidance systematically in a backward progression. Their task analysis of the steps and the teacher guidance included: (1) placing the spoon handle in the child's dominant hand with the teacher holding her same hand over the child's grasp; (2) guiding the spoon into the food, scooping food, and lifting the spoon 1 inch above the bowl; (3) guiding the spoon to a point 2 inches from the child's mouth; (4) opening the child's mouth by applying gentle pressure on the chin; (5) guiding the spoon into the child's mouth; (6) guiding the child's hand in upward and outward directions to remove the food against the child's upper teeth or lips. An interruption-extinction procedure was used whenever an incorrect response occurred during fading or when the child resorted to eating with his hands. That is, the child was not allowed to put food into his mouth if he made an error while getting the food (used his hand, did not complete the step from which assistance has been faded, etc.). Instead the teacher emptied the food from his spoon or hand, cleaning the child if necessary, and began the 6-step sequence again. The systematic fading of manual guidance proceeded as follows:

When training by manual guidance was first introduced, the teacher guided the child through all six of the steps. Whenever the sequence was completed correctly on three successive assisted trials, the child's hand was guided through one less step on the next assisted trial. Whenever an assisted trial was not completed correctly, it was interrupted and another guided trial was begun, which included an additional guided *step. Whenever a step was eliminated* not guided, *added* guided *eliminated and added on three consecutive trials, the child's hand was guided through a point between that step and the next lower step (e.g., if step three was being added and eliminated, on the following trial the child's hand was guided to a point halfway between the bowl and her mouth). (p. 69)*

Totally unguided trials were used after correct completions to probe the amount of independent performance.

This combination of manual guidance and interruption-extinction led to almost perfect independent performance after 9 meals. However, O'Brien and his colleagues found that a maintenance training procedure which consisted of interruption-extinction was essential to keep the child from reverting back to eating without a spoon.

Azrin and Armstrong (1973) used a slightly different physical assistance (graduated guidance) and fading procedure they called "hand-to-shoulder fading with constant contact." Napkin, glass, spoon, fork, and knife usage were taught with this method, although one at a time and in this simple-to-complex order. To apply hand-to-shoulder fading with consistent contact a teacher would

Begin guidance by having the trainer mold his hand around the student's and guide an entire response. As the student grasps the utensil himself, guidance is progressively reduced at the hand with a gentle touch. The locus of guidance is then faded up the arm to the forearm, elbow, upper arm then shoulder and upper back, always maintaining light touch unless more guidance is required. This constant contact serves as a reminder to the student that inappropriate responses will be prevented. (p. 11)

During this prompt-fade procedure, the trainer applied only enough movement assistance "to get a response going" and only enough restraint to stop an error. Verbal praise, specific to what the student was doing, was given throughout each training trial. "Mini-meals" were served hourly so that many training sessions were possible. Initially, if needed, two trainers worked with a single learner—one to guide the utensil hand while the other guided the student's "lap hand" and head to prevent errors. In combination with these intensive training methods, Azrin and Armstrong (1973) applied overcorrective maintenance procedures for errors made once a student learned to spoon-feed (or fork, etc.). For example, after a student was able to eat with a particular utensil, spills made with that implement were cleaned up by the student. These restitutions were followed by a few positive practice trials. Therefore, spills from an overfilled spoon were first cleaned by the student and then he was expected to practice scooping very small amounts of food into his spoon. With this intensive mini-meal procedure, most of the

11 students learned correct utensil usage in 5 days with a few requiring 12 days of training.

Both intervention procedures described actually consist of a complex combination of precise techniques to schedule sessions, to shape, prompt, fade, and maintain correct responses, and to punish, ignore, and prevent errors. Most teachers may not be able to apply such intensive interventions unless additional staff or volunteers are trained. However, simpler combinations of procedures have been effective when applied systematically (Barnard & Powell, 1972; Berkowitz, Sherry, & Davis, 1971; Christian et al., 1973; Song & Gandhi, 1974).

Eating with a Fork

Although the fork grasp may be modified and its manipulation to pick up food is different from spoon scooping, the procedures for teaching fork usage are essentially identical to those for spoon usage (Azrin & Armstrong, 1973; Nelson et al., 1975). Fork usage should not be taught until after the child has mastered the spoon. The finger-hold, palm-up grip pictured at the top of Figure 7.15 is probably the best to teach for spearing and lifting food with a fork. Later, when fork cutting is taught, the grip will be modified as illustrated and held in a sideways position against the food (Nelson et al., 1975). To teach the spearing and lifting motions, precut chunks or cubes of food will be necessary, avoiding soupy food more appropriate for eating with a spoon. Azrin and Armstrong (1973) taught the use of one utensil at a time and did not present combinations of utensils until the use of all utensils were learned.

Knife Usage

Table knives may be used (1) to transport a spread, such as butter, from one place to another, (2) to spread a substance on food, (3) to cut breads while holding the food with one hand, (4) to push foods onto a fork, and (5) in combination with a fork to cut meat, vegetables, or other foods. These skills are taught and learned in this order. Knife cutting is not mastered in the normal child until the fourth or fifth year.

As with the instruction of spoon and fork usage, Nelson et al. (1975) found that modeling was less effective than the use of physical guidance during both instruction and correction of errors. O'Brien and Azrin (1972) and Ferneti et al. (1974) employed three types of assistance to teach various knife usages and faded the assistance from manual guidance and instruction backward to modeling and instruction, to instruction only, and finally to no verbal reminders. If modeling is to be successful, the

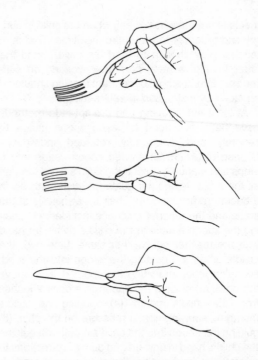

FIGURE 7.15   *Correct grips for holding a fork to eat (top: palm-up finger grip) and to cut (center), and for spreading with a knife (bottom)*

Source: G. L. Nelson, J. D. Cone, and C. R. Hanson, Training correct utensil use in retarded children: Modeling vs. physical guidance. *American Journal of Mental Deficiency*, 1975, *80*, 115.

learner must be attentive to the demonstration and ready to imitate. The effectiveness of modeling is increased with imitative learners if they have already learned the behavior through shaping and physical guidance procedures.

To simplify knife and fork cutting, a teacher may want to teach the "continental" style which does *not* necessitate switching the fork to the nondominant hand. To teach severely retarded individuals this method, Azrin and Armstrong (1973) first provided precut meat chunks and directed students to hold their forks in the dominant hand with fork tines pointed downward to spear the food. Then students were instructed to pick up the knife in the nondominant hand and use a sawing motion while stabilizing the meat with the fork held tines downward. The Project MORE program for eating (Ferneti et al., 1974) suggests teaching the learner to switch the implement from hand to hand; however, they do not provide performance data to support the success of this recommendation with the severely handicapped.

Table manners and related mealtime skills

Many inappropriate behaviors which prevent or interfere with self-feeding may occur during mealtime. For example, if a student is allowed to steal food or eat with his hands, there is little reason for that individual to learn or use the more difficult skills of utensil usage. Time out from eating contingent upon the occurrence of such inappropriate table behavior has been an effective means of improving mealtime behavior in retarded individuals (Barton et al., 1970; Christian et al., 1973; O'Brien & Azrin, 1972; Song & Gandhi, 1974). For some individuals a 30-second removal of the food tray constitutes an aversive consequence strong enough to eliminate food stealing, food throwing, "pigging" or mouth stuffing, eating with hands, and inappropriate utensil usage. With certain behaviors (food stealing), as with some students, tray removal is ineffective and instead, the individual is removed from the room for a period of time or for the remainder of the meal—procedures which quickly result in an elimination of misbehaviors (Barton et al., 1970). Another successful method to reduce occurrences of eating with fingers is that of stoppiing or interrupting the behavior before the individual is able to eat, removing the food from his hands, cleaning his hands, and manually guiding correct spoon usage (Azrin & Armstrong, 1973; O'Brien & Azrin, 1972). This interruption-extinction procedure prevents the child from reinforcing his own inappropriate responses. Finally, overcorrection and positive practice, described earlier, have been used to eliminate spilling and food and utensil throwing (Azrin & Armstrong, 1973).

After the basics of self-feeding and utensil usage are taught, a teacher should consider expanding mealtime instruction to include mixed utensil usage, opening milk cartons, rotation eating (consuming small portions of the different foods included in the meal in an alternating pattern), the use of salt and pepper and other condiments, passing and serving food, and other basic table manners. This advanced self-care instruction could be followed by basic cooking techniques, kitchen care, and dishwashing (described more fully in Chapter 11).

The MORE eating program (Figure 7.11, Ferneti et al., 1974) and Bender and Valletutti (1976) provide task analysis and suggestions for teaching these more advanced skills. Instruction of these skills is carried out systematically if a teacher analyzes the skill; carries out objective measurements of student performance before, during, and after intervention; determines appropriate prompting and reinforcement procedures; uses realistic instructional materials and settings; and programs for skill maintenance and skill generalization to other eating situations (restaurants, home, etc.).

Dressing Skills

In the normal child the ability to undress and dress oneself is learned during the first six years of life with the complicated skill of shoe tying learned last (see Table 7.1). The manipulation of eating utensils and buttoning, snapping, buckling, zipping, lacing, and shoe tying involve refined eye-hand coordination and precise finger dexterity with controlled finger-thumb opposition. Dressing is more difficult than undressing for normal children as well as for handicapped individuals (Minge & Ball, 1967) as are buttoning, tying, snapping, etc. as compared to unbuttoning, untying, and unsnapping.

Programs to teach dressing skills to severely handicapped individuals have involved the use of prompting combined with shaping, backward chaining, and praise and food reinforcers. During short, daily training sessions, undressing usually has been taught before dressing and with one garment instructed at a time beginning with loose-fitting socks, shirts, and pants and, if part of the program, proceeding to buttons, laces, snaps, zippers, and belts (Ball, Seric, & Payne, 1971; Bensberg, 1965; Bensberg et al., 1965; Colwell, Richards, McCarver, & Ellis, 1973; Martin, Kehoe, Bird, Jensen, & Darbyshire, 1971; Minge & Ball, 1967). Although these combinations of training methods have been successful with the moderately and severely retarded, improvement in the dressing skills of institutionalized, profoundly retarded individuals taught by these traditional operant methods has been gradual with learning being time-consuming and often temporary (Ball et al., 1971; Minge & Ball, 1967). This final section of the chapter describes dressing skill assessment and training procedures with suggestions for improving instructional conditions so that learning may be optimized for even the most handicapped individual.

Assessment procedures

Dressing assessment involves the observation of an individual's performance with a variety of garments with or without the application of increasing amounts of assistance whenever a failure is observed. For example, the buttoning checklist described earlier (Figure 7.1) allows the examiner to give assistance after the student has been unsuccessful so that the value of various prompts (verbal/gestural and modeling) might also be assessed. The second example of a buttoning assessment device based upon task analysis of that skill (Figure 7.3) allows the teacher to observe success or failure to perform but without the provision of prompts. Regardless of whether the assessment device allows one to evaluate the effectiveness of prompts upon performance, it is essential that each task be stated in observable terms with specific directions for administration so that with repeated applications the teacher is giving the same test and comparable results are obtained. While teacher-made assessment devices frequently are employed to measure entry skills and monitor learning, a variety of criterion-referenced, informal tests and checklists exist which may be of equal value (Ball et al., 1971; Balthazar, 1971; Behavioral Characteristics Progression, 1973; Bender & Valletutti, 1976; Copeland et al., 1976; Fredericks et al., 1975; Henderson & McDonald, 1973; Linford et al., 1972; McCormack, Hamlet, Dunaway, & Vorderer, 1976; Somerton & Turner, 1975, etc.). Two of these are reviewed briefly.

The dressing subscale of the *Balthazar Scales of Adaptive Behavior* (Balthazar, 1971) illustrated in Figure 7.16 employs a seven-point scoring system by which points earned are proportionate to the independence demonstrated in dressing and undressing. For each item the learner initially is instructed by words and gestures to remove or put on, to fasten or unfasten, etc., each article of clothing or fastening. If the child does not begin or complete the task, a demonstration is given and additional assistance is provided in a step-by-step manner whenever resultant performance stops or errors occur. Therefore the learner is given credit for imitating a demonstration, for performing more than or less than half the task, and even for only cooperating by positioning his limbs. The amount of time allowed for performance at each level of prompt is specified in Table 7.6 as well as the score awarded for various performances. A child's ability to remove and put on pants, shoes, and shirts is evaluated separately from skills in buttoning, zipping, buckling, lacing, and tying. To increase its usefulness, the teacher will need to extend the Balthazar scale score sheet to include coats, hats, mittens, boots, bras, pantyhose, ties, etc. Although it may take some practice to obtain reliable results with the *Bal-*

thazar Dressing Scale, the teacher who does so will procure information relevant to selection of effective teaching strategies for each individual assessed.

Copeland et al. (1976) provides a less-structured checklist assessment of dressing skills (Figure 7.17) as well as a detailed listing of steps to monitor performance during the instruction of each dressing subtask (Figure 7.18). Their checklist allows the teacher to make note of the child's particular method of completing each task (e.g., ineffectively uses flip-over method for jacket)—information which will be useful when devising a teaching procedure.

Assessment may include the related skills of discriminating front from back and inside-out from right-side-in, hanging clothes, and putting away clean and dirty clothing, using a mirror to check appearance and adjust clothing, selection of clothes suitable to various occasions, seasons, and weather conditions, and discriminating between clean and dirty (ripped, wrinkled, etc.) clothing.

Although these skills will be taught only after an individual acquires the basics of dressing and undressing, each ability represents more advanced levels of independence in self-care—relevant goals for the older handicapped individual. Assessment procedures also should include the measurement of skill maintenance (using the skill once learned) and generalization (using the skill in various settings—in the school locker room, at home, and during summer camp—and under changing conditions—lacing boots as opposed to shoes, buttoning side and back buttons, etc.).

With dressing as with eating skills, when assessing the entry abilities of physically handicapped students it will be of particular value to obtain the assistance of a physical or occupational therapist. Once again positioning and support are of utmost importance and when appropriately provided will allow a more accurate measurement of the child's ability to dress or assist in dressing tasks (Campbell et al., 1977; Finnie, 1975). The related fine motor skills of grasping and releasing when complicated by deformities, contractures, or spasticity may need medical evaluation. These examinations will assist the teacher in determining realistic goals for dressing skills and whether adaptive equipment or modified clothing will increase independence.

Teaching the student to look at his hands when he tries to remove, put on, or fasten clothing is another important area which may be assessed as needing instruction. To obtain baseline perfor-

DRESSING SCALES   Date: _____

DRESSING TALLY SHEET

Total Score   MALE   FEMALE

ARTICLE/ACTIVITY	SCORE		ARTICLE/ACTIVITY	SCORE	
	Right	Left		Right	Left
Shoes			**Shoes**		
PUT ON Shoes	1____	2____	PUT ON Shoes	1____	2____
Tighten Laces	3____	4____	Tighten Laces	3____	4____
Tie—single bow	5____	6____	Tie—single bow	5____	6____
TAKE OFF Shoes	7____	8____	TAKE OFF Shoes	7____	8____
Untie—start with a single bow	9____	10____	Untie—start with a single bow	9____	10____
Socks			**Socks**		
PUT ON Socks	11____	12____	PUT ON Socks	11____	12____
TAKE OFF Socks	13____	14____	TAKE OFF Socks	13____	14____

ARTICLE/ACTIVITY	SCORE	ARTICLE/ACTIVITY	SCORE
Pants		**Pants or Skirt**	
PUT ON Pants	15____	PUT ON Pants or Skirt	15____
Fasten	16____	TAKE OFF Pants or Skirt	16____
Zip Up	17____	**Briefs**	
Put Belt On	18____	PUT ON Briefs	17____
Fasten Belt	19____	TAKE OFF Briefs	18____
TAKE OFF Pants	20____	**T-Shirt/Undershirt**	
Unfasten	21____	PUT ON T-Shirt	19____
Unzip	22____	TAKE OFF T-Shirt	20____
Take Belt Off	23____	**Blouse**	
Unfasten Belt	24____	PUT ON Blouse	21____
Briefs		Button	22____
PUT ON Briefs	25____	TAKE OFF Blouse	23____
TAKE OFF Briefs	26____	Unbutton	24____
Shirt		**Dress**	
PUT ON Shirt	27____	PUT ON Dress	25____
Button	28____	Zip Up	26____
TAKE OFF Shirt	29____	TAKE OFF Dress	27____
Unbutton	30____	Unzip	28____
T-Shirt/Undershirt		**Other:**	
		Brassiere	
PUT ON T-Shirt	31____	PUT ON Brassiere	29____
TAKE OFF T-Shirt	32____	TAKE OFF Brassiere	30____
TOTAL SCORE	____	TOTAL SCORE	____

FIGURE 7.16 *A Balthazar scale for adaptive behavior in dressing*

Source: E. E. Balthazar, *Balthazar Scales of Adaptive Behavior for the Profoundly and Severely Mentally Retarded, Section 1*. Champaign, Ill.: Research Press, 1971.

mance, students may simply be asked to follow the cue "Look at this" while the teacher touches a garment, button, or zipper. If attending is deficient, contingent praise, pats, and possibly small food reinforcers on a more continuous schedule initially will be a necessary means to strengthen eye-hand behavior.

Selection of teaching targets

After examining the student's baseline performance, instructional targets will be selected. The teacher should consult the developmental se-

quence in order that developmentally easier skills are targeted and taught before more difficult dependent skills. Therefore, instruction in removal of a garment will precede instruction in putting on that same garment. Depending upon the amount of time allowed for instruction, a student may receive training on a variety of targets simultaneously. Because it is easiest and often necessary to dress or undress completely during the day (gym, bedtime, etc.) a teacher and parent might determine undressing and/or dressing performance targets for underwear, pants, shirts, shoes, and socks as well as jackets or sweaters.

TABLE 7.6   *Summary of the scoring procedure for the dressing-undressing scale of the Balthazar Scales of Adaptive Behavior*

Score	Dressing/Undressing Performance	Testing Procedure
6	Perfect and independent	Give command and gesture, then wait 10 seconds for student to initiate. After student *finishes*, score and record time needed to complete task.
5	Imperfect but independent (e.g., shirt on backwards)	
4	Demonstration provided	If no progress is made for a second period and task still is incomplete, repeat command and gesture accompanied by a demonstration (put shirt on student, then remove). Repeat command and allow 1 minute to complete first step before giving any physical assistance.
3	Partially assisted (less than half of steps)	
2	Primarily assisted (more than half of steps)	
1	Cooperative (e.g., holds arm out for shirt sleeve)	In subsequent steps, if needed give command and allow 10 seconds for progress to begin. If no progress or if student stops, help student through that step. Remember to give student an opportunity to perform each step in every sequence listed in the manual.
0	No participation	

If undressing has been mastered and the student is capable of grasping and releasing small objects, instruction could begin in unbuttoning and unzipping. As discussed in the motor skills chapter, instructional objectives may be delineated for fine motor or manipulation abilities. Because improvement in the manipulative skills of grasp and release, finger-thumb opposition, and eye-hand coordination will positively influence a student's readiness to operate clothes fasteners, such fine motor activities should be scheduled before attempting to teach buttoning, zipping, etc. Finally visual attention during the dressing task may be targeted for instruction (Martin et al., 1971) as well as comprehension of clothing names. Learning of both skills will tend to speed attainment of dressing targets.

General elements of instruction

Teaching Times and Place

To maximize positive transfer of skills, it is wise to teach dressing in the places (bathroom, bedroom, locker room, coat area) and at least at the times when dressing skills are needed. However, to guarantee an unhurried training session, a teacher must schedule sufficient time before the activity for which dressing and undressing are being carried out. If adequate time is alloted, the teacher will not be tempted to overprompt in an effort to avoid being late for that activity.

Shorter training sessions of 10 to 20 minutes should be scheduled at various times throughout each day rather than longer single sessions or sporadic training less than daily. However, Azrin, Schaeffer, and Wesolowski (1976) successfully employed 3-hour sessions with profoundly retarded students where attention was prolonged by an intensive reinforcement and prompting procedure.

Teaching Materials

When instructing the beginning self-dresser, success can be made more attainable by modifying the clothing used during teaching. For example, some studies have employed simple clothing two sizes larger than the child's usual size and without zippers and buttons (elastic waist bands, pull-over shirts) (Azrin et al., 1976; Minge & Ball, 1967). Others suggest color coding or marking clothes: the outside or front of the shirt is marked with colored tape, the right side of both shoestrings is red and the left is white (1 red and 1 white shoestrings are cut in half and each red half is joined with a white half to make the coded shoestrings).

If large buttons and button-holes (snaps, zippers with large tabs) are taught first, the manipulation of smaller fasteners will be learned more quickly. Some teachers have attached strings to front and back zippers to make pulling easier.

For some children who lack the necessary muscle control, more long-term clothing adaptations

Child's name: Date: Pretest of Dressing Skills	Independent	Verbal Assistance	Physical Assistance	Description of Method Child Uses to Complete the Task
Undressing trousers, skirt 1. Pushes garment from waist to ankles 2. Pushes garment off one leg 3. Pushes garment off other leg				
Dressing trousers, skirt 1. Lays trousers in front of self with front side up 2. Inserts one foot into waist opening 3. Inserts other foot into waist opening 4. Pulls garment up to waist				
Undressing socks 1. Pushes sock down off heel 2. Pulls toe of sock pulling sock off foot				
Dressing socks 1. Positions sock correctly with heel-side down 2. Holds sock open at top 3. Inserts toes into sock 4. Pulls sock over heel 5. Pulls sock up				
Undressing cardigan 1. Takes dominant arm out of sleeve 2. Gets coat off back 3. Pulls other arm from sleeve				
Dressing cardigan flip-over method 1. Lays garment on table or floor in front of self 2. Gets dominant arm into sleeve 3. Other arm into sleeve 4. Positions coat on back				
Undressing polo shirt 1. Takes dominant arm out of sleeve 2. Pulls garment over head 3. Pulls other arm from sleeve				
Dressing polo shirt 1. Lays garment in front of self 2. Opens bottom of garment and puts arms into sleeves 3. Pulls garment over head 4. Pulls garment down to waist				
Undressing shoes 1. Loosens laces 2. Pulls shoe off heel 3. Pulls front of shoe to pull shoe off of toes				
Dressing shoes 1. Prepares shoe by loosening laces and pulling tongue of shoe out of the way 2. Inserts toes into shoe 3. Pushes shoe on over heel				

FIGURE 7.17   *Test of dressing skills*

Source: M. Copeland, L. Ford, and N. Solon, *Occupational Therapy for Mentally Retarded Children*. Baltimore: University Park Press, 1976, p. 95.

Name: John   Trainer: Session number: 4

Date: July 2, 1974   Task: Dressing polo shirt   Trials completed: 4/5

Trials

Subtasks	1	2	3	4	5	6	7	8	9	10
1. Holds shirt bottom open with right hand on cue	+	+	+	+	+					
2. Inserts left hand into shirt	+	+	+	–	+					
3. With right hand pulls shirt over left hand so hand comes through sleeve	A	A	A		A					
4. Brings left hand to red cue	A	A	A		A					
5. Holds shirt bottom with left hand on red cue	A	A	A		A					
6. Inserts right hand into shirt and through sleeve	A	A	A		A					
7. Pulls shirt over head	A	A	A		A					
8. Pulls shirt down	A	A	A		A					
9.										
10.										
	R	R	R		R					

Code: + = independent; A = assistance; – = failed; R = reward.

FIGURE 7.18   *Training data sheet for putting on a polo shirt.*
Source: M. Copeland, L. Ford, and N. Solon, *Occupational Therapy for Mentally Retarded Children.* Baltimore: University Park Press, 1976, p. 94.

may be necessary to encourage independence. "Velcro" fasteners might replace buttons or simply be sewn beneath nonworking buttons; loose raglan sleeves, knitted fabrics, loafer shoes, elastic waistbands, and tubular socks without heels will present fewer dressing problems (Finnie, 1975).

While button, snap, and zipper boards or dolls with such clothing seem to be useful instructional materials, skill generalization may be a problem for the severely handicapped learner. The buttoning task becomes quite different when buttoning another's buttons, and zipping up a zipper attached to a horizontal board is not the same as looking down upon a worn zipper. Teachers are advised to make minimal use of such materials or to replace them with "dress-up" or regular clothes with enlarged fasteners. As long as a training wooden shoe is positioned with toe facing away from the child, lacing and tying practice with this material does not result in transfer problems.

Basic methods to teach self-dressing

Encouraging Active Participation

Prior to teaching the learner his first independent steps in self-dressing, it is good practice to encourage active participation when the parent or teacher is dressing or undressing the child. Active participation means extending hands, arms, or feet in anticipation of being dressed or undressed, looking at or reaching for garments and body parts which are named and gestured toward by the teacher, and cooperating by moving limbs into or out of garments held by the teacher, as well as not resisting limb movement during dressing.

In order to teach these beginning dressing skills, the teacher must create an unhurried, positive atmosphere during dressing times. Clothes should be pointed to and labeled repeatedly during the process with simple phrases used to describe the dressing activity (e.g., "Let's put on your shirt"). If the child's attention is not directed toward a particular garment before it is put on or removed, the teacher should prompt attention by turning the child's head, moving the garment into the child's view or shaking the garment. At this time the garment should be labeled and the looking behavior reinforced with praise, hugs, noise toys (e.g., music box for a few seconds), or bits of food if necessary.

Once the learner demonstrates more visual attending to the teacher and garment, a teacher could prompt the child to move her limbs in the appropriate manner. During dressing this is done by holding the garment next to the corresponding limb (e.g., sock by foot), when the child is attending and physically prompting movement of that limb in the direction of the held garment. Getting the learner to push limbs into (or pull out of) is done by pushing the garment onto the extended limb in short, gently abrupt movements allowing the child opportunity to push (or pull away from) between movements. Any beginning efforts made by the learner should be encouraged.

The position of the child during dependent dressing should allow plenty of support, especially if the individual is weak in balance, unable to stand or sit, or demonstrates lack of muscle control such as with the cerebral palsied individual. Finnie (1975) suggests that the younger athetoid child and the spastic child be laid tummy down across the teacher's lap to decrease the tendency to stiffen which is encouraged by a backlying position. As the physically handicapped individual grows larger, lying on one side will prevent the head from bending forward. If the child has some head and neck control, it might be best to support him from the back in a sitting position but at the hips with knees apart and bent and trunk well forward to maintain balance. Slippery sitting surfaces or pants should be avoided so that some friction exists between the child's buttocks and the seat, assuring stability. Once again the teacher is advised to consult the advice of a physical or occupational therapist so that the teaching position may be individually prescribed. Additionally, Campbell et al. (1977), Finnie (1975), and Sternat, Messina, Lyon, and Nietupski (1977), are useful references.

Finnie (1975) provides some guidelines for dressing the cerebral palsied child:

1. Assist the learner to dress or undress the more affected arm or leg first.
2. Working from behind the seated child, try to position him symmetrically so the head is centered; this will allow more uniform ease in bending the limbs on both sides.
3. If a child has fallen too far forward while in a supported seated position, help him to a more upright angle (but still well forward) *before* beginning to dress.
4. To decrease stiffening of the foot and toes, bend the child's leg prior to putting on shoes and socks.
5. Straighten the child's arm before putting on a sleeve; avoid pulling his fingers to get the arm through the sleeve as this causes the elbow to bend.
6. If a pillow is placed beneath the hips and head when changing diapers then the task of bending the hips and knees and keeping the knees together becomes easier. (pp. 94–95)

Taking Off and Putting on Garments

The most common method for teaching a severely handicapped individual to undress or dress involves backward chaining. In this procedure the teacher first analyzes the dressing sequence into a series of small steps as in Figure 7.18. Then the individual is asked to remove the garment and is physically assisted through all the steps except the last step (e.g., removes T-shirt from remaining hand). At this point the teacher encourages the learner to perform the last step by one or more of the following procedures: giving a direction ("Take off your shirt") while gesturing or touching the garment, demonstrating the last step on the learner or on the teacher and allowing the learner to imitate, or applying varying amounts of physical assistance. Praise and tangible reinforcers are given after completion of this last step. Training continues on this step until the learner carries out the last step without any assistance. Then training is directed toward the next to the last step by providing assistance and gradually fading it over trials. The learner continues to perform learned steps without help. Reinforcement is provided after the undressing (or dressing) chain is completed. Gradually the learner learns each successive step in the chain until a single garment can be removed when requested. As illustrated by Figure 7.19, these general methods have been used to teach moderately and severely retarded individuals to undress as well as to dress (Baldwin, Fredericks, & Brodsky, 1973; Ball et al., 1971; Bensberg, 1965; Bensberg et al., 1965; Colwell et al., 1973; Linford et al., 1972; Martin et al., 1971; Minge & Ball, 1967).

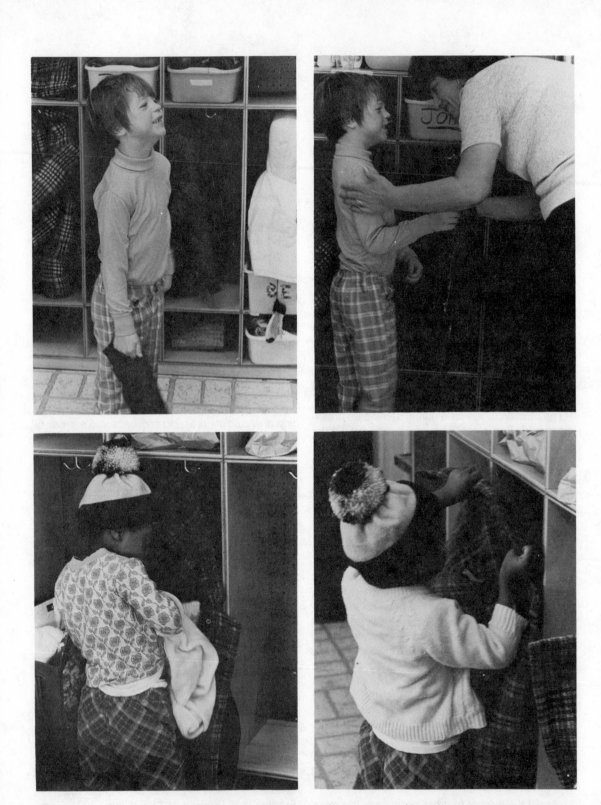

FIGURE 7.19   *Learning to remove and hang up one's coat and sweater independently will require some verbal demonstrative instruction by the teacher as well as lots of praise for improvements in performance. Soon John will be as independent as Glynis in his ability to remove and hang up a coat.*

Forward chaining which may be used to teach these same dressing skills has been applied less often (Azrin et al., 1976). The decision to use forward or backward chaining rests upon an understanding of the two processes, the skill being taught, and the performance of the student (Copeland et al, 1976). Forward chaining, described more fully in Chapter 3, progresses from teaching the first step to the second, third, and so on in a manner similar to that described for backward chaining. One difference occurs with the timing of reinforcement; although praise is given after successful performance of the teaching step, more extensive reinforcement is provided at the end of the chain after the student is assisted through all the unlearned steps. If a student's baseline performance reveals more success early in the dressing or undressing chain, then forward chaining may proceed more quickly than backward chaining. However, backward chaining has the advantage of associating reinforcement with task completion. As discussed earlier for spoon usage, both forward and backward chaining also may be used together to teach dressing skills. Forward chaining is employed at the beginning of the dressing or undressing sequence and advances forward while backward chaining starts at the end and proceeds backward over successive teaching sessions.

If the teacher elects to instruct one undressing skill at a time using forward or backward chaining, it is important that each daily session begin with a review of the step just mastered rather than a new step. Assistance would be provided for the learned step, if needed, then faded before trying to teach the next step in the chain. The number of steps into which a chain is divided may be increased if a student demonstrates difficulty when prompts are faded on any single step. Also at this early stage of dressing instruction, loose, simple clothing should be used, preferably without zippers, hooks, or buttons. If fasteners are present on the clothing, these should be opened and closed for the student since training at this stage is focused on the less-complicated skills of clothing removal and replacement.

Because the methods just described take weeks or months to produce functional dressing skills, Azrin et al. (1976) developed a concentrated method for rapid teaching of these skills to profoundly retarded students. Dressing skills were taught after undressing skills had been mastered. However, each student learned to remove (and put on) five garments from outer- to underwear as an entire sequence (shoes, socks, pants, underpants, and shirt)

rather than learning to remove one garment at a time. If a student demonstrated difficulty with one or two of the five garments, intensive training centered primarily on these garments. Seven students taught by this method learned to put on and remove all five garments after a median training time of 10 hours or over 2 days.

This rapid success resulted from a combination of intense training techniques: long instructional sessions (3 hours), forward rather than backward chaining, extensive use of manual guidance early in learning which was graduated in intensity to match the student's responsiveness, systematic application and fading of prompts, continuous use of praise and stroking contingent upon any effort to follow instructions or guidance, the requirement of visual attention to the task, and the initial involvement of two trainers so that praise, stroking, and manual guidance could be provided. Azrin and his co-workers employed slip-on clothing without fasteners which initially was two sizes larger than the student's regular clothes. After only touch assistance was needed to begin performance of the dressing or undressing chain, clothing one size smaller was substituted. Students were taught to dress and undress while seated and to use both hands for all dressing movements. Prompts were gradually increased until successful performance occurred:

The first instruction for each garment was simply verbal. If a few seconds passed with no action, the trainer pointed at or touched the garment. After a few seconds, the instruction was repeated and the trainer molded the student's hands around the garment. If a student still was not participating, the trainer then described each movement the student was to make as he guided the hands through the necessary motion. The instructions were very specific. This procedure provided multisensory information: verbal, visual, auditory, and tactual. (p. 30)

After manual guidance was faded for a garment, the student was encouraged to perform with pointing and instructional cues provided every 10 seconds as needed. If the response was not completed in 1 minute, manual guidance was reapplied. Some students, especially during early acquisition, resisted manual guidance. Although the trainer's hands were cupped around the student's who in turn held the garment, the student was not forced to respond. After the student relaxed his resistance, manual guidance was gently reinstated. As with methods to teach toileting and eating, Azrin and his co-workers have combined some of the best elements from the teaching technology to produce a dressing instructional procedure that has yielded successful and swift results with profoundly retarded learners. While this method was not tested with physically handicapped, retarded learners, such a rich combination of instructional elements applied under the direction of a physical or occupational therapist has potential for producing some level of skill development (Azrin et al., 1976, p. 33).

Fasteners

Skills in unfastening should be mastered before fastening. When oversized fasteners, visible to the learner, are used as the teaching materials, instruction probably increases in complexity across the following skills: zipping (with front opening zipper already securely attached at bottom), snapping (large, plastic snaps), buttoning, hooking, buckling. Learning to align the zipper tab with the zipper end on a front opening jacket and to fasten buttons, snaps, or hooks located out of direct view is difficult for the handicapped as well as for the normal learner and will be taught after mastery of the simple fasteners. Copeland et al. (1976) and Linford et al. (1972) provide useful task analyses of these skills with suggestions for teaching. For example, zipping unconnected front-opening jackets may be divided into 7 steps which Copeland suggests be chained in a forward direction.

1. First the learner grasps zipper tab and moves zipper slider with the dominant hand to the bottom of the track.
2. Then the pin is grasped between nondominant finger and thumb and the pin is inserted into the slider (while holding onto both sides of the closure at the bottom).
3. The pin is pushed firmly into the slider box.
4. Nondominant hand grasps both sides of closure at bottom with thumb placed across zipper box (held through step 6).
5. With dominant hand the zipper tab is grasped.
6. Zipper tab is pulled up to top stop.
7. Zipper tab released and pushed with index finger to lock into position.

Some teachers will prefer subdividing the first two steps while others may elect not to teach the last step of locking the zipper. If a pull string is added to the zipper tab, the task becomes somewhat easier and the steps are modified slightly.

As illustrated by this example, hand dominance influences the teaching procedure. Hand domi-nance, if unknown, can be determined by simple observation during eating and play. Also the learner may be handed objects at his midline while noting how often right- and left-hand grasps are used. (Chapter 6, motor skills, provides additional comment on hand dominance.) To illustrate the importance of hand dominance, the belt buckling task becomes easier if the learner is taught to grasp the buckle with the dominant hand and the strap with his other hand (Copeland et al., 1976). However, with the changing position of buttons and snaps, the matching of dominant hand to the logically dominant side of the task may create a problem. The position of buttons and button holes as well as bottom-fitting (under snap) and top-fitting snaps (over snap) tends to be one way on boy's clothing and the opposite for girls. In boy's clothing buttons are on the right edge and holes on the left while bottom-fitting snaps are on the right and the top-fitting half is positioned on the left edge of a garment. The opposite arrangement occurs with girl's clothing. Since it may be easier to teach a child to grasp buttons as well as bottom-fitting snaps in the dominant hand (Copeland et al., 1976) boy's clothing would provide the appropriate arrangement for right handers while girl's clothing would be more suited to left handers. However, it is true that each sex must learn to fasten their corresponding clothing and perhaps learning both arrangements is best. Because the research is scanty in this area, teachers are directed to begin girls and boys on their own clothing regardless of dominance and fastener arrangement but to check that all beginning learning takes place with the same arrangement of buttons, holes, and snaps. Once one arrangement is mastered, training could be provided with the opposite arrangement. However, if a child appears to be making slow progress during early learning and his hand dominance is not matched to the position of buttons on his clothing, the teacher may want to try the opposite arrangement.

Shoe Tying

Baldwin et al. (1973), Copeland et al. (1976), Linford et al. (1972), and Martin et al. (1971) describe two nontraditional methods of teaching shoe tying to handicapped learners. The "rabbit ear" method involves tying a single knot, then forming two loops which are then tied together in another single knot (Figure 7.20). Martin and his co-workers employed another procedure to teach the same skill: (A) tying a single knot, (B) tying a second knot which is not pulled tight, (C) making one loop by inserting one lace end into the hole between the knots, (D) pulling

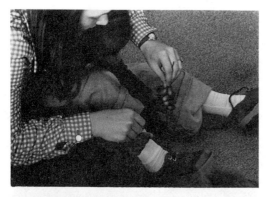

FIGURE 7.20 *This teacher is using a backward chaining procedure to teach her student the traditional method of shoe tying. Jayne verbally instructs and manually helps Maude as needed with each step: tying a simple knot, making a loop with one lace, wrapping the free lace around the loop, switching position of fingers, pulling the second loop out through the opening, and pulling both loops tight. Note that in the bottom picture, which illustrates the last step, Jayne has faded out her manual assistance by letting Maude tighten the bow on her own.*

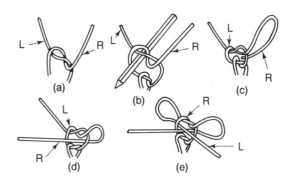

FIGURE 7.21 *Diagram of steps for tying a bow. The letters "L" and "R" indicate the hands (left or right) of the subject that are holding the laces at the head of the arrows.*

Source: G. L. Martin, B. Keogh, E. Bird, V. Jensen, and M. Darbyshire, Operant conditioning in dressing behavior of severely retarded girls. *Mental Retardation*, 1971, *9* (3), 29.

The traditional method (single knot, form loop with one lace, wrap free lace around loop, etc.) appears to be recommended less often for teaching handicapped learners. This could be because of its nonsymmetrical formation as compared with the two untraditional methods—each lace is manipulated in a different way in the traditional method. Regardless of the method selected, the learner should be taught to untie bows and single knots first, then to tie single knots, and lastly to tie bows.

Because of the complexity of shoe tying and the necessity of precise finger control, it may be wise to recommend that some handicapped learners wear nontying shoes and learning time is redirected to skills of a higher priority and with a greater likelihood for success.

Advanced Self-Care Abilities

The subject of this chapter has been basic self-care. However, many field-tested instructional programs for teaching more advanced skills are available to the teacher. The results of successful instruction in hairwashing, toothbrushing, and other aspects of self-care are illustrated in Figure 7.22. Because of limitations of space these programs and related research are not reviewed but references are cited. Behavioral Characteristics Progression (1973), Bender and Valletutti (1976), Copeland et al. (1976), and McCormack et al. (1976) provide useful skill sequences in later self-help skills with descrip-

it to form a small loop, repeating steps (C) and (D) with the second lace end, and (E) grasping both loops and pulling the bow tight. (Refer to Figure 7.21.) While this latter method has data supporting its "learnability" with the severely retarded (Martin et al., 1971), the "rabbit ear" method, though reportedly used with the same population (Baldwin et al., 1973; Copeland et al, 1976; Linford et al., 1972), lacks such data.

FIGURE 7.22   *Handwashing and toothbrushing instruction can begin early and should include teacher demonstration as a primary instructional procedure. More advanced grooming skills can best be taught in conjunction with a physical education program such as swimming. Those skills include showering, hair washing, drying and styling, skin and nail care, and, for girls, hygiene during menstruation.*

tions of appropriate instructional methods. The teacher may consult the following references for teaching toothbrushing and dental care (Abramson & Wunderlich, 1972; Horner, Billionis, & Lent, 1975; Horner & Keilitz, 1975) nose blowing (Ingenthron, Ferneti, & Keilitz, 1975), handwashing (Stevens, Ferneti, & Lent, 1975), use of deodorant (Lewis, Ferneti, & Keilitz, 1975b), complexion care (Keilitz, Horner, & Brown, 1975), hairwashing (Lewis, Ferneti, & Keilitz, 1975a), and sex education (Bender & Valletutti, 1976; Hamre & Williams, 1974; Kempton, 1975).

Summary

This chapter has described procedures to assess and teach the basic self-care skills of independent toileting, eating, and dressing. Developmental sequences for the normal emergence of these abilities were traced with discussion devoted to the relevance of these developmental schedules for teachers of the moderately and severely handicapped. Extensive comment was provided regarding instructional prompts, shaping procedures, and materials with a review of the research on teaching self-care skills to the moderately and severely handicapped.

The extent to which an individual attains independence in the basic self-care skills clearly will influence his or her inclusion in educational programs, social activities, and vocational opportunities and certainly will affect the amount of time available to the parent and teacher and the self-esteem of the individual. The volume of research directed toward self-care instruction has been productive in its provision of methodological guidelines for parents and teachers. If educational programs individualize this information and successfully implement this technology, independence in the basic self-care abilities of the handicapped will be maximized.

Toilet Training Signaling Equipment

Signaling pants and potty chair

1. BRS/LVE Tech. Serv., Inc.
   5301 Holland Drive
   Beltsville, Maryland 20705
   A. Potty Alert (#552–08) $65.00 each
   B. Pants Alert (#552–09) $65.00 each

2. A. Yonovitz
   The University of Texas
   Speech and Hearing Institute
   Health Science Center at Houston
   1343 Moursund
   Houston, Texas 77025
   A. Toilet Alarm $12.50 (unassembled)
   B. Body-Worn Alerting Unit $4.75 (unassembled)
   C. Construction Manual $2.00

3. C. A. Briggs Company
   Cybersonic Division
   P.O. Box 151 Glenside, Pennsylvania 19038
   A. Bleeptone Audible Signaling Device $6.50 (for use with a body-worn alert and as part of a toilet alarm).

Bed signaling equipment

1. Montgomery Ward
   Catalogue Sales
   A. Standard Wet Guard (#53 C 21530) $27.95. Unit with buzzer only. 2 bed packs; battery.
   B. Deluxe Wet Guard (#53 C 21531) $42.95. Unit, 4 bed packs with 2 foil pads, 1 separating sheet; adjustable signal volume, battery.
   C. Replacement kit of 2 foil pad sets (#53 C 21532) $4.95.

2. Sears Roebuck
   Catalogue Sales
   A. Lite-Alert Buzzer (#8A1165) $42.95
   B. Extra bedding Set (#8A1172) $4.95

Adaptive Equipment: Chairs and Self-Care Assistive Devices

Commercial catalogs

1. Abbey Medical Equipment Co.
   Medical Catalog Sales Department
   13500 South Figueroa Street
   Los Angeles, California 90061

2. Be OK Self Help Aids
   Fred Sammons, Inc.
   Box 32
   Brookfield, Illinois 60513

3. Cleo Living Aids
   3957 Mayfield Road
   Cleveland, Ohio 44121

4. Contourpedic Corporation
   1106 Edgewater Ave.
   Ridgefield, N.J.

5. Ortho-Kinetics, Inc.
   1225 Pearl Street
   Waukesha, Wisconsin 53186

6. J. A. Preston Corporation
   71 Fifth Avenue
   New York, New York 10003

7. Skill Development Equipment Co.
   1340 North Jefferson
   Anaheim, California 92807

References

1. *A Manual for Cerebral Palsy Equipment.* Chicago, Ill.: National Society for Crippled Children and Adults, Inc., 11 South LaSalle Street.
2. N. R. Finnie, *Handling the Young Cerebral Palsied Child at Home.* New York: E. P. Dutton, 1975.
3. R. B. Hofmann, *How to Build Special Furniture and Equipment for Handicapped Children.* Springfield, Ill.: Charles C Thomas, 1970.
4. H. L. Kaminetz, *The Wheelchair Book; Mobility for the Disabled.* Springfield, Illinois: Charles C Thomas, 1969.
5. E. Lowman, & J. L. Klinger, *Aids to Independent Living: Self-Help for the Handicapped.* New York: McGraw-Hill, 1969.
6. I. P. Robinault, *Functional Aids for the Multiply Handicapped.* Hagerstown, Md.: Medical Department, Harper & Row, 1973.
7. M. Zimmerman, *Self-Help Devices for Rehabilitation: Part I.* Dubuque, Iowa: William C. Brown, 1958.
8. M. Zimmerman, *Self-Help Devices for Rehabilitation: Part II.* Dubuque, Iowa: William C Brown, 1965.

References

Abramson, E. E., & Wunderlich, R. A. Dental hygiene training for Retardates: An application of behavioral techniques. *Mental Retardation,* 1972, *10*(3), 6–8.

Azrin, N. H., & Armstrong, P. M. The "mini-meal"—A method for teaching eating skills to the profoundly retarded. *Mental Retardation,* 1973, *11*(1), 9–11.

Azrin, N. H., Bugle, C., & O'Brien, F. Behavioral engineering: Two apparatuses for toilet training retarded children. *Journal of Applied Behavioral Analysis,* 1971, *4,* 249–253.

Azrin, N. H., & Foxx, R. M. A rapid method of toilet training the institutionalized retarded. *Journal of Applied Behavior Analysis,* 1971, *4,* 89–99.

Azrin, N. H. & Foxx, R. M. *Toilet training in less than a day.* New York: Simon & Schuster, 1974.

Azrin, N. H., Schaeffer, R. M., & Wesolowski, M. D. A rapid method of teaching profoundly retarded persons to dress by a reinforcement-guidance method. *Mental Retardation,* 1976, *14*(6), 29–33.

Azrin, N. H., Sneed, T. J., & Foxx, R. M. Dry bed: A rapid method of eliminating bedwetting (enuresis) of the retarded. *Behavior Research and Therapy,* 1973, *11,* 427–434.

Azrin, N. H., Sneed, T. J., & Foxx, R. N. Dry-bed training: Rapid elimination of childhood enuresis. *Behavior Research and Therapy,* 1974, *12,* 147–156.

Baldwin, V. L., Fredericks, H. D. B., & Brodsky, G. *Isn't it time he outgrew this? or, A training program for parents of retarded children.* Springfield, Ill.: Charles C Thomas, 1973.

Ball, T. S., Hendricksen, H., & Clayton, J. A special feeding technique for chronic regurgitation. *American Journal of Mental Deficiency,* 1974, *78,* 486–493.

Ball, T. S., Seric, K., & Payne, L. E. Long-term retention of self-help skill training in the profoundly retarded. *American Journal of Mental Deficiency,* 1971, *76,* 378–382.

Baller, W. R. *Bed-wetting: Origins and treatment.* New York: Pergamon Press, 1975.

Balthazar, E. E. *Balthazar scales of adaptive behavior for the profoundly and severely retarded, Section 1.* Champaign, Ill.: Research Press, 1971.

Barnard, K. E., & Powell, M. L. *Teaching the mentally retarded child, a family care approach.* St. Louis: C. V. Mosby, 1972.

Barton, E. S., Guess, D., Garcia, E., & Baer, D. M. Improvement of retardates' mealtime behaviors by timeout procedures using multiple baseline techniques. *Journal of Applied Behavior Analysis,* 1970, *3,* 77–84.

Behavioral characteristics progression, Palo Alto, Calif.: Vort Corporation, 1973.

Bender, M., & Valletutti, P. J. *Teaching the moderately and severely handicapped,* Vol. I. Baltimore: University Park Press, 1976.

Bensberg, G. J. (Ed.), *Teaching mentally retarded children.* Atlanta: Southern Regional Educational Board, 1965.

Bensberg, G. J., Colwell, C. N., & Cassel, R. H. Teaching the profoundly retarded self-help activities by behavior shaping techniques. *American Journal of Mental Deficiency,* 1965, *69,* 674–679.

Berkowitz, S., Sherry, P. J., & Davis, B. A. Teaching self-feeding skills to profound retardates using reinforcement and fading procedures. *Behavior Therapy,* 1971, *2,* 62–67.

Bollard, R. J. & Woodroffe, P. The effect of parent-administered dry-bed training on nocturnal enuresis in children. *Behavior Research & Therapy,* 1977, *15,* 159–165.

Campbell, P. H., Green, K. M., & Carlson, L. M. Approximating the norm through environmental and child-centered prosthetics and adaptive equipment. In E. Sontag (Ed.), *Educational programming for the severely and profoundly handicapped,* Reston, Va.: Division on Mental Retardation, Council for Exceptional Children, 1977.

Christian, W. P., Hollomon, S. W., & Lanier, C. L. An attendent operated feeding program for severely and profoundly retarded females. *Mental Retardation,* 1973, *11* (5), 35–37.

Cohen, M. A., Gross, P. J., & Haring, N. G. Developmental pinpoints. In N. G. Haring & L. J. Brown (Eds.), *Teaching the severely handicapped* (Vol. 1). New York: Grune & Stratton, 1976.

Colwell, C. N., Richards, E., McCarver, R. B., & Ellis, N. R. Evaluation of self-help habit training of the profoundly retarded. *Mental Retardation,* 1973, *11*(3), 14–18.

Coote, M. A. Apparatus for conditioning treatment of enuresis. *Behavior Research and Therapy,* 1965, *2,* 233–238.

Copeland, M., Ford, L., & Solon, N. *Occupational therapy for mentally retarded children.* Baltimore: University Park Press, 1976.

Doleys, D. M., & Arnold, S. Treatment of childhood encopresis: Full cleanliness training. *Mental Retardation,* 1975, *13*(6), 14–16.

Edmonds, M. H. New directions in theories of language acquisition. *Harvard Educational Review,* 1976, *46,* 175–198.

Ellis, N. R. Toilet training the severely defective patient: An S-R reinforcement analysis. *American Journal of Mental Deficiency,* 1963, *68,* 98–103.

Ferneti, C. L., Lent, J. R., & Stevens, C. J. *Project MORE: Eating.* Bellevue, Wash.: Edmark Associates, 1974.

Finnie, N. R. *Handling the young cerebral palsied child at home* (2nd ed.). New York: E. P. Dutton, 1975.

Foxx, R. M., & Azrin, N. H. Dry pants: A rapid method of toilet training children. *Behavior Research and Therapy,* 1973, *11,* 435–442. (a)

Foxx, R. M., & Azrin, N. H. *Toilet training the retarded: A rapid program for day and nighttime independent toileting.* Champaign, Ill.: Research Press, 1973. (b)

Foxx, R. M., & Azrin, N. H. *Toilet training in less than a day.* New York: Simon & Schuster, 1974.

Fredericks, H. D. B., Baldwin, V. L., Grove, D. N., & Moore, W. G. *Toilet training the handicapped child.* Monmouth, Ore.: Instructional Development Corporation, 1975.

Gesell, A., & Amatruda, C. S. *Developmental diagnosis: Normal and abnormal child development.* New York: Harper & Row, 1947.

Giles, D. K., & Wolf, M. M. Toilet training institutionalized severe retardates: An application of operant behavior modification techniques. *American Journal of Mental Deficiency,* 1966, *70,* 766–780.

Gold, M. W. *Meeting the needs of the handicapped.* Paper presented to the National Bicentennial Conference on Vocational Education, Minneapolis, Minnesota, October 11, 1976.

Groves, I. D., & Carroccio, D. F. A self-feeding program for the severely and profoundly retarded. *Mental Retardation,* 1971, *9*(3), 10–12.

Hamre, S., & Williams, W. Family-life curriculum. In L. Brown, W. Williams, & T. Crowner (Eds.), *A collection of papers and programs related to public school services for severely handicapped students,* Vol. IV. Madison, Wis.: University of Wisconsin, 1974.

Henderson, S. & McDonald, M. *Step-by-step dressing.* Champaign, Ill.: Surburban Publications, 1973.

Herreshoff, J. K. Two electronic devices for toilet training. *Mental Retardation,* 1973, *11*(6), 54–55.

Holser-Buehler, P. The Blanchard method of feeding the cerebral palsied. *American Journal of Occupational Therapy,* 1966, *20,* 31–34.

Horner, R. D., Billionis, C. S., & Lent, J. R. *Project MORE: Toothbrushing.* Bellevue, Wash.: Edmark Associates, 1975.

Horner, R. D., & Keilitz, I. Training mentally retarded adolescents to brush their teeth. *Journal of Applied Behavior Analysis,* 1975, *8,* 301–309.

Hundziak, M., Maurer, R. A., & Watson, L. S. Operant conditioning in toilet training of severely retarded boys. *American Journal of Mental Deficiency,* 1965, *70,* 120–124.

Ingenthron, D., Ferneti, C. L., & Keilitz, I. *Project MORE: Nose blowing.* Bellevue, Wash.: Edmark Associates, 1975.

Jones, G. H. The behavioral treatment of enuresis nocturna. In H. J. Eysenck (Ed.), *Behavior therapy and the neuroses,* Oxford: Pergamon Press, 1960.

Keilitz, I., Horner, R. D., & Brown, K. H. *Project MORE: Complexion care.* Bellevue, Wash.: Edmark Associates, 1975.

Kempton, W. *Sex education for persons with disabilities that hinder learning: A teacher's guide.* Belmont, Calif.: Wadsworth, 1975.

Lemke, H., & Mitchell, R. D. Controlling the behavior of a profoundly retarded child: A self-feeding program. *American Journal of Occupational Therapy,* 1972, *26,* 261–264.

Levine, M. N., & Elliot, C. B. Toilet training for profoundly retarded with a limited staff. *Mental Retardation,* 1970, *8*(3), 48–50.

Lewis, P. J., Ferneti, C. L., & Keilitz, I. *Project MORE: Hair washing.* Bellevue, Wash.: Edmark Associates, 1975. (a)

Lewis, P. J., Ferneti, C. L., & Keilitz, I., *Project MORE: Use of deodorant.* Bellevue, Wash.: Edmark Associates, 1975. (b)

Linford, M. D., Hipsher, L. W., & Silikovitz, R. G. *Systematic instruction for retarded children: The Illinois program. Part III: Self-help instruction.* Danville, Ill.: Interstate, 1972.

Lohman, W., Eyman, R., & Lask, E. Toilet training. *American Journal of Mental Deficiency,* 1967, *71,* 551–557.

Lovibond, S. H. The mechanism of conditioning treatment of enuresis. *Behavior Research and Therapy,* 1963, *1,* 17–21.

Lovibond, S. H. *Conditioning and enuresis.* New York: Macmillan, 1964.

Macey, P. G. *Mobilizing multiply-handicapped children: A manual for the design and construction of modified wheelchairs.* Lawrence, Kans.: Division of Continuing Education, University of Kansas, 1974.

Mahoney, K., VanWagenen, R. K., & Meyerson, L. Toilet training of normal and retarded children. *Journal of Applied Behavior Analysis,* 1971, *4,* 173–181.

Marshall, G. R. Toilet training of an autistic eight-year-old through conditioning therapy: A case report. *Behavior Research and Therapy,* 1966, *4,* 242–245.

Martin, G.L., Kehoe, B., Bird, E., Jensen, V., & Darbyshire, M. Operant conditioning in dressing behavior of severely retarded girls. *Mental Retardation,* 1971, *9*(3), 27-30.

McCormack, J. E., Hamlet, C. C., Dunaway, J., & Vorderer, L. E. *Educational evaluation and planning package, Vol. 1,* Medford, Mass.: Massachusetts Center for Program Development and Evaluation, 1976.

Meuller, H. Facilitating feeding and pre-speech. In P. Pearson & C. Williams (Eds.), *Physical therapy services in developmental disabilities.* Springfield, Ill.: Charles C Thomas, 1972.

Meuller, H. Feeding. In N. R. Finnie (Ed.), *Handling the young cerebral palsied child at home.* New York: E. P. Dutton, 1975.

Minge, M. R., & Ball, T. S. Teaching of self-help skills to profoundly retarded patients. *American Journal of Mental Deficiency,* 1967, *71,* 864–868.

Mowrer, O. H., & Mowrer, W. M. Enuresis: A method for its study and treatment. *American Journal of Orthopsychiatry,* 1938, *8,* 436–459.

Nelson, G. L., Cone, J. D., & Hanson C. R. Training correct utensil use in retarded children: Modeling vs. physical guidance. *American Journal of Mental Deficiency,* 1975, *80,* 114–122.

O'Brien, F., & Azrin, N. H. Developing proper mealtime

behaviors of the institutionalized retarded. *Journal of Applied Behavior Analysis,* 1972, *5,* 389–399.

O'Brien, F., Bugle, C., & Azrin, N. H. Training and maintaining a retarded child's proper eating. *Journal of Applied Behavior Analysis,* 1972, *5,* 67–73.

Osarchuk, M. Operant methods of toilet behavior training of the severely and profoundly retarded: A review. *Journal of Special Education,* 1973, *7,* 423–437.

Pipes, P. *Nutrition in infancy and childhood.* St. Louis: C. V. Mosby, in press.

Schmidt, P. Feeding assessment and therapy for the neurologically impaired. *AAESPH Review,* 1976, *1*(8), 19–27.

Seiger, H. W. Treatment of essential nocturnal enuresis. *Journal of Pediatrics,* 1952, *40,* 738–749.

Sloop, W. E., & Kennedy, W. A. Institutionalized retarded nocturnal enuretics treated by a conditioning technique. *American Journal of Mental Deficiency,* 1973, *77,* 717–721.

Smith, D. D., & Smith, J. O. Research and application of a prototypic model for instructional material development. In N. G. Haring (Ed.), *A program project for the investigation and application of procedures of analysis and modification of behavior of handicapped children: Annual report.* National Institute of Education Grant OEG–0–70–3916 (607), 1974.

Somerton, M. E., & Turner, K. D. *Pennsylvania training model: Individual assessment guide.* King of Prussia, Pa.: Regional Resources Center of Eastern Pennsylvania for Special Education, 1975.

Song, A. Y., & Gandhi, R. An analysis of behavior during the acquisition and maintenance phases of self-spoon feeding skills of profound retardates. *Mental Retardation,* 1974, *12*(1), 25–28.

Stainback, S., Healy, H., Stainback, W., & Healy, J. Teaching basic eating skills. *AAESPH Review,* 1976, *1*(7), 26–35.

Sternat, J., Messina, R., Lyon, S. & Nietupski, J. Curricular suggestions for teaching severely handicapped students selected clusters of head control skills. In E. Sontag (Ed.), *Educational programming for the severely and profoundly handicapped.* Reston, Va.: Division on Mental Retardation, Council for Exceptional Children, 1977.

Stevens, C. J., Ferneti, C. L., & Lent, J. R. *Project MORE: Handwashing.* Bellevue, Wash.: Edmark Associates, 1975.

Sugaya, K. Survey of the enureses problem in an institution for the mentally retarded with emphasis on the clinical psychological aspects. *Japanese Journal of Child Psychiatry,* 1967, *8,* 142–150.

Utley, B., Holvoet, J., & Barnes, K. Handling, positioning, and feeding the physically handicapped. In Sontag, E. (Ed.), *Educational programming for severely and profoundly handicapped.* Reston, Va.: Division on Mental Retardation, Council for Exceptional Children, 1977.

Uzgiris, I. C., & Hunt, J. McV. *Assessment in infancy: Ordinal scales of psychological development.* Urbana, Ill.: University of Chicago Press, 1975.

VanWagenen, R. K., Meyerson, L., Kerr, N. J., & Mahoney, K. Field trials of a new procedure for toilet training. *Journal of Experimental Child Psychology,* 1969, *8,* 147–159.

VanWagenen, R. K., & Murdock, E. E. A transistorized signal-package for toilet training of infants. *Journal of Experimental Child Psychology,* 1966, *3,* 312–314.

Yates, A. J. *Behavior therapy.* New York: John Wiley, 1970.

Note

1. Training Resource Center, *Toilet Training Equipment.* Unpublished manuscript, 1973. Available from Training Resource Center, Longley School, Mansfield Training School, Mansfield Depot, Connecticut 06251.

Introduction to Chapter 8

In this next chapter the instructional task becomes even more difficult—the assessment and teaching of social skills. The task is difficult because social behavior is not at all "self-contained." That is, the skills we call "social" overlap extensively with physical movement abilities, reasoning and communication, and even the skills of self-help, daily living, and vocational activity. The goals for instruction will include not only the building of adaptive social behaviors but also the elimination of maladaptive behaviors that interfere with appropriate interaction with others.

One visible trait that frequently characterizes the children and adults we work with, setting them off from the less handicapped, is their deficiencies in social behavior. Deficiencies may appear anywhere along the sequence of social development from smiling and reaching toward the caregiver, to the various emerging forms of play (isolate, parallel, and social play), appropriate imitation of others, and finally social conversation and the pursuit of friendship. At times deficiencies in social behavior are accompanied by inappropriate behavioral excesses —rocking, hand staring, self-injury—and incongruous social interactions—hitting others, food and toy stealing, exhibitionism.

Fortunately strategies to develop social interaction and social responsibility with the severely handicapped have been empirically applied in classroom settings. These include teaching students to play (Boer, 1968; Bradtke, Kirkpatrick, & Rosenblatt, 1972; Keeran, Grove, & Zachofsky, 1969), to ask questions of adults and peers (Twardosz & Baer, 1973), to verbalize current events to others (Keilitz, Tucker, & Horner, 1973), to reduce social isolation (Allen, Hart, Buell, Harris, & Wolf, 1964; Kirby & Toler, 1970; Milby, 1970), to understand the concept of personal property (Bloom, Armstrong, Longhi, & Follett, 1971), to increase smiling at oth-ers (Hopkins, 1968), to stop stereotypic behavior (Repp, Deitz, & Speir, 1974), to curb and control physical aggression (Foxx & Azrin, 1971), and to eliminate inappropriate sexual behavior such as dis-robing (Foxx, 1975) while learning appropriate ways to interact with members of the opposite sex (Vockell & Mattick, 1972).

In Chapter 8, Wes Williams and his colleagues present at least two frameworks within which to conceptualize the development of social skills. These frameworks concern the emergence of social interaction and the development of leisure time skills. They provide the teacher with guidelines for assessment and instruction so that socialization programs may be implemented for students demonstrating severe impairment in social skills.

References

Allen, K. E., Hart, B., Buell, J. S., Harris, F. R., & Wolf, M. M. Effects of social reinforcement on isolate behavior of a nursery school child. *Child Development,* 1964, *35,* 511–518.

Bloom, B., Armstrong, J., Longhi, P., & Follett, R. New instructional program teaches personal property concept to trainable children. *Teaching Exceptional Children,* 1971, *3,* 195–200.

Boer, A. P. Application of a simple recording system to the analysis of free-play behavior in autistic children. *Journal of Applied Behavior Analysis,* 1968, *1,* 335–340.

Bradtke, L. M., Kirkpatrick, W. J., & Rosenblatt, K. P. Intensive play: A technique for building affective behaviors in profoundly mentally retarded young children. *Education and Training of the Mentally Retarded,* 1972, *7,* 8–13.

Foxx, R. M. The use of overcorrection to eliminate the public disrobing (stripping) of retarded women. *Behaviour Research and Therapy,* 1975, *13,* 1–9.

Foxx, R. M., & Azrin, N. H. Restitution: A method of eliminating aggressive-disruptive behavior of retarded and brain-damaged patients. *Behaviour Research and Therapy*, 1971, *10*, 15–27.

Hopkins, B. L. Effects of candy and social reinforcement, instructions and reinforcement schedule learning on the modification and maintenance of smiling. *Journal of Applied Behavior Analysis*, 1968, *1*, 121–129.

Keeran, C. V., Grove, F. A., & Zachofsky, T. Assessing the playground skills of the profoundly retarded. *Mental Retardation*, 1969, *7* (3), 29–32.

Keilitz, I., Tucker, D. J., & Horner, R. D. Increasing mentally retarded adolescents' verbalizations about current events. *Journal of Applied Behavior Analysis*, 1973, *6*, 621–630.

Kirby, F. D., & Toler, H. C. Modification of preschool isolate behavior: A case study. *Journal of Applied Behavior Analysis*, 1970, *3*, 309–314.

Milby, J. B. Modification of extreme social isolation by contingent social reinforcement. *Journal of Applied Behavior Analysis*, 1970, *3*, 149–152.

Repp, A. C., Deitz, S. M., & Speir, N. C. Reducing stereotypic responding of retarded persons by the differential reinforcement of other behavior. *American Journal of Mental Deficiency*, 1974, *79*, 279–284.

Twardosz, S., & Baer, D. M. Training two severely retarded adolescents to ask questions. *Journal of Applied Behavior Analysis*, 1973, *6*, 655–661.

Vockell, E., & Mattick, P. Sex education for the mentally retarded: An analysis of problems, programs, and research. *Education and Training of the Mentally Retarded*, 1972, *7*, 129–134.

Teaching Social Skills

This chapter was written by **Wes Williams,** University of Vermont; **Sue Hamre-Nietupski,** University of Wisconsin; **Ian Pumpian,** University of Wisconsin; **Jaci McDaniel-Marx,** University of Wisconsin; and **Jill Wheeler,** Madison Public Schools.

This chapter was supported in part by Special Projects Training Grant PR# 451AH6 to the University of Vermont; Grant OE G–0–73–6137 to the University of Wisconsin, Madison, from the U.S. Department of Health, Education, and Welfare, U.S. Office of Education, Bureau of Education of the Handicapped, Division of Personnel Preparation; and in part by funds from Federal Contract OEC–0–74–7993 to the Madison Public Schools.

This chapter is divided into two major sections. The first presents selected considerations related to teaching social skills to severely handicapped individuals. The second major section describes how the authors have incorporated those considerations into an instructional program.

For purposes of this chapter, the term "social" is an adjective which characterizes interactions among people. Any time people interact with others they are manifesting social skills. However, we do not limit ourselves to delineating procedures for teaching individuals to appropriately interact with others; we also include procedures for teaching in-dividuals to engage in activities by themselves (isolative activities). The frequency, time, and places individuals engage in isolative activities affect the frequency, time, and places for their interactions with others. Furthermore, isolative activities, when appropriate, usually occur within a particular social context.

Findings from Related Research

Although many severely handicapped individuals can be taught self-help, language, motor, and basic vocational skills, they often do not perform acceptably in home living, recreational, and vocational settings because of inadequate social skills (e.g., Goldstein, 1964; Seeley, 1971). Social skills can be taught or altered through systematic environmental manipulations (e.g., Azrin & Lindsley, 1956; Buell, Stoddard, Harris, & Baer, 1968; Kale, Kaze, Whelan, & Hopkins, 1968; Kirby & Toler, 1970; Koegel, Firestone, & Kramme, 1974; Milby, 1970; Morris & Dolker, 1974; O'Connor, 1969; Paloutzian, Hasazi, Striefel, & Edgard, 1971; Quilitch & Risley, 1973; Stokes, Baer, & Jackson, 1974; Updegraff & Herbst, 1933; Wahler, 1967; Whitman, Mercurio, & Caponigri, 1970). However, as noted in a review by Wehman (1977), the role of specific instructional procedures such as verbal directions, modeling, manual guidance, and external reinforcement have not been clearly identified for teaching social skills.

Many studies have applied various procedures for decreasing or eliminating undesirable social behaviors such as rumination, tantrums, physical aggression (Berkson & Landesman-Dwyer, 1977) by means of withdrawing social reinforcement after the performance of the undesired behavior (extinction); isolating the individual after the performance of an undesirable behavior (time-out); reinforcing an activity which is incompatible with the performance of an undesirable behavior; and punishing the individual for performing an undesirable behavior. In some cases, decreasing undesirable behaviors may result in the spontaneous increase of play behaviors. Koegel, Firestone, Kramme, and Dunlap (1974) studied appropriate toy play of two autistic children with high occurrences of self-stimulatory behavior. They found that when they punished self-stimulatory behaviors (by sharply saying "No" and briskly slapping or briefly holding the part of the child's body that was performing the self-stimulatory behavior), the behavior decreased and spontaneous play with toys increased. However, other studies (e.g., Baumeister & Rollings, 1976) report that decreasing one undesirable behavior may result in the increase in another undesirable behavior. To prevent this problem, programs designed to decrease an undesirable behavior should always be accompanied by a program designed to increase a desirable behavior which may be substituted for the undesirable behavior.

A number of studies have documented procedures to teach severely handicapped individuals elementary social skills. Studies by Wehman, Karan, and Rettie (1976), Kazdin and Erickson (1975), and Hopper and Wambold (1976) report increasing severely handicapped individuals' actions on play materials by manually guiding, modeling, and reinforcing actions with toys and games. Increases in desirable play activities were accompanied by decreases in stereotypic and self-abusive behaviors. Several studies have reported teaching cooperative play skills to severely handicapped individuals. Paloutzian et al. (1971) used modeling to teach children to pull peers in wagons, roll a ball cooperatively, and share play materials. In another study, Whitman et al. (1970) employed physical guidance and modeling to teach two severely handicapped children to roll a ball back and forth.

In a review of the research on recreation programs for the mentally retarded, Wehman (1977) summarizes strategies that have been reported in the literature for teaching cooperative play and social interactions to severely handicapped individuals.

1. A child can be paired with an adult trainer and trained in different play situations.
2. A child can be paired with a higher functioning, although still retarded, peer who engages in appropriate play.
3. A child can be paired with a nonretarded peer who engages in appropriate play.
4. Two equivalent (low functioning) peers can be paired and trained by one or more trainers.
5. A group of severely handicapped children can be integrated with nonretarded peers.
6. Any of the previous combinations can be utilized and different types of reinforcement given, i.e., points, edibles, or praise for instances of cooperative play.
7. Environmental arrangements preceding the onset of play session may be manipulated through toy selection, room size or background music. (p. 26)

The definition of social skills in research studies has, however, been limited. Only a few studies (e.g., Nietupski & Williams, 1974; Wehman, 1977; Williams, Pumpian, McDaniel, Hamre-Nietupski, & Wheeler, 1975) have defined a broad range of social skills and describe procedures for teaching severely handicapped individuals to perform them. One reason for the paucity of research in this area is the complexity of social activities. This leads to difficulties in defining, teaching, and measuring skills related to the activities. A basic framework for defining and teaching social skills (Hamre-Nietupski & Williams, 1976; Williams, Pumpian, McDaniel, Hamre-Nietupski, & Wheeler, 1975) is given below.

Basic Components of Isolative and Cooperative Social Activities

Social activities which primarily involve individuals engaging in isolative activities may be described as consisting of at least four basic components:

1. *Initiating* isolative activities at appropriate times and in appropriate places.
2. *Selecting and locating* a toy, game, or object appropriate for an independent activity (e.g., students go to free-time cabinet and select an activity).

3. *Sustaining* an appropriate activity with the selected toy (e.g., completion of a puzzle, completion of a page, completion of a work task).
4. *Terminating* the activity properly (e.g., cleaning up the play area, putting away work materials).

Social activities which involve individuals interacting extensively with others (e.g., associative and cooperative social activities) may be conceived of as consisting of at least five basic components:

1. *Recognition* of the appropriate *time* and *place* for a social interaction.
2. *Initiating* interactions.
3. *Receiving* requests for interactions.
4. *Sustaining* interaction.
5. *Terminating* interactions.

Initiating an interaction involves asking another individual to participate in an activity, such as, "Do you want to listen to records?" Receiving a request for an interaction requires that the recipient determine whether he desires and can participate in an activity and either accept or decline the invitation. Sustaining an activity involves participating in the activity. Terminating an activity means the participants must determine that an activity is over, that they want to do something else, and/or that the time allotted for the activity has expired. The participants should then indicate that the activity is over and perform any necessary tasks involved in terminating it, such as putting the records away and saying "See you later."

Students should learn to independently perform skills related to these basic components across motor, language, academic, self-care, and recreational tasks which occur throughout their day. For example, students may be taught to recognize when it is break-time and then independently initiate the preparation for break-time activities, receive initiations for social interactions which revolve around the break, sustain break activities, and terminate break activities.

Most individuals engage in and/or may be taught to engage in social activities within the initiate, receive, sustain, and terminate framework. However, the behaviors students perform to initiate, receive, sustain, and terminate interactions should be selected on the basis of their current functioning levels. Students who are motorically impaired or nonverbal may be provided an alternative means to respond in social interactions. The matrices in Figure 8.1 describe some alternatives for severely and multiply handicapped students in social interactions.

Let us use a specific case to illustrate the use of this interaction matrix. For example, Dan is a 14-year-old, severely multiply handicapped boy. He has oral-motor handicaps which currently make speech an unrealistic goal for him. Dan is nonambulatory, but has good head control and visual tracking skills. He has limited use of his arms and hands, but can grossly manipulate objects. Dan's motor problems with his arms and hands do not make sign language a viable alternative for him. Our social goals for Dan could include:

Initiate: Dan will look at and point to objects and people to initiate an interaction. Eventually it is planned to teach him to use a communication board.

Receive:
  Accept: Dan will accept initiations to engage in an activity by nodding his head up and down.
  Decline: Dan will decline initiations to engage in an interaction by shaking his head from side to side.

Sustain: Dan will be taught to engage in isolative and cooperative activities such as block play, puzzle play, bubbles, ball activities. Each activity will be task analyzed and taught through manual guidance and modeling.

Terminate: Dan will be taught to terminate an interaction by looking away to indicate "done."

This sequence of social behaviors (initiate, receive, sustain, and terminate) is oversimplified and only approximates the exchange among persons interacting socially. Most social situations involve a great deal more "give and take" among the participants in terms of gestures, humor, small talk, gossip, "emotion," "affect," and general conversation. However, teaching individuals who are first acquiring these skills to socially interact requires that the interaction process be structured and simplified initially to facilitate measurement and teaching. Once students learn to perform this simple sequence of responses with others who are also learning, then instruction would shift to include peers demonstrating more complex levels of social interaction. With prompting from adults, peers may model basic skills and the complexities and subtle nuances involved in social activities (Morris & Dolker, 1974; Wahler, 1967).

To facilitate learning through peer modeling, any unpleasant characteristics of students such as tantrums, hitting, and bad breath should be decreased; attentive skills may have to be shaped so that stu-

INITIATE

RECEIVE

	Accepts Initiation	Declines Initiation
Nonvocal 1. Looks at object and/or person 2. Reaches for object and/or person 3. Smiles at object and/or person 4. Points to object and/or person 5. Points to picture of object and/or person on a communication board 6. Uses sign language to initiate	**Nonvocal** 1. Looks at object or person 2. Reaches for object or person 3. Smiles at object or person 4. Shakes head yes 5. Uses communication board to indicate "yes" 6. Uses sign language to indicate "yes"	**Nonvocal** 1. Looks away 2. Pushes object or person away 3. Frowns 4. Shakes head no 5. Uses communication board to indicate "no" 6. Uses sign language to indicate "no"
Vocal 1. Vocalizes at an object and/or person 2. Says the name of an object and/or person 3. Asks "Do you want to _____?", "Would you _____?", "Please _____," and so on.	**Vocal** 1. Makes a sound which indicates "yes" 2. Says "yes"	**Vocal** 1. Makes a sound which indicates "no" 2. Says "no" 3. Says "no, some other time" and/or suggests an alternate activity

SUSTAIN

TERMINATE

SUSTAIN	TERMINATE

Chooses an activity appropriate to the skill level of the individual, such as:
 	
  balls
  blocks
  logs
  paddle ball
  bubbles
  table games
	Nonvocal
	
	1. Looks away
	2. Pushes object or person away
	3. Uses communication board to indicate "done"
	4. Uses sign language to indicate "done"
	
	Vocal
	
	1. Says "done," "see you later"

FIGURE 8.1   *Sample social interaction matrices*

dents may benefit from peer instruction; and rudimentary initiation, receiving, sustaining, and termination skills may have to be taught by adults. In some cases it may not be necessary to use extraordinary procedures to teach all the complex behaviors involved in social activities (Wahler, 1967; Nietupski & Williams, 1974). That is, once students learn the basic social skills and begin engaging in social interactions, the natural contingencies in such interactions may shape the subtle nuances involved in social activities. A potential advantage of this instructional strategy is that peers facilitate the acquisition, maintenance, and generalization of social skills and control of social situations is shifted from adults to peers. Such a shift of control follows the "normal developmental" pattern.

Self-regulatory skills

In addition to basic social skills, the ability to function in social situations also involves thinking critically, determining relevant information, and acting on information independently. Williams, Brown, and Certo (1975), in stating their position on independent functioning in social situations, write,   ·

> Individuals labelled severely handicapped are often referred to as externally controlled. That is, persons in authority usually tell them what skills to perform; how and when to perform the skills; if they perform the skills correctly or incorrectly; if they perform the skills incorrectly, how to rectify the errors etc. While responding appropriately to specific cues provided by persons in authority is the responsibility of all adults, there are situations in which performance is crucial but in which persons in authority are not present. In such situations it appears that severely handicapped individuals are particularly deficient and therefore quite vulnerable. One way to compensate for such a deficit is to teach specific skills, and then insure that those skills can be performed appropriately across environmental configurations without specific verbal cues being provided by persons in authority. Perhaps the following will elucidate.
>
> Undoubtedly, there are thousands of situations in adulthood which require responding specifically to verbal or other cues provided by persons in authority. However, there are also situations which require that adults engage in a response or series of responses in the absence of cues to respond provided by persons in authority (e.g., when a person is presented with a burning sofa; when a person is alone and cuts a finger; when a person is lonely or lost; when shopping for food or clothing). If a person responds appropriately when persons in authority are not providing specific cues to respond, that person may be construed as manifesting self-initiated performance skills. Obviously self-initiated performance skills are crucial to the independent functioning of severely handicapped individuals.
>
> Finally, there are situations which require that a person engage in a series of responses, evaluate the correctness of the responses, and, if necessary, correct mistakes without being verbally cued by an authority figure. For example, if a person is confronted with a burning sofa, he/she might smother it with a throw rug, check to see if

it is still smoking, and, if necessary, pour water on it.

It has been our experience that many classroom activities designed for severely handicapped students have not included manipulations that allow individuals to: a) perform skills in the absence of cues provided by persons in authority; and b) evaluate and, if necessary, correct errors.

Thus, we are suggesting here that teachers determine if it is appropriate for a particular skill to be performed without specific cues to do so provided by persons in authority. If so, teachers should arrange for such performance. In addition, if it is appropriate that individuals perform a series of responses, evaluate the responses, and, if necessary, correct errors, then teachers should also arrange for such a performance.

In the recent past the writers and their colleagues have made attempts to teach severely handicapped individuals the skills necessary to initiate responses or a series of responses, to evaluate the correctness of the responses made, and if necessary, to correct errors with few if any cues provided by persons in authority. Such skills are referred to here as self-regulation skills. Nietupski and Williams (1974) conceived of rudimentary self-regulation skills as consisting of at least four steps:

1. Detecting or defining the task
2. Arriving at alternative ways to complete the task ◄
3. Implementing an alternative
4. Assessing the outcome of the alternative — if the task is not correctly completed — if task correctly completed, end of task

In the Nietupski and Williams (1974) paradigm, individuals may fail to self-regulate responding because: a) they do not self-initiate steps in the self-regulation strategy; b) they fail to detect or define the task; c) they fail to arrive at an appropriate way to complete the task; d) they fail to implement an appropriate alternative; or e) they fail to evaluate the outcome correctly.

It is suggested here that self-regulation may be incorporated into a curriculum for severely handicapped individuals as follows: When a skill is taught, if practical, the individual should be required to initiate all components of the self-regulation strategy to complete tasks related to that

that skill without verbal cueing from persons in authority. For example, if individuals are acquiring skills related to cooking, they should be required to initiate the preparation of their own meals without verbal cueing from authority figures. Stated another way, whenever a new skill is taught individuals should be required to complete tasks related to the skill, generate alternative ways of completing the task, implement an alternative, and check the appropriateness of the alternative implemented. Self-regulation strategies should not be taught as segmented or isolated curriculum entities but as internal parts of all activities in which students participate.

Hopefully, if educators in conjunction with parents and other concerned persons can teach students to perform situationally appropriate skills without specific direction to do so, we will more closely approximate the longitudinal objective of independent adult functioning. (pp. 133–135)

The initiate, receive, sustain, and terminate paradigm may be used as a basic framework for conceptualizing social activities. However, as suggested by Wehman (1977), studies on the "normal" development of social activities which describe the learning of sustained cooperative play, should be considered when designing a social skills instructional program. These studies and their implications for teaching are discussed next.

Developmental Analysis of Social Activities

There is a body of developmental literature which divides the development of social skills into various stages or levels (e.g., Ellis, 1973; Parten, 1932; Piaget, 1952). Obviously, all developmentalists do not agree on how many critical levels there are, on the operational definitions of the levels, on the chronological order of the levels, and so on. However, the levels delineated by Parten (1932) are fairly representative of the literature and have been documented by Gesell (1940) and Barnes (1971).

Levels of social activities

Autistic level. Child shows little or no awareness of others or of environment; engages in self-stimulatory behavior; head banging, slapping, rocking, eye-pressing, and so on.

Unoccupied level. Child shows some awareness of the environment but makes no attempt to interact with it; sits, walks aimlessly; looks around room or out of window; may observe activities of others from a distance or for a few seconds.

Independent level. Child plays with toys or objects, but in an isolated manner; makes no attempt to interact with others.

Observing level. Child approaches others and observes their activities without any attempt at involvement; may attempt to sit near others without interacting with them; observation of others must be of a sustained nature.

Attempted interaction level. Child initiates some attempt at interaction with others; attempts to engage in same activity or occupy same location; vocalizes to get attention of others; interaction can be positive or negative, e.g., hitting or pushing another, but, if negative, should not be merely self-defensive.

Parallel interaction level. Child plays independently, but in a way which brings him closer to others; may utilize same toys, e.g., playing side by side in sandbox; plays *beside* rather than with others; devotes full awareness to the activity of the other child.

Associative interaction level. Child plays with others but activity does not require mutual participation; may play with same materials, borrowing and lending; exchanging play materials; following one another with trains or wagons; engaging in similar activities.

Cooperative interaction level. Child interacts with others in activity which necessitates mutual participation; plays ball with others; plays on swings with one child pushing, and so on.

Although this sequence has *not* been validated for handicapped populations, it may be useful in documenting changes in social behaviors. For example Williams, Pumpian, McDaniel, Hamre-Nietupski, and Wheeler (1975) operationally defined each level of the hierarchy and then observed students engaging in social activities and scored the level of social activity using the data sheet shown in Figure 8.2. To evaluate level of social activities they first described what behaviors the student was engaged in, such as staring into space, playing with clay, and so on. Next, the social activity level was scored as autistic, unoccupied, independent, observing, attempted interaction, parallel interaction, associative

Behaviors	Duration of Behavior	Level of Social Activities Behavior
1.		
2.		
3.		
4.		
5.		

FIGURE 8.2   *Assessment sheet for social activities*

interaction, or cooperative interaction. The duration of a behavior was measured so that the percentage of time engaged in each behavior could be calculated. First the total time engaged in all behaviors was summed. To calculate the percentage of time engaged in, for example, playing with clay, the total time was divided into the time spent playing with clay. This information provided basic data on behaviors engaged in by students and whether they socially interacted at isolative or cooperative levels. Periodic observation and measurement of students' social activity levels may be used to assess and document changes in the behaviors engaged in and level of social interaction.

The Parten levels do not indicate that during early development children interact with parents or adults primarily and therefore that adults have primary control of their behavior. Over time, peers interact more with the individual and exert greater increments of control over the individual's behavior, until in many cases peers exert more control and interact more with the individual than do adult authority figures (Harris, Wolf, & Baer, 1964; Hartup, 1964; McCoy & Zigler, 1965).

This cursory analysis indicates that an individual's social activities typically change from isolative to parallel to cooperative and from social activities primarily controlled by adults to those controlled by peers. Although this description oversimplifies the developmental emergence of social activities, it provides a background for the discussion which follows.

Normative Analysis of Social Activities

The fact that an individual's social activities change over time and the usual direction of the change is useful information. However, even though the developmental literature suggests that cooperative social activities eventually supersede some isola-

tive social activities, this information is not sufficient for developing social skill programs for severely handicapped individuals. The developmental literature does not clearly specify: (A) the frequency that individuals engage in the various levels of social activities; (B) the appropriate time and place to engage in a social activity; (C) the chronological age (CA) appropriate for various tasks (e.g., games, work tasks, community survival tasks) related to social activities; and (D) how one might adjust the normal developmental sequence to suit the handicapped learner.

Individuals typically engage in all levels of social activities (e.g., autistic, unoccupied, isolative, observational, attempted interactions, parallel, associative, and cooperative). For instance, most adults spend time engaged in autistic activities such as strumming their fingers and tapping their toes. However, it is not appropriate for individuals to engage frequently in activities at only one social activity level. In addition, some social activities, if engaged in frequently, have more socially "deviant" connotations than others. An individual who displays autistic activities at a high rate may be considered to be more "deviant" than an individual who engages in cooperative activities frequently.

The appropriateness of social activities also should be determined in relation to time and place. Before implementing a program to teach selected social skills to severely handicapped individuals, the frequency, times, and settings in which those skills are to be performed should be determined. If the objective of an instructional program is to teach individuals social skills appropriate to a vocational setting, a recreational setting, or a home-living setting, first assess what social skills are needed in those settings and then teach those skills.

A normative analysis of social activities may be accomplished through using the data collection format depicted in Figure 8.2. To determine what social skills are typically performed in a specified setting, measure the behaviors, the level of social activity (e.g., isolative, cooperative, and so on), and the duration of these behaviors. The goals of a student's educational program may then be set in relation to teaching the student to engage in the observed behaviors at the appropriate social activity level (e.g., isolative and cooperative) for an acceptable period of time.

In considering what social skills an individual should be taught, it is essential to delineate the difference between considerations related to developmental or "normative" analysis and appropriate social skill instructional objectives. Developmental analysis indicates that individuals participate in autistic, unoccupied, isolative, attempted, parallel, associative, and cooperative social activities and in that order. However, in many instances it may not be realistic or necessary to implement instructional programs for each level of social activity at appropriate frequencies, times, and places. For example, once individuals have learned the skills involved in cooperative and isolative activities, they should engage in observational, attempted, and parallel activities without intensive instruction, because the skills involved are components of cooperative and isolative activities. Similarly, autistic and unoccupied activities should also occur without training. In addition, teaching isolative and cooperative activities should significantly affect the frequency, time, and place when autistic, unoccupied, parallel, and associative activities are manifested. The more frequently individuals engage in cooperative activities, the less frequently they may engage in autistic and unoccupied activities.

Given these considerations, it would be wise to teach individuals cooperative activities and to attempt to decrease excessive performance of isolative activities (Eckerman, Whatley, & Kutz, 1975; Smith & Connally, 1972). The objective should be to teach individuals to engage in a range of isolative and cooperative social activities at the appropriate frequencies, times, and places. This general rule simplifies the normative analysis of social activities so that we need to be primarily concerned with what isolative and cooperative activities a student should be able to engage in for reasonable durations of time.

Selection of Tasks for Teaching Social Skills

The development of a program to teach social skills requires prior assessment of the student's baseline or current skills. For individuals who demonstrate

only autistic behaviors, the teaching objective would focus upon a variety of isolative and cooperative activities. There are many ways to determine an individual's functioning levels in various skill domains. If students are already participating in the classroom, their observed social skill levels can be used as baseline indicators of their current social skills. Later the tasks being taught in ongoing programs can be restructured so that they constitute the social skills tasks. For example, if an individual is learning basic motor tasks (e.g., rolling, turning, grasping), he/she may be taught to initiate, receive, and terminate interactions which revolve around these tasks.

Task selection and the student's age

Because the functioning levels of severely handicapped students are quite discrepant from their chronological ages, a problem in task selection may arise. Activities selected to suit an individual's functioning level probably will not be suited to his or her chronological age (CA). These tasks are likely to be perceived by others as "retarded" or "different." However, if CA-appropriate tasks are too sophisticated in terms of the required motor or language abilities, a student's performance is likely to be unsuccessful. This may lead the student to prefer simpler tasks. As the student grows into adolescence, an increasing sensitivity to the perception of others often causes rejection of these simpler tasks and a preference for activities enjoyed by their normal age peers. Unfortunately because these tasks involve skills the handicapped individual is often deficient in, this participation is unsatisfying and may lead to frustration and failure.

One should teach social activities through tasks which are adjusted to the individuals' functioning levels. Ellis (1973) suggests that tasks which are not easy or too sophisticated for individuals are not appropriate. However, tasks just at or above the individuals' current functioning levels should be more interesting and act to pace skill development. It is the teacher's responsibility to remain aware of the chronological and skill level discrepancies in a severely handicapped classroom, first by selecting activities which are both popular and suited to a student's CA and second by simplifying these tasks to match the student's skills. For example, the rules and content of common games such as darts, "Old Maid," jacks, and "Bingo" can be changed to match individuals' functioning levels and, as the individuals' functioning levels increase, the rules of the game can be made increasingly more sophisticated. "Bingo" may be made into a picture match-to-sample game where one student holds up a picture and the players select a matching picture which is placed on top of its match on a 9- or 16-square playing card. As the students learn more skills, letters, numbers, and words may be substituted for pictures.

Leisure time activities and social skill instruction

By viewing the emergence of play skills and socialization as being dependent upon increasing amounts of adaptive behavior, Wehman (1976b; 1977) proposes guidelines for the selection of leisure time activities suited to severely handicapped children, adolescents, and adults. Figure 8.3 illustrates 5 tiers or categories of leisure skills: action on play material, passive leisure activity, game activity, hobby activity, and active socialization. While each category requires more sophisticated adaptive be-

havior, subclassifications within each category also represent more advanced forms of that activity tier.

Tier I concerns the development of play which progresses from isolative and simple to cooperative and more abstract. Tiers II (Passive Leisure) and IV (Hobby Activity) represent constructive isolative activities which, though easily performed alone, may serve as a basis for social interaction. To the extent that passive leisure or spectator activities expand from the home environment to community settings, the participant increases the likelihood that the isolative activity will facilitate active socialization. Hobby activities serve not only to occupy leisure time but may also develop responsibility, provide an outlet for expressing creativity, and promote enjoyment. Tiers III (Game Activity) and V (Active Socialization) automatically require social interaction. In the case of game-playing activities, opportunities are provided to practice cooperation and to interact competitively. The category of active socialization begins with simple visitation of peers and extends to purposeful seeking of new acquaintances. Instruc-

INCREASING COMPLEXITY OF ACTIVITY →

MORE ADVANCED LEVELS OF ADAPTIVE BEHAVIOR ↑

TIER V Active Socialization	Has a friend over to visit	Goes out with friends other than family	Goes to mixed-sex parties	Dates members of opposite sex	Joins social clubs or organizations
TIER IV Hobby Activity	Engages in art and craft activity	Keeps scrapbook or collection	Cares for pet	Engages in outdoor activity, i.e. hiking, bike riding	—
TIER III Game Activity	Engages in simple imitation games	Plays ball-related games	Engages in match recognition table games	Engages in table games needing academic skills	—
TIER II Passive Leisure	Turns on radio or television	Plays record player; chooses records	Looks/reads magazines and books	Goes to movie theater	Attends variety of sports/entertainment
TIER I Action on Play Materials	Acts on toy or limited play materials	Plays independently on wide range of materials	Plays with peers cooperatively	Engages in symbolic play	—

FIGURE 8.3   *A leisure time activities curriculum*

Source: P. Wehman, A leisure time activities curriculum for the developmentally disabled. *Education and Training of the Mentally Retarded*, 1976b, *11*, 309–313.

tion within a few of Wehman's subclassifications is described in more detail to illustrate the value of such a framework for selecting instructional tasks and for targeting social behavior. The earliest type of leisure activity at Tier I consists of visually attending to, smiling at, vocalizing to, reaching for, and touching objects and people. It must be emphasized that mastery involves a student's *self-initiated* interaction with objects and people, unprompted by verbal or physical cues provided by the educator. Once the learner consistently self-initiates a specified response (pounding, putting together, pushing, etc.) with a given toy, the criterion for performance of that social skill has been met.

To assess what objects, events, and people a student interacts with, a reinforcement sampling procedure may be used. As described in Chapter 3, the student is presented objects one at a time. The teacher demonstrates the use of each toy. Next, the item is placed in front of the student and it is noted whether the student attends to or touches it, how long this interaction occurs, and the form of the interaction. Student preference for items is assessed by presenting the student with a set of 4 or 5 items. Again, we note how long the pupil interacts with each item and the specific behavior. On the basis of the Premack Principle (Premack, 1959), we categorize the items a student frequently interacts with as high preference items (potential reinforcers) and those that are infrequently interacted with as low preference items.

If students interact with only a few items or with none, we begin by increasing the number of items, with which they interact. Interactions are taught by arranging the student's environment so that reaching for, touching, or looking at items are reinforced by a pleasant result (music being played, a squeeze toy squeaking, or a person smiling). Physical guidance and modeling are used to teach an interaction and then are faded out. As a general rule, when teaching the first subclassification of each tier or category, select objects, play materials, television shows, games, or individuals that are especially liked or "intrinsically" reinforcing (i.e., an action performed on the objects should produce an interesting auditory and/or visual effect). Students who are self-initiating interactions with objects and people are taught to respond to the objects and people in a more sophisticated manner. (Chapters 4 and 5 elaborate upon these procedures.) The items students frequently interact with are selected for this program and instead of just looking at, reaching for, and touching them, they are taught to use them,

such as eat with the spoon, drink from the cup, roll the ball, spin the top, shake the rattle, pound the drum, turn the handle on the music box, and so on. Before teaching students to use objects, first list the subskills involved in the functional use task and sequence the subskills from easy to hard. Next use modeling and physical guidance to teach each subskill.

In addition, students who demonstrate a preference for selected items also should be taught to indicate their wants and needs (initiate interactions) by consistently expressing that they want to interact with one object or person when presented a choice among several. The following sequence may be used to teach initiations.

1. The teacher presents one object, person, and/or event and facilitates the student looking at, reaching for, touching, smiling at, and so on with the object by pairing the object or person with a pleasant event such as food or music.

2. The teacher terminates the event, such as stops squeaking the toy, turns off the record player, stops singing, takes the food away, and asks "Do you want more?"

3. The teacher waits for the student to emit the desired response such as smiling, making a vocalization, or reaching for the object. When the student emits the desired response, the teacher presents the event again, such as turns on the record player, sings, squeaks the toy, or provides more food.

4. The teacher presents at least 2 objects, people, or events from step 3, says "This is a ———and this is a ———," "Show me what you want." When the student points to/reaches for/looks at the object for a specified period of time, the teacher provides the natural consequence associated with the object, person, or event, such as turns on the record player, squeaks the toy, sings, or gives the student a taste of the food. Student choice may be controlled by pairing a high preference item with a low preference item. When the student consistently produces the desired response to obtain the high preference items, she/he has learned a means to obtain a desired object or a desired end—a basis for many aspects of later social and language development.

Play behavior at more advanced levels includes initiating interactions by looking at or reaching for an item; accepting initiations for interactions by looking and reaching; declining interactions by looking away, pushing the item away; sustaining interactions by using objects in a socially appropriate manner or playing a game such as peek-a-boo with a person; and terminating interactions by looking away or pushing the item away. To teach these behaviors, the student's social interaction program is integrated with gross and fine motor components of a curriculum which teach reaching, grasping, visual tracking, and object manipulations.

Speech or nonvocal forms of communication become an important component of a social interaction program in that they represent more efficient methods of initiating, receiving, and terminating social interactions than do looking and reaching behavior. For example, to teach students to initiate interactions, they may be taught to answer "What do you want?" questions. This may be done by presenting a high preference toy, such as bubbles, and a low preference toy, such as blocks, and asking, "What do you want?" The student is taught to indicate what she/he wants by naming the object, signing its name, or by pointing to a corresponding picture, depending upon the student's vocal ability. When the student spontaneously uses language to express a want or need, she/he has learned to initiate rudimentary social interactions. This component of the social interactions program is integrated with a student's expressive language program (Guess, Sailor, & Baer, 1976).

Once students have been taught to follow basic directions through their language program, they may be taught to play simple table games or cooperative activities at Tier III. Table games may be constructed using the language, math, and reading skills a student has just learned and is still reviewing. For example, if students have learned to label objects and to count, the game may involve rolling dice, counting the number of dots displayed, and moving that many squares on a game board. Each square of the gameboard may depict a picture of an object. For students to remain on that square they must correctly label the picture. Other less complex activities include rolling a ball to members of the group; building a construction from blocks, Tinker Toys, or play logs; placing cut-outs on a felt board; matching pictures or objects; etc. These simple games provide not only the opportunity to teach beginning cooperative interaction but also enable overlearning or review of basic concepts.

At this level of social learning, objectives will center upon a number of behaviors related to the specific difficulty of the game activity.

1. Taking turns or learning to wait while another performs and to perform on cue while others in the group wait.
2. Sharing a single set of materials.
3. Remaining at the table or with the group until the activity is over.
4. Visually following the activity as it moves from one participant to another.
5. And, for some activities, completing a product (block tower, all pieces in a form board, etc.).

Integrating social skill instructing into the total curriculum

Ideally a social skills instructional program should be incorporated into an already existing, developmentally based, longitudinal curriculum starting at zero ability level and continuing through advanced levels or secondary programs. The developmental curriculum should provide a framework for the total educational process with objectives in at least the areas of motor, communication, community survival, self-help, functional academics, and social skills. Furthermore, the curriculum should provide a basis for assessing an individual's skill levels, determining instructional objectives, and assessing progress toward specified goals.

The developmental curriculum should correlate all learning areas (e.g., motor, social, academic, communication, community survival), making it possible to design school days to approximate real life and to teach skills relevant for the handicapped individual. Such a curriculum should oppose present programming strategies of teaching isolated bits and pieces of living which are incidental, rather than integral, parts of an individual's life.

When employing this developmental curriculum model to implement instructional programs, 3 or 4 objectives are determined for each curricular area. Instructional tasks are then designed to incorporate target objectives from as many of the curricular areas as is possible. For example, if a student's objectives include use of wet sponge and broom and dustpan, asking for objects in three-word sentences ("I want ———"), completing assigned job, and cooperating with peers, the student could be taught these skills in relation to the task of cleaning up the lunch table and floor after lunch. Another student capable of cooperative interaction would be selected to help. In addition to teaching the specified daily living, language, and prevocational abilities, the social skills of initiating, receiving, and terminating interactions which naturally revolve around the clean-up process could be taught. As illustrated in the final portion of this chapter, the social skills involved in the instructional activity are analyzed so that learning the tasks also involves learning the social skills inherent in completion of the tasks.

Instructional Procedures

Decelerating inappropriate behaviors

Social interactions involve verbal and nonverbal exchange between at least two people. Individuals who frequently engage in inappropriate behavior (e.g., body rocking, teeth grinding) and/or isolate themselves from others will not readily learn to socially interact. One of the first objectives of an educational program should be to decrease inappropriate and isolative behaviors. The following steps may be followed when designing and implementing a program to decelerate inappropriate and isolative behaviors.

1. Perform a descriptive analysis of the student's behavior; observe the student in structured (e.g., instructional programs) and unstructured (e.g., play) situations and describe everything the student does, including what events precede and follow a student's behavior.

2. From the descriptive analysis, specify the behaviors to be accelerated, such as manipulating objects, and behaviors to be decelerated, such as body rocking, teeth grinding, and hand flapping. Define the behaviors. That is, define behaviors in terms that allow them to be measured.

3. Perform a functional analysis of the behaviors of concern. The following format may be used:

Antecedent Event	Behavior	Subsequent Event

Observe the student in structured and unstructured situations and note each occurrence of the operationally defined behaviors and what events precede and follow the behavior. (Chapter 2 provides more detail in techniques of behavior measurement.)

4. Analyze the data and attempt to determine if specific antecedent events are evoking a behavior and if specific subsequent events appear to be maintaining the behavior.

5. Design a program to decelerate the behaviors that cause concern by changing the events which precede and follow the behaviors. The procedures of reinforcing incompatible behaviors, withdrawing reinforcement for undesirable behaviors, isolating an individual for performing undesirable behaviors, and punishment described in Chapter 3 may be employed to decelerate behavior.

As mentioned earlier, it is often ineffective to decrease an undesirable behavior without teaching the student an alternative such as playing with objects. Programs to decrease undesirable behavior should be run concurrently with programs to increase appropriate behaviors. In some cases teaching a student to interact with objects and people which are incompatible with self-stimulation and isolative behavior will decrease such behaviors without a program focused directly on decelerating the behaviors. The aim of behavior modification programs should be on positive goals; that is, building new behavior. *Never* focus a program solely on decelerating behavior.

Teaching social skills

Social skills may be taught through object proximity in conjunction with verbal directions, modeling, and manual guidance. The objective of a social interaction program is for students to self-initiate interactions. Instructional procedures may be ordered according to the level of intervention provided from the most to the least intervention.

1. Manual guidance
2. Modeling
3. Verbal directions
4. Object proximity and appropriate task selection

Object Proximity

The physical placement of objects and materials may elicit spontaneous responses to them (Quilitch & Risley, 1973). Research with profoundly retarded adolescents and adults indicates that object proximity significantly increases their physical actions on objects (Wehman, 1976a). As described previously, materials which produce a visual and/or auditory effect when acted upon should be chosen. Studies by Wehman (1976a) and Williams, Pumpian, McDaniel, Hamre-Nietupski, and Wheeler (1975) indicate that severely and profoundly handicapped individuals demonstrate some preference for interacting with items such as paddleballs, bubble blowers, View Masters, balls, and Lincoln Logs. However, further research is needed in this area.

In addition, the types of tasks available to individuals will influence and, in some cases, determine whether individuals engage in isolative or cooperative activities (Hake & Vukelich, 1973; Kawin, 1934; Quilitch & Risley, 1973; Updegraff & Herbst, 1933; Van Alstne, 1932; Zimmerman & Calovini, 1971). If tasks applicable to isolative activities but not very applicable to cooperative activities (e.g., clay) are the only tasks available, individuals will more readily participate in isolative activities. On the other hand, if only tasks which are applicable to cooperative activities are available (e.g., cooperative games), individuals will be more likely to engage in cooperative activities.

Verbal Directions, Modeling and Manual Guidance

The instructional procedures of verbal direction, modeling, and physical guidance are described in detail in Chapter 3. There is support for using these procedures to teach moderately to profoundly handicapped students social skills. Wehman (1976a) investigated the efficacy of toy proximity, verbal directions, and modeling on the independent leisure time activities of three severely and profoundly handicapped individuals. It was found that, by themselves, toy proximity and modeling each resulted in substantially higher levels of independent play activity relative to the individual's initial level of play. However, a combination of verbal directions plus modeling resulted in the highest levels of independent play.

There is support for pairing higher-functioning peer models and adult models with severely and profoundly handicapped learners to teach cooperative (Morris & Dolker, 1974) and independent play (Paloutzian et al., 1971). For example, Knapczyk and Peterson (Note 1) (1975) found that trainable students substantially increased their rates of cooperative play when "normal" models were present.

When severely handicapped students do not follow verbal directions and/or are nonimitative, they may be taught social skills through manual guidance. Manual guidance should be faded gradually until students perform a skill independently. Caution

should be taken when using manual guidance. Fading manual guidance before the behavior is well established may result in the loss of that behavior. However, excessive use of manual guidance leads to dependence on the teacher and may result in lack of self-initiated behavior.

When teaching the social skills of independent interaction with an object, the following sequence may be adhered to.

1. Place the materials in close proximity to the student. If proximity does not produce the desired interaction, go to step 2.
2. Verbally direct the student to interact. If verbal directions do not produce the desired interaction, go to step 3.
3. Model the desired interaction and verbally direct the student. If modeling and directions do not produce the desired interaction, go to step 4.
4. Manually guide the student through the desired interaction.
5. Cycle through steps 1 to 5 until the students emit the desired interaction when the only cue is material proximity.

Programming for skill generalization and maintenance

Social skills should be performed across tasks, people, settings, and cues to respond. Social skills which are performed only in the classroom have little value. Several strategies may be employed to facilitate skill generalization, maintenance, and self-regulatory skills (Wehman, 1971; Williams, 1973; Williams, Brown & Certo, 1975).

1. Initially provide one-to-one instruction and gradually increase the physical distance between the student and teacher until the targeted skills are performed with no teacher present.
2. Initially provide one-to-one instruction and gradually fade in higher functioning peers who may serve as models. Gradually increase the distance between the teacher and students until the targeted skills are performed with no teacher present.
3. Systematically vary requirements until the student performs the targeted skill in different settings, when provided with different cues to respond, and in the presence of different teachers.
4. Include the student's family and peers in social interaction programming so that teaching and

reinforcement may be provided in additional settings. (pp.16, 35)

In the final pages we will describe a social skills program incorporating the information and skills we have discussed so far.

A Social Skills Instructional Program

This section describes a social interaction program which was developed and implemented in two public school classrooms for severely handicapped students (Hamre-Nietupski & Williams, 1976; Williams, Pumpian, McDaniel, Hamre-Nietupski, & Wheeler, 1975). The program was intended as a demonstration and this section presents the framework derived for conceptualizing and teaching social skills.

The following guidelines were adhered to in designing the program.

1. Focus instructional programs on building appropriate social behaviors. Eliminate or decelerate inappropriate behaviors such as public masturbation or petting, inappropriate physical aggression, rumination, and so on. Teach appropriate social behaviors which are incompatible with the inappropriate behaviors.
2. Teach social skills as an integral part of each component of a total curriculum. Teach students the skills of initiating, receiving, sustaining, and terminating social interactions in relation to every task in which they participate. That is, use the procedures of task analysis, modeling, priming, chaining, and fading to teach the social skills involved in motor, communication, academic (e.g., math, reading), prevocational, home-living, community survival, and recreational tasks.
3. Prior to implementing a social skills instructional program use such procedures as parent conferences, questionnaires, group home and work setting surveys, task analysis, and naturalistic observations to assess the social skills students currently display and to predict those needed in future situations.
4. Teach social skills through tasks (e.g., work tasks, games) that are matched to students' functioning levels in such areas as motor skills, cognition, and language.
5. Whenever possible, pair students learning social skills with students who can model social skills.

This will facilitate learning the complexities and subtle nuances involved in social activities.

The social interactions program was implemented in two self-contained classrooms (designated A and B). In Class A, the 6 students, 4 female and 2 male, ranged in CA from 12 to 17 years; IQ's ranged from 38 to 52. Class B was constituted during the school year. Consequently, some students were transferred in and out of the class during programming. Thus, of the 9 students, only 5 received sustained instruction. Of these 5, 3 were male and 2 were female. Their CA's ranged from 13 to 18 years and IQ's ranged from 39 to 42.

Preprogram assessment

Prior to implementing the social skills program, the social skills the students exhibited in home and school environments were assessed. Figure 8.4 depicts the data collection sheet employed.

To collect data, the teacher observed each student's performance on selected tasks at least 4

Name _____   Date _____

Tasks →					
Inappropriate					
Initiate Appropriate					
With Whom					
Inappropriate					
Receive Appropriate					
From Whom					
Inappropriate					
Sustain Appropriate					
Duration					
Inappropriate					
Terminate Appropriate					

FIGURE 8.4   *Social interaction data collection sheet.*

times in a 2-week period. The teacher noted the task, whether the student initiated the task appropriately and with whom, whether the student appropriately received social interaction from others and from whom, whether the student appropriately sustained the interaction and for how long, and whether the student appropriately terminated the interaction. When scoring sustained activity, the teacher noted: the duration of the activity; the level of social play —autistic (AU), unoccupied (U), independent (I), observing (O), attempted interaction (AI), parallel (P), associative (A), or cooperative (C). In an attempt to estimate what social skills students exhibited at home, the teacher filled out a data sheet with parents during a conference.

This program focused on the social skills used in relation to recreational tasks. It was felt that the social skills exhibited during free time on recreational tasks would provide the best measure of spontaneous and independent performance of social skills. Table 8.1 provides a summary of data collected during free time on students S_1 and S_5.

Analysis of the data presented in Table 8.1 helped determine the skills each student needed to learn. For example, the data indicated Student 5 (S_5) needed to learn at least the following skills:

1. In 4 play sessions S_5 made no initiations to other S_s; this is an important social interaction skill because it leads to cooperative play; therefore, the number of initiations needed to be increased.
2. In relation to #1 above, S_5 engaged in isolative play 75% of the time and in observational play 25% of the time; S_5 spent *too much* time engaged in isolative play and needed to be taught cooperative social skills.
3. S_5 engaged in only two different activities; it was

a goal of the program to increase the number of games and activities in S_5's repertoire.

4. S_5 engaged in appropriate toy play 66% of the time, *but* engaged in inappropriate play 33% of the time; another goal of the program was to increase appropriate play so that S_5 would engage in it almost 100% of the time.
5. S_5 engaged in an activity for an average of 9.5 minutes; this indicated that S_5 was able to sustain an activity.
6. Finally, S_5 appropriately terminated an interaction 100% of the time, indicating no problem in regard to termination with an activity or object. *However, S_5 never engaged in cooperative play and therefore it is uncertain as to whether S_5 had the skills to appropriately terminate an activity with another student.*

As previously noted we focused primarily on teaching social interaction skills in relation to simple games. Games to teach social interactions were selected by matching the skills required to play games to the student's functioning levels. Both isolative and cooperative games were made available to the students. The social skills and games each student was taught were also selected on the basis of observation of the students' game and social skills in natural settings; information obtained from parents; and a survey of the recreational social skills needed in the students' potential future living environments (e.g., group homes). When teaching students new games and social interaction skills, students were paired with students who had already learned the skills to help minimize teacher intervention. With some prompting, skilled students were able to teach unskilled students many of the skills. Procedures for facilitating peer-peer instruction are described in the procedure section.

TABLE 8.1   *Summary of free time data*

	Initiate	Receive	Time per Activity	Level of Toy Play	Level of Social Play	Average Time per Activity	Terminate
S_1	5 play sessions 4 initiations 100% approp.	no opportunity to receive	records 33% cards 50% book 17%	100% approp.	parallel 33% cooperative 67%	7.16 min. per activity	100% approp.
S_5	4 play sessions 0 initiations	1 initiation from others 100% approp.	butterflies 25% cootie 75%	33% inapprop. 66% approp.	observational 25% isolative 75%	9.25 min. per activity	100% approp.

Designing specific programs

Selected tasks and the social interaction skills of initiating, receiving, sustaining, and terminating related to the tasks were analyzed and the sequence of skills students should perform was described. Condensations of task analyses for "View Master" (isolative leisure time activity), "Old Maid" (cooperative leisure time activity), and "Setting the Table" (home living activity) are presented below.

"View Master"

1. Student *recognizes* that it is free time.
2. Student *initiates* by going to game shelf and finding the View Master and reels.
3. Student finds a spot near a light or window.
4. Student takes reel out of envelope.
5. Student puts the reel in the View Master with the top of reel sticking out.
6. Student looks into View Master.
7. Student pulls trigger to view each of the 7 pictures.
8. After viewing each reel the student takes reel out of the View Master and puts it back in the appropriate envelope.
9. Student *terminates* playing with the View Master by putting it and reels away in the appropriate place.

"Old Maid"

1. Student A *appropriately asks* Student B to play "Old Maid."
2. Student B *appropriately accepts or declines* the invitation.
3. Students get "Old Maid" cards.
4. Students find an appropriate play area.
5. Student A or B decides to be the dealer.
6. The dealer shuffles the cards.
7. The dealer passes out the cards.
8. Students hold cards in hands or place them in a card rack if they can't hold all the cards.
9. Students match the pairs in their hands and place them on the table, face up.
10. Students draw cards from each other's hands.
11. Students match drawn cards to cards in their hands and place matches face up on the table.
12. Students continue play until one student is left with the Old Maid.
13. Students *terminate* the game by stating appropriate comments, and putting "Old Maid" cards away in their appropriate place.

"Setting the Table"

1. Student A *recognizes* that it is time for lunch.
2. Student A appropriately *initiates* setting the table by telling the teacher that he/she will set the table.
3. Student A *appropriately asks* Student B to help set the table.
4. Student B *appropriately accepts or declines* the request to help set the table.
5. Student A divides up the task of setting the table by requesting Student B to perform half the tasks of
   a. putting out plates
   b. putting out knives, forks, and spoons
   c. putting out napkins
   d. putting out glasses
   e. pouring milk or water
   f. putting out pepper, salt, butter
   g. putting out food.
6. Student B *appropriately* accepts or declines each request delineated in step 5.
7. Student A and/or B *terminate* the table setting task by noting that all jobs are done and calling the rest of the class to lunch.

Measuring skill acquisition

Direct and continuous data were collected on the students' acquisition of tasks and the social skills involved during instructional intervention. To collect direct and continuous data during instructional intervention, a data sheet was constructed with rows that corresponded to each skill in the task. As students progressed through the chain of skills, the teacher would score '+' if students performed a skill without the aid of verbal directions, models, or manual guidance; a "VD" if students performed a skill after a verbal direction; "M" if students performed a skill after the teacher modeled it; and a "P" if students had to be physically guided through a skill. Each instructional trial was defined as starting when students performed the first skill of a sequence. The subsequent instructional session then focused on the unlearned skills. When students could perform the sequence of skills without any verbal directions, models, or manual guidance on three successive trials, they were considered to have learned the sequence of skills.

The social skills of initiating, receiving, sustaining, and terminating social interaction were taught in relation to every task (e.g., home living, academic, prevocational) which occurred throughout the day. However, it was not possible to collect data across all tasks. We selected target tasks and measured skill acquisition only on those tasks. Our primary target tasks were recreational, as we felt they involved the most spontaneous and independent use of social skills. Three to four target tasks were chosen per student. As the social skills involved in a task were incorporated into the task analysis, acquisition of the task involved the acquisition of social skills.

Instructional procedures

To teach students to perform, correctly and in sequence, the skills delineated by each task analysis, the teacher would permit them to progress through the chain of skills without intervening until they made an error. At this point, the teacher first verbally prompts the correct response (e.g., say, "Deal the cards"). If prompting failed to produce the correct response, the teacher modeled the correct response and the skill in the sequence which preceded the error response; then the students were encouraged to imitate the model. The skill *before* the error response was modeled as a cue for the correct performance of the response on which students erred. If modeling failed to produce the correct response, the teacher manually guided students through the skill which preceded the error response and the response on which students erred. These three instructional procedures, at increasing levels of assistance to the learner, were employed whenever learner errors occurred. When one level of assistance failed to produce the correct performance by the learner, the teacher intervened with the next level until the learner's performance was correct. Then the teacher gradually faded this instructional support by employing a simpler level of assistance and finally no assistance at all.

Instructional phases

Instruction on each task analysis was divided into phases. The following is a brief description of how instruction of the social skills involved in games was divided.

Phase I

During this phase students were taught to socially interact and play a game with the teacher. We felt that learning the games or tasks was a prerequisite

to learning the social interactions which revolve around them. The teacher modeled proper initiation and termination skills, but students were not required to perform these skills until Phase II.

It should be emphasized that students were given a "choice" as to whether or not they wanted to play a particular game or with an object. However, students were not allowed to waste time by doing nothing at all. They were, however, encouraged to engage in many different activities. In some cases it was necessary to intervene when students engaged in an activity too frequently or too infrequently and at time to coax a student to play a game with the teacher.

While teaching the game, the teacher verbally and physically directed the student through each step of the game or activity. However, after students were able to play the game, they were taught to direct the teacher. This was accomplished when the teacher asked the student what to do next and/or by not following the directions of the student or the rules of the game. For example, if the teacher and student were playing "Old Maid" and it was the teacher's turn, the teacher would ask, "What do I do now?"; the student could respond, "Pick a card." The teacher might respond by picking a card from his/her own hand, and the student should say, "No, pick a card from my hand."

There are several reasons the authors feel that being able to direct others is a necessary skill. Individuals who have learned selected social skills can then teach games and social skills to peers with fewer social skills. Secondly, once students have the skills to play the game and act upon their environment, they should increase their frequency of appropriate social behavior. Finally, being able to direct others should increase students' abilities to control their own environment and not allow others to inappropriately manipulate them.

Phase II

In this phase the environment was structured to facilitate students' use of social interaction and game skills taught in Phase I. For cooperative games, the teacher instructed one of the students to ask another student to play a particular game. A student who had learned the game and social interaction skill was paired with a student who had not. The teacher observed the initiation between the students and intervened only when the students initiated or accepted/declined the initiation inappropriately. In case of error, the teacher modeled the proper behavior for the students and had them repeat the initiation following the model. The students then continued the response chain (i.e., getting the game materials, deciding on a play area, setting up the game, playing the game, and terminating the game). Again, the teacher observed the students' responses and only intervened when students inappropriately performed. If an error occurred, the teacher provided a verbal prompt for the correct response and, if necessary, modeled and/or primed the response. Peer instruction was encouraged.

In Phase II, for isolative games, the teacher provided opportunities for students to play a game, play with an object, and/or suggested that they play with a game or object.

Phase III

This phase was designed to teach further performance and/or modification of games and social skills learned in Phases I and II. Organizing tournaments, offering special prizes, altering rules, increasing or decreasing the number of students participating, and changing the location of the activity are a few modifications that were employed.

As previously stated, we primarily targeted instructional intervention with recreational tasks. The program was in effect only for the last 3 months of the school year. Skill acquisitional data indicated that 9 students progressed through Phases I, II, and III of "Old Maid," 4 students progressed through Phases I, II, and III of "Bingo," 6 students progressed through Phases I, II, and III of darts, and 2 students progressed through Phases I and II of "Cootie."

All students in Class A participated in a "Bingo" tournament which lasted 4 days. The teacher was the banker and ran the tournament for a half hour each day. Every time students got "Bingo," they recorded it on a tournament chart. On the fourth and last day of the tournament, the 2 students with the most wins had a play-off for the championship. Both students received ribbons. We felt this was an excellent learning experience for them in that they learned to accept that only one person can win while others must lose.

For Class B, an "Old Maid" tournament was organized as a Phase II activity. The student who won the most games within a week's time was taken to a restaurant for lunch. It was the students' responsibility to initiate and receive invitations to play these tournament games. Although no initiations to play

"Old Maid" were demonstrated before the tournament, there were 41 separate initiation and receptions to play during the tournament.

Observation indicated that students in Class B were interested in darts. Therefore, it was decided that darts should be taught. When students completed Phases I and II of darts, Phase III included a round-robin tournament. This tournament was constructed to afford students the opportunity to challenge the winner on any given day to play darts the following day. Making such arrangements prior to performing the activity is a demonstration of a sophisticated and highly appropriate social interaction.

Summary

Social activities may be conceptualized as consisting of various levels: autistic, unoccupied, independent, observing, attempted interaction, parallel interaction, associative interaction, and cooperative interaction. When developing a social skills instructional program, the primary instructional focus involves the determination of the appropriate times, places, and frequency associated with various isolative and cooperative activities. The social skills involved in most activities generally consist of initiating, receiving, sustaining, and terminating an activity. These basic social skills should be taught in relation to tasks natural to the student's typical daily activities—motor tasks, communication tasks, academic tasks (e.g., math, reading), prevocational tasks (e.g., workshop activities), home living tasks (e.g., lunch and snack-time activities), and so on. A social skills instructional program should not be a separate curriculum area taught in a specified daily time slot; it should be an integral part of all tasks students are learning.

References

Azrin, N. H., & Lindsley, O. R. The reinforcement of cooperation between children. *Journal of Abnormal and Social Psychology*, 1956, *52*, 100–102.

Barnes, K. Preschool play norms: A replication. *Developmental Psychology*, 1971, *5*, 99–103.

Baumeister, A. A., & Rollings, J. P. Self-injurious behavior. In N. R. Ellis (Ed.), *International review of research in mental retardation* (Vol. 8), New York: Academic Press, 1976.

Berkson, G., & Landesman-Dwyer, O. Behavioral research on severe and profound mental retardation. *American Journal on Mental Deficiency*, 1977, *81*, 428–455.

Buell, J., Stoddard, P., Harris, F., & Baer, D. M. Collateral social development accompanying reinforcement of outdoor play in a preschool child. *Journal of Applied Behavior Analysis,* 1968, *1,* 167–173.

Eckerman, D. O., Whatley, J. L., & Kutz, S. L. Growth of social play with peers during the second year of life. *Development Psychology,* 1975, *11,* 42–50.

Ellis, M. *Why people play.* Englewood Cliffs, N.J.: Prentice-Hall, 1973.

Gesell, A. *The first five years of life.* New York: Harper, 1940.

Goldstein, H. Social and occupational adjustment. In H. Stevens & R. F. Heber (Eds.), *Mental retardation: A review of research.* Chicago: University of Chicago Press, 1964.

Guess, D., Sailor, W., & Baer, D. M. *Functional speech and language training for the severely handicapped* (Parts 1 and 2). Lawrence, Kans.: H & H Enterprises, 1976.

Hake, D. F., & Vukelich, R. Analysis of the control exerted by a complex cooperation procedure. *Journal of the Experimental Analysis of Behavior,* 1973, *19,* 3–17.

Hamre-Nietupski, S., & Williams, W. Teaching selected sex education and social skills to severely handicapped students. In L. Brown, N. Certo, K. Belmore, & T. Crowner (Eds.), *Madison's alternative for zero exclusion: Papers and programs related to public school services for secondary age severely handicapped students* (Vol. 6). Madison, Wis.: Madison Public Schools, 1976.

Harris, F. R., Wolf, M. M., & Baer, D. M. Effects of adult social reinforcement on child behavior. *Young Children,* 1964, *20,* 8–17.

Hartup, W. W. Friendship status and the effectiveness of peers as reinforcing agents. *Journal of Experimental Child Pyschology,* 1964, *1,* 154–162.

Hopper, C., & Wambold, C. An applied approach to improving the independent play behavior of severely mentally retarded children. *Education and Training Center,* 1976, *2,* 1–18.

Kale, R. J., Kaze, J. H., Whelan, P. A., & Hopkins, B. L. The effects of prompts and reinforcement on the modification, maintenance, and generalization of social responses. *Journal of Applied Behavior Analysis,* 1968, *1,* 307–314.

Kawin, E. The function of toys in relation to child development. *Childhood Education,* 1934, *11* December, 122–124.

Kazdin, A. F., & Erickson, L. Developing responsiveness to instruction in severely and profoundly retarded residents. *Journal of Behavior Therapy and Experimental Psychiatry,* 1975, *6,* 17–21.

Kirby, F. D., & Toler, H. C. Modification of preschool isolate behavior: A case study. *Journal of Applied Behavior Analysis,* 1970, *3,* 309–314.

Koegel, R. L., Firestone, P. B., Kramme, K. W. & Dunlap, G. Increasing spontaneous play by suppressing self-stimulation in autistic children. *Journal of Applied Behavior Analysis,* 1974, *7,* 521–528.

McCoy, N., & Zigler, E. Social reinforcer effectiveness as a function of the relationship between child and adult. *Journal of Personality and Social Psychology,* 1965, *1,* 604–612.

Milby, J. B. Modification of extreme social isolation by contingent social reinforcement. *Journal of Applied Behavior Analysis,* 1970, *3,* 149–152.

Morris, R. J., & Dolker, M. Developing cooperative play in socially withdrawn retarded children. *Mental Retardation,* 1974, 12(6), 23–28.

Nietupski, J., & Williams, W. Teaching severely handicapped students to use the telephone to initiate selected recreational activities and to respond to telephone requests to engage in selected recreational activities. In L. Brown, W. Williams, & T. Crowner (Eds.), *A collection of papers and programs related to public school services for severely handicapped students* (Vol. 4). Madison, Wis.: Madison Public Schools, 1974.

O'Connor, R. D. Modification of social withdrawal through symbolic modeling. *Journal of Applied Behavior Analysis,* 1969, *2,* 15–22.

Paloutzian, R. F., Hasazi, J., Streifel, J., & Edgard, C. L. Promotion of positive social interaction in severely retarded children. *American Journal of Mental Deficiency,* 1971, *75,* 519–524.

Parten, M. Social play among preschool children. *Journal of Abnormal Psychology,* 1932, *28,* 136–147.

Piaget, J. *The origins of intelligence in children.* New York: Norton, 1952.

Premack, D. Toward empirical behavioral laws: I. Positive reinforcement. *Psychological Review,* 1959, *66,* 219–233.

Quilitch, R. H., & Risley, T. R. The effects of play materials on social play. *Journal of Applied Behavior Analysis,* 1973, *6,* 573–758.

Seeley, M. S. *An experimental evaluation of sociodrama as a social habilitation technique for mentally retarded adolescents.* Unpublished doctoral dissertation, University of Wisconsin, 1971.

Smith, P. K., & Connally, K. Patterns of play and social interaction in preschool children. In N. G. Blurton Jones (Ed.), *Ethological studies of child behavior.* London and New York: Cambridge University Press, 1972.

Stokes, T. F., Baer, D. M., & Jackson, R. L. Programming the generalization of greeting responses in four retarded children. *Journal of Applied Behavior Analysis,* 1974, *7,* 599–610.

Updegraff, R., & Herbst, E. K. An experimental study of social behavior stimulated in young children by certain play materials. *Pedagogical Seminary and Journal of Genetic Psychology,* 1933, 372–391.

Van Alstne, D. *Play behavior and choice of play materials of preschool children.* Chicago: University of Chicago Press, 1932.

Wahler, R. G. Child interactions in free field settings. Some experimental analyses. *Journal of Experimental Child Psychology,* 1967, *5,* 278–293.

Wehman, P. Effects of different environmental conditions in leisure time activity of the severely and profoundly handicapped. In O. Karan, P. Wehman, H. Renzaglia, & R. Schutz (Eds.), *Habilitation practices with the severely developmentally disabled.* Madison, Wis.: University of Wisconsin Rehabilitation Research and Training, 1976. (a)

Wehman, P. A leisure time activities curriculum for the developmentally disabled. *Education and Training of the Mentally Retarded,* 1976, *11,* 309–313. (b)

Wehman, P. *Helping the mentally retarded acquire play skills: A behavioral approach.* Springfield, Ill.: Charles C Thomas, 1977.

Wehman, P., Karan, D. C., & Rettie, C. Developing independent play in three severely retarded women. *Psychological Reports,* 1976, *39,* 995–998.

Whitman, T. L., Mercurio, J. R., & Caponigri, V. Development of social responses in two severely retarded children. *Journal of Applied Behavior Analysis,* 1970, *3,* 133–138.

Williams, W. Procedures that enhance the maintenance and generalization of induced behavioral change. *Catalogue of Selected Documents in Psychology,* Spring, 1973.

Williams, W., Brown, L., & Certo, N. Components of instructional programs for severely handicapped students. In L. Brown, T. Crowner, W. Williams, and R. York (Eds.), *Madison's alternative for zero exclusion: A book of readings* (Vol. 5). Madison, Wis.: Madison Public Schools, 1975.

Williams, W., Pumpian, P., McDaniel, J., Hamre-Nietupski, S., & Wheeler, J. Teaching social interaction skills to severely handicapped students. In L. Brown, T. Crowner, W. Williams, & R. York (Eds.), *Madison's alternative for zero exclusion: A book of readings* (Vol. 5). Madison, Wis.: Madison Public Schools, 1975

Zimmerman, L. D., & Calovini, G. Toys as learning materials for preschool children. *Exceptional Children,* 1971, *37,* 642–654.

Notes

1. Knapczyk, D., & Peterson, N. *Social play interaction of retarded children in an integrated classroom environment.* Unpublished paper, University of Indiana, Developmental Training Center, Bloomington, Indiana, 1975.

Introduction to Chapters 9 and 10

The next two chapters concern the instruction of functional math and reading. The only purpose of teaching functional academics to the moderately and severely handicapped is to expand their independence in the activities of daily living, recreation, and vocations. In order to achieve this purpose, you, as their teachers, must resist the traditional methods. When working to "functionalize" learned skills, your instructional materials need to be realistic; most workbooks, readers, commercial charts, flashcards, and dittoed worksheets are not practical because your students cannot relate the materials to the desired skills. Instead you will need materials such as newspapers, street signs, price tags from stores, and movie tickets. You will be unable to remain within the four walls of your classroom if you expect your students to reach the goals of functional skill development. For example, students who have learned the basics of counting money must next be taught to count out and receive change in a store. They must be given opportunities to use pay telephones, vending machines, and coin-operated washers and dryers. Students who recognize a small sight vocabulary need to use those reading skills in the operation of electric appliances, the location of restrooms and exits, food labels in large supermarkets, office signs in public buildings, the completion of application forms, the location of names, numbers, and addresses in telephone books, and the comprehension of directions on simple packaged foods. Academic skills need to be taught to the moderately and severely handicapped in the context of their functional use.

Both chapters take the position that reading and math skill development progresses in a logical, identifiable sequence from easy to more difficult levels. The authors note that this sequence does not differ from that followed by nonhandicapped learners, except that the steps often need finer analysis when applied to handicapped learners thereby creating more subskills and more instructional steps.

A functional academics program will necessitate that you employ small group instruction and continous skill measurement because your students will exhibit a wide range of ability levels. Students must learn to work independently on tasks because there are likely to be more instructional groups than there are instructors. In addition, students must learn to locate their own work areas and materials, to remember what they are expected to do during independent work periods, and to know what they can do once they have completed assigned work. For these behaviors to be learned you must have an organized classroom, a schedule that allows adequate time for daily instruction, and a workable system to manage, modify, and maintain student behavior.

9

Teaching Math Skills Using Longitudinal Sequences

This chapter was written by **Weston Williams,** University of Vermont; **Peggy Coyne,** Madison Public Schools; **Clarence De Spain,** Madison Public Schools; **Fran Johnson,** Madison Public Schools; **Nancy Scheuerman,** Madison Public Schools; **Jacalyn Stengert,** Madison Public Schools; **Barbara Swetlik,** Madison Public Schools; **Robert York,** University of Vermont.

This chapter was supported in part by Special Projects Training Grant PR# 451AH6 to the University of Vermont, and Grant OE–G–O–73–6137 to the University of Wisconsin, Madison, from the U.S. Department of Health, Education, and Welfare, Office of Education, Bureau of Education of the Handicapped, Division of Personnel Preparation; and in part by funds from Federal Contract Number OEC–O–74–7993 to the Madison, Wisconsin, public schools.

In a large part because of recent judicial and legislative actions, the educational rights of the moderately and severely handicapped are now being realized. Since many states mandate or allow public education for handicapped children from the time of their identification until they reach the ages of 21, instructional programs should reflect this longitudinal commitment. Educational programs for handicapped children should be founded upon long-term, developmentally sound sequences of skills. Such long-term skill sequences should lead from essentially no competence (or an individual's current level of functioning) to the competencies necessary for independent functioning within that individual's community. Skill instruction by means of longitudinal skill sequences will be illustrated by a math skills sequence developed for moderately and severely handicapped students in the Madison public schools, Madison, Wisconsin. About 75 moderately and severely handicapped students and 10 teachers have been involved in this project.

Skill Performance Across Tasks and Materials

Before discussing the teaching of math skills it may be helpful to discuss teaching skill performance across tasks and materials. A task is a specified situation in which a particular response should occur. For example, placing pegs in a board and tracking a slowly moving rattle are tasks since they are specified situations which require a particular response of different colors, sizes and shapes.

Through tasks individuals may learn concepts. The tasks of sorting objects such as pennies or buttons into groups of 5 may teach individuals the concept of "5." Almost all tasks involve the teaching of concepts, i.e., teaching individuals to sort environmental events along specified dimensions such as color, shape, size, and quantity. For instance, to set the table individuals must differentiate spoons from forks. To solve most math problems individuals must learn to sort sets of items according to quantity.

Individuals may also learn operations or response classes through tasks. The tasks of counting pennies, balls, and pencils may teach individuals the operation of counting. Almost all tasks involve operations or response classes such as "*give me* ball," "*give me* cup," "*pull* wagon," "*pull* truck," and so on. Individuals use operations to demonstrate knowledge of concepts. For instance, the operation of counting may be used to demonstrate knowledge of the concept of "5."

It must be emphasized that teaching always focuses upon tasks. Individuals' mastery of concepts and operations is always inferred from their performance on a number of tasks. After individuals have been taught to "count" across a number of materials (e.g., count balls, count jacks, count pennies), we can infer that they know the operation or the response class of counting. If these individuals appropriately use the operation of "count" across a variety of tasks, we assume they can use it across most tasks.

If the tasks used for teaching a skill are functional in individuals' natural environments, then the skill should be functional. For instance, the concept of "cup" could be taught through tasks which require individuals to touch various cups which are intermixed with other objects on the classroom work table. This task is relatively nonfunctional. A functional means of teaching the concept "cup" would be to have individuals sort cups from other items while putting away dishes, to sort cups from noncups while setting the table, to drink from a cup, and so on.

This chapter is concerned with teaching students to perform math or quantity-related tasks. On the basis of their performance across a number of tasks we may infer that they know concepts such as sets, one-many, one-to-one correspondence, equivalence, and so on. We stress teaching math concepts and operations through useful or functional tasks so that the newly acquired skills are functional.

Overview of the Math Skill Sequence

We initially attempted to teach moderately and severely handicapped students skills such as rational counting, numeral recognition, and matching a quantity to a numeral. The students' performance soon indicated that such skills represented too high an initial skill level and were nonfunctional for them. Students did not readily acquire the skills and, when they did acquire them, these skills were not used functionally in their environments. As a result, the students did not maintain or generalize the use of these skills.

This failure led us to redesign the math skill sequence. There is evidence that there is an inherent and empirically verifiable order to skills in math sequences (Resnick, Wang, & Kaplan, 1973). There is also evidence that learners who have been labeled retarded learn math skills in the same sequence as nonretarded learners (Spradlin, Cotter, Stevens, & Friedman, 1974). The order of skills commonly found in commercially available elementary school texts and materials developed for moderately and severely handicapped individuals generally follow a similar sequence.

The math skill sequence we have used with moderately and severely handicapped students is similar to sequences used in preschool and elementary-school programs and to the sequences found in other curricula developed for moderately and severely handicapped individuals (Fredericks, 1976). However, most commercially available math curricula do not apply directly to moderately and severely handicapped students because they provide insufficient opportunities for practice and instruction of skills; they often employ large group and worksheet instructional formats; they use abstract tasks to teach skills instead of concrete functional tasks; and they teach math skills through more complex levels of receptive and expressive language.

The math skill sequence described here differs from most commercially available sequences in that each skill is broken into more component skills; the skill sequence is adaptable to nonverbal students; the sequence starts with lower skills, such as imitation and functional object use; and we stress teaching each skill through functional tasks. Another major difference between our math curriculum and commercially available curricula is the emphasis on teaching students to solve functional math problems through the operation of one-to-one correspondence. Students who have not yet learned to count, recognize numerals, and associate a quantity with a numeral may be taught to solve many functional math problems by aligning objects in one-to-one correspondence. For example, to set the table a student may first count the number of place settings and then count out the appropriate number of plates and cups. A student who has not yet learned to count may solve the same functional math problem through providing each place setting with a plate and cup. When the student has established a one-to-one correspondence between the place settings and the plates and cups, the table is correctly set. The emphasis on one-to-one correspondence provides those students with severe skill deficits a method for solving functional math problems. As the overview of our skill sequence illustrates, students can initially be taught to solve many functional math problems through one-to-one correspondence. Thus, this chapter highlights one-to-one correspondence as an especially powerful and useful math skill to teach severely handicapped students. In later components of the sequence students are taught to use counting and numeral ordering skills to solve the same problems.

Figure 9.1 portrays the math curriculum scope and sequence chart. All the skills taught in the sequence are listed vertically (functional object use, imitation, sets, one-many, one-to-one correspondence, etc.). The objectives within each skill are listed horizontally.

As indicated in the chart, the objectives of various skills often may be taught concurrently. For instance, a student could be learning objectives 3, 4, 5 of "Sets" concurrently with objectives 1, 2, 3 of "One-many." The sequence is *not* linear in that the students do *not* first learn sets, then one-many, then one-to-one correspondence, and so on. The students are concurrently taught skills for which they have mastered the prerequisites. Table 9.1 provides an outline of the math skill sequence.

The sequence outlined in Table 9.1 is a framework for assessing students and developing instructional programs. It is not a prescription for automatic use with all students. The sequence must be adapted to meet individual student needs. In addition, the sequence should be continuously revised in relation to student performance within it. In the following paragraphs we briefly describe selected components of the skill sequence and procedures to make the math skills immediately functional. This does not attempt to detail every objective or detail every subcomponent of each objective, but merely to present an overview.

Teaching Procedures

This section will expand a few of the teaching procedures not evident from the detailed objectives listed in Table 9.1. First when teaching quantity concepts, the arrangement of the items to be operated on should be carefully sequenced. To teach math skills which involve aligning objects in one-to-one correspondence, equivalence, and more and less, we progress through the easy to hard sequence listed below.

1. Vertical arrays of items presented in one-to-one correspondence.

2. Horizontal arrays of items presented in one-to-one correspondence.

3. Mixed arrays of items students move objects into vertical arrays.

4. Linear arrays of items presented in one-to-one correspondence.

5. Mixed arrays of items students move objects into vertical or horizontal arrays.

For example, in the first step of the one-to-one correspondence component a teacher presents a set of objects (e.g., cups) in a vertical arrangement or array (⋮), then gives students a set (e.g., cups) with an equal number of members and teaches the students to align members of the sets in one-to-one correspondence (e.g., give each cup a cup). The next component of this step teaches students to align functionally related objects (e.g., glasses and straws, cups and saucers, napkins and placemats) in an arrangement which manifests one-one-one correspondence by means of tasks occurring daily in the classroom and at home; for example, setting the table, passing out crayons, passing out milk at lunch, placing a paper cup in each hole of a cupcake tin. Before going to the second step in the skills sequence (D-2), the teacher may present additional identical objects and then functionally related objects but use progressively more difficult arrangements: horizontal, linear, etc.

A. Prerequisites
   1. Imitation   1
   2. Functional Object Use   1
   3. Play   1

B. Sets   1 2 3 4 5 6 7 8 9

C. One-many   1 2 3

D. One-to-one correspondence   1

E. Equivalence   1 2

F. More and less
   1. More   1
   2. Less   1
   3. More/less   1
   4. Conservation of number   1 2 3 4 5 6

G. Counting forward
   1. Rational   1 2 3 4 5 6
   2. Rote   1 2 3
   3. Numeral recognition   1 2
   4. Matching numerals to quantities   1
   5. Matching quantities to numerals   1
   6. Ordering numerals   1 2 3 4 5 6 7 8
   7. Ordering quantities   1
   8. Writing numerals   1 2

H. Addition (Equation)
   1. Objects   1 2
   2. Numerals and objects   1
   3. Numerals and lines   1
   4. Numerals   1
   5. Fingers   1
   6. Facts   1

I. Story problems
   1. One-to-one correspondence   1
   2. X + Y = 2   1
   3. X + 2 = Y   1

FIGURE 9.1   *Scope and sequence chart.*

Source: Chart adapted by permission from W. Williams, P. Coyne, F. Johnson, N. Scheuerman, B. Swetlik and R. York. Skill sequences and curriculum development: Application of a rudimentary developmental math skill sequence in the instruction and evaluation of severely handicapped students. In N. Haring and L. Brown (Eds.), *Teaching the Severely Handicapped* (Vol. 2). New York: Grune & Stratton, 1977, p. 71.

TABLE 9.1   *Math skill sequence outline*

A. *Prerequisites*

1. *Imitation*. Students should imitate responses which are required in the math sequence, such as manipulating objects, imitating sounds, and/or imitating sign language gestures. (Objective 1) (Refer to Chapter 5 for instructional procedures).

2. *Functional object use*. Students should demonstrate the socially appropriate use of objects common to their home and school environments, such as drink from a cup, eat with a spoon, and roll a ball. (Objective 1) (Refer to Chapter 5 for instructional procedures).

3. *Play*. Students should spontaneously and appropriately interact with common objects and people. (Objective 1) (Refer to Chapters 5 and 8 for instructional procedures).

B. *Sets* (Prerequisite: Students should appropriately use or play with the objects used in the sets program.)

Sort objects (model). Students should sort objects, such as forks and spoons, when the teacher points and directs them, "Put the forks here and the spoons here," and then demonstrates sorting one fork and one spoon. (Objective 1)

Task sequence:
1. Sort unlike and unrelated items such as blocks and bears.
2. Sort unlike but related items such as cups and saucers.

Sort objects (no model). Students should sort objects, such as forks and spoons, when the teacher points and directs them, "Put the forks here and the spoons here." (Objective 2)

Task sequence:
1. Sort unlike and unrelated items such as spoons and buttons.
2. Sort unlike but related items such as paper and pencils.

Identify a set of objects (model)

Receptive. Students should indicate the correct set when the teacher models the response (points and says, "These are spoons") and then directs them to "Show me the spoons." (Objective 3a)

Expressive. Students should label objects (verbally or nonverbally) when the teacher models the response (says "These are spoons") and then asks "What are these?" (Objective 3b)

Identify a set of objects (no model)

Receptive. Students should indicate the correct set when the teacher directs them to "Show me the spoons." (Objective 4a)

Expressive. Students should label a set when the teacher asks "What are these?" (Objective 4b)

Identify a set of 2 unlike objects (model)

Receptive. Students should indicate the correct set of 2 unlike objects when the teacher models the response (points and says, "This is a spoon and fork") and then directs them to "Show me the spoon and fork." (Objective 5a)

Task sequence:
1. Unlike but related items such as cup and saucer.
2. Unlike and unrelated items such as button and cup.

Expressive. Students should label a set of 2 unlike objects when the teacher models the response (says "This is a spoon and fork") and then asks, "What are these?" (Objective 5b)

Task sequence:
1. Unlike but related items such as cup and saucer.
2. Unlike and unrelated items such as pencil and penny.

Identify a set of 2 unlike objects (no model)

Receptive. Students should indicate the correct set of 2 unlike objects when the teacher directs them to "Show me the fork and spoon." (Objective 6a)

TABLE 9.1   *Continued*

Task sequence:
1. Unlike but related items such as cups and saucers.
2. Unlike and unrelated items such as balls and spoons.

Expressive. Students should label a set of 2 unlike objects when the teacher asks, "What are these?" (Objective 6b)

Task sequence:
1. Unlike but related items such as cups and straws.
2. Unlike and unrelated items such as blocks and bears.

Make sets of 2 unlike objects (model). Students should make a set of 2 unlike objects when the teacher models the response (e.g., makes a set of spoon and fork) and directs them to "Give me a spoon and fork." After the students make the set, they should label it. (Objective 7)

Task sequence:
1. Unlike but related items such as spoons and forks.
2. Unlike and unrelated items such as buttons and blocks.

Make a set of 2 unlike objects (no model). Students should make a set of 2 unlike objects when the teacher directs them to "Give me spoon and fork." After the students make the set, they should label it. (Objective 8)

Task sequence:
1. Unlike but related items such as spoons and forks.
2. Unlike and unrelated items such as bears and cups.

Sort objects by color, size, and form. Presented a set of objects which can be made into 3 separate sets on the basis of color, size, and form, the students should sort the set when the teacher directs them to ' Sort by color/size/form." After the students sort the objects, they should label the dimension (e.g., red-yellow, big-little, circle-square) they sorted along. (Objective 9)

C. *One-Many* (Prerequisite: Sets, sort objects—no model.)

Identify sets of one and many (model)

Receptive. Students should indicate the correct set when the teacher models the response (points to the correct set) and then directs them to "Show me one/many." (Objective 1a)

Expressive. Students should label a set as having one or many objects when the teacher models the response (says "This is one/many") and then asks, "Is this *one* or *many*?" (Objective 1b)

Identify sets of one and many (no model)

Receptive. Students should indicate the correct set when the teacher directs them to "Show me one/many." (Objective 2a)

Expressive. Students should label a set as having one or many objects, when the teacher asks, "Is this *one* or *many*?" (Objective 2b)

Take one or many objects from a group. Presented a set of 6 objects and asked to "Take one" or "Take many," students should take one or many. After taking one or many objects, students should indicate one or many when asked, "Does your set have one or many?" (Objective 3)

D. *One-to-One Correspondence* (Prerequisite: Sets, sorting objects—no model.) Students should align their set of objects (e.g., cups) in one-to-one correspondence with the teacher's set (e.g., saucers) and when—

1. Their set is equal to the teacher's set; student indicates that there are "enough."
2. Their set has fewer objects than the teacher's set; student indicates there are "not enough" and they need "more."
3. Their set has more members than the teacher's set; student indicates that they have "too many" and they need to "take away."

TABLE 9.1   *Continued*

Students who have learned to count objects should indicate how many more they need or how many should be taken away. (Objective 1)

Task materials should progress from those that are easily aligned to unrelated objects: like items, functionally related items, and unlike and unrelated items. The arrangement of teacher's and student's sets is sequenced in an easy to difficult order: vertical, horizontal, linear, then mixed arrays.

E. *Equivalence* (Prerequisite: One-to-One Correspondence.)

Identify equal sets

One-to-one correspondence: Students should use the operation of one-to-one correspondence to match equal sets and place an equals sign between the sets when the teacher presents sets, such as ⊡ ⊡ ⊡ ⊡ , and directs the students to "match the sets which are equal." (Objective 1a)

Rational counting. Students who have learned to count objects and to order numerals should count the objects in the sets and determine that, for example, a set of 3 equals a set of 3 to match equal sets. After students indicate that the sets are equal, the teacher asks, "How can you tell?"; the students should use the operation of one-to-one correspondence to check and if necessary correct their answers. (Objective 1b)

Make equal sets

One-to-one correspondence. Students should use the operation of one-to-one correspondence to make their set equal to the teacher's when the teacher directs them to "Make your set *equal* to my set." The teacher alternates providing the student with a set equal to hers, less than hers, and more than hers. Students should indicate that the sets are "equal" ("enough") or "not equal" ("not enough") and they need more or "not equal" ("too many") and they must remove some. (Objective 2a)

Rational counting. Students who have learned to count objects and to order numerals should count the objects in teacher's set and count out the correct number of objects to make their set equal to the teacher's. After students indicate that the sets are equal, the teacher asks, "How can you tell?"; the students should use the operation of one-to-one correspondence to check and if necessary correct their answers. (Objective 2b)

F. *More and Less* (Prerequisites: Equivalence, rational counting.)

1. *More*

   One-to-one correspondence. When presented 2 unequal sets and asked, "Which set has more?", students should match the objects in the sets in one-to-one correspondence, point to the set with at least one object left unmatched and indicate "more." (Objective 1a)

   Rational counting. Students who can count objects and order numerals should count the number of objects in each set to determine which set has more. Then students can indicate that, for example, 5 is more than 4. After determining which set has more, the teacher asks, "How can you tell?"; the students should use the operation of one-to-one correspondence to check and if necessary correct their answers. (Objective 1b)

2. *Less*

   One-to-one correspondence. When presented 2 unequal sets and asked "Which set has less?", students should match the objects in the sets in one-to-one correspondence, point to the set with no objects left unmatched, and indicate "less." (Objective 1a)

   Rational counting. Students who can count objects and order numerals should count the number of objects in each set and indicate that, for example, 4 is less than 5 to determine which set has less, the teacher asks, "How can you tell?"; the students should use the operation of one-to-one correspondence to check and if necessary correct their answers. (Objective 1b)

3. *More/less.* When presented 2 unequal sets of objects and asked, "Which set has *more/less*?", students should use the operation of one-to-one correspondence or rational counting to determine which set has more or less. (Objective 1)

TABLE 9.1   *Continued*

4. *Conservation of number of objects in 2 sets* (Prerequisite: ordering numerals.)

Spacing change in each set. Students should use the operation of one-to-one correspondence or rational counting to determine that 2 sets of objects are equal or not equal. After the teacher changes the spacing of the objects in both sets but maintains equal distance between the objects (⋮ ∴ ⋮ → ⋮ ∴ ⋮), the students should indicate that the sets are still equal or not equal. (Objective 1)

Spacing change in one set. Students should use the operation of one-to-one correspondence or rational counting to determine that 2 sets are equal or not equal. After the teacher changes the spacing of the objects in one set (⋮ ∴ ⋮ → ˙∴˙), the students should indicate that the sets are still equal or not equal. (Objective 2)

Object added to each set. Students should use the operation of one-to-one correspondence or rational counting to determine that 2 sets are equal or not equal. After the teacher adds an object to *each* set, the students should indicate that the sets are still equal or not equal. (Objective 3)

Object added to only one set. Students should use the operation of one-to-one correspondence or rational counting to determine that 2 sets are equal or not equal. After the teacher adds an object to *only one* set, the students should indicate that sets which were equal are not equal and sets which were not equal are equal. (Objective 4)

Object removed from each set. Students should use the operation of one-to-one correspondence or rational counting to determine that 2 sets are either equal or not equal. After the teacher removes an object from *each* set, the students should indicate that the sets are still equal or not equal. (Objective 5)

Object removed from only one set. Students should use the operation of one-to-one correspondence or rational counting to determine that 2 sets are either equal or not equal. After the teacher removes an object from *only one* set, the students should indicate that sets which were equal are not equal and sets which were not equal are equal. (Objective 6)

G. *Counting Forward* (Prerequisite: One-Many)

1. *Rational*

Counts horizontal and vertical arrays of 1–5 objects. Students should count objects by assigning a sound or gesture to each one when presented a set of 1–5 objects in a horizontal (...) or vertical (⋮) array and asked "How many?" (Objective 1)

Counts varied arrays of 1–5 objects. Students should count objects by assigning a sound or gesture to each one when presented 1–5 objects in a varied array (˙ ˙ ˙˙) and asked "How many?" (Objective 2)

Counts objects in horizontal and vertical arrays of 1–20 objects. Students should count objects by assigning a sound or gesture to each one when presented 1–20 objects in horizontal or vertical arrays and asked "How many?" (Objective 3)

Counts out a specified number of objects from a group. Students should count out the correct number of objects when presented a varied array of 1–20 objects and directed to "Count out (*number*)." (Objective 4)

Counts objects in crooked arrays. Students should assign a sound or gesture to each object when presented objects in varied arrays (˙ ˙ ˙˙) and asked "How many?" (Objective 5)

Counts objects which appear and disappear. Students should tally each object's appearance and then count their tallies to count objects which appear and then disappear, such as cars going down the highway. (Objective 6)

2. *Rote* (Prerequisite: Rational counting—counts 1–20 objects.)

Counts from 1 to a number. Students should count from 1 to a number when the teacher directs them to "Count from 1 to (*number*)." (Objective 1)

TABLE 9.1   *Continued*

Indicates number counting from. Students should indicate the number they are counting from and then count from the correct number after the teacher directs them to "Count from (*number*) to (*number*)" and asks, "What are you counting from?" (Objective 2)

Indicates number counting from and to. Students should correctly indicate what number they are counting from and to and then count from and to the correct numbers after the teacher directs them to "Count from (*number*) to (*number*)," and then asks, "What are you going to count to?" (Objective 3)

3. *Numeral matching, recognition, and labeling* (Prerequisite for objectives 2a and 2b: Rational counting—counts 1–20 objects.)

   Matching. Students should match numerals by aligning identical number cards ("Show me the number card that looks like this card.") (Objective 1)

   Receptive. Students should indicate the appropriate numeral when asked "Show me (*number*)." (Objective 2a)

   Expressive. Students should label numerals when the teacher holds up a number and asks, "What is this?" (Objective 2b)

4. *Matching numerals to quantities* (Prerequisite: Numeral recognition and rational counting—counts 1–20 objects.) Students should count out the correct number of objects when presented a numeral and directed to "Count out this many." (Objective 1)

5. *Matching quantities to numerals* (Prerequisite: Matching numerals to quantities.) Students should find the correct numeral when presented a set of objects and directed to "Show me this many." (Objective 1)

6. *Ordering numerals* (Prerequisites: Rote counting, matching numerals to quantities, and matching quantities to numerals)

   Order numerals (number line and verbal prompt). Students should order numerals (e.g., 3, 1, 2 → 1, 2, 3) by matching the numerals to a number line when directed to "Put the numerals in order" and the teacher prompts the response by saying "One, two, three . . . ." (Objective 1)

   Order numerals (verbal prompt). Students should order numerals without the aid of a number line when directed to "Put the numerals in order" and the teacher prompts the response by saying "One, two, three . . . ." (Objective 2)

   Order numerals. Students should order numerals when directed to "Put the numerals in order." (Objective 3)

   Counts to determine missing numerals. Students should indicate which numerals are missing from a number line (e.g., 1, 2, ____, 4, ____, 6) by counting to determine the missing numerals when directed to "Count, which numbers are missing?" (Objective 4)

   Determine missing numerals without counting. Students should indicate which numerals are missing from a number line without counting to determine the missing numerals when asked, "Which numbers are missing?" (Objective 5)

   Touch and indicate numbers which come before/after on a number line. Students should touch a number line and label numbers which come before and after a specified number when the teacher says, "Touch the number that comes *before/after* (____). What number comes before/after (____)?" (Objective 6)

   Indicate numbers which come before/after on a number line. Students should indicate which numbers come before/after a specified number on a number line when asked, "What number comes before/after (____)?" (Objective 7)

   Indicate numbers which come before/after or are less/more than another number. Students should indicate what number comes before/after or is less/more than a specified number without the aid of a number line when asked, "What comes before/after (____)" or, "What number is more/less than (____)?" (Objective 8)

TABLE 9.1   *Continued*

7. *Ordering quantities* (Prerequisite: Ordering numerals.) Students should count the number of objects in sets and determine which sets have more/less to order unequal sets of objects from least to most when directed to "Order the sets." (Objective 1)

8. *Writes numerals* (Prerequisites: Rational counting—counts 1–20 objects.)

Single numerals (model). Students should copy models of printed numerals when asked "Write (____)." (Objective 1)

Single numerals (no model). Student should write numerals when asked "Write (____)." (Objective 2)

After students have learned to write numerals, they should indicate the answer to math problems by writing the answer.

H. *Addition* (Prerequisites: Ordering numerals, ordering quantities)

1. *Objects*

Join sets. Students should join 2 sets of objects when the teacher says, "This is a set of (____) and this is a set of (____), plus/join the sets." (Objective 1)

Join sets and count how many. Students should count the number of objects in each of 2 sets, join the sets, and indicate how many objects are in the joined set when the teacher says, "How many objects are in each set? Plus/join the sets. How many objects are there?" (Objective 2)

2. *Numerals and objects.* Students should solve problems of the form $\boxdot + \boxdot = \square$ by matching a numeral to each quantity $\underset{1}{\boxdot} + \underset{2}{\boxdot} = \square$, moving the objects from the factor boxes (joining the sets) to the sums box $\underset{1}{\square} + \underset{2}{\square} = \underset{3}{\boxdot}$, and then reading the equation, for example, "One plus two equals three." (Objective 1)

3. *Numerals and lines.* Students should solve problems of the form $// + / = \underline{\quad}$ by matching a numeral to each quantity $\underset{2}{//} + \underset{1}{/} = \underline{\quad}$, counting the number of lines on the left side of the equation, making the sides of the equation equal by drawing the number of lines counted on the left side of the equation on the right side of the equation $\underset{2}{//} + \underset{1}{/} = \underline{///}$, matching the quantity in the sums box to a numeral $\underset{2}{//} + \underset{1}{/} = \underset{3}{\underline{///}}$, and then reading the equation, for example, "Two plus one equals three." (Objective 1)

4. *Numerals.* Students should solve problems of the form $1 + 2 = \underline{\quad}$ by matching a quantity to each numeral $1 + 2 = \underline{\quad}$, counting the number of lines on the left side of the equation, making the sides of the equation equal by drawing the number of lines counted on the left side of the equation on the right side of the equation $\underset{/}{1} + \underset{//}{2} = \underset{///}{\underline{3}}$, and then reading the equation. (Objective 1)

5. *Fingers.* Students should solve problems of the form $2 + 3 = \underline{\quad}$ by holding up the number of fingers indicated by the second numeral of the equation (3), counting from the first numeral of the equation (2), counting each finger held up (3, 4, 5), writing down the last number counted (5) in the sums box, and then reading the equation. (Objective 1)

6. *Facts.* Students should quickly indicate the answer to problems of the form $3 + 4 = \underline{\quad}$ without the use of lines or fingers. After stating the answer, students should use lines or fingers to check and if necessary correct their answers. (Objective 1)

TABLE 9.1   *Continued*

I. *Story Problems.*

1. *One-to-one correspondence.* Students should use the one-to-one correspondence operation to solve problems presented in a story problem format. (Objective 1)

2. $X + Y =$ _____ . Students should use finger addition problem-solving skills to solve problems of the form $2 + 2 =$ _____ presented in a story problem format. (Objective 1)

3. $X +$ _____ $= Y$. Students should use finger addition problem-solving skills to solve problems of the form $2 +$ _____ $= 4$ presented in a story problem format. (Objective 1)

The equivalence program extends the skills acquired in one-to-one correspondence by teaching that the equals sign is an alternative way of expressing the concept of "enough," taught during one-to-one correspondence. Students are taught to solve equivalence problems in two ways. First, they are taught to match the objects in each set in one-to-one correspondence and indicate that the sets are "equal" or matched." Second, students who can count and order numerals are taught to count each set and indicate that, for example, "3=3." Then the students are asked how they can tell that the sets are equal and have to demonstrate that their answers are correct by using one-to-one correspondence. If students indicate that 3=3 and both sets did not contain 3 members, they often are not corrected. Instead, when asked how they can tell, they line up the objects in one-to-one correspondence and can easily see that they have made a mistake and how they can correct it. Since we all frequently make mistakes, it is important to teach students procedures for checking their answers instead of always setting up situations where errors do not occur. Students were taught to use equivalence skills in such functional situations as dealing cards so that everyone had an equal number and choosing equal teams for relay races.

The reader is referred to Table 9.1 for the order and detail of instructional procedures to teach the concepts of sets, one-many, one-to-one correspondence equivalence, more-less, counting forward, addition, and story problems. The prerequisite skills however receive more attention in earlier chapters —imitation and functional object use are covered in Chapter 5, while play is discussed in Chapter 8.

Advantages of the Use of Long-Term Developmental Skill Sequences

The use of long-term developmental skill sequences, as outlined for math skills in Table 9.1, has at least four advantages.

1. Developmental skill sequences should help minimize the disruptive effects on education programs resulting from changes in teachers and administrators.

2. Traditionally, students have been grouped on such dimensions as CA, general labels (e.g., trainable, autistic, learning disabled), presence of physical handicaps, IQ scores, and achievement test scores. Such dimensions rarely provide enough information to be relevant to instructional programming. In a skill sequence model students can be grouped on the basis of the skills they have mastered and the skills they should be taught next.

3. Readiness in a skill sequence model consists of mastery of the requisite skills to enable the learning of more advanced skills. Within this model a teacher does not simply wait for a student to be "ready" to learn a skill but teaches the requisite skills.

4. Skill sequences can facilitate the development of more efficient curricula. That is, if teachers carefully monitor student performance, they can obtain data which indicate the order in which skills are most readily acquired and which skills must be broken into smaller subskills. The cycle of constructing a skill sequence, monitoring student performance, revising the skill sequence, monitoring student performance should lead to more efficient and valid curricula. Through such monitoring we can effectively progress from "normal" developmental skill sequences, logically derived notions of skill sequences, and psychological laboratory research to empirically valid curricula.

Adapting the Skill Sequence to Individual Student Needs

A skill sequence provides a set of learning objectives around which instructional programs of many types may be organized. A skill sequence is *not* a statement of how to teach a skill but rather a statement of what is to be taught. The teacher must precisely describe what is to be taught before determining how to teach target skills. Finally, in order to select target skills the teacher must examine the student's entry skills. The sequence serves as a checklist for the assessment process.

Math skills have a logically built-in order. All students should learn math skills in basically the same sequence. The math skill sequence should be adapted to the individual needs of students with motor, vision, auditory and/or communication handicaps. The math skill sequence may be adapted by using instructional procedures which are most effective with individual students; allowing students to indicate knowledge of math skills through responses in their repertoire (e.g., sign language, communication boards); individualizing tasks and materials; reformulating instructional objectives; and task analyzing the component skills of the sequence.

Selecting instructional procedures

Math skills may be taught through such procedures as modeling, physical guidance, shaping, fading, cuing, verbal directions, and chaining. Instructional procedures which have been demonstrated to be effective with individual students should be selected for teaching math skills. When designing a math instructional program, the contexts (e.g., play activities, group instruction, individual instruction, highly structured drills) which have in the past resulted in efficient skill acquisition for individual students should be employed. Generally, we have used highly systematic procedures based on applied behavior analysis, such as those described in Chapters 2 and 3.

To teach math skills we have used the instructional procedures of verbal directions, modeling, cuing, and manual guidance described in Chapter 3. These instructional procedures may be designated as performance levels, with no instruction being the highest performance level and manual guidance the lowest. The performance levels may be quantified: 4, no instruction; 3, verbal directions; 2, modeling; 1, cuing. 0, manual guidance.

Student progress in the acquisition of a skill is determined by calculating the average performance level used per trial each day. A student's average performance level should progress toward 4, or responding under the control of appropriate stimuli and independently of teacher assistance.

The basic instructional procedure we have used to teach math skills is:

1. Cue the student to attend to the task, such as, "Tom, listen."

2. Present the task *materials* such as printed numerals in mixed order: 1, 4, 5, 3, 2.

3. Cue the student to attend to the appropriate task dimension, such as saying, "Tom, look at these," while pointing to the numerals to be ordered from 1 to 5.

4. Direct the student to respond to a cue such as, "Put the numbers in order."

5. Evaluate the student's response.

   5.1 Correct response: Praise the student and score 4.

   5.2 Incorrect response:

      5.2.1 Verbal direction: The teacher provides a verbal direction such as, "Tom, two, *three,* four." If the student performs correctly, score 3. If the student performs incorrectly, go to 5.2.2 and model the response.

      5.2.2 Model: The teacher models ordering the numerals and cues the student to imitate the model. If the pupil performs correctly, score 2. If the student performs incorrectly, go to 5.2.3 and cue the response.

      5.2.3 Cuing: At this point the cuing procedures of movement, position, redundancy, and match-to-sample described in Chapter 3 may be employed. For example, when teaching a student to order the printed numerals 1, 3, 5, 4, 2, we present a number line as a match-to-sample cue. The teacher points to the number line and says, "Look at this, 1, 2, 3, 4, 5," while pointing to each numeral on the number line. On subsequent trials the number line is faded out by presenting shorter number lines such as 1, 2, 3, 4, then 1, 2, 3, and so on. If the initial cuing does not result in correct performance, the teacher may provide additional cuing such as pointing to 1 on the number line and then pointing to the student's printed numeral 1, pointing to 2 on the number line and then pointing to the student's printed numeral 2. If the student performs correctly, score 1. If the student performs incorrectly, go to 5.2.4 and manually guide the student through the correct response.

      5.2.4 Manual guidance: Manually guide the student through the correct response and score 0.

6. Continue to cycle through steps 1 to 5 until the student has acquired the skill.

Students should master math skills, not merely acquire them. They should be taught to perform skills across at least 3 functional tasks, 3 materials, 3 cues to respond, 3 people, and 3 settings. One of the functional tasks should be one which occurs at home; one of the cues to respond should be one used by a parent; one of the people should be a parent; and one of the settings should be home. This criterion for mastery insures that skills learned at school are transferred to home and mandates that educators work as partners with parents in designing, implementing, and evaluating educational programs.

Initially it may be instructionally efficient to focus on teaching students to perform a math skill on one task, given one response cue, in one setting, in the presence of one person. When a student can perform a skill in such a limited situation, he has acquired a skill.

After students have acquired a skill, they should be taught to perform the skill proficiently. As used here, proficiency involves correctly performing the skill and performing it at a specified rate. Students may be able to count coins but if they cannot count them at a specified rate they will not be able to make change efficiently when purchasing at the store. Proficiency rates for skills may be estimated by sampling adult rates of performance and then multiplying the rate by 75%. As a rule of thumb, we have found that 75% of normal rate often serves as a realistic guide for moderately to severely handicapped individuals. After students have acquired a skill they may become proficient if the educator contingently reinforces rate of correct performance. Games and races which require correct and rapid skill performance are excellent vehicles for building rates. Instructional tasks may be transformed into races in which students race to beat their previous rate, the rates of peers, and/or the rate of the teacher to earn a reinforcer.

Concurrently, with building skill proficiency, skill mastery should be taught. To teach skill mastery the teacher derives a list of functional tasks the student may perform the skill on, cues which should commonly evoke the skill, settings in which the skill should be performed, people who will typically cue the response, and teaches and/or verifies that the pupil can perform the skill across at least those functional tasks, cues to respond, settings, and people.

Adapting response requirements

Many moderately and severely handicapped students have limited speech. Most math skill sequences and curricula typically require that students use speech as a response mode, making them inappropriate for some students. The teacher of these students needs a sequence of math skills which may be adapted to either verbal or nonverbal students.

In the sets component of the math skills sequence, students who can classify objects according to their functional use (e.g., consistently demonstrate the intended function of objects) may be taught the gestures or the words associated with the objects or both. For instance, students who functionally use a variety of cups and thus know a rudimentary concept of cup may be taught that the things they drink from are called "cups." We teach students alternative ways of labeling or representing the concept of cup. That is, gestures for cup, the word "cup," and the object itself may all represent the same concept.

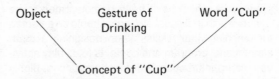

Object   Gesture of   Word "Cup"
                Drinking

                Concept of "Cup"

During periods when eating, drinking, and washing are scheduled, we have been successful in teaching the words and gestures associated with ball, comb, spoon, cup, washcloth, and toothbrush. Before using objects, students are required to make the gesture involved in using the objects: for ball, a throwing movement may be used; for comb, a combing movement may be used; or for toothbrush, a brushing movement may be used. Objects from daily activities (e.g., eating, dressing, bathing) appear to be the most appropriate for initial instruction. Success is realized when students learn to use a gesture to request an object.

As teaching progresses, the similarity between the gesture representing the object and the functional movement from which the gesture was derived should decrease. Students learn to use abbreviated hand movements or gestures. This is a schematization of the gesture called "denaturalization" (Lee, Note 1, 1973). Thereafter, for example, the whole combing movement does not need to be used for comb and a partial gesture may be used for drinking. As instruction progresses, students learn to use a standard sign language, such as American Sign Language.

In addition to "denaturalization," progressive instruction should lead to response generalization. That is, the gesture is used to request an object out of the context in which it was taught. For instance, students learn to use the gesture to request a different cup in a different setting—using the gesture for cup in the kitchen where it was taught and at the snack time to request a cup of juice. Generalization of gestures from the original functional use and from the context in which they were taught appears to be one development of symbolization.

We attempt to facilitate words becoming symbols for concepts in a similar fashion to gestures. That is, students are taught to say the object label before obtaining an object. Response generalization occurs when the word is used to request an object out of the context in which it was taught. For instance, students may use the word "ball" in the play area to obtain a big red ball, and the word "ball" on the playground to request a blue ball or even to request a ball when no ball is present.

We have also taught nonverbal students to use pictures of objects and later printed words as an alternative system of expressive language. Objects, spoken words, gestures, printed words, and pictures which represent the same class of objects (concept) may be called equivalent operations.

When selecting nonverbal operations for comprehension instruction, initially select nonverbal operations that provide an opportunity for students to interact with task materials, such as "show me," "take." Nonverbal students should be taught to use such expressive modes as signing and communication boards to label math concepts. In addition, the type of expressive output required of students in a math program should be appropriate to the individual student's mean length of utterance. That is, students who typically use 1-word utterances should be required to use 1-word utterances and students who use 3-word utterances should be required to use 3-word utterances when responding to math tasks. The math skill sequence should be adapted to students by selecting verbal and nonverbal operations which are readily available within a student's repertoire for demonstrating knowledge of math skills.

Adapting tasks and materials

Many tasks and materials may be used to teach a skill. As previously described, a task is a specified situation in which a particular skill should occur. For example, aligning cups and saucers in one-to-one correspondence is a task. One-to-one correspondence may be taught through multiple tasks such as aligning cups and straws, pencils and paper and so on. Different materials may be used within a task. A student may be taught to align cups and saucers of different color, shape, and size in one-to-one correspondence. Williams, Brown, and Certo (1975) suggest that teachers select tasks and materials using the following criteria: (A) their functional use to the student; (B) their accessibility or frequency of occurrence in the environment of the student; (C) their reinforcement value to the student; (D) their facilitation of discrimination learning; (E) their applicability to repeated practice during skill acquisition; and (F) their facilitation of future skill maintenance.

It is difficult to devise tasks which meet all these criteria. Rather a teacher seeks tasks which when combined meet the criteria. By drawing from 3 basic categories of tasks, this combination of instructional activities can be devised: (1) functional activities; (2) games; and (3) repeated practice tasks.

Functional activities. Functional activities are tasks which students need to perform frequently in daily living. For instance, sorting may be taught through activities of daily living such as putting boots on the floor and coat on a hook while undressing, putting the blocks on one shelf and puzzles on another shelf while cleaning up, and so on. Skills are often not maintained when only infrequent use is required. Teaching students to perform skills through frequently occurring activities of daily living should enhance maintenance.

Games. Frequent use and practice of skills can be assisted through incorporating the skill into a game or play activity. When skills are integrated into games, the process of skill maintenance is made fun for students. For instance, one-to-one correspondence skills may be maintained through review sessions or through games, such as musical chairs, which require students to use the skill in the context of play.

Repeated Practice Tasks. Skill acquisition is usually facilitated through frequent sessions which provide each student with many response opportunities during instruction. Many games and functional tasks (e.g., passing out milk during snack) permit only one or two response opportunities for a limited number of students each day. In most cases it is necessary to use tasks that can be frequently presented and provide repeated opportunities for responses and instruction. In addition, repeated practice tasks may often be designed to facilitate discrimination learning. Examples of the task can be presented that attempt to make the essential stimulus characteristics (e.g., number, form, size) easy to discern. It may be difficult to highlight these same characteristics as they occur within functional tasks and games, for instance, when teaching students to label numerals, it may be difficult to emphasize the forms of the numerals as they appear on price tags. In most cases repeated practice tasks need to be used in conjunction with functional tasks and games to facilitate generalization and fade reliance upon cues.

It is important to select and sequence tasks according to the representational levels of the task materials. There are four basic material representational levels: (1) real objects; (2) photographs and representations of objects, such as toy animals; (3) simple pictures, such as line drawings, flannel items, and workbook pages; and (4) complex pictures, such as those found in magazines.

A skill should initially be taught in relation to real objects and events, then the student should progress to performing the skill in relation to photographs and object representations, simple pictures, and, finally, complex pictures. For example, when teaching students to count rationally, first teach them to count real objects, then progress to object representations (such as toy animals) and objects depicted in photographs. Next, teach students to count objects depicted in simple line drawings, and, finally, teach them to count objects represented in magazine pictures.

Reformulating instructional objectives

Although the importance of precisely formulating instructional objectives cannot be overemphasized, as Goodstein (1975) points out, precisely formulated instructional objectives have inherent limitations when developing instructional programs for students with moderate and severe handicaps. For instance, if an objective states that students should verbally label objects, an alternative objective may have to be formulated for nonverbal students. Similarly, objectives may have to be revised for physically impaired deaf, or blind students.

As instructional objectives become more precisely formulated, there exists a parallel need to formulate more alternative objectives. As listings of alternative objectives become more numerous, *the ability of the teacher to use the listings of objectives to make sequencing decisions for curriculum planning becomes more limited. (Goodstein, 1975, p. 2)*

If because of a sensory or motor impairment, an objective is not appropriate for a student, adapt the objective to meet the student's needs. Goodstein (1975) describes a matrix teaching system which is useful in adapting instructional objectives. When adapting an instructional objective, alternative teacher output modes, alternative student input modes, alternative student responses, and cognitive level of materials may be selected.

The four dimensions and the alternatives delineated in each dimension combine to form matrices of instructional interactions. The matrices facilitate the formulation of alternative objectives or tasks to meet the motor, sensory, and communication impairments of severely handicapped students. Within a matrix teaching system, it is possible to delineate sequences through which most students should progress and to select alternative teacher output modes, student input modes, student response modes, and representational levels of materials from the matrices when adapting objectives or tasks to meet the specific needs of individual students.

To illustrate the use of these matrices, consider the teacher who requests a student to count a group of 5 straws by saying, "Count these straws and tell me how many there are." These instructions and the expected student response may be classified within the corresponding matrix. Teacher output would be verbal, unless the counting response was also modeled making the output verbal *and* motoric. Student input would be auditory and visual—listening to the directions and looking at the straws. The student response mode for a verbal student would be motoric and verbal while the materials are real, familiar objects. If the student had been auditorally, visually, or motorically impaired, adjustment would be necessary in the teacher's output. Functional modes of student input could be tapped, as well as the response mode; i.e., the student could express a reaction to the task requests and materials.

We are typically concerned with teaching students such skills as counting, adding, subtracting, and so on. However, in some cases because of our current lack of knowledge and technology, we fail to teach students such skills even after providing intensive instructional intervention. In addition, if a moderately or severely handicapped student is provided his first educational program at the age of 19, time restraints may arbitrarily limit the skills we can teach him. When faced with such challenges we can translate specific behaviors (counting and addition) into their functions and then derive alternatives for those behaviors which will accomplish the same function.

For example, one math-related function students should learn is purchasing items at stores. To perform this function students should learn to determine how much money they have. This function may be performed by counting by ones to count pennies, counting by fives to count nickels, counting by hundreds to count dollars, and so on. An alternative would be to provide students with money counters, such as those used by banks, in which pennies are piled in a slot long enough to correspond to units of 100. Students should also learn to sum the cost of individual items. This function may be performed by addition or by using a hand calculator. Another function students should learn is to determine whether they have enough money to pay for the items. This function may be accomplished through subtracting the money on hand from the total cost of the items or by using a hand calculator or number line.

The vehicle we provide a student for performing a function should be the most chronological age appropriate, normal, and least restrictive possible. A vehicle for performing a function is restrictive if it requires the presence of specified devices or restricts the student from performing the function in specified environments. Relative to these guidelines, hand calculators and money counters are less viable alternatives for counting money than addition and subtraction skills. We should teach students functional alternatives such as using hand calculators only after we have exhausted the possibility of teaching them addition and subtraction. A key point in setting educational objectives is that we must not be handicapped in our ability to derive functional alternatives that meet the students' individual needs.

Task Analyzing Component Skills

Skill sequences may also be adapted to individual needs by adding or deleting component skills. First, each component skill of the sequence is stated as an instructional objective tailored to students' individual vision, speech, auditory, and motor needs, then the objective is broken into a separate sequence of component skills. For example, if rational counting, rote counting, and numeral recognition are selected, instructional objectives are written for each with adjustments for individual students' handicaps. Next, task analysis, as described in Chapter 2, is used to subdivide each objective into a series of component skills leading from the students' entry level to mastery of the objective.

Developing a Math Program Around Relevant Tasks

An important step in developing an instructional program based upon relevant tasks is to delineate functional tasks, games, and repeated practice tasks through which the skill may be taught. Some potential functional tasks for the sets component of the math skill sequence are sorting food items at snack time (e.g., put the milk on the shelf and cookies on the table); sorting objects when setting up or cleaning up an activity (e.g., put the puzzles on the shelf and the balls in the box); joining (adding) sets when cleaning up or setting up an activity (e.g., put the paint and the crayons on the table; put the paper and scissors on the floor).

Some potential games for teaching sets are board games which require the students to draw a card and move their markers to the next square on the board which matches the card, and grab bag, which requires students to draw an object from a bag and then label it. Selected tasks which are applicable to repeated practice are sorting or making sets of objects (e.g., blocks and toy bears) at the classroom worktable; sorting or making sets of flannel items; and sorting or making sets of pictures. Students should be systematically required to use the math skills throughout the day. The following is a sample daily routine for teaching and requiring students to use the skills of one-many and one-to-one correspondence.

Opening Tasks

One-to-one correspondence tasks. The bulletin board is divided into a present and absent section. Each student has a name card and name cards are sorted into the appropriate section of the bulletin board. To teach one-to-one correspondence, ask a student to take roll (or you take roll) by giving one name card to each student. If there are too many name cards, someone is absent. In this instance reading and naming classmates are being taught concurrently with one-to-one correspondence. Picture name cards may be used instead of words.

Another section of the bulletin board is devoted to a job board with pictures of the various jobs (e.g., watering plants, feeding fish). A check is placed next to each job that has been completed. During opening activities students can ascertain whether all jobs have been completed by determining whether each job has a check. In this case home living skills (jobs) and cooperating (everyone has a job) are being taught concurrently with one-to-one correspondence.

One-many tasks. During attendance the students can be asked if one or many students are present or absent. Students may be also asked to bring one or many crayons, pieces of paper, etc., with them for a special activity.

Math Class Tasks

During math class repeated practice tasks are presented.

One-to-one correspondence tasks. Some one-to-one correspondence tasks are requesting students to give each flannel circle a flannel star; to give each cup a saucer; to give each paintbox a brush; and to give each piece of candy a penny.

One-many tasks. Some one-many tasks are presenting a set of one apple and a set of many apples and requesting students to touch, point to, take the set with one or many; presenting pictures of one comb and many combs and requesting students to point to the set with one or many; and pointing to a set of objects and asking students if the set has one or many objects.

Language Tasks

In language some students may be learning the functional use of objects (drink from cup, eat with spoon, stir with spoon, eat from bowl). Others may be learning to demonstrate nonverbal comprehension of object labels (presented with objects and the cue, "Take a spoon," the student takes a spoon), or to label objects (asked "What is this?" or "What do you want?", students indicate, verbally or nonverbally, the object name). These language skills may be taught through such tasks as tea party play. During the course of the tea party the students are requested to demonstrate functional object use or receptive comprehension of object labels or to label objects. Students can also be requested to "give each classmate a cup" to demonstrate one-to-one correspondence and receptive comprehension of the label "cup."

Snack Time Tasks

Snack time is a variation on the tea party activities of the language period. Students are asked to give each classmate a napkin, to bring one or many cartons of milk from the kitchen, to indicate whether they want one or many pieces of cookie, etc.

Recess Tasks

Students can be asked to take to the playground one or many balls, jump ropes, etc. In addition, games such as musical chairs could be played to teach one-to-one correspondence.

Prereading Tasks

One-to-one correspondence. While looking at pictures, students can be asked to indicate whether each person in the picture has a hat on, whether every bear has feet, etc.

One-many. Some one-many tasks are requesting students to bring one or many pencils, crayons, pieces of paper, to reading class; and while looking at pictures, students can be asked to indicate whether there are one or many dogs, cats, policemen in the picture.

Math skills can be taught and used throughout most daily activities. These limited examples attempt to illustrate that math skills should *not* be taught in isolation but should be taught in relation to other skills (language, reading, recreation, social) if they are to be functional, to be maintained, and to generalize.

Advanced Math Skills

We have concentrated on the initial math skills to illustrate the functionality of math skills for severely and moderately handicapped students. The skill sequence does not differ greatly from math skill sequences in use in most preschools and elementary schools and the sequences which may be found in commercially available curricula for the moderately and severely handicapped. The difference is the emphasis upon teaching the operation of one-to-one correspondence and upon insuring that the math skills taught are functional. As teachers of the severely handicapped we cannot afford to assume that isolated skills taught to students in instructional settings will be used in their daily lives. The math skill sequences used by regular educators to teach such advanced skills as column addition, volume, subtraction, money, time telling, and the calendar have applicability to moderately and severely handicapped students. However, we have to adapt them to the particular needs of severely handicapped students by (A) adapting instructional procedures (e.g., using more systematic and intensive procedures); (B) adapting response requirements (e.g., allowing for verbal and nonverbal responses); (C) adapting instructional tasks (e.g., teaching skills through functional tasks, games, play and repeated practice tasks); (D) formulating or reformulating instructional objectives; and (E) task analyzing component skills of the sequence. With this approach, we have successfully taught moderately handicapped students advanced math skills.

Space does not permit a lengthy discussion of teaching advanced math skills to severely and moderately handicapped students. However, skill sequences and instructional programs from a number of sources may be readily adapted to the particular needs of severely handicapped students (Bereiter & Engelmann, 1966; Brown, Crowner, Williams, & York, 1975; Brown, Williams, & Crowner, 1974; Engelmann, 1969; Engelmann & Engelmann, 1966; Peterson, 1973; Resnick et al., 1973).

Assessment

Finally, we will briefly discuss an assessment model (DeSpain, Williams, & York, 1975) that has been developed for use with the math skill sequence (Figure 9.2). The model stresses controlled initial assessment with variations encouraged as teaching strategies are developed. Mastery is assumed to have occurred only after teachers can record evidence of functional skill use across materials, tasks, cues, persons, and settings. In this model, if students can perform a skill but fail to use it functionally, they have not completely mastered the skill.

The model basically consists of seven steps:

1. Box A: Before assessing students formally, become familar and comfortable with them. Informally assess what environmental events control a student's behavior. Use information from this informal assessment to determine optimal assessment conditions.
2. Box B: Assessment: Level I. Assess one or more objectives from the skill sequence under optimal but controlled conditions. If students fail the objective, go to Box D (Assessment: Level II); if they pass, go to Box H (Check for Functional Use).

3. Box D: Assessment: Level II. If students could not perform the skills required by an objective in Level I assessment, assess students' behavior under varied conditions to determine under what conditions (e.g., cues, models, prompts, reinforcement) they can perform the skills. Use information from this assessment to develop an instructional strategy (Box F).
4. Box F: Teach students the target skills.
5. Box H: Assess student mastery of skills. First verify that they can use the skill in the performance of functional tasks which frequently occur (e.g., setting the table, dressing). If they use the skill across functional tasks, formally check skill performance across persons, materials, settings, and language cues (Box I).
6. Box I: Verify student performance of skills across persons, materials, settings, and language cues.
7. Box J: Review (reassess) student skill performance.

A. Determination of Optimal Assessment Conditions

In order to make a valid assessment of a student's performance on a given objective, we provide conditions that will evoke the student's optimal performance. It is important to become familiar and comfortable with students before formally evaluating them. The evaluation situation should be pleasant, facilitating a valid assessment of the student's skills. With new students it is often necessary to spend several days playing with them and presenting assessment tasks informally. During the informal assessment, attempt to determine:

1. The optimal *setting* for administering the assessment (e.g., perhaps the table where students usually perform tasks).
2. The *person* who is most likely to evoke optimal performance from the students.
3. *Materials* familiar to the students which should potentially insure optimal performance.
4. Potential *reinforcers* which have encouraged performance in the past.
5. *Language cues* to which the students have demonstrated they can correctly respond.
6. A *style* of task presentation that elicits optimal performance from the students (e.g., the teaching style of the *teacher* for whom the students work well—play/unstructured, competitive/gamelike, etc.).

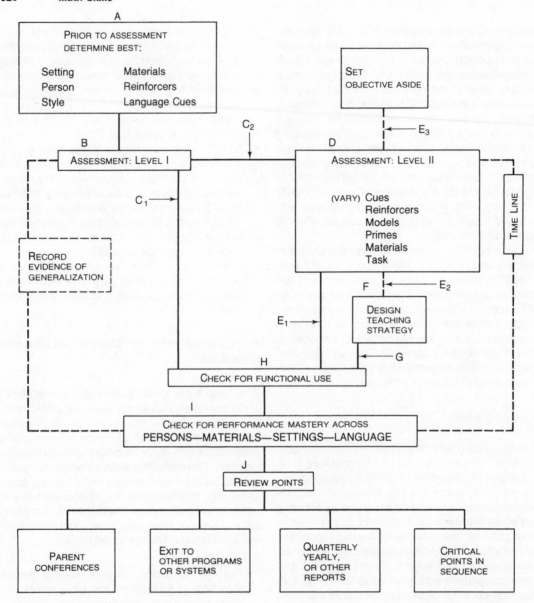

FIGURE 9.2   *Maze evaluation program: assessment phase*

B. *Assessment: Level I*

Once the potentially optimal conditions have been determined, an assessment of selected objectives is administered under conditions which are controlled but which should elicit optimal performance. (Chapter 2 describes how to design assessment procedures.) Only administer tests on objectives for which students have demonstrated either through previous test performance or data from their ongoing math program that they have the prerequisite skills. For instance, if students do not perform the operation of rational counting or one-to-one correspondence, they lack the prerequisite skills for equivalence, more/less, ordering numerals, and addition, and it is not necessary to assess their performance in these skill areas.

When evaluating a particular skill area (e.g., sets, one-many, rational counting), it may be advantageous to test the highest objective in the skill area first. If students fail on 2 consecutive trials, alter the procedure (note on the data sheet that you are switching to a Level II procedure) and try to evoke the correct response any way you can (e.g., model, prime, change the instructional cue, change the materials, change the reinforcement). If students respond correctly to a Level II procedure, note on the data sheet what alternatives did and did not evoke correct response. Then move to the next lower objective in the sequence. Follow this procedure until you arrive at an objective which students perform correctly.

C. First Decision Point (C_1 or C_2)

(C_1) If the student performs the objective(s), the decision (C_1) is to move to an assessment of skill mastery (H, I, J) but at a later date. (C_2) If the student does not perform the objective in Level I, the decision (C_2) is to move immediately to Level II of assessment D.

D. Assessment: Level II

If students could not perform skills at Level I, Level II requires the evaluator to assess students' performance under varied conditions (e.g., varied *cues, reinforcers, models, primes, materials, tasks*) in an attempt to determine under what conditions the student can correctly perform a skill. The students' performance in various conditions should be carefully recorded. Information from the Level II assessment may be used to devise a teaching strategy.

E. Second Decision Point (E_1, E_2, or E_3)

(E_1) If Level II assessment indicates the students can correctly perform a skill across varied conditions, skill mastery may be assessed (H, I, J). (E_2) If students can at least partly perform the skills required under varied conditions, such as verbal prompts, modeling, and cuing, the conditions which produce correct performance are incorporated into a teaching strategy (F) for the students. (E_3) If it is found that students cannot perform the skills required by the objective under any conditions, the decision (E_3) is to set the objective aside until the student has mastered the prerequisite skills.

F. Teaching Strategy

Whoever is charged with designing students' programs should use the data from the Level II assessment to design and implement an appropriate instructional program. Intervention and measurement strategies similar to those described in Chapters 2 and 3 should be designed.

G. Third Decision Point

When students demonstrate that they have learned the skills required by the objective through an instructional program, functional use and skill mastery is assessed.

H. Functional Use

The most critical feature of the model is the assessment of students' functional use of a skill. The teacher, with assistance from students' parents or guardians, should report in what functional tasks students can perform a skill. The report should indicate what cues the performance of tasks (e.g., the task itself, verbal language cues), what the tasks are, and the date. Both parents and teachers should have a similar data sheet and when they observe students independently perform a skill on a functional task, they should record the cue, task and setting, and date. The recording format in Figure 9.3 appears to be appropriate. If the data indicate that over time a student performs a skill across functional tasks, people, settings, and language cues, then a formal test of skill mastery across these dimensions should be implemented (I).

I. Confirmation of Skill Performance

Student performance of a skill across a variety of selected persons, materials, settings, and language cues is formally assessed by outside evaluators, such as a school psychologist. Skill mastery is confirmed when several persons have verified that the student can perform a skill under various conditions.

J. Review Points

Student mastery of skills should be periodically assessed, reassessed, and reported. The assessment, reassessment, and reporting of skill mastery should coincide with (A) parent conferences, (B) quarterly and/or semester periods, and (C) the students' mastery of selected critical curriculum objectives. When any one of the events (A, B, C) occurs, teachers should use their data on students' skill acquisition and, if appropriate, student performance on a formal evaluation of skill mastery to list at least:

1. For what people a student performs the skill.
2. In what settings a student performs the skill.
3. Across what materials a student will perform the skill.
4. In response to what language cues a student will perform the skill.

Skill		School	Home	Other
Less	tasks cues dates			
More	tasks cues dates			
Equivalence	tasks cues dates			
1-to-1 correspondence	tasks cues dates			
One-many	tasks cues dates			
Sorting	tasks cues dates			

FIGURE 9.3   *Recording form for assessment of skill use.*

5. Across what functional tasks a student has demonstrated that he can perform the skill.

This information can then be used for the following purposes:

1. Reporting to parents and the school system on a student's progress.
2. Assessing a student's rate of progress.
3. Evaluating the skill sequence. If data from many students indicate that most students are requiring an unusual amount of instruction to master a skill, it may be that the skill sequence fails to delineate appropriate prerequisites or instructional procedures necessary for the acquisition of that skill.
4. Evaluating the effectiveness of a teacher's program. If a teacher is moving the students through skills at an unusually rapid pace, the teacher may request that the instructional program be closely evaluated to determine why it is unusually effective so that others may emulate it. Conversely, if the data indicate that students are mastering few or no skills, a teacher may request that a more successful teacher help restructure the program or that a curriculum specialist evaluate the program.

Generalization and Rate of Learning Place

Concurrent to and following instruction of a skill (F), persons in the students' environment should be aware of the instructional objectives and record (anecdotally) any evidence of generalization of the skill being taught.

There should be emphasis on recording the rate of student progress through the sequence. Information on what skills students can perform and student acquisition rates can be used instead of traditional testing (e.g., IQ, achievement tests). We believe this information will be more valid and viable than information gleaned through traditional evaluation.

Conservation of Accumulated Data

Finally, the model lends itself to the conserving (storing and retrieving) of critical data and provides potentially useful data to all who have use for it (parents, teachers, administrators, psychologists).

In our judgment the evaluation model has the following attributes:

Validity. The model is valid because it measures actual student performance through criteria-based objectives under optimal student performance conditions.

Reliability. The model is reliable since it provides for confirmation of student performance across persons, settings, and materials.

Generalizability. The model is generalizable since it can be adapted for use across the total of the student's environment.

Ecological. The model is ecological since it insures functional performance of skills across the total of the student's environment.

Conserving. The model conserves since it allows for an orderly recording of achievement and rate of achievement for every student so that retrieval of information is easily achieved.

Flexible. The model is flexible since it encourages all key figures in the student's environment to be evaluators.

This assessment model should be applicable to many skill sequences (e.g., language, play, self-care, reading). We expect that it provides basic principles and concepts of assessment, but these principles and concepts must be adapted to particular circumstances.

Summary

In summary, this chapter describes a math skill sequence and specific applications to moderately and severely handicapped students. Although most students learn these skills in the same order, at times the sequence must be adapted to an individual student's needs. This can be accomplished by adjusting the response requirements, the instructional tasks and procedures, reformulating instructional objectives, and task analyzing component skills of the sequence. If math skills are taught through functional tasks and games which frequently occur in the students' environments, the students will be more apt to generalize the skills. Math skills are not merely academic nor are they irrelevant if they are taught through functional tasks such as counting money, setting the table, and passing out food at snack time.

References

Bereiter, C., & Engelmann, S. *Teaching disadvantaged children in the preschool.* Englewood Cliffs, N.J.: Prentice-Hall, 1966.

Brown, L., Crowner, T., Williams, W., & York, R. (Eds.), *Madison's alternative for zero exclusion: A book of readings* (Vol. 5). Madison, Wis.: Madison Public Schools, 1975.

Brown, L., Williams, W., & Crowner, T. *A collection of papers and programs related to public school services for severely handicapped students* (Vol. 4). Madison, Wis.: Madison Public Schools, 1974.

DeSpain, C., Williams, W., & York, R. Evaluation of the severely retarded and multiply-handicapped: An alternative. In L. Brown, T. Crowner, W. Williams, & R. York (Eds.), *Madison's alternative for zero exclusion: A book of readings* (Vol. 5). Madison, Wis.: Madison Public Schools, 1975.

Engelmann, S. *Preventing failure in the primary grades.* Chicago: Science Research Associates, 1969.

Engelmann, S., & Engelmann, T. *Give your child a superior mind.* New York: Simon & Schuster, 1966.

Fredericks, H. D. *The teaching research curriculum for moderately and severely handicapped.* Springfield, Ill.: Charles C Thomas, 1976.

Goodstein, H. A. Assessment and programming in mathematics for the handicapped. *Focus on Exceptional Children,* 1975, *7* (7), 1–11.

Koegel, R. L., & Covert, A. The relationship of self-stimulation to learning in autistic children. *Journal of Applied Behavior Analysis,* 1972, *5,* 381–387.

Peterson, D. *Functional mathematics for the mentally retarded.* Columbus, Ohio: Charles E. Merrill, 1973.

Resnick, L., Wang, M., & Kaplan, J. Task analysis in curriculum design: A hierarchiacally sequenced introductory mathematics curriculum. *Journal of Applied Behavior Analysis,* 1973, *6,* 679–710.

Spradlin, J. E., Cotter, V. W., Stevens, C., & Friedman, M. Performance of mentally retarded children on pre-arithmetic tasks. *American Journal of Mental Deficiency,* 1974, *78,* 397–403.

Williams, W., Brown, L., & Certo, N. Components of instructional programs for severely handicapped students. In L. Brown, T. Crowner, W. Williams, & R. York (Eds.), *Madison's alternative for zero exclusion: A book of readings* (Vol. 5). Madison, Wis.: Madison Public Schools, 1975.

Note

1. Lee, P. Co-active movement with deaf-blind children. In J. L. Horsley and W. J. Smith (Eds.), *New techniques for working with deaf-blind children.* Denver: Mountain Plains Regional Center for Services to Deaf-Blind Children, 1973.

10

Functional Reading

*This chapter was written by **Martha E. Snell,** Department of Special Education, University of Virginia.*

The educational goals for the moderately and severely handicapped center upon useful skills that enable increasing amounts of independence in the tasks of daily living. Teachers of these students must operationalize these goals in order that their curricula systematically build such skills. To do this a teacher must ask how much reading ability is necessary to achieve a functional skill.

Many would quickly state that a basic "protective" vocabulary should be readily recognized and understood by the student. This set of words would include certain street signs (stop, walk, don't walk, etc.), building signs (danger, men, women, open, push, exit, entrance), and other cautionary words (poison, do not enter, private, danger) as well as their standard pictorial representations (i.e., the international sign system). The number of protective words would vary considerably from teacher to teacher as would the words themselves. Other teachers would expand this list and include words pertaining to days and months, name and address, cooking, shopping, entertainment, and employment. This expansion quickly transforms a list of 15 to 50 words into one the size of a small dictionary. For example, the Oregon State curriculum for

teachers of the trainable (*Curriculum-Cumulative Progress Report,* Note 1, page 1) in the cooking category lists 52 verbs and adjectives from recipes: "wash," "cook," "cut," "saute," "scramble," "soft boil," "hard boil," "scrape," "poach," etc. Then there are still food words, utensil words, and all the common adjectives, adverbs, conjunctions, prepositions, and so on commonly found in even the simple cookbooks. In short, while a list of cautionary vocabulary words may tend to be shorter than functional vocabulary lists, both sets of reading vocabulary lack specific definition, and their actual content is related to variables of school district, teacher philosophy, and the student's specific vocational preparation and daily living curriculum.

Some teachers would dodge the question altogether and state that reading instruction is unrealistic for this population, that it is too complex a skill, and that success will not be forthcoming. Class time, they say, would be spent more profitably on other, less academic skills. This attitude is reflected by Kirk's words (1973):

In general, trainable children do not learn to read from even first grade books. Their ability is limited to reading and recognizing their names, isolated words and phrases, common words used for their protection, such as "danger", "stop", "men", "women" and other signs which they encounter in a community. Some trainable children with special abilities can learn to read. Most who learn to read, however, are probably educable mentally retarded children. (p. 231)

Kirk's comments represent the position that the task of reading is reliant upon mental abilities far beyond the capabilities of those functioning in the moderate and severe ranges of mental deficiency (Apffel, Kelleher, Lilly, & Richardson, 1975).

Fortunately, there has been a reasonable amount of research demonstrating successful procedures to teach reading to the moderately and severely handicapped. However, as with other complex skills, (1) the handicapped pupil's success is clearly a product of the teacher's ability to analyze and program instruction; (2) the pupil's progress is usually slower than for learners with no mental or emotional handicap; and (3) the ultimate level of ability is less for handicapped as compared with normal learners. None of these three characteristics need prevent the development of reading as a useful skill.

This chapter will analyze the task of reading and its measurement, will set forth guidelines to determine realistic long-term goals in reading instruction for the moderately and severely handicapped learner, will discuss implications of research for teaching reading to this special population, and will review the content of specific reading programs successful with these learners. (Because the cognitive aspects of handwriting instruction are so closely related to learning to read, the behavioral components leading to writing and their placement in the reading progression will be included in the task analysis section.)

Terminology

Before delving into instructional methods, a few terms require further definition. The description "functional" is commonly applied to describe the orientation of skill development for the severely handicapped. As it applies to reading vocabulary lists or to literacy, it takes on somewhat different meanings.

Functional Literacy

This term refers to minimal but practical competency in reading, indicating an ability to react appropriately to the daily reading and writing demands of modern life. These demands include the use of checks and bank statements; completion of appli-

cations for jobs, driver's license, Medicaid, Social Security number, etc.; reading recipes, maps, personal letters, categorized listings such as the Yellow Pages and the want ads, food labels, warranties, and so on. In Figure 10.1, Lichtman (1974) lists common printed materials representative of activities related to practical life activities.

The question of what level of reading is synonymous with functional literacy has caused great debate in recent years (Harman, 1970) with educators identifying from fourth- up to seventh-grade skills as minimal competency levels (Duffy & Sherman, 1977). However, most researchers are unanimous in agreeing upon the prevalence of the problem. The Survival Literacy Study (Heckler, Note 2, 1970) estimated that 13% of Americans are unable to complete common forms without making mistakes on 10% of the form's blanks, and one-third of these individuals make errors on more than 30% of the form. For example, 34% of those interviewed had trouble reading a simplified Medicaid application and 8% could not accurately complete a driver's license form. While the exact overlap between functional illiterates and those classified as severely educationally handicapped or mentally retarded is unknown, it is probably considerable because of the recency of effective instructional methods in reading for this population.

Realistic tools to measure functional literacy are still being developed and validated (Lichtman, 1974; Nafziger, Thompson, Hiscox, & Owen, 1975; Stricht, Caylor, Kern, & Fox, 1972). Traditionally the tests used to assess reading ability in the grade school have been applied inappropriately to test unskilled adults. Although these tests do tap the necessary abilities of word recognition and comprehension and moniter an individual's type of reading errors and rate, practical reading tasks are omitted and test content often is geared to children. Because it is essential that teachers of the severely handicapped be able to assess functional literacy, this topic will be expanded in a later section of the chapter.

Functional Reading

Although the definition of "functional reading" is not specific across users, it is quite similar to "functional literacy" but has more frequent use by special educators. Brown and Perlmutter (1971) define functional reading as "discrete and observable motor responses to printed stimuli" (p. 75), such that the student would learn two responses for any given

1	2	3	4	5
Signs and Labels	Schedules and Tables	Maps	Categorized Listings and Indices	High-Interest, Factual Narrative
Road Signs*	T.V. Guide*	City/Street	Yellow Pages	Sports Events
Clothing Tags	Bus Schedule	Road*	Book Indices	News Report
Medicine Labels	Train/Plane Schedule	Global	Want Ad*	Narcotics Article*
Billboards	Work/School Schedule	Weather	Dictionary	

6	7	8	9
Illustrated Advertisements	Technical Documents	Sets of Directions	Fill-in Blank Form
Department Store	Conditional Sales Contract	Recipe (Pizza)*	Banking Forms
Yellow Pages	Insurance Policies	Use of Tools/ Machinery/ Equipment	Job Application*
Food Store*	Guarantees		Car Registration
Magazine	Apartment Lease*	Sewing with Pattern	Credit Application
			Hospital Entry Form

*For each of these representative reading activities, detailed task analyses have been prepared, including terminal tasks and enabling tasks.

FIGURE 10.1   *Categories of commonly used printed materials.* [Items marked with an asterisk are included in a test of functional literacy: Reading/Everyday Activities in Life (R/EAL). The test is presented so that its appearance clearly resembles its actual printed form.]

Source: M. Lichtman, The development and validation of R/EAL, an instrument to assess functional literacy. *Journal of Reading Behavior*, 1974, *6*, 172.

printed stimulus: to read the word and to indicate the word's meaning in an observable way. "Functional" dictates the practical nature of the vocabulary taught, but its difficulty range as judged by grade level and its exact content is less clear than that covered by the term "functional literacy." Brown and his colleagues emphasize that the goal of functional reading instruction is a skill that enables survival in our word-dependent community—making the term synonymous with functional literacy. Although the term does *not* prescribe teaching methods, it is true that a "whole word" or visual approach is commonly associated with functional reading. Students are taught to memorize words through repeated drill without placing emphasis upon sentence context, structural, or letter sound

cues (Brown, Huppler, Pierce, York, & Sontag, 1974).

Cautionary or Protective Vocabulary

This term includes that small set of warning words which, if recognized and understood as they normally appear on labels or signs in public places, serve to warn the reader of potential risks. This set consists of words like "Danger," "Keep out," "Poison," "Don't Walk," "Walk," and the associated symbols (skull and crossbones to symbolize poisonous substances) or sign cues (red, hexagonal stop signs). If a teacher elects to instruct only a protective vocabulary, most of the words included in a functional vocabulary or recognized by a functional literate would *not* be taught. Therefore, although the instructional task is less extensive, the resultant reading skill is far less practical.

Learning to Read—A Task Analysis

Underlying all successful instruction is a clearly defined understanding of the learning task. When the task is a complex one, such as reading, the analysis is difficult. If handwriting and written expression are added as logical extensions of reading, the complexity is multiplied. This section of the chapter borrows heavily from the work of others to describe a sequence of subtasks leading to reading and writing skills. The fine motor aspects of handwriting skills are not covered here but rather the behavioral components leading to writing skills and their placement within the reading progression. Chapter 6 outlines the physical considerations in the teaching of handwriting. The reader is referred also to the portions of Chapters 2 and 3 that detail behavior measurement, task analysis, and learning principles; these teaching skills serve as the basic tools for structuring learning into small, ordered steps, bolstering learning with the necessary cues and prompts, strengthening responses with an external motivation system, and measuring the learning stage and the extent of learning in each stage from acquisition and fluency to maintenance and generalization.

The analysis of a learning task relies upon the analyst's conceptualization of how the task is learned. Even with the simpler motor chains like handwashing, any given task analysis will vary from teacher to teacher; the detail in the steps, their order, and the method employed to achieve task completion will change depending upon the student performing the task, the materials used, and the teacher doing the analysis. With complex learning tasks like reading, many more conceptualizations of how the skill is acquired are possible. The task analyst must determine what visual, auditory, and visual-auditory stimuli need to be discriminated, the corresponding responses, and the order of instruction.

This section describes three overlapping analyses of reading. The first is the simplest but has been demonstrated to be successful with retarded learners (Sidman, 1971; Sidman & Cresson, 1973). This learning process may be labeled a *whole word* or look-say approach in that it involves auditory and visual matching of pictures (their spoken and printed labels) and words (both spoken and printed). The second analysis is actually a series of simple analyses of specific *functional tasks* (Lichtman, 1972) such as interpreting the directions on a macaroni and cheese mix box. The task analysis simply evaluates the reading and direction-following skills. After the learner has mastered a set of vocabulary words, these functional task analyses suggest learning activities consistent with the development of useful reading skills. While the whole-word instructional analysis details the steps to teach simple word acquisition, the functional analysis suggests steps for directing the learner to practically apply reading skills in everyday activities.

By necessity, the third analysis of reading is very detailed because it recognizes that reading involves both visual and auditory association and discrimination tasks as well as visual memory and sequencing. Reading is not simply a process of visual memorization. The third analysis of reading describes the behaviors necessary to take the learner from a performance level of no reading skills to a level of functional literacy—fluent reading at approximately the fourth-grade level with reading comprehension and an active use of word recognition strategies (Duffy & Sherman, 1973; Smith, Smith, & Brink, 1977). Although many of the earlier portions of this *functional literacy task analysis* have been successfully applied to the mildly and moderately mentally retarded (and will be reviewed in a later section of this chapter), it is not clear how many of the remaining reading behaviors can be mastered by the moderately or severely handicapped. Because of the success in reading reported in the literature with this population, the presentation of this complex task analysis as a guide for performance assessment and instruction is justified.

The selection of a task analysis (simple or complex) to guide reading instruction will depend upon many variables. The teacher must consider the learner's current performance in the prerequisite skills, the learner's chronological age or the number of schooling years that remain, and, depending upon the student's age, her vocational potential (if a younger learner), or her current need for reading in daily living and vocational activities (if an older learner). For students weak in receptive language, reading instruction is obviously inappropriate. Other students with a good receptive repertoire will learn best if teaching is limited to a whole-word approach. And for some, if instruction begins early enough and prerequisite skills are evident, the goal of functional literacy may be achieved by following a more complex analysis to guide learning.

TABLE 10.1   *Skills prerequisite for reading and handwriting instruction*

Handwriting[a]	*Reading*
Fine motor dexterity and visual-motor coordination which allows one to:	Basic language and sensory prerequisites:
1. Show hand preference	1. Intact visual and auditory sensory mechanisms[b]
2. Hold and grasp a writing implement with or without adaptation (built-up handle, etc.)	2. The ability to respond to classroom stimuli which control and direct the learner's attentiveness
3. Move a pencil on a paper and make marks with purposeful control (i.e., up, down, and circular movements which ideally are under control of verbal direction)	3. Meaningful receptive repertoire
	4. A repertoire of vocal responses (repeating words, matching sounds and words, etc.) under the learner's immediate control[b]
4. Make or copy straight lines (vertical and horizontal) and circles; then cross, square, and rectangle	5. Word associations leading to context cues
	6. The ability to match identical geometric shapes
5. Copy simple letters (V, H, T, O); then print capital initials of own name	7. When given sounds in pairs that are identical or clearly different, the ability to identify each pair as same or different

[a]Handwriting is regarded as a fine motor and cognitive ability which is not synonomous with written expression; given the necessary response adaptations (e.g., scan control typewriter), written expression is possible without any of the above visual-motor skills.
[b]While these behaviors are not mandatory, their absence necessitates the analysis of a more complex learning task with possible modifications in stimulus presentation format and response mode.
Source: Adapted from Cohen, Gross, and Haring (1976); Duffy and Sherman (1973); Smith, Smith, and Brink (1977); Staats (1968).

Prerequisites

One of the essential cognitive precursors to reading is a *large receptive repertoire of meaningful words* without which "reading" could be conditioned but would remain meaningless. Reading and writing are abstract symbol systems whose entire meaning rests upon their corresponding verbal interpretation. As Staats (1968) has stated:

> *Bringing a vocal response under the control of a printed word stimulus imparts no additional functions to the printed word stimulus than just that— unless the vocal response (or the stimulus it produces) has already acquired other functions (meanings). If the vocal response already has other functions, that is, elicits other responses, then bringing the vocal response under the control of the printed word will impart these "functions" to the word according to the learning principles involved. At this point, the individual will read the printed word with comprehension. (p. 508)*

Table 10.1 summarizes commonly identified, basic prerequisites to successful reading and handwriting instruction. If the learner is physically handicapped (manual dexterity, vision, or hearing),

this alone does not eliminate the goal of learning to read or to express oneself in print. It does require, however, that the response modes of the learner be modified. For example, a motorically impaired student may learn to use a headwand-operated typewriter or a scanning aid (Harris-Vanderheiden & Vanderheiden, 1977) in place of handwriting, while manual communication would serve as an alternate response system during reading instruction with deaf individuals; and braille, though a complex tactual symbol system in itself, would replace printed words for the blind reader.[1]

The mental and emotional handicaps present in our students act to deter learning in both known and controllable ways as well as in unknown ways. Research pertaining to what is known and controllable for this population in the instructional process will be

1. Response mode adjustments are major considerations in the instructional process for learners with physical impairments. However they are beyond the content limitations of this chapter. The reader is referred to Vanderheiden and Grilley (1976) and Vanderheiden and Harris-Vanderheiden (1977) for alternate nonvocal response modes appropriate to the motorically impaired, to Berger (1972) for a multimodal approach with deaf retarded, and to *Learning Steps* (1976) for deaf-blind learners.

reviewed following the discussion on task analysis and testing.

Whole word approach

Sidman (1971) and Sidman and Cresson (1973, p. 521) viewed the task of learning to read as making a transfer from learned auditory-visual stimulus equivalences (teacher says "cat," student selects card with "cat" printed on it) to the purely visual equivalences that define simple reading comprehension (teacher shows student the word "cat" and student selects the cat picture from a group of choices). According to them, the learning barriers

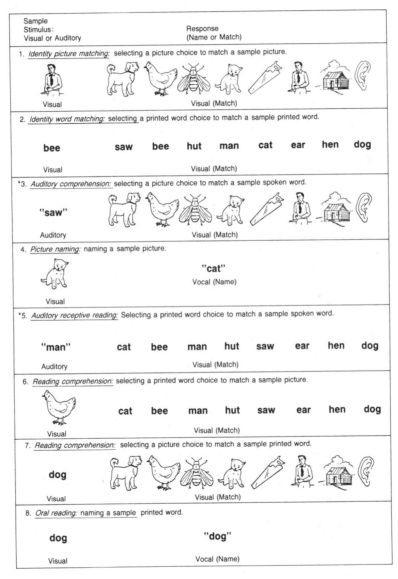

FIGURE 10.2   *A task analysis of learning to read by a whole word process* (Sidman, 1971; Sidman & Cresson, 1973)

Once tasks 3 and 5 were mastered, subjects demonstrated successful learning transfer to tasks 6, 7, and 8 — they demonstrated reading comprehension and oral reading without direct instruction on these skills.

Source of pictures: L. M. Dunn, *Peabody Picture Vocabulary Test.* Circle Pines, Minn.: American Guidance Services, 1959.

for most mentally retarded individuals who have been unsuccessful in learning to read *does not* concern the ability to understand spoken words (auditory comprehension, task 3 in Figure 10.2) or to name pictures (task 4). These individuals generally master both tasks. However difficulties occur in the ability to "break through the 'sound barrier,' " as Sidman puts it or to transfer from auditory comprehension and picture naming to visual reading comprehension (tasks 6 and 7) and oral reading (task 8) (Sidman, 1971, p. 6). Sidman (1971) and Sidman and Cresson (1973) proposed and then demonstrated that if severely handicapped learners *first* were taught all of tasks 1 through 4 in which they were deficient (1, picture matching; 2, word matching; 3, auditory comprehension; and 4, picture naming) and *second* were taught auditory receptive skills (task 5), then reading comprehension skills (tasks 6 and 7) and oral reading (task 8) emerged without any additional training directly on these tasks.

The learners in these research studies were functioning in the moderately and severely retarded range, demonstrated some skills in tasks 1 through 4 before teaching began, but essentially had no skills in tasks 5 through 8. They could not write, but were familiar with the automated teaching machine on which the teaching and testing was done. All 3 students learned to read 20 simple words after receiving instruction in the first 5 tasks listed in Figure 10.2. The majority of instruction was directed toward task 5 (auditory receptive reading) while tasks 2 and 3 (word matching and auditory comprehension) required a lot of instruction for 2 of the 3 students. The exact amount of instruction needed to teach these skills is difficult to quantify because it was sporadic; instruction ranged from one month of sessions for 1 student to a school year with sessions scheduled 1–3 times per week for another.

Depending upon the student's baseline performance in all the tasks, instruction began on one of the first 5 tasks and continued until the student had learned all 20 words at a given task level. Then instruction moved up to the next task in the first 5 tasks. The match-to-sample tasks (1, 2, 3, 5, 6, 7) were similar except that the sample stimulus in tasks 1, 2, 6, and 7 was visual while in tasks 3 and 5 it was auditory. Visual samples appeared in an automated central window on the teaching machine which, when pressed by the learner, caused the outer circle of 8 choices to be lighted. Auditory samples were spoken over a speaker followed by the 8 visual choices. In both cases, the student was to press the matching choice. In the 2 naming tasks (4 and 8) the center stimulus was lighted but outside choice panels remained blank since the task involved naming the stimulus rather than matching to a sample.

This method of teaching reading does not involve letter-sound association. Instead the emphasis is upon the whole word as a meaningful unit without any analysis of its parts. The main focus of instruction involves associating a spoken word with its printed word match (step 5), after prior visual discrimination of printed word similarities (step 2) and auditory comprehension of words (step 3). This analysis of a whole word approach is more complete than other definitions of the same method; some whole word methods go from picture naming directly to oral naming of words with modeled prompts, a rather large shift in task complexity; other visual methods focus primarily on word-object matches followed by word-reading drill. Two studies, which will be reviewed later (Hawker, 1968; Hawker, Geertz, & Shrago, 1964), suggest that steps 6 (picture stimulus–word choice) and 7 (word stimulus–picture choice) be reversed. This change would program the first task of reading comprehension to involve a choice between meaningful items (pictures) rather than items with low meaning (words). More comparative study is needed to know whether all 8 instructional steps in their present order represent the most efficient way to teach words without any letter-sound analysis.

Functional reading tasks

Another way to approach the task analysis of reading is to examine directly examples of reading encountered in common everyday situations, such as are listed in Table 10.1. Bender, Vallettutti, and Bender (1976) suggest that this examination include 10 primary categories of emphasis. For these categories they identify 116 specific examples regarded as essential functional reading activities. These categories and their subobjectives are listed in Table 10.2.

Once such a list has been generated, the rationale for including each objective should be examined so that unnecessary ones might be eliminated. Next the instructional sequence should be determined. For some objectives there will be a logical order for instruction which is dictated by the easy-to-hard relationships among objectives as well as by the dependencies of some tasks upon others. For example, before teaching a student to interpret a

TABLE 10.2 *Functional reading tasks and subobjectives*

1. *The student will identify important personal data when he sees it written* (p. 27). (For example, name, address, telephone number, social security number.)

2. *The student will respond appropriately to written information and markings on watches, clocks, and other dials and gauges* (pp. 36–37). (For example, identifies time by hour and half hour; operates the following: kitchen timer, electric toaster, refrigerator dial, electric can opener, stove, electric fry pan, oven dial, electric percolator, blender, electric mixer, dishwasher, automatic clothes washer and dryer, vacuum cleaner, iron, thermostat, electric fan, air conditioner, shaver, hair dryer, alarm clock, heating pad, electric blanket, television set, radio, record player, dials and switches on toys, cassette tape recorder, drill press, and self-service elevators; uses a food scale, bathroom scale, and telephone; and pays the correct fare on a taxi meter.)

3. *The student will respond appropriately to written information on safety signs, size labels, price tags, and other signs and labels* (pp. 59–60). (For example, reads signs for bathrooms, public buses, and traffic directions; recognizes warning signs identifying places as dangerous or recognizes information on packages, clothing care labels, and content identification labels; identifies correct value of stamps needed to mail letters, "Push," "Pull," "Entrance," "Exit," "In," "Out," and other signs found in public buildings, detour signs, and cost of admission at facilities open to the public; recognizes type of store or business by reading key words on signs, cooking and storing directions, cleaning instructions found on household cleaning and laundry agents, office and store hours, and public telephones; uses the size of packages to estimate quantity of foods and other substances found in various containers; and locates the mailboxes and doorbells of friends and relatives.)

4. *The student will respond appropriately to instructions written in simple notes* (p. 81). (For example, identifies names and titles of family members and acquaintances, objects common to student's home and school, basic action verbs, prepositions, numbers 1 to 10, time written in numerals, and amounts of money up to $100 written as numerals.)

5. *The student will locate needed information from simple charts, diagrams, maps, and menus* (pp. 88–89). (For example, identifies present and future dates on a calendar; locates key information on posters and informational charts; and uses hand drawn maps to get around school and community; uses bus maps, subway map, simple diagrams to assemble objects and make arts and crafts projects; and uses a menu to order meals.)

6. *The student will locate needed information from directories, schedules, and bulletin boards* (pp. 95–97). (For example, locates telephone numbers in personal and standard telephone directories, apartment numbers of acquaintances by using apartment house directories, office numbers by using office building directories, foods and other items in supermarkets by using supermarket directories, times of departures and arrivals using bus, train, and airplane schedules, and desired store floor by using department store directories; and identifies times of mail pickups on mailbox schedules and food and food prices on cafeteria bulletin boards.)

7. *The student will correctly carry out simple directions written on packages, machinery, equipment, games, toys, and items that are to be assembled* (p. 103). (For example, operates vending machines and coin-operated washers and dryers and follows the directions for preparing simple packaged foods, for playing with simple games and toys, and for objects to be assembled.)

8. *The student will respond appropriately to key words found on employment forms and other simple blanks and forms* (pp. 115–116). (For example, prints or writes name, address, telephone number, social security number, birthdate, and indicates sex, marital status, bank account number, correct amount of money, previous employment, and date on appropriate places on blanks and forms.)

9. *The student will respond appropriately to written information found on bills, work time cards, check stubs, and market receipts* (p. 123). (For example, pays bills by due date on bill and provides correct amount; identifies and varifies gross pay, net pay, and deduction information found on pay check stubs; checks market receipts to determine if charges are correct; checks to determine if work time-card information is correct.)

10. *The student will identify help wanted ads, printed advertisements, correspondence, and other written materials and will seek the assistance of a responsible person to decode written and printed material he is unable to read* (p. 132). (For example, identifies common abbreviations found in help wanted ads.)

Source: Italicized tasks from M. Bender, P. J. Valletutti, and R. Bender, *Teaching the Moderately and Severely Handicapped* (Volume III). Baltimore, Md.: University Park Press, 1976.

bus schedule or a television guide (objective 6), it is essential that the student be able to read times, the days of the week, and have or develop a sizable sight vocabulary of words commonly used in television show titles and streets and places in the community. Therefore time recognition (objective 2) and days of the week (objective 5) would be taught first. Another consideration for sequencing the objectives relates to the specific daily living and vocational needs of a given student. If a student lives in a boarding house, reading tasks related to cooking could be postponed while others may be of more immediate importance (e.g., operating automatic washers or dryers, use of bus schedules, and reading street signs relevant to pedestrians). For younger students living at home, functional reading instruction also should be tied to activities the student performs regularly at home and school so practice opportunities are created and the motivation for learning is maximized.

Listing and ordering general objectives that directly relate to functional reading activities are not synonomous with a task analysis but rather precede task analysis. Once a particular objective or small set of objectives has been informally selected as relevant for a student, each must be analyzed to identify (1) how the terminal behavior will be measured, (2) the enroute instructional objectives leading to achievement of the terminal objective, (3) the instructional order of those enroute objectives, and (4) the entry requirements or the skills *prerequisite* to the first enroute objectives.

Lichtman (1972) used a flow chart format to display her task analyses of the reading comprehension and direction-following skills involved in some everyday activities. Task analyses were made to determine the reading, writing, and comprehension skills involved in one representative material from each of the many categories of common printed materials listed in Figure 10.1. Then criterion-referenced tests were constructed to measure an individual's functional use and understanding of each of these nine materials: want ads, food store advertisement, television guide, road sign, road map, recipe, apartment lease, job application form, and high-interest, factual article on narcotics.

In Figure 10.3 the task analysis for following directions on a packaged pizza box is shown. An examination of the analysis reveals 8 enroute objectives with an instructional sequence roughly identified from botton to top by the 3 horizontal levels of objectives. Therefore, the 2 bottom objectives would be taught first and at the same time, although

in different sessions with each being measured separately. Furthermore, the 8 enroute objectives must be stated in measurable terms so performance corresponding to each objective can be evaluated. For example, the lower left-hand objective concerns the recognition and selection of ingredients and utensils needed to carry out the package instructions. A test of these skills might be constructed like that in Figure 10.4. The student's performance indicates a need for additional practice with specific review on reading the two words "can opener" and "cloth" and locating these objects without verbal reminders. Once criterion is met (95–100% correct performance on 2 consecutive tests), the teacher may plan to teach additional enroute objectives in the task analysis employing the same packaged mix. At the same time other simple packaged mixes may be employed to teach generalization of the skill just learned—recognition and selection of ingredients and utensils called for in the package directions.

If reading instruction for the moderately handicapped does *not* include functional applications of skills such as suggested by Bender, Valletutti, and Bender's extensive objective list and by Lichtman's functional literacy tasks, it is unlikely that reading skills will be used outside the classroom. However, a teacher must also employ a procedure to teach the reading abilities underlying each practical life activity. Task analyses of the practical life activity will identify the reading content, the comprehension involved, and behaviors related to carrying out the activity but will *not* supply an understanding of how to teach the visual and auditory elements involved in word recognition. Therefore a teacher must select or carry out an evaluation of the learning steps involved in word recognition abilities. This could be a simple analysis such as Sidman's (1971) or a more complex process as will be discussed next.

Functional literacy: Reading with word recognition and comprehension skills

In comparison to Sidman's whole word method, many additional skills must be learned in order to apply word recognition strategies to new words and to read with comprehension at a fourth-grade level of reading. In other words, learning to read at the level of functional literacy is a far more comprehensive chore than acquiring a small set of sight words via the whole word procedure. Contrasting an analysis of the learning process involved in achieving functional literacy with that involved in the functional application of these skills reveals another large difference in complexity. That is, Lichtman's flow charts and Bender et al.'s (1976) objectives detour the question of *how* reading skills are first acquired. Instead they analyze the abilities involved in survival reading activities such as filling out applications, reading a movie or television schedule, and cooking from a recipe.

As shown in Figure 10.5, a comprehensive analysis of learning to read has to meet at least 3 broad objectives: first, it must consider both visual and auditory elements; second, it must program for more than simply visual discrimination learning (i.e., visual memory and sequencing, auditory discrimination, sound-symbol association and sound-symbol association with meaningful clues); and third, it must sequence the skills for learning so that the learner with little or no ability to read is taught the basic readiness skills and may progress systematically to the initial mastery stage when the less efficient techniques of visual discrimination and memory are supplemented by a choice of word recognition strat-

egies as the means to "attack" new words (Duffy & Sherman, 1973). So that the skills listed in Figure 10.5 are understood, definitions and examples of prerequisite word recognition skills are listed in Table 10.3.

Prerequisite Word Recognition Skills

The student who is learning the prerequisite word recognition skills actually will be building 7 smaller skills, each of which is either primarily a visual task leading to recall and recognition of words or is an auditory task leading to letter and sound association and context awareness. How the student is taught these skills depends upon the type of learning task involved. When teaching *discrimination*, the teacher will direct the learner to note differences between stimuli; when teaching *memory*, the teacher will instruct the learner in various remembering strategies; *sequencing* tasks require that the learner direct his attention to the ordering of stimuli and employ memory strategies to retain that order;

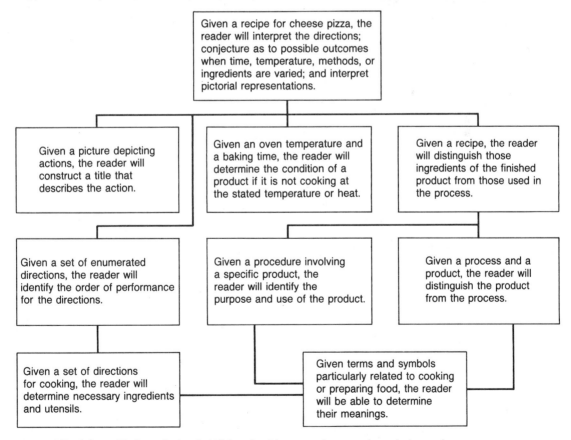

FIGURE 10.3   *Task analysis of skill involved in preparing a packaged pizza mix*

Source: M. Lichtman, *Reading/Everyday Activities in Life, Examiner's Manual*. New York: CAL Press, 1972, p. 22.

Name Nancy   Examiner Susan

Date 9-12-77   Situation Classroom Kitchen

Measurement: Baseline 2 Maintenance Generalization

Objective: enroute terminal Given a set of directions for cooking, the reader
will determine the necessary ingredients and utensils.

Conditions: *Utensils:* measuring cup, bowl, fork, pizza pan, can opener,
cloth to cover bowl. *Ingredients:* 1/2 c. warm water, grease, flour.
Appian Way pizza mix is used. All items in kitchen, but put away.

Criterion: 95—100% correct responses on 2 consecutive tests. Then recycle
objective for generalization (jello mix, canned soup, macaroni and
cheese mix); check pizza mix performance one month after criterion
(maintenance).

KEY: V = verbal instructions, M = model, P = physical assistance, + = correct unassisted, P = prompted
response, – = incorrect response, NR = no response; numbers indicate order of responses when
more than one response is given by student.

Behavior	Prompt				Performance				
1. Gets utensils	V	M	P		+	P	–	NR	
a. measuring cup					✓				
b. bowl					✓				
c. fork					✓				
d. pan				"That's not the right opener."	✓				
e. can opener	✓					2 ✓	1 ✓		bottle opener
f. cloth	✓			"What will you cover it with?"		2 ✓		1 ✓	
Score	100%				67%	(33%)	16%	16%	
2. Gets ingredients									
a. 1/2 c. warm water					✓				
b. grease					✓				
c. flour					✓				
d.									
e.									
f.									
Score					100%				

FIGURE 10.4   *Probe form for one enroute objective leading to the functional reading skill of compre-
hending and carrying out directions on a packaged food mix (e.g., pizza, cake, gelatine
mix)*

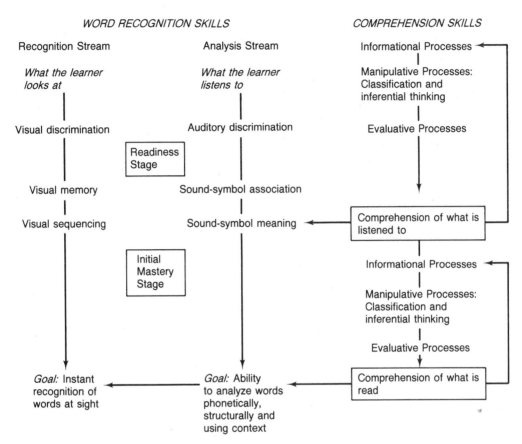

FIGURE 10.5   *Word recognition and comprehension skills leading to functional literacy*
Source: Modified from G. G. Duffy and G. B. Sherman, *How to Teach Reading Systematically*. New York: Harper & Row, 1973, p. 136.

when the task involves an *association,* the teacher will build on the learner's visual and auditory discrimination skills and direct the student's attention to connecting one type of stimulus (letter sound) to another (letter).

Because of the complexity of the task, other analyses of reading (Gagne, 1965; Smith, 1976; Smith et al., 1977; Staats, 1968) do not correspond exactly. Not only does the wording of the steps, their number, and detail vary from one analysis to another, but their order and the type of learning targets specified also tend to differ in ways reflecting the analyst's orientation toward learning itself. Duffy and Sherman's (1977) task analysis (Table 10.4) is presented because of its clarity, its comprehensiveness, its adaptability as an assessment and an instructional guide, and its goal of functional literacy suitable for some moderately handicapped learners.

Word Recognition Skills

To read fluently, a student must be able to instantly recognize a large number of words as well as quickly determine new words through sound analysis and context clues. Since fluency is the goal of this second stage of learning, the talents developed by the learner in the auditory analysis stream are combined and utilized as specific analysis techniques. The three different techniques are *phonetic analysis* or sounding out words; *structural analysis* or the recognition of meaning units in words such as parts of compound words, prefixes, suffixes, and parts of contractions; and *context analysis* or using the meaning of the sentence and preceding sentences to determine an unknown word. While the first two skills rely mainly upon the learner's auditory sense, context analysis is comprehension—a skill

TABLE 10.3   *Examples of prerequisite word recognition skills*

Prerequisite Word Recognition Skills	Exemplifying Behaviors[a]
Visual Discrimination—noting visual differences between geometric shapes, letters, and words.	"When given three geometric figures that are exactly alike and one that is clearly different, the learner will mark the one that is different." (p. 89)
Visual Memory—remembering the visual form and orientation of geometric figures, letters, and words. (May require a writing response mode.)	"When given a few seconds to examine a geometric figure, the learner will reproduce from memory, to the satisfaction of the teacher, a figure just like it." (p. 93)
Visual Sequencing—remembering the left-to-right order of letters and noting the first and last letter of a word.	"When presented with a card having his or her name printed on it, the learner will point to the first letter and to the last letter in his or her name." (p. 101)
Auditory Discrimination—noting differences in the beginning and ending sounds of words and in identifying specific beginning and ending sounds.	"Given spoken pairs of words, the learner will say 'Yes' if the words begin alike and will say 'No' if they do not begin alike." (p. 128)
Sound-Symbol Association—establishing connections between alphabet letters (consonants and vowels) and the sounds they produce. Requires auditory discrimination.	"Given a stimulus word beginning with either *m* or *d* and a group of three other words one of which begins with *m* or *d*, the learner will pair the two words beginning with the same letter sound." (p. 135)
Sound-Symbol Meaning—using both letter-sound correspondence and the source of context to identify unknown words. Requires auditory discrimination and sound-symbol connection.	"When given an oral sentence with one word missing and being cued for the missing word with a card having printed on it the first letter of that word (*m, d, l, c, s, h*), the learner will say a word that fits the context and begins with that letter." (p. 147)

Source: G. G. Duffy and G. B. Sherman, *Systematic Reading Instruction* (2nd ed.). New York: Harper & Row, 1977.

less dependent upon a single sense and more cognitive in nature.

Phonetic analysis includes three subskills: letter-sound correspondence, phonetic generalization, and syllabication (Duffy & Sherman, 1973). The prerequisite letter-sound associations focus upon single consonants and some consonant blends and digraphs[2] but do not teach symbol-sound associations for vowels. "Letter-sound correspondence" at this point in the development of reading skill focuses upon analyzing vowel sounds. In order to analyze the sound a vowel makes, one must know the letters that surround that vowel in any given word. Because a single vowel may have many sound associations depending upon the word it is in, one cannot identify its associated sound apart from seeing its position in a word. Instruction of vowel-sound correspondence proceeds in two stages. First the student is taught to recognize short-vowel phonograms[3] (*at, et, ot, ut, it*, etc.) within known words (*cat, pet, cot, nut, sit*) and then she is taught to replace the initial consonant with another to make a new word (*bat, set, rot, hut, pit*). Later the student learns to replace the final consonant in words containing known phonograms with another consonant or a digraph to make new words with new phonograms (*cat-cap, can; met-men, mesh*).

In the English language there are some fairly consistent rules of sounding similar letter combinations in similar ways. These are called "phonetic generalizations." Examples of these include the silent *e* (evident in the pronunciation of *smile, make, joke, ride, hole, cake, woke, while*) and the two vowels

---

2. A "blend" refers to the sound combination resulting from the adjacent consonants without loss of either sound's identity, for example, *bl*ue, *str*ike. A "digraph" refers to 2 letters in succession which when pronounced represent a single sound rather than a blending of both letter sounds, for instance, *sh*oe, *th*irty.

3. A "phonogram" is a pronounceable sound unit beginning with a vowel (*ing, at, ot*) frequently found at the end of a word which may be combined with various initial consonants, consonants blends, or digraphs to make new words (*sing, bring, thing*).

TABLE 10.4   *Sequential list of skills leading to functional liter*

Cluster I

I. A. Sight Words (SW)

SW1.   When given three geometric figures that are exactly alike
learner will mark the one that is different. (89)

SW2.[a]   When given a few seconds to examine a geometric figure,
ory, to the satisfaction of the teacher, a figure just like it

SW3.   When shown a circle, square, triangle, diamond, and rectar
each geometric form in turn. (95)

SW4.   When presented with a card having his or her name printe
say his or her name. (98)

SW5.   When given a list of five names of students in the class, the learner will identify her or his name
by drawing a circle around it. (99)

SW6.   When presented with a card having his or her name printed on it, the learner will point to the
first letter and to the last letter in his or her name. (101)

SW7.[a]   When given a few seconds to examine his or her name, the learner will reproduce it from
memory to the satisfaction of the teacher. (103)

SW8.   When given three letters that are exactly alike and one that is clearly different, the learner will
mark the one that is different. (104)

SW9.   Then presented with a card having a letter printed on it, the learner will point to the left, right,
top, and bottom parts of the letter. (105)

SW10.[a]   When given a few seconds to examine a letter, the learner will reproduce the letter from memory,
to the satisfaction of the teacher. (107)

SW11.   When presented with a random group of alphabet letters in lowercase, the learner will point to
and name each letter in turn. (108)

SW12.   Given three numerals from 1 to 10 that are exactly alike and one that is clearly different, the
learner will mark the one that is different. (110)

SW13.[a]   When given a few seconds to examine a numeral, the learner will reproduce if from memory,
to the satisfaction of the teacher. (111)

SW14.   When presented with a card having a numeral printed on it, the learner will point to the left, right,
top, and bottom parts of the numeral. (112)

SW15.   When presented with a random group of numerals, the learner will point to and name each
numeral in turn. (113)

SW16.   When given three letters that are exactly alike and one that is somewhat similar, the learner will
mark the one that is different. (115)

SW17.   Given a flash presentation of each of the following frequently confused letters, the learner will
say the name of the letter within one second. The letters to be tested are *b, d, u, v, m, n, p, q,
w, i, j.* (116)

SW18.[a]   When given a few seconds to examine a letter that is easily confused with other letters, the
learner will reproduce the letter from memory, to the satisfaction of the teacher. (118)

I. B. Word Analysis (WA)

WA1.   When directed to close his or her eyes and listen to rhythms tapped by the teacher, the learner
will reproduce the rhythm. (119)

WA2.   When directed to close his or her eyes and listen to three words spoken by the teacher, the
learner will reproduce the words in the sequence in which they were given. (122)

WA3.   When directed to close his or her eyes and listen to three words spoken by the teacher, the
learner will repeat the first word and the last word spoken by the teacher. (124)

WA4.   Given a polysyllabic word spoken by the teacher in which the initial sound unit has been omitted,
the learner will repeat the word correctly and supply the missing sound. (125)

WA5.   Given spoken pairs of words, the learner will say "Yes" if the words begin alike and will say "No"
if they do not begin alike. (p. 128)

s in pairs that either rhyme or do not rhyme, the learner will say "Yes" if the pair
and will say "No" if the pair does not rhyme. (132)

a polysyllabic word spoken by the teacher in which a medial sound unit has been omitted
distorted, the learner will repeat the word correctly supplying the missing sound. (134)

Given a stimulus word beginning with either *m* or *d* and a group of three other words one of
which begins with *m* or *d*, the learner will pair the two words beginning with the same letter
sound. (135)

WA9. Given spoken words, beginning with *m* or *d* sounds, the learner will identify the beginning letter
as *m* or *d*. (137)

WA10. When given a stimulus word beginning with either *l* or hard *c*, and a group of four other words
one of which begins with *l* or hard *c*, the learner will pair the two words beginning with the
same letter. (141)

WA11. When given spoken words beginning with *l* or hard *c* sounds, the learner will identify the beginning letters as *l* or *c*. (143)

WA12. When given a stimulus word with either *s* or *h* at the beginning and a group of three other words
one of which begins with *s* or *h*, the learner will pair the two words beginning with the same
letter. (144)

WA13. When given spoken words beginning with *s* or *h* sounds, the learner will identify the beginning
letter as being either *s* or *h*. (146)

WA14. When given an oral sentence with one word missing and cued for the missing word with a card
having printed on it the first letter of that word (*m, d, l, c, s, h*), the learner will say a word that
fits the context and begins with that letter. (147)

WA15. When given a stimulus word beginning with the *t, b,* or *p* sounds and a group of three other
words, one of which begins with the *t, b,* or *p* sounds, the learner will pair the two words beginning with the same sound. (151)

WA16. When given spoken words beginning with the *t, b,* or *p* sounds, the learner will identify the beginning letters as *t, b,* or *p*. (153)

WA17. When given a stimulus word beginning with the *w, r,* or *f* sounds and a group of three words,
one of which begins with the *w, r,* or *f* sound, the learner will pair the two words beginning with
the same sound. (154)

WA18. When given spoken words beginning with the *w, r,* or *f* sounds, the learner will identify the beginning letters as *w, r,* or *f*. (156)

WA19. Given a stimulus word beginning with the hard *g, k, j,* or *n* sounds and a group of three other
words one of which begins with the hard *g, k, j,* or *n* sounds, the learner will pair the two words
beginning with the same sound. (157)

WA20. When given spoken words beginning with the hard *g, k, j,* or *n* sounds, the learner will identify
the beginning letters as *g, k, j,* or *n*. (159)

WA21. When given an oral sentence with one word missing and cued for the missing word with a card
having printed on it the first letter of the missing word (*t, b, p, w, r, f, g, k, j,* and *n*), the learner
will say a word beginning with that letter that fits the context of the sentence. (160)

I. C. Information Gathering (IG)

IG1. When given content words that have been identified by the teacher, the learner will use each
word correctly in an oral sentence. (162)

IG2. When given words containing known roots and *-ed, -ing,* and *-s* endings, the learner will use each
word correctly in an oral sentence. (165)

IG3. When given two objects and function words that signal position (*to, at, in, on, out, here, there,
by, from, over, into, upon, away, near*), the learner will position the two objects in relation to
each other according to the relationship signaled by the function words contained in the teacher's
oral directions. (168)

Cluster I (continued)

I. D. Manipulative Thinking (MT)

MT1.   When given pairs of words, the learner will state the way in which the two words are related. (171)

MT2.   When given a short story problem read orally by the teacher, the learner will provide a solution that is implied but not stated. (174)

I. E. Evaluative Thinking (ET)

ET1.   When given oral material containing factual and fanciful information with which the learner has experience, the learner will state whether the information is factual or fanciful and tell why. (177)

Cluster II

II. A. Sight Words (SW)

SW1.   When given a stimulus lowercase letter, the learner will match it with its uppercase counterpart. (181)

SW2.   When given a few seconds to examine a word, the learner will pick out another word having the same initial consonant from a group of four words. (182)

SW3.   When given three words that are exactly alike and one that is clearly different, the learner will mark the one that is different. (184)

SW4.   When given three words that are exactly alike and one word that is somewhat similar, the learner will mark the word that is different. (185)

SW5.[a]   When given a few seconds to examine a short word, the learner will reproduce the word from memory, to the satisfaction of the teacher. (187)

SW6.   When given a fraction of a second to examine each of ten flashcards having printed on them words he or she selected as wanting to learn to read, the learner will pronounce each word within one second. (188)

SW7.   When given a fraction of a second to examine flashcards having printed on them the words *yes, no, I, and, the, a, to, was, in, it, of, my,* and *he,* the child will pronounce each word within one second. (194)

SW8.   When given sentence frames created by the teacher and the words the learner recognizes at sight printed on cards, the learner will point to and name the word that completes the sentence frame. (195)

SW9.   When given cards with words printed on them he or she has learned to pronounce at sight, the learner will, when directed to, point to the first letter and then to the last letter in each of these words. (198)

SW10.   When given part of a sentence frame created by the teacher and the words he or she recognizes at sight printed on cards, the learner will place certain word cards in an order that completes the sentence and will read the sentence. (199)

SW11.   When given a fraction of a second to examine flashcards having printed on them the color words (*white, black, red, blue, green,* and *yellow*), the learner will pronounce each word within one second. (201)

SW12.   When given a fraction of a second to examine flashcards having printed on them the number words from one to ten, the learner will pronounce each word within one second. (202)

SW13.   When given five known sight words in which the first letter is printed in lowercase, the learner will match each word with the same word when the first letter is printed in uppercase. (203)

SW14.   When given a fraction of a second to examine flash cards having printed on them the words *here, fast, to, me, at, come, see, help, home, work, down,* and *up,* the learner will pronounce each within one second. (204)

SW15.   When given a page of writing and directed to point to the first word and last word in a line of print and to the first word and last word on a page, the learner will instantly do so. (205)

Cluster II (continued)

II. A. Sight Words (SW) (continued)

SW16. When given a fraction of a second to examine flashcards having printed on them the following words, the learner will pronounce each within one second. (207)

that	is	go	we	have	what	dog
had	are	you	did	ride	something	ball
out	not	little	make	said	do	with
look	who	funny	for	this	want	will

II. B. Word Analysis (WA)

WA1. When given a word spoken by the teacher in which each of the syllabic units has been isolated, the learner will recognize and repeat the word by fusing these units together into a normally spoken cadence. (208)

WA2. When given a word spoken by the teacher in which each of the letter sound units have been isolated, the learner will recognize and repeat the word by fusing the isolated sounds together into a normal spoken cadence. (211)

WA3. When given stimulus words ending with the *m, d, l,* or voiceless *s* sound and a group of three other words one of which ends with the *m, d, l,* or voiceless *s* sound, the learner will pair the two words ending with the same sound. (212)

WA4. When given spoken words ending with *m, d, l,* and voiceless *s* sound, the learner will identify the ending letters as *m, d, l,* or *s*. (214)

WA5. When given stimulus words ending with *b, f, g, n, p, t,* or *v,* and a group of three other words, one of which ends with the *b, f, g, n, p, t,* or *v* sound, the learner pairs the two words ending with the same sound. (215)

WA6. When given spoken words ending with *b, f, g, n, p, t,* or *v* sounds, the learner will identify the ending letters as *b, f, g, n, p, t,* or *v*. (218)

WA7. When given a stimulus word beginning with the *q, v, y,* or *z* sounds, and a group of three other words one of which begins with the *q, v, y,* and *z* sounds, the learner will pair the two words beginning with the same sound. (219)

WA8. When given spoken words beginning with the *q, v, y,* or *z* sounds, the learner will identify the beginning letter as *q, v, y,* or *z*. (221)

WA9. When given an oral sentence with one word missing and cued for the missing word with a card having printed on it the first letter of that word (*q, v, y,* or *z*), the learner will say a word beginning with that letter that fits the context of the sentence. (222)

WA10. When given a stimulus word beginning with the *sh* or voiceless *th* digraphs and a group of three other words, one of which begins with the *sh* or voiceless *th* sound, the learner will pair the two words beginning with the same sound. (224)

WA11. When given spoken words beginning with the *sh* or voiceless *th* sounds, the learner will identify the beginning letter as *sh* or *th* . (226)

WA12. When given an oral sentence with one word missing and cued for the missing word with a card having printed on it the *sh* or *th* digraphs, the learner will say a word beginning with that digraph that fits the context of the sentence. (227)

WA13. When given a stimulus word beginning with the *ch, wh,* or voiced *th* sounds and a group of three other words, one of which begins with the *ch, wh,* or the voiced *th* sounds, the learner will pair the two words beginning with the same sound. (229)

WA14. When given spoken words beginning with the *ch, wh,* or voiced *th* sounds, the learner will identify the beginning letters as *ch, wh,* or *th*. (231)

WA15. When given an oral sentence with one word missing and cued for the missing word with a card having printed on it the digraph with which the word begins (*ch, wh,* or *th*), the learner will say a word beginning with that digraph that fits the context of the sentence. (233)

WA16. When given a stimulus word having a short *a, e, i, o,* or *u* as the medial sound and a group of three other words one of which has a short *a, e, i, o,* or *u* as the medial sound, the learner will pair the two words having the same medial sound. (234)

WA17. When given spoken words with either the sound of the short vowel *a, e, i, o,* or *u* in the middle, the learner will identify the middle letters as *a, e, i, o,* or *u*. (236)

Cluster II (continued)

II. B. Word Analysis (WA) (continued)

WA18. Given known words composed of the vowel consonant phonograms *-at, -et, -it, -ot, -ut,* the learner replaces the first consonant in each known word with another consonant or digraph and pronounces the new word. (238)

WA19. When given words he or she pronounced in the previous objective, the learner replaces the final consonant of the known word with another consonant or digraph and pronounces the new word. (242)

WA20. When given key words either introduced in the previous two objectives or identified during the course of this objective, the learner will change either the beginning or the ending of the words and pronounce the new words. (244)

WA21. When given words the learner has previously learned to recognize at sight, he or she will change the medial vowel in a short vowel phonogram and pronounce the new word. (246)

WA22. When given a stimulus word ending with the *ck* sound and a group of three other words one of which ends with the *ck* sound, the learner will pair the two words that end with the *ck* sound. (247)

WA23. When given a spoken word, the learner will point to the letters *ck* if the word ends in the *ck* sound. (249)

WA24. When given words he or she pronounced in previous objectives, the learner will replace the final consonant sound in these words with the *ck* and pronounce the new word. (250)

WA25. When given words he or she has previously analyzed or learned to recognize at sight, the learner will add the structural ending *-ed, -ing,* or *-s* and pronounce the new words. (251)

II. C. Information Gathering (IG)

IG1. When given content words identified by the teacher, the learner will use each word correctly in an oral sentence. (255)

IG2. When given the compound words he or she will be asked to identify in print in the next cluster of skills, the learner will use each correctly in an oral sentence. (256)

IG3. When given oral sentences containing the function words *she, some, you, we, they, who, me, I, my, he, it, him, us, her, the, his, our, any, your,* and *their,* the learner identifies the antecedent for each pronoun. (257)

IG4. When given an oral sentence containing a word unknown in meaning and a direct definition clue to the word's meaning, the learner will state the meaning of the unknown word. (259)

II. D. Manipulative Thinking (MT)

MT1. When given a list of four words, the learner will group together those that belong together and explain his or her system for classifying them. (261)

MT2. When given a short story read orally by the teacher and three possibilities about what will happen next, the learner will select the most likely outcome. (263)

II. E. Evaluative Thinking (ET)

ET1. When given the beginning of an oral sentence and three oral phrases with which to complete the sentence, the learner will choose the phrase that makes the most sense. (264)

Cluster III

III. A. Sight Words (SW)

SW1. When given a fraction of a second to examine flashcards having printed on them the following words, the learner will pronounce each within one second. (267)

show	know	too	hot	like	saw	ask
car	paint	take	from	but	then	on
get	word	around	your	went	us	father
cat	she	tree	birthday	away	about	new
all	sit	good	soon	book	fun	house

Cluster III (continued)

III. A. Sight Words (SW) (continued)

SW2. When given a flash presentation of words the learner frequently confuses, he or she will pronounce each word correctly within one second. (268)

SW3. When given words that he or she recognizes instantly, the learner will create and read a single-sentence story using these words. (269)

III. B. Word Analysis (WA)

WA1. When given a stimulus word beginning with one of the consonant blends, *br, cr, dr, fr, gr, tr,* or *pr* and a group of three other words, one of which begins with a blend *br, cr, dr, fr, gr, tr,* or *pr,* the learner will pair the two words beginning with the same consonant blend. (271)

WA2. When given spoken words beginning with the *br, cr, dr, fr, gr, tr,* or *pr* sounds, the learner will identify the beginning letters in each word. (274)

WA3. When given an oral sentence with one word missing and cued for the missing word with a card having printed on it the blend with which the word begins (*br, cr, dr, fr, gr, tr, pr*), the learner will say a word beginning with that letter blend that fits the context of the sentence. (275)

WA4. When given words he or she has learned previously, the learner will substitute the blends *br, cr, dr, fr, gr, tr,* and *pr* in the initial position and pronounce the new word. (277)

WA5. When given an oral presentation of a stimulus word beginning with the consonant blends *bl, cl, fl, pl, gl,* or *sl* and a group of three other words, one of which begins with the blends, *bl, cl, fl, pl, gl,* or *sl,* the learner will pair the two words beginning with the same consonant blend. (278)

WA6. When given spoken words beginning with the *bl, cl, fl, pl, gl,* and *sl* sounds, the learner will identify the beginning letters in each word. (281)

WA7. When given an oral sentence with one word missing and cued for the missing word with a card having printed on it the blend with which the word begins (*bl, cl, fl, pl, gl,* or *sl*), the learner will say a word beginning with the letter blend that fits the context of the sentence. (282)

WA8. When given words previously learned, the learner will substitute the blends *bl, cl, fl, pl, gl,* and *sl* in the initial position and pronounce the new words. (284)

WA9. When given a spoken stimulus word ending with the *ng* sound and a group of three other words, one of which ends with the *ng* sound, the learner will pair the two words that both end with the *ng* sound. (285)

WA10. When given a spoken word, the learner will point to the letters *ng* if the word ends in the *ng* sound. (287)

WA11. When given words pronounced in previous objectives, the learner replaces the final consonant sounds in these words with the *ng* sound, substitutes initial sounds he or she knows, and pronounces the new words. (288)

WA12. When given compound words composed of two unknown words, the learner will pronounce the compound words. (289)

III. C. Information Gathering (IG)

IG1. When given content words that have been identified by the teacher, the learner will use each word correctly in an oral sentence. (290)

IG2. When given the contractions he or she will be asked to identify in print in the next cluster of skills, the learner will use each contraction correctly in an oral sentence and name the words from which each contraction is derived. (292)

IG3. When given function words that signal various relationships, the learner will use each correctly in an oral sentence. (293)

IG4. When given oral sentences with words or phrases out of position, the learner will orally repeat the sentence with all words in the correct position. (294)

IG5. When given an oral sentence containing a word unknown in meaning and an experience clue to the word's meaning, the learner states the meaning of the unknown word. (296)

IG6. When given a short oral paragraph, the learner will recall details about the paragraph in response to the teacher's oral questions. (298)

Cluster III (continued)

III. D. Manipulative Thinking (MT)

MT1. Given an oral list of 12 words, the learner will classify each word according to three categories provided by the teacher. (301)

MT2. When given a short oral paragraph, the learner will select an appropriate title for the paragraph from among three choices. (302)

MT3. When given an oral paragraph and a question about the paragraph that requires inferential thinking, the learner will supply details that are implied by not stated in the paragraph. (305)

III. E. Evaluative Thinking (ET)

ET1. When given a short oral story containing an unlikely reference to time and sequence, the learner will identify the event that does not fit and tell why. (307)

Cluster IV

IV. A. Sight Words (SW)

SW1. When given a fraction of a second to examine flashcards having printed on them the following words, the learner will pronounce each within one second. (309)

girl	by	bear	them
turn	as	please	cage
picture	boy	their	there
any	balloon	which	day
talk	before	her	pull
after	how	build	tomorrow
head	off	old	again
eye	been	am	our

SW2. When given a flash presentation of words the learner frequently confuses, he or she will pronounce each word correctly within one second. (310)

SW3. Given words that he or she recognizes instantly, the learner creates and reads a single-sentence story using these words. (311)

IV. B. Word Analysis (WA)

WA1. Given a known word composed of the vowel-consonant photograms *-en, -in,* or *-an,* the learner will replace the initial consonant in each word with another consonant, digraph, or blend he or she knows and pronounces the new word. (313)

WA2. Given a stimulus word beginning with the consonant blends *sk, sw, sm, sn, sp,* or *st,* and a group of three other words, one of which begins with *sk, sw, sm, sn, sp,* or *st,* the learner will pair the two words beginning with the same sound. (314)

WA3. When given words beginning with the *sk, sw, sm, sn, sp,* and *st* sounds, the learner will identify the beginning letters in each word. (317)

WA4. When given an oral sentence with one word missing and cued for the missing word with a card having printed on it the blend with which the word begins (*sk, sw, sm, sn, sp,* or *st*), the learner will say a word beginning with the letter blend that fits the context of the sentence. (318)

WA5. When given key words learned in previous objectives, the learner will replace the initial consonants with an *s-* blend and pronounce the new words. (320)

WA6. When given a spoken stimulus word ending with the *st* sound and a group of three words one of which ends with the *st* sound, the learner will pair the two words that end with the *st* sound. (321)

WA7. When given a spoken word, the learner will point to the letters *st* if the word ends in the *st* sound. (323)

WA8. When given words pronounced in previous objectives, the learner will replace the final consonant sound with the *st* sound, substitute initial sounds he or she knows, and pronounce the new words. (324)

WA9. When given the contractions *I'm, can't, won't, I'll, don't, isn't, he's, it's, I've, you're, we've,* and *let's* printed on cards, the learner will pronounce each contraction and identify the two words that make up the contraction. (325)

Cluster IV (continued)

IV. C. Information Gathering (IG)

IG1. When given content words identified by the teacher, the learner will use each word correctly in an oral sentence. (326)

IG2. When given words containing the suffixes -'s, -est, -ly, -er, and -y, the learner will use each word correctly in an oral sentence. (328)

IG3. When given a short paragraph with four happenings signaled by the function words *first, next, then,* and *finally,* the learner will number the four statements in the order in which they happened in the story. (329)

IG4. When given a sentence containing an unknown word and in which a clue to the word's meaning is provided by an example, the learner will state the meaning of the unknown word. (330)

IV. D. Manipulative Thinking (MT)

MT1. When given a four-part analogy frame in which the first two words are related and the third word is paired with a blank, the learner will complete the frame by supplying a word that relates the second pair of words in the same way the first two words are related. (331)

MT2. Given a sentence to read, the learner matches the sentence with a title that expresses the main idea of the sentence. (332)

MT3. When given a paragraph to read and three possibilities about what happened next in the story, the learner will select the most likely outcome. (333)

IV. E. Evaluative Thinking (ET)

ET1. When given pairs of sentences that are identical except for one word, the learner will state whether the different word in the sentence makes him feel more positive or more negative about the topic being discussed. (335)

Cluster V

V. A. Sight Words (SW)

SW1. When given a fraction of a second to examine flashcards having printed on them the following words, the learner will pronounce each within one second. (339)

give	money	would	oh	shoe
color	turtle	more	many	animal
hurry	were	read	could	people
should	find	miss	own	into
hair	does	thought	hello	friend
push	store	feet	took	bird
right	next	good-bye	over	nothing
street	every	school	morning	song
ready	an	catch		

SW2. When given a flash presentation of words the learner frequently confuses, he or she will pronounce each word correctly within one second. (340)

SW3. When given words he or she recognizes instantly, the learner will create and read a single-sentence story using these words. (341)

V. B. Word Analysis (WA)

WA1. When given a known word composed of the phonograms -and, -end, -ight, -old, and -ind, the learner will replace the initial consonant with another consonant, consonant blend, or digraph and pronounce the new word. (343)

WA2. When given a known word containing a double *e* in the medial position, the learner will replace either the initial or final letter with other letters and pronounce the new words. (344)

WA3. When given a known one-syllable word containing the -ay combination, the learner will replace the initial consonant with another letter and pronounce the new word. (345)

WA4. When given a known one-syllable word ending in -ell or -ill, the learner will replace the initial consonant with another letter and pronounce the new word. (346)

Cluster V (continued)

V. B. Word Analysis (WA) (continued)

WA5. When given a known one-syllable ending in *-all*, the learner will replace the initial consonant with another letter and pronounce the new word. (348)

WA6. When given words he or she has previously analyzed or learned to recognize at sight, the learner will add the structural endings *-'s, -est, -ly, -er,* and *-y* and pronounce the new words. (349)

V. C. Information Gathering (IG)

IG1. When given content words identified by the teacher, the learner will use each word correctly in an oral sentence. (350)

IG2. When given words containing the prefixes *dis-* and *un-*, the learner uses each word correctly in an oral sentence. (351)

IG3. When given a sentence that states a cause-effect relationship and in which a function word has been omitted, the learner selects the appropriate function words from two choices that are provided. (352)

IG4. When given a series of sentences containing ending punctuation, the learner orally reads each sentence with the correct voice intonation and states the varying meanings signaled by punctuation at the end of each sentence. (353)

IG5. When given sentences containing a word unknown in meaning and in which a clue to the word's meaning is provided by either a synonym or an antonym, the learner will state the meaning of the unknown word. (356)

IG6. When given a paragraph to read in which the details can be classified together, the learner will recall the details from the story in response to questions from the teacher. (357)

V. D. Manipulative Thinking (MT)

MT1. When given a list of phrases, the learner will sort the phrases into three categories and label each category. (358)

MT2. When given a list of words and four possible story titles, the learner will sort the phrases into three categories and select one title that would be appropriate for all three categories. (359)

MT3. When given a paragraph in which the mood is implied and in which a word has been omitted, the learner will select a word that describes the mood from a choice of two words provided. (361)

V. E. Evaluative Thinking (ET)

ET1. When given a paragraph and the main idea, the learner will identify the details in the paragraph that are irrelevant. (362)

Cluster VI

VI. A. Sight Words (SW)

SW1. When given a fraction of a second to examine flashcards having printed on them the following words, the learner will pronounce each within one second. (365)

even	window	write	chair	behind	pony
wagon	woman	along	bee	pocket	TV
zoo	airplane	penny	picnic	toy	letter
under	food	stopped	story	live	enough
dress	sister	party	lost	open	boy
rocket	peanut	maybe	grass	better	rabbit
began	never				

SW2. When given a flash presentation of words that the learner frequently confuses, he or she will pronounce each word correctly within one second. (366)

SW3. When given the words he or she recognizes instantly, the learner will create and read a single-sentence story using these words. (367)

VI. B. Word Analysis (WA)

WA1. When given a known word illustrating the silent *e* vowel principle, the learner will correctly pronounce other words illustrating the silent *e* principle. (369)

WA2. When given a known word illustrating the two-vowels-together principle, the learner will correctly pronounce other words illustrating this principle. (373)

WA3. When given a known one-syllable word ending in a vowel, the learner will correctly pronounce other syllable units ending in a vowel. (375)

WA4. When given a known word illustrating the two-vowels-together principle as it applies to the *ow* combination, the learner will correctly pronounce other words illustrating this principle. (376)

WA5. When given words containing the *ou* and *ow* diphthongs, the learner will correctly pronounce other words containing these diphthongs. (377)

WA6. When given spoken stimulus words ending with either the *-nd,* the *-nt,* or the *-nk* sounds and a group of three other words of which one ends with either the *-nd,* the *-nt,* or the *-nk* sounds, the learner will pair the two words that end in the same sound. (379)

WA7. When given three cards that have the letters *nd* printed on one, the letters *nt* on another and the letters *nk* on the third and a spoken stimulus word that ends in either the *-nd,* the *-nt,* or the *-nk* sounds, the learner will point to the letter card having printed on it the letters with which the word ends. (380)

WA8. When given words he or she pronounced in previous objectives, the learner will replace the final consonant sound of these words with the *-nd,* the *-nt,* or the *-nk* sound and pronounce the new words. (382)

WA9. When given known sight words, the learner will pronounce these words when they are prefixed by *dis-* and *un-*. (383)

VI. C. Information Gathering (IG)

IG1. When given content words identified by the teacher, the learner will use each word correctly in an oral sentence. (384)

IG2. When given words containing the prefixes *im-, in-,* and *re-,* the learner will use each word correctly in an oral sentence. (385)

IG3. When given a paragraph containing a compare-contrast relationship, the learner identifies both the relationship and the function words that signal the relationship. (386)

IG4. When given a group of sentences containing direct quotations, the learner will read only the words to be said by the speaker. (388)

IG5. When given written sentences in which the subject and predicate phrases are out of order, the learner will arrange the phrases in the correct order and orally read the sentence. (389)

IG6. When given a sentence containing a word unknown in meaning to the learner and in which a clue to the word's meaning is provided through inference, the learner will state the meaning of the unknown word. (390)

IG7. When given a paragraph containing details about who, what, when, and where, the learner will recall these details from the story in response to questions from the teacher. (391)

VI. D. Manipulative Thinking (MT)

MT1. When given three stories, the learner will answer correctly the teacher's questions regarding relationships between the central characters in the three stories. (392)

MT2. When given the title of a possible story and a series of possible details, the learner will select the details that would be appropriate for the title and explain his or her reason for classifying them with the title. (393)

MT3. When given a paragraph in which the character's emotional reaction is implied, the learner will select the correct emotion from a choice of three. (394)

VI. E. Evaluative Thinking (ET)

ET1. When given a series of advertising claims, the learner will identify the propaganda words used in each advertisement. (396)

Cluster VII

VII. A. Sight Words (SW)

SW1. When given a fraction of a second to examine flashcards having printed on them the following words, the learner will pronounce each within one second. (399)

only	today	also	end	felt
bigger	full	sure	listen	lion
table	poor	quiet	air	bread
done	draw	slow	triad	Mrs.
love	doll	match	ear	apple
wild	break	wash	family	careful
brother	near	keep	Mr.	heavy
once	child	believe	most	together
busy	orange	upon	because	milk

SW2. When given a flash presentation of words that the learner frequently confuses, he or she will pronounce each word correctly within one second. (400)

SW3. When given words he or she recognizes instantly, the learner will create and read a single-sentence story using these words. (401)

VII. B. Word Analysis (WA)

WA1. When given a known word that illustrates the vowel-consonant-consonant-vowel principle of syllabication and in which both medial consonants are heard, the learner will correctly pronounce other words illustrating the principle. (403)

WA2. When given a known word containing the *ar* and *or* combination, the learner will pronounce other words containing these combinations. (408)

WA3. When given a known two-syllable word ending in *-er,* the learner will correctly pronounce other two-syllable words ending in *-er.* (409)

WA4. When given a known word composed of the *-ire* combination, the learner will replace the initial consonant with another consonant, blend, or digraph and correctly pronounce the new word. (411)

WA5. When given compound words composed of two known words, the learner will correctly pronounce the compound words. (412)

VII. C. Information Gathering (IG)

IG1. When given content words identified by the teacher, the learner will use each word correctly in an oral sentence. (413)

IG2. When given words containing the suffixes *-less, -al,* and *-ful,* the learner will use each word correctly in an oral sentence. (414)

IG3. When given a sentence in which nouns are set off by commas in a series arrangement, the learner will identify the series of things referred to in the sentence in response to the teacher's questions. (415)

IG4. When given a sentence containing a word unknown in meaning and in which a clue to the word's meaning is provided through the mood conveyed, the learner will state the meaning of the unknown word. (416)

IG5. When given paragraphs each of which contains context clues for intonation patterns and ends with the same sentence, the learner will repeat the last sentence with the correct intonation pattern. (417)

IG6. When given a paragraph in which the details either precede or follow the main idea, the learner identifies the details and states how they support the main idea. (420)

VII. D. Manipulative Thinking (MT)

MT1. When given a paragraph to read that has details that can be classified together, the learner will classify the details and select an appropriate title for the paragraph. (421)

MT2. When given a multiparagraph selection in which the author's theme is implied but not stated, the learner states an appropriate theme. (423)

Cluster VII (continued)

VII. E. Evaluative Thinking (ET)

ET1. When given three reports of a happening, the learner will identify the writer of the report and describe how the author's use of biased words helped him or her to determine authorship. (424)

Cluster VIII

VIII. A. Sight Words (SW)

SW1. When given a fraction of a second to examine flashcards having printed on them the following words, the learner will pronounce each within one second. (427)

post	quick	bowl	father	honey	noise
already	both	breakfast	elephant	large	held
move	quite	country	kept	field	fire
paw	bump	circus	wonder	early	clothes
arrow	climb	warm	caught	floor	roar
hurt	war	board	egg	umbrella	roll
voice	always	uncle	else	piece	

SW2. When given a flash presentation of words that the learner frequently confuses, he or she will pronounce each word correctly within one second. (428)

SW3. When given the words he or she recognizes instantly, the learner will create and read a multiple-sentence story using these words. (429)

SW4. When given a fraction of a second to examine flashcards having printed on them the following words, the learner will pronounce each within one second. (431)

wolf	world	worm	cried	pennies	sign
splash	spring	station	turkey	across	bottom
automobile	deer	buy	dear	lie	answer
calf	learn	log	soft	beautiful	care
heard	year	carry	soup	squirrel	wear
cover	cross	through	thought	brought	vegetable
watch	monkey	engine	front	great	left
minute					

SW5. When given a flash presentation of words the learner frequently confuses, he or she will pronounce each word correctly within one second. (432)

SW6. When given words he or she recognizes instantly, the learner will create and read a multiple-sentence story using these words. (433)

VIII. B. Word Analysis (WA)

WA1. When given a known word illustrating the vowel-consonant-vowel principle of syllabication in which the first vowel might be either long or short, the learner will correctly pronounce other words that illustrate this principle. (435)

WA2. When given a known word illustrating the short *y* principle, the learner will correctly pronounce other two-syllable words containing the short *y*. (436)

WA3. When given a two-syllable word with an unaccented *a* in the initial position, the learner will correctly pronounce other two-syllable words illustrating the same principle. (438)

WA4. When given a known word composed of the *-ew* combination, the learner will replace the initial consonant with another consonant, blend, or digraph and correctly pronounce the new word. (439)

WA5. When given a stimulus word beginning with the *str* or *thr* consonant combinations and a group of three words of which one begins with the *str* or *thr* sounds, the learner will pair the two words beginning with the same sound. (440)

WA6. When given spoken words beginning with the *str* or *thr* sounds, the learner will identify the beginning letters in each word. (442)

Cluster VIII (continued)

VIII. B. Word Analysis (WA) (continued)

WA7. When given a written sentence with one word missing, and cued for the missing word by the letter combinations with which that word begins, the learner will say a word beginning with that letter combination that fits the context of the sentence. (443)

WA8. When given words composed of the *str* and *thr* combinations and other phonetic elements known to him or her, the learner will correctly pronounce the words. (445)

VIII. C. Information Gathering (IG)

IG1. When given content words identified by the teacher, the learner will use each word correctly in an oral sentence. (446)

IG2. When given a sentence containing a word unknown in meaning and in which a clue to the word's meaning is provided through a summary clue, the learner will state the meaning of the unknown word. (447)

IG3. When given a short paragraph in which a word in the last sentence should be stressed to obtain the exact meaning, the learner will identify the word to be stressed and emphasize that word when reading the paragraph orally. (448)

IG4. When given a multiparagraph selection, the learner will recall details from each paragraph in response to questions from the teacher. (450)

VIII. D. Manipulative Thinking (MT)

MT1. When given a paragraph containing details that can be classified into three categories, the learner will classify the details and state one title for the paragraph that reflects all three categories of details. (451)

MT2. Given a multiparagraph selection in which details are implied, the learner will supply such details in response to questions asked by the teacher. (452)

VIII. E. Evaluative Thinking (ET)

ET1. When given two reports about the same event, the learner will identify which is factual and which is opinionated and will identify the words that signal opinion. (454)

ᵃHandwriting skill objectives.
Source: G. G. Duffy and G. B. Sherman, *Systematic Reading Instruction* (2nd ed.). New York: Harper & Row, 1977, pp. 89–454.

together–one syllable rule (*boat, plain, rain, wheat, goat, leaves, suit*). Although these rules are not universally true, they are consistent enough to be learned as patterns to attend to in unknown words.

"Syllabication" is the third part of phonetic analysis—strategies to analyze sound units in an unknown word as a means of identifying that word. The purpose of syllabication is to break large multisyllable words into smaller, more, manageable sound units. The instructional progression for teaching the various syllabication patterns (for example, vowel-consonant-consonant-vowel: *until, almost, after;* vowel-consonant-vowel: *even, between, tiger*) is *first* to teach auditory discrimination of the number of sound units, *then* to teach visual discrimination of the particular pattern of vowels and

consonants and the rule for dividing a word into single sound units, and *finally* to teach generalization of the rule across many unfamiliar words with various patterns of letters.

Whereas in phonetic analysis the learner focuses attention on sound units to unlock unknown words, in *structural analysis* the learner must direct attention to those parts of the word that signal meaning as a method to analyze unknown words. Units of meaning that the student is taught to attend to include:

1. Root words plus inflectional endings, such as *-s, -ed,* and *-ing*
2. Root words plus suffixes, such as *-ness, -able,* and *-ly*

3. Prefixes plus the root word (*un-happy*)
4. Parts of compound words (*back pack*)
5. Parts of contractions (*couldn't = could not*) (Duffy & Sherman, 1973, p. 169)

In order to use structural analysis the reader must be able to look at unknown words and discover known parts, to recognize the root word either instantly as a sight word or by sounding it out, to sound the prefix, suffix, or the other portion of the compound, and finally to blend the parts together as one word.

Context analysis allows the reader to determine unknown words from the meaning of the known words and the clues provided by known letter sounds. Context analysis requires that the student read for meaning and, with the assistance of letter-sound correspondence, guess unknown words. When context clues are used without letter-sound analysis or vice versa, guessing often is inefficient. For example, the unknown word in the sentence "She put the [UNKNOWN WORD] on her head" could be *cap, hat, helmet, scarf, shampoo,* etc. If an initial sound clue is recognized, (*s* . . .) identity becomes more likely. Additional phonetic or structural clues (i.e., *s . . . f*) may be employed along with context to increase this likelihood (final consonant, syllabication prefixes, etc.).

High Utility Words

A few comments should be made regarding high utility words or those words most frequently encountered in beginning reading. To determine which words to teach in a functional literacy reading program when only a limited number will be taught requires an awareness of word frequency. Word lists such as Fry's list of 300 "Instant Words" (Fry, 1957, 1972), the Dolch list of 200 words (Dolch, 1950), and the revised Dale list of 769 useful words (Stone, 1956)—all represent efforts to compile the most frequently appearing words in beginning reading material. Duffy and Sherman (1977) selected words common to the Fry, Dolch, and Stone lists as the most frequently appearing, and therefore most useful, words. Most of these words are taught during the readiness phase. Next, they classified words by their phonetic and structural elements (i.e., compound words, words with the *sh* digraph, and those with the *at* phonogram), ordered each classification in terms of its frequency, eliminated words composed of infrequently occurring elements, and matched groups of words with objectives to teach

those words. Words illustrating a certain phonetic or structural element are taught at the time their corresponding rule is taught, whereas some frequently appearing but irregular words (those not employing the identified elements) are taught as sight words. In addition, some regularly spelled words (such as *cat* and *pen*) are taught in the prerequisite skills unit as sight words and are used again later as examples of phonetic or structural generalizations. In all, the reader who completes the prerequisite and word recognition skill units learns to recognize or analyze more than 900 words.

Comprehension Skills

While decoding new words is the most obvious half of reading, comprehension of what has been read is what ultimately makes the skill functional. Most standardized and informal reading tests assess a reader's comprehension by asking factual, vocabulary, and inferential questions about a passage read silently or aloud. In essence, these tests attempt to test comprehension—a skill that rests primarily upon the student's ability to conceptualize, to classify or determine relationships between concepts, and to answer factual questions about or make inferences from what is read. According to Duffy and Sherman's (1977) task analysis, teaching comprehension skills means the instruction of informational, manipulative, and evaluative processes. While this instruction would parallel rather than follow instruction in prerequisite and word recognition abilities, it logically proceeds from the informational to the evaluative processes in a hierarchical order. For any given reading selection comprehension activities must begin at the literal level—does the reader understand the factual content of what was read? If, as shown in Figure 10.5, the learner is in the stage of reading readiness and cannot read enough to apply developing comprehension skills to a reading selection, listening comprehension is taught.

The informational processes which permit the reader to comprehend the basic facts contained in a selection include (1) word meaning skills, (2) understanding relationships, (3) contextual prediction, and (4) factual recall. For the functional reader, "concepts" or word meaning centers upon "content" and "function" words. Content words have a known referent and carry the meaning of a sentence, for example, "Christmas," "mask," "dock," and "wishbone." However, the specific meaning of a content word is related to its particular use in a sentence context (e.g., "The man dove from the *dock*"; "Don't *dock* me for being late").

Function words describe the relationship between other words in a sentence; these relationships include (1) cause and effect ("since," "because," "if," "then"), (2) chronological sequences ("during," "after," "finally," "first," "then," "later"), (3) contrast-comparison ("much more than," "either-or," "although," "like"), (4) pronouns and their antecedents ("they" = John and the boys; "her" = Mary's), and (5) prepositions that refer to positional or time relationships ("across," "but," "on," "off," "between," "until," "among," "from").

Both function and content words are taught in 3 steps: first, provide an experience that serves as a basis for understanding the concept; second, identify the defining characteristics of the concept; and third, associate the word label with the concept. Since functions words show relationships rather than the more "visible" referents of content words, they are often more difficult concepts to teach. Therefore function words should always be taught in spoken or written contexts rather than isolated from content words. Understanding relationships between ideas read builds directly upon an understanding of the function and content words learned earlier. Once the student has learned the meaning of function words such as "because," "after," "next to," and many content words at an appropriate vocabulary level, then she is taught to verbalize relationships among concepts. This is done by a variety of instructional activities—arranging pictures to retell a known story, completing analogies, and looking for sequential relationships, cause and effect, use, and composition similarities in sets of pictures, etc.

Contextual prediction, a skill that can only accompany fluent reading, allows the reader to predict the unknown elements of a paragraph or sentence from what has been read. For example, the student who may not recognize the word *escalator* could understand its meaning from the following sentence: "It's fun to ride an escalator because it's like a moving staircase." Contextual predictions also may be made from the clues of word order, punctuation, and intonation.

A final element of the informational processes includes factual recall, or memory. Once the reader has learned to identify the important facts, retention of these facts is necessary before comprehension develops into higher forms, manipulative and evaluative processes.

At the second level of comprehension, readers learn to manipulate ideas mentally. They are able to see relationships between facts, to grasp the main idea of a selection, and to make inferences from facts—to "read between the lines." Both these mental operations enable readers to expand their comprehension beyond the literal level.

Duffy and Sherman (1977) describe the third type of comprehension attained by functionally literate readers as an evaluative process. Readers learn to use their past experiences as a measure to judge the content of a selection and to recognize words that reflect the author's bias, mood, stereotype, or intent.

It is not known to what extent moderately handicapped learners may be taught comprehension skills beyond the basic level of information gathering. Advanced comprehension requires recognition of main ideas, mental classification, inference, and evaluation of content, skills which are far more abstract than simply understanding and remembering the literal meaning of a passage. The primary purpose of teaching moderately handicapped individuals to read is to facilitate their independence in the activities of daily living and employment. Since the bulk of these activities requires reading for information, instruction will be directed toward these basic comprehension abilities.

Tasks analysis selection and instructional goals

If one views reading as a dual complexity of visual and auditory skills leading to word recognition abilities *and* understanding and thinking skills leading to comprehension, then many more instructional steps are required than if the task of learning to read were to be analyzed simply as a look-say process. Unlike the whole-word task analysis, it is not known how many of the instructional steps contributing to word recognition and comprehension may be achieved by the moderately handicapped learner. Some steps have been tested and found successful with this population. The supporting studies are reviewed in this chapter. The recency of systematic reading instruction for the moderately handicapped learner contributes to our difficulty in evaluating the validity of this complex task analysis for these learners.

Despite validity problems, each task analysis supplies useful guidelines for teaching and testing the handicapped learner. Reading prerequisites for all three analyses are the same. The beginning elements of visual discrimination and initial mastery of sight words are identical to the whole-word approach. Therefore a teacher may start readiness instruction without having to select a particular analysis of reading. Then, depending upon the student's success and the number of remaining schooling years for the student (i.e., the speed with which the student must achieve the *minimal* reading objective of a small cautionary vocabulary), a teacher will elect either (1) to continue to add sight words, limiting them to the essential protective vocabulary and giving particular attention to functional comprehension, or (2) to work toward the goal of functional literacy. The latter goal would necessitate following a complex task analysis (e.g., Duffy & Sherman, 1972; Resnick & Beck, 1976; Smith, 1976) in part or total, while directing comprehension activities and reading materials toward the functional reading tasks (e.g., Bender et al., 1976; Lichtman, 1974).

Assessment

Traditional Tests

Traditional methods of reading assessment include the presentation of a series of graded word lists and paragraphs with comprehension questions asked on the content of the paragraphs. The levels of difficulty correspond to grade levels beginning with preprimer and primer levels (first part of first grade) and progressing through first grade, second grade, third grade, and so on. Many tests allow two difficulty levels in the early grades so that the student's ability may be more closely pinpointed. Selections read aloud by the pupil are followed carefully by the examiner with all errors coded by their particular type (words omitted, substituted, misread, etc.) for later analysis of word recognition weaknesses. After reading the paragraph aloud, the student is asked factual, inferential, and vocabulary questions; responses are scored and recorded by the teacher before proceeding to the next graded paragraph. Although there are a multitude of systems for measuring performance on informal reading inventories,[4] one example of this procedure for scoring and recording word recognition and comprehension performance is illustrated in Figure 10.6.

In addition to the diagnostic information obtained on a student's word recognition and comprehension abilities, test data may be used to determine three levels of reading ability based upon the student's word recognition responses (percentage of words correctly read) and comprehension responses (percentage of questions answered correctly). These levels range from nearly error-free to an error frequency of 1 word recognition mistake every 10 or fewer words. They are referred to as the "independent reading level," the "instructional reading level," and the "frustration reading level." (See Table 10.5) Some tests suggest that the student be read a series of graded paragraphs by the examiner and then asked comprehension questions so that an "independent listening level" may be calculated. Listening level is generally at a higher grade level than the frustration level of reading.

The use of graded word lists and paragraphs to determine the percentage of correct word recognition and comprehension ability and resultant reading and listening levels will have value for teachers of the severely handicapped only if the students tested have some reading ability. For these students, testing will be limited primarily to selections from primer to fourth- or fifth-grade levels, although hearing comprehension may be higher for some students. If reading inventories of this type are used, it is of utmost importance that the content of the paragraphs reflect interest levels appropriate for the student. Since most tests draw primary-level selections from materials geared to young children, a teacher will need to seek out paragraphs from graded high interest–low vocabulary materials[5] (e.g., *Checkered Flag Series, SRA Pilot Library Series, Reader's Digest Skill Builders*, etc.) or construct graded selections with content suitable to the student's social age.

Word Lists

Word list tests may be made easily from graded lists of high utility words (e.g., Dolch, 1950; Fry, 1957, 1972; Stone, 1956) as illustrated in Figure 10.7. The rules for giving an informal test on words in isolation are generally similar from test to test. Because the goal of word recognition is *instant* recognition, words are first systematically presented in 1-second exposures; all error responses are repeated under

---

4. For additional reading or formal and informal methods of reading assessment the reader is referred to Bond and Tinker (1957), Duffy and Sherman (1973), Gillespie and Johnson (1974), Johnson and Kress (1965), Spache (1976), and Silvaroli (1973).

---

5. For title and publisher information on high interest–low vocabulary materials refer to Appendix C in Duffy and Sherman (1977) and to Appendix 1 in Gillespie and Johnson (1974).

Notation System (Duffy & Sherman, 1973, p. 38)

A pupil might make many kinds of word identification errors. In recording his errors, you should use a notation system that distinguishes one type of error from another because your analysis of his strengths and weaknesses depends on the patterns of errors he makes. A suggested notation system follows:

/ = hesitates before pronouncing words. Although infrequent or very brief hesitations may not be significant, frequent and lengthy hesitations indicate that the reader is not sure of the next word or that he is sounding out the word to himself. Such hesitations indicate that he does not know the word well; it is a pronunciation error.

bottom = does not know the word and it has to be pronounced for him by the teacher

the = substitutes an incorrect word for the printed word

little = repeats the word twice. This is an error because the pupil is unsure of the next word. He re-peats the preceding word or words in hopes that the unknown word will come to him.

in the = inserts a word that does not belong

there = starts to pronounce the word incorrectly but corrects himself. This is an error despite the fact that he corrects himself because it indicates that his initial perception of the word was inac-curate.

was = omits a word

= ignores punctuation

Reading Inventory Example

The following test results employ the above notation system and reflect a student's oral reading perfor-mance on selections taken from the *Durrell Analysis of Reading Difficulty* (Durrell, 1955).

First Grade (21 words)

Muffy is a little yellow kitten.
She drinks milk.
She sleeps on a/chair.
She does not like to get wet.

___+__ 1. What color was the kitten?
___+__ 2. What does she drink?
___+__ 3. Where does she sleep?
___+__ 4. Why doesn't Muffy like to go out on rainy days?
         (Duffy & Sherman, 1973, p. 39)

___0__ Number word recognition errors   ___0__ Number comprehension errors

__100__ % word recognition   __100__ % comprehension

Second Grade (51 words)

A *big* little black dog ran away from home. He played with two big dogs. They ran away from him. It began to rain. He/went under a tree. He wanted to go home, but he did not/know the way. He saw a boy he knew. The boy took him home.

big dog- 1. Who ran away from home?
___+__ 2. How many other dogs did he play with?
___+__ 3. Why did the dog go under the tree?
___+__ 4. What did the dog want then?
___+__ 5. Whom did he see?

FIGURE 10.6   *Example of a student's oral reading performance on graded paragraphs from the* Durrell Analysis of Reading Difficulty *(Durrell, 1955).*

Sources: G. G. Duffy and G. B. Sherman, *How to Teach Reading Systematically*. New York: Harper & Row, 1973, pp. 38–40; D. D. Durrell, *Durrell Analysis of Reading Difficulty*. New York: Harcourt, Brace and Jovanovich, Inc., 1955, p. 4.

_____+_ 6. How did he get home?

       (Duffy & Sherman, 1973, p. 39)

_____/_ Number word recognition errors   _____0_ Number comprehension errors

_____98_ % of word recognition   _____83_ % comprehensions

Third Grade (55 words)

Six boys put up/a tent by the side of the river. They took/things to eat with them. When the sun went down,/they went into the/tent to sleep. In the night, a cow came and began to eat/grass/around the tent. The boys were/afraid. They/thought it was a bear.

_____4–_ 1. How many boys went camping?

NEAR A LAKE –2. Where did they put up their tent?

_____+_ 3. What did they take with them besides their tent?

_____+_ 4. What did the boys do when the sun went down?

_____+_ 5. What came around their tent in the night?

_____+_ 6. What was the cow doing?

_____+_ 7. What did the boys think the cow was?

       (Duffy & Sherman, 1973, p. 40)

_____5_ Number word recognition errors   _____0_ Number comprehension errors

_____91_ % word recognition   _____72_ % comprehension

Fourth Grade (71 words)

Henry goes to a/large lake in/summer. Last/summer, a/motor/boat sank near his/house. The/boat had ten men in it. The man who was/running the boat brought it very close to the shore when the/water was low. He hit a big/rock/under/water. It made a hole in the/bottom of the boat. The/water came in very/fast. All of the/men swam to shore.

TO THE LAKE + 1. Where does Henry go in summer?

_____+_ 2. What happened near his house?

_____+_ 3. What kind of boat was it?

_____+_ 4. What did the boat hit?

_____–_ 5. How fast did the water come in?

_____–_ 6. How many men were in the boat?

RESCUED – 7. What happened to the men on the boat?

       (Duffy & Sherman, 1973, p. 40)

_____11_ Number word recognition errors   _____3_ Number comprehension errors

_____85_ % word recognition   _____57_ % comprehension

Summary of Results

Grade level of test material	Word recognition	Comprehension
First	100%	100%
Second	90%	83%
Third	91%	72%
Fourth	85%	57%

The student's independent reading level is first grade.

His instructional reading level is second grade.

His frustration reading level is third grade.

FIGURE 10.6   *Continued*

TABLE 10.5   *Levels of reading and listening ability*

Ability Level	Word Recognition (% of words correctly read)	Comprehension (% of questions answered correctly)	Behavioral Characteristics	Purpose of Level
Independent Reading Level	98–100%	90–100%	Level at which learner reads comfortably and with good comprehension; marked by expressive oral reading, observation of punctuation, and absence of lip movement, finger pointing, vocalization, head movement	Home work, worksheets and independent reading for enjoyment and information should be at this level
Instructional Reading Level	95%	75%	Makes 1 error every 20 words while only 3/4 of the content is understood; similiar characteristics as independent level	Level at which student can profit from directed reading instruction
Frustration Reading Level	90% or less	50% or less	Makes 1 error every 10 words or less while only half or less of the content is understood. May be marked by word-by-word reading without rhythm, lack of interest, pointing and lip movement, poor use of context cues	Material at this level of difficulty should be avoided
Independent Hearing Comprehension Level	Not applicable	75%	Highest level at which student satisfactorily understands materials read to him	Guide to level for verbal instruction and materials read to student; an index of student's level of speaking vocabulary and language structure

untimed conditions. The simpler words are tested first, followed by more difficult lists.

If a teacher desires to teach a limited vocabulary of highly functional or protective words, informal tests may be simply constructed for lists composed of such words (e.g., *Curriculum-Cumulative Progress Report,* 1972; Otto, McMenemy, & Smith, 1973). Because such lists are difficult to grade, no estimates of grade reading levels will be obtained. However, since a criterion-referenced test such as a word list test or the oral reading of a paragraph may be constructed to measure exactly what is being taught, these tests are the most meaningful tools to monitor learning. Estimates of reading ability measured in often inexact grade levels are far less helpful in determining specific instructional targets and in measuring performance changes. In fact, in an extensive survey of high interest–low vocabulary reading materials used frequently by special education teachers, Lavely, Lowe, and Follman (1975) analyzed the accuracy of each publisher's grade level selections from all levels of each

reading series examined. They found that the majority of publishers had assigned grade levels much lower than their actual difficulty and that most books in a series did not gradually increase in difficulty. Therefore, the use of such texts with their present difficulty designations to determine a student's reading levels would produce meaningless results.

Criterion-Referenced Tests

If an instructional objective is stated in observable terms and contains all the essential elements (conditions, behavior, and criteria), then a criterion-referenced test may be constructed to measure an individual's performance of the skill specified by the objective. This type of testing, referred to as "criterion referenced," does not compare a person's performance to a peer group, as with norm-referenced tests, but rather to an arbitrary criterion specified by the teacher. Because such tests are matched closely to what is being taught, they provide a means to measure the effectiveness of a given

General Instructions:

The following steps should be followed to give an informal test of an individual's ability to recognize frequently used words (Dolch, 1950) in isolation of phrase or sentence context.

1. *Preparing word cards.* Type in primary-sized type or print clearly the high utility words selected for each grade level on separate 3 × 5 inch cards. A minimum of 25 words should be selected for at least each of the following grade levels: preprimer, primer, first, second, third.
2. *Ordering the words.* Order the words by level from preprimer on with a matched listing on which to score the student's responses (see test pages).
3. *Flashed exposure.* Make sure that the student is ready and attending; flash the words to the student one at a time allowing a 1-second exposure to each word. Unless you have information that the student "reads well" at levels above preprimer, start with preprimer words. The best method of flashing words is to hold a blank card over the word and move it up (or down), then back down after 1 second. Another way involves the use of a card with a window-opening in it or a tachistoscope.
4. *Scoring flashed words.* If the word is correctly read in the flashed condition, score a + in the appropriate blank and go to the next word. Immediate self-corrections are scored as incorrect because it indicates that the student's initial perception of the word was not accurate. If the word is not attempted, score a NR for no response to the word. For misread words, write the incorrect response in the blank. These mistakes will be analyzed after the test to detect any patterns in the student's incorrect responses.
5. *Untimed exposure.* Whenever an error is made in a flashed exposure, record the student's performance, then repeat the trial, allowing sufficient time (10 seconds) for the student to examine and analyze the word.
6. *Scoring untimed words.* The student's response to the untimed condition is listed in the untimed column: + for correct, NR for no response, and for errors the misread word is placed in the blank.
7. *Test ceiling.* Testing is stopped as soon as the student misses 10% (or more) at a given grade level (i.e. 2 of 20 words, 4 of 40, etc.). However, if one is interested in obtaining a larger baseline, one may test beyond a 10% error level as long as adequate reinforcement is made available.
8. *Determination of reading levels.* The results of a word list test can be used only to *roughly estimate reading levels* and tend to underestimate these levels because reading words in isolation is more difficult than in context. However, the highest grade level at which 98–100% of the words were correctly read may be regarded as an estimate of the student's independent reading level; 95% corresponds to instructional level and 90% or less signifies frustration level.

Informal Word Recognition Test of Dolch Basic Words in Isolation

Name _____ Examiner _____

Date _____ School _____

	Pre-Primer			Primer			First Grade	
	Flashed	Untimed		Flashed	Untimed		Flashed	Untimed
1. and	_____	_____	1. all	_____	_____	1. after	_____	_____
2. run	_____	_____	2. am	_____	_____	2. again	_____	_____
3. up	_____	_____	3. are	_____	_____	3. an	_____	_____
4. down	_____	_____	4. at	_____	_____	4. any	_____	_____
5. where	_____	_____	5. ate	_____	_____	5. as	_____	_____
6. it	_____	_____	6. black	_____	_____	6. ask	_____	_____

FIGURE 10.7 *Informal word recognition test of Dolch Basic Words in isolation*

Source: E. W. Dolch, *Teaching Primary Reading.* 2nd ed., Champaign, Ill.: Garrard Press, 1950.

	Pre-Primer			Primer			First Grade	
	Flashed	Untimed		Flashed	Untimed		Flashed	Untimed
7. come	____	____	7. do	____	____	7. by	____	____
8. red	____	____	8. eat	____	____	8. could	____	____
9. yellow	____	____	9. four	____	____	9. every	____	____
10. big	____	____	10. get	____	____	10. fly	____	____
11. see	____	____	11. good	____	____	11. from	____	____
12. away	____	____	12. he	____	____	12. give	____	____
13. I	____	____	13. like	____	____	13. going	____	____
14. me	____	____	14. must	____	____	14. had	____	____
15. make	____	____	15. new	____	____	15. has	____	____
16. blue	____	____	16. no	____	____	16. her	____	____
17. help	____	____	17. now	____	____	17. him	____	____
18. one	____	____	18. on	____	____	18. his	____	____
19. for	____	____	19. our	____	____	19. how	____	____
20. a	____	____	20. out	____	____	20. just	____	____
21. little	____	____	21. please	____	____	21. know	____	____
22. funny	____	____	22. ran	____	____	22. let	____	____
23. go	____	____	23. saw	____	____	23. live	____	____
24. three	____	____	24. she	____	____	24. may	____	____
25. two	____	____	25. soon	____	____	25. of	____	____
26. to	____	____	26. that	____	____	26. old	____	____
27. said	____	____	27. there	____	____	27. once	____	____
28. my	____	____	28. they	____	____	28. open	____	____
29. the	____	____	29. this	____	____	29. pretty	____	____
30. look	____	____	30. too	____	____	30. put	____	____
31. here	____	____	31. under	____	____	31. round	____	____
32. is	____	____	32. want	____	____	32. some	____	____
33. in	____	____	33. was	____	____	33. stop	____	____
34. find	____	____	34. well	____	____	34. take	____	____
35. can	____	____	35. what	____	____	35. them	____	____
36. you	____	____	36. white	____	____	36. then	____	____
37. not	____	____	37. who	____	____	37. think	____	____
38. we	____	____	38. will	____	____	38. walk	____	____
39. jump	____	____	39. with	____	____	39. were	____	____
40. play	____	____	40. yes	____	____	40. when	____	____
TOTAL	____	____	TOTAL	____	____	TOTAL	____	____
PERCENT CORRECT	____	____	PERCENT CORRECT	____	____	PERCENT CORRECT	____	____

FIGURE 10.7   *Continued*

	Flashed	Untimed		Flashed	Untimed
1. always			1. about		
2. around			2. better		
3. because			3. bring		
4. been			4. carry		
5. before			5. clean		
6. best			6. cut		
7. both			7. done		
8. buy			8. draw		
9. cold			9. drink		
10. does			10. eight		
11. don't			11. fall		
12. fast			12. far		
13. first			13. full		
14. gave			14. got		
15. goes			15. grow		
16. green			16. hold		
17. its			17. hot		
18. made			18. hurt		
19. many			19. if		
20. off			20. keep		
21. or			21. kind		
22. pull			22. laugh		
23. read			23. light		
24. right			24. long		
25. sing			25. much		
26. sit			26. myself		
27. sleep			27. never		
28. tell			28. only		
29. their			29. own		
30. these			30. pick		
31. those			31. seven		
32. upon			32. shall		
33. us			33. show		
34. use			34. six		
35. which			35. small		
36. why			36. ten		
37. wish			37. today		

FIGURE 10.7   *Continued*

	Flashed	Untimed
38. work	_____	_____
39. would	_____	_____
40. write	_____	_____
TOTAL	_____	_____
PERCENT CORRECT	_____	_____

_____ independent reading level

_____ instructional reading level

_____ frustration reading level

	Flashed	Untimed
38. together	_____	_____
39. try	_____	_____
40. warm	_____	_____
TOTAL	_____	_____
PERCENT CORRECT	_____	_____

Comments on student's word analysis methods:

FIGURE 10.7 *Continued*

teaching program by monitoring changes in the student's performance over time.

To construct criterion-referenced tests to measure various reading skills, the teacher begins by task analysing the skill and writing instructional objectives matched to the terminal and enroute behaviors revealed by the task analysis. (Refer to Figure 10.3 where a daily living skill involving reading was task analyzed, i.e., following the instructions on a packaged pizza mix [Lichtman, 1972].) A test was constructed (Figure 10.4) to measure one of the enroute objectives (collecting utensils and ingredients specified in the instructions) and a criterion for that objective was established.

Informal test construction and resultant teaching will result in less trial and error if one begins with a task analysis already validated with the moderately handicapped. Such is the case with the whole word analysis (Sidman, 1971; Sidman & Cresson, 1973). Once a specific set of words has been selected, a student may be given informal tests constructed to measure each of the 8 tasks listed in Sidman's whole word method analyses (Figure 10.2). For example, to test task 2, "identity word matching," one would first specify the instructional objective in more precise terms: "when shown a printed word sample stimulus, the student will select the single printed word match from a choice of eight printed words (hat, man, dog, cow, box, cat, bed, hen) with 100% correct performance for three successive, randomly ordered tests on all eight words." Next, the testing materials must be made (2 sets of printed word cards) and the testing directions and procedure stated (e.g., "Look at this card," sample stimulus word placed in front of student; "Now, find the word that matches this one in this group of words"; teacher places all 8 choices in random or-

der below the sample word in front of student. Finally a simple recording form and daily performance chart or graph needs to be devised so results can be recorded accurately and progress toward achieving criterion can be monitored over time.

The complex task analyses of Duffy and Sherman (1977), Smith (1976), and Smith et al. (1977) do not have published applications with a moderately handicapped student population. (Smith et al. (1977) *do* describe the validity of their criterion-referenced tests for general school and special project, or educationally delayed, populations.) However, both objective lists contain criterion-referenced tests for each objective, thereby easing the teacher's task. One of these tests and its corresponding objectives is presented in Table 10.6. Notice that the order of stimuli and/or the sample of specific stimuli tested may be varied to avoid memorization of one small set of test responses. This is an important consideration since tests are repeated at least twice (pretest or baseline and posttest), if not more often.

Testing for Functional Use of Skill

At some point after informal testing reveals that a skill is close to meeting criteria, additional practice and testing should be provided using realistic materials and in applied situations to ensure the expansion of skills still impracticable for functional reading. Many of the discrete skills listed in the Duffy and Sherman (1977) sequence exemplify this problem—by themselves they are not directly applicable at home, in the community, or in a vocational setting (e.g., matching the letters *t, b,* and *p* to spoken words beginning with these consonants). However the same discrete skills are necessary elements for building reading ability. In addition, it is

TABLE 10.6   *Sample criterion referenced test of reading skills*

I. Cluster I, Sight Words

Objective 10

The performance objective. Given a few seconds to examine a letter, the learner will reproduce the letter from memory, to the satisfaction of the teacher.

The pretest. Prepare ten flashcards, with each card having one letter of the following sequence: *q, s, a, e, y, m, l, v, b.* Flash each for the count of three. Then direct the learner to reproduce it. The criterion for mastery is teacher judgment concerning the accuracy of each reproduction. Size is not a criterion.

Caution: It is not necessary at this time for the learner to be able to name the letters, because naming is tested later.

The posttest. The pretest may be used also as the posttest.

Source: G. G. Duffy, and G. B. Sherman, *Systematic Reading Instruction* (2nd ed.). New York: Harper & Row, 1977, p. 107.

true that learning progresses best if during the early instruction of a skill the teaching task is held constant (materials remain the same, no change in stimuli presented and response requested) (Gagne, 1965; White & Haring, 1976). In fact, White and Haring suggest that during this acquisition phase of learning, the instructional task remain unchanged until the student responds correctly, without any assistance, about two-thirds of the time. Once this point is reached, it is essential that generalization training be programmed *in addition to* working with the basic task until the skill is fluently or proficiently performed and the criterion is met.

As applied to reading, generalization training may mean changing from less realistic materials (word cards, sentence building charts, word family wheels) to some of the common printed materials listed in Table 10.1 (e.g., magazines, newspaper food ads, classified want ads, telephone book listings, slides taken of street signs, building directories, and bathroom signs, the writing on appliances and food boxes, and so on). If instruction was begun with more functional materials, then additional applications could be programmed. For example, the probe in Figure 10.4 suggests that after criterion is

met for selecting utensils and ingredients necessary for making a pizza mix, the student will be taught (and tested on) the same skill using gelatine mix, canned soup, and possibly a packaged macaroni and cheese mix. Besides changing materials, the teaching and corresponding testing situation may change from a classroom with a familiar teacher to a grocery store, a department store, a restaurant, a street corner, or a workshop with a variety of individuals requesting from the student the same reading skill or a combination of learned reading skills. All of the objectives listed earlier by Bender et al. (1976) as well as Lichtman's (1974) development of tasks to assess functional literacy provide curriculum guidelines for building generalized reading skills with a functional orientation. Informal test construction is done in the same way as for examining less applied reading skills except the conditions (materials, setting, individuals present) and the behaviors will be functional in nature.

Besides teacher-made tests of functional skill use, there are currently available some tests of adult functional literacy, 36 of which recently have been summarized and evaluated by Nafziger, Thompson, Hiscox, and Owen (1975). Among the instruments reviewed are informal reading tests, criterion-referenced tests, and standardized tests. Lichtman's (1972) test, *Reading/Everyday Activities in Life (R/EAL)*, is a criterion-referenced instrument which could be used by a classroom teacher to collect performance data on such skills as the ability to read want ads, to understand a lease, to complete an application form, and to read traffic signs. Some of the testing materials are illustrated in Figure 10.8. Three additional criterion-referenced tests assess similar types of applied writing and reading skills such as filling out a check, ordering by mail, using a phone book, and addressing a letter. These are the *Adult Performance Level Functional Literacy Test* (Northcutt, Kelso, & Barron, 1975), the *Basic Reading Skills Mastery Test*, and the *Wisconsin Test of Adult Basic Education.*

Implications of Research for Teaching the Basic Components of the Reading Task

Materials and procedures for reading programs that do not use the research findings on the basic components of the reading task lead to error-ridden guesswork. However, this is not uncommon among authors and publishers of elementary school materi-

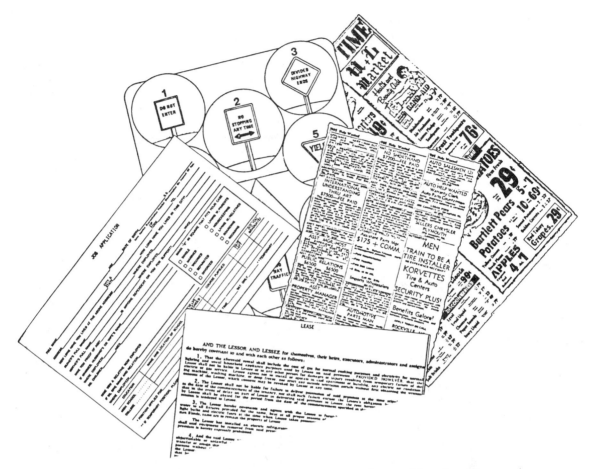

FIGURE 10.8   *Examples of testing material used in Lichtman's test of functional literacy*
Source: M. Lichtman, *Reading/Everyday Activities in Life*. New York: CAL Press, 1972, pp. 2, 10, 12, 16, 18.

als (Coleman, 1970). Consistent with the reading task analyses already reviewed (Duffy & Sherman, 1977; Sidman, 1971; Smith et al. 1977), the more logical and, in the long run, the more efficient approach to creating reading programs begins with isolating the components of associational learning involved in the reading task. Both Sidman's tasks, outlined in Figure 10.2, and Duffy and Sherman's breakdown of word recognition and comprehension skills (Figure 10.5) attempt to identify these components of associational learning. The components of reading acquisition that have been isolated (Samuels, 1971) include *attention, visual* and *auditory discrimination, short-* and *long-term memory,* and *mediation* (the often covert ability to act upon, classify, or analyze information or perceived stimuli for the purpose of establishing organizational systems or solving problems). The second step in the development of reading programs is to seek "empirically based information on the training and sequencing of the essential subskills" (Bilsky, Evans, & Martin, 1975, p. 359).

This two-step procedure of producing empirically based instructional methods in reading is even more essential when the learners are moderately and severely handicapped. This is because of the widespread evidence that deficiencies exist in the mentally retarded individual's ability to attend (Zeaman & House, 1963), to remember on a short-term basis (Ellis, 1970), and to mentally organize material into categories (Spitz, 1966, 1973). This section of the chapter describes the teaching implications of studies that have examined with moderately retarded learners the components of learning to read.

Principles for creating optimal learning conditions

An extensive review of the learning research with retarded populations allowed Denny (1966) to define 7 instructional conditions which maximize learning for these students. As you already know, success in reading tasks relies upon skills of attention, discrimination (visual and auditory), memory (long- and short-term), and mediation. The purposes of these maximizing practices are (1) to make the relevant stimuli more obvious, (2) to decrease the tendency for error, (3) to provide informative consequences to the learner for every response, and (4) to encourage retention and skill generalization. To the extent that these principles result in these 4 outcomes, their application to reading instruction for the moderately handicapped will facilitate attending, discrimination, memory, and mediation. The principles are described in order of importance.

1. *Prevent uncorrect responses early in learning and increase the number of correct responses made by the learner.* This principle calls for two types of teaching during the initial stage of learning —prompting to promote the correct response, thereby reducing errors and allowing the learner many opportunities to repeat the same behavior in the presence of the relevant stimuli. Chapter 3 clearly defines the range of prompts that may be employed to reduce a student's uncertainty in responding; these include decreasing the number of choices to make a discrimination task easier, physical guidance, intercepting and stopping errors, redundancy cues or temporary pairing of one dimension with the correct choice (color coding, size, or position cuing), match-to-sample cues, modeling a vocal or gestural response for the learner to imitate, or physically cuing a response by tapping near or looking at the correct choice. Once these prompts have served to establish the correct behavior, they must be gradually faded. Delay procedure (Touchette, 1971; see Chapter 3) has been a useful technique for the errorless elimination of prompting cues with severely retarded individuals.

2. *Provide the learner immediately with knowledge of the accuracy of her response.* This principle states that if a correct response is made, inform the learner as soon as the response has been completed; if an error is made, let the learner know in a nonaversive manner. Trials resulting in error should be repeated with prompting. If *noncompliancy* is suspected as the cause of error (i.e., the student's response level is approaching criterion and the error is more indicative of a refusal to respond rather than uncertainty), a time out may be used as a conse-

quence for errors. While the presentation and the absence of tangible reinforcers serve to signal a correct or an error response, it will be necessary to verbally affirm correct responses if reinforcement is not being given continuously (e.g., "Good, that's right! The *B* goes with the *baseball* picture").

The use of *Language Master* recording–playback machines (Bell and Howell Company) to drill word recognition is a good example of immediate response feedback. Words or sentences are written on special cards that have a strip of magnetic tape on the bottom. The cards are placed into a track in the *Language Master* and a voice prerecorded onto the tape reads the word as a check for the student.

3. *Whenever possible, provide the learner with differential feedback—feedback relevant to the meaning of the concept being taught.* This principle states that word meaning be emphasized to promote comprehension. When teaching positional prepositions, familiar nouns, and verbs, it would be important to have the learner perform each action or pair an object or picture with the word. The reading procedures that Brown and his colleagues have employed with the moderately handicapped illustrate this principle well. For example, Brown et al. (1974) taught students to read action verbs by first requiring that they perform the action to indicate understanding and later match the word to a picture. These techniques will be presented in more detail in the next section of the chapter.

4. *To facilitate discrimination of the relevant stimuli and appropriate transfer of a learned response, first randomize all the irrelevant stimulus cues (e.g., the color, size, or position of an object, picture, or written word) and then program opportunities for stimulus generalization.* All the prompts that were employed to "get a response going" during early learning need to be faded gradually so the student discriminates the stimuli in the presence of which a particular behavior is appropriate. For example, a teacher may have used red color cuing, as did Egeland and Winer (1974) with inner-city preschool children, to highlight the distinctive feature of similar letter pairs:

R–P   Y–V   C–G   K–X

Then using a match-to-sample, visual discrimination task, the teacher would say, "See this letter? [*R*] Now find all the letters that look the same in this group [*P R R P P R P*]." The color highlight certainly would emphasize the relevant feature of the letter and reduce the tendency for errors. However, until the color cue is faded, the child may simply be matching red marks with other red marks and not attending to the letter differences. Fading of cues is essential in order that the discrimination occur but it must be done slowly or the student will become confused. Egeland and Winer (1974) found that 10 successive reductions of the red cue from bright red to no red cue at all enabled the children to master the discrimination without error.

Stimulus generalization is a somewhat opposite learning procedure. The learner who already discriminates the relevant stimuli must expand this discrimination to include a broader class of stimuli. For example, once a student reads "Men" and "Women" without assistance at criterion, it is important that this skill be generalized to the same words and to words with similar meaning despite variations in size, placement (on doors, walls, outside the classroom rather than word cards), and configuration, (MEN, Gentlemen, Men, BOYS).

5. *To promote long-term retention, a student should be provided with opportunities to overlearn —repeated practice or review distributed over time rather than massed into a brief time period.* Some educators refer to this procedure as a maintenance period of learning which begins *after* a student has achieved performance criterion. Review activities are most efficient if they are scheduled at spaced intervals (once a week, monthly, etc.) during a school year (as well as the summer).

6. *Keep the student's motivation for performance and interest in the task at high level.* Motivating students is important throughout all stages of learning. However, because motivation may be achieved in different ways (task novelty, reinforcement amount and schedule), one should be careful to match the method of motivation with the stage of learning (White & Haring, 1976). During the acquisition stage the immediate provision of reinforcers on a fairly frequent schedule is the best means to keep performance high. At this point in learning it would not be appropriate to change the task materials or requests significantly, since the student is likely to become confused. However, during the generalization stage, task novelty is the primary mechanism for increasing interest because external reinforcers should have been added to an infrequent schedule.

All the classroom studies in which moderately and severely handicapped learners have been taught reading skills have employed contingent positive reinforcement. Bijou, Birnbrauer, Kidder, and Tague (1966), Staats (1968), and two studies with nonretarded populations (Staats & Butterfield, 1965; Staats, Minke, Finley, Wolf, & Brooks, 1964) established the importance of a strong motivational system upon the development of on-task behavior, reading, and other academic skills. These and more recent studies have frequently employed token economies in which marks or marbles (exchangeable for back-up reinforcers at a later time) were awarded for identified behaviors. Bijou et al. (1966) identified 3 rules for the effective use of tokens in a classroom reading program for retarded students: "(1) The marks must be given as soon as possible consequent to the specific behaviors to be strengthened. (2) They must be given for increasingly larger units of behavior. (3) They must be given simultaneously, or almost so, with social stimuli from the teacher" (pp. 516–517).

Discussed more fully in Chapter 3, the techniques for reinforcer selection, scheduling, and classroom use are relevant to effective reading instruction of the moderately handicapped learner.

7. *Determine the easy-to-hard sequence underlying the development of a skill, so that instruction begins with the prerequisites and gradually builds toward more difficult goals.* This practice is an especially common recommendation when teaching the handicapped learner. Sequential building relies upon the teacher's knowledge of developmental sequences and the ability to accomplish accurate task analyses, careful baseline and ongoing assessment, and precise determination of instructional targets from assessment data.

Implications of basic reading research with retarded learners

Even though the more basic research in reading with moderately and severely retarded subjects is not carried out in classroom settings, it has produced important educational implications for task structure or instructional format, the stimulus or teaching materials, and the provision of reinforcement. To present these implications efficiently, several studies will be annotated along with a summary of related recommendations.

Task Structure

Bilsky, Evans, and Martin (1975) investigated the effect of task format on the ability of mildly to severely retarded subjects to discriminate between the similar letters of "b" and "d." Tasks were presented to different groups in a variety of ways in two studies: (1) 4-choice matching ("Find the one that looks like this," *b – b d d d*); (2) 2-choice matching ("Find the one that looks like this," *d – b d*); (3) 4-choice oddity ("Find the one that does not look like the others," *b d d d*); and (4) 2-choice discrimination ("Find the one that is right and gives you the candy" [e.g., "b" is correct], student sees: *b d.*) They found that with 2-choice discrimination tasks none of the students learned to visually discriminate between the letters while both the match-to-sample formats and the oddity format resulted in discrimination learning. In a second study they learned that a match-to-sample task arrangement employing redundancy in its choices (*b – d b d d*) as compared with no redundancy (*b – b p d g*) did not make the discrimination easier for retarded learners. Also when the choices (*b d d d* or *b g d p*) were delayed, that is, were presented after the sample letter (*b*) had disappeared, the subject learned to discriminate more slowly than when both the stimulus and the choices were present simultaneously (*b – b g d p*) and visual memory was not required.

Implications of the Bilsky et al. (1975) study for promoting optimal learning in visual discrimination reading tasks are as follows:

1. Avoid 2-choice discrimination tasks because of their difficulty; do not present 2 unknown stimuli with an unmeaningful request or no request at all and expect the student to learn that one choice is correct and leads to reinforcement and the other is incorrect. Avoid using worksheets or teaching tasks with students that make a choice response if either the preceding directions or printed stimuli or all of the choices are not meaningful to the student. For example, if the teacher holds up 2 or more last name cards and asks a student who *does not* recognize her last name to choose "her" card, the student will probably guess. Because of the low number of choices she will be right half of the time without ever learning a visual discrimination.

2. To facilitate visual discriminations, use match-to-sample arrangements (*cat – bat cat toy cot*) or oddity tasks (*bat bat cat bat*). Both task formats make correct responding more probable because the skills of matching and of selecting the single different stimulus are easier than selecting a choice from 2 (or more) different stimuli with no directions or unmeaningful directions.

3. The use of redundancy in the choices of a match-to-sample match ($\triangle$ – $\square$ $\square$ $\square$ $\triangle$) may be more distracting than when all alternatives are different ($\triangle$ – $\square$ $\bigcirc$ $\times$ $\triangle$). Retarded learners do not readily make use of redundancy in the choices, and for some it is distracting.

4. To teach visual discrimination skills, first use simultaneous match-to-sample tasks in which the sample is presented along with the choices and no memory is required. Later teach the same discrimination on a delayed basis; that is, the choices follow the presentation of the sample. This will strengthen the discrimination in preparation for a more difficult task such as an auditory association with the same visual stimulus. For example, task A should precede task B.

A. "Look at this word" (teacher points to BOY on left). "Now find the same word over here" (teacher points to choices).

BOY	BAT	BALL	BOY	TOY

B. "Look at this word and remember what it looks like" (teacher exposes card BOY). "Now find the same word you just saw" (teacher places 4 word cards in front of the student).

BAT	BALL	BOY	TOY

Hawker (1968) and *Hawker, Geertz, and Shrago (1964)* investigated the effects of (1) instructional procedure (prompting or confirmation), (2) grouping of response choices (same or different concepts), and (3) method of stimulus presentation (word-pictures or picture-words) on 96 moderately to severely retarded individuals' ability to learn and retain a list of 8 words (e.g., horse, duck, table, chain, pie, etc.). The task itself was a simultaneous match-to-sample arrangement of words and pictures. Some learners had word samples and 4 picture choices ([horse]– [picture: pie] [picture: table] [picture: train] [picture: horse]), and others had picture samples and 4 word choices ([picture; horse] – [pie] [table] [train] [horse]). In the earlier study (Hawker et al., 1964), some students were given picture response choices that were all in the same class, such as all animals or all foods; whereas for the different-concept group, all the choices were from different classes (e.g., pie, horse, table, ball). In the *prompting* teaching procedure the response choice was coded with a red arrow and the student was instructed to point to that item, then back to the matching stimulus and say the word aloud; students did not make errors in the prompting condition. In the *confirmation* condition, students were shown the stimulus and instructed to point to the choice that was the same as the stimulus. If they made the correct choice, they were reinforced and asked to point to the word and say it aloud. If they made an incorrect choice, they were asked to try another choice until they were correct. Learning for all subjects was tested on recognition probes (a multiple choice of words) and on recall probes (words alone) after each of the 8 teaching sessions and 1 week later.

Although students made some errors under the confirmation procedure and none in the prompted procedure, neither procedure was superior to the other and both resulted in similar learning. Whether the picture choices were in the same class or a different class from the stimulus made no difference. It was felt that students did not attend to the similarity or difference; so that when incorrect response choices were in different categories from the stimulus (*duck – pie duck table train*), the task was not any easier. It was clear from the results that a task becomes easier to learn if the response choices have high meaningfulness for the student. Students in the word stimulus—picture choice condition learned to read the words more quickly than those with a picture stimulus and word choices. This was because the picture choices were meaningful and the word choices were not. Finally, because students were taught to *recognize* (to select the correct choice from 4 choices) rather than to *name* (read) single words, they showed no noticeable forgetting when given a recognition test a week after training, but did poorly on a word-naming test.

Four teaching implications for sight word instruction of the moderately retarded may be drawn from the work by Hawker and his coworkers.

1. The use of prompting or confirmation in a multiple-choice (picture-word or word-picture) sight vocabulary task will promote learning. Both are good techniques; prompting reduces error and cues the correct choice, while confirmation provides the learner with immediate feedback and task repetition until the correct choice is made. It is likely that a combination of prompting and confirmation would produce even faster learning.

2. If multiple-choice tasks are used to teach sight words, it is not important whether the choice pictures are of the same category as the stimulus picture. This makes little difference to a retarded learner. The category each picture choice belongs to should *not* be confused with visual similarity between the picture choices (e.g., pie, circle, ball, plate). Visual similarity *is* likely to make the task more difficult.

3. In multiple-choice (match-to-sample) tasks, position the items most meaningful to the learner as the choices rather than as the sample. Therefore use pictures for the choices and a word as the stimulus *before* teaching the picture-word multiple-choice task. It is interesting to note that Sidman's task analysis (1971) does not demonstrate this easy-to-hard sequence; in Figure 10.2, the order of steps 6 (picture-word match) and step 7 (word-picture match) should be reversed according to Hawker's findings.

4. Match your probe to the reading skill you are teaching; for example, word list tests are harder than multiple-choice recognition tests and will underestimate a student's skill to recognize words that go with pictures or pictures that go with words.

Dorry and Zeaman (1973, 1975) also attempted to teach a simple reading vocabulary to 35 nonreading moderately and severely retarded individuals who were all able to label pictures corresponding to the vocabulary words. They experimented with 4 training procedures for the purpose of determining which procedure resulted in the most learning. In the *standard procedure,* the subject was shown slides of a single vocabulary word and its picture and was asked to say what was on the slide. Slides were repeated so that half of the 8 words were each seen in one session a total of 6 times in random order; then the student was immediately tested on the first 4 words by being asked to read each word. The second 4 words were taught in the same way with an immediate test. Finally word list 1 was tested again followed by a repeat test of list 2 (delayed tests). Standard procedure consisted simply of viewing repeatedly the pairs of pictures and their printed labels.

In the *faded* procedure students began with the same picture-word pair slides but during training the pictures were gradually faded from very clear to hardly visible by the end of training on each list. The order of the 4 different picture-word slides was varied but picture fading proceeded from visible to not visible. As with all groups these students were also asked to say the stimulus word for each slide and the order of teaching and listing was the same: train on list 1, test on list 1; train on list 2, test on list 2; retest on lists 1 and 2.

The *mixed* procedure incorporated some properties of fading out the picture. That is, the training slides for each word alternated regularly over trials from a word-picture slide to a word slide and back.

Describing the mixed training method, Dorry and Zeaman (1975) stated:

This sequence mimics three properties of fading: (a) it reduces generalization from training to test by interpolating test trials (word alone) among the training trials, (b) it provides a mixture of noncontingent (word-picture) trials and contingent (word) trials, and (c) it forces attention to the word on (word) trials, since these trials can be viewed as extreme instances of picture-fading. (p. 712)

The last teaching procedure was a control condition not meant to be effective. Control students were simply shown alternating slides of pictures alone and words alone (e.g., P_1, W_1, P_4, W_4, etc.).

The results clearly showed that the faded training procedure produced the *most* learning, followed in effectiveness by the mixed procedure, the standard procedure, and the very ineffective control procedure which resulted in almost no learning. Although all students performed better on the immediate test, when they did not have to remember, than they did on the delayed test, the order of procedural effectiveness on the delayed tests was still clearly the same. The Dorry and Zeaman (1973, 1975) studies suggest the following classroom practices:

1. If pictures are used as part of a procedure to teach a learner to read (verbally label) a printed word, learning will be greatest if the picture stimulus is always presented with the word stimulus and, over trials, the picture is gradually faded away. The learner should verbally label the picture-word pair on every trial.

2. If picture fading of some type is not used in sight-word instruction, learning will be poor. This is because nothing in the standard pairing approach (word-picture pairs with no picture fading) guarantees that the learner will attend to the word. To be correct she simply must label the picture. On the other hand, fading the picture gradually decreases the picture's salience, resulting in more attention to the word. In the mixed procedure the learner's attention also is directed to the word on the "word only" trials, although attention to the word is less orderly.

The decision of whether to teach reading by an analytic (whole word) approach or by a synthetic (small parts of word) approach is a debated topic for normal as well as handicapped learners. A synthetic program starts by teaching the learner to associate single letter sounds with letters. A whole word program which starts by teaching the whole word and then presents single letter sounds may produce

more rapid initial learning than a synthetic approach. However, the whole word learner must be taught new words because he is not likely to transfer or decode new combinations of previously introduced letters. *Neville and Vandever (1973)* matched normal 6- and 7-year-olds with mild to moderately retarded persons of the same mental age and taught half of each group to read simple words written in a contrived alphabet somewhat analogous to the Roman alphabet:

$$a = ① \quad c = ⊖ \quad f = ⊓ \quad t = ⊔$$

The contrived alphabet was used to guarantee that high frequency words (e.g., "fan," "get") could be taught without any instances of prior knowledge. Each child had two 45-minute, teaching-testing sessions. On the first day, 6 words were taught, after which the subjects were tested on those 6 plus 4 similar transfer words. On the second day, they were taught 8 words followed by a test of the 8 and 4 more transfer words.

In the whole word method words were presented in word families (e.g., fog, hog; get, met) in the following way:

1. One word (in contrived alphabet letters) was shown on a screen, pronounced, and used in a sentence.
2. Subjects were asked to count the number of letters.
3. Subjects' attention was drawn to tall letters and letters below the line.
4. A second word from the same word family was introduced (steps 1–3).
5. The two words were compared with configuration outlines (e.g., fog) which students were encouraged to use as an aid.
6. Students found words in booklets that matched spoken words and were given feedback.
7. The remaining word pairs were introduced in a similar manner.
8. All words were reviewed.
9. All instructed words and new transfer words were tested—words were read aloud (e.g., "fog," "get," etc.) and students circled the printed word that corresponded to the spoken word from a choice of words.

Synthetic instruction was started with the presentation of several letters and proceeded as follows:

1. Several letters were shown on the screen and their sound pronounced first in isolation and then in a word.

2. The letters were combined to form words.
3. Students found words in a booklet that matched words on screen.
4. Review was given on each of the letter sounds.
5. Words were presented orally and students sounded each out silently, then matched the corresponding word in their booklet.
6. Words were tested as in the last step of the whole word procedure.

The test results indicated that both retarded and nonretarded synthetic learners learned more words and were able to read transfer words more often than subjects taught by the whole word approach. In addition, there was no difference in the amount of learning or transfer between retarded and the MA-matched nonretrarded students except by the instructional procedure they received.

The major implication of Neville and Vandever's (1973) study, despite its short intervention time and the use of a contrived alphabet, was that a synthetic method was more successful than a whole word method in teaching retarded learners a strategy to decode both instructed and new words. This study presents evidence somewhat contradictory to *traditional* practice—that a whole word approach is simpler than an analytic or "phonetic" approach for moderately handicapped learners. The results provide more support for starting reading instruction early and for teaching both the visual *and* auditory component skills so that the goal of functional literacy might be achieved.

Stimulus Materials

A number of studies have examined various ways of presenting letters and words to moderately handicapped learners that have affected their rate of learning. In the first study to be reviewed, the investigators were interested to learn whether special printing would facilitate learning. "Symbol accentuation" is a term used by *Miller and Miller (1968)* and defined as the conveyance of meaning by printing the letters of a particular word in a way that characterizes its meaning. For example, one could accentuate the letters of the word "candy" by coloring them with red and white stripes, the word "run" could be written with letters that slant forward, "up" written with the "p" raised above the line, and "look" with "o"'s that symbolize eyes ("lóók"). In two studies with a total of 48 mild to severely retarded individuals (mean IQ in the moderate range), Miller and Miller found that accentuated words were more rapidly learned.

In the *accentuated* condition the student saw the accentuated word and heard an explanation of its meaning ("This word is *candy*. A candy cane has red stripes," p. 202). The word was flashed quickly for a few seconds either by flipping a flashcard from the accentuated side to its conventionally written side or, in a later study, by alternating projected, overlapping slide images of the conventional form ("look") with the accentuated form ("lóók") 2 times per second for 15 seconds. In *conventional* training, no accentuated symbols were used but the meaning statement was still given. Even though the amount of time the word was viewed and the number of printed word–spoken word pairings were kept the same in both conditions, students in the accentuated condition still learned to read the conventional form faster.

Miller and Miller's study demonstrates the importance of (1) emphasizing meaningful cues as a memory strategy and (2) novel and interesting task presentation. Symbol accentuation (SA) must not be equated with picture-word pairs; they are different in many ways. Most importantly, words cued with SA still have the same basic form as their conventional word partner, while pictures do not incorporate the letter shapes of their printed label. This means that when the learner looks at an SA word, she is already attending to letter shape and position while being reminded of a familiar association of meaning. The clever use of SA and conventional word alternation forced the learner to attend more closely to the conventional form and served to fade the SA cues.

It is true that most words cannot be easily accentuated making symbol accentuation a very limited teaching technique. However, SA may be useful for two types of handicapped learners: with beginning readers, SA is an interesting way to teach an initial, small set of content sight words; and with older, nonreading students, SA might provide a quick and effective means to teach certain protective words (e.g., "stop," "poison," "entrance," "push," "pull," "walk," etc.).

Drinkwater (1972) reported that category words selected by the experimenter ("move," "wear," and "food") were learned more quickly by moderately retarded students when the words were taught with pictures they preferred (boy sliding down slide, a watch, a hot dog) rather than with nonpreferred illustrations (boy walking, pair of school shoes, a potato). The implications from this simple study are clear. If task materials are interesting and have high meaning association for the learner, then attention for those materials will increase. At the same time, the probability is increased that an association between meaningful picture stimuli and nonmeaningful printed stimuli will be made and remembered.

Vandever and Neville (1974) reported a specific variation of their earlier study comparing whole word (visual emphasis) and synthetic (letter-sound emphasis) approaches to reading instruction. They examined the effect of various visual cuing procedures upon the word recognition skills of mildly retarded and nonretarded readers of the same chronological age (7 years). The same contrived alphabet used in their earlier study was employed to insure that the children could not read any of the training words before instruction. Three cuing procedures were used to teach different groups the same set of 8 words. Except for different letter cues, the basic instructional procedure for all 3 cuing techniques was a whole word approach.

The first 2 conditions emphasized word configuration both in their instructional procedures, by calling attention to word shape, and in their cue. While *outline cues* simply employed a thin black line following the up-and-down shape of the letters, *contrast cues* used the same outline but each word was set against a black background that followed the configuration contour. For example, in the experimental orthography the word "fat" with an outline cue appeared as follows: ⊓ ⊕ ⊔; in the contrast condition it was presented as ⊓ ⊕ ⊔. While the *letter cue* condition simply underlined each word (⊓ ⊕ ⊔), the instruction for learners in this treatment was directed toward the "distinctive features" of each word's initial and final letters rather than to word shape. The student's attention was also drawn to the tall letters and those extending below the line. All three groups learned 1 word at a time, matched words presented on a screen to words in their booklets, and reviewed learned words.

The results showed that while all the same-aged normal students learned more words, they were not affected by cuing condition. The retarded subjects taught with the letter cue recognized more words on a multiple-choice recognition test than did those learning with outline or contrast configuration cues. These findings suggest the following recommendations:

1. For young retarded learners who generally do not know what visual cues to look for when learning

to read words, it is more effective to emphasize individual letter cues (position in word, ascending or descending parts, etc.) rather than word shape cues.

2. Cuing by shape or configuration outlines, whether they be simple line outlines or more obvious contrasting outlines, should be avoided. Configuration cues are not very utilitarian word-recognition strategies because many different words have identical shapes even though the ascending and decending letters may be different (e.g., "pad," "put," "got," "yet").

Classroom Reading Instruction

Applied research, reading programs, and materials

To the extent that classroom procedures to teach reading meet the following criteria, moderately handicapped students will learn functional reading skills more quickly: (1) derive their content from accurate task analyses (whether they be complex or simple), (2) incorporate functional materials and generalization activities, and (3) structure tasks to facilitate learning. This section describes reading programs which not only have been used in classroom settings with the moderately handicapped but also incorporate 2 or all 3 of these criteria. Some of the programs were developed for slow learners but have been successful in varying degrees with the moderately handicapped learner. Others were developed specifically for use with the moderately handicapped. These latter reading programs may be divided roughly into 2 types: visually oriented or emphasizing a whole word approach and synthetic (phonetic) or emphasizing both visual and auditory elements.

It is true that some traditional remedial methods of teaching reading have been applied to mildly and moderately handicapped students. The research on the effectiveness of these methods is often inconclusive (Gillespie & Johnson, 1974). These techniques have included the language experience approach (Stauffer, 1970), the Fernald method (also called VAKT for its visual, auditory, tactual, and kinesthetic emphases) (Fernald, 1943), Montessori's method (Montessori, 1912), various basal series procedures, and some programmed reading textbooks (e.g., *Sullivan Programmed Readers,* Buchanan, 1968). For more about these programs and their use with retarded learners, the reader is referred to their original references and to Gillespie and Johnson (1974) and Otto et al. (1973).

Rebus, Edmark, and Distar reading program

Of these three commercially available programs, the Edmark Reading Program (1972) is the only one developed specifically for the mildly and moderately retarded nonreader (Bijou et al., 1966; Birnbrauer, Wolf, Kidder, & Tague, 1965). Because each program is very different in its approach and goals, they are described separately.

Peabody Rebus Reading Program

The Peabody Rebus Reading Program (Woodcock, Davies, Clark, 1969) grew out of an experimental program that compared 6 different procedures for teaching young, mildly retarded children (Woodcock, 1968). Since that time it has been modified and used to teach non-English–speaking and hearing-impaired children, preschool through first-grade children in regular grades, and Head Start classes. Its primary characteristics are the use of rebuses (pictures or symbols) to represent words prior to the introduction of printed words.

The rebuses introduced in the first two books are shown in Figure 10.9. After completing the two initial

FIGURE 10.9   *Rebus vocabulary for the two introductory books in the Peabody Rebus Reading Program*

Source: R. W. Woodcock, C. O. Davies, and C. R. Clark, *The Peabody Rebus Reading Program Supplementary Lesson Kit: Manual of Lessons*. Circle Pines, Minn.: American Guidance Service, 1969, back cover page.

programmed books the child learns a vocabulary of 68 words and can decipher a series of rebuses arranged in a left-to-right manner with a normal down-the-page and page-to-page progression. Because the workbooks have a programmed format (Figure 10.10), they provide the student with immediate feedback on each response and advance in small steps with gradually increasing difficulty. In this readiness phase of learning (the first two books), the student is exposed to the use of picture and context clues and structural analysis involving the *-ing* verb ending, the possessive *-'s,* and plural *-s*

word endings. In the third book and two accompanying readers, the transition process between traditional orthography and the rebuses takes place. Spelled words are gradually substituted for the rebuses by first being colored cued and paired with smaller rebuses, then spelled words appear alone but are color cued to a word key at the top of each page. At the end of the transition, the student can read 172 words, with 122 of them being spelled words, and has been exposed to beginning sound-letter associations involving initial consonant sounds and some vowel-consonant combinations.

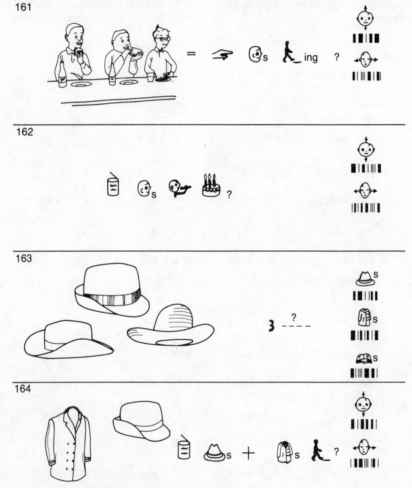

FIGURE 10.10   *Example response frames from the second programmed workbook in the Peabody Rebus Reading Program*
Student reads frame, responds by touching a damp eraser to the markings below his selected answer in the right-hand column; color-changing inks provide immediate feedback to student—green means "correct," red means "try again."

Source: R. W. Woodcock, *Introducing Reading, Book Two, Peabody Rebus Reading Program*, Circle Pines, Minn.: American Guidance Services, 1967, Frames 161–164.

The standardized picture vocabulary enables the learner to represent to himself the necessary paired associates of sound and written form, taking advantage of the child's well-developed language skills.

Additional examples of picture-symbol materials. The use of standardized picture systems with accompanying words *to substitute* for reading skills is quite different from those which are intended *to teach* reading. Recalling Dorry and Zeaman's research (1973, 1975) reported earlier, one could compare a more permanent picture-word system to the standard treatment in which word and picture are viewed repeatedly without any picture fading. As you may remember, this teaching practice produced very little reading ability because the learner focused attention on the picture, not the word. Instruction that employs picture-word pairing will lead to reading only if the pictures are faded out, thereby directing the learner's attention away from the picture to the word. The more gradual the fading, the better the learning (Dorry & Zeaman, 1975). The Peabody Rebus program incorporates gradual fading of its picture symbols.

Chapter 11 discusses a picture system meant to substitute for reading rather than to teach reading. If such a system is standardized, the nonreading handicapped adult would be able to consult picture reference books for recipes, reminders on clean-up procedures, and the steps in common daily activities, thereby reducing the dependency upon memory or nonhandicapped adults. The international sign symbols used to mark restrooms and code traffic signs are meant to serve as permanent word-picture pairs to facilitate comprehension for foreigners and nonreaders. A final example of a permanent picture-word system are the Bliss symbols (Bliss, 1965). Bliss symbols, some of which are illustrated in Figure 10.11, have been used effectively as communication systems for nonvocal, severely physically handicapped individuals (Vanderheiden & Grilley, 1975). Although each symbol card has the corresponding printed word on it, the word is meant primarily to remind readers of the symbol's meaning.

A wide variety of cookbooks do exist which employ various levels of picture symbols meant to either substitute for reading or to aid the poor reader (*Cooking with Betty Crocker Mixes,* 1970; *Easy Menu Cookbook,* 1974; Kaman, 1974; Reed, 1973; Staples: 1975). Staples provides some useful guidelines for the development of picture recipes based upon the results of a project to teach recipes, basic nutrition, and cooking to moderately and severely retarded students. She found that three difficulty levels of picture instructions were needed to match

FIGURE 10.11   *A cerebral palsied, mentally retarded child using Bliss Symbols as a means for nonvocal communication*

Source: G. Vanderheiden, and K. Grilley, *Non-vocal Communication Techniques and Aids for the Non-vocal, Severely Handicapped.* Baltimore, Md.: University Park Press, 1976, p. 129.

the varying skill levels of reading, attending, and memory encountered in a moderately and severely handicapped group. However, recipes at all levels were introduced with instruction. At *level one,* the directions were the simplest with generally not more than 2 pictures per page. At this level every utensil, ingredient, and action is pictured with only a few words. In Figure 10.12, part of a level-one, 8-page recipe on making orange juice is illustrated. At level one, red and green traffic lights are useful to mark beginning and end of a recipe. *Level two* incorporates a utensil guide so that easy reference may be made to needed utensils; rather than picturing each spoon, bowl, etc. everytime, the recipe would state, for example, "For utensils needed, see utensil reference guide; page 1A, page 1B, page 7A, page 7B, page 8" (p. 24). This refers the cook to pictures of a wooden spoon, a paring knife, a measuring cup, etc., in the utensil guide. In level two, more than one step may be described per page, the recipes are often more difficult, and more words are relied upon. The *third level* of difficulty is exemplified by two pages from a casserole recipe in Figure 10.13. As can be seen, this level depends more upon words but uses pictures for reinforcement. There may be 6–8 ingredients pictured per page or 3–4 direction steps.

Staples (1975) provides additional suggestions for efficient and nonconfusing use of picture-word directions. Although her guidelines are directed toward the development of recipes, they have direct implications for the development of other picture-word directions.

1. The finished product should be on the first page of an instruction booklet.
2. All ingredients (and utensils for level one) should be illustrated next.
3. Arrows should be employed to describe the direction of a movement (mixing, turning can opener, plugging in an appliance).
4. Steps are more easily followed if listed from top to bottom rather than left to right.
5. All pages should be numbered beginning with the front title page.
6. Stencils should be used to standardize pictures; a picture is best if it corresponds to the object's actual size (cup and spoon measures); color photographs or container labels corresponding to the actual brands used provide the most realistic pictures.

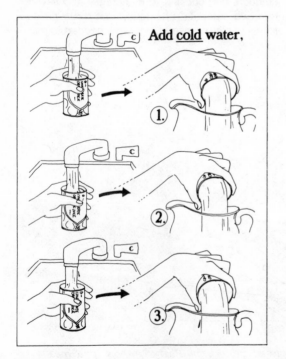
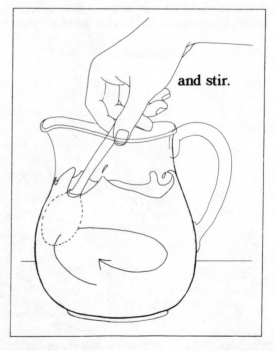

FIGURE 10.12   *The last 2 pages from an 8-page, level 1 (least complex) picture recipe on making orange juice from frozen condensed juice*

Source: K. S. Staples, *Cooking from Pictures.* Fargo, N. D.: North Dakota State University, 1975, pp. 20–21.

7. Picturing glass bowls, cups, and pitchers allows the illustration of their visible contents and avoids the use of cut-away pictures.

8. Time and temperature are clearly pictured by the use of shaded clocks and dials (Figure 10.13).

Because many severely handicapped individuals cannot read and others will not learn to read beyond a small protective vocabulary, the development of simple, standardized picture-cued direction guides for vocational and daily living activities represents an immediate materials need. Considerations important in meeting this need are discussed more fully in Chapter 11.

Edmark Reading Program

The Edmark Reading Program (1972) was developed by Sidney Bijou over a 10-year period with mildly and moderately retarded students at Rainier School in Washington (Bijou et al., 1966). Its instructional method is whole word and uses a programmed response format for one-to-one word recognition instruction. As with Distar, the teacher's script is supposed to be followed carefully so that error and correct responses are handled in a set manner, consistent with operant principles of learning. The program teaches a 150-word vocabulary of high utility words. The word-recognition program progresses from gross visual discrimination tasks (pictures and geometric shape matching) to finer and finer discriminations (single letters and word matching) in readiness for reading. Once a word is introduced and learned through the word-recognition programmed task, the student is provided with independent activities that allow the functional use of learned words. Direction books (Figure 10.14) request that the student locate and arrange pictures according to printed directions (e.g., "man on horse," "man in car"). In the Picture/Phrase Matching lessons, a student selects word and phrase cards to place beside their appropriate picture (Figure 10.15). Finally Story Book lessons center upon reading words the student is already independently capable of decoding.

Edmark has the advantages of being based upon supportive research, progressing in a sequential manner, incorporating learning principles, providing opportunity for functional use of reading, requiring no special training for its use, and allowing the teacher to monitor a student's progress closely. Its disadvantages include its expense, the lack of supplemental reading materials, and the fact that word-recognition lessons are expected to be taught on a

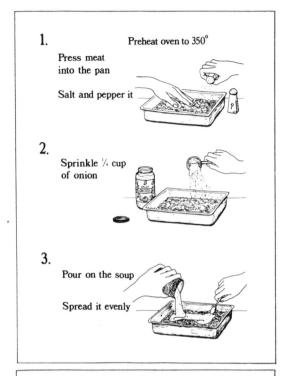

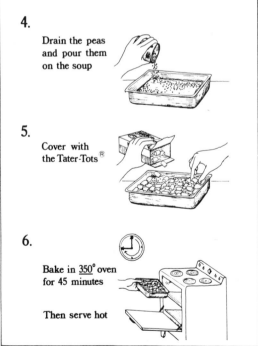

FIGURE 10.13   *Two pages of a 3-page, level 3 (most difficult) casserole recipe*

Source: K. S. Staples, *Cooking from Pictures.* Fargo, N. D.: North Dakota State University, 1975, pp. 38–39.

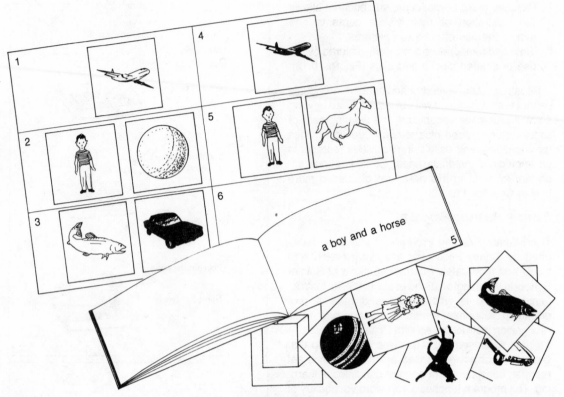

FIGURE 10.14   *Direction Books: An independent reading activity in which the student reads the words on each page of directions, selects the corresponding picture from a group with a variety of distractor pictures, and places the pictures on the appropriate section.*

Source: *Edmark Reading Program* (Direction Book, Set B, Book 7). Seattle: Edmark Associates, 1972.

one-to-one basis. (Limited informal application of this program with groups of 2 and 3 students by the author suggests that this latter requirement may not be essential.)

Distar Reading Program

Designed to teach reading to slow learning and lower-income preschool children, the Distar Reading Program (Engelmann & Bruner, 1969) also was developed from an empirical base and incorporates many of the principles for systematic learning (Bereiter & Engelmann, 1966). The program places particular emphasis upon the instruction of sound-symbol association, sound blending, rhyming, and sequencing, and left-to-right visual progression. First, learners are taught to pronounce a set of 20 individual sounds, then they learn to sound out words ("say words slowly") and to blend words by saying them fast. To simplify word-sounding tasks, Distar teaches a set of 9 visually and audibly distinct phonemes. These nontraditional letters (e.g., a

joined-together *th*) are used in words to represent sounds distinct from other sounds made by the same letters.

Instruction is done primarily in small, ability-matched groups and is characterized by moving in small steps and being fast-paced, lively, and dense with reinforcement and feedback from the teacher. Hand signals are used frequently by the teacher to ensure that group responses begin and end together, to direct attention to visual stimuli, and to pace sound-blending activities.

Englemann (1967) states that Distar reading instruction is not only appropriate for mentally retarded learners but should be begun early—at a mental age of four.

The major implication of our work seems to be that children with relatively low mental ages (initially less than four years) can learn to read if the instruction is adequately geared to give them instruction in all of the subskills demanded by the

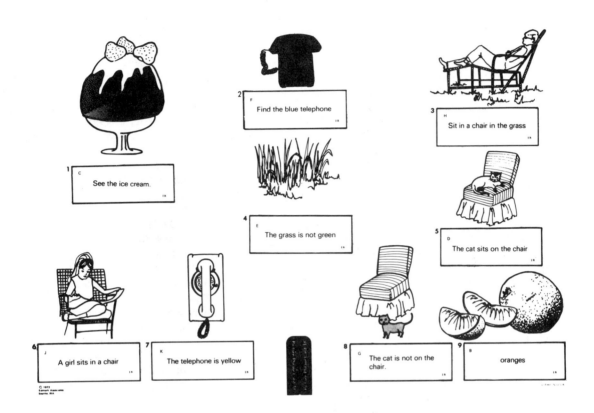

FIGURE 10.15   *Picture/Phrase Cards: An independent reading activity in which the student looks at the pictures on each section of the card, selects the appropriate word or phrase to label each picture from a group of phrases, and places the phrase card in the corresponding box under each picture.*

Source: *Edmark Reading Program* (Picture/Phrase Card 18). Seattle: Edmark Associates, 1972.

complex behavior we call reading. Furthermore, virtually all children with mental ages of four or over can learn to read. Their progress is relatively slow, but all can progress from one subskill to the next until they are reading. With the emphasis on subskills, the teacher is in a position to know what skills a child has not learned. She therefore knows which skills to work on. When a child masters a given skill, the teacher can proceed to the next one. (p. 199)

Despite the assurances provided by Engelmann's words, it is not clear how slow a moderately retarded or otherwise handicapped student will progress through the Distar program and how many of the subskills will be mastered. Results of a few studies examining the effectiveness of the Distar, Edmark, and Rebus programs are described next.

Effectiveness of the Peabody Rebus, Edmark, and Distar reading programs with the moderately retarded

All three programs have been reported as being successful in teaching some reading skills to mentally retarded individuals at mild and moderate levels (*Rebus:* Apffel, et al., 1975; Woodcock, 1968; *Edmark:* Bijou et al., 1966; Birnbrauer, et al., 1965; Lent, 1968; Vandever, Maggart, & Nasser, 1976; *Distar:* Apffel et al., 1975; Engelmann, 1967; Williamson, 1970). Unfortunately few comparative studies exist which allow critical evaluation of each program's effectiveness and the identification of ways to match students to programs.

At the beginning and end of a school year, Vandever et al. (1976) pretested and posttested the word-recognition skills of 15 primary level classes for mildly retarded students. During the year 5 randomly selected classes were taught reading with the Edmark Reading Program, 5 with the Sullivan Programmed Readers (Buchanan, 1968), and 5 with the Merrill Linguistic basal series (Fries, Wilson, & Rudolph, 1966). Two word-recognition tests were used with each of the 3 groups; 1 test was composed of the first 150 words taught by a group's respective reading program and the other test was meant to measure reading transfer by testing a list of 50 words (15 words on this list were those common to all 3 programs and included on the first 150-word test, and the remaining 35 words were selected from the first 114 words on the Dolch list [Dolch, 1950] as those *not* appearing in any of the 3 programs). Children who recognized more than 50 words on the pretest were eliminated from the study.

The Edmark program previously discussed teaches a 150-word vocabulary by using a whole word, highly structured, programmed approach. Merrill Linguistic Readers (Fries et al., 1966) make use of learning words as members of word families (e.g., "mat," "fat," "pat," "sat"). Although the Linguistic Readers emphasize group instruction by the whole word approach, students are taught to attend to and contrast the distinctive features of separate letters (e.g., above or below the line) with the words initially presented in capital letters only. Sullivan Programmed Readers (Buchanan, 1968) take synthetic or phonetic approaches to teaching reading. Workbooks are programmed and present tasks involving question answering and sentence and word completion with multiple choices. The Sullivan series emphasizes sound-symbol associations with generalization of letter-sounding skills to phonetically regular words.

Analysis of the test data revealed that students taught in the Edmark program recognized significantly more words on their 150-word test (an average of 49 words) than did those taught with either the Sullivan (average of 31 words) or the Merrill series (average of 39 words). However, all groups did equally poorly on the 50-word transfer test, mastering only about 20% of the words. The authors drew two important conclusions with related recommendations for classroom teachers.

1. While Edmark was shown to be the most effective reading program of the three for mildly retarded students, its requirement of individual instruction demands that (A) peer tutoring or unpaid classroom volunteers supplement professional teaching staff so that one-to-one instruction is possible, and (B) classroom staff be skilled in behavior management techniques in order that the individualized instruction and independent work required by the Edmark program is feasible.

2. Unlike Edmark, the Merrill and Sullivan series teach words only of specific linguistic patterns. Because of this characteristic, the authors stated, "It may be particularly important, therefore, that children introduced to reading in a Merrill or Sullivan program complete the basic parts of that program before the attempt is made to transfer them to a more traditional basal reading program" (p. 32).

Apffel et al. (1975) closely monitored, rather than compared, the performance of 60 moderately to severely retarded students, aged 10 to 14, in two reading programs for one school year (Distar and Rebus). Regular measurement of performance was made every 4 weeks using the reading program's own evaluation device. Student progress was recorded in terms of correct and error rates in relation to the difficulty level of the program in which a student was participating. While some students in both programs did not succeed, a majority made fair to good progress. Some students in both programs advanced to more conventional reading instruction; by contrast, some students needed "recycling" or repetition of lessons in their assigned instruction group, and others were reassigned to less-advanced groups depending upon the trends visible in their correct and error rate performance in relation to the program's pace. The authors concluded that, "These results give further evidence of the ability of the moderately retarded to cope with academic instruction. It is not suggested that all such children will profit from it, but clearly some can" (p. 235).

While it is unquestionably true that more systematic, applied research is called for before conclusions may be drawn comparing the effectiveness of the Distar, Rebus, and Edmark reading programs with moderately handicapped individuals, there appears to be adequate evidence supporting the notion that a large fraction of these learners can learn to read when instructed in one of the three programs.

Structured whole word teaching methods

Some examples of highly structured whole word teaching methods have already been discussed; a few were laboratory examples, most of which involved the use of some automated teaching equipment (Dorry & Zeaman, 1973, 1975; Hawker, 1968; Hawker et al, 1964; Sidman, 1971; Sidman & Cresson, 1973). Other studies (Bijou et al., 1966; Birnbrauer, Kidder, & Tague, 1964; Birnbrauer, et al., 1965), which laid the foundation for the Edmark reading program, were carried out systematically in classrooms with mild- and moderate-handicapped students. In addition, Brown and his colleagues have reported a series of successful variations of the whole word approach; these are described briefly along with a final example of a structured, visually directed reading program not supported by published data.

Work by Brown and Colleagues

Brown and Perlmutter (1971) defined functional reading as "discrete and observable motor responses to printed stimuli" (p. 75). This instructional definition included the presentation of printed stimuli (words or sentences) followed by 2 student responses: reading the printed stimuli and demonstrating comprehension (e.g., by carrying out the actions indicated, by matching a word to its pictured referent).

In the first of 3 studies, Brown and Perlmutter (1971) taught 7 moderately retarded teenagers to read 9 sentences, a total of 71 words. The students were instructed in 2 small groups; each student received a total of 60 instructional hours. During this period, instruction was ordered according to the following steps with performance measured before step 1 and after each step marked with an asterisk. All students were assessed on their ability to label single words, read sentences, and demonstrate reading comprehension by the following directions stated in each sentence.

1. Teaching students to label single words
   A. Word card presented (Set I)
   B. Teacher labels word; student repeats
   C. Teacher model is faded; training continues until criterion is reached on set being taught (criterion equalled 3 consecutive correct responses)
   D. Set II taught to criterion with steps A–C, while Set I is reviewed
   *E. Set III taught to criterion with steps A–C, while Sets I and II are reviewed
2. Teaching students to read words in sentences
   A. Present sentence
   B. Teacher reads sentence word by word as each word is pointed to in order; students repeat sentence

*C. Teacher model is faded; training continues until criterion is reached
3. Teaching students to demonstrate reading comprehension
   A. Teacher reads each sentence and points to location directed by sentence (e.g., "The penny is on top of the box")
   B. Teacher reads 1 of the 9 sentences; student carries out directions or indicates listening comprehension until criterion is reached (modeling prompts are used as needed, then faded)
   *C. Repeat step B with remaining sentences to criterion
   D. Student reads 1 sentence and carries out directions or demonstrates reading comprehension until criterion is reached (modeling prompts are used as needed, then faded)
   *E. Repeat step D with remaining sentences to criterion.

As with their other studies, this study employed a response controlled progression. That is, students were not advanced to a level of more difficult instruction until criterion performance was attained at each earlier measured step. If the task analysis upon which instruction is based has small and properly sequenced steps leading to the target behavior and the measurement of performance is accurate, then students should progress through instructional steps with minimal amounts of error. In addition, instruction in this and other studies was characterized by contingent reinforcement, immediate feedback, error correction, prompts early in learning, and easy-to-hard learning sequences—all of which are features that promote optimal learning.

Brown et al. (1974) report the results of a program to teach 3 moderately retarded children to functionally read 5 action verbs ("color," "touch," "run," "walk," and "sit"). Their instructional procedure, which was successful, involved the following steps. As each behavior was taught, it was measured so that progression in the program was controlled by the student's performance.

1. Baseline measurement
   A. Demonstrating spoken verb comprehension by performing action (e.g., "*Walk* to the chair.")
   B. Labeling the different actions illustrated in pictures
   C. Demonstrating spoken verb comprehension by pointing to appropriate picture

D. Reading 5 printed verbs
E. Performing action indicated by a printed verb
2. Teaching student to demonstrate comprehension of spoken verbs by carrying out requested action
3. Teaching student to label action pictures
4. Teaching student to demonstrate comprehension of spoken verbs by selecting a picture that illustrates that verb
5. Teaching student to label verb word cards
6. Teaching student to select a picture illustrating a printed verb
7. Teaching student to perform action specified by a printed word.

In another study employing similar whole word methods, Brown, Jones, Troccolo, Heiser, Bellamy, and Sontag (1972) report a procedure by which 2 moderately retarded 5-year-olds learned to read 12 objective-noun phases (e.g., "big cup," "little cup," "red crayon", "blue crayon"). The instructional steps were as follows with progression through the steps dependent upon a student's measured performance in each step.

1. Baseline measurement
   A. Labeling objects
   B. Labeling printed words
   C. Labeling words and touching corresponding object
2. Labeling objects
3. Reading printed stimuli for objects learned in step 2
   A. With teacher model
   B. Without teacher model
4. Reading printed stimuli and touching corresponding object
5. Second baseline measurement
   A. Verbally labeling objects and their descriptors (e.g., "What is that?" "Yes, that is milk, but what kind of milk is it?")
   B. Reading adjective-noun phrases
   C. Reading adjective-noun phrases and touching the corresponding object
6. Labeling objects with descriptors (adjective-noun phrases)
7. Reading printed stimuli for adjective-noun phrases learned in step 6
   A. With teacher model
   B. Without teacher model
8. Reading printed stimuli and touching corresponding object with appropriate description.

Data for both students indicated not only similar learning patterns but that as the student learned to read increasing numbers of words, fewer trials were needed to reach criterion for each additional word.

Brown's studies provided valuable evidence that the successful laboratory findings with whole word reading instruction for moderately retarded learners hold true even in applied classroom settings. Classroom comparisons between Sidman's more detailed whole word method, Dorry and Zeaman's whole word plus picture fading techniques, and Brown's definition of the whole word method would produce valuable information.

Curriculum-Cumulative Progress Report: Functional Reading Program

Oregon's state curriculum for teachers of the moderately and severely retarded (*Curriculum-Cumulative Progress Report,* Note 1) outlines a whole word instructional program that employs prompts to reduce errors, immediate feedback, overlearning, and generalization training. Although no supportive data are reported, its procedures do align well with the instructional principles and research implications outlined earlier. Although a protective vocabulary was taught with this procedure, it could also be used to teach high utility sight words. The following steps represent the general instructional progression employed with each new word, although additional training suggestions have been added to increase procedural clarity. Throughout teaching, correct and error responses respectively are followed with positive reinforcement or repetition with assistance and correction. For example, in the matching tasks, student responses may be handled in the following ways. *Correct responses:* praise and repeat answer (e.g., "Yes they both say MEN"). *Error responses:* repeat with some assistance; increase assistance only as is needed to evoke the correct response (e.g., reduce choices, use color cuing, etc.).

The student's word recognition performance is measured with flashed cards before and after teaching for all old and new words taught.

1. *Matching*
   Place 4 word cards in front of the student. (MEN, WOMEN, EXIT, ENTRANCE).
   A. Give the student a second MEN word card. Say "Match MEN, find the word that looks the *same* as this."
   B. Repeat with other 3 cards, 1 at a time.
2. *Receptive Reading*
   Select 1 word from the set of training words to begin with. This same word will be taught in steps 2–6 before any of the other words are taught in those steps.

A. Place 1 word card in front of the student (MEN). Say "Point to MEN."

B. Place two words in front of the student (the same correct choice and 1 distractor: MEN PUSH) and repeat for the same word.

C. Repeat for the same word with 3 choices, 2 of which are distractors.

3. *Oral Reading*

Hold up card for word taught in step 2 and ask "What does this say?" (MEN)

4. *Comprehension (receptive reading)*

Place 4 word cards in front of student. Ask (for male student): "If you needed to go to the bathroom you would look for the sign that says MEN. Which sign would you look for?"

5. *Generalization to New Settings*

Tape the MEN and WOMEN word cards to the respective bathroom doors (over existing signs). Ask (for male student): "If you needed to go to the bathroom which sign would you look for?" Then ask, "What does that sign say?"

6. *Generalization from Word Cards to New Configurations*

Locate bathroom doors with the words MEN and WOMEN printed on them (or use slides). Repeat question in step 5.

After student performs step 6 without errors On first training word, repeat steps 2 through 6 with each additional word in the set of 3 to 4 new training words (WOMEN, EXIT, ENTRANCE). Drop back to matching step if student makes errors in step 2. Adjust comprehension and generalization requests, settings, and materials as appropriate to the target word (e.g., reword questions for males and females with words MEN and WOMEN; locate building signs marking ENTRANCE and EXIT to teach these words).

Testing and review: Introduce a new set of 3–4 words and teach as described above. Use old words as distractors. Review old words on a regular basis both during teaching sessions and by testing. When testing, record the student's first response but provide feedback as done during teaching so that testing provides an opportunity for maintenance training.

Teachers using the program are directed to alternate positions of the word-card choices whenever more than one choice is used to avoid reinforcing positional responses.

In Chapter 2, the graph employed to illustrate cumulative graphing techniques (Figure 2.14) represents data collected for a group of 3 moderately handicapped students who had been taught a small set of protective words using these instructional steps. Various worksheets involving matching, receptive reading, writing, picture labeling, and comprehension were used to reinforce and extend reading skills.

Synthetic or phonetic approach

Many researchers have recognized the limitations that whole word methods put upon reading achievement. Brown et al. (1974) comment,

It is quite probable that the whole-word method of teaching reading, at least as it has been discussed here can result in substantial gains in reading achievement. However, it is doubtful that teachers will, by the use of this method, teach their students to read every word, every verb conjugation, and every plural and abbreviation that the students must learn. Hopefully it should be unnecessary to do this. Effective methods of teaching word-attack skills, phonetic, etc., must be delineated and verified empirically for use with this level student. (p. 58)

In order to achieve most of the functional reading goals described by Bender et al. (1976), it seems necessary that the moderately handicapped reader must learn some of the word-recognition skills outlined earlier.

Some of the laboratory research already cited or described (Neville & Vandever, 1973; Staats, 1968) as well as some applied research with moderately retarded populations (Apffel et al., 1975; Vandever et al., 1976) and mildly handicapped learners (Lahey, Weller, & Brown, 1973; Lovitt & Hurlburt, 1974) have indicated the success of teaching readers to analyze words by sound, sight, and context rather than to read by sight alone. Two additional applied studies will be reviewed briefly with some attention given to their techniques for teaching the functional application of phonics.

Direct Approach to Decoding (DAD)

Richardson, Oestereicher, Bialer, and Winsberg (1975) summarize an experimental program that was successful in teaching phonetic word-recognition skills to nonreaders. DAD was used with small group instruction and incorporated a criterion progression through the following four teaching steps:

1. Letter sounds: Student learns to associate a sound with single isolated letters *(p, s, m)*.

2. Sound blending: Student learns to listen to sequences of sounds learned in step 1 (/p/, /an/) and to blend sounds to make words ("pan").
3. Phonetic analysis and blending: Student learns to look at printed words that were learned by blending (step 2) and to say each sound in sequence and then read the word.
4. Word reading: Student learns to look at, quickly analyze, and read new words in rapid succession.

While Richardson et al.'s (1975) program has been demonstrated successful, more research would be valuable to assess its comparable effectiveness with other sound-based reading programs as well as total reading achieved by DAD "graduates" as compared with students learning by a whole word approach.

Teaching Word Recognition Skills of Picture Cues, Context Cues, and Initial Sounds

Entrikin, York, and Brown (1975) report a well-defined sequence of objectives directed toward the instruction of elementary word recognition strategies: the use of picture cues, context cues, and initial consonant sounds to determine an unknown word. Three moderately retarded, 10-year-old students with varying amounts of motoric handicaps met the following 6 entry criteria for training and demonstrated successful use of basic word recognition strategies with unknown words.

1. Imitation of teacher-provided consonant sounds.
2. Rudimentary speech.
3. A sight vocabulary of at least 50 words.
4. Left to right eye movement when reading.
5. A reliable and valid yes-no response.
6. A basic understanding of logical and absurd relationships. (Entrikin et al., 1975, p. 451)

The content of the instruction program is summarized by the detailed objectives that follow. For more definition of teaching procedure, the reader is referred to the original report (Entrikin et al., 1975).

Phase I: When students are presented with a printed word they cannot label and four pictures that represent objects and actions with differing initial consonant sounds, they will determine the label of the unknown word by finding and labeling the picture which represents the object or action with the same initial consonant sound.
Part 1 –Teaching students to label object pictures and describe action pictures.

Part 2 –Teaching students to sound consonants presented on flashcards.
Part 3a–Teaching students to touch the first letter (color coded) in printed words.
Part 3b–Teaching students to touch the first letter (not color coded) in printed words.
Part 4 –Teaching students to sound initial consonants in selected printed words.
Part 5 –Teaching students to label object pictures, to describe action pictures, and to make the initial consonant sounds of the objects and actions represented in the pictures (e.g., Q–"What is this?" A–*"(ball)"* Q–"What is the first sound in *(ball)*" or Q–"What is the *(boy)* doing?" A–*"(running)"* Q–"What is the first sound in *(running)*?").
Part 6 –Teaching students to label object pictures, to describe action pictures, and to make the initial consonant sounds of the objects and actions presented in those pictures (e.g., Q–"What is this?" A–*"(ball)"* Q–"What is the first sound in that word?" or Q–"What is the (boy) doing?" A–"(running)" Q–"What is the first sound in that word?")
Part 7 –Teaching students to make the initial consonant sounds of objects and actions represented in pictures (e.g., "What is the first sound in this?").[a]
Part 8 –Teaching students to touch the appropriate object or action picture in response to a consonant sound stated by the teacher (e.g., "Touch the thing that begins with (bb).").[b]
Part 9 –When students are presented with a printed word they cannot label and four pictures that represent objects and actions with differing initial consonant sounds, they will determine the label of the unknown word by finding and labeling the picture which represents the object or action with the same initial consonant sound.

Phase II: When students are presented with a worksheet containing sentences composed of words they can label but which are missing one

---

[a]Parts 5 and 6 differ in that the teacher repeats object labels and action descriptions in Part 5 but does not do so in Part 6. In part 7, neither the teacher nor the student labels object pictures or describes action pictures.
[b](bb) as in boy.

word in the subject, verb or object position (e.g., the ———hit the ball. The boy————the ball. The boy hit the————.) and three printed words above each sentence, they will mark the one word that logically completes the sentence.

Part 1 –Teaching students to label object pictures and describe action pictures.

Part 2 –When students are presented with eight sets of two pictures one component of each set depicting an absurd action (e.g., teacher combing hair with toothbrush) and the other component depicting a logical action (e.g., teacher combing hair with comb) and the question, "Does this picture make sense?", they will respond "yes" to pictures of logical actions and "no" to pictures of absurd actions.

Part 3 –When students are read sentences which are logical or absurd following the question, "Does this sentence make sense?" they will respond "yes" to logical sentences and "no" to absurd sentences.

Part 4a–When students are presented with a printed sentence read by the teacher with one word missing in the object position (e.g., The boy hit the————.) and three object pictures, they will touch the one picture that represents the object which logically completes the sentence.

Part 4b–When students are presented with a printed sentence read by the teacher with one word missing in the verb position (e.g., The boy————the ball.) and three action pictures, they will touch the one picture that represents the verb which logically completes the sentence.

Part 4c–When students are presented with a printed sentence read by the teacher with one word missing in the subject position (e.g., The————hit the ball.) and three object pictures, they will touch the one picture that represents the subject which logically completes the sentence.

Part 4d–When students are presented with a printed sentence read by the teacher with one word missing (e.g., The———— the ball. The boy————the ball. The boy hit the————.) and three object or action pictures, they will touch the one picture that represents the subject, verb or ob-

ject which logically completes the sentence.

Part 5 –When students are presented with a printed sentence read by the teacher with one word missing in the subject, verb or object position (e.g., The———— hit the ball. The boy————the ball. The boy hit the————.) and three printed words, they will touch the one word which logically completes the sentence.

Part 6 –When students are presented with a worksheet containing sentences composed of words they can label but which are missing one word in the subject, verb or object position (e.g., The————hit the ball. The boy————the ball. The boy hit the————.) and three printed words above each sentence, they will mark the one word which logically completes each sentence.

Phase III: When students are presented with a worksheet containing sentences composed of words they can label with the exception of one underlined word in the subject, verb or object position and four pictures above each sentence, they will determine the label of the underlined word by marking and naming the one picture which represents the object or action (A) with the same initial consonant sound as the underlined word and (B) which logically completes the sentence.

Part 1 –Teaching sentences to label object pictures and describe action pictures as they are presented on worksheets.

Part 2 –When students are presented with a worksheet containing sentences composed of words they can label with the exception of one underlined word in the subject verb or object position and four pictures above each sentence, they will determine the label of the underlined word by marking and labeling the one picture which represents the object or action (A) with the same initial consonant sound as the underlined word and (B) which logically completes the sentence. (Entrikin et al., 1975, pp. 451–454)

Not only does Entrikin et al. (1975) provide useful prerequisite and instructional guidelines for teaching fundamental word attack skills to the moderately handicapped learner but also this study provides classroom data to support the relevance of Duffy and Sherman's (1972) task analysis for some learners in this population of students.

Summary

Learning to read is one of the more complex school tasks that most students master in their elementary years. For moderately and severely handicapped learners this same task is enormously more complicated partly because of their weaknesses in attending, memory, and other thinking skills. More visible reasons for a lack of reading skills concern poor instruction (e.g., failure to teach prerequisite skills, excessive errors early in learning, an absence of generalization training with functional materials in realistic settings), not enough instruction, and a philosophy that the curriculum for these students should not include reading instruction.

Fortunately there is adequate information concerning the sequence of skills that underlie word recognition and comprehension. In addition, the evidence provided by basic and applied research with moderately and severely retarded learners justifies the policy that teachers begin prerequisite or readiness instruction early and systematically direct their teaching toward the goal of functional literacy. For older students demonstrating (1) no repertoire of sight vocabulary or (2) deficiencies in understanding spoken language, alternate instructional goals for reading should be selected. The first priority for students who have poor comprehension of spoken language is language instruction, *not* reading instruction, since verbal language understanding must precede written language. If the older student does have a strong receptive language repertoire but recognizes few sight words, then, in the remaining school years, instruction should be directed toward learning to recognize and understand at least a protective vocabulary. For these students reading instruction will be taught by a whole word approach. Because their reading ability will be very limited, these students should be taught to use pictoral cues in directions and picture reference books on a long-term rather than a temporary basis.

References

Apffel, J. A., Kelleher, J., Lilly, M. S., & Richardson, R. Developmental reading for moderately retarded children. *Education and Training of the Mentally Retarded*, 1975, *10*, 229–236.

Basic reading skills mastery test. Bloomington, Ind.: Services for Educational Evaluation, Inc.

Bender, M., Valletutti, P. J., & Bender, R. *Teaching the moderately and severely handicapped* (Volume III). Baltimore, Md.: University Park Press, 1976.

Bereiter, C. & Engelmann, S. *Teaching disadvantaged children in the preschool*. Englewood Cliffs, N.J.: Prentice-Hall, 1966.

Berger, S. A clinical program for developing multimedia response with atypical deaf children. In J. McLean, D. Yoder, & R. Schiefelbusch (Eds.), *Language intervention with the retarded*. Baltimore, Md.: University Park Press, 1972.

Bijou, S. W., Birnbrauer, J. S., Kidder, J. D., & Tague, C. Programmed instruction as an approach to teaching of reading, writing, and arithmetic to retarded children. *Psychological Record*, 1966, *16*, 505–522.

Bilsky, L. H., Evans, R. A., & Martin, P. Relative effectiveness of various letter discrimination procedures in directionality pretraining. *American Journal of Mental Deficiency*, 1975, *79*, 259–266.

Birnbrauer, J. S., Kidder, J. D., & Tague, C. Programmed reading from a teacher's point of view. *Programmed Instruction*, 1964, *3*, 1–2.

Birnbrauer, J. S., Wolf, M. M., Kidder, J. D., & Tague, C. Classroom behavior of retarded pupils with token reinforcement. *Journal of Experimental Child Psychology*, 1965, *2*, 219–235.

Bliss, C. K. *Semantography.* Sydney, Australia: Semantography Publications, 1965.

Bond, G. L., & Tinker, M. A. *Reading difficulties: Their diagnosis and correction* (2nd ed.). New York: Appleton-Century-Crofts, 1967.

Brown, L., Huppler, B., Pierce, L., York, B., & Sontag, E. Teaching trainable-level student to read unconjugated action verbs. *Journal of Special Education*, 1974, *8*, 51–56.

Brown, L., Jones, S., Troccolo, E., Heiser, C., Bellamy, T., & Sontag, E. Teaching functional reading to young trainable students: Toward longitudinal objectives. *Journal of Special Education*, 1972, *6*, 237–246.

Brown, L. & Perlmutter, L. Teaching functional reading to trainable level retarded students. *Education and Training of the Mentally Retarded*, 1971, *6*, 74–84.

Buchanan, C. D. *Teacher's guide to programmed reading* (Book 1, Series 1, rev. ed., Sullivan Associates Program). St. Louis: Webster Division, McGraw-Hill, 1968.

Cohen, M. A., Gross, P. J., & Haring, N. G. Developmental pinpoints. In N. G. Haring & L. J. Brown (Eds.) *Teaching the severely handicapped* (Vol. 1). New York: Grune & Stratton, 1976.

Coleman, E. B. Collecting a data base for reading technology. *Journal of Educational Psychology Monograph*, 1970, *61* (4, Pt. 2), 1–23.

Cooking with Betty Crocker mixes (large type edition), Minneapolis: General Mills, 1970.

Denny, M. R. A theoretical analysis and its application to training the mentally retarded. In N. R. Ellis (Ed.), *International review of research in mental retardation* (Vol. 2). New York: Academic Press, 1966.

Dolch, E. W. *Teaching primary reading* (2nd ed.) Champaign, Ill.: Garrard Press, 1950.

Dorry, G. W., & Zeaman, D. The use of a fading technique in paired-associate teaching of a reading vocabulary with retardates. *Mental Retardation*, 1973, *11* (6), 3–6.

Dorry, G. W., & Zeaman, D. Teaching a simple reading vocabulary to retarded children: Effectiveness of fading and nonfading procedures. *American Journal of Mental Deficiency*, 1975, *79*, 711–716.

Drinkwater, B. A. The significance of affect in verbal learning by subnormal children—An exploratory study. *Australian Journal of Psychology*, 1972, *24*, 327–329.

Duffy, G. G. & Sherman, G. B. *Systematic reading instruction* (2nd ed.). New York: Harper & Row, 1977.

Duffy, G. G. & Sherman, G. B. *How to teach reading systematically*. New York: Harper & Row, 1973.

Dunn, L. M. *Peabody picture vocabulary test*. Circle Pines, Minn.: American Guidance Service, 1959.

Durrell, D. D. *Durrell analysis of reading difficulty*. New York: Harcourt, Brace & Jovanovich, 1955.

Easy menu cookbook, Bristol, Ind.: Elkhart Jaycees-Auxiliary of the Elkhart Jaycees, 1974.

Edmark reading program: Teacher's guide. Seattle: Edmark Associates, 1972.

Egeland, B., & Winer, K. Teaching children to discriminate letters of the alphabet through errorless discrimination training. *Journal of Reading Behavior*, 1974, *2*, 143–150.

Ellis, N. R. Memory processes in retardates and normals. In N. R. Ellis (Ed.), *International review of research in mental retardation* (Vol. 4). New York: Academic Press, 1970.

Englemann, S. Classroom techniques: Teaching reading to children with low mental age. *Education and Training of the Mentally Retarded*, 1967, *2*, 193–201.

Engelmann, S. & Bruner, E. C. *Distar reading: An instructional system*. Chicago: Science Research Associates, 1969.

Entrikin, D., York, R., & Brown, L. Teaching trainable level multiply handicapped students to use picture cues, context cues, and initial sounds to determine the labels of unknown words. In L. Brown, T. Crowner, W. Williams, & R. York (Eds.), *Madison's alternative for zero exclusion: A book of readings* (Volume 5). Madison, Wis.: Madison Public Schools, 1975.

Evans, R. A., & Bilsky, L. Discrimination training on the identification of reversible letters by EMR adolescents. *American Journal of Mental Deficiency*, 1972, *77*, 169–174.

Fernald, G. *Remedial techniques in basic school subjects*. New York: McGraw-Hill, 1943.

Fries, C. C., Wilson, R., & Rudolph, M. K. *Merrill linguistic reader*. Columbus, Ohio: Charles E. Merrill, 1966.

Fry, E. Developing a word list for remedial reading. *Elementary English*, 1957, *33*, 456–458.

Fry, E. *Reading instruction for classroom and clinic*. New York: McGraw-Hill, 1972.

Gagne, R. M. *The conditions of learning* (2nd ed.). New York: Holt, Rinehart & Winston, 1965.

Gillespie, P. H., & Johnson, L. *Teaching reading to the mildly retarded child*. Columbus, Ohio: Charles E. Merrill, 1974.

Harman, D. Illiteracy: An overview. *Harvard Educational Review*, 1970, *40*, 226–243.

Harris-Vanderheiden, D., & Vanderheiden, G. C. Basic considerations in the development of communicative and interactive skills for non-vocal severely handicapped children. In E. Sontag, J. Smith, & N. Certo (Eds.), *Educational programming for the severely and profoundly handicapped*. Reston, Va.: Council for Exceptional Children, Division on Mental Retardation, 1977.

Hawker, J. R. A further investigation of prompting and confirmation in sight vocabulary learning by retardates. *American Journal of Mental Deficiency*, 1968, *72*, 594–598.

Hawker, J. R., Geertz, U. W., & Shrago, M. Prompting and confirmation in sight vocabulary learning by retardates. *American Journal of Mental Deficiency*, 1964, *68*, 751–756.

Johnson, M. S., & Kress, R. A. *Informal reading inventories*. Newark: International Reading Association, 1965.

Kaman, M. *Cooking activities for retarded children*. Nashville, Tenn.: Abingdon Press, 1974.

Kirk, S. A. *Educating exceptional children* (2nd ed.). Boston: Houghton Mifflin, 1972.

Lahey, B., Weller, D., & Brown, W. The behavior analysis approach to reading: phonics discriminations. *Journal of Reading Behavior*, 1973, *5*, 200–206.

Lavely, C., Lowe, A. J., & Follman, J. Actual reading levels of EMR materials. *Education and Training of the Mentally Retarded*, 1975, *10*, 271–275.

Learning steps: A handbook for persons working with deaf-blind children in residential settings. Sacramento, Calif.: Southwestern Regional Deaf-Blind Center, California Office of State Printing, 1976.

Lent, J. N. Mimosa cottage experiment and hope. *Psychology Today*, 1968, *52*, 51–58.

Lichtman, M. *Reading/everyday activities in life. Examiner's manual*. New York: CAL Press, 1972.

Lichtman, M. The development and validation of R/EAL, an instrument to assess functional literacy. *Journal of Reading Behavior*, 1974, *6*, 167–182.

Lovitt, T. C., & Hurlburt, M. Using behavior-analysis techniques to assess the relationship between phonics instruction and oral reading. *Journal of Special Education*, 1974, *8*, 57–72.

Miller, A., & Miller, E. Symbol accentuation: The perceptual transfer of meaning from spoken to printed words. *Journal of Mental Deficiency*, 1968, *73*, 200–208.

Montessori, M. *The Montessori method*. New York: Stokes, 1912.

Nafziger, D. H., Thompson, R. B., Hiscox, M. D., & Owen, T. R. *Tests of functional adult literacy: An evaluation of currently available instruments*. Portland, Ore.: Northwest Regional Educational Laboratory, 1975.

Neville, D., & Vandever, T. Decoding as a result of synthetic and analytic presentation for retarded and nonretarded children. *American Journal of Mental Deficiency*, 1973, *77*, 533–537.

Northcutt, N. *Adult performance level functional literacy test*. Austin, Tex.: Division of Extension, University of Texas at Austin.

Northcutt, N., Kelso, C., & Barron, W.E. *Adult functional competency in Texas*. Austin, Texas: University of Texas Press, 1975.

Otto, W., McMenemy, R. A., & Smith, R. J. *Corrective and remedial teaching* (2nd ed.). Boston: Houghton-Mifflin, 1973.

Reed, F. S. *A special picture cookbook*. Lawrence, Kans.: H & H Enterprises, 1973.

Resnick, L. B., & Beck, I. L. Designing instruction in reading: Interaction of theory and practice. In J. T. Guthrie (Ed.), *Aspects of reading acquisition*. Baltimore, Md.: Johns Hopkins University Press, 1976.

Richardson, E., Oestereicher, M., Bialer, I., & Winsberg, G. Teaching beginning reading skills to retarded children in community classrooms: A programmatic case study. *Mental Retardation*, 1975, *13* (1), 11–15.

Samuels, S. J. Success and failure in learning to read: A critique of the research. In F. B. Davis (Ed.), *The literature of research in reading, with emphasis on models*. New Brunswick, N. J.: Graduate Schoool of Education, Rutgers University, 1971.

Sidman, M. Reading and auditory-visual equivalences. *Journal of Speech and Hearing Research*, 1971, *14*, 5–13.

Sidman, M., & Cresson, O., Jr. Reading and cross modal transfer of stimulus equivalences in severe retardation. *American Journal of Mental Deficiency*, 1973, *77*, 515–523.

Silvaroli, N. J. *Classroom reading inventory* (2nd ed.). Dubuque, Iowa: Wm. C. Brown, 1973.

Smith, D. E. P. *A technology of reading and writing, Volume I: Learning to read and write, a task analysis*. New York: Academic Press, 1976.

Smith, J. M., Smith, D. E. P., & Brink, J. R. *A technology of reading and writing, Volume 2: Criterion referenced test for reading and writing*. New York: Academic Press, 1977.

Spache, G. D. *Diagnosing and correcting reading difficulties*. Boston: Allyn & Bacon, 1976.

Spitz, H. H. The role of input organization in the learning and memory of mental retardates. In N. R. Ellis (Ed.), *International review of research in mental retardation* (Vol. 2). New York: Academic Press, 1966.

Spitz, H. H. Consolidating facts into the schematized learning and memory system of educable retardates. In N. R. Ellis (Ed.), *International review of research in mental retardation* (Vol. 6). New York: Academic Press, 1973.

Staats, A. W. *Learning, language, and cognition*. New York: Holt, Rinehart & Winston, 1968.

Staats, A. W., & Butterfield, W. Treatment of nonreading in a culturally deprived juvenile delinquent: An application of reinforcement principles. *Child Development*, 1965, *36*, 925–942.

Staats, A., Minke, K., Finley, J., Wolf, M., & Brooks, L. A reinforcer system and experimental procedure for the laboratory study of reading acquisition. *Child Development*, 1964, *35*, 209–231.

Staples, K. S. *Cooking from pictures*. Fargo, N.D.: North Dakota State University, 1975.

Stauffer, R. G. *The language-experience approach to the teaching of reading*. New York: Harper & Row, 1970.

Stone, C. R. Measuring difficulty of primary reading material: A constructive criticism of Spache's measure. *Elementary School Journal*, 1956, *6*, 36–41.

Stricht, T. G., Caylor, J. S., Kern, R. P., & Fox, L. C. Project REALISTIC: Determination of adult functional literacy skill levels. *Reading Research Quarterly*, 1972, *1*, 424–465.

Touchette, E. P. Transfer of stimulus control: Measuring the moment of transfer. *Journal of Experimental Analysis of Behavior*, 1971, *15*, 347–354.

Vanderheiden, G., & Grilley, K. *Non-verbal communication techniques and aids for the non-vocal severely handicapped*. Baltimore, Md.: University Park Press, 1975.

Vandever, T. R., Maggart, W. T., & Nasser, S. Three approaches to beginning reading. *Mental Retardation*, 1976, *14*(4), 29–32.

Vandever, T. R., & Neville, D. D. Letter cues vs. configuration cues as aids to word recognition in retarded and nonretarded children. *American Journal of Mental Deficiency*, 1974, *79*, 210–213.

White, O. R., & Haring, N. G. *Exceptional teaching*. Columbus, Ohio: Charles E. Merrill, 1976.

Williamson, F. *DISTAR Reading—Research and experiment*. Urbana, Ill.: University of Illinois, 1970.

Wisconsin test of adult basic education. Madison, Wis.: Rural Family Development Program, University Extension, University of Wisconsin.

Woodcock, R. W. *Introducing reading. Book two, Peabody rebus reading prog*. Minn: Circle Press, American Guidance Services, 1967.

Woodcock, R. W. The Peabody-Chicago-Detroit reading project: A report of second year results. In J. R. Block (Ed.), *i.t.a. as a language arts medium*. Hempstead, N.Y.: The i.t.a. Foundation, Hofstra University, 1968.

Woodcock, R. W., Davies, C. O., & Clark, C. R. *The Peabody rebus reading program supplementary lessons kit:*

Manual of lessons. Circle Pines, Minn.: American Guidance Service, 1969.

Zeaman, D., & House, B. J. The role of attention in retardate discrimination learning. In N. R. Ellis (Ed.), *Handbook of mental deficiency.* New York: McGraw-Hill, 1963.

Notes

1. *Curriculum-cumulative progress report.* Salem, Ore.: Mental Health Division, Community Mental Retardation Section, 1972.

2. Heckler, M. M. How many Americans read well enough to survive? *Congressional Record,* Nov. 18, 1970, 38036–38–40.

Introduction to Chapter 11

A list of all the daily living skills which should be taught to moderately and severely handicapped young adults would probably begin with using a telephone, elementary cooking, kitchen safety, washing dishes, using a vacuum, table setting, bed making, purchasing food, ordering simple meals in a restaurant, basic yard care, emptying trash, and so on. To identify all relevant daily living skills for the moderately and severely handicapped by simply brainstorming without guidelines leads to uneven skill identification (some skills are broadly defined, e.g., elementary cooking, and others are specifically pinpointed, e.g., washing dishes), overemphasis of some skills (e.g., relating to food preparation), and omission of other skills (e.g., use of money, leisure time).

A more efficient procedure for organizing and detailing the range of daily living skills involves the use of adaptive behavior tests such as the TMR Performance Profiles (DiNola, Kaminsky, & Sternfield, 1963) or the 1974 revision of the AAMD Adaptive Behavior Scale (Lambert, Windmiller, Cole, & Figueroa, 1975) described in Chapter 1. The table on the next page lists most of the Adaptive Behavior Scale items which directly pertain to daily living skills. Excluded were the advanced self-care skills (personal hygiene, table manners, etc.), vocational activity items, and items in the test category of numbers and time. Some of you may prefer to include time telling as a daily living skill. Also excluded were the more difficult to measure skills of self-direction (initiative, attention, persistence) and responsibility. The extent to which these abilities are developed directly affects the performance of daily living skills and could be clearly specified and included in this category. Because of the interdependency of daily living skills upon basic skill and preacademic skill development, there is no clear line of division between the beginning of the daily living skill area and the

end of other areas of skill development (e.g., self-care and functional academics). Therefore, your organization of which skill belongs in the daily living category and which belongs in other categories is relative to the rest of your curricular organization and to the priorities set for your particular community. Your classification system is valuable to the extent that it allows you to conceptualize and systematically keep track of all the relevant areas of a curriculum for the moderately and severely handicapped.

Once you have selected an organization system and have classified the relevant skills of daily living into subcategories, you will need to apply your talents in task analysis to each subskill before pupil assessment and instruction can begin. In this next chapter Chuck Spellman and his colleagues at Project MESH (Model Education for the Severely Handicapped) in Parsons, Kansas, illustrate this process. They provide detailed analyses of simple cooking skills which serve their teachers both as assessment tools and as teaching plans. In addition, they describe an exciting instructional alternative for nonreading students—the use of pictures as operational guides and informational references for the severely handicapped.

For at least two very good reasons this chapter does not begin to provide detail for all the daily living skills which you will need to teach your students. First, as we have already seen, the task would be voluminous! Just to catalogue all daily living skills and to analyze their steps would be a lengthy process and, more than likely, the results would not be widely useful for teachers. This latter point relates to the second reason: the situational characteristics of any given geographical region, specific community, and the classroom and home of the particular student will greatly affect the exact nature of each daily living skill. If the student's home does not have

Items on the AAMD Adaptive Behavior Scale (1974 Rev.) pertaining to daily living skills

Category I:	Independent Functioning
	A. Care of clothing (hangs clothes, polishes shoes, etc.)
	B. Travel
	1. Sense of direction (walks around home, yard, or several blocks from home without getting lost)
	2. Public transportation (rides city bus, subway, taxi on long/short or familiar/unfamiliar journeys)
	C. Other independent functioning
	1. Telephone
	2. Miscellaneous
	a. Goes to bed unassisted
	b. Eats moderately
	c. Knows simple postage rates
	d. Looks after personal health (e.g., changes wet clothing)
	e. Handles simple injuries
	f. Knows how and where to obtain doctor's/dentist's help
Category II:	Economic Activity
	A. Money handling and budgeting
	1. Money handling (uses money, makes change, uses banks, etc.)
	2. Budgeting (saves for a purpose, budgets fares, etc.)
	B. Shopping skills
	1. Errands (goes with/without note, goes to one/several shops)
	2. Purchasing (shops with supervision, makes minor purchases, buys all own clothing, etc.)
Category VI:	Domestic Activity
	A. Cleaning
	1. Room cleaning
	2. Laundry (washes, dries, folds, irons)
	B. Kitchen
	1. Table setting
	2. Food preparation (simple food requiring no cooking, mixes, complete meal)
	3. Table clearing
	C. General domestic activities
	1. Washes dishes
	2. Makes bed
	3. Helps with household tasks
Category VIII:	Self-Direction
	A. Leisure time
	1. Organizes leisure time simply (e.g., watch T.V., listen to radio, etc.)
	2. Has hobby
Category IX:	Responsibility
	A. Personal belongings (amount of care taken and frequency)

a telephone, devoting much instructional time to this skill would be unwise. If the community is urban and subways are the easiest mode of public transportation, bus riding instruction may be omitted from the curriculum. In addition, characteristics of the student will affect the task selected for instruction and the instructional procedure. You will need to know what task-relevant abilities and deficiencies the student already demonstrates (e.g., attention, verbal skills, fine motor abilities) and what particular values and needs are present in the student's home because both will influence (1) what skills are taught,

(2) the teaching priorities, (3) how many teaching steps a task is divided into, (4) what types of antecedent conditions (teacher's directions, prompts, instructional materials) and response consequences (feedback, reinforcement, etc.) to program, and (5) whether skill maintenance and generalization can be naturally carried out in the home.

It is true that we must aim for generalized daily living skills (a term discussed in depth by Bob Horner and Tom Bellamy in their later chapter on vocational skill instruction). Generalized skills are those that an individual can employ despite changes in the task materials and the setting where performance occurs, while making the necessary adaptations in response as the materials and setting stimuli change. In order to build generalized skills you must slowly yet systematically vary stimuli and the response requirements, beginning with the form of the response that is most easily performed by the student and using the materials that are most familiar. In time, with successful performance you will teach variations of the response in new settings with a variety of materials. For example, when teaching grocery shopping, start in a store closest to the school, which will facilitate repeated practice. Initially you will want to limit and maintain the same shopping list until the student learns the store arrangement and is able to recognize each item on the list. You may find it helpful to provide the student with a picture direction book (such as described by Chuck Spellman in the next chapter) or some type of prosthetic shopping aid. Nietupski, Certo, Pumpian, and Belmore (1976) taught students to use a card listing specific common shopping items in an order corresponding to the arrangement of the particular store. By teaching the students to buy a particular size of a product, students were able to estimate the cost of their purchases with the device and stay under $5.00. Later, depending upon the student's success in a program to teach grocery shopping, you may want to shop in a number of grocery stores so that the students learn to locate and purchase food regardless of whether they shop in the corner grocery, the A & P, or the Safeway.

Besides taking care to select relevant daily living skills, to task analyze them, and to begin with the familiar form of the task before programming skill generalization, you will need to incorporate some general instructional principles to facilitate learning (Denny, 1966). These may be stated briefly as follows, but are more carefully described in Chapter 10.

1. Structure the teaching program so that during the early or acquisition stage of learning the student
   A. Has plenty of opportunities to perform the targeted behavior.
   B. Makes little or no errors.
2. Provide the learner with immediate knowledge of the accuracy of his performance. When errors do occur, provide another opportunity to perform with the smallest amount of assistance needed to correct the performance.
3. Program for skill generalization so that the learner is taught to perform the skill in the situations where the skill is ultimately expected to occur.
4. Make use of overlearning or review activities so that the skill is maintained once acquired. Schedule overlearning so that it is spaced regularly across the school year rather than massed into a short period.
5. Be concerned with the student's demonstrated interest in the task and, when performance drops or plateaus too soon or apparent motivation appears to be lacking, reexamine the reinforcers you are using as well as modify elements of the task to create novel variations.
6. Before teaching, determine the underlying easy-to-hard sequence of the skills involved in the task. If the daily living skill depends upon successful performance of other basic skills (motor, self-care, language, cognitive, social) or preacademic skills (math, reading, writing, etc.) you must first understand how these skills are learned before you can generate a task analysis. This task analysis needs to be field-tested and perhaps rewritten so that learning is programmed in an easy-to-hard order.

In addition to these general teaching principles you may want to consult references to programs which have reported successful field-testing. These primarily include the work of Jim Lent and his Project MORE colleagues (Lent & McLean, 1976; see also specific references provided in the self-care chapter) and Lou Brown at the University of Wisconsin and his students and colleagues (Brown, Williams, & Crowner, 1974; Brown, Crowner, Williams, & York, 1975; Brown, Certo, Belmore, & Crowner, 1976; Haring & Brown, 1977). Brown's programs cover many skills including sex education, use of the telephone, use of the "Yellow Pages," grooming skills, learning to ride a public bus, and supermarket shopping. Additionally, a useful three-volume curriculum guide has been written by Bender and Valletutti (1976) which provides objectives and teaching activities for the instruction of daily living skills.

References

Bender, M., & Valletutti, P. J. *Teaching the moderately and severely handicapped* (Volumes 1, 2, 3). Baltimore, Md.: University Park Press, 1976.

Brown, L., Certo, N., Belmore, K., & Crowner, T. (Eds.). *Selected papers related to secondary programming with severely handicapped students* (Volume 6). Madison, Wis.: Madison Public Schools, 1976.

Brown, L., Crowner, T., Williams, W., & York, R. (Eds.). *Madison's alternative for zero exclusion: A book of readings* (Volume 5). Madison, Wis.: Madison Public Schools, 1975.

Brown, L., Williams, W., & Crowner, T. (Eds.). *A collection of papers and programs related to public school services for severely handicapped students* (Volume 4). Madison, Wis.: Madison Public Schools, 1974.

Denny, M. R. A theoretical analysis and its application to training the mentally retarded. In N. R. Ellis (Ed.), *International review of research in mental retardation* (Volume 2). New York: Academic Press, 1966.

DiNola, A. J., Kaminsky, B. P., & Sternfeld, A. E. *TMR performance profile*. Ridgefield, N.J.: Educational Performance Associates, 1963.

Haring, N. G., & Brown, L. J. *Teaching the severely handicapped* (Volume 2). New York: Grune & Stratton, 1977.

Lambert, N., Windmiller, M., Cole, L., & Figueroa, R. *AAMD adaptive behavior scale, public school version* (1974 Rev.). Washington, D.C.: AAMD, 1975.

Lent, J. R., & McLean, B. M. The trainable retarded: The technology of teaching. In N. G. Haring & R. L. Schiefelbusch (Eds.). *Teaching special children*. New York: McGraw-Hill, 1976.

Nietupski, R., Certo, N., Pumpian, I., & Belmore, K. Supermarket shopping: Teaching severely handicapped students to generate a shopping list and make purchases functionally linked with meal preparation. In L. Brown, N. Certo, K. Belmore, & T. Crowner (Eds.), *Selected papers related to secondary programming with severely handicapped students* (Volume 6, Part 1). Madison, Wis.: Madison Public Schools, 1976.

11

Pictorial Instruction: Training Daily Living Skills

*This chapter was written by **Charles Spellman,
Terry DeBriere, Donna Jarboe, Susan Campbell,**
and **Cynthia Harris,** Project MESH, Bureau of Child
Research, University of Kansas.*

Oral and written language plus other standard symbol systems are available to most persons for obtaining information. For certain types of handicaps, such as visual or hearing impairment, standard language systems have been developed to allow the person to acquire information from unimpaired senses. Braille, for example, is a symbol system for persons who have severe visual impairments. Persons with severe hearing impairments may use manual signing as a language system. The development of alternate symbolic language systems has provided a means to circumvent the debilitating effects of hearing and visual deficits. Once symbols are validated, they become standardized and are adopted by formal educational programs, industry, and society. The educational system readily incorporates new symbol systems into a curriculum whenever these generic skills are needed by students in fields such as music, mathematics, engineering, and computer science.

Many mentally handicapped persons are functionally deaf and blind with respect to gaining information from available symbol systems. They present a unique problem because they have no information obtaining system such as Braille or sign language to aid them once formal training has been terminated or exhausted.

Without a functional symbol system, persons with moderate to severe handicaps will forever remain dependent on human trainers and memory. There are few published textbooks for use by severely handicapped students. Most available instructional material is designed to be read by the trainer, not the student, thus perpetuating the severely handicapped person's dependency.

In recognition of this problem, the Model Education for Severely Handicapped (MESH) project developed a symbol system based on pictures to allow students to independently obtain information from instructional material. This program is discussed in detail later. First we shall consider the implications of independently obtained information as it applies to formal education programs for the moderately and severely handicapped student.

This chapter was supported in part by Project MESH, a demonstration school operated pursuant to a contract (United States Office of Education OEG–0–74–7991) from the Bureau of Education for the Handicapped, United States Office of Education, Department of Health, Education, and Welfare, to the University of Kansas, Bureau of Child Research, Parsons, Kansas 67357.

Generic Skills

Most people receive a variety of informal and formal learning experiences from which they ultimately acquire the daily living skills necessary to live independently. Living in a continually changing society requires constant reapplication of previously learned experiences to new tasks which have never been specifically trained.

Formal education and training programs usually teach an individual both specific isolated skills and generic conceptual operations applicable to other tasks. Almost no training is required for most persons to learn to wash their clothing at a commercial laundromat or to operate kitchen appliances. Indeed, it would be unreasonable and unnecessary to expect formal education programs to identify and provide specific skill training for each task required in daily living.

Society does not expect nonhandicapped persons to be trained specifically for every task or even to remember everything required to complete a task. When need is sufficient for an alternate symbol system, one is developed to reduce the amount of specific training necessary to complete new tasks. For example, it would be virtually impossible to use written instructions to communicate all information at the level of precision necessary to construct a new building. Blueprints, however, yield the needed level of information. Existing word-based symbol formats would be cumbersome, time consuming, and generally inefficient as the sole method of conveying information required by engineers, carpenters, electricians, and plumbers. Instead of relying on an inefficient format, a new system was devised. Workers in building trades developed blueprints and plans to describe construction techniques and materials. Once they have learned the operation of reading blueprints and mastered specific construction skills, workers can generalize these skills to build many different structures without additional training.

Skill-Based Curriculums

To date, most curriculum approaches for moderately and severely handicapped students depend on a skill-based developmental model. Skill-based developmental models such as those proposed by Bijou (1963; 1966; 1971), Horner (Note 1), and Roos (1970) are predicated on the assumption that

by teaching all the skills and behaviors of the next highest level of retardation, the person becomes less retarded. For example, by teaching the severely retarded to perform the behaviors required of a moderately retarded person, the severely retarded person becomes moderately retarded. This model suggests that retardation is not static and one could be trained to move from profoundly retarded developmental levels to nonretarded levels of development. The task then is to provide each retarded student with a sequence of instructional programs that teach the skills and behaviors required to advance his development to the next level.

As described in the first two chapters of this book, numerous attempts have been made to identify and analyze the skills required to live independently in the community. The developmental model suggests that by analyzing complex behaviors into their simpler components and then teaching each component, students can reach higher levels of development. This analytic approach to curriculum selection provides a starting point and rationale for deciding what to teach. Without the analytic approach, accomplishing complex goals would be virtually impossible. It does, however, make two assumptions: (1) that all the specific skills can be identified analytically, and (2) that the requirements of the complex behavior remain fairly stable over a given period of time.

The first assumption is probably correct. After a number of approximations, every major skill necessary to live independently in the community probably could be identified. But once these skills are identified, empirically verified, and made available to the consumer, would educators have the resources to identify the prerequisite behaviors, complete a task analysis, provide environmental support, and develop the instructional materials, assessment forms, baseline procedures, teaching procedures, measurement systems, and generalization procedures? Would there be sufficient teachers and time to instruct all of the needed skills?

Even if all these resources were available, would the sum of the simpler behaviors be equal to the whole? Does being trained to cook specific meals, clean the house, and pay bills assure survival in the community? Or does survival depend upon being able to complete novel tasks, without training, by interpreting new information and applying it to the complex and ever-changing demands of our environment? In the process of learning each skill necessary to live independently, normally developing persons also learn something about gaining new information and retrieving seldom-used information. In the synthesis of learning each skill, we also learn many underlying generic skills, the most important being that of learning how to learn new behaviors. Developing a functional system for gaining and using a variety of sources of information is a critical process which is not explicitly addressed in the skill-based developmental models proposed to date.

A skill-based developmental model also assumes that the requirements for complex behavior remain fairly stable over a given period of time. Even a casual review of technological advances during the past 30 years, however, indicates that the skills required for living today differ greatly from those needed in the past. This variable alone suggests that an individual who can use a variety of information sources has a greater likelihood of adapting to the constantly changing demands of society. Development of a curriculum which teaches both sufficient specific developmental skills and basic generic skills thus represents a critical but difficult challenge for those working with severely and profoundly handicapped students. Difficult, complex problems, however, evade effective experimental analysis far less frequently than experimenters evade complex problems (Harlow, 1957).

Pictorial Instruction: One Approach to Training Daily Living Skills

In developing a survival skill curriculum, the Model Education for Severely Handicapped (MESH) project attempted to develop a system to teach both specific developmental skills and generic skills. Since persons with severe handicaps cannot use many of the existing symbol systems to obtain new information, picture books were developed as an instructional format. While not a revolutionary approach, the rationale for the books was that once a student has learned to gain information from them, the books could remain a reference source after graduation. Picture books currently in use are crude approximations of a potentially powerful training strategy for teaching many behaviors required to live in society.

After using a pictorial instruction book as a training format, the Project MESH staff noted that some students quickly learned to use the pictures as cues for completing the training program. However, some students, especially the younger or more severely handicapped ones, learned to use pictures as cues only after many trials. Others never seemed to utilize the picture cue system.

Pictures alone were not always a sufficient cue for behavior for three reasons:

1. Many action verbs and adjectives were difficult to illustrate in a line drawing or photograph.
2. The existing picture books did not have all the symbols required to complete some tasks.
3. Some students were not previously trained to translate symbols into actions.

Because of these constraints, the instructional strategy required that the teachers use verbal cues, demonstrations, and/or physical assistance in addition to the picture/symbol cues. Because some students could not translate symbols as cues to perform a behavior, another program and teaching strategy—a picture reading program—was established to teach students to "read" pictures, or to translate pictures into actions.

Picture reading

Pictorial instructions are the heart of the strategy for teaching daily living skills at Project MESH. Yet picture reading is not a mandatory skill for students beginning the daily living skills curriculum. Picture reading is designed as a component skill which aids in learning the daily living skills and is thus taught concurrently.

The picture reading program begins with a pretest to determine whether the student can select an object on the basis of a picture alone. Three trials are given for each of 14 objects tested by presenting pictures of the objects. Objects pictured in the pretest are a glass, cup, saucer, plate, fork, knife, spoon, napkin, spool of thread, scissors, pin cushion, thimble, Tinker Toy wheel, and Tinker Toy j-joint. These 14 were chosen because they are some of the objects used in other daily living skills programs. The student's responses indicate how many pictures he associates with their actual referent (see Figure 11.1).

The pretest includes three steps:

Step 1. Three objects, for instance, a plate, napkin, and glass, are placed on the table in front of the student being tested. The teacher is seated across the table.

Step 2. The teacher holds up a picture cue card of one of the 3 objects and asks the student to indicate which object is pictured on the card by se-

FIGURE 11.1   *Picture reading pretest*

lecting the corresponding object from the table. No feedback is provided the student as to the correctness of his choice. Each of the 14 objects is tested 3 times in trials of 3 objects each. Objects are arranged and pictures presented in random order throughout the pretest.

Step 3. After each trial, the teacher marks a data sheet with a plus or minus indicating whether the student correctly identified the object. An object the student recognizes 2 out of 3 times, for example, would show 2 pluses and 1 minus.

Once the pretest is completed, the data from all trials are analyzed to determine which objects the student recognized most often. If the student responded correctly on all 3 trials for an object, no training is needed because these results are interpreted to mean that the student will match the object only to its corresponding picture. If, however, the student recognized the object 2 out of 3 trials or less, training is indicated for the object. The trainer then determines which 4 objects were missed least often and those 4 are the first to be taught. This practice rests upon the assumption that there is a higher probability that the student will learn these items more rapidly because of either preference or familiarity with the object. If several objects rank the same, the trainer arbitrarily chooses which will be trained first.

Once the first 4 objects have been selected, training that incorporates a delay procedure begins.

1. Three objects are placed randomly in front of the student, who is then shown a picture of a cup, for example. Simultaneously, the teacher says the student's name to gain his attention and points to the object (cup). On the first 2 trials for each object, the teacher points to the correct choice simultaneously with presentation of the pictures.

2. After the first 2 trials, the picture is presented and the pointing cue is delayed 1 second. The 1-second delay is used for the third and fourth trials, then the delay is prolonged to 2 seconds for the fifth

and sixth trials, 3 seconds for the seventh and eighth, and 4 seconds for the ninth and tenth trials.

3. The eleventh and twelfth trials, plus all trials after that, include a 5-second delay until the student anticipates the teacher's action and picks up the correct object before the pointing cue is given.

For all correct responses, an appropriate reinforcer is delivered immediately. If the student makes an incorrect choice, the trainer decreases the time delay to the point where the student made the last correct response. Touchette (1971) used a similar procedure, but at first continued to increase the time delay (before the cue was given) after each trial. Touchette (Note 2) later recommended that his strategy be modified so that the time delay is held at 5 seconds.

4. The training criterion for each object is 10 out of 10 correct responses. That is, the student must select the correct object 10 consecutive times before the pointing cue in order to complete training; trials on other objects would be interspersed with the 10 criterion trials.

5. Once criterion has been achieved on an object, it is replaced with another until all 14 objects have been trained. Previously trained objects are interspersed with later training as a review. Sufficient data have not been accumulated to determine how often the reviews are needed, but Striefel (1974) has suggested that newly learned objects should be reviewed at the start of each training session for about 15 sessions. At least 5 newly learned objects should be reviewed during each session after a sufficient number have been trained. If more than 5 objects have been reviewed at 15 sessions, then the trainer should randomly choose among them for the objects to be reviewed at following sessions.

After all 14 objects have been learned, the student is taught to select 2 pictured objects in a left-to-right sequence and then to perform a pictured action with the 2 objects. If, for example, a saucer and cup are the objects, the task is to pick up first the saucer, then the cup, and to place the cup on the saucer as it is represented on the picture cue card. To begin, 4 objects are placed on the table in front of the student. The teacher presents the first picture cue card (Figure 11.2A) showing the 2 objects in sequence. The student is to select the objects in sequence—first the one on the left, then the one on the right. If the student does not select them in sequence, the teacher provides a prompt. Initially the prompt is physical guidance, then it is faded to a prompt requiring imitation—pointing to the correct choice. The point cue is eliminated by using the time delay procedure. The student selects the objects, placing them in front of him in the order shown on the card. The teacher next presents a second cue card which represents an action to be performed (Figure 11.2B). Physical assistance is given if necessary. The position of the objects on the cue card indicates how the objects are to be manipulated.

To insure that the student is using the sequence on the picture cue card and not memorizing which object to select first, another picture card, containing the same objects but in reverse order, is presented randomly in place of the first picture card (Figure 11.2C). Once the student can select 2 objects in sequence and perform the designated action, he learns to choose 3 objects in sequence,

then 4, 5, and 6. Because the longest single sequence of actions trained in the picture reading program requires 6 objects, the number of objects in this initial training period has not been expanded. Also, fewer than 6 objects in sequence are required for the beginning programs in cooking and domestic skills.

As the tasks become more complex, they are presented in more steps. For instance, after 3 objects have been selected in sequence (Figure 11.3A) a card is presented indicating an action to be performed with 2 of the objects (Figure 11.3B). Then the third object is incorporated on another card presented to illustrate the final placement of all 3 objects (Figure 11.3C).

The picture reading program described in this chapter is but one strategy which could be used to teach students how to gain information from picture symbols. A number of other training strategies should be explored to determine the most efficient methods of teaching the basic discrimination skills needed to acquire information from a picture/symbol format.

Meal preparation

The Project MESH programs use pictorial instruction books for meal preparation. Meal preparation is a complex area for training because of the number

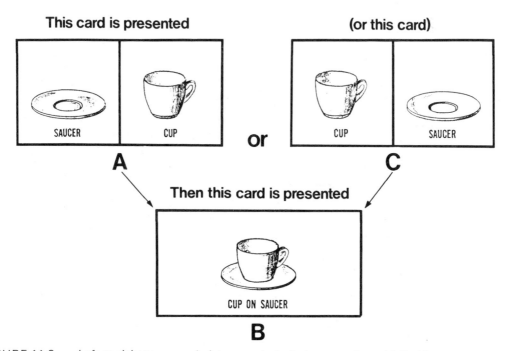

This card is presented

SAUCER   CUP

A

or

(or this card)

CUP   SAUCER

C

Then this card is presented

CUP ON SAUCER

B

FIGURE 11.2   *Left-to-right sequenced picture cards depicting an action with 2 objects*

This card is presented   (or this card)   (or this card)

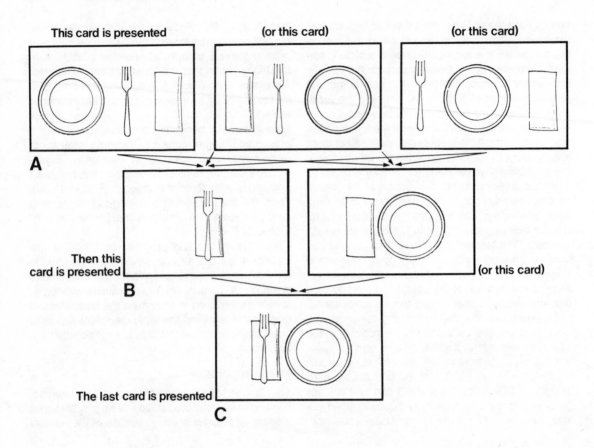

A

Then this
card is presented

B   (or this card)

The last card is presented

C

FIGURE 11.3   *Left-to-right sequenced picture cards depicting an action to be performed with 3 objects*

and scope of skills necessary to cook balanced meals. Even a nonhandicapped cook occasionally adds too much salt or leaves out a critical ingredient. Fixing daily meals is made more complicated for the severely handicapped because there are few procedures or instructional materials available which provide appropriate instructions and recipes for cooking.

In order to prepare balanced meals regularly, one must master meal planning and food preparation skills such as:

1. Deciding what food combinations to prepare.
2. Deciding how much food needs to be prepared.
3. Selecting the proper ingredients and utensils for preparation.
4. Measuring ingredients and combining them according to recipe directions.
5. Using utensils and appliances properly.
6. Timing how long a food item should be cooked.
7. Setting oven and burner temperatures.

8. Timing the overall preparation of several foods so all items are ready at the same time.
9. Applying these skills to a wide variety of foods.

Several programs exist to teach meal preparation to the mildly and moderately retarded (Farran, Note 3; Kahan, 1974; Steed, 1974), but only a few programs are for the severely retarded (Bellamy, 1975; Brown, Bellamy, & Sontag, 1971; Robinson-Wilson, 1976). Farran's (Note 3) program, which has convincing supportive data, consists primarily of a task analysis and teaching strategy. The program, however, does not teach students to follow recipe directions. Hence it relies on the teacher as the primary source of information. The other four programs contain a strategy for teaching the student to read recipes.

Kahan's (1974) and Steed's (1974) programs provide simplified recipe directions. The first uses pictorial cues, but relies heavily upon written words, whereas the second makes more extensive use of picture symbols and places less emphasis on written cues. Their methods of simplifying directions are significant, but the degree of complexity in both programs makes them unusable for most moderately and severely retarded people. Brown et al. (1971) require students to learn a basic sight word vocabulary while applying sight word skills in learning to follow recipes. Both the Project MESH and the Robinson-Wilson (1976) program utilizes picture recipe books, a task analysis, a teaching strategy, and a data system.

At Project MESH, an attempt is being made to develop a systematic meal preparation program. Some of the programs also have intensive supplementary training procedures branching from the linear sequence of instructional steps. These intensive training sessions are employed with students demonstrating difficulty on steps in the regular program which mandate fine discriminations such as setting oven temperature or small motor movements such as opening a milk carton. Those students receive approximately 5 intensive training trials on the problem steps before each of the regular training sessions. The premise for these extra trials is that additional practice on the difficult steps will decrease the time necessary to train the skill. By following the intensive training trials within the regular program, the problem steps are learned in the context of the program.

Teaching the generic skills of interpreting recipe directions is a vital component of the meal preparation program—even a skilled cook may refer to a recipe for the exact amount of a particular ingredient, the oven temperature, or the cooking time. When preparing a new dish, a recipe becomes the primary source of information. Other general components of the meal preparation program include the cooking skills (e.g., stirring) and techniques (e.g., boiling) themselves. One of the program's goals is for students to learn not only a specific skill, such as cooking beans, but the processes involved which also can be used in cooking other foods.

Both generic components of the program (i.e., following instructions and learning cooking techniques) must be learned well enough to generalize to other programs. For students who have completed several of the MESH cooking programs, the number of trials to criterion decreases as they advance to other programs, even though these programs are more difficult. Despite the number of variables involved, students appear to be learning how to gain information more efficiently.

Because cooking balanced meals is so complex, 3 main subobjectives were identified and the cooking program was divided into preparation of food items, meal planning, and shopping. To date, efforts have concentrated primarily on teaching food preparation because food preparation could probably be maintained more easily by its natural consequences than could meal planning or shopping. Another consideration was that meal planning could be readily circumvented by providing monthly menus. Therefore, the student who could not plan meals could still live independently if someone provided a menu and the ingredients needed to prepare these meals.

Food Preparation

The pretest does not require that the student follow the task analyzed sequence or make use of the recipe book, although it is available. Instead the student is simply requested to prepare a food, for example chocolate milk, and then is shown where each item needed in the preparation is located. If the student completes the pretest without help, he proceeds to the next program. If not, training begins.

In training, the student is required to use the picture recipe book and perform steps in the sequence specified by the task analysis. For example, the teacher begins by saying to the student, "I would like you to make a glass of chocolate milk, please." The first step in each program is for the student to open the book. If the student does not initiate or complete the step within 5 seconds, the teacher provides a verbal cue ("Open the book, please") and gestures toward the book. The 5-second limit is based on a clinical decision that 5 seconds is sufficient time to motivate a response. If the step is not completed then, the teacher demonstrates; if the student still does not complete the step, the teacher provides physical assistance.

The teaching procedures used in the cooking programs are similar to the Project MORE teaching strategy (Lent, 1974) which was designed to provide the minimum level of assistance necessary for the student to complete each step in the program. In this teaching strategy the student may be provided with up to 4 levels of assistance: no help, verbal cue, demonstration, and physical assistance. If the student does not complete the step correctly without help, he is given a verbal cue. If he does not respond to this level of assistance, he is given a demonstration which, if he does not imitate, is followed by physical assistance.

The teaching strategy in the cooking programs

incorporates the same 4 levels of assistance with some modification in all levels except demonstration. For the "no help" level of assistance, the students can use the picture symbols as a cue. During the verbal cue level of assistance, a gesture is paired with the verbal cue. The verbal cue is later dropped, leaving only the gesture which is next faded. For students who require physical assistance, the amount of assistance is faded across trials. In other words, the teacher provides not only the minimum level of assistance but also the minimum amount of assistance within each level. Criterion for completion of the tasks is 3 successive trials without error and with no assistance from the teacher. The student's performance and the amount of assistance needed during each teaching session is recorded on the data sheet which corresponds to a task analysis of the skill.

Examine the chocolate milk program recipe book, task analysis, and sample data provided in Figures 11.4 and 11.5. As the student proceeded through a training session, the trainer recorded the type of assistance the student required to complete each step (physical assistance, 0; demonstration, 1; verbal cue, 2; without assistance, 3). At the end of the session, the trainer (1) recorded the number of steps the student performed without assistance, (2) recorded the number of crucial steps (asterisked steps) the student performed without assistance, and (3) calculated the percentage of correctly performed crucial steps for the purposes of graphing. Exit criterion for training is 3 out of 3 consecutive sessions with 100% of all crucial steps performed without help. In the sample data of Figure 11.4 the individual met this performance criterion and exited from training into maintenance on November 6. Exit criterion for the maintenance program is 3 out of 3 consecutive maintenance probes with 100% of all crucial steps correct, which was achieved for the chocolate milk program on May 21, 1976. As shown in the sample data of Figure 11.4, the maintenance probes should be spread over at least a 3-month period.

Consistent with the format of the picture reading program, the second page of the recipe book illustrates the objects needed to complete the next blocks of instructions. The student must point to the first object pictured, then find the object in its storage space in the kitchen. Picture representations of the contents of drawers, cupboards, and the refrigerator are attached to storage areas. The student uses a match-to-sample strategy whereby he matches the picture in the book to the picture on the cupboard to identify the location of pictured objects.

Objects are selected in the left-to-right sequence, with the last object being the first used in the following action instruction. The object itself then can serve as an additional cue for the next step. From left to right on the first page of the chocolate milk book (Figure 11.5) are shown a spoon, a can of instant chocolate, a glass, and a carton of milk. After the student locates the objects in that order, the next step is to use the last object, in this example: the milk—"Open the milk carton," then, "Pour a glass of milk." The last page pictures a double action performed in a left-to-right order: adding a spoonful of chocolate and then stirring the milk. As with other steps, assistance is provided only as needed, improvements in performance are rewarded, and performance data are recorded for each teaching trial. Similar to the chocolate milk recipe book, although more complex, the hot dog recipe book and its corresponding task analysis are illustrated in Figures 11.6 and 11.7.

Meal Planning and Shopping

Programs for meal planning and shopping, which are being developed, are presented as ideas rather than validated training programs. These programs are described briefly to show their logical development from the picture book format used in preparing meals.

A strategy for teaching students to plan and prepare balanced meals is first to teach the student to prepare meals following a preplanned menu. The menu is a chart showing pictures of foods to be prepared for each meal. The pictures on the chart are the same as the pictures on the cover of the picture recipe books. The student is taught to look at the menu and then select the corresponding recipe book for that meal. Next, the student prepares the meal, using the recipe books if needed. Finally, the student is taught to mark an "X" beside each item after it is prepared. The first part of the strategy is conceptually similar to the chore charts used in the housekeeping program described in the following section.

In the next part of the program the student is taught to plan the menu. Planning a nutritionally balanced menu is extraordinarily complex. Determining balanced menus for the personnel of day care centers and nursing homes to follow is currently a major effort for the Bureau of Child Research, University of Kansas. Nutrition is not just a matter of selecting one food from each of the four

MESH *Model Education for the Severely Handicapped*

Data Sheet

Scoring Summary:

3 - Without Assistance
2 - Verbal Cue
1 - Demonstration
0 - Physical Assistance
Number of Steps Correct - Number of Steps Student Made a Score of '3' on for Session
Number of Crucial Steps Correct - Number of Asterisked Steps Student Made a Score of '3' on for Session
% of Crucial Steps Correct - Compute the number of crucial steps correct out of the total crucials possible.

Program ___ Chocolate Milk ___

Student ___ M.G. ___ Date ___

Trainer ___ J.D. ___ Reinforcer _SOCIAL/MILK_

Materials Needed: A spoon, a glass, milk (quart size) and instant chocolate

Task Statements: 1. "Wash your hands, please."
2. "Make a glass of chocolate milk, please."

	10/11/75	10/13	10/14	10/16	10/23	10/29	10/31	11/3	11/4	11/6	2/8/76	3/4/76	5/21/76			
Number of Steps Correct	2	7	12	17	16	17	18	20	20	20	20	19	20			
Number of Crucial Steps (*) Correct *12 POSSIBLE*	0	5	7	9	10	8	10	12	12	12	12	12	12			
% of Crucial Steps Correct	0	42	58	75	83	66	83	100	100	100	100	100	100			

											M	M	M			
1. Open the recipe book	2	2	2	3	3	3	3	3	3	3	3	3	3			
★2. Get out a spoon.	2	2	2	3	3	3	3	3	3	3	3	3	3			
★3. Get out the chocolate	1	2	2	2	3	3	3	3	3	3	3	3	3			
★4. Get out a glass	1	3	3	2	2	2	3	3	3	3	3	3	3			
★5. Get out the milk carton	1	3	3	3	3	3	3	3	3	3	3	3	3			
6. Turn the page	2	2	2	3	2	2	3	3	3	3	3	2	3			
★7. Open the milk carton	1	3	3	3	3	3	3	3	3	3	3	3	3			
★8. Pour the milk into the glass	2	2	3	3	3	3	3	3	3	3	3	3	3			
9. Fill it full	2	2	2	3	3	3	3	3	3	3	3	3	3			
10. Put the milk away	2	2	3	3	3	3	3	3	3	3	3	3	3			
11. Turn the page	2	2	3	3	2	3	3	3	3	3	3	3	3			
★12. Pick up the spoon	2	3	3	3	3	3	3	3	3	3	3	3	3			
★13. Pry open the chocolate	1	2	2	3	3	3	3	3	3	3	3	3	3			
★14. Get a large spoonful of chocolate	1	1	2	3	3	3	2	3	3	3	3	3	3			
★15. Put it in the glass	2	3	3	3	3	3	3	3	3	3	3	3	3			
★16. Stir	2	2	3	3	2	3	3	3	3	3	3	3	3			
★17. Stir until it's mixed	2	2	2	2	3	2	2	3	3	3	3	3	3			
18. Put the spoon into the sink	2	3	3	3	3	3	3	3	3	3	3	3	3			
19. Put the chocolate away	3	2	3	3	3	3	3	3	3	3	3	3	3			
20. Close the recipe book	3	3	3	3	3	3	3	3	3	3	3	3	3			
21.																
22.																
23.											MAINTENANCE	MAINTENANCE	MAINTENANCE			
24.																
25.																
26.																
27.																
28.																

FIGURE 11.4   *Data sheet and task analysis of steps in chocolate milk program*

FIGURE 11.5   *Chocolate milk recipe book*

basic food groups but must take into consideration factors such as quantity of nutrient, desirability, methods of preparation, the menu cycle, cost of foods, etc. (Risley, Note 4). At the very least, however, it seems feasible to teach students to plan a weekly menu by choosing from different picture cards representing preplanned meals.

Although the task is independent of meal planning, once a student has learned to follow picture recipes to prepare a meal, he could be trained to prepare a shopping list. A simple method would be to have a picture card which corresponds to the ingredients in the picture book. Students could then be taught to match the cards with items in the kitchen. If the item is available, then the card would be returned to the file. Cards representing items not in stock would become the student's shopping list.

Students have been provided with picture shopping lists to see whether they could locate and select the items in a local grocery store. The students were first escorted on shopping trips to purchase the weekly supplies needed for the cooking and housekeeping programs. Next the students were provided several picture cards of items they were to locate and place in the shopping cart. In the last step, they were given a picture shopping list as they entered the store and instructed to locate the items

and bring them to the checkout stand. Even with these very informal strategies, some of the students were able to complete the task. The teachers were confident that, with more intensive and systematic training, most of the students could be taught to identify items needed to complete a preplanned menu, prepare the shopping list, locate the items in the store, place them in the shopping basket, and go through the checkout lines.

Housekeeping

As in the cooking programs, a picture book is used as an instructional format for teaching housekeeping skills. The picture book format was suited to the cooking program because the books could serve as a reference source after graduation. The reminder system for housekeeping duties needs to include not only a "how to" booklet but also a method of specifying when to perform a task, which often requires that a person identify and respond to subtle cues, such as the amount of dust on furniture, film on windows, or dirt on a floor. The system being developed at Project MESH to help the students determine when to perform a housekeeping task consists of a weekly schedule (Figure 11.8) showing which tasks should be completed by each student

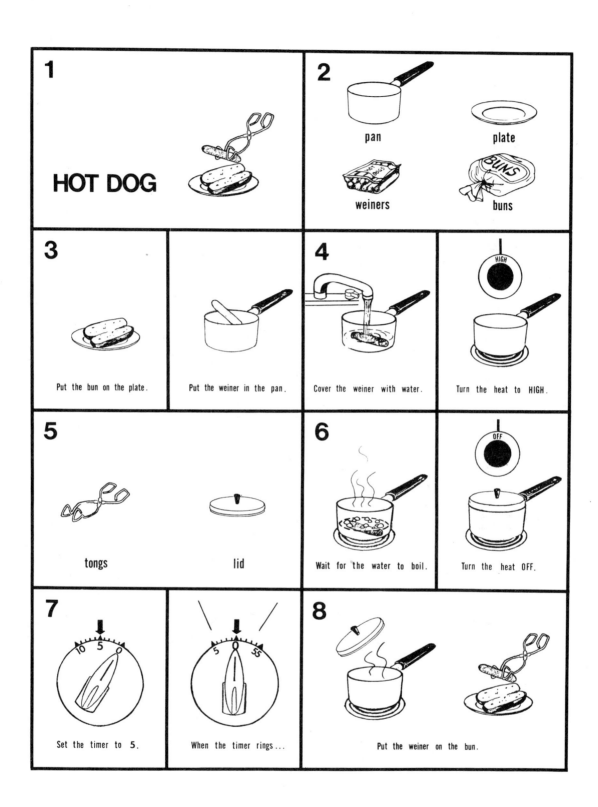

1 HOT DOG

2 pan   plate   weiners   buns

3 Put the bun on the plate.

Put the weiner in the pan.

4 Cover the weiner with water.

Turn the heat to HIGH.

5 tongs   lid

6 Wait for the water to boil.

Turn the heat OFF.

7 Set the timer to 5.

When the timer rings...

8 Put the weiner on the bun.

FIGURE 11.6   *Hot dog recipe book*

MESH Model Education for the Severely Handicapped
Data Sheet

Scoring Summary:

3 - Without Assistance
2 - Verbal Cue
1 - Demonstration
O - Physical Assistance
Number of Steps Correct - Number of Steps Student Made a Score of '3' on for Session
Number of Crucial Steps Correct - Number of Asterisked Steps Student Made a Score of '3' on for Session
% of Crucial Steps Correct - Compute the number of crucial steps correct out of the total crucials possible.

Program: Hot Dog Program
Student: S.H.   Date: 9/8/76
Trainer: J.D.   Reinforcer: SOCIAL/HOT DOG
Materials Needed: Large saucepan and lid, weiners, plate, buns, tongs and timer (condiments)
Training Time
Task Statements: 1. "Please wash your hands." 2. "Please make a hot dog."

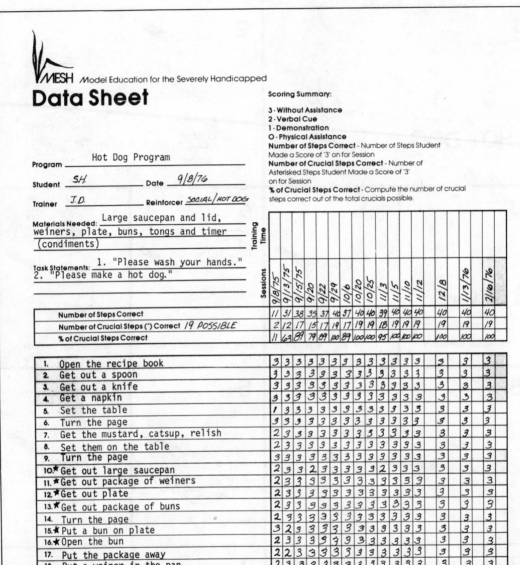

	9/8/75	9/13/75	9/15/75	9/20	9/22	9/29	10/6	10/20	10/25	11/3	11/5	11/10	11/12	12/8	1/3/76	2/10/76
Number of Steps Correct	11	31	38	35	37	40	37	40	40	39	40	40	40	40	40	40
Number of Crucial Steps (*) Correct (19 POSSIBLE)	2	12	17	15	17	19	17	19	19	18	19	19	19	19	19	19
% of Crucial Steps Correct	11	63	89	79	89	100	89	100	100	95	100	100	100	100	100	100
1. Open the recipe book	3	3	3	3	3	3	3	3	3	3	3	3	3	3	3	3
2. Get out a spoon	3	3	3	3	3	3	3	3	3	3	3	3	3	3	3	3
3. Get out a knife	3	3	3	3	3	3	3	3	3	3	3	3	3	3	3	3
4. Get a napkin	3	3	3	3	3	3	3	3	3	3	3	3	3	3	3	3
5. Set the table	1	3	3	3	3	3	3	3	3	3	3	3	3	3	3	3
6. Turn the page	3	3	3	3	3	3	3	3	3	3	3	3	3	3	3	3
7. Get the mustard, catsup, relish	2	3	3	3	3	3	3	3	3	3	3	3	3	3	3	3
8. Set them on the table	2	3	3	3	3	3	3	3	3	3	3	3	3	3	3	3
9. Turn the page	3	3	3	3	3	3	3	3	3	3	3	3	3	3	3	3
10.* Get out large saucepan	2	3	3	2	3	3	3	3	3	2	3	3	3	3	3	3
11.* Get out package of weiners	2	3	3	3	3	3	3	3	3	3	3	3	3	3	3	3
12.* Get out plate	2	3	3	3	3	3	3	3	3	3	3	3	3	3	3	3
13.* Get out package of buns	2	3	3	3	3	3	3	3	3	3	3	3	3	3	3	3
14. Turn the page	2	3	3	3	3	3	3	3	3	3	3	3	3	3	3	3
15.* Put a bun on plate	3	2	3	3	3	3	3	3	3	3	3	3	3	3	3	3
16.* Open the bun	2	3	3	3	3	3	3	3	3	3	3	3	3	3	3	3
17. Put the package away	2	2	3	3	3	3	3	3	3	3	3	3	3	3	3	3
18. Put a weiner in the pan	2	3	3	3	3	3	3	3	3	3	3	3	3	3	3	3
19. Put the package away	3	3	3	3	3	3	3	3	3	3	3	3	3	3	3	3
20. Turn the page	3	2	3	3	3	3	2	3	3	3	3	3	3	3	3	3
21.* Cover the weiner with water	1	2	3	3	2	3	2	3	3	3	3	3	3	3	3	3
22.* Put the pan on the burner	2	3	3	3	3	3	3	3	3	3	3	3	3	3	3	3
23.* Turn the heat to HIGH	1	2	2	3	3	3	2	3	3	3	3	3	3	3	3	3
24. Turn the page	2	3	3	3	2	3	3	3	3	3	3	3	3	3	3	3
25.* Get out the tongs	1	3	3	3	2	3	3	3	3	3	3	3	3	3	3	3
26.* Get out the lid	1	2	2	3	3	3	3	3	3	3	3	3	3	3	3	3
27. Set them by the stove	2	3	3	3	3	3	3	3	3	3	3	3	3	3	3	3
28. Turn the page	3	3	3	3	3	3	3	3	3	3	3	3	3	3	3	3

FIGURE 11.7   *Data sheet and task analysis of steps in hot dog program*

Program ___Hot Dog Program___

Student ___S.H.___ Date ___9/8/76___

Trainer ___J.D.___ Reinforcer ___SOCIAL/HOT DOG___

Materials Needed: ___See Page 1___

Task Statements: ___See Page 1___

Training Time

Sessions	9/8/75	9/13/75	9/15	9/20	9/22	9/29	10/6	10/20	10/25	11/3	11/5	11/10	11/12	12/8	1/13/76	2/6/76	
29. ★ Wait for the water to boil	2	3	3	2	3	3	3	3	3	3	3	3	3	3	3	3	
30. ★ When it does, put the lid on	2	2	3	3	3	3	3	3	3	3	3	3	3	3	3	3	
31. ★ Turn the burner OFF	2	2	3	2	3	3	3	3	3	3	3	3	3	3	3	3	
32. Turn the page	2	3	3	2	3	3	3	3	3	3	3	3	3	3	3	3	
33. ★ Set the timer	2	3	3	3	3	3	3	3	3	3	3	3	3	3	3	3	
34. ★ Turn it to '5'	1	1	3	2	3	3	3	3	3	3	3	3	3	3	3	3	
35. ★ Wait for the timer to ring	2	3	3	3	3	3	3	3	3	3	3	3	3	3	3	3	
36. Turn the page	2	3	3	3	3	3	3	3	3	3	3	3	3	3	3	3	
37. ★ Pick up the tongs	1	3	3	3	3	3	3	3	3	3	3	3	3	3	3	3	
38. ★ Put the weiner on the bun	3	3	3	3	3	3	3	3	3	3	3	3	3	3	3	3	
39. Put tongs in the sink or pan	2	3	3	3	3	3	3	3	3	3	3	3	3	3	3	3	
40. Close the recipe book	2	3	3	3	3	3	3	3	3	3	3	3	3	3	3	3	
41.																	
42.																	
43.																	
44.														MAINTENANCE	MAINTENANCE	MAINTENANCE	
45.																	
46.																	
47.																	
48.																	
49.																	
50.																	
51.																	
52.																	
53.																	
54.																	
55.																	
56.																	
57.																	
58.																	
59.																	
60.																	
61.																	
62.																	
63.																	
64.																	
65.																	
66.																	
67.																	
68.																	
69.																	
70.																	
71.																	
72.																	

Sheet _2_ of _2_

Carry All Scoring Data Back To Sheet One

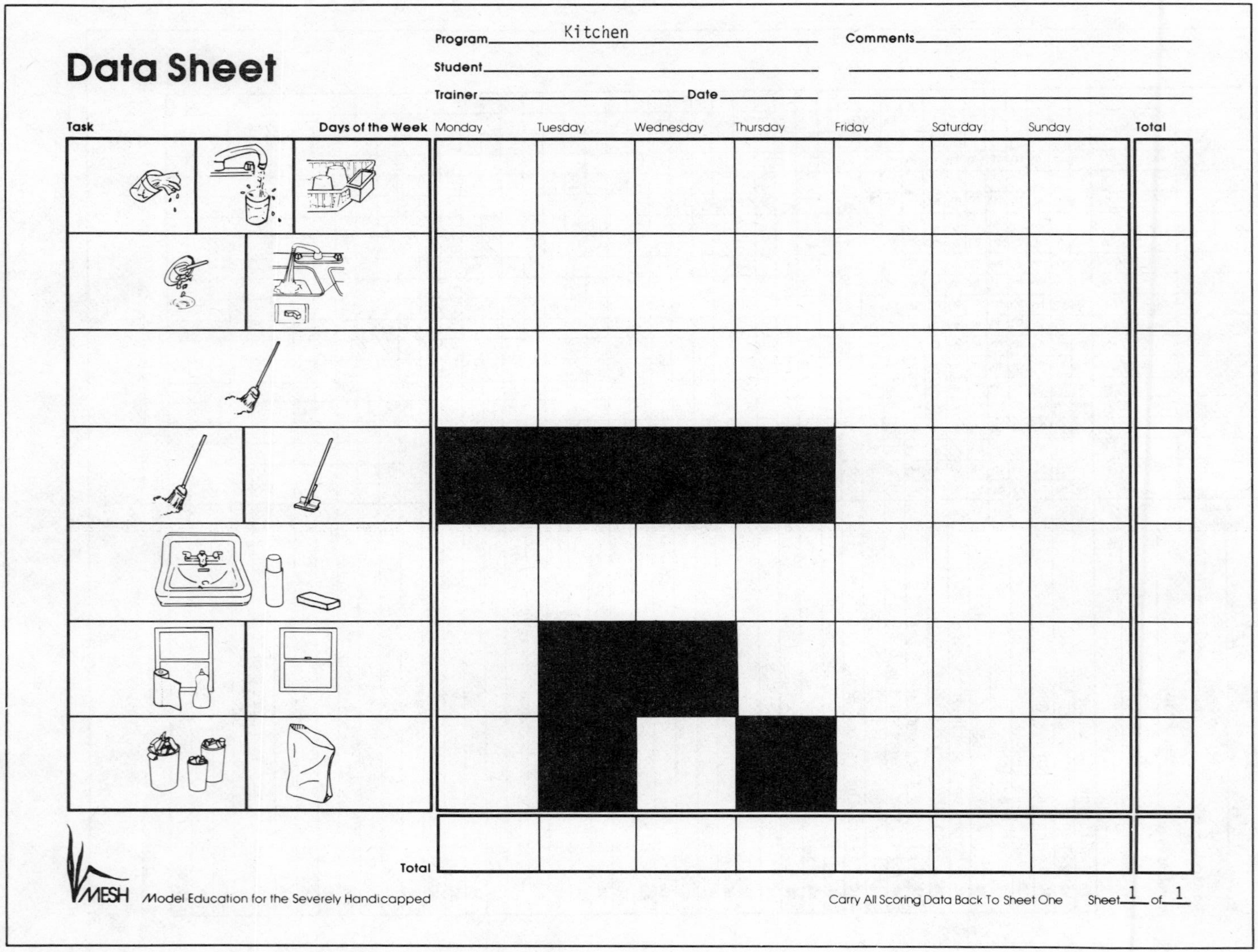

FIGURE 11.8   *Weekly schedule of housekeeping tasks*

Data Sheet

Program __Bedroom__

Student _____

Trainer _____ Date _____

Comments _____

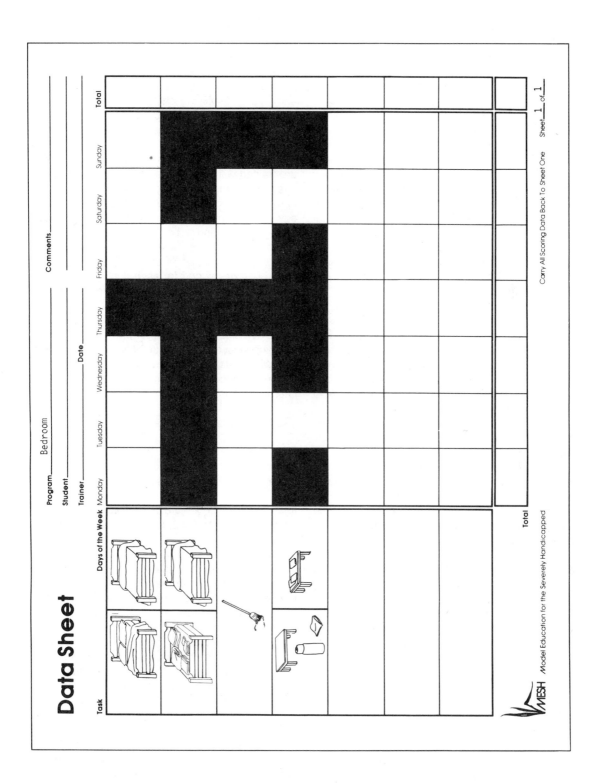

Task	Days of the Week	Monday	Tuesday	Wednesday	Thursday	Friday	Saturday	Sunday	Total
Total									

Carry All Scoring Data Back To Sheet One

MESH   Model Education for the Severely Handicapped

on each day rather than teaching them to identify subtle cues. These charts establish what tasks must be completed on a specific day. For example, making beds and washing dishes might be listed daily, whereas others such as sweeping would be shown perhaps twice a week, and changing the linens weekly. To remember which days (or at what time) a task should be done, the student can rely on a daily, weekly, or monthly schedule. Functionally, this strategy resembles an appointment book, daily reminder list, or schedule of events used by many busy people to recall tasks to be accomplished. Note that the housekeeping schedule depicted in Figure 11.8 reflects that used by a teacher and students during training and therefore may not logically match a typical housekeeping routine.

The tasks are represented pictorially in a vertical column at the left of the chart with days of the week listed horizontally at the top. The pictures on the chart are the same as on the front cover of the corresponding instruction book. A blank square indicates a task needs to be completed. The student consults the chart, sees which task is to be done, performs the task, and marks an "X" in the corresponding square. When the daily tasks are completed, the teacher checks the student's work to make sure the task has been done properly.

Students begin using the chart after completing the training in at least 3 of the housekeeping skills listed on their chart. Thereafter for these skills the students are not required to use the picture books. If they do not remember how to complete a task or have forgotten a step in the task, they are directed to refer to the picture book as a reminder. If the teacher determines that the task has not been completed correctly, the student is asked to use the picture instruction book for the next trial. If the student cannot complete the task with the book, he is retrained to meet criterion level of performance.

Although this approach does not require a student to interpret the environmental cues concerning when to perform the task, it does offer a system for use by the student once he has been graduated from school. This approach provides handicapped people with a reminder and a reference system which does not require constant supervision.

Housekeeping skills taught at Project MESH are sweeping (with a broom), emptying trash, bedmaking, mopping, dusting, window cleaning, toilet cleaning, changing linens on a bed, using a vacuum cleaner, scouring, dishwashing, and disposal of garbage. Cleaning duties encompass those needed in a living room, bedroom, bathroom, and kitchen.

Simulated training areas are available for each of these rooms at Project MESH.

In addition to these skills, care of clothing is also included in the housekeeping training areas. Skills for clothing care include hanging clothes, sorting and folding, polishing shoes, using an automatic dryer, using an automatic washer, handwashing clothes, ironing flat pieces, ironing jeans, ironing shirts, hanging laundry, using a coin-operated washer, and using a coin-operated dryer. All skills are trained with procedures similar to the teaching strategy for the meal preparation program, incorporating the modified Project MORE teaching strategy combined with picture books. Attempts have been made to find actions common among tasks and to present these actions in a uniform format with a consistent set of symbols. Task analyses have been developed for each duty.

As in the meal preparation program, duties are taught on an easiest-first basis with preference given tasks common to various duties. Emptying trash, for example, is an easy task common to cleaning most rooms. Unique housekeeping chores —making beds, changing linens, washing dishes, or cleaning the toilet—are harder skills and are taught later in training.

Teaching Strategy

As with the recipe books, the pretest trial and first training trial for the housekeeping program are the same, except that in the pretest students do not use a picture instruction book and are not required to follow an exact sequence in finishing a chore. If the student is able to finish the task successfully, he advances to the next program. If the student cannot complete the job, training is started.

Training requires that the student follow a picture instruction book and do each step as indicated by the task analysis. The teacher starts by telling the student, "I would like you to sweep the floor, please." Opening the book is the first step for each program. As in the cooking trials, the student is given 5 seconds to open the book before the teacher provides a verbal cue to "Open the book, please " and points to the book. If the student fails to respond, physical assistance is provided.

Objects needed to complete the instructions are shown on the first page of the picture instruction book for a housekeeping skill. A broom, dust pan, and wastebasket are pictured on the first page of the book for sweeping with a broom. This format is identical to the one used in the cooking program.

First, the student points to the pictured object, and then he goes to its storage space which is marked by pictorial cues. A match-to-sample strategy is used to locate the needed objects which are chosen in a left-to-right order with the last one being the first used in the next action instruction. From the left in the sweeping program are a wastebasket, dust pan, and broom. The student uses the last object (broom) and sweeps, then he sweeps into the dust pan and finally empties the dust pan into the wastebasket.

Small group instruction

One major advantage of the picture instruction system is that it facilitates small group instruction. Instead of a one teacher per student model, this approach allows one teacher to supervise individualized training programs for several students at the same time. In both the housekeeping and cooking programs, most students are assigned to the training area in small groups. The students are assigned tasks so that the teacher can allocate the majority of attention to one student at a time during the training session. The teacher is available to provide assistance to the others if needed and to evaluate the final product of the assignment. This is accomplished by assigning all but one student from the group to tasks for which they need very little assistance. Such tasks would be ones the students have already completed but on which they need to be evaluated intermittently to insure that the initial training was maintained, or ones in which acquisition training is nearly completed. In the maintenance training sessions the students may refer to their picture book if necessary, but are not required to complete the steps in the exact order described in the task analysis. Students who have nearly completed the acquisition training are those who can complete the task with the picture book but who have not met the final criterion of 3 successive trials without error. Both the teacher and reference books are available if assistance is needed.

While students are working independently on their assigned tasks, the teacher can attend to one student who is working on an assignment that requires a great deal of teacher assistance. Once this student has completed his task, he is assigned to a task which requires less teacher assistance. This approach allows each student intensive training for a portion of each session and allows the students to work with less supervision during the remaining portion of each session. Some students will require direct supervision during the entire session and may need additional one-to-one sessions until they are able to complete the tasks independently.

Obtaining Picture Books

Plans are being made to disseminate some of the picture cookbooks developed by Project MESH through a commercial distributor of instructional material. At present, however, the primary source of picture books for training daily living skills is the individual teacher. If you decide to make your own picture books, these suggestions will be of use:

1. Task analyze the skill you wish to train.
2. Use line drawings or photographs to illustrate the task. Often a picture will represent more than one step in the task analysis.
3. Make use of copying equipment to have several books available.
4. Paste pictures onto cardboard or file cards for added strength.
5. Cover the pages with clear contact paper or mylar sheets so that they are washable.
6. Use loose-leaf rings to bind the pages together.
7. Copy the MESH data sheet or design one to suit your own needs, but do not attempt to use this teaching strategy without a data collection procedure.

Generalization

A housekeeping program taught only at school can be successful in training students to complete the tasks at school, but there is no assurance these skills will be used in another environment. Differences in equipment, furniture, room arrangement, and locations of particular items needed to perform a task cannot be standardized. Thus the wall charts and instructional material described previously should be used in the student's home and in as many other environments as possible. Parents should be encouraged to have students perform the housekeeping skills they learn in school.

This requires that school personnel adapt the program as needed for home use. Detergent, for example, likely would be stored in a different location at home than at school and might be a different brand. A picture for detergent may need to be placed on the appropriate cupboard or closet at home to mark the storage place if the student needs this location assistance. For some students specific training might need to be completed in the home environment. However, some would be able to complete the tasks once they knew where to locate the items or after minor changes have been made to accommodate the program to the home.

Where a student lives once he has graduated from public schools will depend upon his level of development and the options available in the community. A variety of group homes, supervised apartments, and other less restrictive home environments are being developed in many communities. Although one cannot predict with certainty what will be available to the student or at what level he eventually will function, schools can increase the probability a student will live in a less-restricted environment by training him to be more competent in completing housekeeping tasks.

In one example, a student named Marcus was discharged from an institution at the age of 18 and placed in a foster home while completing vocational training. Classified as moderately handicapped, he had lived in an institution all his school life and had completed most of the housekeeping and some cooking programs available at Project MESH. In a follow-up interview with his foster parent, the teacher found Marcus had pleasantly surprised the parent by emptying trash, making his bed, cleaning the toilet, and generally using all his cooking and housekeeping skills.

Another example of the application of the housekeeping program involved moderately to severely handicapped young adults living in a group home where MESH housekeeping programs were being field tested. The houseparent reported that the students followed the daily chore chart to remind them of assigned tasks. Awakening late one morning, the houseparent discovered beds already made and breakfast almost ready. Job charts and picture books similar to these cooking and housekeeping programs also have been used in a sheltered workshop for vocational training in janitorial services and for a variety of assembly and industrial jobs. Though limited, these experiences do suggest the system described in this chapter has application after students leave the public school programs.

Self-help

Some daily living skills cannot readily be trained through picture reading materials. The food preparation and housekeeping skills previously discussed adapted well to the picture reading format. Other daily living skills, including self-help abilities, are presently trained using a skill-based curriculum approach. When the potential of the picture reading approach is more fully explored, some of these skills may also be trained in this manner.

Certain self-help skills, such as toileting, locomotion, and self-feeding, are critical to both the student and the educational system. The absence of these skills drastically reduces training time and affects trainer attitudes toward the student. The critical nature of these skills warrants the expenditure of a considerable amount of staff training time until the necessary behaviors are acquired and used appropriately by the student.

Other self-help skills, including dressing, showering, and grooming, do not affect the overall system so significantly and therefore do not require concentrated training time. These skills can be developed gradually at the appropriate place and time at which they normally occur. Self-help skills often are not a prerequisite to other skill areas. Therefore, staff training time can be spent on other skills (e.g., language, vocational, academic) with self-help being trained concurrently.

Specific programs for training self-help skills are not provided herein, as several excellent sources of programs are available (Anderson, Hodson, & Jones, 1974; Guess, Sailor, & Lavis, 1975; Spradlin & Spradlin, 1976; Tucker, 1974). These and other programs are discussed in detail in Chapter 7. Although self-help skills are obviously necessary for daily living, they are only a part of the total repertoire required to live independently.

Limitations and Future Implications

The instructional procedures and suggestions described in this chapter represent an initial effort to develop an instructional format for training which may be generalized to specific survival skills. The picture symbol system supplies one alternate instructional model for those students who have not learned to use more conventional information systems for acquiring new skills. Once students learn how to use the picture cue and reminder systems, they can profit from individualized small group instruction and are less dependent upon a trainer. If a student forgets how to complete the task, he can refer to the instructions to complete the problem step.

One major disadvantage of the picture instruction

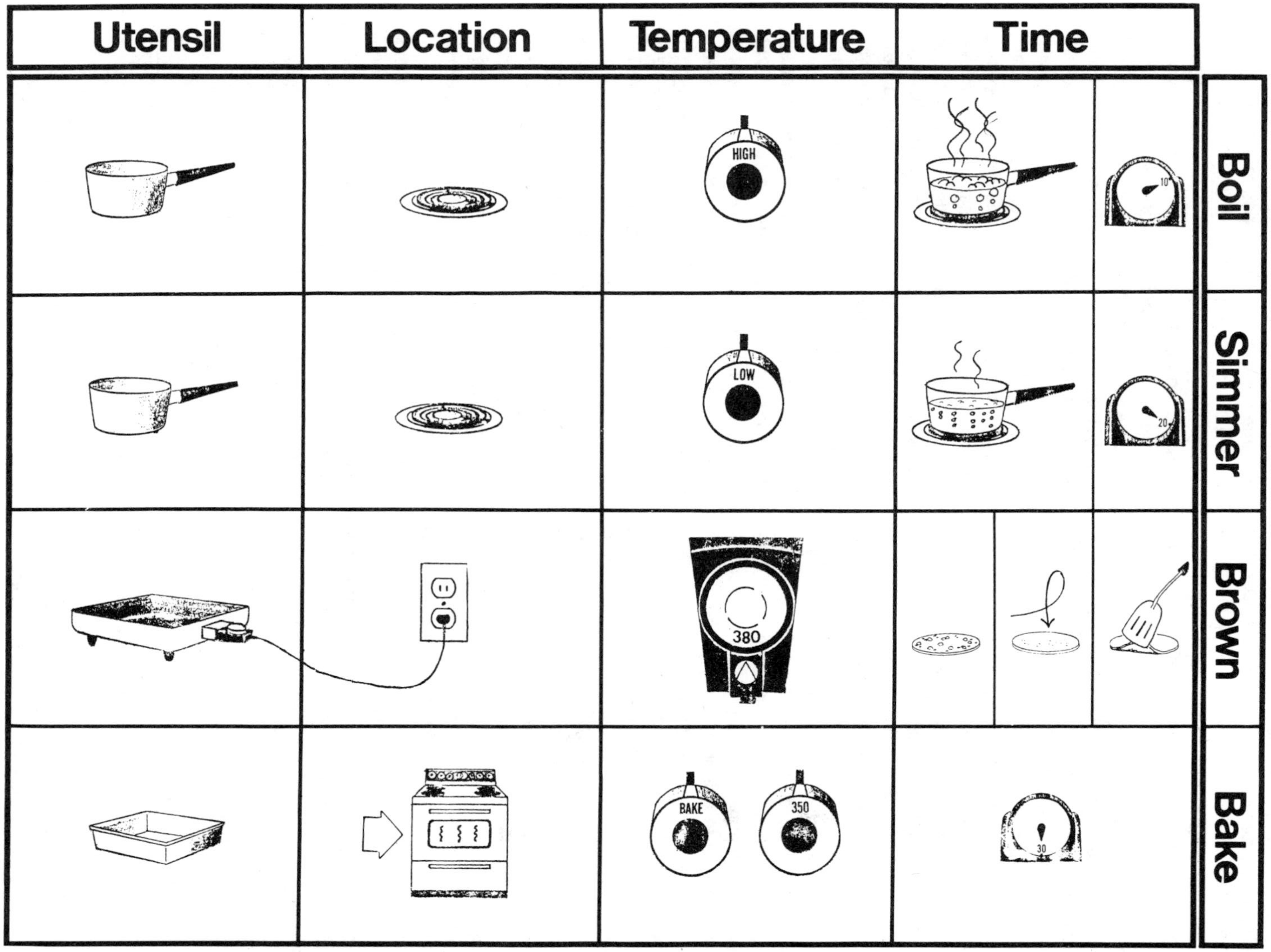
Utensil
Location
Temperature
Time
Boil
Simmer
Brown
Bake
HIGH
LOW
380
BAKE
350
10
20
30

FIGURE 11.9 *Standardized symbols for boil, simmer, brown, and bake* teaching strategy is the amount of time required to teach picture reading skills to some students. A number of the students learned to use pictures without specific training while enrolled in the housekeeping, cooking, and/or vocational training programs. Others, however, were unable to gain information from picture books prior to completing the picture reading program. For students who successfully complete the picture reading program, the cost in training time is potentially offset by the student's ability to use picture instructions to more rapidly learn many new critical survival skills.

Not all of the students have successfully completed the picture reading programs and a few have not learned even the first step in this program, which is object-to-picture discrimination. Continued effort needs to be invested to develop strategies which will enable these students to gain information from a sequence of pictures and symbols. The ability to make such basic discriminations is a necessary component in many language, reading, math, daily living, and vocational training programs. If students are not trained to gain information from symbols, many will remain forever dependent upon a human trainer for new information and will be required to remember indefinitely a number of different tasks.

Another disadvantage of this strategy for instruction is that there are neither standard rules governing what symbols to use nor rules concerning the syntactic arrangement of these symbols. The system, therefore, lacks the universality of most existing symbol systems. Without these standards, each teacher or program writer must create his own symbols and decide how these symbols are to be organized. If teachers were asked to develop instructional programs using picture symbols for boil, simmer, brown, and bake, for example, there could be as many symbols as there are teachers.

Suppose these same teachers had access to the mythical *Handbook and Rules for Standard Symbols for Non-Readers* (1980) and that this document contained symbols such as those found in Figure 11.9. Instead of each teacher's creating a different symbol for boil, simmer, brown, and bake, assume that they described the processes by the utensil needed, location, temperature, and the amount of cooking time required. One could speculate that with this information the instructional programs developed by one teacher would be useful for students from another classroom who had been taught to interpret these symbols while learning to prepare other food items.

Without standardization, the system described in this chapter is a limited strategy. If standard symbols and formats were developed for use by teachers and other program writers, manufacturers could be encouraged or required to print instructions in the same format. If this should occur, many persons who have not learned to read instructions adequately would have an alternate method of gaining information. Severely handicapped adults in the future could conceivably interpret the instructions found on commercially produced cake mixes, change the batteries in a new hearing aid, or "read" the instructions on the wall of the local laundromat. Many manufacturers and businesses now use a variety of picture instructions for simplification and as a source of information for customers who have difficulty reading printed words. They would likely welcome a publication that standardized the symbols and thus made their products more useful to consumers.

The emphasis of this chapter has been on an alternate communication system; however, this alternate system is not intended as a replacement of other forms of communication training. Students should be taught to use as many receptive communication systems as possible so they will be able to gain information from many different sources. One of the major needs for the future is to develop a complete communication system to teach severely handicapped students in an order from simple to hard: language, picture reading, and reading. There are a number of reading and language training strategies for persons with severe handicaps, but these programs are not specifically designed to parallel each other.

The curriculum for severely handicapped students of the future should not consider these 3 generic skills (language, picture reading, and reading) as separate entities. Instead picture reading and reading should be treated as advanced components of a communication curriculum and should be designed so that each skill facilitates learning the next more difficult skill.

References

Anderson, D. R., Hodson, G. D., & Jones, W. G. (Eds.). *Instructional programs for the severely handicapped student.* Springfield, Ill.: Charles C Thomas, 1974.

Bijou, S. W. Theory and research in mental (developmental) retardation. *Psychological Record,* 1963, *13,* 93–110.

Bijou, S. W. A functional analysis of retarded development. In N. R. Ellis (Ed.), *International review of research in mental retardation* (Volume 1). New York: Academic Press, 1966.

Bijou, S. W. What psychology has to offer education now. *Journal of Applied Behavior Analysis,* 1971, *3,* 65–71.

Brown, L., Bellamy, T., & Sontag, E. *The development and implementation of a public school prevocational training program for trainable level retarded and severely emotionally disturbed students* (Volume 1). Madison, Wis.: Madison Public Schools, 1971.

Cohen, M., Gross, P., & Haring N. G. Developmental pinpoints. In N. G. Haring & L. J. Brown (Eds.), *Teaching the severely handicapped* (Volume 1). New York: Grune & Stratton, 1976.

Guess, D., Sailor, W., & Lavis, L. *Educational technology for the severely handicapped: A comprehensive bibliography.* Topeka, Kans.: Robert R. Sanders, 1975.

Harlow, H. F. Experimental analysis of behavior. *American Psychologist,* 1957, *12,* 485–490.

Kahan, E. H. *Cooking activities for the retarded child.* Nashville, Tenn.: Abingdon Press, 1974.

Lent, J. R. *How to do more—A manual of basic teaching strategy.* Bellevue, Wash.: Edmark Associates, 1974.

Robinson-Wilson, M. A. Picture recipe cards as an approach to teaching severely retarded adults to cook. In G. T. Bellamy (Ed.), *Habilitation of the severely and profoundly retarded: Reports from the specialized training program,* Monograph, 1976, 99–108.

Roos, P. Trends and issues in special education for the mentally retarded. *Education and Training of the Mentally Retarded,* 1970, *5,* 51–61.

Spradlin, J. E., & Spradlin, R. R. Developing necessary skills for entry into classroom teaching arrangements. In N. G. Haring & R. L. Schiefelbusch (Eds.), *Teaching special children.* New York: McGraw-Hill, 1976.

Steed, F. R. *A special picture cookbook.* Lawrence, Kans.: H & H Enterprises, 1974.

Striefel, S. *Behavior modification: Teaching a child to imitate.* Lawrence, Kans.: H & H Enterprises, 1974.

Touchette, P. E. Transfer of stimulus control: Measuring the moment of transfer. *Journal of the Experimental Analysis of Behavior,* 1971, *15,* 347–354.

Tucker, D. *Skill acquisition program bibliography.* Lawrence, Kans.: Camelot Behavioral Systems, 1974.

Notes

1. Horner, R. D. *Training needs critical to each level of retardation: Profound to borderline.* Unpublished manuscript, University of Kansas, Bureau of Child Research, October 1972.
2. Touchette, P. E. Personal communication, 1975.
3. Farran, I. Program available through Rocky Mountain Special Education Instructional Materials Center, Greeley, Col.: University of Northern Colorado, 1974.
4. Risley, T. R. *An empirical basis for nursing home meal service,* Department of Health, Education, and Welfare grant application, 1976.

Introduction to Chapters 12, 13, and 14

In the next three chapters you will read information basic to vocational preparation of the severely handicapped. Traditionally the special teacher has had little to do with vocational training in special education, and few teachers know much of the mechanics and economics of a workshop. Vocational preparation of the mildly handicapped usually has been the responsibility of a few individuals at the senior-high level or of a vocational rehabilitation counselor. Similarly, teachers of the moderately handicapped or higher functioning trainable students have had minimal involvement with a workshop program, if one was available at all. The severely handicapped (often the lower functioning students in classes for the trainable) generally could expect no vocational training component in their curriculum since it is only recently that models and funds for this training has been available.

When you stop and reflect on these practices, they are quite the opposite from what they should be—that those individuals who are the least self-sufficient should be abruptly and often briefly dumped into a vocational training program or not provided with one at all. These practices have re-sulted in many young adults with nothing to do upon completion of school, except perhaps to enroll in a nonprofitable activity center with no alternatives for vocational training. Their schooling comes to an end with little or no provision for a vocational future.

While these practices have not disappeared, more generous funds for developing vocational training programs are now available; a supply of successful data-based models for vocational training of the severely handicapped exists; and subsequent remunerative employment has been demonstrated possible for this population. In the first chapter of this section on vocational skill development, Pete Flexer and Andy Martin provide extensive information on the rehabilitation and production components of the workshop. Next, Rob Horner and Tom Bellamy describe a model for training generalized vocational skills. Finally, Marc Gold and Dave Pomerantz debate the relevant issues pertaining to prevocational training of the severely handicapped. Because of the common lack of knowledge among teachers (including perhaps you) about vocational skill training, these three chapters have been devoted to this topic.

12

Sheltered Workshops and Vocational Training Settings

This chapter was written by **Robert W. Flexer** and **Andrew S. Martin,** Research and Training Center in Mental Retardation, Texas Tech University.

Preparation of the handicapped for employment is an area of rehabilitation which can be of short or long duration and can take place during any of several developmental periods. Career education, the broadest concept to describe employment preparation, attempts to address all of the person's educational, psychological, social, and vocational needs related to choosing and preparing for remunerative work from the primary grades through the post-secondary level. Other terms are used for more specific activities. "Vocational education," used in public-school settings, and "vocational training," a term used in state vocational rehabilitation agencies, often refer to skills training with a trade orientation, for example, carpentry and auto mechanics. This type of skill training usually requires formal preparation and/or extensive on-the-job training.

To function in a job successfully and to meet expectations in a work environment, the handicapped must also possess behaviors other than those required to perform the tasks of an occupation. Work habits and work attitudes—for example, adequate interpersonal relations with supervisors and co-workers and the ability to remain on task for

sustained periods of time—are also important considerations in preparing the handicapped for the work world. Providing the handicapped with experience to meet the social and personal demands of work environments and to conform to industrial routines is most commonly known as "work adjustment training" (Greenleigh Associates, Note 1).

For the developmentally disabled—those, such as the severely retarded, who have significant handicaps from birth—prevocational training is a prerequisite for entering a program focusing on work behavior of any kind. This type of training includes both rudimentary work skills, such as manipulation of objects, and community living skills (Baroff, 1974). (If the developmentally disabled do not have adequate living arrangements and survival skills for nonwork settings, performance at work will be affected adversely.) Home living, travel, money and time management, and leisure skills are a few of the areas for which the handicapped often need intensive, developmental training.

State vocational rehabilitation (VR) agencies have played a central role in the vocational rehabilitation of handicapped persons. In addition to underwriting fees to facilities for vocational skill and work adjustment training, state VR agencies have provided monies for medical and restorative rehabilitation, maintenance for living expenses while in a rehabilitation program, counseling, and the necessary tools for job performance, among other services.

In order to be eligible for vocational rehabilitation services, clients must meet three criteria:

1. There must be a physical or mental disability.
2. The disability must present a substantial handicap to employment.
3. The provision of vocational rehabilitation services must render the client employable, either competitively or in a sheltered situation.

Prior to 1950, assessment to determine eligibility was based mainly on medical evaluation, psychometrics, and interviews and histories by vocational counselors (Nelson, 1971). With the mentally retarded, these traditional techniques of assessment were inadequate to determine employability.

Consequently, the Vocational Rehabilitation Amendments of 1954 and 1965 provided for the development of programs and services for the mentally retarded with special emphasis on sheltered workshop facilities and staff. With these additional funds, state VR agencies became a major source of support for programs for the retarded. This aid in the expansion of sheltered workshop services for the retarded was in the form of fees for diagnosis, evaluation, work adjustment, and vocational training services provided to clients and of grants for building, modifying, and expanding existing facilities, equipment, and staffing. The 1965 amendments also created a special category of evaluation whereby 6–18 months could be used to determine employability. Increased federal funding from the legislation instigated the movement toward transition sheltered workshops—where the emphasis was on rehabilitation services and vocational training for competitive employment. Moreover, sheltered workshops increased 104% from 1969 to 1974 (Greenleigh Associates, Note 1).

For the most part, however, this increased activity on the part of state VR agencies was directed mainly at individuals above IQ 50 (National Association of Retarded Citizens, 1976a). Many state rehabilitation agency administrators and staff, as well as facility personnel, lacked experience in dealing with the severely handicapped, and there evolved a practice in vocational rehabilitation of screening out the "nonfeasibles"—persons who are not expected to be made more employable through rehabilitation services. During this period of change in sheltered workshops, voluntary agencies, such as the National Association of Retarded Citizens and the United Cerebral Palsy Associations, sought community services for the more severely handicapped who were ineligible for workshop training programs (for example, see Tobias & Cortazzo, 1963).

The main service which developed from this effort was the activity centers. The major focus of activity centers was the provision of a group setting for personal, social, and vocational development, while work for pay was viewed as primarily therapeutic rather than as a means of support. Over the next several years, the growth of activity centers was great; Cortazzo (1972) surveyed the country and reported that activity centers in the United States had increased from 68 in 1964 to 422 in 1971. The bulk (85%) of the programs responding to Cortazzo's survey indicated that work preparation was a goal of the center, hence the new assignation, Work Activity Center.

More recent legislation has provided more support for the development of vocational programs for the severely handicapped. The Vocational Rehabilitation Act of 1973 placed a priority on service to people who are severely disabled. The Developmental Disabilities Services and Facilities Construction Act (1970) is directed at serving the severely handicapped who have generally been judged unsuitable for rehabilitation services because of the severity of their disability. Under this act, sheltered workshops and work activity centers can obtain funding for special projects on transportation, housing, recreation, and contract procurement, among other things. The Vocational Education Act of 1968 specifies that 10% of the federal funds allocated to states must be used to provide vocational education services to the handicapped. The Education for All Handicapped Children Act of 1975 requires that all schools provide free, appropriate education for all children, regardless of the severity of their handicapping condition. Appropriate education for handicapped persons includes preparation for the world of work. Finally, numerous federal and state agencies are committed to providing funding for special projects aimed at improving service delivery and rehabilitation and educational practices for the severely handicapped population.

The next section will deal with types of sheltered employment—additional physical, psychological, or social support and assistance is usually required because of the extent of limitations imposed by the severe disability—to be followed by more specific information on facilities, methods, and techniques for the severely handicapped.

Types of Sheltered Employment Programs

In the past, the usual practice in state vocational rehabilitation agencies was to obtain a vocational evaluation from a rehabilitation facility to determine appropriate vocational programming for clients. Vocational evaluation reports typically provide three options to the vocational rehabilitation counselor for planning eventual placement: competitive employment, sheltered employment, and no vocational potential. Brolin (1976) made an additional distinction in the competitive category—between "competitive" and "competitive with sheltered features." The assumption for this distinction is that although the severely handicapped may find jobs in the competitive labor market, some accommodation in work environment will need to be made for the limitations of the severely handicapped person. Most severely handicapped clients will require some kind of sheltered arrangement in which to perform remunerative work. The following discussion delineates the primary distinctions among the three major types of sheltered employment for severely handicapped persons: extended employment programs, work activity center programs, and competitive employment with sheltered features.

Sheltered workshops came into being to extend the function of existing institutions, such as the educational system, the church, moral improvement societies, health organizations, social welfare agencies, public and private vocational rehabilitation agencies, and the business and industrial sectors of the nation (Nelson, 1971). Although the history of workshops reflects many influences, central to all workshops then and now has been the goal of providing work programs and the benefits that come from work to the handicapped. In 1968 a definition of sheltered work was issued by the National Association of Sheltered Workshops and Homebound Programs (now the International Association of Rehabilitation Facilities):

A sheltered workshop is a non-profit rehabilitation facility utilizing individual goals, wages, supportive services, and a controlled work environment to help vocationally handicapped persons achieve or maintain their maximum potential as workers. (p. 2)

Although workshops can be classified according to types of disabilities, age groups, types of work performed, or sponsoring authority, the most common classification has been based on the type of service performed for the handicapped (Greenleigh Associates, Note 1). The transitional workshop attempts to place the handicapped into competitive employment after a period of evaluation, work adjustment, and/or vocational training. The extended employment workshop provides remunerative or profitable work to the more severely handicapped person who is considered unable to compete in the open labor market. The transition program usually provides a structured program of work adjustment or vocational training for which fees are received from the state vocational rehabilitation agency. Rehabilitation services in an extended employment program are primarily supportive to the objective of achieving successful employment within the workshop, and fees from agencies are not provided (National Association for Retarded Citizens, 1976b).

Both types of programs are often in the same facility for ease of operation. Programs which provide both extended work programs and comprehensive rehabilitation services are often referred to as rehabilitation facilities, whereas the term *sheltered workshop* is reserved for programs which concentrate on remunerative work.

Work activity center (WAC) programs are another form of sheltered work and are usually designed and operated with the more severely handicapped worker in mind, particularly the severely retarded and cerebral palsied person. The main distinction between the work activity center and the extended employment program is that the WAC provides services to clients whose "physical and/or mental impairment is so severe as to make their productive capacity inconsequential" (Fishler, 1976, p.2). The clients of WACs need compensatory prevocational and vocational education and training programs, are of postschool age, and are not developmentally prepared to enter a sheltered workshop program. By contrast, day activity centers provide a "developmental" program of structured training for the most severely and profoundly multiply impaired individuals who are unprepared to profit from the vocational orientation of a WAC program (National Association of Retarded Citizens, 1976a).

Another useful distinction among kinds of sheltered workshop programs is the classification of the Wage and Hour Division of the Department of Labor for subminimum wage work programs for the handicapped (Greenleigh Associates, Note 1). Four types of subminimum wage arrangement for the handicapped are allowed:

1. *Regular work programs* (extended employment programs) must provide at least 50% of the minimum wage to all clients.
2. *Work activity programs* are operated for clients who make less than 50% the minimum wage.
3. *Evaluation and training programs* have no requirements for level of payment.
4. *Individual rates* are provided for particular clients who may be in one of the first two programs and not meet the program wage requirements.

Facilities which have regular work programs and evaluation and training programs are usually called rehabilitation facilities. Other facilities may be a combination of regular work programs and work activity programs, or they may operate as free-standing regular work programs or work activities centers. All the facilities which provide regular work programs, work activities programs, or both are often referred to simply as sheltered workshops.

The concept of competitive employment with sheltered features is relatively new to the rehabilitation community. These programs take one of two general approaches to the training and placement process. One approach, the enclave, consists of handicapped persons who function as working units under special supervision (Pomerantz & Marholin, 1977). Groups of severely handicapped are trained and placed as crews in outdoor maintenance, building maintenance and cleaning, or some phase of production in factories. Trainers and supervisors ensure adequate production and accuracy of work, and such programs are generally publicly funded to subsidize the costs of the rehabilitative functions of training and special supervision.

Another approach to sheltered competitive employment has been referred to as trainer-advocate programs (Bucks County Public Schools, Note 2). In these programs, full-time training-placement staff find potential jobs for severely handicapped clients in competitive industry. After arranging a job tryout with an employer, the trainer-advocate works at a job until a thorough knowledge of skills and demands of the job is obtained. These data are then used to develop a training program for a severely handicapped client. After training, the staff person stays on the job, supervising the client, until employer criteria of performance are met. After one year of operation, the Bucks County program successfully placed 14 of 23 clients who took an average of 70 hours to train and who earned $2.13 per hour (Bucks County Public Schools, Note 2).

Finally, a less common approach to training the severely handicapped with transportation problems includes home employment.

Organization and Administration in Sheltered Workshops

Redkey (Note 3) has outlined several trends in sheltered work programs of the last 10 years which provide some perspective into the present situation:

1. Workshop programs have greatly multiplied in number.
2. Workshops have been more widely used to provide services to mentally retarded clients.
3. Workshops have become less concerned with work and more concerned with services.
4. Workshops have become more dependent on state rehabilitation agencies for money.

In fact, a recent survey by Greenleigh Associates (Note 1) supports the observations of Redkey. They reported that:

1. The number of certificated workshops increased 104% from 1969 to 1974.
2. Approximately half the clients in sheltered workshops are mentally retarded.
3. Approximately half of the clients in sheltered workshop programs are referrals from state rehabilitation agencies, and the agency pays fees to the workshop for the provision of rehabilitation services. The rehabilitation and business practices of sheltered workshops have been greatly affected by these changes, and the roles and operations of sheltered workshops have recently become very controversial in rehabilitation circles because of the implications of these changes.

Sheltered work and rehabilitation programs can provide one or some combination of three types of programs: evaluation and training for competitive employment (the transition function), extended employment, or work activities. Greenleigh Associates (Note 1) found that 38% of the facilities in their survey had extended employment programs whereas only 24% were free-standing work activity centers. The remaining 38% had both types of programs. Approximately half (46%) of all the survey facilities conducted programs of evaluation and training for competitive employment.

There are two basic components to the organization of any sheltered workshop. Sheltered workshops provide rehabilitation services to handicapped clients through the medium of work and also need to operate as businesses to obtain and produce the work used as a rehabilitative device. Conducting an effective business enterprise allows the workshop to create the demands of a work environment (Nelson, 1971). In performing a rehabilitation function the workshop attempts to accommodate the handicapped person's limitations but gradually and progressively adjusts the client to greater demands. Workshop programs need to have these dual abilities and to keep the two functions in balance in order to be effective. Figure 12.1 shows a schematic of this duality as it operates in sheltered workshops. Nelson (1971) and Salkind (1971) provide extensive discussion of this duality in the organization and operations of sheltered workshops.

In Figure 12.1, handicapped people are shown coming to the sheltered workshop needing certain rehabilitation services, and business is shown as having labor needs. Handicapped people are then put to work on materials provided by business. The end products are wages for the handicapped and/or increases in their functioning levels or abilities through the work and finished products for business.

It is a common criticism of sheltered workshops that they are not effective businesses. Greenleigh Associates (Note 1) stated that the extended employment and work activity programs were among the weakest aspects of vocational programming for the severely handicapped and reported that the median wage of work activity clients is only 25¢ per hour. Workshops do not have the business acumen and industrial know-how to bid and produce competitively, which results in payment of less than industrial wages to their workers (Conley, 1972). Pomerantz and Marholin (1977) provide a discussion of the "disincentives" in the rehabilitation service delivery system for effective business practices and vocational programming.

At least three suggestions have been provided to help make workshops more effective businesses.

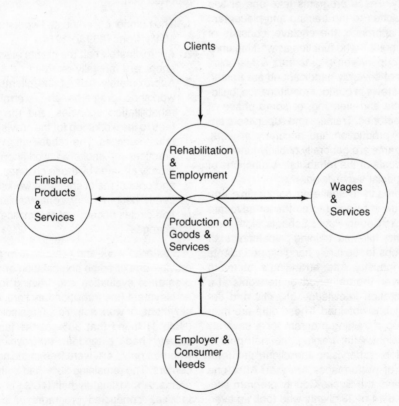

FIGURE 12.1   *Diagram of workshop duality*

Source: Adapted from J. E. Walthall and H. D. Love, *Habilitation of the Mentally Retarded Individual*. Springfield, Ill.: Charles C Thomas, 1974, p. 79.

Pomerantz and Marholin (1977) advocate specialization in the type of subcontract obtained by workshops through concentration on one type of product —for example, electrical equipment. They claim that workshops could invest in the necessary equipment for profitable contracts, develop expertise in production designs, and invest in training a skilled corps of workers because of the carryover of task requirements from contract to contract. Government subsidies for the hidden rehabilitative cost of extended employment and work activities are viewed by many as essential to effective business operation for sheltered workshops (Greenleigh Associates, Note 1). Contract development is improved when several workshops form an association. Greenleigh Associates (Note 1) claim that associations should eliminate competition among sheltered workshops since it enables them to obtain larger contracts.

Bellamy, Inman, and Horner (1977) provide an interesting organizational model for dealing with the contract problem and resultant business inefficiency. With several satellite workshops forming an alliance with a core of technical consultants and program advisers in business, industrial engineering, and vocational training, all workshops involved have access to much needed assistance which is usually unavailable or too expensive for small workshop operations. Moreover, these satellite workshops are serving the severely retarded.

Staff positions in sheltered workshops fall along the lines of the rehabilitation and business functions. Business and production personnel include the production manager, contract procurement officer, and sometimes an industrial engineer. Rehabilitation personnel consist of psychologists, social workers, vocational evaluators, counselors, and work trainers. Floor supervisors usually perform in both roles because they are responsible for meeting daily production quotas and supervising the handicapped clients. The workshop director is responsible for making the two parts fit, thereby enabling the workshop to be an effective business and rehabilitation facility at the same time. For the interested reader, Salkind (1974) provides a description of training for workshop directors.

Most sheltered workshops are private, nonprofit corporations. Workshops usually get started because some interested group or person sees a need for workshop services for the handicapped. Broad-based community support is sought, much planning is done, and a survey of need is conducted. A board of directors is chosen, and procedures of incorporation are followed. Application for certification must be made with the Wage and Hours Division of the Department of Labor. The National Association of Retarded Citizens has published two free booklets, *A Guide to Establishing an Activity Center for Mentally Retarded Persons* and *Planning and Organizing a Sheltered Workshop for Mentally Retarded Persons,* on planning and establishing work-oriented facilities. The International Association of Rehabilitation Facilities is another good source of information.

Standards and guidelines for developing workshop goals and measuring program effectiveness are essential to the operation of a sheltered workshop. Three national accreditation organizations are appropriate for sheltered workshops. The Accreditation Council for Facilities for the Mentally Retarded evaluates and administrates standards for facilities serving the mentally retarded; the Commission on Accreditation of Rehabilitation Facilities accredits a wide variety of rehabilitation facilities including sheltered workshops; the National Accreditation Council is concerned with facilities for the blind and other visually handicapped persons. State agencies of rehabilitation also have certification groups; and state licensing bodies may also administer standards for sheltered workshops.

Vocational Evaluation and Training of the Severely Handicapped

Rehabilitation facilities and sheltered workshops are the primary resources for providing vocational services to the severely handicapped adult. There are resources available in public school programs for the severely handicapped adolescent and young adult, but these services are mainly modifications of programs in community facilities or are in some type of cooperative arrangement with community facilities. Therefore, categories of services will be discussed generally, with the understanding that the information pertains to both public school and community facilities providing vocational services.

Services of vocationally oriented facilities and programs are of two general types: basic program (work-related) services and supportive services. All workshops perform some type of evaluation of work behavior and some kind of paid work (Greenleigh Associates, Note 1). Typical workshops usually have a delivery system which combines several of the basic services with several of the supportive services. In this section, an overview of past and current practices in evaluation is given, with special attention to considerations for the severely handicapped. Vocational training is then discussed.

Vocational evaluation

Vocational evaluation, as defined by the U.S. Department of Health, Education, and Welfare (1971), is "the appraisal of the individual's capacity including patterns of work behavior, ability to acquire occupational skills, and the selection of appropriate vocational goals" (p. 1). Attempts are generally made to determine work potential and preferences in a work or simulated work environment. The major techniques of evaluation are standardized tests, work samples, and situational assessment.

Standardized psychological tests are designed to measure such things as dexterity, perception, personality, achievement, interests, and aptitude. Although the vocationally oriented tests (except for interest tests designed specifically for the mentally retarded) were originally developed to aid in matching a person's abilities to the requirements of jobs, this approach has met with little success with the retarded because these clients usually score below the norms established on populations of normal intelligence. These standardized tests have been used in several research studies to predict vocational adjustment or success. The studies are rather consistent in demonstrating the general lack of utility of these tests for predicting practical criteria of performance and success.

Another major category of standard tests is the rating scale. These scales are generally used to assess clients' social and personal adjustment and work-related behaviors in relation to the demands of the work environment. Such factors as attitude toward work, work habits, interpersonal relations, and work tolerance are common attributes evaluated by such scales. Also, comprehensive batteries of standardized tests have been designed for use with the mentally retarded. In these batteries, psychological tests, rating scales, and other factors such as physical capacity are combined.

Work samples are a "mock up"—a close simulation—of an actual industrial operation, not different in essentials from the kind of work a potential worker would be required to perform on an ordinary job (Neff, Note 4). The work sample approach is an attempt to wed the standardization of mental testing with realism—if you want to evaluate work behavior, observe people at work—of the job analysis approach. Neff points out the many problems of the

work sample approach, not the least of which is constant change in the way jobs are performed. In reference to the way evaluation is conducted with the mentally retarded, Gold (1973) commented:

> In summary no attempt has been made to distinguish between acquisition and performance, i.e., between learning ability and production ability. Equally important, no attempt has been made to make the evaluation period fruitful to the client in terms of the development of the skills which are being evaluated. If anything is gained from the evaluation period, it is usually adjustive in nature with the clients often spending many hours or days being nonproductive and not learning new skills. It is also possible that many retarded clients, who are in a work setting for the first time, develop inappropriate concepts regarding work, which are based on nonproductivity and low-level tasks and which are reflected in future performance. Current prediction and evaluation procedures and tests as they are presently conducted are not very successful. (p. 113)

See Timmerman and Doctor (Note 5) and Cobb (1972) for additional discussion of evaluation and prediction.

Although Gold's points are widely accepted as dogma by many, work samples which are carefully set up to simulate actual jobs can be helpful in determining what are realistic possibilities for the client (Salkind, 1971). Work sampling can also assist in occupational choice. However, work samples do not provide useful data on the interaction between supervisor and worker and on the effects of wages, social factors, working conditions, and coworker relations.

The remaining major area of vocational evaluation is situational assessment. A job(s) tryout is the most common form of situational assessment. It can be used to evaluate the individual's capacity to adjust to the social demands of work and work environments as well as to assess and develop motivation, preference, or aptitude for a specific job or vocational alternative. In the job tryout method, the individual is placed in a controlled work environment and closely observed in order to determine the nature of her response to the setting—including response to peers, various modes of supervision, and various types of work tasks (Gellman, 1970).

Several recent developments in the field of evaluation show some potential for use with the severely handicapped. For example, Leslie (1976) described a battery of tests which were developed to determine client capability in an industrial work environment. After collecting information on physical requirements of numerous types of machine controls and observing actual production tasks, devices were developed to measure reach capability, ability to control machine controls, and capability for assembly tasks. On the basis of a client profile of capability, job modification devices were designed by engineering personnel and 23 severely handicapped, cerebral palsied clients were placed in competitive and sheltered jobs using the machine adaptations.

The *Trainee Performance Sample* is a work sample with emphasis on evaluation of training needs (Bellamy & Snyder, 1976). Even though recent success in training the severely retarded has demonstrated the feasibility of services affecting rehabilitation outcome, decisions about individual treatment, placement, or caseload acceptance will still have to be made by vocational rehabilitation counselors and institution administrators. The *Trainee Performance Sample* attempts to predict the amount of training time which clients will need to learn particular tasks, thereby indicating the level of investment in training resources.

Another approach to evaluation which shows some promise for application to severely retarded groups is the identification of discrete behaviors which are relevant to many kinds of work and take into account areas of difficulty experienced by many retarded individuals (Whelan, 1974). A developmental work skills training kit described by Whelan is a collection of tasks meeting the above criteria and providing evaluative information for use in program design to remediate deficits which would prevent vocational placements.

Behavior observation in work settings is another situational evaluation technique which has relevance for evaluation of severely handicapped clients. Behavior observation requires pinpointing a precise description of behavior as well as allowing specification of the rate of a particular behavior. For both positive and negative behaviors, observation provides baseline data which are essential to the development of individual program plans. The Research and Training Center at the University of Wisconsin at Stout is in the process of developing an observational approach for classification and recording of vocational behaviors in sheltered workshop settings. This approach should be applicable to programming for the severely retarded.

The most widely used technique of evaluation for the severely handicapped is task analysis. By breaking tasks into small discrete steps, evaluation can determine client strengths and weaknesses relative to the components of the task in question. Several individuals and groups concerned with vocational programming for the severely handicapped, particularly the retarded, have applied techniques of task analysis to evaluation and training (Bellamy, 1976; Gold, 1976; Karan, Wehman, Renzaglia, & Schutz, 1976; Martin & Flexer, Note 6).

Vocational training

The training of the severely handicapped is a rapidly growing area in the field of rehabilitation. The term *habilitation* is frequently used when referring to training the severely handicapped to underscore that for the severely handicapped, especially the severely developmentally disabled, many if not most of the skills being trained are being encountered by clients for the first time. Whereas rehabilitation usually refers to retraining, or reorganizing skill patterns, the severely developmentally disabled individual may never have been exposed to many of the skills and attitudes which most of us take for granted.

One perplexing problem encountered by sheltered workshop staff in working with severely retarded clients is that most of their clients have little concept of the value of money. In a milieu which utilizes remunerative work as one of its primary rehabilitative agents, a client who is more satisfied with 5 nickels than a $10 bill can present quite a problem.

There is evolving from recent research a training technology specifically aimed at those persons who not very long ago were classified as "too severely handicapped to have any rehabilitation potential." One of the factors which has facilitated this growth is an attitude change, which began with several researchers and is now spreading to practitioners who work with the severely disabled. In part, this change in attitude means that instead of saying, "These people (the severely handicapped) cannot learn and cannot be trained," we are now saying, "We have not been competent enough to teach. The failing is not with the severely handicapped, but with us." It is necessary to note that until this attitude began to change, researchers and practitioners were not motivated to invest heavily in the time or money necessary to search for and develop effective training strategies for the severely handicapped. It was easier, and still is, to discount the severely handicapped person's chances of learning anything useful and to move on the lower risk clients.

Much of the rehabilitation training research has been with the severely developmentally disabled, specifically the severely and profoundly mentally retarded. This may be in part because mental retardation is defined, in the main, as an inability to learn, and researchers in that field were already familiar with some of the techniques which showed promise. The research into more effective training methods has been varied, but the research of most interest to sheltered workshops has tended to concentrate in three primary areas: vocational skill training, production-oriented training, and training for work adjustment or work-related skills.

Vocational Skill Training

The emphasis on vocational skill is an obvious one, and some big gains have been made in this area. Much of the work has aimed at demonstrating that severely handicapped, especially severely retarded, clients could acquire and retain complex assembly skills. Studies by Bellamy, Peterson, and Close (1975), Crosson (1969), Friedenberg and Martin (1977), Gold (1972), Irvin (1976), Irvin and Bellamy (1976), and Martin and Flexer (Note 6), to mention just a few, have amply demonstrated that severely and profoundly retarded individuals can acquire complex vocational tasks requiring multiple discrimination of form, color, color-form compounds, size and orientation, "fine motor dexterity," multiple limb coordination, judgment, and the use of intricate tools. These researchers have also demonstrated the lack of correspondence between a worker's measured intelligence (IQ) and the probability of, or speed of, acquiring a complex skill (Gold, 1976; Martin & Morris, 1977). The degree of disability or the presence of multiple disabilities (Gold, 1976) is an extremely poor predictor of a person's ability to acquire complex vocational tasks.

Production Oriented Training

An area which has been of concern to workshop personnel and to researchers has been the question of how to get a client's work speed up to or close to industrial standards and how to keep it there once he or she has acquired the task. Research on rate acquisition and maintenance has ranged from more efficient job methods and work station design (Martin & Flexer, Note 6) and improved use of task analysis (Bellamy et al., 1975; Gold, 1972, 1976) to strengthening reinforcing con-

sequences for high production rates (Bellamy & Sontag, 1973; Brown, Van Deventer, Perlmutter, Jones, & Sontag, 1972; Crosson, 1969; Huddle, 1967; Trybus & Lacks, 1972; Zimmerman, Stuckey, Garlick, & Miller, 1969). Whatever the particular strategies being investigated, or the theoretical orientation of the researcher, research findings have enabled the sheltered workshop to achieve its purpose; the successes of applied research run counter to the view of workshops as a dumping ground or industrial baby-sitting service for the severely retarded or physically handicapped client. Techniques are available and are being refined to do something positive with that client. Techniques are available for training complex skills; and once the skill has been mastered, additional techniques are available to increase quantity and quality of production output.

Training for Work Adjustment

A persistent problem for practitioners serving the severely retarded concerns those skills which, while often hard to specify precisely, define what we mean by "work adjustment." The examples mentioned earlier of a client with no concept of money or one who can acquire tasks easily but who is so distractable that he or she disrupts the entire workshop illustrate this problem. Work adjustment skills and work attitudes can be viewed as necessary and equal adjuncts to work skills in the vocational habilitation of the severely handicapped individual.

Work adjustment research is for the most part not so advanced as training research. This is in large measure because the variables are more elusive and harder to define. The orientation of work adjustment researchers is as straightforward as those in other areas. Behavior in a work situation, concepts of money, a viable work ethic, and interaction with peers and supervisors in a work setting are skills which can be learned by the severely handicapped when strategies become available to train them. That the severely retarded client does not display these skills spontaneously should come as no surprise when one considers that the same low expectations which held that the severely developmentally disabled could not acquire complex work skills also mandated that they could never be good money managers or have long attention spans.

Recent studies have shown that the severely retarded can be trained to increase uninterrupted work time and at the same time decrease interfering behaviors which distract other workers (Martin & Flexer, Note 6). These and other studies have used training (and hence reinforcing) incompatible behaviors as a technique to increase acceptable work place behavior. The use of behavioral graphs (Jens & Shores, 1969) and videotape feedback of performance (DeRoo & Haralson, 1971) have been applied to train the client in work performance awareness and self-management. Techniques for training retarded clients with no prior work experience to become effective goal setters show promise as do techniques to teach more generalized attitudes toward work.

Training technology research with the severely handicapped worker is available to the practitioner in ever-increasing amounts. Several recent reviews, such as *Habilitation of Severely and Profoundly Retarded Adults* (Bellamy, 1976) and *Educational Programming for the Severely and Profoundly Handicapped* (Sontag, 1977), and publications such as the *AAESPH Review* published by the American Association for the Education of the Severely/Profoundly Handicapped are bringing the results of training methods research to the practitioner with little delay. If the results of the past several years are any guide, the field of training for the severely handicapped can anticipate stimulating and exciting times ahead.

Business and Industrial Practices in Sheltered Workshops

The discussion which follows, while applicable to all sheltered workshops, pertains most directly to an extended employment workshop in which clients can be expected to remain for relatively long periods of time. As stated earlier, the primary goal of such a shop is to provide opportunity for steady, meaningful, remunerative employment for workers who are unlikely candidates for employment in community job situations.

Classification of work types

Three basic types of work are generally undertaken by sheltered workshops: contracting with industry, prime manufacture, and reclamation or salvage operations. Each of these types of work has its advantages and disadvantages.

Contracting

Contracting, or subcontracting as it is also called, is a long-standing business practice in the United States. Dolnick and Musolf (1963) describe some of the reasons why this is so:

1. Additional facilities and labor are needed because of insufficient work and storage space, inadequate labor supply, insufficient machinery, and emergency delivery schedules.
2. The work is outside the normal activities of the contractor.
3. The contractor does not wish to use highly skilled or highly paid personnel on jobs requiring lower skill levels.
4. The cost of contracting is less than the cost of performing the work in-house.

The range of contract jobs is extremely broad, from folding boxes to assembling electronic components. Even though contracting is the primary source of work in most workshops, most contract work is tedious, repetitive work which requires little or no training and is the lowest paying contract work available (Gold, 1973; Greenleigh Associates, Note 1; Pomerantz & Marholin, 1977).

The reasons for the simple level of most contract work appear to be due as much to the low expectations of the workshop staff and persons responsible for procuring contracts as they are to industry's unwillingness to contract with sheltered workshops for more complex and lucrative contracts. To date, organized labor has not raised serious objections when higher paying contracts are awarded to sheltered workshops. That labor unions may raise serious objections has been more of a rationalization for not seeking these contracts than a reality. Additional reasons are identified by Gold (1973): Workshop personnel have no confidence in clients' ability to perform accurately on anything but simple repetitive tasks; clients are perceived by community members as capable of only menial, nuisance-type work; procurement officers do not have contacts established for complex contracts except where a limiting bias has already been established; shops are not equipped in terms of staff, attitude, equipment, or know-how to handle the increased quality control and production demands of such contracts.

Prime Manufacturing

Prime manufacturing involves the design, production, and marketing of a product. It is often seen as a highly desirable way to avoid the slack-period problems associated with the seasonal and short-run contracts typical in many workshops. The visible benefits which can accrue to a workshop engaged in prime manufacturing are usually outweighed by the less obvious problems involved. Prime manufacturing requires a completely different workshop orientation, and a workshop staff with this expertise is rare. Two areas of critical importance in prime manufacturing are marketing and industrial and human engineering.[1] The Greenleigh Associates study (Note 1) surveyed the business training and experience of sheltered workshop staffs and found that they had the least background in personnel management, marketing, and industrial or human engineering (Greenleigh Associates, Note 1). Most sheltered workshops, as presently constituted, are not equipped to handle the engineering and marketing problems necessary to make prime manufacturing a viable business enterprise. Many workshops, however, notably those organized by National Industries for the Blind, have had successful prime manufacture operations for a number of years. With the proper management and marketing expertise, prime manufacture can be successfully adapted to sheltered work settings.

Salvage or Reclamation Operation

Salvage or reclamation operations are among the most profitable of workshop operations (Greenleigh Associates, Note 1). They may be done on a contract basis for a particular firm (e.g., reclaiming silver from telephone relays) or may be operated more like prime manufacturing, in which case a workshop purchases or collects salvageable material and performs salvage/reclamation with the products to be sold to the highest bidder. Used computer cards have been utilized and mechanics' grease rags made from discarded clothing. Salvage and reclamation operations are highly desirable workshop operations in that they are labor intensive, have low overhead, provide a wide variety of work experiences, have little or no danger of spoilage, and are usually long term in nature. If these types of operations have any particular drawbacks, it may be that they often require considerable storage floor space. "Prime reclamation" requires some careful canvassing of local markets and sources of salvageable materials as well as a sales force to promote the product, especially for a commodity with competition (such as grease rag reclamation competing with rag suppliers).

A fourth category of work done by workshops is the provision of services such as janitorial and grounds-keeping services. These activities would

include all of the work programs which operate out of sheltered facilities.

The contracting process

The first major step before contract negotiation is contacting industry to procure contracts for bidding. The most successful method is for the workshop to employ a person solely for this purpose. The statement is often made that "for what a contract procurement person would cost us we could hire two more trainers." However, so important is contract procurement that a shop almost cannot afford *not* to have a contract procurement person.

Making Contact with Industry

Regardless of who does the procurement, there are a number of sources for pursuing contract jobs which should be mentioned. These sources derive from a study of contract procurement practices (Dolnick & Musolf, 1963) and are listed in order of their importance to contract procurement persons.

Industrial directories. Industrial directories of most benefit to workshops are those published by local chambers of commerce. Local and national directories can be checked for applicability and usefulness at local libraries before purchase. National directories include *Thomas Register of American Manufacturers, MacRae's Blue Book, Dun and Bradstreet Million Dollar Directory, Dun and Bradstreet Little Market Directory, Moody's Industrial Directory,* and *Standard and Poor's Directory.*

Board member recommendations or leads. The participation of board members can significantly aid a workshop's contract procurement. Individual board members can make the activities and availability of the workshop known professionally within their own companies and those of business associates. Board members can also assist in the development of sales and promotional literature.

Personal knowledge of the business community. All contract procurement persons, and most workshop supervisors, use their knowledge of the surrounding business and industrial community to develop sources for contracts. Those who are most successful not only rely on past associations and knowledge but actively study the community, its buying and selling practices, new businesses, and labor markets. It is the procurement person's duty

---

1. Industrial and human engineering training refers to skills and training in time and motion studies, human factors in job design to reduce fatigue and motions required, work flow design and standards for lighting, seat, and bench design, and design of special tools and equipment.

to remain well informed of all local business news that affects possible contracts for the workshop.

Direct mail advertising and publicity. The degree of success of mail advertising and radio and television publicity for sheltered workshop contracting is the same as for any other commercial enterprise. That is, the success of an advertisement is directly related to the quality of the advertising material. If the materials are honest, well presented, direct, and professional, the reader may take time to read the message. Bad copy or poor presentation rarely gets anyone's attention, or, if it does, it is probably negative. Responses to advertising or publicity can frequently lead to very positive results when pursued aggressively by the procurement staff. While additional sources of business leads are utilized, the above sources are most preferred by contract procurement officers.

Door-to-door solicitation. Also known as "cold canvass," door-to-door solicitation is the most difficult type of selling and the one least favored by the contract procurement persons surveyed.

State and federal business. State and federal government agencies purchase many thousands of items each year, and workshops which are equipped and staffed for prime manufacture are often good candidates to sell to these markets. Products sold to the federal government, and the eligibility of workshops to produce them, are regulated and implemented through the Statutory Committee for Purchase from the Blind and Other Severely Handicapped. Until 1971, only the blind participated in this system of sheltered contracting, but with the amendment of the Wagner-O'Day Act in 1971, the mentally retarded and other severely handicapped are included. The basic steps involved in becoming a prime supplier for government-purchased items are:

1. Identification of items feasible for production by workshops (these are usually items or commodities listed in the *Federal Supply Catalogue*). This is primarily the responsibility of NISH (National Industries for the Severely Handicapped) and NIB (National Industries for the Blind), two national nonprofit organizations set up to represent the interests of workshops.

2. Matching federal government requirements with workshop capability. On-site evaluation of the workshop is accomplished by NIB or NISH as part of this process.

3. An initial feasibility study lists production requirements, capital required, space, manpower, storage, equipment, and cost estimates.

4. The workshop develops specific cost data and submits a proposed pricing structure which is reviewed by NISH and transmitted to the Statutory Committee.

5. The Statutory Committee approves a "fair market price," after which a formal request is submitted to this committee to place the item on the *Federal Procurement List*. The items listed on the *Federal Procurement List* are reserved for purchase from a specific designated workshop; the price is not the low bid but an established price based on "fair market costs" and profit, and there is no annual rebidding. Subject to its performance, the workshop designated retains its exclusive sole source status indefinitely.

A number of state governments have sole-source legislation patterned after the Wagner-O'Day provisions, and the procedures are similar. Most state procurement programs are based on lowest bid rather than fair market price, and specific state statutes should be checked by workshops concerned.

The Contract Bidding Process

Whatever process is used to make initial contacts or secure leads, the most important phase of the contract procurement process is bidding. This area is one which deserves a great deal of careful attention but unfortunately usually receives the least. An improperly bid contract can be a financial albatross around the workshop's neck, demoralizing and contributing to an overall impression that workshops are not very good businesses. Some of the problems with contract bidding arise out of the low esteem as businesses with which many workshop staffs view themselves. They regard the contracts they do receive as charity instead of business. Most problems arise from a lack of knowledge about negotiations and the legal implications of contracting. A full discussion of all of the factors to be considered and a review of contract law is beyond the scope of this chapter. However, there are some essential aspects of bidding which necessitate discussion.

Know your workshop. The first aspect of contract bidding which must be taken into account is a careful study of the workshop. The actual and anticipated labor pool must be accounted for along with its present level of training in regard to the anticipated contact. The skill level of the workshop staff must be assessed to determine if the requisite skills are present to conduct the training, work station layout, and jigging necessary for the to-be-bid contract. Is adequate floor space available for work and storage? Can the work force handle increased production demands without the staff becoming fill-in workers? Questions such as these require close examination.

Method analysis. The method analysis is the first part of a general task analysis which should be done for any job, whether for bidding or for training purposes. The method analysis enables selection of the "best" method for accomplishing a given job. The term *best* is deceptively simple to use in this context because of the duality of most workshop functions and the philosophy and business acumen of the workshop staff. The assumption is that the *best method,* determined from a business standpoint, is the one which leads to high production at minimum production costs and utilizes automation appropriate to achieve these goals. Because workshop staff and teachers usually have limited business experience, with little or no industrial or human engineering training (Greenleigh Associates, Note 1), production methods used to fulfill workshop contracts are frequently inefficient from a business standpoint (Gold, 1973; Greenleigh Associates, Note 1; Pomerantz & Marholin, 1977). The severely handicapped need superior job methods to help compensate for their disabilities (Pomerantz & Marholin, 1977). The rationalization is frequently encountered that the methods, however inefficient they may be, are necessary because of the rehabilitation function of the workshop. However, rehabilitation of clients does not require poor job design. Training clients to work with inefficient hand methods while industry is using automated methods is not serving the best interests of the workshop client. If clients are going to develop into motivated, productive workers, they should be able to utilize all available technologies which will assist them in achieving maximum, high-quality output.

In order to accomplish an effective method analysis, another activity must be carried out simultaneously—the design of the work station and any jigs or aids to facilitate production or quality control. Outside help should be sought in this area if expert personnel are not available on the staff. Such persons must have a thorough knowledge of the principles of motion economy, human factors, and human engineering and the nature and characteristics of the clients in the workshop.

Jigs, work aids, and job redesign. The use of jigs, work aids, and job redesign deserve careful attention because of the dual function (rehabilitation and employment) served by most workshops. *Jigs* and *work aids* are specialized pieces of equipment designed to aid in the accomplishment of a particular task. More precisely, in the authors' definition of the words: A jig is a piece of equipment designed as part of the work station to aid all workers doing a particular task, whereas a work aid is an even more specialized piece of equipment such as a special chair, platform, or tongue-operated switch which is custom designed to aid a single worker. *Job redesign* means rearranging the sequencing or content of a job in order to make it easier for the handicapped worker. The purposes of the particular workshop and the weight given to each of the functions (rehabilitation and employment) are considerations in deciding how extensive the use of jigs, work aids, or job redesign should be. For extended employment shops, widespread use should be made of any technology which will speed production. In transitional shops, extensive use of jigs or job redesign may be counterproductive if clients are expected to progress shortly to competitive employment where these aids are not available. Even within extended employment shops, jigs and work aids should not be thought of as substitutes for training even though in many cases designing a work aid may be easier than designing a training curriculum.

The method analysis must determine whether the job should have an assembly-line design or not. The beneficial effects of job simplification, or breaking jobs into small components, have been widely demonstrated in workshop operations (Bellamy, 1976; Gold, 1973; Martin & Flexer, Note 6). However, the motivational aspects of an unsimplified or an enriched job (i.e., fewer workers, more decisions, more work variety) in comparison to simplified jobs have not been explored in workshop applications.

Time study. Time study is used to calculate direct labor costs. Additional uses include measuring improvements in client performance and evaluating alternate task methods, job station designs, and work flow designs. There are many different systems available for time study of jobs and shop operations; and it is obvious that the more familiar the practitioner is with the different systems, the more effective time study will be as a tool in contract bidding and shop operations. At the very minimum, the workshop operations staff should be familiar with calculating direct labor costs based on the *net* over-all time per unit method (Rogers, 1963) which provides an approximate and quick estimate of the total base time per unit. It is unfortunate that too many shops base direct labor charges solely on the net time measure because their skills in time study are lacking. An example of the step for calculation of net time is provided below.

1. Set up a work station for the operation including all materials, tools, and jigs.

2. Have a nonhandicapped staff member perform the operation at a comfortable pace—one that he or she could maintain for a long period of time. The person doing the time study should observe the activity with a stopwatch (preferably a decimal hour watch, but a regular stopwatch will suffice). The timer counts how many operations are performed (or products completed) in a given length of time. Experience with net time calculations show that the longer the interval, the more accurate the estimate of the total base time. Accuracy is also increased if several workers are timed and an average of their time taken.

3. After the number of operations per unit time has been recorded, the standard time, or net time, can be converted into labor costs by applying a labor standard (a wage-per-hour figure). As an example, suppose three staff members each worked for 30 minutes and the number of ballpoint pens assembled by each in that time was:

Worker	Rate per 1/2 hour
A	70
B	75
C	65

Average = 70 per 30 minutes or 140 per hour

Based on a $2.30 minimum hourly wage, the direct labor cost per unit is:

$$\frac{\$2.30}{140} = .0164 \text{ or } 1.64¢ \text{ per pen}$$

Since cost and prices are usually quoted per 100 or 1000 units, this would be:

$1.64 per 100 units; $16.40 per 1000 units

4. When using these figures to calculate pay rates rather than labor costs, it should be remembered that if workshop employees are paid hourly wages, they must be paid at the same rate as workers in industry. This means that if the industrial worker (who assembles approximately 140 pens per hour) is paid at the rate of $2.30, the handicapped worker who assembles only 70 pens per hour would be paid at a rate adjusted for production —$1.15 based on $2.30 per hour rate for 140 pens per hour. If workshop employees are paid on a piecework basis, they must be paid the same piece rate as workers in industry—in this case 1.64 cents per pen (after Dolnick & Musolf, 1963).

Calculation of overhead. Overhead represents all expenses in operating the workshop other than the direct labor and materials for the contract job. Miscalculation of overhead expenses can cause a business to lose money, prestige, and profitable contacts. Subsidized shops frequently ignore or give short shrift to this aspect of contract bidding in the mistaken belief that since they are subsidized, the contractor should not be charged for his share of the operating expenses of the shop while that workshop is working for him. It is also false economy to trim overhead in order to keep a bid low. It presents a picture of poor business management in the workshop. Some of the items to be considered in calculating overhead costs are administrative costs (salaries), supervisory costs, rent (or mortgage payments), taxes (property, social security), electricity, heating, water, insurance, depreciation on buildings and equipment, telephone, office supplies, and record-keeping expenses—outside audits, consultant expenses, rehabilitation service costs. These overhead costs must be prorated according to the percentage of time and space allocation which the contract being bid upon will require of the total time and space available.

Additional cost considerations. Additional cost factors which may frequently be overlooked but must be accounted for in any workshop operation are:

1. Safety training and equipment. As workshops increasingly extend rehabilitation services to more severely handicapped clients, and as less severely impaired clients move into community job placements, workshops will find that safety devices and programs which previously may have been sufficient are no longer adequate. Severely developmentally disabled clients with few verbal skills may require more than warning signs and posted areas. Guards may have to be posted where signs once would suffice, and additional safety equipment, programs, and consultants may well be required.

2. Spoilage. This factor must be taken into account in any type of operation, whether prime manufacturing or contracting. Spoilage costs (the costs of

materials which are broken or ruined while clients are learning a job) are often considered as one of the "extra costs" associated with the rehabilitative nature of the workshop, but they must not be ignored. They are likely to increase with more severely handicapped clients unless training is instituted over and above on-the-job training (which is where most of the spoilage costs come from).

3. *Equipment down-time.* This factor is frequently overlooked in workshop bidding procedures. It is especially critical if the equipment being used is specialized or adapted for handicapped clients. If specialized jigs have been constructed for a particular job, it must be kept in mind that jigs break down as do machines. Backups must be available on short notice. Before "one-of-a-kind" pieces of equipment are utilized, or special modifications are made to only one piece of equipment in a shop, thought must be given to what steps to take in the event that the equipment breaks in the middle of a production run. Broken equipment is no excuse for a missed delivery date.

The other major category of costs, material costs, is not discussed since it is applicable primarily to prime manufacturing shops. In calculating material costs, consultant advice should be sought.

When all relevant costs have been assembled, the workshop is in a position to offer a bid. The workshop procurement person should add up the costs and arrive at a figure.

	Per 100	Per 1000	Per 10,000
Labor (from time study)	1.64	16.40	164.00
Materials (contractor supplied)	0	0	0
Set up (tools and jigs)	10.00	10.00	10.00
Tools and equipment	15.00	30.00	45.00
Overhead (100% of labor)	1.64	16.40	164.00
Total cost	28.28	72.80	383.00
Profit margin (8%)	2.26	5.82	30.64
Total price	30.54	78.62	413.64
Price per 100	30.54	7.86	4.14

This chapter permits only a brief description of the procedures used to establish a base for contract bidding. Additional cost factors are certainly involved. Very precise time study procedures, not de-

scribed here, are available, and task breakdown and production design are broad enough topics to warrant being termed "fields of study." The reader is urged to explore these areas much more fully in order to appreciate the precision which can be brought to the area of contract bidding, thereby avoiding a "best guess" process. The reader is referred to *Contract Procurement Practices of Sheltered Workshops* by Dolnick & Musolf (1963) for an excellent overview of contract bidding procedures.

Record Keeping

Some record keeping is mandated by law. Applications for exemption from certain wage and hour laws require that the workshop substantiate client production figures and earnings. The basic records which will be required are client attendance, hours worked on each job operation, and production on each operation (Dolnick & Musolf, 1963). Additional records which can materially aid in the bidding process can be derived from the partial list of costs included in the discussions of overhead and additional costs. These records should be reviewed and updated at least monthly so that bids may accurately reflect rising costs for building space, utilities, salaries, transportation, and the myriad of other costs. Currently costs change so rapidly that figures used only 6 months earlier may be gross underestimates.

Workshop space utilization and layout

Proper workflow within the workshop is required to meet production deadlines, to reduce the amount of supervision needed, and to facilitate client morale. An inefficient plant design can lead to bottlenecks in production, pileups of parts and materials, and an unpleasant work setting. Workshops frequently are physical plants that were not designed to be manufacturing operations. Often they are former school buildings, quonset huts, church basements, or partially renovated office buildings. In order to use these facilities, a knowledge of workflow processes and proper workshop space utilization (or the use of specialists in optimum space utilization) is imperative. The first step of physical plant design requires a working knowledge of drawing workflow diagrams (simple pictures of how parts move around the workshop during the manufacturing process). For example, one workshop trainer began practicing workflow studies in the kitchen of her home and was quickly amazed at how inefficiently the kitchen was arranged and stocked for the types of work performed—aesthetically pleasing, but operationally inefficient. Not much could be done about the location of major appliances or doorways, but after rearranging the foods, dishes, pots and pans, and cleaning materials, she was amazed at how much easier the work seemed and how many fewer steps were required.

Summary

This chapter has described a wide range of topics related to vocational training. The teacher or counselor unconcerned with the daily operations of a workshop may ask what benefit could accrue from a deeper study of these topics. Anyone teaching severely handicapped persons, children or adults, must work within a team of professionals in order to promote their maximum educational or vocational development. In many if not most cases, these maximum levels are determined by the skills of the people who teach the severely handicapped whether they be classroom teachers or workshop staff. Many of the skill areas discussed in this chapter have a direct relationship to classroom instruction. Knowledge of other vocational information, while not directly applicable to classroom settings, will enable the teacher to take a more active part in preparing handicapped individuals to leave the classroom for an active vocational life.

Acknowledgments

The authors wish to express sincere appreciation to Jim Newbery for his assistance in background research, to Carol Sigelman and Jerry Parham for their editorial comments and assistance, and to LaDonna Martin and Elizabeth Mathews for their preparation of the manuscript.

References

Baroff, G. S. *Mental retardation: Nature, cause, and management.* Washington, D.C.: Hemisphere, 1974.

Bellamy, G. T. (Ed.). *Habilitation of severely and profoundly retarded adults.* Eugene, Ore.: Rehabilitation Research and Training Center in Mental Retardation, University of Oregon, 1976.

Bellamy, G. T., Inman, D. P., & Horner, R. H. *Design of vocational habilitation services for the severely retarded: The specialized training program model.* Eugene, Ore.: Center on Human Development, University of Oregon, 1977.

Bellamy, G. T., Peterson, L., & Close, D. Habilitation of the severely and profoundly retarded: Illustrations of competence. *Education and Training of the Mentally Retarded,* 1975, *10,* 174–187.

Bellamy, G. T., & Snyder, S. The trainee performance sample: Toward the prediction of habilitation costs for severely handicapped adults. In G. T. Bellamy (Ed.), *Habilitation of severely and profoundly retarded adults.* Eugene, Ore.: Rehabilitation Research and Training Center in Mental Retardation, University of Oregon, 1976.

Bellamy, G. T., & Sontag, E. Use of group contingent music to increase assembly line production rates of retarded students in a simulated sheltered workshop. *Journal of Music Therapy,* 1973, *10,* 125–136.

Brolin, D. E. *Vocational preparation of retarded citizens.* Columbus, Ohio: Charles E. Merrill, 1976.

Brown, L., Van Deventer, P., Perlmutter, L., Jones, S., & Sontag, E. Effects of consequences on production rates of trainable retarded and severely emotionally disturbed students in a public school workshop. *Education and Training of the Mentally Retarded,* 1972, *7,* 74–81.

Cobb, H. V. *The forest of fulfillment.* New York: Teachers College Press, 1972.

Conley, R. *The economics of mental retardation.* Baltimore: Johns Hopkins University Press, 1972.

Cortazzo, A. *Activity centers for retarded adults.* Washington, D.C.: President's Committee on Mental Retardation, 1972.

Crosson, J. E. A technique for programming sheltered workshop environments for training severely retarded workers. *American Journal of Mental Deficiency,* 1969, *73,* 814–818.

DeRoo, W. M., & Haralson, H. L. Increasing workshop production through self-visualization on videotape. *Mental Retardation,* 1971, *9*(4), 22–25.

Dolnick, M. M., & Musolf, F. A. *Contract procurement practices of sheltered workshops.* Washington, D.C.: U.S. Government Printing Office, 1963.

Fishler, A. L. *Development of work programs for the multihandicapped.* New York: Professional Services Program Department, United Cerebral Palsy Association, 1976.

Friedenberg, W. P., & Martin, A. S. Prevocational training of the severely retarded using task analysis. *Mental Retardation,* 1977, *15*(2), 16–20.

Gellman, W. Adapting the rehabilitation workshop to the needs of the disadvantaged. In W. H. Button (Ed.), *Rehabilitation, sheltered workshops and the disadvantaged: An exploration in manpower policy.* Ithaca, N.Y.: Cornell University Press, 1970.

Gold, M. W. Stimulus factors in skill training of retarded adolescents on a complex assembly task: Acquisition, transfer and retention. *American Journal of Mental Deficiency,* 1972, *76,* 517–526.

Gold, M. W. Research on the vocational habilitation of the retarded: The present, the future. In N. R. Ellis (Ed.), *International review of research in mental retardation* (Volume 6). New York: Academic Press, 1973.

Gold, M. W. Task analysis of a complex assembly task by the retarded blind. *Exceptional Children,* 1976, *42,* 78–84.

Huddle, D. Work performance of trainable adults as influenced by competition, cooperation and monetary reward. *American Journal of Mental Deficiency,* 1967, *72,* 198–211.

Irvin, L. K. General utility of easy to hard discrimination training procedures with the severely retarded. *Education and Training of the Mentally Retarded,* 1976, *11,* 247–250.

Irvin, L. E., & Bellamy, G. T. Manipulation of stimulus features in vocational skill training of the severely retarded: Relative efficacy. In G. T. Bellamy (Ed.), *Habilitation of severely and profoundly retarded adults.* Eugene, Ore.: Specialized Training Program and Rehabilitation Research and Training Center in Mental Retardation, University of Oregon, 1976.

Jens, K., & Shores, R. Behavioral graphs as reinforcers for work behavior of mentally retarded adolescents. *Education and Training of the Mentally Retarded,* 1969, *4,* 21–26.

Karan, O., Wehman, P., Renzaglia, A., & Schutz, R. *Habilitation practices with the severely developmentally disabled* (Volume 1). Madison, Wisc.: Research and Training Center in Mental Retardation, University of Wisconsin–Madison, 1976.

Leslie, J. H. Wide battery of tests measures disabled workers for industrial roles. *Rehabilitation World,* Autumn 1976.

Martin, A. S., & Morris, J. L. *Development of a general purpose vocational assessment technique.* Annual Progress Report. Lubbock, Tex.: Research and Training Center in Mental Retardation, 1977.

National Association of Retarded Citizens. *A guide to establishing an activity center for mentally retarded.* Washington, D.C.: U.S. Government Printing Office, 1976a.

National Association of Retarded Citizens. *Planning and organizing a sheltered workshop for mentally retarded persons.* Washington, D.C.: U.S. Government Printing Office, 1976b.

National Association of Sheltered Workshops and Homebound Programs. *Proceedings of annual meeting,* October 1968.

Nelson, N. *Workshops for the handicapped in the United States.* Springfield, Ill.: Charles C Thomas, 1971.

Pomerantz, D., & Marholin, D. Vocational habilitation: A time for change. In E. Sontag (Ed.), *Educational programming for the severely and profoundly handicapped.* Reston, Va.: Council for Exceptional Children, Division on Mental Retardation, 1977.

Rogers, H. B. Time study. In Dolnick, M. M. (Ed.), *Contract procurement practices of sheltered workshops.* Washington, D.C.: U.S. Government Printing Office, 1963.

Salkind, I. Economic problems of workshops. In R. Lamb (Ed.), *Rehabilitation in community mental health.* San Francisco: Jossey-Bass, 1971.

Salkind, I. The training of workshop directors. In R. E. Hardy & J. G. Cull (Eds.), *Administrative techniques of rehabilitation facility operations.* Springfield, Ill.: Charles C Thomas, 1974.

Sontag, E. (Ed.). *Educational programming for the severely and profoundly handicapped.* Reston, Va.: Council for Exceptional Children, Division on Mental Retardation, 1977.

Tobias, J., & Cortazzo, A. D. Training severely retarded adults for greater independence in community living. *Training School Bulletin,* 1963, *60,* 23–37.

Trybus, R. J., & Lacks, P. B. Modification of vocational behavior in a community agency for mentally retarded adolescents. *Rehabilitation Literature,* 1972, *33*(9), 258–266.

U.S. Government Printing Office. *Standards for rehabilitation facilities and sheltered workshops* (U.S. Department of Health, Education, & Welfare, Publication No. [SRS] 72–25010, Rev. Ed.). Washington, D.C.: Author, 1971.

Walthall, J. E., & Love, H. D. *Habilitation of the mentally retarded individual.* Springfield, Ill.: Charles C Thomas, 1974.

Whelan, E. The "scientific approach" in the practical workshop situation. In H. C. Gunzburg (Ed.), *Experiments in the rehabilitation of the mentally handicapped.* Southampton, England: Camelot Press, 1974.

Zimmerman, J., Stuckey, T., Garlick, B., & Miller, M. Effects of token reinforcement on productivity in multiply handicapped clients in a sheltered workshop. *Rehabilitation Literature,* 1969, *30,* 34–41.

Notes

1. Greenleigh Associates. *The role of the sheltered workshop in the rehabilitation of the severely handicapped.* Report to the U.S. Department of Health, Education, and Welfare, Rehabilitation Services Administration, 1975.
2. Bucks County Public Schools. *Methods in vocational education: Program report to Pennsylvania Department of Education.* Doylestown, Pa.: Bureau of Vocational, Technical, and Continuing Education, 1974.
3. Redkey, H. *A way of looking at sheltered workshops for the 1970's.* Stout, Wisc.: Stout Vocational Rehabilitation Institute, University of Wisconsin, 1975.
4. Neff, W. S. *Problems of work evaluation.* Paper presented at the convention of the American Personnel and Guidance Association, Minneapolis, Minnesota, 1965.
5. Timmerman, W. J., & Doctor, A. C. *Special applications of work evaluation techniques for prediction of employability of the trainable mentally retarded* (Reprint series no. 11). Stryker, Ohio: Quadco Rehabilitation Center, 1974.
6. Martin, A. S., & Flexer, R. W. *Three studies on training work skills and work adjustment with the severely retarded.* Lubbock, Tex.: Research and Training Center in Mental Retardation, Texas Tech University, 1975.

13

Issues in
Prevocational Training

*This chapter was written by **Marc W. Gold,** Institute for Child Behavior and Development, University of Illinois at Champaign-Urbana; and **David J. Pomerantz,** Department of Special Education, State University College at Buffalo.*

The provision of vocational and prevocational training to all individuals, regardless of handicapping conditions, is a challenge for the fields of special education and rehabilitation. Vocational training presents unusually difficult programmatic questions because the content of relevant curricula is not easily determined. No areas of instruction are purely vocational or purely nonvocational. Furthermore, the world of work is so diverse that no standardized objectives fit all cases and no curriculum is universally appropriate. In this chapter, we address the issue of defining vocational tasks in the hope of stimulating the planning of vocational curricula and programs. Several general strategies for vocational programming are suggested.

Preparation of this chapter was supported by NICHHD Program Project Grant No. HD05951 to Institute for Child Behavior and Development, University of Illinois at Champaign-Urbana.

Defining Vocational Skills and Vocational Education

How can a behavior be defined as a "vocational behavior" or "skill"? Are certain skills, such as those concerned with technical matters (e.g., handling machinery), "vocational" as compared with skills which are "social," "academic," "daily living," etc.? Such a definitional scheme does not hold up to close scrutiny (Parker, 1971). Many people have technical skills but use them as a hobby rather than a vocation (e.g., the weekend mechanic). Others are unskilled in technical matters but are vocationally successful. Obviously, any work setting involves communication skills, daily living and self-help skills, transportation skills, etc., as well as the specific tasks peculiar to a particular job. All socially appropriate behaviors are needed in the work world and are just as much "vocational" as they are any other arbitrary classification. There can be no topographical definition of a vocational task.

In order to understand vocational activity, it may be more fruitful to look at the effects of work in our society. Some major consequences of working are (1) financial support, (2) opportunities for social interaction, (3) opportunity to gain the respect of others, (4) opportunities to enhance skills in chosen areas, and (5) personal satisfaction (Terkel, 1974).

As a general statement, most working behavior is controlled by at least some, and possibly all, of these outcomes. The executive who hates the pressures of his job but enjoys the salary would probably leave if his salary were drastically reduced. The musician who is committed to writing and performing new materials is likely to leave the world of music altogether if forced to write and play only background music.

Although different jobs may require completely different skills to be performed in different kinds of settings, the functional relationships involved in working behavior have some degree of uniformity within the society. By emphasizing these functional relationships, vocational educators are most likely to meet the needs of handicapped students. Parker (1971) suggested that vocational education is training for gainful employment. This appears to be a straightforward and useful outlook, particularly if the term *gainful* is considered in a broad sense, encompassing the outcomes of work listed above. The first outcome of working (i.e., financial support) might, however, be weighted more heavily than the others because it may lead directly to the other outcomes (Ryan, 1971). Thus, for the purposes of this chapter, let us define *vocational skills* as those which enable an individual to earn a living and other normative reinforcers associated with working.

Problems Concerning Vocational Opportunity

At present, most individuals labeled as moderately, severely, or profoundly retarded work in sheltered employment if they work at all. The tasks performed in sheltered workshops and work activity centers are generally extremely simple, unimportant in industry, and nonremunerative (Gold, 1973; Greenleigh Associates, Note 1; Pomerantz & Marholin, 1977). In fact, many of these tasks are so low level that training is rarely needed nor particularly useful (Levy, Pomerantz, & Gold, 1977). Commonly, vocational and prevocational training programs use the same kinds of tasks as models and introduce sheltered workshoplike activity as the core of the curriculum. But is this vocational education? According to the definition used in this chapter, it is not. The performance of low-level tasks as the end product of a training program provides no access to financial independence. These tasks are not useful in competitive employment (Greenleigh Associates, Note 1) and generally pay considerably below the minimum wage rate in sheltered employment. Furthermore, it is difficult to see how the performance of such tasks could produce continuing skill development in any area, gain the respect of others, or lead to a sense of personal satisfaction. The disturbing conclusion which must be reached is that few moderately, severely, or profoundly retarded persons are currently engaged in vocational activity. School and rehabilitation programs which rely on the nonvocational tasks currently performed by handicapped workers are implicitly accepting and maintaining the status quo.

Opening opportunities: An orientation for vocational education

The educator who is involved in vocational programming must gear his or her efforts toward the upgrading and expanding of the retarded individual's opportunities in the world of work. Otherwise there is no purpose to prevocational or vocational programming. Training must be used as a strategy for increasing opportunity. For example, placement in competitive industry might be established as the objective for a prevocational program. With such a concrete target, training could be provided in situations that are actually relevant and important for reaching that target. Skills which are tied to specific opportunities (e.g., getting along with a particular supervisor, performing certain job skills) would be taught. Little time would be wasted in training ill-defined hypothetical constructs which may not even exist and are not likely to enhance usable skills (e.g., "eye-hand coordination," "figure-ground").

A second goal of prevocational programming to broaden vocational opportunities includes major changes in the sheltered workshop. Training can be used to demonstrate to those in charge of habilitation programs and to people in industry that the students can perform higher level, more remunerative work if such work is available. In both cases, a social change activity (obtaining jobs or better workshop contracts) is paired with effective training to meet a predetermined educational objective.

Guidelines for vocational education strategies

The following are general considerations in devising strategies to open vocational opportunities; each of the issues mentioned should be examined specifically, taking into consideration the particular resources and problems of the home community.

1. *Do skills which are taught have current utility and at the same time represent a future-oriented change strategy?* Part of the utility of the concept of vocational skill is that it causes teachers and curriculum planners to view students' activities as related to some life goal or activity that will be performed in adulthood. This perspective leads to the development of long sequences of lessons, in some cases years long. If we are to have severely and profoundly handicapped individuals, for example, operating farm implements, we must task analyze the operation of this equipment and the skills which are prerequisite to such operation. The result would, it is to be hoped, be the identification of specific skills which may eventually be elaborated into machinery operation skills and which might even be taught to 4-year-olds. Caution must be taken, however, to ensure that the skills which are taught contribute to the successful existence of the student at the present time. If we fail to consider the long-range outcomes of our programs, too much time is spent teaching behaviors that have their only relevance in the school setting or during childhood. Conversely, ignoring current utility of skills leads to an inappropriate allocation of training time to information which can be used only in conjunction with a great deal of other information; and students end up with a great deal of unusable information.

If the future-oriented change strategy is well designed, there should be little problem identifying curriculum content which is both consistent with the goal of the strategy and currently useful to students. School programs should be designed (1) to create the need to train vocational skills in students by stimulating work opportunities in communities, and (2) to follow through by providing the skills necessary to take advantage of these newly opened opportunities. The strategy should be kept specific (e.g., secure 10 jobs in the food-processing factories in town within 1 year). Similarly, the curriculum derived from the strategy should be a sequence of specific, clearly defined skills rather than vague constructs. For example, particular machine operation and factory maintenance skills which correspond to existing jobs in the target factories would be defined and analyzed into component skills.

In the context of a change strategy, training is most likely to meet students' current needs if target behaviors include some "competencies" rather than an exclusive focus on supposedly "normal" characteristics (Gold, 1975). "Competence" refers to a set of skills which is valued by society and not freely available. Competencies do not develop in nonhandicapped or handicapped individuals without training. Once they have been developed, however, an individual has something to offer society (i.e., the work world, for the purposes of this discussion) and is in a position of strength when he applies for a job. If a program turns out competent students, it can engineer change by demonstrating the students' ability to successfully engage in vocational activity. A young adult trained to operate one type of duplicating machine is obviously not skilled in operating all such machines. However, if the competence is demonstrated to a potential employer who needs an operator of duplicating machinery, the feasibility of training the student on other machines should be evident. Rather than asking for employment "handouts," the vocational programmer is selling competent labor.

A similar strategy is to obtain verbal commitments from businesspersons to consider for employment any individual who demonstrates specified skills. Training could then be directed in these skill areas, and a follow-up visit to the potential employers would be arranged when the skills are mastered. Such a procedure (1) gets "your foot in the door," always an important part of getting a job, (2) indicates that you can be trusted to fulfill commitments, and (3) demonstrates the students' work potential and receptivity to training.

Finally, the educator interested in vocational programming should attempt an analysis of employers' needs in the local community. By reading management literature and classified ads, talking to businesspersons, and any other means available, the educator must identify skills or worker characteristics that are truly needed and valued. Significant increases in vocational opportunity for handicapped individuals will occur when they are prepared to meet some real employment needs.

A first step might be to identify the types of industries operating in the community. What kinds of jobs exist within these industries? More specifically, what kinds of skilled, semiskilled, and unskilled jobs are common within an industry and are found in all factories or warehouses related to that industry? It is not uncommon for certain jobs to be characterized by high turnover rates over extended periods of time. Such jobs are ideal targets for job placement programs. If certain industrial settings are more receptive than others to the prospect of hiring trained handicapped workers, these settings should be job analyzed in more detail. After several successful placements, the supervisors and workers might be willing to share their positive experiences with more hesitant employers.

Analysis of industry in a community is by no means limited to factories and production settings. What special features of the community contribute to the economy? In tourist areas, for example, the vocational educator could approach hotels and motels which might employ maids and related maintenance staffs. If students are appropriately trained, perhaps they will be hired during peak tourist seasons when the need for labor is highest. Once the students demonstrate that they are competent and reliable, it is possible that they will be retained on a year-round basis. Similarly, students trained in farm-related jobs might begin with a temporary placement during the spring or fall. Quality labor is always appreciated, and further opportunities should open once it is demonstrated that the handicapped worker is an asset.

2. *Does the change strategy operate within the values of the business world as well as the values of the helping professions?* Traditionally, appeals on behalf of the handicapped have asked for kindness and charity for "those who are less fortunate." The slogan "hire the handicapped," for example, implies that employers should change their hiring criteria, moving away from the workers who best meet their needs to those who need special help and favors. It is unreasonable and short-sighted to expect business interests to behave in a manner incompatible with the patterns that developed and maintain their current position in society. Rather, change efforts should purposefully arrange consequences to match business interests, which would make business more likely to extend opportunities to handicapped persons. Potential employers should be made aware of the assets of handicapped workers as well as aversive consequences for not integrating a labor force. Examples of positive and aversive consequences to business include worker reliability (cost savings from reduced turnover) and potential loss of government contracts resulting from the potential legal action taken if handicapped persons are systematically excluded from a labor force (*Federal Register,* 1976). In placement activities, a vocational program should demonstrate to employers an understanding of the business world and make sensible arguments in business terms (Kelly & Simon, 1969). Those who implement a strategy for integrating and changing sheltered workshops must understand industry and know how to estab-

lish efficient production systems before they can expect to secure better contracts (Gold, 1973; Stroud, 1970; also refer to Chapter 12).

A teacher can enhance the chances of placing students into competitive jobs by keeping data bearing on the reliability and competence of students. Attendance records, acquisition data for vocational skills which have been taught, and records of time needed to train the more difficult skills should be organized into a "package presentation" for potential employers. A concise and clear presentation indicates to the employer that he is talking with people who know their business and can deliver on the promises being made. A data-based presentation may be especially effective because it speaks in terms used in the business world, not in the generalities and subjective labels which have traditionally dominated education and the social services.

3. *Does the program capitalize on existing community resources?* Unfortunately, some of the educators responsible for vocational programming know very little about the world of work. In the past, there has been little effort to obtain occupational information because low expectations prevented consideration of most kinds of jobs for students with special needs. This suggests that the fields of vocational education and special education must begin to work together (Gold, Note 2; Phelps, 1977). There is evidence that such an alliance is beginning to form (Chaffin & Clark, Note 3). For the present, however, programmers must make a concerted effort to familiarize themselves with a broad range of occupations. When target occupations have been selected (i.e., those job areas at which change strategies will be aimed), it is the programmer's responsibility to become knowledgeable about these jobs. Educators must move out from the confines of the school building and open lines of communication with those who recruit, employ, and train workers. The people who know the content of target jobs (i.e., requisite skills) have the information and materials to make great contributions to developing vocational curricula. Those of us whose expertise is in the teaching process (i.e., how, rather than what, to teach) must go to them for help.

4. *Are program criteria explicit?* The ambiguously stated objectives of current prevocational and vocational programs are not conducive to the achievement of any meaningful outcome. The intended result of a training program must be clearly delin-

eated. Not only must target behaviors and skills be clearly defined, but the conditions in which these skills are to be performed should also be stated. For example, rather than simply specifying the operation of a buffing machine as the training goal, the programmer should indicate criteria for quality and quantity of performance; the locations where work will occur; the people likely to be around the worker; and the quality of supervision that can be expected. The problem which arises is that complex criteria based on natural environmental conditions present an almost insurmountable challenge to the trainer. It is difficult enough to teach complex skills without worrying about the intricacies of the situations in which the skills must be performed. For this reason, we suggest two criteria be established prior to the initiation of training. Criterion I is an arbitrary point at which it can be assumed that the student has learned the skill. Criterion II is defined as demonstration of the skill in the situation where it is ultimately expected to occur (Gold, 1976).

Using these two criteria, the programmer can separate two equally vital tasks: establishing control over behavior and ensuring that control is exercised by the natural environment. There are some situations in which it is desirable to combine both tasks by teaching directly in the Criterion II situation or by training natural reinforcement agents (e.g., parents) to work with the student. With such a direct approach, there is little reliance on generalization. Teaching students to use public transportation provides a good example of a circumstance in which direct training in the Criterion II situation is advisable. The trainer cannot accurately simulate the buses and street corners that comprise Criterion II in this case, and generalization is most unlikely (Emshoff, Redd, & Davidson, 1976). Therefore, the trainer should "take to the streets" and slowly proceed through the sequence of skills needed by an individual who wishes to use the bus system.

Similarly, the operation of expensive machinery peculiar to one factory would be trained directly in the factory. It is not feasible for the school program to purchase similar machinery because of the cost and the existence of only one or two jobs related to the machinery. Rather than teaching the use of other machines and hoping for generalization, instruction would occur after the job is secured in the Criterion II setting. In this case, however, the teacher could establish a Criterion I and shift to Criterion II after the machine operation skills are acquired. For example, he could train during the least busy work shift, thereby reducing distraction

and competition from activity around the machinery. When the task is reliably performed under these conditions, the student would be introduced into the shift that he will actually work.

When it is extremely difficult to establish control in the Criterion II setting, or it is impractical to use the Criterion II setting for training, the programmer must design an instructional situation which (1) is conducive to training or establishment of behavioral control and (2) is no more discrepant from Criterion II than is absolutely necessary. Under the artificial conditions that are established, skills are taught until the student demonstrates reliable performance. At this point, Criterion I has been achieved. For example, in handling money, when the student can make change without error 5 consecutive times, the trainer can reasonably assume that the basic skill is intact. At this point, generalization to Criterion II conditions must be actively programmed (Pomerantz & Redd, Note 4). In this example, the student's handling of money might be monitored in a crowded store and additional training implemented if the target skills are not exhibited in the appropriate form or at the appropriate times.

Programming generalization to Criterion II has been accomplished by varying irrelevant aspects of the instructional environment or by gradually fading to Criterion II conditions after the target behavior has been established. If only a single trainer has conducted the program, newly acquired skills may be restricted to the presence of that trainer (Reiss & Redd, Note 5). Similarly, instruction in a single setting (Wahler, 1969), with a specific series of prompts (Rincover & Koegel, 1975), or with a single set of instructional materials (Redd, 1972) may inhibit generalization to Criterion II. Using more than one trainer (Reiss & Redd, Note 5) or multiple settings and materials (Emshoff et al., 1976) may enhance performance in Criterion II. For example, several supervisors might be asked to participate in teaching janitorial skills within a work setting. In this way, the student is more likely to respond appropriately to instructions from all people to whom he is responsible than if one supervisor or teacher conducts all training. Alternatively, a program similar to the one employed by Pomerantz and Redd (Note 4) could be initiated. In such a program, critical differences between the training and Criterion II settings are identified. Artificial aspects of training are then gradually eliminated and natural Criterion II characteristics are introduced into the instructional setting. An extremely difficult assembly task might be color-coded in order to facilitate acquisition. The color cues would be removed eventually, however, because the actual materials on the job do not contain reliable color cues.

Opening Opportunity Through Training

All of the programmatic questions which have been raised are important. All vocational education strategies, however, rest on the assumption that useful work skills can be taught to handicapped students. From our perspective, such an assumption is reasonable if the teacher is able to carefully analyze the skills and tasks needed for vocational activity.

Content task analysis

Content task analysis is a term used in our instructional system to mean breaking a task into teachable components (Gold, 1976). "Teachable" is determined by the skills of the teacher and the skills of the learner. There are a variety of reasons for a content task analysis. Perhaps the most important is that the trainer or teacher must develop intimacy with the task. One principal reason why many handicapped individuals learn so little is that their teachers have failed to recognize the distinction between being able to do something and being "intimately familiar" with that same thing. Take as an example a rather trivial task found in both work and nonwork settings, the dropping of one's pants to go to the bathroom. The task is one that everyone performs. How much do we really know about this task? Where are the feet positioned in relationship to the toilet before beginning the process? Is it done the same every time? When the pants are first touched, which hand is used and exactly where is it placed? Is a palmer grasp used, or the thumb and forefinger? Are the pants touched in any place or does the thumb go to the exact place every time? If the pants have a zipper, are they first unzipped or unbuttoned? Are the outer garment and undergarment lowered simultaneously, or one at a time? How far are the garments dropped, above the knees or down to the ankles? Few individuals could answer these questions about a task that they have performed thousands of times. Furthermore, task intimacy is not necessarily indicated even for somebody who can answer all of these questions. What are the possible alternative ways of performing each of these functions? Are there methods of performing this task that are different from the one

that you use for yourself, that are more efficient and effective for the people you are responsible for training? Many tasks, of course, are not so familiar.

When we develop a task analysis for an industrial task or some other task that we have never seen before, we have no already existing method of our own to bias our decisions. We proceed step by step through each component of the task and, being unfamiliar with it, inspect and become intimate with the components. What results from this process of careful inspection is the content task analysis, or the listing of the steps into which the task has been arbitrarily divided. It is to be hoped that these steps represent teachable components. The notion that a component is teachable is really a hypothesis. It is proven during the training process when we find out which steps are, in fact, being acquired and which are not. The size of the divisions (i.e., how many steps) depends on preconceived notions regarding the capabilities of the learner. The same task can be divided into any number of components. For example, to teach a person to add the numbers 2 and 3, we might give a single instruction such as "Take 2 objects; put them together with 3 more; then count the new total." Such an instruction represents a very weak training strategy involving a content task analysis of 3 steps. To use this strategy the teacher must assume that the learner has a well-developed repertoire of entering behaviors. Alternatively, one could teach $2 + 3$ by including steps for the concepts of the numbers 2 and 3, the concept of "putting things together," how to count, etc. Anybody with experience in teaching knows that some "clinical judgment" or sensitivity to the needs of individual students is important. Perhaps these terms can be understood, at least partly, as the ability to make subtle discriminations regarding the number of component steps needed for each student. Such discriminations are indeed important. If we divide a task into an unnecessarily large number of components, efficiency is lost, and even more seriously, the task can become tedious and aversive to the student. If each component is too large (i.e., too few steps), the student will not acquire the skill. The ability to make these subtle discriminations can be developed by (1) preparing many content task analyses and implementing the training that they generate, (2) knowing the intended student population, and (3) revising the content task analysis when necessary (Gold, 1976).

Assessment. Since the above statements indicate the need to know student characteristics, some discussion of the issue of assessment is in order. Behavioral assessment can be helpful in certain situations to determine priorities about what to teach. If such assessment is to be genuinely useful to the trainer, however, it must focus on the specific behaviors prerequisite to the target task. Assessment of general behavioral constructs is not seen as particularly useful. These general types of assessment usually result in limiting a teacher's expectations and willingness to teach relatively difficult skills. They provide little specific information on whether a learner is ready to acquire a particular task. The focus, then, should be on task-specific assessment. In order to conduct such assessment, intimacy with the task is necessary because the trainer must know enough to be able to identify the specific behaviors needed to begin lessons on the target task.

Identifying necessary prerequisite skills for a particular task is another important reason for a content task analysis. It forces the task analyst to identify what is expected of the learner upon entering the situation. It is interesting to note that the more the task analyst knows about the task, the fewer prerequisites needed by the learner. As the task analyst learns the intricacies of the task, the behaviors needed by the learner become more and more apparent. It is common to conclude from the development of a content task analysis that there are skills and lessons that need to be completed before a learner may enter the planned situation. When writing a content task analysis for time telling, for example, it becomes obvious that recognition of numerals from 1 to 12 is a necessary prerequisite. It is also clear that the clock is not the best place for teaching numeral recognition. The content task analysis signals the trainer to assess whether the intended learners recognize numerals from 1 to 12 and, if not, to have lessons on this (and other prerequisites) before entering the time-telling lesson. The logical extension of a content task analysis leads to a long sequence of lessons in those cases where many prerequisites are identified. In other cases, content can be acquired without mastering other skills in advance of the particular one being taught. In this sense the content task analysis has an almost diagnostic function of signaling what the trainer must look for in terms of prerequisite skills.

There is another diagnostic aspect to content task analysis. Most training begins with some opportunity for the learner to demonstrate what he already knows about the task. Either the task is presented for him to do, it is demonstrated once for

the learner to copy, or something else happens that allows the learner to show what he knows. When the learner can perform the task perfectly, that is obvious also. Most learners know something about most of the tasks that we teach them. Watching such a learner proceed through a task, after a content task analysis has been done, allows the trainer to clearly identify which components of the task the learner does and does not know. This is very helpful in focusing on what needs to be taught and evaluating how training is proceeding.

The data collection system which has been used in our research on skill training relies on the content task analysis. As illustrated below, each step in the analysis is written across the top of a data sheet. Positioned vertically are the training trials. During each cycle (i.e., trial) the trainer marks a symbol for correct, error, or correct with assist. Thus, in reviewing a data sheet the trainer knows the precise components of the skills that have been mastered or are causing problems. Errors should decrease with each additional trial. In some cases, however, they do not and revisions in the content task analysis (i.e., smaller steps) must be made.

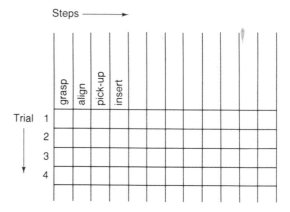

Cycle constancy. Another important reason for doing a content task analysis relates to the concept of cycle constancy. *Cycle constancy* is a term used in industry to describe a production situation in which the worker's series of motions are consistent each time he does whatever he does. Without a content task analysis it is almost impossible to clearly evaluate whether or not a series of motions is consistent each time an individual performs the task. Cycle constancy is a critical variable for training individuals who have been labeled severely or profoundly retarded. Establishing an invariant set of operations as the initial condition for training makes sense with this population. We have found in our research that moving from a cycle constant circumstance to a more generalized set of circumstances is more efficient than trying to teach the generalized set in the initial stages of training. Similarly, in manual tasks, the content task analysis allows the trainer to demand consistent use of the left and right hands, thereby making constant the movement cycle of the task. Random switching of hands makes acquisition of complex skills less efficient.

Example of content task analysis. One sample content task analysis is shown below to clarify the procedure. Purpose, materials, prerequisites, and how to teach the content are covered separately in this system.

Task: Winding bobbin of sewing machine

1. Release thread for spool
2. Place spool of thread on spool pin
3. Pull thread with left hand to thread guide hook
4. Wrap thread around hook (from back to front, ¾ revolution) and drop thread
5. Pick up bobbin with right hand (holes on top)
6. Put thread through one of the holes in bobbin (from under side)
7. Hold thread with right thumb on top of bobbin
8. Hand wrap thread around bobbin axle (2 full revolutions)
9. Place bobbin on winder spindle with holes up
10. Push bobbin to right to engage winder
11. Release coupling wheel (turn top to bottom, counterclockwise)
12. Step on foot control—lift foot when bobbin is full (machine will stop automatically when bobbin is full)
13. Push bobbin to left (disengage winder)
14. Retighten coupling wheel (turn clockwise)

The complexities of various tasks become evident when a content task analysis has been done. We have found two general qualities of tasks that, when identified, add considerably to our ability to design powerful training procedures. We refer to these as "information" and "judgment."

Information and Judgment

In the past, decisions about which tasks could and could not be taught to retarded individuals were based on estimates of the individuals' potential to learn (see Wolfensberger, 1967; Gold, 1973). This practice was plagued by inappropriately low expectation levels of training personnel (Gold, 1975). One contribution of a systematic task analysis approach is that it provides criteria for making such decisions on the basis of task characteristics and available training methods. That is, there are parameters which signal the trainer about the "teachability" of various tasks. An important example is the distinction between what we call *information* and *judgment*. This distinction has proven especially valuable in planning instructional methods for tasks that do not have cycle constancy (e.g., social skills). "Information" is discrete, dichotomous, and absolute. "Information" refers to situations in which a set of correct responses can be clearly specified. "Judgment" is not discrete. "Judgment" is used in circumstances in which there is a range of correct responses without discrete boundaries.

The distinction between information and judgment is sufficiently important to warrant a few examples. Take the task of putting 1-inch wooden cubes into a box. If you take one cube at a time and place it in the box, exactly 300 will fill the box. That is information. If there are 301, then one sticks up; 299, there is a 1-inch hole. That is information. If a supervisor says to a worker, "Hey, man, I'm not going to pay you to put one cube at a time in that box, just put all that stuff in there," the task changes. It turns out that, depending on how the cubes lie when thrown in, anywhere from 260 to 285 cubes fill the box. There is no exact number or even an exact appearance that says too few or too many cubes have been put in. It is a range of correctness without discrete, definable boundaries and as such comprises a judgmental task.

The difference between information and judgment is critical for several reasons. The first is that instructional technology is quite sophisticated for teaching information but provides little help for teaching judgment. In fact, the most common, systematic way to teach judgment is to restrict the range of acceptable performance. The learner is then given feedback which restricts his performance within these close boundaries, thus increasing the probability that subsequent performance will fall within the broader true range.

The second reason for distinguishing between information and judgment concerns job selection. For individuals with moderate, severe, and profound mental retardation, how can we "meaningfully" assess which jobs and which workers might go together? Looking at the information and judgmental aspects of tasks and jobs is quite revealing. For example, what is the simplest job in a gas station?: pump jockey, the person hired for $2 an hour to take care of the pumps. Let us look at this job from the perspective of hiring and training a person who is labeled severely retarded. Informational aspects of this job include squeezing the handle until certain numbers show up on the pump, taking the handle and putting it back on the pump, walking over to the window, collecting money from the customer, and returning proper change according to the amount of money listed on the pump. Judgmental aspects of this job include cleaning the windshield, conversing with the driver, giving directions, and cleaning the pump area. The job of pump jockey includes several critical tasks which are judgmental and very difficult to teach to someone who finds it difficult to learn.

Now let us look at the job of mechanic, which pays more than four times that of pump jockey. We estimate that a mechanic spends approximately 40% of his time in disassembly, 20% on diagnosis and evaluation, and about 40% on reassembly, correcting all of the problems. Disassembly for most things done by a mechanic is a semiskilled operation. Let us take a brake job as an example. The first two operations are judgmental, putting a car up on jacks and taking off the hubcaps. Now come the informational parts of this job: placing a small stool at the left front wheel; getting an air hose; taking an impact wrench off the wall and connecting the hose up to it; setting it for removal; putting it to each lug nut and removing each of the nuts; pulling the wheel off and setting it down; removing the dust cap on a front wheel bearing; removing the cotter pin, nut, and bearing; and pulling the drum off. To continue the job, the mechanic removes the springs, removes the shoes, takes the 7/16-inch wrench and removes the brake line, takes the same wrench and removes 4 bolts and the wheel cylinder, putting all these parts into a bucket. All of these steps are informational and, with readily available instructional procedures, we can teach them to individuals with severe and profound mental retardation. In the meantime the $14-an-hour mechanic has gone ahead and spent that 40% of his time putting other brake jobs together.

The information-judgment aspect of content task analysis indicates that jobs which have always been considered simple may present complex training problems. Other jobs which are seemingly more difficult involve many informational steps that can be readily taught. As Gold (1976) emphasized, the decision to teach or not teach any task to the severely/profoundly handicapped must be based on whether or not that task can be analyzed into teachable components rather than on some general feeling about the difficulty of the task. The concepts of information and judgment help the trainer to arrive at this decision.

Conclusion

Analyses of the world of work and vocational needs of the handicapped indicate the necessity for improvement in vocational education programs. The curriculum content must be designed to give students functional skills and the opportunities to use these skills in meaningful jobs. Once a curriculum is established, content analyses of specific tasks can be performed. Decisions regarding the particular skills to be emphasized in training and the instructional methods to be used should be made on the basis of what is learned from content task analyses.

References

Emshoff, J. G., Redd, W. H., & Davidson, W. S. Generalization training and the transfer of treatment effects with delinquent adolescents. *Journal of Behavior Therapy and Experimental Psychiatry,* 1976, *7,* 141–144.

Federal Register, April 16, 1976, *41*(75), 16147–16155.

Gold, M. W. Research on the vocational habilitation of the retarded: The present, the future. In N. R. Ellis (Ed.), *International review of research in mental retardation* (Volume 6). New York: Academic Press, 1973.

Gold, M. W. Vocational training. In J. Wortis (Ed.), *Mental retardation and developmental disabilities: An annual review* (Volume 7). New York: Brunner/Mazel, 1975.

Gold, M. W. Task analysis of a complex assembly task by the retarded blind. *Exceptional Children,* 1976, *43,* 78–84.

Kelly, J. M., & Simon, A. J. The mentally handicapped as workers. *Personnel,* 1969, *46*(5), 58–64.

Levy, S. M., Pomerantz, D. J., & Gold, M. W. Work skill development. In N. G. Haring & L. J. Brown (Eds.), *Teaching the severely handicapped* (Volume 2). New York: Grune & Stratton, 1977.

Parker, S. *The future of work and leisure.* London: McGivvon & Kee, 1971.

Phelps, L. A. *Instructional development for special needs.* Urbana, Ill.: University of Illinois, Department of Vocational and Technical Education, 1977.

Pomerantz, D. J., & Marholin, D. Vocational habilitation: A time for change in existing service delivery systems. In E. Sontag, N. Certo, & J. Smith (Eds.), *Educational programming for the severely handicapped.* Reston, Va.: Council for Exceptional Children, Division of Mental Retardation, 1977.

Redd, W. H. Attention span and generalization of task-related stimulus control: Effects of reinforcement contingencies. *Journal of Experimental Child Psychology,* 1972, *13*(3), 527–539.

Rincover, A., & Koegel, R. L. Setting generality and stimulus control in autistic children. *Journal of Applied Behavior Analysis,* 1975, *8,* 235–246.

Ryan, W. *Blaming the victim.* New York: Viking Press, 1971.

Stroud, R. R. *Work measurement in rehabilitation workshops: Time study and predetermined motion time systems.* Regional Rehabilitation Research Institute, University of Maryland, College Park, 1970, Technical Monograph No. 2.

Terkel, S. *Working: People talk about what they do all day and how they feel about what they do.* New York: Pantheon, 1974.

Wahler, R. G. Setting generality: Some specific and general effects of child behavior therapy. *Journal of Applied Behavior Analysis,* 1969, *2,* 239–246.

Wolfensberger, W. Vocational preparation and occupation. In A. A. Baumeister (Ed.), *Mental retardation: Appraisal, education, and rehabilitation.* Chicago: Aldine, 1967.

Notes

1. Greenleigh Associates. *The role of the sheltered workshop in the rehabilitation of the severely handicapped.* Report to the U.S. Department of Health, Education, and Welfare, Rehabilitation Services Administration, 1975.
2. Gold, M. W. *Meeting the needs of the handicapped.* Paper presented to the National Bicentennial Conference on Vocational Education, Minneapolis, Minn.: October 11, 1976.
3. Chaffin, J. D., & Clark, G. M. *Proceedings of organizing for cooperation: A multiagency conference.* Sponsored by Rehabilitation Services Administration, Kansas City, Mo.: July, 1973.
4. Pomerantz, D. J., & Redd, W. H. *Programming generalization through stimulus fading in one-to-one instruction with retarded children.* Unpublished manuscript, University of Illinois, 1977.
5. Reiss, S., & Redd, W. H. Suppression of screaming behavior in an emotionally disturbed, retarded child. *Proceedings of the American Psychological Association,* 1971, 741–742.

14

A Conceptual Analysis of Vocational Training

*This chapter was written by **Robert H. Horner** and **G. Thomas Bellamy,** University of Oregon.*

Teaching or training involves the manipulation of antecedent and consequent events to alter the probability that a particular response will follow a particular stimulus. This applies to teaching a child to produce a certain sound when presented with a letter, to teaching a college student the step-by-step process necessary for solving a calculus problem, or to teaching a severely retarded adult to complete a small parts assembly task. The child is to respond in the presence of a letter, the college student when given a calculus problem, and the retarded adult when presented with the unassembled parts of a task. If prior to instruction the learner did not perform correctly when presented with relevant stimuli and if after instruction she consistently does respond correctly, we infer that learning took place (Ellis, 1972).

The goal of most teaching, however, is not just to teach specific responses to specific stimuli but to teach skills that extend beyond the examples and setting used in instruction. Becker and Engelmann (1977) refer to this goal as teaching a "general case." "A general case has been taught when, after instruction on some tasks in a particular class, any task in that class can be performed correctly" (p. 1). The child produces appropriate sounds when presented with letters that are bigger, different in color, or in a different typeface from those seen in training. The college student uses the skills acquired during training to solve calculus problems never before encountered. The retarded adult uses skills (e.g., use of a screwdriver) acquired during training on one task to correctly assemble parts of other tasks. In each case skills acquired in the presence of one stimulus are performed in new or different contexts.

The value of teaching the general case to individuals learning to read or solve academic problems is obvious to educators (Engelmann, 1969). The importance of teaching the general case in vocational training with the severely retarded, however, has not been so obvious. The ability of the severely retarded to learn specific vocational skills is well documented (Bellamy, Peterson, & Close, 1975; Gold, 1972, 1976; Hunter & Bellamy, 1976; Jacobs, 1976; Martin & Flexer, Note 1), yet the adaptability of these responses remains unassessed. The purpose of this chapter is to explore the relevance of teaching the general case as described by Becker,

Preparation of this review was supported by grants from the U.S. Department of Health, Education, and Welfare, Developmental Disabilities Office, Region X, and the Bureau of Education for the Handicapped, Research Branch.

Engelmann, and their associates (Becker & Engelmann, 1977; Becker, Engelmann, & Thomas, 1975; Engelmann & Bruner, 1969; Engelmann & Carnine, 1969; Engelmann & Osborn, 1970) for vocational training with the severely and profoundly retarded. This chapter describes a model of vocational training and discusses the utility of the programming approach of Becker and Engelmann in light of this model.

A Vocational Training Model

Completion of most vocational tasks available to workshops involves repeated performance of a specific sequence of responses, or an *operant chain*. Each response in the chain must follow certain task-relevant stimuli and must be performed to an acceptable criterion. Training a severely retarded worker to complete the task involves teaching the precise topography of each response required by the task and bringing these under control of relevant stimuli.

Response topography

The topography of a response describes the specific movements or manipulations the worker must perform. Response topographies required by vocational tasks frequently involve grasping an object between the thumb and index finger, holding a tool with fingers and palm, rotating the hand, applying pressure with fingers, and flexing and relaxing biceps and triceps to lift and reach. The way in which these motor responses are combined defines the response being learned. For example, the response "tightening a screw with a screwdriver" is a function of many changes in muscle tension. Whereas the normal worker might be taught all of the aspects of this response simultaneously, a severely retarded worker may require instruction in the specific topography of each reaching, grasping, turning, and releasing aspect of the response. Training is incomplete if a worker has not learned to perform all required response topographies.

For some workers, a physical handicap or lack of dexterity may result in a particular response topography being extremely difficult or impossible to perform. For these workers at least two options exist. One involves the use of prosthetic task manipulation (i.e., fixtures or jigs); the other is extensive training in muscle control. Fixtures can be used to simply change the response demands of a task. Figure

14.1 shows a fixture constructed at the Specialized Training Program, a subcontract workshop for severely and profoundly retarded adults at the University of Oregon. This fixture allows a worker to use both hands to manipulate a screwdriver rather than using one hand to hold the assembly and the other to operate the screwdriver. By changing the response demands of the task, the fixture allows this worker to perform the task with response topographies that appeared easier for him.

The second option involves direct training of required movements. Recent research on biofeedback (Inman, in press) may be relevant to difficult training problems. This research suggests improved muscle control may be trained by manipulating the feedback a worker receives about the tension of his or her muscles. Further research in this area is currently needed to develop more practical vocational applications.

Stimulus control

To complete a task accurately a worker must not only perform the responses required by the task but perform those responses in a specific sequence. For appropriate sequencing to occur, the responses must each be under control of task-relevant stimuli. To the extent that this stimulus control exists, there will be a high likelihood that each set of task-relevant stimuli will be followed by the appropriate response.

Stimulus control describes the extent to which an antecedent stimulus functionally alters the probability of a conditioned response (Terrace, 1966). Two criteria have been identified as sufficient for development of stimulus control: (A) the learner's atten-

FIGURE 14.1   *Fixture used to assist adapter assembly by a severely retarded adult*

tion to relevant stimuli within the task and (B) differential reinforcement for correct responses (Skinner, 1969; Terrace, 1966). This suggests that stimuli of a work task will come to control task-relevant responses (A) if those stimuli are attended to by the worker and (B) if they set the occasion for reinforcing consequences when an appropriate response occurs.

An application of these stimulus control principles can be seen in the cam switch actuator pictured in Figure 14.2. The actuator is an oscilloscope part assembled by workers in the Specialized Training Program. The 77 steps required to assemble the cam are provided in Table 14.1. Steps 68–73 involve placing a .15 cm x 2.22 cm sheet metal screw in the only remaining hole on the cam housing and screwing it tight. This part of the task can be viewed as a response chain with 6 links or discriminated operants: (1) pick up a screw, (2) put the threaded end of the screw in the hole, (3) pick up the screwdriver by the handle, (4) put the point of the screwdriver in the head of the screw, (5) rotate the screwdriver in a clockwise direction until the screw is tight, and (6) put the screwdriver down. Each of these responses is cued by a task-relevant discriminative stimulus (S^D). The stimuli produced by performing the first response act as the S^D for

performing the second response. This pattern continues with the second response producing the S^D for the third, and so forth until the task is complete. The greater the probability of each response when its S^D is presented, the greater the degree of stimulus control that exists. Each response is defined by a particular topography and a criterion. The topography indicates how the response is to be performed. The criterion operationally defines the effect the response has on the environment (e.g., the criterion for rotating the screwdriver is met when the screw is tight). The task is learned when each of the six S^Ds in the chain is very likely to be followed by the appropriate response.

Figure 14.3 illustrates the chain of stimulus-response relationships that occur as this small task is performed. The empty hole in the cam housing and the loose screw serve as the discriminative stimuli (S^D), which set the occasion for picking up the screw (R_1). The criterion for this response is met when the worker is holding the screw in her hand. The stimuli provided by seeing and feeling the screw in hand also function, however, as the discriminative stimuli (S^D_2) for putting the screw in the hole (R_2). The criterion for this response is met when the threaded end of the screw is in the hole. The screw in the hole functions as the discriminative

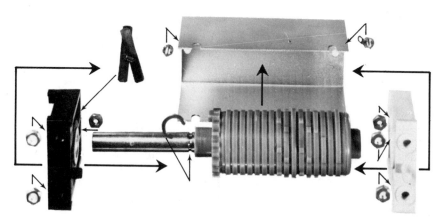

FIGURE 14.2   *Exploded and assembled views of a cam switch actuator #105–0465–00*

TABLE 14.1   *Task analysis for cam switch actuator #105–0465–00*

S^D	Response
1. 17 bins filled with task parts, tools	Move marker to bin 1
2. Marker in front of bin 1	Pick up one black bearing
3. Bearing in hand	Place on table with flange facing up and knob away
4. Bearing on table, flange up, knob away	Move marker to bin 2
5. Marker in front of bin 2	Place 2 large nuts on spots in front of marker
6. Nuts on spots	Pick up needle-nose pliers
7. Pliers in hand	Put 1 large nut in tip of pliers
8. Nut in pliers	Seat nut in open slot of bearing
9. Nut seated	Put other large nut in tip of pliers
10. Nut in pliers	Seat nut in remaining open slot of bearing
11. Nut seated	Rotate bearing so flange faces down
12. Flange down	Move marker to bin 3
13. Marker in front of bin 3	Pick up one small nut in tip of pliers
14. Nut in pliers	Seat nut in open slot of bearing
15. Nut seated	Put pliers on table
16. Pliers on table	Place bearing in jig, knob in right hole, flange facing left
17. Bearing in jig	Move marker to bin 4
18. Marker in front of bin 4	Pick up barrel
19. Barrel in hand	Place tongue of barrel into bearing, red notch visible through roller hole
20. Barrel in bearing	Move marker to bin 5
21. Marker in front of bin 5	Pick up retaining ring and place on apron, points facing away
22. Ring on apron	Pick up ring tool with writing facing up
23. Tool in hand	Slide tool over ring until ring holds
24. Ring in tool	Seat ring onto groove in barrel tongue
25. Ring seated	Put ring tool on table
26. Ring tool on table	Pick up pliers
27. Pliers in hand	Move marker to bin 6
28. Marker in front of bin 6	Use pliers to pick up 1 roller
29. Roller in pliers	Place roller in roller hole
30. Roller seated	Move marker to bin 7
31. Marker in front of bin 7	Pick up spring and place in pliers with black mark up
32. Spring in pliers	Rotate jig so barrel tongue faces away
33. Tongue facing away	Place spring in bearing
34. Spring seated	Move marker to bin 8
35. Marker in front of bin 8	Pick up spring and place in pliers with black mark up
36. Spring in pliers	Place spring in bearing on top of previous spring
37. Spring seated	Move marker to bin 9
38. Marker in front of bin 9	Pick up white bearing and place on table with knob away, holes facing up
39. Bearing on table	Move marker to bin 10
40. Marker in front of bin 10	Place 2 large nuts on spots in front of marker
41. Nuts on spots	Pick up pliers
42. Pliers in hand	Put 1 large nut in tip of pliers
43. Nut in pliers	Seat nut in 1 of the upper open slots in bearing
44. Nut seated	Put other large nut in tip of pliers
45. Nut in pliers	Seat nut in remaining upper bearing slot
46. Nut seated	Move marker to bin 11
47. Marker in front of bin 11	Put 1 small nut in tip of pliers

TABLE 14.1   *(Continued)*

S^D	Response
48. Nut in pliers	Seat nut in bottom bearing slot
49. Nut seated	Put pliers down
50. Pliers on table	Place bearing in jig, knob down, nuts facing in, barrel in bearing hole
51. Bearing in jig	Move marker to bin 12
52. Marker in front of bin 12	Pick up 1 case
53. Case in hand	Place case over bearings and barrel open end down, case lips in bearing slots
54. Case seated	Move marker to bin 13
55. Marker in front of bin 13	Pick up 1 lip washer
56. Lip washer in hand	Place lip washer over casing hole above white bearing, lip up
57. Lip washer over casing hole	Move marker to bin 14
58. Marker in front of bin 14	Pick up 1 screw
59. Screw in hand	Place screw threads in casing hole above white bearing
60. Screw in hole	Pick up torque screwdriver
61. Screwdriver in hand	Place nose of screwdriver in head of screw
62. Screwdriver in screw	Press down and rotate screwdriver in a clockwise direction until screw is tight (indicating 3 pounds of pressure)
63. Screw is tight	Place screwdriver on table
64. Screwdriver on table	Move marker to bin 15
65. Marker in front of bin 15	Pick up 1 flat washer
66. Washer in hand	Place washer over casing hole above blade bearing
67. Washer over casing hole	Move marker to bin 16
68. Marker in front of bin 16	Pick up 1 screw
69. Screw in hand	Put the threaded end of the screw in the hole
70. Screw in hole	Pick up screwdriver by the handle
71. Screwdriver in hand	Put the point of the screwdriver in head of screw
72. Screwdriver in screw	Rotate screwdriver in a clockwise direction until screw is tight
73. Screw is tight	Put the screwdriver down
74. Screwdriver on table	Move marker to bin 17
75. Marker in front of bin 17	Pick up 1 plastic bag with open end facing up
76. Bag in hand	Place completed cam in bag
77. Cam in bag	Place cam and bag in box and raise hand

stimulus (S^D_3) for the next response (R_3), picking up the screwdriver. Performance of this response produces stimuli (S^D_4) which cue the next response (R_4) and so on, until the worker completes the task and lays down the screwdriver. At this point the chain ends, and a reinforcer (S^{R+}) in the form of food, praise, tokens, or wages typically is delivered. The reinforcer, delivered at the end of the chain, serves to maintain control of each response in the chain (Kelleher, 1966). As the chain develops, additional reinforcement is provided by the fact that

each S^D within the chain comes to function as a reinforcing consequence for the previous response (e.g., S^D_2 serves as a conditioned reinforcer for R_1 and S^D_3 serves to reinforce R_2, etc.). To achieve this situation the chain must terminate with a reinforcer (S^{R+}) as indicated below.

Within this model, (A) each response is cued by a different S^D; (B) each response has a criterion which defines the next S^D; (C) each S^D serves both to reinforce the previous response and to set the occasion for the next response; and (D) mainte-

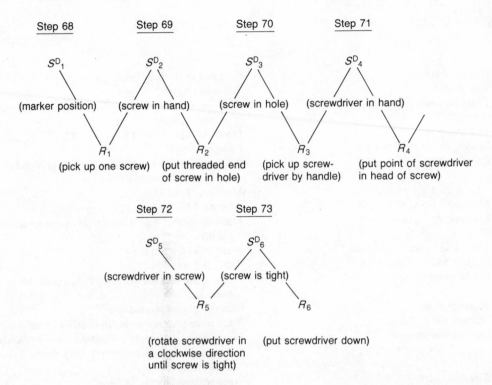

FIGURE 14.3   *Operant chain defined by steps 68–73 of task analysis for cam switch actuator #105–0465–00*

nance of the entire chain is dependent upon the terminal reinforcer.

Development of an operant chain is typically accomplished through a systematic application of shaping, fading, and differential reinforcement procedures. Successive approximations of desired responses are differentially reinforced, and trainer assistance in the form of physical priming, modeling, and verbal cues is gradually decreased (Bellamy, Inman, & Schwarz, in press; Screven, Straka, & LaFond, 1971).

Utility of the Model

Vocational training procedures based on this or similar models have been used to teach an impressive array of tasks to severely retarded workers (Bellamy et al., 1975; Crosson, 1967; Gold, 1976; Martin & Flexer, Note 1). However, retarded workers must not only learn vocational skills but often must learn these skills quickly. The time necessary for training a worker is especially important when industrial demands (e.g., short-lived contracts) require that several successive tasks be learned over a short time period. The cam switches assembled at the Specialized Training Program workshop are of a wide vari-

ety (see Figure 14.4). Though similar in many respects, each requires some unique responses. It is not uncommon for the contractor to require that a new cam be learned and a substantial quantity assembled within a 4-day period. A significant factor in a retarded worker's ability to respond to demands such as these will be the degree to which skills learned on one task transfer to other tasks with similar response requirements.

The question this raises is how learning within one stimulus context affects later performance in another. This is not an issue unique to training the severely retarded. It has been addressed in a variety of reports on transfer of training (Gray & Fygetakis, 1968; House & Zeaman, 1960), development of learning sets (Harlow, 1949; Sahakian, 1970), and stimulus generalization (Lovaas, Koegel, Simmons, & Long, 1973; Terrace, 1966). This research has generally emphasized the effects of similarity among stimuli in the training and transfer tasks. If two tasks require similar responses (e.g., threading nuts on bolts) and the stimuli cuing these responses are similar (e.g., unassembled nuts and bolts), then training on the first task will generally facilitate acquisition of the second. This research emphasizes

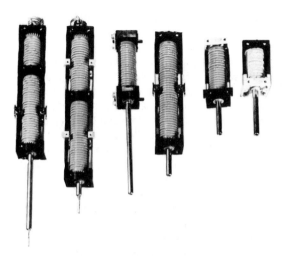

FIGURE 14.4 *Six different cam switches assembled at the Specialized Training Program*

the effects of task variables. It suggests a worker should be assigned successive tasks which have common stimulus characteristics serving as discriminative stimuli for common responses if the time required to train later tasks is of concern. This could involve, for example, assigning a series of circuit boards to a worker (Merwin, 1974). Many circuit board tasks provide similar polarity, position, or match-to-sample cues for similar component insertion responses.

An alternative analysis of the effects that learning one task have on acquisition of other tasks emphasizes the effects that training procedures have on facilitating positive transfer. This approach is the focus of the present chapter. It builds from an operant model of response acquisition and the educational movement toward direct instruction (Becker et al., 1975; Carnine & Bateman, 1977).

Becker and Engelmann (1977) maintain that performance on novel tasks is functionally related to two variables: (A) the similarities between the new task and previously learned tasks and (B) the extent to which the general case was taught in previous training. A general case can be taught with respect to classes of stimuli or classes of responses. When a general case is taught with respect to a class of stimuli, a *concept* has been taught. When a general case has been taught with respect to a class of responses, an *operation* has been taught (Becker, 1971; Becker & Engelmann, 1977; Becker et al., 1975). If vocational training with the severely and profoundly retarded is to provide viable work skills,

trainers will need to identify and teach the concepts and operations required by the tasks which an individual is likely to encounter.

Concepts

Within any universe of stimulus instances, unique classes of stimuli can be identified. The members of a particular class of stimuli are identified by the common stimulus characteristics they possess. Members of the stimulus class "crescent wrenches" may vary across characteristics such as texture, size, position in space, smell, and many more, but they are all objects with a crescent wrench shape (see Figure 14.5). If an individual is taught to perform a particular response (e.g., pick up, adjust, or any other response) when presented with a crescent wrench, and after training with some crescent wrenches responded in the same way to all members of the class "crescent wrenches," we could say she had learned the general case or the "concept." The "concept" is defined by the stimulus characteristics uniquely common to members of that class. Each stimulus possessing the relevant set of characteristics is an *instance* of that concept. Any stimulus not possessing all the relevant characteristics is a noninstance of that concept.

Defining a concept based on stimulus characteristics unique to instances of that concept allows differentiation between instances and noninstances of the concept within any universe of objects or stimuli. The degree of specificity with which the stimulus characteristics need to be labeled, however, are dictated by the similarity between instances and noninstances in the stimulus universe. If noninstances are considerably different from instances, discrimination of instances and noninstances can be made on the basis of only a few relevant stimulus characteristics. Instances of the concept "crescent wrench" can be discriminated from a universe of crescent wrenches, coats, axe handles, pencils, and glue very easily because there are several obvious stimulus differences between crescent wrenches and all other members of this universe. To identify crescent wrenches, a learner

FIGURE 14.5 *A crescent wrench*

needs to attend to the meta! construction or the shape or the adjustability of the objects. However, if the universe consisted of crescent wrenches, pliers, pipe wrenches, and socket wrenches, the stimulus characteristics necessary to define an instance of "crescent wrench" would require more detailed specification; only the shape of the various objects provides a reliable means of identifying members of the concept "crescent wrench."

A second characteristic of concept analysis is that identification of an instance requires a double discrimination process. When presented with all members of a stimulus universe and asked to specify which are instances of a particular concept, the learner must (A) discriminate which stimulus characteristics are relevant for identifying instances and (B) use those relevant characteristics to identify which elements of the universe meet the stimulus requirements of an instance. In the above example, identification of all instances of "crescent wrench" would require that the learner (A) attend to shape characteristics of objects while ignoring size, color, orientation, and position characteristics and (B) examine each member of the universe and respond only to those shaped like crescent wrenches.

The dual discrimination analysis of concept learning may be a valuable method of identifying relationships between a worker's error patterns and training procedures. A worker who consistently performs incorrectly may be either attending to irrelevant stimulus dimensions or simply failing to discriminate instances from noninstances along the relevant dimensions. It is possible these two potential sources of error will require different strategies for remediation.

Concept analysis expands the model of vocational tasks as response chains. In concept teaching, responses are conditioned to classes of stimulus characteristics rather than specific stimuli. A response in the chain no longer follows a particular S^D but any S^D from a stimulus class (S^D_i). In a response chain where specific responses are under concept control, each S^D in the model is replaced by a stimulus class.

The way in which concept learning expands the versatility of conditioned responses can be seen by examining a small part of the cam switch assembly. Figure 14.4 shows 8 different bearings used in assembling cam switches at the Specialized Training Program. The bearings differ in shape, color, and construction material. Each bearing is made of molded plastic or metal and at least one flat surface contains several holes. These holes vary in shape, size, location on the bearing, and depth. Three or four of these holes in each bearing form slots into which a .15 x .45 cm hex nut fits snugly. As is apparent in Figure 14.4 these slots vary in their position on the bearing and in their overall configuration.

One response in assembly of a cam switch is to place a hex nut in each empty slot of two or three different bearings. If this hex nut insertion response were brought under control of specific stimuli associated with a single slot in the first bearing in Figure 14.6, it is likely that some trainees would not per-

FIGURE 14.6   *Eight bearings used in assembly of different cam switches*

form the behavior in response to stimuli provided by other slots on that bearing or by slots in other positions on different bearings. In the formulation of vocational tasks as simple response chains, the stimuli controlling the next insertion response could be very specific, as indicated below:

$$S^D_1$$

(Bearing number one with an empty hex nut slot in the upper left corner)

$$R_1$$

(Insert hex nut in slot)

If this same response is under control of a concept, any stimulus which was an instance of the concept "empty slot" would control the response. The unique stimulus characteristics defining instances of the concept are (A) a cam bearing and (B) an empty hex slot of the appropriate size. Bearing size, shape, color, or position in the cam and location of the slot in the bearing are all irrelevant. If the response "place a hex nut in the open hex slot" is under control of a concept, the stimuli controlling the response could vary across all irrelevant dimensions. All stimuli with the relevant characteristics would form a stimulus class (S^D_i) with any member of that class controlling placement of the hex nut.

$$S^D_i$$

(*Any* bearing with an empty hex nut slot in any position)

$$R_1$$

(Place hex nut in slot)

Teaching Concepts

Concept teaching involves the manipulation of antecedent and consequent events in an effort to change the probability that an individual will emit certain responses only in the presence of instances of a concept. To achieve this end: (A) present a set of instances and noninstances rather than a single instance; (B) ensure that, within the set of instances and noninstances, instances share all the relevant stimulus characteristics and noninstances possess none or only some of the relevant characteristics; (C) vary irrelevant stimulus characteristics (this will facilitate responding only to relevant characteristics); (D) when several relevant characteristics are required to define a concept, present the characteristics in a cumulative fashion, starting with only one, then adding a second, a third, etc. (require the learner to meet a response criterion at each level of this cumulative progression); (E) provide differential reinforcement for appropriate responses.

An oversimplified example of teaching a concept can be seen in a task demanding that hex nuts, regardless of size and color, be sorted from a bin of hex nuts, square nuts, bolts, washers, and clamps.

The concept being taught is "hex nut." To teach the concept "hex nut": (A) present the worker with both hex nuts (instances) and bolts, washers, square nuts, and clamps (noninstances) during training trials; (B) instances should all share the common characteristics of being six-sided, flat, and having a threaded hole in the middle; noninstances should possess none or only some of these characteristics; (C) when training the worker to respond to instances of the concept "hex nut," do not use just one hex nut—use several that are of different size and color so the worker learns that size and color are not relevant characteristics; (D) if a more complex sorting task requires the worker to sort out only brass hex nuts, first teach the order to sort hex nuts from nonhex nuts, next teach sorting of brass hex nuts from nonbrass hex nuts and then sorting of brass hex nuts from all the other parts; (E) throughout the teaching process, reinforce the worker only when she responds in the presence of hex nuts. Ignore or correct all incorrect responses.

Concept teaching is a logical extrapolation of traditional procedures for teaching discriminations. As in discrimination training, differential reinforcement is used to obtain stimulus control of specific responses. In concept training, however, those responses are not brought under the control of a specific stimulus but of a set of stimulus characteristics. The major difference between teaching concepts and traditional discrimination training is the particular manipulation of antecedent events. Concept teaching requires presentation of both a greater number and more varied set of training examples.

Teaching concepts is advantageous if the learner will need to perform newly acquired skills when presented with stimuli not experienced in the training setting. Retarded adults in vocational workshops have generally performed specific task-related responses to specific task-related stimuli. As workers are expected to perform multiple tasks and use training received on one task to facilitate performance on other tasks, additional attention will need to be given to the programming variables affecting concept learning.

Operations

An *operation* is defined by the common response characteristics of a set of responses under stimulus control (Becker & Engelmann, 1977). An individual response is not an operation; rather, it is an instance of an operation. The operation itself is defined by the common effect, or characteristics, of the response class. Just as concepts are defined by the common characteristics of stimuli, so operations are defined by the common effect, or characteristics, of the response class.

The operation "writing" might include response instances of writing letters, writing memos, writing with a pencil, or writing with a pen. These responses are under stimulus control and have the common effect of producing words on a page. Similarly, the operation "soldering" can be seen as a class of responses which have a common effect and are under stimulus control. Any set of responses which begins with separated objects and ends with objects being soldered together would be an instance of the operation "soldering." The response class defining soldering would be comprised of all possible sets of responses which begin with separated objects and end with objects connected by solder.

As with most vocationally viable operations, any instance of soldering will involve a set of responses (i.e., reaching for the soldering iron, picking up the soldering iron, placing the iron on the object(s) to be soldered, etc.). Becker and Englemann identify these responses as *component operations.* Each is under separate stimulus control and is a member of a response class with a common effect. For example, lifting the soldering iron would be an instance of the component operation "picking up an object." Becker et al. (1975) have noted the importance of component operations for programming. They imply that a long-term objective for individuals involved in vocational training must be the identification of a minimum number of responses that can be used as building blocks for a maximum number of vocational operations.

A response class can be under stimulus control of a single discriminative stimulus or under control of a concept. If a concept is taught, any member of a stimulus class will set the occasion for a specific response. In operation learning a stimulus will set the occasion for any instance of a class of responses. When the two are combined, any of a class of stimulus instances will set the occasion for a particular class of responses. When teaching the general task "put this object on that object," both concepts and operations are involved. The object concepts for the task must be learned and a set of responses having the common effect of object A ending up on object B will be learned. The learner comes to discriminate the relevant stimulus charac-

teristics which define the concepts, of which objects A and B are instances, and also learns that appropriate responding is dictated not by particular responses but by the common effects of responding across trials (i.e., object A ending up on object B).

One operation required in assembling a cam switch involves placement of a retaining ring. Figure 14.7 shows two different cams which require this operation. In each case a tool is used to place a retaining ring on a groove in the cam barrel. In each case the effect of this response is that the bearing is fastened to the cam barrel. The way in which the ring is placed, however, varies for the two cams. In cam 7A the closed side of the ring is placed on a groove in the tool and the tool is then used to push the ring around the groove; in cam 7B the open end of the ring is held by two points on the tool and the tool is used in a plierlike fashion to spread the ring and place it in the groove. The set of responses required for placing the ring in the second cam differ significantly from those in the first. Both sets of responses, however, produce a common effect (i.e., ring snaps into groove, fastening the bearing to the barrel). This common effect suggests that placement of the ring on cam 7A and placement of the ring on cam 7B are members of a response class (placement of retaining rings) which defines a single operation.

The addition of operations to the model of a response chain greatly expands the versatility of the model. The designation of a particular response R is replaced by a class of responses R_a which define the operation. A response chain composed of concepts and operations (such as that required for

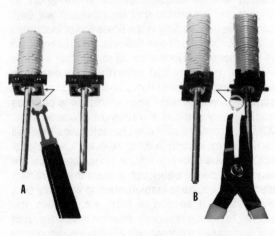

FIGURE 14.7   *Two instances of the operation "placement of retaining ring"*

placement of retaining rings) contains a wide variety of stimulus and response possibilities, all of which comprise a conditioned sequence of behavior.

Within this model, presentation of any member from the stimulus class *i* will set the occasion for a response from the response class *a*. This response will be consequated by a stimulus from the stimulus class *j* and that stimulus will also set the occasion for a response from the response class *b*. This response will be consequated with a reinforcer (S^{R+}). In general this model represents a generalized response chain in which concepts and operations are learned.

Teaching Operations

Procedures for teaching operations follow logically from those described for teaching concepts: (1) the learner is presented with task-relevant stimuli and prompted to perform appropriately; (2) differential reinforcement and corrections are used to define the relevant response effects; (3) a sequence of responses is required which systematically contrasts the effects of the operation being taught from those of alternate operations. Prill (Note 2) applied these procedures to teach the operation of using a socket wrench to a severely retarded adult: (1) she presented the worker initially with one task which required that the correct socket head be selected from 8 different sizes, fit onto a socket handle, and used to remove a hex nut; (2) if the worker performed correctly, he was praised. If he performed incorrectly, he was corrected; (3) several additional tasks were presented which varied in size, position, and orientation of the nut or bolt. These tasks allowed comparison across tasks of the common effects of the different responses. Even though the worker had to find a socket size he had not used

before and manipulate the wrench in a novel position on new tasks (e.g., from the side rather than the top), he was able to perform accurately with little or no training after learning the first few tasks. This demonstrates the worker's acquisition of the operation of using a socket wrench to remove a nut or bolt.

Implications for Vocational Training

Teaching the general case with respect to concepts and operations appears to have several possible implications for vocational habilitation of the severely retarded. Of particular relevance is the potential impact teaching the general case may have on procedures for vocational training, task analysis, and prevocational programming.

Vocational Training

Severely retarded adults have been taught a variety of vocational skills in workshop programs. However, the competitive industrial community in which these workshops must function places additional demands on training procedures. To be successful, workers generally need to learn a variety of tasks. In addition, this learning frequently must be completed in a short time period. Teaching the general case may be one way of responding to these demands.

Several concepts and operations can be identified as likely to be required on tasks available to a workshop. This list includes the performance of operations (e.g., rotating a nut until tight or using a screwdriver or soldering iron) or differential response to concepts (e.g., placing the curved side

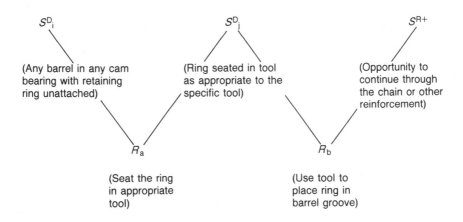

S^{D}_{i} S^{D}_{j} S^{R+}

(Any barrel in any cam bearing with retaining ring unattached)

(Ring seated in tool as appropriate to the specific tool)

(Opportunity to continue through the chain or other reinforcement)

R_{a} R_{b}

(Seat the ring in appropriate tool)

(Use tool to place ring in barrel groove)

up) (Gold, 1972) or matching assembly steps to pictures of the completed task (DeBriere, Note 3).

Teaching such concepts and operations generally requires more time than does instruction on the specific requirements of a single task, since more examples are used to discriminate instances from noninstances. Practically, therefore, the extra time required to teach a concept or operation will be justified only when there is a reasonable likelihood that it will facilitate performance on later tasks the worker might encounter inside or outside the workshop. To determine whether to teach specific skills or the general case involves some estimation of the behavioral requirements of future tasks. Frequently it is possible to identify concepts and operations that apply across tasks, especially when a variety of similar tasks, like circuit boards (Merwin, 1974), cable harnesses (Hunter & Bellamy, 1976), or cam switches are available. Once concepts and operations are identified in such tasks, systematic instruction can be designed to teach not just specific instances of a concept or operation but the general case. For instance, if several soldering jobs are anticipated, a worker could be taught not just one soldering task but several different tasks, each of which involves different responses and different stimuli but each of which results in two parts being soldered together. In this way, the adaptability of a severely retarded worker's skills to realistic work settings might be enhanced.

Training which emphasizes acquisition of concepts and operations also may assist the workshop staff in assessing which workers are able to learn new tasks quickly. By comparing the generalized skills learned by workers with the skills required by different tasks, a meshing of task demands and worker competencies can be made. While this would be but one of the variables to consider in assigning a worker to a task, it could be a useful one for workshops dealing with many short-term contracts.

Task analysis

Another implication teaching the general case has for training severely retarded people is in the construction of task analyses. The term *task analysis* has been used to label a variety of pretraining and training procedures. It is used here simply to indicate the breakdown of a task into component steps and the sequencing of those steps. The component steps generally indicate the responses required by the task. They are in effect the *R*'s in an operant chain:

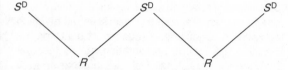

Each of these responses, however, is also one instance of an operation, and following training will be under control of some specific stimulus or of a concept. If training is being conducted not just to develop skill on the specific task at hand but to train a generalized skill, then the task analysis should indicate not simply a response for each step but the characteristics of the class of responses (i.e., operation) which are acceptable. Similarly, the trainer should be aware of the characteristics of the class of stimuli (concept) that must come to control responding.

The advantage of utilizing concepts and operations in task analysis is readily apparent in a task which requires soldering. Acceptable solder connections seldom result from repetition of exactly the same movements on task after task. Rather, a class of responses must be taught which is under the stimulus control of characteristics of the melting solder. By specifying this class of responses and its common effect (an acceptable solder connection), the task analysis becomes a much more accurate reflection of actual task demands than would be possible if the analysis were limited to simple responses.

Analysis of a task into concepts and operations has two functions. The first pertains to the way tasks are designed for production. Most tasks can be performed in a variety of different ways. In selecting an assembly method from these options, one relevant concern might be the extent to which concepts and operations were utilized to reduce the number of different movements or discriminations required. For example, the ballpoint pen shown in Figure 14.8 can be assembled by preparing the upper and lower sections of the pen separately and then putting them together as shown in 14.8A. This approach requires a variety of dissimilar responses. An alternative approach, shown in 14.8B, requires only two operations (pick up and put on) which are performed with each part. By designing the task to be performed in this latter fashion, several responses with a similar effect are performed. It is likely this approach would facilitate training of the pen assembly.

A second benefit which occurs when a task is analyzed into concepts and operations is that the

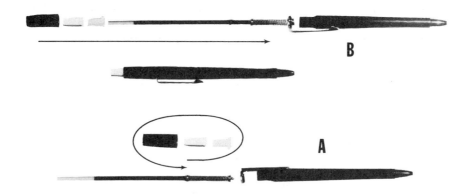

FIGURE 14.8   *Two ways of assembling a ballpoint pen*

trainer gains a clear picture of the range of examples the worker will need to experience in order to acquire a generalized skill. When the objective is to teach a generalized skill, this range will typically extend beyond the stimuli available in any one task. If the training is designed to make use of previous acquisition of concepts and operations, the task analysis will indicate the range of examples within a task that need to be experienced. The range of examples will be a function of the number of irrelevant stimuli or response characteristics that must be varied to facilitate performance of certain responses in certain stimulus contexts.

Prevocational programming

Many facilities serving the severely retarded define their goals in terms of preparing their clients for vocational placement. Typically, skills are taught which are identified as prerequisites for entering a sheltered workshop. These frequently range from simple tasks, such as sorting or folding, to training in language, self-help, and community living skills. Labeling these skills as prerequisites for vocational training implies that individuals incapable of performing these skills will not be able to master complex vocational tasks. Current research assessing the vocational potential of the severely retarded has clearly indicated that many such "prevocational" skills are not necessary precursors of remunerative vocational employment (Bellamy et al., in press). Workers with very little language, minimal self-help skills, and no previous vocational preparation have been able both to learn complex tasks and to perform them consistently over long periods of time (Bellamy et al., 1975; Bellamy, Inman, & Yeates, Note 4). It is becoming increasingly clear that while

these "prevocational" skills are valuable in their own right, they need not be classified as prerequisite skills.

Research demonstrating the competence of severely retarded adults to perform complex vocational tasks opens up new alternatives for prevocational facilities. The focus can now shift to training skills that will be directly functional in anticipated vocational settings. This creates a need to both identify those skills most commonly used in workshops and then teach them. Given, however, that the specific vocational placement of any one worker is difficult to predict, it will not be sufficient to simply teach a worker to perform one task or two. Those tasks may or may not be useful to the worker upon placement. From the viewpoint of teaching the general case, it would seem more functional to identify the most commonly used concepts and operations the worker may encounter and teach them as generalized skills.

This approach involves a two-step process. First, a workshop or school program needs to assess the tasks that are available within its specific area. Then, the concepts and operations most used across those tasks need to be identified. While this list would vary from region to region, it might include operations involving tool use (e.g., screwdriver, pliers, soldering iron) or basic assembly (e.g., putting on, screwing a screw or bolt, using a bin set-up to sequence parts for assembly).

However, even if a worker can perform some of these task-relevant operations when she enters a vocational setting, a certain amount of training will be required. It is likely that concepts and operations which are most useful to such a worker would relate to knowing how to obtain information in a training setting. Bellamy, Oliver, and Oliver (in press) suggest that matching a sample is one such operation. This would fit with literature indicating the value of teaching generalized imitation skills in language training (Sloane & MacAulay, 1968). Other operations that may facilitate training include following physical primes, physical or verbal cues, requesting assistance, and following instructions.

As prevocational workshops and public school programs for the severely retarded become more involved in training complex vocational tasks, there will be an increasing need to identify the specific skills a curriculum should address. While this analysis should be sensitive to the requirements of local communities (i.e., rural vs. urban), it should also identify concepts and operations which are useful across a wide range of vocational settings.

A prevocational program for the severely retarded will need not only to identify relevant skills but to implement programming procedures which maximize the utility of skills that are learned. This programming involves defining concepts and operations that are relevant to vocational performance, sequencing these to identify longitudinal instructional objectives, and then designing specific materials to teach each concept and operation. Becker et al. (1975) provide an excellent summary of this process in their discussion of academic skills. Operations should be taught not just as specific manipulations of specific objects but as a set of responses, any of which is appropriate if a certain effect is obtained. Similarly, the operations learned will be most useful if they are applied across a class of stimuli with common characteristics (a concept) rather than limited to specific stimuli.

For example, in teaching the operation of manipulating parts to match samples, the teacher must do more than teach the learner to match one particular object to a model. Teaching the general case would require that a number of different tasks with different stimuli be presented. The specific responses necessary to match a model (i.e., rotate, turn over, place next to, etc.) will change depending upon the characteristics of each sample. The effect of the responses, however, will always be to manipulate one part so it matches a sample. To the extent that the matching response is performed across a variety of stimuli, the match-to-sample operation would be under control of a concept. Training of this nature could greatly facilitate the worker's ability to adapt to a workshop environment in which match-to-sample procedures are used to train new tasks. It is suggested here that teaching the general case with respect to concepts and operations such as those required for matching-to-sample may better equip a worker for active employment than training on one or two simulated tasks.

Conclusion

The vocational potential of severely retarded individuals is being repeatedly confirmed, and the need for well-structured programming of vocational training is apparent. Since many workshop tasks require generalized as well as specific vocational skills, careful consideration should be given to programming and training procedures. Research assessing acquisition of reading and arithmetic skills with disadvantaged children has focused on similar programming needs (Abt Associates, 1976; Becker & Engelmann, 1977; Stallings, 1975). The techniques developing from this research have impressively demonstrated the importance of teaching concepts and operations. The teaching of concepts and operations in vocational settings may be as advantageous as proponents of direct instruction feel they are for teaching reading and arithmetic. These potential advantages surely warrant further empirical assessment.

References

Abt Associates. *Education as experimentation: A planned variation model* (Volume 3). Boston: Author, 1976.

Becker, W. C. *An empirical basis for change in education.* Chicago: Science Research Associates, 1971.

Becker, W., & Engelmann, S. Systems for basic instruction: Theory and application. In T. A. Brigham & A. C. Catania (Eds.), *Applied behavioral research.* New York: John Wiley & Sons, 1977.

Becker, W., Engelmann, S., & Thomas, D. *Teaching: A course in applied psychology.* Chicago: Science Research Associates, 1971.

Becker, W., Engelmann, S., & Thomas, D. *Teaching 2: Cognitive learning and instruction.* Chicago: Science Research Associates, 1975.

Bellamy, G. T., Inman, D., & Schwarz, R. Vocational training and production supervision: A review of habilitation techniques for the severely and profoundly retarded. In N. Haring and D. Bricker (Eds.), *Teaching the severely and profoundly handicapped* (Volume 3). Columbus: Charles E. Merrill, in press.

Bellamy, G. T., Oliver, P. R., & Oliver, D. D. "Operations" in vocational training for the severely retarded. In C. Cleland, L. Talkington, & J. Schwartz (Eds.), *Research on the profoundly retarded: A conference proceedings* (Volume 3). Austin, Tex.: Western Research Conference, in press.

Bellamy, G. T., Peterson, L., & Close, D. Habilitation of the severely and profoundly retarded: Illustrations of competence. *Education and Training of the Mentally Retarded,* 1975, *10,* 174–186.

Carnine, D., & Bateman, B. Direct instruction—DISTAR. In N. Haring & B. Bateman (Eds.), *Teaching the learning disabled child.* Englewood Cliffs, N. J.: Prentice-Hall, 1977.

Crosson, J. *The experimental analysis of vocational behavior in severely retarded males.* Final report, Grant No. OEG32–47–0230–6024. Washington, D. C.: Department of Health, Education and Welfare, 1967.

Ellis, H. C. *Fundamentals of human learning and cognition.* Dubuque, Iowa: Wm. C. Brown, 1972.

Engelmann, S. *Conceptual learning.* San Rafael, Calif.: Dimension, 1969.

Engelmann, S., & Bruner, A. *DISTAR reading level I.* Chicago: Science Research Associates, 1969.

Engelmann, S., & Carnine, D. *DISTAR arithmetic level I.* Chicago: Science Research Associates, 1969.

Engelmann, S., & Osborn, J. *DISTAR language level I.* Chicago: Science Research Associates, 1970.

Gold, M. W. Stimulus factors in skill training on a complex assembly task: Acquisition, transfer and retention. *American Journal of Mental Deficiency,* 1972, *76,* 517–526.

Gold, M. W. Task analysis of a complex assembly task by the retarded blind. *Exceptional Children,* 1976, *43*(20), 78–84.

Gray, B., & Fygetakis, L. The development of language as a function of programmed conditioning. *Behavior Research and Therapy,* 1968, *6,* 455–460.

Harlow, H. F. The formation of learning sets. *Psychological Review,* 1949, *56,* 52–65.

House, B. J., & Zeaman, D. Transfer of discrimination from objects to patterns. *Journal of Experimental Psychology,* 1960, *59,* 298–302.

Hunter, J., & Bellamy, G. T. Cable harness construction for severely retarded adults: A demonstration of training technique. *AAESPH Review,* 1976, *1*(7), 2–13.

Inman, D. P. Gaining control over tension in spastic muscles. *Proceedings of the ninth Banff conference on behavior modification.* New York: Brunner/Mazel, in press.

Jacobs, J. W. Retarded persons as gleaners. *Mental Retardation,* 1976, *14*(6), 42–43.

Kelleher, R. T. Chaining and conditioned reinforcement. In W. K. Honig (Ed.), *Operant behavior: Areas of research and application.* New York: Appleton-Century-Crofts, 1966.

Lovaas, O. I., Koegel, R. L., Simmons, J. Q., & Long, J. S. Some generalization and follow-up measures on autistic children in behavior therapy. *Journal of Applied Behavior Analysis,* 1973, *6,* 131–165.

Merwin, M. R. The effect of pretraining upon the training and transfer of circuit board assembly skills of retarded adults (Doctoral dissertation, University of Illinois, 1974). *Dissertation Abstracts International,* 1974, *35* (12), 6136B.

Sahakian, W. S. *Psychology of learning: Systems, models and theories.* Chicago: Marlan, 1970.

Screven, C., Straka, J., & LaFond, R. Applied behavioral technology in a vocational rehabilitation setting. In W. Gardner (Ed.), *Behavior modification in mental retardation.* Chicago: Aldine, 1971.

Sloane, H. N., & MacAulay, B. D. (Eds.). *Operant procedures in remedial speech and language training.* New York: Houghton-Mifflin, 1968.

Skinner, B. F. *Contingencies of reinforcement: A theoretical analysis.* New York: Appleton-Century-Crofts, 1969.

Stallings, J. Implementation and child effects of teaching practices in Follow Through classrooms. *Monographs of the Society for Research in Child Development,* 1975, *40*(7–8, Serial No. 163).

Terrace, J. S. Stimulus control. In W. K. Honig (Ed.), *Operant behavior: Areas of research and application.* New York: Appleton-Century-Crofts, 1966.

Notes

1. Martin, A. S., & Flexer, R. W. *Three studies on training work skills and work adjustment* (Monograph No. 5). Lubbock, Texas: Texas Tech University, Research and Training Center in Mental Retardation.
2. Prill, N. *Evaluation of a procedure for teaching tool use operations to a severely retarded person.* University of Oregon, 1977.
3. DeBriere, T. *Meaningful institutional training.* Paper presented at the American Association on Mental Deficiency Annual Convention, Chicago, Illinois, June 1976.
4. Bellamy, G. T., Inman, D., & Yeates, J. *Workshop supervision: Evaluation of a procedure for production management with the severely retarded.* University of Oregon, 1977.

Introduction to Chapter 15

New parents of severely handicapped children stand on a precarious ledge. Unable to accept and understand at first, they naturally must want to reject.

> It is not true that retarded (brain damaged, idiot, feeble-minded, emotionally disturbed, autistic) children are the necessary favorites of their parents or that they are always uncommonly beautiful and lovable, for Derek, our youngest child, is not especially good-looking, and we do not love him at all. (We would prefer not to think about him. We don't want to talk about him.) (Heller, 1966, p. 334)

Only later can they gain their balance and perhaps grow to accept the child as one with handicaps.

> I take him everywhere with me; if people don't like it, it's up to them to close their ears and walk away. He's got a right to be on this earth as much as they have. (Hannam, 1975, p. 47)

As teachers we often refer to the students in our classroom possessively as "our kids." Yet during a student's years in school, we, as teachers, are responsible for only about 20% of that student's waking hours. By comparison 80% of the student's life is under the influence of the home—parents, siblings, relatives, family friends—the neighborhood, and the community. The home influence has a greater advantage than simple frequency, it tends to be consistent for most children; that is, interactions are with a small, constant number of family members. By contrast the school's influence fluctuates from one teacher to another every year and across a variety of classroom aides, supplementary staff, and classmates.

My point is that often we hastily claim to understand the parents of our handicapped pupils, to know what feelings they have about their child's "backwardness." We may categorize them nonchalantly into accepting and rejecting parents and we may think we know what the 80% year-in-and-year-out influence and responsibility is, but we cannot easily know this. Our aim must be to foster and cultivate such understanding.

In this next chapter Ann Turnbull discusses the power of positive teacher-parent interactions. She purposefully avoids the term "parent training." While it is true that some parents may allow us to share with them our talents in teaching the handicapped, it is more often that we need to occupy a variety of other roles. The most common role involves listening rather than telling, to understand what most of us have not actually experienced—the day-to-day trials of having a severely handicapped child. Another role is to answer questions as best we can on the causes of handicaps and the reasons for "peculiar" behaviors, such as self-stimulatory behavior or the absence of speech. Other interactions with parents may consist primarily of trying to establish trust between the parent and the school. Yet for all of us a new role has arrived. With the passage of P.L. 94–142, we must set instructional goals for students with the help of their parents and discuss with them ways to achieve these goals and to maintain and generalize that learning once it has been acquired. As you read "Parent-Professional Interactions" your concept of the potential ties that may be established between the teacher and the home will expand and come into better focus.

References

Hannam, C. *Parents and mentally handicapped children.* Baltimore, Md.: Penguin, 1975.

Heller, J. *Something happened.* New York: Ballantine, 1966.

15

Parent-Professional Interactions

This chapter was written by **Ann P. Turnbull,** Assistant Professor, Division of Special Education, University of North Carolina at Chapel Hill.

As we have labeled handicapped children, have we also labeled their parents. Our motivations in labeling the child have been a positive (if somewhat misguided) effort to identify, clarify, and categorize, so that specialized services—remediation, education, and treatment—be developed to meet his special needs.

Has our labeling of parents also been positively motivated? Frequently used terms such as "rejecting," "overprotective," "unrealistic," and "unaccepting" are not positive words. They are words that separate, isolate, even discredit and discount. On the basis of such labels, we have been quick to prescribe counseling, therapy, training, and removal of the child from the home. Have these prescriptions or treatments been based, primarily, on the fact that the parents are parents of a handicapped child? Does this fact alone indicate the existence of pathology? Have such directions been taken only because the family did not agree with our diagnosis or act upon our recommendations?

Have we, while being very aware of apparent shortcomings, coupled this awareness with the belief that these parents should: support and justify our services in the community; lobby for legislation; accept our programming for the child without question; be appreciative of the efforts we make on their behalf; and, in short, be superparents?

Have we as professionals working in a field that traditionally has been child centered, unwittingly cast parents into the role of adversary, object of pity, inhibitor of growth, or automatic misfit, while expecting them to perform in a way expected of no other parents? Have we been too quick to focus on weakness and too slow to recognize the normality of the behaviors we see? (Cansler, Martin, & Valand, 1975, p. 9)

The above quote raises issues that have in the past characterized many of the interactions among parents of moderately and severely handicapped children and educational professionals. It is important to be aware of some of the problems which have interfered with positive parent-professional relationships in order to fully understand the current emphasis on establishing a new partnership among parents and professionals.

Parents have often been analyzed, criticized, and blamed for the problems of their handicapped children. In the past, many parents were encouraged to place their handicapped child in a residential institution immediately after diagnosis. The implicit message in this professional advice was that rearing the child required coping skills and attitudes which the parent did not possess.

Some educational programs have required parental involvement in ways such as serving as an aide in the classroom, attending therapy sessions, following through on training at home, and attending formal training sessions to learn new child management skills. If parents became overwhelmed with all their extra responsibilities, they have in instances been viewed as unresponsive and uncaring. The mother who fights for services for her severely retarded, multihandicapped child might be turned down by every agency she contacts. If she, herself, rejects her child, she may be viewed by professionals as in need of psychiatric help.

Some attempts to establish interaction among educational professionals and parents have been doomed to failure from the beginning. Some causes of failure are related to an unwillingness to listen to the parents' concerns or to respond to problems in their order of priority. Parents who are wondering where their next meal is coming from are unlikely to be very interested in a teacher's making a home visit to explain the principles of positive reinforcement. One parent trainer was describing his home-based training program for low-income parents. He commented, "On the first visit to the parents' home, we spend about five minutes making small talk and listening to their problems. Then we introduce our new parent training manual and ask them to turn to Chapter One. . . ." This trainer questioned why he had such a low rate of parents who consented to finishing the prescribed 12 sessions of weekly home visits. His hypothesis was that the parents were not concerned about the development of their child.

Some parents of handicapped children describe their interactions with professionals as characterized by a superiority (professional)-inferiority (parent) status. One parent involvement program used the slogan "Parents are Educable." In the jargon of special education, the literal translation of this slogan is "Parents have IQs roughly between 55 and 70." Of course, this was not the intent of the slogan; yet parents viewed it as an insult to their capabilities.

Just as professionals have sometimes slighted parents of moderately and severely handicapped children, the attitudes and behavior of parents have also contributed to negative interactions. There is no easy way to tell a mother and father that their child is substantially handicapped. Some parents

want to hear the hard facts; others want to be eased into facing the reality. Professionals might carefully choose their words with the greatest sensitivity, yet still offend the parents. Sometimes parents are unforgiving and do not stop to realize the difficult position in which the professional is placed. They might vent their anger to the professional and/or discuss the professional's "gross lack of sensitivity" to their family and friends. Frequently parents of handicapped children have been highly critical of the professionals with whom they and their children have worked. Professionals are sometimes totally or socially excluded from interest groups in the community on the grounds that it is impossible for them to understand the feelings and needs of parents of handicapped children. Tight cliques are sometimes formed by parents with the primary goal of ostracizing and criticizing professionals. There are situations in which parents have fought long and hard for services for their handicapped child; after the services are found and the child is receiving an appropriate education, the parents continue their intensive advocacy to the point that minor issues become the basis for major confrontation. This type of advocacy posture is likely to lead to unhealthy interactions among parents and professionals.

Why has the important relationship of parents and educational professionals been frequently counterproductive in the past? Negative interactions have largely resulted from a lack of awareness and sensitivity of both groups to the other's roles and responsibilities. Only in the last decade has significant national attention been focused on the importance of a parent-professional partnership based on mutual respect and decision making. Some of the reasons contributing to the recognition of the importance of this partnership include

1. The experimental evidence that parents can positively influence the development of their children through teaching them at home (Baker & Heifetz, 1976; Brophy, 1970; Denhoff & Hyman, 1976; Haynes, 1976; Hess & Shipman, 1965; Wiegerink & Parrish, 1976).

2. The encouraging results of early intervention in ameliorating the developmental deficits associated with moderate and severe handicaps (Bereiter & Englemann, 1966; Karnes, Wollersheim, Stoneburner, Hodgins, & Teska, 1968; Tjossem, 1976.)

3. The success of parents in bringing litigation to establish the educational rights of their children (Mills v. Board of Education, 1972; Pennsylvania

Association for Retarded Children v. Common-wealth of Pennsylvania, 1972).

4. The resulting federal legislation, P.L. 94–142 (Education for All Handicapped Children Act), which sets forth clear standards for parental involvement in the educational process. Since P.L. 94–142 provides statutory guidelines for the interaction among parents and educational professionals, the 6 major principles of the legislation will be reviewed in regard to the specification of parental rights and responsibilities. The implementation of these rights and responsibilities will provide the basis for new relationships among educational professionals and parents.

P.L. 94–142: Parent Rights and Responsibilities

P.L. 94–142 was passed by Congress in November 1975. Its essential purpose is to insure that all handicapped children are provided with a free, appropriate education at public expense. The six major principles included in the legislation which contribute to the provision of a free, appropriate public education include

1. Zero reject
2. Nondiscriminatory assessment
3. Individualized education programs
4. Least restrictive alternative
5. Procedural due process
6. Parent participation

The regulations adopted to implement each principle clearly set forth requirements for parental involvement. These requirements for parental involvement are summarized for each principle (*Federal Register*, 1977). They provide the foundation for many of the interactions among educational professionals and parents.

Zero reject

Zero reject assures that all handicapped children will be provided with a free, appropriate public education. Timelines were set which require states to provide full educational opportunity to all handicapped children between the ages of 3 and 18 by no later than September 1, 1978, and to all handicapped children between the ages of 3 and 21 by no later than September 1, 1980. There is an exception to this requirement and that is that states do not

have to provide educational services to students between the ages of 3 through 5 and 18 through 21 if a state law or practice or a court order is inconsistent with the requirements of educating these age groups.

The legislation requires that each state education agency (SEA) and local education agency (LEA) conduct an annual child-find program to identify, locate, and evaluate all handicapped children residing in their jurisdiction who are in need of special education and related services. Federal aid to SEAs and LEAs who comply with the requirements of P.L. 94–142 must be used first for two "service priorities." These priorities include (1) all handicapped children receiving no education and (2) handicapped children within each disability area with the most severe handicaps who are not receiving an adequate education.

When no suitable program is available for a handicapped child in the LEA serving the jurisdiction in which he resides, the LEA may refer him for placement in a private program. In these instances, the private program must meet all requirements of P.L. 94–142 and the LEA must assume full financial responsibility for the room, board, and educational expenses (not medical expenses) of the handicapped student.

Not only must handicapped students be admitted to school, they must also be provided with a relevant and appropriate curriculum. This issue will be discussed in the section on individualized education programs.

The implication of the zero reject requirements for parents of moderately and severely retarded children is that they can be assured that educational services must be provided. With the service priorities covering handicapped children previously excluded from school and the more severely handicapped children, parents of moderately and severely retarded students are in the best position to receive appropriate services for their child. In the past, negative interactions have occurred among educational professionals and parents when parents were put in the position of having to beg for programs and then often feeling the frustration of finding no publicly financed programs. Private school placements have resulted in tremendous financial burdens for parents which have led to feelings of further alienation from the public schools. Many educators have experienced similar frustration in wanting to provide for moderately and severely handicapped children but realizing the constraints posed by school budgets. Zero reject requirements will create new relationships among educational professionals and parents based on the premise that appropriate educational services will be provided at public expense. Interactions can be initiated at the point of defining what types of curriculum and services constitute an appropriate education rather than at the point of deciding whether or not the school will provide services for the handicapped student.

Nondiscriminatory assessment

The legislative requirements related to nondiscriminatory assessment focus on insuring that evaluation procedures are broadly based, fairly administered, and given only with the informed consent of parents. Obtaining informed consent of parents throughout the evaluation process will be discussed in the section on due process. In regard to using evaluation procedures that are broadly based and fairly administered, requirements specify that tests must be sensitive to cultural factors (e.g., administered in the child's native language, validated for the specific purpose for which they are used) and that a variety of measures be used (a minimum of two tests, information from sources other than tests including information concerning physical condition, sociocultural background, and adaptive behavior in home and school). In order to gather this information on the child's cultural background and functioning at home, parents must contribute information during the evaluation process. Although not specifically required by P.L. 94–142, parents may be members of the evaluation team which is charged with the responsibility of interpreting educational data. If they are not formal team members, the educational professionals on the evaluation team should conduct a parent conference or solicit information from parents, possibly through a questionnaire on topics such as physical condition, sociocultural background, and adaptive behavior.

Parents have other rights related to evaluation, such as challenging the appropriateness of particular evaluation data and obtaining formal evaluations on their child from private sources to be considered in making placement decisions. Since these rights are classified as procedural safeguards, they also will be discussed in the section on due process.

Thus, P.L. 94–142 extends fuller opportunities to parents to be involved in the collection and interpretation of evaluation data. As parents participate in the evaluation process, they begin to interact with professionals in making important educational decisions. No longer are parents merely recipients of evaluation information collected on their child. The intent of P.L. 94–142 is to assert their right for active participation.

Individualized education programs

The individualized education program (IEP) is a primary mechanism set forth by P.L. 94–142 to insure that handicapped children are provided with a meaningful education appropriate to their needs and abilities. The required components of the IEP include

1. A statement of the child's present level of educational performance
2. Annual goals expected to be achieved by the end of the school year
3. Short-term instructional objectives (written in measurable terms) which represent the intermediate steps between the present level of performance and the attainment of the annual goal
4. Special education and related services needed by the student
5. The date of initiating and terminating the services
6. A specification of the extent of time the student will participate in the regular educational program
7. Evaluation procedures (criteria and schedules) for determining on at least an annual basis whether the short-term objectives are being met

IEPs must be developed at the beginning of the year for all handicapped students receiving special education. For a handicapped child not receiving special education, a meeting must be held to develop the IEP within 30 days of the determination that the child is handicapped. The required participants on the IEP committee include

1. An LEA representative, other than the child's teacher, who is qualified to provide or supervise special education services
2. The child's teacher or teachers who have direct responsibility for implementing the IEP
3. One or both of the child's parents
4. The handicapped child, when appropriate

When the child is classified as handicapped for the first time, the evaluator or a representative familiar with evaluation results must also attend the IEP committee. Other individuals may also be included on the committee at the discretion of the parent or LEA.

The implications of parental involvement in developing the IEP are tremendous. This requirement brings parents to the forefront in specifying what constitutes an appropriate curriculum for their child and significantly influences the interactions of educational professionals and parents in mutual decision making and shared responsibility. Some parents of handicapped children have complained in the past that the educational professionals working with their child did not solicit their opinions or consider the needs which they felt were most pressing for their child. The IEP conference provides an opportunity for parents to state what they want for their child. In a recent IEP conference, the parent of a moderately retarded child questioned why her child was being taught to verbally label prehistoric animals. The parent asked the teachers what type of job they expected the child to have as an adult. The teachers replied that they had never really considered job opportunities for the child, since he was only 10. To the teachers, 10 seemed young; to the parents, reaching the age of 10 meant that almost one-half of his formal educational experiences were completed. As the meeting progressed, it was clear that the parents were specifying objectives related to achieving independence as an adult (telling time, reading survival words, sex education) which were different from the more traditional curriculum proposed by the teachers. Through sharing evaluation data, goals for the child, and special problems, a curriculum was devised which met the approval of all parties involved.

In addition to helping to specify curriculum objectives, membership on the IEP committee provides an opportunity for parents to request services which they believe their child needs, share relevant information on their child's functioning at home which was not included in the evaluation phase, participate in making the placement decision, and specify what type of responsibility they are willing to assume in implementing the IEP. The parents may agree to follow up at home on the objectives which are currently being taught at school either by directly working with their child or by locating a volunteer or tutor, assuming full responsibility for teaching certain objectives, serving as an aide in the classroom in helping the teacher, or assuming other responsibilities. Parents have different interests, skills, periods of available time, and levels of energy. In specifying the type of involvement the parent will have in his child's educational program, it is important to make individual arrangements according to the needs and interests of the parents.

The educational professionals on the IEP committee must insure that all communication at the conference is understandable to the parent. This means that an interpreter must be provided for parents who are deaf or whose native language is other than English. If it is impossible for parents to attend a meeting, their participation in IEP development can be achieved by an individual or conference telephone call.

In order for parents to fully participate as an IEP committee member, educational professionals have a responsibility to inform them of this opportunity and to create an atmosphere at the conference characterized by respect and open communication. The LEA should initially inform all parents of handicapped children of the requirements of P.L. 94–142 and of the necessity for them to participate in the IEP conference. Since many parents of handicapped students are totally unfamiliar with this new educational approach, the purpose of the IEP needs to be fully explained in order to prepare parents for their membership on the committee. With the initial implementation of IEPs, teachers of moderately and severely handicapped children should consider scheduling a group parent meeting as close to the beginning of the school year as possible to discuss the nature of IEPs, emphasize the importance of parental involvement, and prepare parents for their role in the actual IEP development. Strategies which could be used at the group meeting by the teacher include discussing the legislative requirements for the IEP and then role-playing an IEP conference with a parent who has agreed ahead of time to participate. Teachers might give parents a list of questions to be thinking about before the conference such as:

What skills would you most like your child to learn?
Are there concerns about your child's functioning at home that could be addressed by work at school?
What aspects of your child's behavior do you believe need to be improved?
What do you believe to be your child's strengths and weaknesses?
What methods have you found to be effective in rewarding and punishing your child?
To what extent does your child interact with children in the neighborhood?
What are your feelings about providing opportunities for your child to interact with nonhandicapped children?

By providing a list of these questions ahead of time, parents will have an opportunity to think about the kind of comments they would like to make at the IEP conference. Teachers might also want to schedule the IEP conferences with individual parents at the group meeting and to assist in working out any logistical problems such as transportation.

According to P.L. 94–142, the only exception to parental involvement in the IEP conference is in instances in which parents refuse to be involved. In these cases, school officials are required to provide documentation of attempts to encourage the parents to be involved including detailed records of telephone calls, copies of letters, and/or visits to the parent's home or place of employment.

The membership of parents on IEP committees strongly influences the interactions of parents and professionals. They must meet at the beginning of the school year to define the child's total educational program. If all parties agree that the IEP is appropriate, implementation of the specified instructional objectives and educational services is initiated. Since parents know what to anticipate in terms of progress, they are in a position to monitor implementation. Monitoring can result in increased accountability for both the professionals and parents. Some IEP committee meetings will not result in complete consensus. If either the professionals or parents object to the opinions of the other to the point of being deadlocked, either party may initiate a due process hearing as a method of resolving the conflict. One point of conflict is likely to be the related services needed by the student. For example, parents may have the opinion that their severely handicapped child needs daily physical therapy. The professional members of the IEP committee might disagree (perhaps for the reason that they know it is impossible for the school to provide such intervention). If consensus cannot be reached, the IEP cannot be officially approved. Thus, either party could initiate a due process hearing to resolve the conflict. The P.L. 94–142 requirements related to IEPs clearly result in curriculum decisions being a shared responsibility among professionals and parents rather than the singular responsibility of professionals.

Least restrictive alternatives

The requirements of P.L. 94–142 state that to the maximum extent possible, handicapped children, including those in public or private facilities, should be educated with children who are nonhandicapped.

Removing handicapped children from regular school environments should occur only when the nature or severity of the handicap is such that education in regular classes, with the use of supplementary aids and services, cannot be successfully achieved. The decisions as to placement are made by the IEP committee. Thus, parents interact with professionals in making the decision as to what constitutes the most appropriate environment for their child.

There are significant implications of the least restrictive doctrine for parents of handicapped children. For example, consider the parents who institutionalized their child shortly after birth and never established strong ties with the child. At age 15, the institution recommends that the child be returned to his family based on the concept of least restriction. The parents may be psychologically unable to provide a home for their child and to make the tremendous adjustments posed by deinstitutionalization. Presently, the legal assumption is in favor of parental custody; yet many parents are unprepared to discharge their duties (Turnbull & Turnbull, 1975). Educational models must be established which focus on preparation for both the handicapped individual and his family who are in the midst of the deinstitutionalization process (Turnbull, Tyler, & Morrell, Note 1). Parents of institutionalized children are organizing into interest groups in many states for the purpose of halting deinstitutionalization until community alternatives are developed. The most careful interaction is needed among professionals and parents in planning the movement of moderately and severely retarded children from residential institutions to community environments to insure that the process is systematic, manageable for the family, and sensitive to the unique needs of the handicapped child.

Many parents of handicapped students also have concerns about the placement of their children in regular education programs. Parents who are dissatisfied with the teacher's responses are encouraged to report their opinions to school officials and parent advocacy groups. This example points to the need for professionals and parents to cooperatively devise a systematic plan for moving handicapped students from more restrictive to less restrictive environments. Parents might serve on system advisory boards or participate in the process of specifying needs and identifying strategies to meet the needs. Paul, Turnbull, and Cruickshank (1977) describe a procedure for collaborative planning among professionals and parents regarding mainstreaming and point out the roles and responsibilities of both groups. Since it is both educationally sound and legally required that parents be involved in the process of making placement decisions, the positive interaction of professionals and parents on this important task is crucial to successful programming.

Due process

Due process can be viewed as a means for holding both professionals and parents accountable for the educational decisions they make on behalf of the handicapped child. Basically, due process safeguards include the requirements stated below.

1. Parental consent must be obtained before the preplacement evaluation is conducted. Evaluation is defined as a procedure used to determine whether a child is handicapped and to identify the nature of special education services which are needed. According to the regulations, parental consent must be obtained only when selective testing procedures are used with an individual child, not for basic tests administered to all children in a school, grade, or class.

2. Parents of a handicapped child may examine all relevant records with respect to the identification, evaluation, and educational placement of the child.

3. Parents may obtain an independent evaluation (an evaluation conducted by a certified or licensed examiner who is not employed by the school system and who does not routinely provide evaluations for the SEA or LEA) and have it considered by the system in determining what constitutes a free, appropriate public education for the child.

4. Written notice must be provided to the parents before initiating or changing the identification, evaluation, or educational placement of a child or the refusal to make such a change. The notice must meet the following criteria: (A) a description of the action proposed or refused including an explanation concerning the rationale for the decision, a description of other options considered, and reasons why the other options were rejected; (B) a description of each evaluation procedure, record, or report upon which the decision was based; and (C) a description of any other factors related to the agency's decision.

Further requirements specify that the notice must be written in language understandable to the general public and in the native language or other mode of communication of the parent (if not, the notice must be translated orally into the parents' native

language or some other mode of communication must be used). In essence, the educational agency must insure that parents understand the content of the notice.

5. The SEA must insure that a child's rights are protected when his parents are unknown or unavailable or when he is a ward of the state. In these cases, a determination must be made as to whether the child needs a surrogate parent, and if necessary, a surrogate parent must be assigned. The surrogate parent has all responsibilities related to representing the interests of the child in obtaining a free, appropriate public education. The surrogate parent must meet the following stipulations: (A) have no interests that conflict with the interest of the child, (B) have knowledge and skill that will insure adequate representation, and (C) not be an employee of the SEA or LEA responsible for providing an education to the child.

6. The parents (including the guardian and surrogate) or the LEA may initiate a due process hearing to present complaints concerning the child's identification, evaluation, placement, or his right to a free, appropriate public education. Any party may be advised by counsel or individuals with expertise related to the education of handicapped students, present evidence, make cross-examinations, obtain a written or electronic verbatim record of the hearing, and obtain written findings of facts and decisions. The hearing officer must not be an employee of the SEA or LEA nor have any personal or professional interests that would bias his or her opinions.

All hearings must be conducted within 45 days after receipt of the complaint except in situations in which all parties agree to an extension. While the proceedings are being conducted, the child should remain in his present educational placement unless the SEA or LEA and the child's parents agree to another placement. If the complaint involves the child's initial admission to public education, the child must be placed in the public school program until the proceedings are completed.

Any party dissatisfied with the findings of the hearing conducted by the LEA may appeal to the SEA for an impartial review of the hearing. If parties are further aggrieved by the decisions of the reviewer, any party may file a civil action in either a state or federal district court.

It is obvious that due process stipulations create significant opportunities for parents to have access to educational information and to influence or change educational decisions. The opportunity for due process hearings provides a system of checks and balances for both the parents and educational professionals. It is common to view due process hearings as adversarial procedures; however, this does not have to be the case. Hearings can provide a forum for deciding what constitutes an appropriate education for a handicapped student and can take into consideration the divergent opinions of the parties involved. It can be a method of protection for both parents and professionals. Due process requirements most certainly provide new opportunities for parents and professionals to interact and to have increased accountability in their interactions. As stated in the first portion of this chapter, many parent-professional relationships have been characterized by a perceived dissatisfaction of the behavior or performance of one party by the other. Due process hearings provide an opportunity to examine these issues of dissatisfaction in an objective and systematic manner. Thus, due process requirements can be viewed as a method of resolving conflict. Undoubtedly due process will influence significantly the interactions of professionals and parents, making both parties more accountable to each other and to the best interests of the handicapped child.

Parent participation

In the P.L. 94–142 regulations pertaining to parent participation, the opportunity is extended to parents to have access to educationally relevant information and to be involved in educational decisions. Such requirements pertaining to the SEA include providing parents with (A) a summary of policies in regard to the storage, release to a third party, and the protection of personally identifiable information; (B) a description of all the rights of parents and children regarding personally identifiable information; and (C) a description of the children on whom the SEA will maintain information, the methods to be used in gathering the information, and the uses to be made of the information.

Parents are entitled to inspect and review all educational records (unless they are prevented from doing so under state laws pertaining to matters such as guardianship, separation, and divorce) within a maximum period of 45 days following their request to record access. They may ask for an interpretation of the information and may make a request that the information be amended. If the agency refuses to amend the information in accordance with the parents' request, the parents must be advised of their right to a due process hearing. The result of the hearing will determine whether or not the information in the record is to be amended. All opportunities

must be made available to parents to review or inspect the records, including providing the parents with copies if they are unable to come to school to review them. Finally, parents may request from the LEA a list of the types and locations of information collected, maintained, or used by the agency.

Access to records can be viewed as another way of equalizing the power to make educational decisions among professionals and parents. Prior to the legal establishment of this parental right, a frequent educational practice has been not to report fully the evaluation results of moderately and severely retarded children to their parents. Some school policies even prevented the release of IQ scores to parents. Another practice has been to write subjective opinions in school records. These opinions can become very debilitating to handicapped individuals as future teachers and employers read them. In the past, there has been limited accountability for professionals, because usually they were the only ones who read the records. By extending the opportunity to parents not only to read their child's records but also to be entitled to an explanation of the contents and to make a request for an amendment, a new forum is established for interaction. Thus, there are no private sanctions which are off-limits to the parent-professional partnership. The implications for professionals of parental access to records are that they will be held accountable for the manner in which they collect and maintain student data.

Prior to releasing personally identifiable information to anyone other than authorized agency officials, parental consent must be obtained. Each agency must train all persons who use personally identifiable information in the state's policies and procedures pertaining to confidentiality and must maintain a current listing of names and positions of employees who have access to the information. The list must be available for public inspection. Further, the agency must inform parents when a need no longer exists for the collection, maintenance, and use of the confidential information; however, parents should also be informed that records may be needed in the future to obtain social security and tax benefits. Upon the request of the parents, all confidential information must be destroyed when it is no longer needed by the agency. A permanent record of the following student data may be maintained: name, address, phone number, grade, attendance record, classes attended, grade level completed, and year completed.

Parent participation is also addressed by P.L. 94–142 by encouraging parental involvement in decision making through participation at public hearings and membership on advisory panels. Prior to the adoption of the annual state program plan, the SEA is required to conduct public hearings at times and in locations that would permit interested parents to attend. A notice of the hearings and the purpose of the plan must be provided in the newspaper or other media with enough advance time to sufficiently inform the public of the upcoming hearing. At the public hearing on the annual program plan, the SEA must provide information on its programs to interested parties and solicit their favorable and critical comments. Prior to the final adoption of the plan, modifications must be made to incorporate the educationally significant public comments. Further, LEAs are required to develop a process for providing parents or guardians of handicapped students the opportunity to participate in the development of the application for P.L. 94–142 funds. After the application is developed, it must be made available to parents and the general public.

The SEA is required to establish an advisory panel with parental representation to establish guidelines for meeting educational needs of the handicapped population and commenting publicly on rules and regulations. Panel meetings are to be open and minutes must be shared. Thus, parents who do not have membership on the panel can still stay informed about and monitor the proceedings of the meetings.

By having public hearings and advisory meetings as arenas for the interaction of professionals and parents, parents are provided with the opportunity to influence the development of policy in initial stages and to monitor the implementation of policy. This provides the opportunity for interaction on system issues, whereas other parental rights, such as membership on the IEP committee, are directed more at interaction around child issues.

From the discussion of parental rights and responsibilities as they relate to the six principles of P.L. 94–142, it is obvious that a parent-professional alliance is the backbone of the provision of a free, appropriate public education to handicapped students.

Development of a Parent Program

In addition to the nature and scope of interactions among professionals and parents established by P.L. 94–142, there are many other ways in which interactions can occur. Many educational programs for moderately and severely retarded children have a concurrent parent program with particular expectations for parental involvement. Regular meetings and activities might be jointly planned by the professionals and parents around issues of mutual concern.

When initially establishing a parent program, one of the most important considerations for the professionals is to tailor the program to the needs and interests of the parents. The importance of meeting individual needs is a concept that applies to adults as well as children. One method of identifying parental needs is to use an assessment form such as the one depicted in Figure 15.1. This form (Cansler, Martin, and Valand, 1975) or one similarly constructed could be completed by parents on the first day of school or could be sent to them by mail. Eliciting parental viewpoints from the beginning sets up a communication pattern characterized by respect for what parents have to say. An outgrowth of this type of communication is tailoring the objectives of the parent program to the preference of parents. Thus, parental interest and active participation are likely to be enhanced.

Parent programs can be described or categorized in many ways. One format for conceptualizing parent programs is to focus on the various roles and responsibilities of parents of handicapped children. These include parenting, teaching, and advocating. The subsequent sections of this chapter focus on each of these areas with emphasis given to various parental roles and responsibilities and strategies to assist parents in meeting these responsibilities.

Parents as parents

Sometimes parent programs tend to overemphasize the roles of parents as teachers of their own children and as advocates for their children but deemphasize their role as parents. To be the parent of a moderately or severely handicapped child requires tremendous emotional adjustments, additional time devoted to parenting responsibilities, and often excess financial burdens in comparison to the cost of rearing nonhandicapped children. Parents can be assisted in carrying out their responsibilities by a program aimed at providing them with support, knowledge, and access to resources. Some of the particular issues that might be addressed include:

1. The adjustment process
2. Socialization for the child
3. Addressing concerns related to siblings
4. Estate planning and guardianship

It is our feeling that a child's progress in school is greatest when staff and family form a cooperative team with common goals. To have an effective family-staff team, parents should be given the opportunity to express what they feel are their expectations and limitations in relation to such a program. Will you please rate the following areas for service according to their importance to you.

	Please check:		
	Not Important	Some Importance	Very Important
1. Training in classroom activities and teaching methods.			
2. Interpretation of test results.			
3. Counseling for family problems.			
4. Suggestions of other available services in the community.			
5. Help with managing behavior of children (temper tantrums, toilet training, eating habits, etc.)			
6. Transportation			
7. Suggestions for home activities for child.			
8. Training for brothers and sisters of child.			
9. Meetings for groups of parents.			
10. Suggestions for inexpensive or home-made learning and play materials.			

What do you think would be the most helpful format for parent-staff contacts? Check one or more.

_____ Group meetings with information-sharing (lecture-discussion) on general areas of interest

_____ Small-group discussion on topics selected by participating parents

_____ Periodic individual conferences between parent(s) and staff member(s). How often?

_____ Visits to families' homes by staff member

_____ Classroom observation and participation by parents

_____ All of the above, depending on need at the time

_____ I do not feel that parents should be involved in child's education program

_____ Other

Thank you for your comments.

Name _____

FIGURE 15.1   *Sample form for parents to rate their needs for service*

Source: D. P. Cansler, G. H. Martin, and M. C. Valand, *Working with Families*. Winston-Salem, N.C.: Kaplan Press, 1976, p. 15.

Adjustment Process

Parents of handicapped children experience tremendous emotional pain in the process from the first recognition that something is wrong with their child until they are at the point of realistically planning for his education. Cansler et al. (1975) discuss the emotional adjustment of parents of handicapped students in three phases: (A) denial; (B) intellectual awareness of the handicap with emotional reactions of anger, guilt, depression, and grief; and (C) intellectual and emotional adjustment.

The process of moving through these stages and adjusting to the fact that a child is handicapped is somewhat different for each parent; yet a commonality found in almost every situation is that parents can be helped by supportive and sensitive friends and professionals during their adjustment (Schlesinger & Meadow, 1976). Educational professionals might work in conjunction with advocacy organizations such as the Association for Retarded Citizens and the Society for Autistic Children in assisting in the development of parent-support groups. The major purpose of such groups is for parents with similar problems to have opportunities to offer support to one another. It can be extremely helpful for parents to know that other parents have similar problems, questions, and concerns. Such support groups often need a facilitator in initial sessions. If parents experience difficulty in discussing their feelings, perhaps a parent speaker or a film dealing with parental adjustment issues could be used as a basis for eliciting reactions. Parents need to be encouraged to express their feelings. Active listening in a nonjudgmental fashion can create a trusting atmosphere for parents (Coletta, 1977). If more intensive support is needed, educational professionals should discuss with the parents the possibility of receiving counseling and might assist them in obtaining these services.

Socialization for the Child

A frequent source of concern for parents of moderately and severely handicapped children is the sometimes negative reaction of the nonhandicapped population toward their child. It can be exasperating for parents to be out in public with their moderately or severely handicapped child and to be aware of stares and sometimes even to receive insensitive questions, such as, "Why does Joe look so funny?" It is difficult to know the most appropriate way to respond in these situations. Some parents are more comfortable in trying to ignore the situations, and others feel strongly that a reply is in order. Schulz (in press) described her typical response to a stranger who stares at her son who has Down's syndrome. She looks squarely at the stranger and says, "You seem interested in my son. Would you like to meet him?" She reports that this comment frequently terminates the staring episodes and creates an opportunity to provide information.

Another problem for parents related to socialization can be in helping their child to be socially accepted by neighborhood peers. Some handicapped children are automatically accepted; others need assistance in making friends. It can be a source of disappointment and feelings of helplessness for parents to see all the other children in the neighborhood frequently playing together if their child remains isolated at home with few friends. Parents might share their experiences and, working with educational professionals, might plan a systematic procedure to help nonhandicapped children be comfortable around and to get to know their child. Such a procedure for increasing socialization should be based on successive approximation and could include the following steps:

1. Invite one or two neighborhood children over to the house to play (the house of the handicapped child). In choosing which neighborhood children to invite first, consideration should be given to choosing children who are already sensitive to individual differences and who have influence with other neighborhood children. The parents of the handicapped child should be available to answer any questions posed by the neighborhood children in regard to the nature of the handicapping condition. For example, one neighborhood peer asked of a new friend who had hydrocephaly, "Why is his head so big?" It is important to have open and honest communication with nonhandicapped children in responding to questions resulting from natural curiosity. The visit should be brief and supervised by the handicapped child's parents. If the handicapped child has any special problems such as seizures, the parents should look for an appropriate time to explain the nature of seizures to the nonhandicapped peers and to again answer their questions.

2. Expand the length of visits with the one or two neighborhood children and begin to phase out the parental supervision.

3. Add a new child to the invitation to visit or to go on a family outing with the handicapped child. Use the older neighborhood friends as models for the new friend.

4. Have the parents of the nonhandicapped peers over to the house to allow them the opportunity of getting to know the handicapped child. Communicate very openly concerning the needs of the handicapped child. (Step 4 may be sequenced before Step 1 in some cases).

5. Ask the parents of the nonhandicapped children if it would be agreeable with them for their children (handicapped and nonhandicapped) to play together at their homes.

6. Reinforce nonhandicapped peers for including the handicapped child in activities away from his house and yard. Encourage independence in the neighborhood.

In resolving the problems of socialization, parents might be interested in having group meetings with educational professionals to collaboratively devise strategies and to role-play particular situations. Further, educational professionals might work with parents in increasing the socialization of their child by assisting them in socialization situations at home.

Addressing Concerns Related to Siblings

The brothers and sisters of handicapped individuals often need special help in understanding their handicapped sibling. Brothers or sisters may have concerns related to the cause of their handicapped sibling's problems, whether their friends will understand, the educational and vocational potential of the sibling, the likelihood of producing a handicapped child themselves, and whether they will have responsibility for their handicapped sibling after their parents die. Parents may request help from educational professionals in knowing how to deal with some of these concerns.

Strategies which might be used by educational professionals include conducting parent meetings with concrete suggestions on ways to handle sibling concerns, setting up a library with books for siblings, organizing a sibling support group, planning for siblings to observe the classroom, and conducting a workshop for siblings of handicapped children enrolled in the educational program. Cansler et al. (1975) include a description of a sibling workshop conducted by the staff of a developmental center serving moderately and severely retarded children. This workshop was a full week in length and included sessions related to the causes of mental retardation, making educational materials, principles of behavior modification, and observation of the classroom program.

Estate Planning and Guardianship

Parents of moderately and severely retarded children understandably have concerns about planning for their child's future. How should their will be devised? Who should they ask to assume the responsibilities of serving as a guardian should one be needed? What is the procedure for appointing a guardian? Should a trust fund be established?

Estate planning and guardianship are embroiled with many intricate issues which must be fully explored before parents make important decisions in regard to their child's future. For example, in many states guardianship is declared on an "all-or-none" basis. In order for a guardian to be appointed, the mentally retarded individual must be declared incompetent by the courts; and such a declaration generally results in the retarded person's losing all of his legal rights and privileges including, as a rule, the power to give consent, vote, obtain a driver's license, enter into contracts, and decide where he will live. A few states have passed limited guardianship legislation which provides degrees of guardianship according to the level of independent functioning of the handicapped individual. In these states, the handicapped person does not have to be declared incompetent to receive the services of a guardian. Since state laws to a large extent determine the most advantageous course of action for a parent to take, the first step in making decisions regarding estate planning and guardianship is to become informed on these topics.

If parents need assistance in exploring these issues, educational professionals and parents might plan a group parent meeting devoted to a discussion of various alternatives associated with estate planning and guardianship. A lawyer and/or a trust officer of a bank might be asked to present information to the group pertaining to state laws and specific options under these laws. A discussion of the pros and cons of various options should be included in the meeting.

Parents who have strong concerns about their moderately or severely retarded child's future may not be able to fully concentrate on his present educational needs. Assisting parents to alleviate future concerns can significantly contribute to helping them fulfill their parenting roles and responsibilities.

Parents as teachers

Parents have been recognized as valuable instructional resources in meeting the developmental and educational needs of handicapped children. Many valid reasons exist for encouraging parents to be teachers of their handicapped child including (1) parents typically are powerful reinforcing agents, (2) parents know their children better than others and generally spend more time with their children than do professionals, (3) the effectiveness of intervention can be increased if parents follow up at home on the skills being taught at school, (4) teaching children at home is cost effective, and (5) parents receive gratification from contributing to the development of their child. To date, the majority of demonstration projects aimed at training parents as teachers have involved early intervention with handicapped infants and preschoolers; however, the procedures involved in the development of these programs are applicable also to parents of elementary-age and adolescent individuals.

Parent-professional interactions may center around preparing parents to teach developmental or academic skills and concepts to their child. The setting of this priority should result from the needs assessment conducted with parents. Some parents become excellent teachers of their handicapped child and other parents are not inclined to develop skills in this area. The individuality of parents requires that their priorities and interests be respected.

Parent-professional interactions in regard to preparing parents as teachers can be structured according to the following models: (1) home training, (2) group training, and (3) classroom helper.

Home Training

One approach to parent training is to work with the parents in their home in teaching them intervention skills. This approach has the greatest utility with parents of preschoolers who are providing direct care to their child during the day. In this situation, the trainer who goes into the home can work with both the parent and the handicapped child and, furthermore, has an opportunity to observe the parent interacting with and teaching the child.

A model home-based instruction program, the Portage Project, was developed by Shearer and Shearer (1976). The Portage Project serves preschool handicapped children who reside in south central Wisconsin. Rather than having a classroom program, all teaching is done in the home by the parents. A home teacher is assigned to each family and has the responsibility of teaching the parents skills in specifying objectives, methods of instruction, and principles of behavior management. The home teacher is assigned 15 families and visits with

each family one day per week for 1.5 hours. During each weekly visit an individualized curriculum is planned for the child in the areas of language, self-help, cognitive, motor, and socialization skills. The project incorporates the following behavioral model:

1. Three behaviors are targeted each week which should be accomplished by the next weekly visit
2. Baseline data are recorded by the home teacher
3. The home teacher models teaching techniques for the parent and then observes the parent teaching the child
4. Written directions are provided to the parents
5. The parents follow through on the teaching sequences during the week
6. The home teacher records post-baseline data to determine if the child has mastered the objectives

When professionals make home visits, basic considerations should be followed such as asking the parents in advance for their permission to visit them in their home, being prompt, listening attentively to the family's concerns when they might conflict with the purpose of the meeting, and respecting the privacy of the family. Many parents of handicapped children feel threatened by home visits and may believe that the visitor (professional) is evaluating their life style or standard of living. Establishing rapport from the beginning is essential to successful home training programs. Giesey (1970) offers valuable "how-to" suggestions for readers desiring more information on the mechanics of home visits.

A drawback to home training often occurs when parents work during the day and are at home only in the evenings. When families are large and live in crowded conditions, the disruptions in the evening can make it virtually impossible to concentrate on training. Another drawback happens in situations in which the handicapped child is in a school-based program during the day. In these circumstances, the training might best be delivered in the same setting as the program attended by the child.

Group Training

Group training of parents in teaching competencies can be conducted in a variety of ways. Bricker and Bricker (1976) trained mothers of handicapped children in the four curriculum areas of language, cognitive, motor, and social development. As a component of the Infant, Toddler, and Preschool Research and Intervention Project, mothers were requested to spend one-half day per week at the center, which provided the educational program to their handicapped child. Mothers attended training groups which met once a week and focused on a single skill. Emphasis in training sessions was given to specifying target behaviors, discussing training strategies, and reviewing evaluation data collected by the mothers. Demonstration sessions were also held in which the mothers' teaching strategies were observed by the trainer. These sessions enabled the trainers to assist the mothers in refining their teaching skills.

Another model for group training of parents is described by Baker and Heifetz (1976). This parent training program is operated as part of a behavior modification residential camp for retarded children (Baker, 1973). Parents meet in groups of 6 to 12 families with a preprofessional trainer. The instructional program is packaged into an assessment booklet and 10 instructional manuals entitled "Basic Skills," "Early Self-Help Skills," "Advanced Self-Help Skills," "Toilet Training," "Beginning Speech," "Speech and Language," "Early Play Skills," "Play Skills," and "Behavior Problems." The preprofessional trainer uses the manuals as the basis for instruction. Each manual includes content related to pinpointing behaviors, teaching principles, using rewards, and recording progress. The practicality of the manuals is enhanced by case studies, explanatory illustrations, and specific program outlines. This model is comprised of 9 training sessions. Parents are provided with a $50 tuition refund if they attend at least 8 of the 9 sessions.

A distinct advantage to group training models is that parents have the opportunity to learn from one another and to share their successes. Many parents benefit from this type of group involvement. In planning group training sessions, it is advantageous to keep groups relatively small (12 persons or fewer) in order to increase the likelihood of meeting individual needs of group members. Professionals and parents should jointly plan sessions in consideration of the schedules of the parents who will be attending. If the majority of the parents work, evening meetings might be the most convenient alternative. The number and frequency of the meetings should be determined according to parent preferences. Practical obstacles, such as baby-sitting and transportation, can prevent parent participation. Planning should be directed at eliminating these problems by working out any necessary car-pools and by arranging for a baby-sitter at the same location as the group meeting so that parents may bring their child. Meetings should use a variety of training strategies

including ones emphasizing active involvement of parents, and evaluation should occur at the conclusion of each session.

One task which should be accomplished in the group training sessions is to devise a procedure that meets the approval of both the educational professionals and the parents in regard to a method of coordinating the instructional program of the handicapped child. It will be more beneficial for efforts at school and home to be simultaneously directed toward the same objectives using similar teaching strategies. This type of coordination leads to greater generalization on the part of the child. Coordination can partly be handled as the professionals and parents work together to develop the child's IEP. Once the IEP is developed, all parties have reached agreement on the appropriate goals and objectives for the child. However, further coordination is required to determine exactly what to teach at a given time. Professionals and parents might agree that weekly or biweekly home activity sheets would be helpful. These activity sheets developed by the teacher could include suggestions as to ways the parents can follow up at home on specific skills and concepts currently being taught at school. It is important for teachers to be reasonable in suggesting activities that can be accomplished within limited time constraints and typically in the absence of special instructional materials.

Group training sessions must be directed at the day-to-day concerns of parents. In order to insure the relevance of training, parents should participate in defining the topics of instruction. As parents recognize that they can be effective teachers of their children, their interest in more advanced training is likely to be increased. Additional guidelines for implementing group training are provided by Cansler et al. (1975) and Auenback (1968).

Classroom Helper

A third alternative for training parents as teachers is to involve them in the classroom program as helpers (e.g., Hayden & Haring, 1976; Wiegerink & Parrish, 1976). Participation in the classroom provides parents with an opportunity to observe their child and other handicapped children in an educational setting and to model the teaching strategies employed by the teacher. An additional advantage to this approach is that it provides the teacher with some valuable assistance.

Parents served as classroom helpers in the Regional Intervention Program (RIP) in Nashville, Tennessee (Wiegerink & Parrish, 1976). In this pre-school program, parents were expected to spend from 6 to 9 hours per week at the program working with their child. The first phase of their involvement included working with their child in individual tutoring sessions or on special behavioral problems under the supervision of a case manager. Parents learned behavioral skills which enabled them to work successfully with their child at home. In addition to learning essential behavior modification skills, information on child development in social, language, and motor areas was shared with parents. As the skills of the child and parent progressed, the handicapped child was transferred to a preschool class in the program. Parents were expected to serve as a volunteer in the class for a 6-month period. This opportunity to be in the classroom enabled parents to learn competencies which prepared them to be effective teachers of their children. At the conclusion of the 6-month volunteer period, some parents assumed other duties in the program such as conducting admission interviews with new families or administering assessment procedures. Parents had a significant role both as providers and recipients of the RIP services.

The classroom participation of parents requires careful and systematic planning. Serving as a classroom helper may be the outgrowth of home-based training or group training sessions. Parents should be given the back-up support to feel confident with this new role. In order to provide this support, educational professionals and parents might jointly establish the expectations for parental involvement. Expectations might differ for individual parents depending upon their schedule, time commitment, prerequisite teaching skills, and interest in being in the classroom.

When parents initially start to work in the classroom, professionals should arrange frequent conferences with parents to answer questions and provide any feedback on their performance. The most careful attention must be given to the interpersonal style of the professional-parent interactions in these conferences. It is important for parents to feel gratification and satisfaction in their new role which results from feelings of being successful. At the same time, the professionals must guide the parents into refining their teaching skills. Parents should be encouraged to participate in a self-evaluation process.

Some working parents will be unable to participate in the classroom program. Alternative methods will have to be developed for increasing their com-petency in working with their children. Home-based instruction and group parent meetings should be considered.

Parents as advocates

Advocacy in regard to handicapped individuals is a popular movement. Advocacy can take many directions but is mainly directed at federal or state laws, state agency regulations, local policies of school boards or county commissioners, community service agencies, potential employers, or other targets. The term *advocacy* has many different meanings; however, it is generally used to refer to advancing or securing the rights and interests of the client.

Interactions among professionals and parents often are advocacy oriented as efforts are made to advance or secure the rights and interests of handicapped persons and their families. A parent program with advocacy as a primary objective might focus on the following areas: (1) legal advocacy, (2) citizen advocacy, and (3) locating professional, community, family, and financial resources.

Legal Advocacy

Legal advocacy may take the form of instituting a lawsuit, lobbying for legislation, participating in a due process procedure, or seeking to influence administrative decisions. Parent-professional coalitions have been extremely successful in advancing the rights of handicapped persons through legal advocacy. Right-to-education litigation (Mills v. Board of Education, 1972; Pennsylvania Association of Retarded Children v. Commonwealth of Pennsylvania, 1972) and the passage of P.L. 94–142 have been the result of these efforts. Additionally, every state has passed mandatory education legislation for handicapped individuals which establishes the right to education at the level of state law. Since legal rights have already been established in regard to the education of handicapped students, the question as to whether continued legal advocacy efforts are necessary is sometimes raised. Unquestionably, legal advocacy for the handicapped population must continue in order to enhance the educational, vocational, personal, and recreational quality of life. Some of the particular issues requiring legal advocacy include mandatory educational services for handicapped individuals between the ages of 3 through 5 and 18 through 21, increased financial appropriations for the education of handicapped students, provision of meaningful career education, increased enforcement of nondiscriminatory employment practices, revision of guardianship legislation in accord with the principle of normalization, and review and revision of sterilization legislation.

Professionals and parents might organize group meetings to explore issues requiring legal advocacy efforts. If there is strong interest in becoming active legal advocates, training sessions should be planned for all concerned parties. The purpose of these sessions would be to define exactly what goals need to be accomplished and to plan strategies for accomplishing these goals. Since many professionals and parents alike are unsure of the most advantageous method of influencing legislation or administrative decisions, the training leader should have direct experience with legal advocacy and be knowledgeable in the organization of advocacy coalitions. Commercial materials may be helpful in preparing professionals and parents for legal advocacy. Biklen (1974) has prepared a manual which could serve as an excellent training tool for legal advocacy groups. Step-by-step procedures are outlined for various strategies of legal advocacy including demonstrations, letter writing, public hearings and fact-finding forums, communication, symbolic acts, negotiation, lobbying, and boycotts. National Association for Retarded Citizens (1973) and Paul, Neufeld, and Pelosi (1977) also provide practical assistance to persons planning advocacy campaigns. Other sources of information in regard to legal assistance and support include

Closer Look
Box 1492
Washington, D.C. 20013

The National Center for Law and the
   Handicapped
1235 North Eddy Street
South Bend, Indiana 46617

Council for Exceptional Children
Governmental Relations Unit
1920 Association Drive
Reston, Virginia 22091

National Center for Child Advocacy
Department of HEW, Office of the Secretary
P.O. Box 1182
Washington, D.C. 20013

American Civil Liberties Union
84 Fifth Avenue
New York, New York 10011

When the decision is made by educational professionals and parents in a particular program that collaborative efforts will be directed toward legal advocacy, communication should be established with other advocacy groups at the local, state, and national level. The previously listed addresses provide national contacts. At the local and state levels, contact should be made with interest organizations (associations for retarded citizens), advocacy councils, interagency coalitions, and special commissions established by local or state agencies to advocate for handicapped individuals. Advocacy efforts which are coordinated and speak with singular purpose for a substantial number of people are likely to be more successful in accomplishing their goals than multiple splinter groups. This kind of effort provides a meaningful forum in which parents and professionals can interact.

Citizen Advocacy

Wolfensberger (1972) describes citizen advocacy as individualized relationships of a short-term or long-term nature that may include formal roles (adoptive parenthood, guardianship) or informal roles (friend). The functions of the advocate will be dependent upon the needs of the client. Citizen advocacy is largely distinguished from other forms of advocacy by the personal relationship between two or more people in overcoming some of the complex life problems associated with handicapping conditions (Turnbull, 1977). Citizen advocacy relationships might be structured so that the advocate spends a specified amount of time with the handicapped individual each week. The shared time might be directed at personal communication about concerns or problems, developing leisure time hobbies, taking advantage of community recreation (swimming, shooting basketball), going shopping, or developing social skills. Citizen advocacy of an informal nature may be likened to Big Brother or Big Sister programs in many communities.

The need for moderately and severely handicapped persons to have personal relationships cannot be overstated. Sometimes in the desire to provide systematic training programs for them, overemphasis is given to skill development and underemphasis to humanistic concerns such as the development of personal relationships with others.

Parents and professionals might jointly establish a citizen advocacy program in a community. They would need to identify interested volunteers to serve as advocates and to provide training to the volunteers in order to prepare them for their advocacy roles. Volunteers might be recruited from civic or service clubs, religious organizations, nearby colleges or universities, senior citizens groups, or from the citizenry at large. Since many volunteers may have had limited previous exposure to handicapped persons, training sessions should involve an overview of handicapping conditions, principles of behavior management, and principles of normalization. The volunteers could be assigned a particular handicapped individual with whom they will develop a relationship considering preferences such as age and degree of disability. After individual assignments have been made, each advocate needs to be provided with more detailed information in regard to their associate such as level of skill development, special interests, and behavioral needs identified by the parents and professionals. This type of background information can enable the advocate to approach the new relationship with confidence. More detailed guidelines are provided to professionals and parents by the Texas Association for Retarded Citizens (1973) in regard to developing a citizen advocacy program.

Locating Professional, Community, Family, and Financial Resources

Many parents of moderately and severely retarded children are unsure of where to go for specialized professional help (pediatricians, speech therapists, physical therapists, ophthalmologists, orthopedists, psychiatrists, dentists, audiologists, and others), community recreation services, religious opportunities, baby-sitting, respite care services, or financial aid. Advocacy efforts are required in helping to locate or sometimes instigate resources and services.

In regard to locating professional help, parent meetings might be scheduled to give an overview of this information. A panel presentation could be made on the topic of obtaining various types of professional services or a representative from an interagency council might speak to the group on the particular services of various agencies set up to provide assistance to handicapped persons and their families. Parents should also be encouraged to share information with one another related to the particular professionals and agencies with whom they have had positive interactions. Educational professionals might start a community service file or directory which would need to be updated regularly. This file or directory could be made available to parents when they have particular questions.

Many parents of moderately and severely retarded children may find that the child is excluded from many community recreation services and religious opportunities. If these are problems, educa-

tional professionals might work with parents in trying to locate services or directly with the personnel of recreation and church programs to increase their awareness of the needs and to prepare them with skills to serve moderately and severely handicapped individuals.

Another major area in which parents often need help is in locating baby-sitting and respite care services. Some parents of moderately and severely retarded children have an extremely difficult time finding persons who feel comfortable and confident in assuming responsibility for their child. Educational professionals might encourage high-school service clubs or community volunteer groups to consider taking on such projects. When lists of baby-sitters and/or respite care providers are generated, professionals and parents might jointly plan and conduct some training sessions on topics such as behavior management, feeding problems, language stimulation, medication, and handling of any special problems. The provision of training can help insure the success of baby-sitters and respite care providers. Parents of children in an educational program might consider setting up a baby-sitting cooperative in which they agree to take care of one another's children. If parents are interested in such a strategy, a group parent meeting might be devoted to planning the logistics.

The final resource which requires advocacy on the part of parents and professionals is locating and obtaining financial aid. There can be extreme excess cost associated with moderate and severe handicapping conditions. Often the lack of awareness of financial resources results in many eligible persons receiving no assistance. This unfortunate situation can be prevented by active advocacy efforts directed at compiling accurate information on available financial resources. Educational professionals and parents might work on a collaborative project of compiling a financial directory. The purpose of this directory would be to identify financial sources including supplemental security income (Social Security Administration), Crippled Children's Services, Easter Seals, and Vocational Rehabilitation. Information should also be compiled on possible income tax deductions related to handicapping conditions. For each source of financial aid, information should be compiled on what constitutes eligibility, including the age of qualifying handicapped individuals, level of family income, type of disability, severity of disability, and manner in which the money can be spent. After the information has been collected, it should be shared with all parents and continually updated to retain its usefulness. If it becomes known that a potential financial source, such as supplemental security incomes, is turning parents away who should qualify for help according to specified regulations, professionals and parents might work together in securing the rights of parents who qualify for support.

Summary

Historically, parent-professional interactions have not been so positive and productive as they might have been. The passage of P.L. 94–142 has established new ground rules for both educational professionals and parents in interacting with one another. Associated with each of the six major principles of P.L. 94–142—zero reject, nondiscriminatory assessment, individualized educational programs, least restrictive alternative, due process, and parent participation—are requirements for shared decision making and responsibility among professionals and parents in insuring that handicapped students are provided with an appropriate education.

In addition to the interaction required by P.L. 94–142, educational professionals and parents frequently interact in parent programs developed as an integral part of the educational services delivered to the handicapped child. Suggestions for such interactions were made according to the various roles and responsibilities associated with being the parent of a handicapped child, such as parents as parents, parents as teachers, and parents as advocates.

Regardless of the particular issue being addressed, the key to successful parent-professional interactions is mutual respect and open communication. Appropriately preparing moderately and severely handicapped individuals with academic, social, emotional, and vocational skills to function in society is a complex process. It requires the best efforts of parents and professionals working together as partners to systematically accomplish mutually defined goals.

References

Auenback, A. *Parents learn through group discussion: Principles and protection of parent group education.* New York: John Wiley, 1968.

Baker, B. L. Camp Freedom: Behavior modification for retarded children in a therapeutic camp setting. *American Journal of Orthopsychiatry,* 1973, *43,* 418–427.

Baker, B. L., & Heifetz, L. J. The Read Project: Teaching manuals for parents of retarded children. In T. D. Tjossem (Ed.), *Intervention strategies for high risk infants and young children.* Baltimore, Md.: University Park Press, 1976. ·

Bereiter, C., & Engelmann, S. *Teaching disadvantaged children in the preschool.* Englewood Cliffs, N.J.: Prentice-Hall, 1966.

Biklen, D. *Let our children go: An organizing manual for advocates and parents.* Syracuse, N.Y.: Human Policy Press, 1974.

Bricker, W. A., & Bricker, D. D. The infant, toddler, and preschool research and intervention project. In T. D. Tjossem (Ed.), *Intervention strategies for high risk infants and young children.* Baltimore, Md.: University Park Press, 1976.

Brophy, J. E. Mothers as teachers of their own preschool children: The influence of socioeconomic status and task structure on teaching capacity. *Child Development,* 1970, *41,* 79–94.

Cansler, D. P., Martin, G. H., & Valand, M. C. *Working with families.* Winston-Salem, N.C.: Kaplan Press, 1975.

Coletta, A. J. *Working together: A guide to parent involvement.* Atlanta, Ga.: Humanics Limited, 1977.

Denhoff, E. & Hyman, I. Parent programs for developmental management. In T. D. Tjossem (Ed.), *Intervention strategies for high risk infants and young children.* Baltimore, Md.: University Park Press, 1976.

Federal Register. Washington, D.C.: U.S. Government Printing Office, August 23, 1977.

Giesey, R. (Ed.). *A guide for home visitors.* Nashville, Tenn.: DARCEE, George Peabody College, 1970.

Hayden, A. H., & Haring, N. G. Early intervention for high risk infants and young children: Programs for Down's syndrome children. In T. D. Tjossem (Ed.), *Intervention strategies for high risk infants and young children.* Baltimore, Md.: University Park Press, 1976.

Haynes, U. B. The national collaborative infant project. In T. D. Tjossem (Ed.), *Intervention strategies for high risk infants and young children.* Baltimore, Md.: University Park Press, 1976.

Hess, R. D., & Shipman, V. C. Early experience and the socialization of cognitive models in children. *Child Development,* 1965, *36,* 869–886.

Karnes, M. B., Wollersheim, J. P., Stoneburner, R. L., Hodgins, A. S., & Teska, J. A. An evaluation of two preschool programs for disadvantaged children: A traditional and a highly structured experimental preschool. *Exceptional Children,* 1968, *34,* 667–676.

Mills v. Board of Education of the District of Columbia. 348 F. Supp. 866 (D.C.D.C., 1972).

National Association for Retarded Citizens. *Action guidelines: Evaluating and monitoring education services for mentally retarded persons.* Arlington, Tex.: National Association for Retarded Citizens, 1973.

Paul, J. L., Neufeld, G. R. & Pelosi, J. W. (Eds.). *Child advocacy within the system.* Syracuse, N.Y.: Syracuse University Press, 1977.

Paul, J. W., Turnbull, A. P. & Cruickshank, W. M. Main-streaming: A practical guide. Syracuse, N.Y: Syracuse University Press, 1977.

Pennsylvania Association for Retarded Children v. Commonwealth of Pennsylvania, 343 F. Supp. 279 (ED. Pa., 1972).

Schlesinger, H. S., & Meadow, K. P. Emotional support for parents. In D. L. Lillie & P. L. Trohanis (Eds.), *Teaching parents to teach.* New York: Walker, 1976.

Schulz, J. B. The parent-professional conflict. In A. P. Turnbull & H. R. Turnbull (Eds.), *Parents speak out: Views from the other side of the two-way mirror.* Columbus, Ohio: Charles E. Merrill, 1978.

Shearer, D. E., & Shearer, M. S. The Portage Project: A model for early childhood intervention. In T. D. Tjossem (Ed.), *Intervention strategies for high risk infants and young children.* Baltimore, Md.: University Park Press, 1976.

Shearer, M. S. A home-based parent training model. In D. L. Lillie & P. L. Trohanis (Eds.), *Teaching parents to teach.* New York: Walker, 1976.

Texas Association for Retarded Citizens. *Citizen advocacy: A manual for local implementation and operation.* Austin, Tex.: Texas Association for Retarded Citizens, 1973.

Tjossem, T. D. (Ed.). *Intervention strategies for high risk infants and young children.* Baltimore, Md.: University Park Press, 1976.

Turnbull, A. P. Citizen advocacy in special education training. *Education and Training of the Mentally Retarded,* 1977, *12,* 166–169.

Turnbull, H. R., & Turnbull, A. P. Deinstitutionalization and the law. *Mental Retardation,* 1975, *13,* 14–20.

Wiegerink, R., & Parrish, V. A parent-implemented preschool program. In D. L. Lillie & P. L. Trohanis (Eds.), *Teaching parents to teach.* New York: Walker, 1976.

Wolfensberger, W. *The principle of normalization in human services.* Toronto, Canada: National Institute on Mental Retardation, 1972.

Note

1. Turnbull, A.P., Tyler, D.K., & Morrell, B.B. *An educational model for deinstitutionalization.* Proceedings of the Council for Exceptional Children Institute on Right to Education, CEC National Topical Conference, 1976.

Introduction to Chapter 16

In this final chapter, Debby and Jim Smith sketch for us a picture of our future horizons in the provision of services for the severely handicapped. Their view is spectacular, and breath-taking in its sweep of topics. Their approach is diverse and includes careful predictions of trends in the prevention of serious handicaps and the conditions which foster them, the inclusion of the handicapped in the normal "swing of life," environmental and architectual barriers and necessary modifications, advances and deficiencies in our teaching methods and curriculum, preparation of personnel from teachers to paraprofessionals, and recent and present legislation and the legal contests that produced our current laws.

As you reflect upon these trends, a multitude of questions will be stimulated. For example, are you aware what Public Law 94–142 actually mandates and what extensive community and state commitments will be requested over the next three years? With some predictions, the solutions are presently at hand, but the problems must wait until geographical distances and personnel shortages are overcome. For example, reflect upon the time delay between the available teaching technologies and their common application in classrooms, on wards, and in homes where the severely handicapped learn. Many of you must have a collection of specific illustrations of this discrepancy.

As you read this chapter, consider that these predictions describe the path on which all of us are walking; and while we may influence our future direction, we will also be influenced by it.

16

Trends

*This chapter was written by **Deborah D. Smith** and **James O. Smith**, Department of Special Education, University of New Mexico.*

The advent of Public Law 94–142 brings to this nation a mandate of education for all. Those children who in the past were excluded from educational services for many reasons are now being brought into the mainstream of American education.

With these children and youth comes a perplexing array of problems and challenges. As is so often true in special education, the children have come to school before either our teachers or our technology is ready.

The formulation of policies, regulations, and procedures that will come to dictate practices are going to derive from basic societal values and judgments. Our leaders, reflecting personal convictions based on their clinical experiences, past research, or other reasons, will affect the quantity and quality of change. Whether this nation creates optimal and diverse environments reflecting continuing and deep commitment of all those concerned remains to be seen.

This text seeks to detail the current status of research and practice with ample suggestions of what can and ought to be. This final chapter seeks to focus on necessary directions that must be taken in the future to assure continuing progress in developing optimal service delivery systems. Each of these directions will be seen as a trend toward the ideal of society's commitment to the worth and dignity of every individual.

Prevention[1]

Over the past decade and a half, the prevention of mental retardation and other disabling conditions has remained of primary concern. During this period of time, medical researchers have learned more about various etiologies which cause mental retardation. This has led to the discovery of ways to prevent and control specific diseases and conditions which frequently lead to retardation.

Generally, the aspects of prevention are divided into four categories which relate to time of occurrence: preconception, pregnancy, delivery, and early childhood. The remainder of this section centers on preventive trends in each period.

Preconception

Mental retardation can be prevented before conception by immunization against disease, proper

---

1. For more in-depth information about etiology, the reader is referred to Robinson and Robinson (1976) and Grossman (1973).

nutrition for the prospective mother, genetic assessment, and the timing of pregnancy to avoid high risk periods of life (onset of pregnancy either too early or too late). Through knowledge of these four kinds of preconception preventive techniques, many trends come to light. Most involve both diagnosis and education.

During this past decade, for example, medical researchers discovered an effective and inexpensive immunization against rubella. Through education and better availability of medical services to the poor, in the future all those who might contract various diseases, such as rubella, which can lead to retardation will be immunized.

Genetic counseling is a concept which is still emerging. As more is learned about those genetic factors which lead to retardation and the diagnostic process is refined through the use of computers and more advanced technology, this educational process will be more available to and used by couples planning a family.

Through the food stamp and other government-sponsored programs, we have already seen an initial effort to attain the goal of guaranteeing proper nutrition to all regardless of economic status. In the future this will have to be coupled with more education about basic nutrition and budgeting if there is to be a reduction in the frequency of retardation due to poor maternal nutrition.

Finally, an important preconception prevention trend already emerging is family planning. The public needs to be educated, and will be in the future, about the increased probability of retardation related to maternal age: either early adolescence or over 35 years. Knowledge that there is an increased risk if child bearing occurs either too early or too late and information about and access to contraception devices will prevent those cases of retardation caused by poor family planning.

Possibly the goal of reducing the frequency of retardation through preconception tactics will require education of the public, which can only be accomplished through restructuring the high-school curricula to include courses on the important aspects of family life: budgeting, nutrition, family planning, child rearing, etc.

Pregnancy

There are many current and future trends which relate to controlling those factors which cause retardation during the pregnancy period. These center on protection from disease, good nutrition, proper medical supervision, diagnosis of the fetus' condi-

tion in high-risk mothers, and parental choice for the termination of pregnancy. Amazingly, 30% of expectant mothers in some rural and urban areas do not see a doctor until delivery (President's Committee on Mental Retardation, 1976b). If the incidence of retardation is to be reduced, increasing emphasis must be given to the delivery of medical services to all expectant mothers. Since maternal malnutrition is a factor which contributes to prematurity and other neurological abnormalities, in the future there must be increased emphasis on public education about the nutritional value of processed foods and the provision of dietary supplements for high-risk pregnant mothers. There should be and will be better availability of medical attention for all those below the poverty level who are expecting children.

There will be a higher frequency of the application of newly developed, safe diagnostic procedures which determine the condition of the fetus. Jacobson (cited in National Association of Retarded Citizens, 1976b) reported that "more than 9,900 laboratory studies of amniotic fluid will be performed this year, a 50 percent increase over 1975" (p. 3). Now that amniocentesis is a safe diagnostic procedure for diagnosing fetal defects, more doctors will use this procedure and, with public education, more will request the application of this diagnostic procedure. If amniocentesis indicates that the fetus is abnormal, in some cases medical supervision can minimize the disabling condition. In most cases, however, the parents will have to decide whether or not to terminate the pregnancy.

Birth

The third time for medical preventive techniques to be applied is at birth. More and more infants will be screened for metabolic disorders such as PKU and endemic cretinism which through dietary and medical control can be prevented from developing into retardation. In the future, infant screening procedures will become routine and even mandatory by state law.

Rh sensitization can be controlled now if, within 72 hours after birth, the mother is injected with gamma globulin which prevents Rh sensitization with future pregnancies. It is apparent that if protection from the Rh problem can be achieved, in the future medical researchers will find and control other conditions which lead to retardation.

The incidence of mental retardation could be reduced if all high-risk mothers were able to give birth with proper medical supervision, so sick infants can receive intensive medical care. This is substantiated by some Oregon data obtained in 1973. There the infant mortality rate was 53.4% for those not delivered in hospitals and 18.4% for those born in hospitals (President's Committee on Mental Retardation, 1976b). Possibly if regional medical facilities staffed by doctors and paramedical personnel appropriately trained in infant care were predominant, a further reduction in retardation would be seen in the near future.

Early childhood

The last group of prevention techniques is basically educational in nature. Parents need and should receive education about the appropriate nutritional needs of infants and should receive dietary supplements if necessary. If metabolic conditions are diagnosed at birth, parents must be trained in the appropriate dietary management for their infants. As more types of these conditions are discovered, more parents will receive this kind of management training. Although great strides have been made to remove environmental hazards, such as lead-based paint, from young children's environments, only a start has been made. The public will need to receive continual education to be able to detect environmental dangers and receive governmental help, if necessary, to have these potential dangers eliminated.

The number of early stimulation programs will be increased in the future. Although severe retardation cannot be eliminated through such projects, certainly more growth and development can be achieved with early training.

The last important cause of retardation which must be prevented has existed for many years but has received a considerable amount of attention only recently. Only through more counseling programs, public education, and crisis facilities will child abuse be eliminated from our society.

Most causes of retardation which manifest themselves during the preconception, pregnancy, and birth periods are the domain of the medical profession. The essence of the trends in these areas was summarized well in *Mental Retardation: Century of Decision* (President's Commission on Mental Retardation, 1976a).

The biomedical problems of reducing the incidence of mental retardation center in human reproduction and the processes of human development. One essential focus of the problem is on the expansion and refinement of scientific knowledge. A second focus is on the advancement of clinical applications of knowledge to diagnosis and treatment of existing pathology. A third is on the development of public health provision for anticipating and intervening in the causal chains that produce mental retardation. (p. 9)

Summary

Here, as for each section of this chapter, an attempt has been made to summarize those trends which we feel will receive considerable attention during the next decade. Those for the area of prevention follow.

1. *National immunization programs* to insure the protection of all people from contagious disease which can lead to retardation.

2. *Advanced medical diagnostic procedures* will be refined through the expansion of basic knowledge and more efficiently analyzed through computers and advanced technology. This will lead to the greater availability of medical information to be used prior to conception in genetic counseling and in planning for medical treatment during and after the pregnancy period.

3. Junior and senior high-school basic course offerings will be enriched and increased so that all will receive *education* on family planning, birth control, consumer awareness, budgeting, nutrition, and child development so that the frequency of retardation caused by poor nutrition, inappropriate maternal age, and child abuse might be reduced.

4. There will be even greater *availability of medical attention* to supervise pregnancies, avoid difficulties at the birth of one child and prevent difficulties with ensuing children, and provide intensive infant care to those infants who so require it immediately after birth.

Inclusion

Many persons would immediately point to the inclusion of severely and profoundly handicapped persons in school programs as a highly visible trend. More fundamental and all too subtle is the trend toward permitting, allowing, or encouraging these persons to be included in *all* aspects of life. Whether we realize it or not, most moderately, severely, and profoundly handicapped persons have been excluded—from our families, from churches, schools, public transportation, community organizations, and, in fact, oftentimes from our thoughts. For example, in a 1970 national study of 616 public organizations, it was found that over half the churches, libraries, and museums did not think that handicapped persons resided in their service area (President's Committee on Mental Retardation, 1976b).

At present, the clearest trend is toward inclusion rather than exclusion. This will take many forms and result in a far more normal, dynamic, and visible life style for these citizens. With mandated inclusion of these children and youth in school programs will come greater acceptance in other community supportive and adjunctive service. A ripple effect will certainly be felt. For example, once the child enters school, she will certainly enjoy some field trips; one field trip may well be the local library—if the library is found to be inaccessible because of architecture design, then discussion begins on removing artificial environmental limitations—and so on, and on it goes. Children in school join after-school functions, e.g., Brownies, Cub Scouts, Boy Scouts, Girl Scouts. Transportation is necessary, requiring review of the accessibility of existing school buses. When these children and youth participate, further ripple effects occur involving the feasibility of taxis, public transportation, and, in fact, all common carriers. This trend of including persons in all facets of life has great ramifications far beyond "attending" a public school for several hours each day. Under inclusion, trends clearly fall into several general categories.

Greater age range for school

Age limitations will continue to be expanded downwards and upwards until society accepts full responsibility of life planning for severely and profoundly handicapped citizens. Parameters such as chronological ages 6 to 18 will become 3 through 21 and eventually infant through young adult (24), and, in time, chronological age will disappear as a criterion for receiving developmental services.

Increased types of educational programs

All possible meaningful developmental services will be brought to bear for the severely and profoundly handicapped. Just "going to school" will appear too restrictive and narrow as developmental services are brought to infants by professionals and parents (and possibly siblings). Inclusion in developmental programs will mean hospital teaching programs, itinerant services, special classes in regular schools

(Smith & Arkans, 1974), special schools, and the full cascade of services so often cited (Deno, 1970; Dunn, 1973; President's Committee on Mental Retardation, 1976b; Reynolds, 1962) as necessary for the exceptional. More and more, these persons will be included in postsecondary programs similar to the currently operating program for mentally retarded persons at Metropolitan State College in Denver, Colorado (Tennessee Chapter, American Association on Mental Deficiency, November 1976). This college program sponsors classes covering money management, communication, human sexuality, leisure time, and transportation.

Inclusion in society and normal life experiences

Severely and profoundly handicapped persons will be included as citizens of our society. This will have a far-reaching impact on the attitudes of those who heretofore regarded the handicapped as "wards," "charges," "patients," or, in extreme cases, as "vegetables." The future suggests that each individual's personal development is an individual right and a societal charge. These persons will become informed as much as possible, be registered where possible, and vote when possible. More and more, the handicapped will represent themselves, suggesting, no doubt, further insightful and meaningful paths for their own continued progress.

These persons will be included in many more activities that relate directly to quality of life. In many instances, this will mean a fuller expression of human sexuality and love, including dating, heterosexual companionship, and marriage among those who may remain dependent.

The moderately, severely, and profoundly handicapped will be included in and enjoy far more leisure time pursuits. One need only see the remarkable film "Like Other People" (Teitelbaum, 1972) to clearly realize how possible it is to restrict, unnecessarily, the total life space of the handicapped. Leisure time pursuits can no longer be regarded as incessant, blaring TV on a ward or mobiles on a crib but rather they must be seen as a full spectrum of things most persons, including you and I, enjoy. This means movies, trips to parks, adapted games, reading and pictorial materials, trips (local, regional, national), and inclusion not just in formal church services but in all other appropriate activities. In some instances, this will mean beer busts, football games, basketball games, and parties—activities all long overdue for these handicapped persons.

Summary

During the next decade, trends pertaining to inclusion center on the following.

1. Only during the past few years have we seen the severely and profoundly handicapped *included in appropriate education programs*. In the future, we will find that *all* children actually are attending schools. Gradually, the age range for these programs will widen, so for many children school will begin at birth and seldom conclude before age 24.

2. The severely and profoundly handicapped will be allowed and encouraged to *become full members of community organizations* which will extend to them the types of normal experiences available to all.

Environments

As we seek to allow each individual a full and continuing participation in all aspects of life, we will see several trends emerge relating to environmental modifications.

Further strides will be made in all modes of transporting nonambulatory persons. Further creativity will be found in designing supportive desks, beds, and educational material presentation formats to allow the physically disabled to learn more readily.

Most important will be sweeping changes in the design of new buildings to be used by all the public. This will include removing architectural barriers that now prohibit many handicapped persons from various pursuits. Important changes are already occurring in modification of various physical plants to allow use by those with physical limitations. These changes include ramps, elevators, special toilet facilities, lowered water fountains, pay telephones, etc.

Another facet of environmental design not often discussed is its effect on behavioral development or control. Arnold Ganges, devoted friend of the handicapped and Seattle architect, noted that the direct effect of newly designed 6-person living units was to reduce the frequency of behavior problems with profoundly retarded persons (President's Committee on Mental Retardation, 1976a). Much more thinking will go into designing environments for the severely and profoundly handicapped that relate to and foster their physical, social, and mental development.

Another trend will be the physical integration of the classroom with occupational and physical therapy. The old idea of a "wing" for P.T., O.T., and speech removes all possibility of on-going, continuing therapeutic development with education. More and more these activities will become a functional whole and will permeate the entire school day (Sternat, Messina, Nietupski, Lyon, & Brown, 1977).

Summary

Two general trends emerge as noteworthy in the area of environmental change.

1. *Open access to all buildings,* civic centers (ranging from governmental to shopping centers), *and modes of transportation* through modification of existing structures and enforced building codes for new structures will occur. To accomplish this, improved comprehensive guidelines will be developed and supported through legislation to insure their implementation.

2. Increased research interests to *determine the influence of environmental structures and organizations on human behavior* must occur so that environments more conducive to education and daily living can be designed.

Curriculum and Methodology

During the past few years, many changes have been noted in both the type and kind of educational experience offered the moderately, severely, and profoundly handicapped. What these individuals are taught has changed as much as how, when, and where they receive instruction. Much of the current thinking about when the handicapped should be taught which skills has been expressed expertly in the earlier chapters of this book. Therefore, only some of these current trends are highlighted here.

Early education

One extremely important trend, probably started in the late 1950s by Kirk (1958) and extended by others (Guskin & Spicker, 1968; Weikart, 1967), has found increasing support and emphasis with the more severely handicapped. Early intervention programs, many even beginning shortly after birth, have indicated that remarkable gains can be made by the handicapped population if careful, systematic training begins in the early months and years. Recently many model infant and early education programs have been developed. For example, the highly acclaimed work at the University of Wisconsin has shown that early intervention can change and maintain positive growth scores in intelligence (Heber, cited in President's Committee on Mental Retardation, 1976b; Heber & Garber, 1971). The Down's Syndrome Project at the University of Washington (Hayden & Haring, 1975) has demonstrated that remarkable growth can be made by this population if systematic training begins early in the child's life and continues on through the school years.

There are several indicators of governmental support and encouragement for the further expansion of early intervention projects for the handicapped. Government support should not only serve to allow for the continuation of the excellent work already begun but also provide the impetus for others to initiate innovative programs. A most encouraging statement indicating governmental support is found in the President's Committee on Mental Retardation's Report to the President (1976a): "The emphasis of public policy is on developing the potential of retarded persons by early identification and intervention through education, social habilitation and vocational training" (p. 3). Such supportive comments found in government reports are certainly encouraging for the future development of the handicapped, but laws which mandate the inclusion of the handicapped in government-sponsored early education programs are even more demonstrative of existing support for early intervention programs for the handicapped. One example of this rests in the 1972 amendment to the Economic Opportunity Act which requires that at least 10% of those children attending Head Start programs be handicapped.

There appears to be a trend for the handicapped to be included in state-supported preschool programs also. A number of states now have mandatory legislation requiring the establishment of preschool programs for the severely handicapped (Haring, 1975). As of 1975, the government estimated that 31 of 42 states responding to a government survey had day training programs for severely handicapped preschoolers. This survey, unfortunately, only tells us that programs exist and are available to severely handicapped youngsters. The data do not indicate how these programs are staffed or what the curriculum comprises. Since, however, only a few years ago practically no state-supported preschool (or even school) programs were available for this population of learners, a positive trend is clearly indicated. The next, of course, is specific attention to the curriculum of these programs and the efficacy of the teaching plans. This trend has

already begun and will receive considerable attention in the next decade.

Pragmatic curricula

The mere availability of programs does not guarantee positive growth and change in student performance. There needs to be a curriculum for each educational program which is practical and which centers on those skills imperative for independent or semi-independent living. With a pragmatic curriculum also must come a verified methodology which insures, as much as possible, that the specified curriculum targets are mastered. In the past, we have seen few successful products of programs for the severely handicapped. This was partly attributable to unrefined teaching skills but more importantly to our lack of expectancy for these students to learn. All too often, we have provided them with an impractical and useless curriculum, poorly conceived and poorly taught. Unfortunately, the situation described in a recent National Association for Retarded Citizens report (1976a) is not so historical as we might wish:

> Because of limited educational opportunities in the past, and the almost inevitable placement of severely and profoundly retarded citizens in large institutions, it might once have been acceptable to teach this population to "walk in line," or "make pot holders," with little concern as to why such skills were taught. Now, though, severely handicapped will be enrolled in public school programs for as long as 21 years. Longitudinal public education, coupled with the goals of the deinstitutionalization and child advocacy movements, compel us to justify the teaching of any specific skill. (p. 14)

As discussed in almost every chapter of this book, the skills to evaluate what a teacher does in the classroom are available and are commonly used. We can determine whether a teacher is successful in helping her students master the skills which she presents. This can be accomplished almost immediately through the use of direct and daily measurement procedures. Unfortunately, many times we do not know whether what is being taught and mastered is truly important to the learner until many years after instruction, when the learner enters society. Therefore, curriculum targets must be carefully scrutinized to insure the feasibility of what is being taught.

Unfortunately, we have no guides to assist us in

identifying the appropriate curriculum targets for the severely handicapped. This is because the "graduates" of our recently initiated early education programs will not reach adulthood for many years; and, therefore, we do not know what the potential of this population really is. As Haring (1975) so aptly stated: "Still, a critical need exists to change any conceptual limitations placed on future growth of the severely/profoundly handicapped: Their potential is practically unknown because effective intervention programs have not existed until recently" (p. 427). It is apparent, therefore, that we will continue to strive to determine the most appropriate, practical curriculum for many years to come. We do not start from a total lack of knowledge, however, for some guides are clear. Much of what is taught to the normal child is not practical for the moderately or severely handicapped. Even the curriculum presented to the moderately handicapped in classes for the trainable may not be suitable for the more severely handicapped learner. As Bijou (cited in National Association for Retarded Citizens, 1976a) points out:

> Teachers must abandon their traditional concepts of curriculum if they are to be successful with severely and profoundly retarded students. They must be trained to deal with a whole range of behaviors that have rarely been the concern of the public schools. The traditional three R's are simply not enough here. Teachers must be prepared to help their students in the world from the moment they wake up in the morning until they go to bed at night. (p. 7)

This educational responsibility is awesome, for the number of curriculum targets which must become long-term and short-term objectives for each student is almost infinite.

Packaged instructional materials

We know from the literature that a vast number of practical skills can be mastered by the profoundly and severely handicapped. To use only some self-help skills as examples, we know that dressing (Ball, Seris, & Payne, 1971; Martin, Kehoe, Bird, Jensen, & Darbyshire, 1971; Watson, 1973), self-feeding (Ferneti, Lent, & Stevens, 1974; Groves & Carroccio, 1971; Spradlin, Note 1), toileting (Foxx & Azrin, 1973; Levine & Elliott, 1970), grooming (Horner, Billionis, & Lent, 1975; Keilitz, Horner, & Brown, 1975; Lewis, Ferneti, & Keilitz, 1975a, 1975b; Treffry, Martin, Samels, & Watson, 1970),

and many more skills can all be mastered in a relatively short period of time by most learners if teachers use systematic instructional procedures. Unfortunately, however, this information primarily appears in research reports, journal articles, and in a few instructional packages, such as those prepared by Project MORE (Ferneti et al., 1974; Foster, Billionis, & Lent, 1976; Horner et al., 1975; Igenthron, Ferneti, & Keilitz, 1975; Kielitz et al., 1975; Lewis et al., 1975a, 1975b; Stevens, Ferneti, & Lent, 1975), and is not always available to assist the teacher who is seeking to help students master these specific skills.

Self-help is not the only skill area where there is a dearth of prepackaged materials to assist teachers in their program planning efforts. Fristoe (1976) found in her national survey that 299 language systems or programs can be identified, but only 39 are commercially available in kit or program format. She found that only 31 of these systems are reported in the literature in either journals or books. The rest are either in preparation or in limited editions. It is hoped that more language development programs written for and verified with the profoundly handicapped will become available in the years to come.

As the students are handicapped, so, too, are the teachers, for there are practically no commercial materials available in any curriculum area which are designed and field-tested with the severely and profoundly handicapped. Because commercial publishers have not developed and manufactured materials for the severely and profoundly handicapped population, teachers are forced to either develop their own materials (Smith, Smith, & Edgar, 1976) or adapt those materials which were created for more able learners and different tasks (Roberts, 1976). As more school programs for severely handicapped students open, there will be a greater demand for relevant and functional materials and, consequently, a better supply of this much needed resource. More realistically, however, the limited potential market will mean a dearth of needed materials for some time to come.

Until appropriate curricular resources are available, a great temptation looms before teachers, one which they must resist. Because of the limited number of commercially available or prepackaged instructional programs, and because teachers do not have enough time for individualized instructional programs for all students for the entire school day, some teachers are tempted to place several students in one curricular activity whether it is warranted or not. It is vital to remember that the decision about what will be taught to students comes before the selection, purchase, or adaptation of the instructional materials. As Roberts (1976) so wisely observed about the relationship between materials and curriculum targets, "This crucial decision should not be dictated by the availability of materials but rather should be determined by the immediate and long term goals of the child" (p. 75).

Multidisciplinary approach

As mentioned earlier, the number and kinds of curriculum targets which become important long- and short-term goals for these students are different from those of other learners. A trend which has started in many states and school districts and which will expand to many, many more in the future is the inclusion of curriculum targets which belong to disciplines other than education. For example, many handicapped youngsters have great difficulty with fine and gross motor skills; some are not ambulatory and have not developed the physical skills of their counterparts. Many of these students need to develop reach, grasp, and release movements. Others are deficient in hand, head, mouth, and tongue movements which are so important for proficiency in self-feeding. For many of these students, their motor reflexes are insufficient; they have poor muscle tone and incomplete reflex motions.

Typically, teachers are not trained to use the equipment or therapy techniques which might enable their students to gain motor abilities necessary for the mastery of daily living skills. There are two disciplines, occupational and physical therapy, whose highly trained specialists can evaluate student performance and plan activities which will expedite the development of these and comparable skills. As more knowledge is gained about physical development, language development, etc., it will become increasingly apparent that classroom teachers cannot develop programs for their students across all curriculum targets without the assistance of specialists from other disciplines.

Unfortunately, at the present time, there are not enough occupational therapists to adequately staff all school settings where the severely and profoundly handicapped are found (Anderson, Greer, & McFadden, 1976). Although the same is true for physical therapists, successful attempts have already been made to have physical therapists serve in itinerant roles (Scarnati, 1971). Possibly, some time in the distant future, there will be an increased emphasis on limiting the demands on the teachers of severely handicapped and enlarging the number of personnel from other disciplines to work with these students. Until that time, the few specialists available will have to serve in consulting roles, leaving the teacher as the implementer of programs established by others.

As other disciplines will work with teachers, teachers will need to work with parents to increase the educational part of the day from 6 hours to the entire day. To accomplish all of the goals which must be mastered, curriculum planning and implementation must be a 24-hour venture. Consistent and comprehensive 24-hour programs can be developed through proper communication between home and school (Odle, Greer, & Anderson, 1976).

Summary

The following highlights the major trends in the curriculum area.

1. There will be an increasing number of *infant and early childhood programs with appropriate curriculum targets* specifically designed for the moderately, severely, and profoundly handicapped population.

2. Curricula will become *more practical and relate to maximal independence of the learner*.

3. A *multidisciplinary approach* to the education of this population is a necessity and will become a reality.

Personnel

Great changes will occur in the training of those persons who, in turn, will directly affect the progress made by the moderately, severely, and profoundly handicapped. It appears that "personnel" will be redefined to include all persons whose contact with the child or youth allows a potential for training and development. We will see more specific efforts made to train natural parents, foster parents, house parents, siblings, teachers, paraprofessionals, therapists, doctors, nurses, and, it is hoped, program administrators.

Family

One trend that is growing in importance is the move toward parent training (Burke & Saettler, 1976; Haring, 1975; Hayden, McGinness, & Dmitriev, 1976; Kroth, 1977; Kroth, 1978; Quick, Little, & Campbell, 1974; Roos, 1975). For many years, parents appeared apart from, rather than a part of, the therapeutic and educational effort. At last, it is apparent that maximal development of the handicapped child must include the parent in a vital and key role. As suggested by others, 24-hour handicapped children need 24-hour programs!

These same ideas of informing and educating the parent as a developmentalist will extend to those serving in a surrogate parent role. Parents, foster parents, and house parents could all profit from demonstrated programs now available. Ample references and papers relating such programs are available (Anderson & Greer, 1976). A specific parent-training program, the Parent Technology System (PTTS), that appears to hold very real promise is detailed by Watson and Bassinger (1974). This verified system has effected changes in youngsters' behavior by reorganizing the social environment in such a way that significant others, particularly parents, utilize systematic reinforcement procedures consistently. After reviewing many studies of parent-training programs, Watson and Bassinger conclude

. . . They provide impressive evidence that child behavior modification programs employing parents as behavior modification technicians have the potential to provide an economical, effective, alternative to existing clinical intervention techniques. (p. 4)

Our expectation is that siblings will receive more attention as possible trainers. Current efforts have been directed more toward furnishing information to develop "understanding" in siblings of the profoundly handicapped. In some cases, the sibling has also been included in training programs with and without the parents (Baker, 1976). Such programs would allow more realistic expectations and consistent management of the child while in the home. One would hope to see further investigation of this area.

Teachers

A most definitive and noticeable trend will be the increasing attention paid to training programs for teachers of the severely and profoundly handicapped. In an already classic article in this field, Sontag, Burke, and York (1973) stated

At this point in time, it is a rare teacher who has been able to acquire all the skills needed to teach severely handicapped students merely from the experiences obtained in his or her college level

special education training programs. Assuming that the previous statement is accurate, then it seems logical that there are very few teachers in the field who have the competencies to teach severely handicapped students and that there are very few, if any, teacher training programs producing teachers with those needed competencies. Thus, most of the new classes arranged for these students will be staffed by untrained teachers. (p. 23)

Further evidence of concerted focus on this problem of the teacher is given by Beth Stephens (1976), past president of the Council for Exceptional Children's Mental Retardation Division, in *Education and Training of the Mentally Retarded:*

What teaching competencies are necessary to provide individually appropriate educational programs? Can traditional special education teacher training models be revised in a way that will provide adequate preparation, or is a reorientation of objectives and techniques required to meet the needs of highly heterogeneous lower functioning pupils. . . . Which is more appropriate, a teacher training or a therapist training model; or will a blending of these with other designs result in the evolution of innovative approaches to staff training? (p. 3)

Without a doubt, the teacher must acquire more skills related to the child's physical development. Present teachers, most of whom were trained to serve mildly handicapped children, are primarily interested in the development and remediation of academics with some emphasis on group management. There will be great strides made in redesigning teacher education programs to include much more emphasis on sensory motor development, physical mobility and coordination, self-care development, language development, and social behavior development (Lucky & Addison, 1974). The teacher will require programs much more influenced by the modalities of physical therapy, by the meaningfulness and practicality of occupational therapy, and by the indispensable basics of speech and language therapy. Further support for this trend and elaboration of the role of the "educational synthesizer" is furnished by Bricker (1976). A nuclear program which represents what the future thrust will be in teacher education is described by Sailor, Guess, and Lavis (1975).

Presently, in the rush to serve, it appears that a great many colleges and universities are initiating new programs to prepare such teachers. Already, the advisability of "everyone getting into the act" has been questioned. Meyen (cited in National Association for Retarded Citizens, 1976a) suggests that a typical special education faculty may not be equipped or prepared to initiate new courses or to develop such new programs. One possible trend would be the development of a network of regional training centers which would allow better use of available resources without denying training possibilities to all service areas. Tawney (Note 2) has even gone so far as to strongly suggest to Bureau for the Education of the Handicapped that measures must be taken now to *limit* the number of training programs, to establish criteria for programs to be developed, and to set a time line for the development of such regional programs as can assure quality training for the teachers of moderately and severely handicapped.

Auxiliary personnel

The trend toward upgrading the skills of paraprofessional persons in line with their responsibilities for human service is long overdue. Many hopeful signs for this trend appear on the horizon. The United States General Accounting Office in a report to the Secretary of Health, Education and Welfare (General Accounting Office, 1976) emphasized the need to prepare and utilize paraprofessionals in the implementation of individualized instruction for the handicapped. The Mental Retardation Division of the Council for Exceptional Children has just added a new department, "Associate Teaching Personnel," which will focus on the roles of those heretofore called "nonprofessional" or "paraprofessional." The journal *Education and Training of the Mentally Retarded* (Galloway & Larsen, 1976) has lent its support to this trend, which should help stimulate as well as publicize worthwhile efforts in this important area.

Evidence of the success of further development of paraprofessional skills is evident in an early program carried out in a state institution with severely/profoundly handicapped children (Guess, Smith, & Ensminger, 1971). In this project, institutional aides functioned very effectively as "language developmentalists" under the supervision of a trained speech clinician. Further evidence of "readiness" for a trend toward paraprofessional development is the remarkable work around the University of Kansas–Kansas Neurological Institute consortium (Tucker, Hollis, Sailor, Horner, Kelly, & Guess,

1976). One need only view the thoroughness and detail of this performance-based curriculum to realize that, once again, we are prepared to do much more on a nationwide basis than we are currently doing. One would hope that developed innovative training programs such as this could be disseminated nationally (Adamson, Note 3) and that regional workshops and training efforts could be begun at once. For a comprehensive treatment of the future role, uses, and training patterns of supportive personnel, the work of Sigelman and Bensberg (1976) should be reviewed.

Another trend grows out of the implications of Public Law 94–142. With "education for all" in its neophytic stage, traditional definitions of education are being challenged and modified. Roos (1971) states

Education is the process whereby an individual is helped to develop new behavior or to apply existing behavior, so as to equip him to live more effectively with his total environment. It should be clear, therefore, that when we speak of education we do not limit ourselves to the so called academics. We certainly include the development of basic self-help skills. Indeed, we include those very complex bits of behavior which help to define an individual as human. We include such skills as toilet training, dressing, grooming, communicating and so on. (p. 2)

Such a definition involves occupational, physical, and speech therapists as more than adjunctive members of a team. A future trend will see increasing emphasis upon the roles and skill development of the physical therapist (Scarnati, 1971; Wilson & Parks, 1970), the occupational therapist (Anderson et al., 1976; Copeland, Ford, & Solon, 1976), and speech clinician (Bricker & Bricker, 1970; Graham, 1976; Gray & Ryan, 1973) in relation to the severely and profoundly handicapped.

Summary

It is clear that many trends center on who works with the handicapped.

There will be more emphasis placed on the *systematic training of all those who interact on a regular basis with the handicapped*. All family members, teachers, educational support personnel, and other professionals will learn how to develop consistently and systematically many diverse skills ranging from social to academic to basic life skills.

Legislation and Litigation[2]

A trend initiated in the late 1960s, reaching full impact in the early 1970s and noted as the most apparent of this decade, is the attempt to change American educational policy through the courts and legislatures. Frustrated in their attempts to secure basic rights for the handicapped through nonlegal channels, various advocacy groups attempted to and succeeded in many cases in changing state laws to extend basic rights to all citizens. When this aim of guaranteeing basic rights through the modification of laws was not successful, litigation was employed and test cases were brought to the courts.

Through these two processes, many rights were obtained for the handicapped. All handicapped persons now have the right to marry, procreate, vote, travel on public conveyances, and have access to public buildings through the removal of environmental barriers. Those handicapped who reside in state institutions shall be free from cruel and unusual punishment, free from servitude (employment without compensation or intent of rehabilitation training), and free from involuntary institutionalization if they are not harmful to self or society. In addition, all school-aged (3 to 21) handicapped persons have the right to free, appropriate educational services. In the following subsections, major landmarks which resulted in changes for the handicapped are discussed according to the process through which these decisions were made.

Litigation

According to Weintraub, Abeson, and Braddock (1971), in the early 1970s there were 7 million school-aged children identified as handicapped, 1 million of whom were not receiving a free public education. Through a series of court cases, an attempt was made to rectify this deplorable situation. The first federal court case was filed in 1971. The now famous Pennsylvania Association for Retarded Children (PARC) vs. Commonwealth of Pennsylvania case resulted in the mandate that all Pennsylvania children between the ages of 6 and 21 attend public school. By 1972, that goal was almost accomplished. In 1972, the Mills vs. the Board of

Education case determined that all children in state-operated residential facilities must receive an educational program. Two other important decisions also resulted from this case. First, all handicapped persons are entitled to a due process hearing before placement can be made into either an educational or residential program. Second, appropriate educational services cannot be denied because of insufficient funding. These two landmark court cases, PARC and Mills, set the trend of using the legal system to shape educational policy. Although this trend began several years ago, the courts will continue to be one major vehicle for obtaining and enforcing the mandate which guarantees basic rights for the handicapped population.

To indicate how comprehensive the courts have been in stating what are basic inalienable rights of the handicapped, Gilhool (1976) summarized the results of the Alabama case, Wyatt vs. Stickney, in this way:

Judge Johnson in that case ruled that citizens residing at state schools and hospitals indeed have certain rights. They have the right to a human physical and psychological environment. They have the right to treatment or, if you will, habilitation, or, if you will, program. They have the right to an individual program fitted to their capabilities, a program which is designed individually and reviewed often and a program which, of course, includes education. They have a panoply of other rights such as the right to privacy, the right to use the telephone and to receive and send letters, and finally the right to receive their programs in the least restrictive setting, that is, in the community or perhaps in the public school rather than in a remote and isolated institution. (p. 14)

The ramifications of these and other court decisions are clear. First, the courts will intervene on behalf of the handicapped when human rights are denied, and the courts are appropriate channels to obtain changes in educational and social policies. By the courts' mandating that handicapped individuals obtain the fruits of their basic rights in a least restrictive environment, the implication is that a number of environmental choices exist. Since many and diverse options are frequently not available, we will need to see a growth in the number and kinds of services available to the handicapped during the next decade. In addition, we will need to develop strategies to determine what is an optimal setting

---

2. For comprehensive reviews of these areas, the following texts should be of assistance: Friedman (1976); Weintraub, Abeson, Ballard, and LaVor (1976).

for individuals and what, in fact, are appropriate educational and social programs to develop the abilities of handicapped individuals.

The notion of due process hearings and the involvement of parents in the development of educational plans for youngsters has been mandated by the courts. The true implications and implementation of this, however, is in an evolutionary state. Clearly, there is and will continue to be a trend for increasing parent involvement on advisory boards and as active agents in educational programs. Merely giving permission for their children to participate in research projects is not the parental role of the future, for we will see them taking more responsibility in the entire implementation and decision-making process regarding the handicapped.

Legislation

Concurrent with the PARC case, a group of activists in the state of Washington succeeded in obtaining the educational mandate for all handicapped children residing in that state. What was accomplished in the courts of Pennsylvania was accomplished in the legislative houses in Washington.

The most significant piece of legislation so far in this decade, however, was passed in 1975 and is called the Education for All Handicapped Children Act (P.L. 94–142). This law requires every state to insure that a free and appropriate education is provided for all handicapped children and youth aged 3–18 by the school year beginning 1978 and 3–21 by the school year beginning in 1980. In addition, the law requires that each handicapped child have an individualized educational program, a written statement of attainable goals, and objectives in accord with the individual's performance levels. The law also requires that nondiscriminatory tests and identification procedures be used for selection, due process hearings be held before placement, all personnel working with the handicapped be qualified and trained appropriately, and the educational program provided be appropriate for each student and be presented in the least restrictive environment possible.

This comprehensive law has many national implications, for it is the law of the land and guarantees basic civil rights to all handicapped children and youth. In the area of personnel preparation, for example, many changes must occur in the near future if all those who work with the handicapped are to be qualified. Certainly an increased use of volunteers will be a part of future educational programs, partic-

ularly when community members possess expert knowledge in areas in which the handicapped need training. This will necessitate new training programs to be developed so these volunteers can be effective in their dealings with the handicapped. Clearly we must see a trend to train paraprofessionals. Although several fine training programs, like that described by Tucker et al. (1976), have been developed, they are not available in sufficient supply. Preservice programs must be developed and provided through adult education, community, and junior colleges. This will necessitate the development of short-term curricula so appropriate training can be guaranteed with a minimal amount of time and expense. In addition, inservice programs must be developed so those already fulfilling paraprofessional roles can have their skills upgraded. Most likely, this will lead to certification, credentials, and employment standards to insure that auxiliary personnel possess at least minimum qualifications.

The Handicapped Children Act also will give rise to an emphasis on parent training. Funding priorities of the Bureau for Education of the Handicapped even provide for monies to be spent in the development and implementation of such programs (Burke & Saettler, 1976). Haring (1975) and Scholls (1978) feel that it is most important to involve parents in the teaching process and that it is imperative that they be given instruction which will facilitate productive interchange with their children. In accord with the act, Haring (1975, p. 430) stated, "it must be emphasized that personnel preparation includes preparing and training parents." Certainly, parent training will lead to greater involvement of this group with the education and treatment of the handicapped. In addition to paraprofessional and parent training, there must be a trend to train teachers in an ever-increasing number of skills in the areas of vocational training, career education, therapeutic recreation, etc. Otherwise, it will not be possible to provide appropriate educational opportunities for their pupils.

Although there are many areas of concern surrounding P.L. 94–142, the most central one rests with the concept of adequate and appropriate education for the handicapped. Burke and Saettler's (1976) statement emphasizes their concern with this concept also: "One issue that will surely test our teachers, administrators and bureaucrats is the 'determination of adequacy.' This issue is the fulcrum upon which the success of P.L. 94–142 will be balanced" (p. 363).

There must be a concentrated effort to set flexible guidelines to judge the appropriateness of treatment programs for each individual. This is not an easy task to be resolved either simply or quickly. There will be difficulties surrounding who determines program adequacy, what components are included, and how evaluation will be conducted. These issues are most difficult to remedy since, "in this nation we do not have a national determination of what an adequate general education is for all children" (Burke & Saettler, 1976, p. 364). It is apparent, therefore, that until such a national standard exists, professionals will have to watchguard the educational process and insist on quality implementation of the Handicapped Children Act of 1975 so the ideals stated there will become a reality.

Summary

The legal system has been used to secure the rights of the handicapped. The major trends seem to be:

1. The *courts and law-making bodies will* continue to *be major vehicles for obtaining change in educational and social policy* affecting the handicapped.

2. More *diverse options for educational service delivery must be developed* so the concept of providing appropriate education to all according to their individual abilities and needs is realized.

3. Considerable amounts of professional effort will be spent in the development of procedural *guidelines to evaluate the appropriateness of educational treatment programs* designed to develop the handicapped.

Conclusion

At last this nation has committed itself to the education and development of *all* of its children and youth. One hopes sincerely that this commitment is intense, long term, and sincere. History tells us that others, dedicated and learned, have made similar commitments which did not endure. Itard, fascinated and intrigued by Victor, labored diligently for years to develop his charge. However, as we know, while Victor improved and developed measurably, Itard abandoned his pursuit and considered his quest a failure. Similarly, Guggenbuhl, a Swiss physician, dedicated his energies and talents to the development of cretins. He created an environment (Abendberg) which was at one time called comparable to the Holy Mount. His program attracted great attention and for many years was praised. Again, however, after his failure "to cure a cretin" and because his institution drifted toward neglect and despair, another highly positive effort came to naught.

Through Samuel Gridley Howe and other idealistic pioneers, our early efforts at developing retarded individuals began with great zeal and positivism. As time passed and numbers increased, the slow, laborious work and limited results took their toll on professional morale and public optimism (Kanner, 1964).

Even today, the spasmodic surge toward mainstreaming has seen failures and returns to special schools and special classes (Keogh & Levitt, 1976). Over-deinstitutionalization has no doubt occurred. Many hurriedly organized, poorly planned group homes have already fallen into disrepute and closed as did Guggenbuhl's Abendberg. Many persons, idealistic and well trained (we thought), have left the severely handicapped after only a short time, speaking of isolation, inability, slow progress, and lack of cooperation. One now finds professionals pondering a "burn out" factor that may be prevalent among personnel who engage with those whose response repertoires are severely limited.

All of this says to us that a serious dilemma presents itself. If "cure" is our goal and "normalcy" is our criterion for this population, a generation of personnel will again approach their tasks with zeal and enthusiasm only to experience ultimate failure by their own and others' judgment. Yet, however, if one accepts, at the beginning, a lesser dream and restricts the developmental potential of individuals because of limited but more attainable goals, a moral and ethical commitment is blunted.

Where will our nation go with all of this? Will we come to recognize the satisfaction that accrues to so many when a severely handicapped child learns to walk *if* he eventually remains unable to walk to *work?* Will we rejoice with each newly gained developmental step if that individual *remains* dependent, though much less so?

This chapter and the trends cited herein are predicated on a societal commitment that we feel is promoted by P.L. 94–142. However, the *intensity* and *duration* of this commitment will be most important if we are to be sustained in a challenging, long-term, and difficult task. Only time can tell whether our programs for the moderately, severely, and profoundly handicapped will move from our "current dream" to an ultimate manifestation that represents our society's "finest hour."

References

Anderson, R. M., & Greer, J. G. (Eds.). *Educating the severely and profoundly retarded.* Baltimore, Md.: University Park Press, 1976.

Anderson, R. M., Greer, J. G., & McFadden, S. M. Occupational therapy for the severely handicapped in the public schools. In R. M. Anderson & J. G. Greer (Eds.), *Educating the severely and profoundly handicapped.* Baltimore, Md.: University Park Press, 1976.

Baker, B. L. Parent involvement in programming for developmentally disabled children. In L. L. Lloyd (Ed.), *Communication assessment and intervention strategies.* Baltimore, Md.: University Park Press, 1976.

Ball, T., Seris, K., & Payne, L. Long-term retention of self-help skill training in the profoundly retarded. *American Journal of Mental Deficiency,* 1971, *76*(3), 378–382.

Bricker, D. D. Educational synthesizer. In M. A. Thomas (Ed.), *Hey, don't forget about me!* Reston, Va.: Council for Exceptional Children, 1976.

Bricker, W. A., & Bricker, D. D. A program of language training for the severely language handicapped child. *Exceptional Children,* 1970, *37,* 101–111.

Burke, P. G., & Saettler, H. The division of personnel preparation: How funding priorities are established and a personal assessment of the impact of P.L. 94–142. *Education and Training of the Mentally Retarded,* 1976, *11,* 361–365.

Copeland, M., Ford, L., & Solon, N. *Occupational therapy for mentally retarded children.* Baltimore, Md.: University Park Press, 1976.

Deno, E. Special education as developmental capital. *Exceptional Children,* 1970, *37,* 229–237.

Dunn, L. M. *Exceptional children in the school.* New York: Holt, Rinehart & Winston, 1973.

Ferneti, C. L., Lent, J. R., & Stevens, C. J. *Eating.* Bellevue, Wash.: Edmark Associates, 1974.

Foster, S., Billionis, C. S., & Lent, J. R. *Feminine hygiene.* Bellevue, Wash.: Edmark Associates, 1976.

Foxx, R. M., & Azrin, N. H. *Toilet training the retarded.* Champaign, Ill.: Research Press, 1973.

Friedman, P. R. *Rights of mentally retarded persons.* New York: Avon, 1976.

Fristoe, M. Language intervention systems: Programs published in kit form. In L. L. Lloyd (Ed.), *Communication assessment and intervention strategies.* Baltimore, Md.: University Park Press, 1976.

Galloway, C., & Larsen, L. Associate teaching personnel. *Education and Training of the Mentally Retarded,* 1976, *11,* 273–280.

General Accounting Office. *Training educators for the handicapped: A need to redirect federal programs* (GAO Report, No. HRD-76–77). Washington, D. C.: U.S. General Accounting Office, September 1976.

Gilhool, T. K. Education: An inalienable right. In F. J. Weintraub, A. Abeson, J. Ballard, & M. L. LaVor (Eds.), *Public policy and the education of exceptional children.* Reston, Va.: Council for Exceptional Children, 1976.

Graham, L. W. Language programming and intervention. In L. L. Lloyd (Ed.), *Communication assessment and intervention strategies.* Baltimore, Md.: University Park Press, 1976.

Gray, R., & Ryan, B. *A language program for the nonlanguage child.* Champaign, Ill.: Research Press, 1973.

Grossman, H. J. (Ed.). *Manual on terminology and classification in mental retardation.* Washington, D.C.: American Association on Mental Deficiency, 1973.

Groves, I. D., & Carroccio, D. F. A self-feeding program for the severely and profoundly retarded. *Mental Retardation,* 1971, *9*(3), 10–12.

Guess, D., Smith, J. O., & Ensminger, E. E. The role of nonprofessional persons in teaching language skills to mentally retarded persons. *Exceptional Children,* 1971, *37,* 447–453.

Guskin, S. L., & Spicker, H. H. Educational research in mental retardation. In N. R. Ellis (Ed.), *International review of research in mental retardation* (Volume 3). New York: International Press, 1968.

Haring, N. G. Educational services for the severely and profoundly handicapped. *Journal of Special Education,* 1975, *9,* 425–433.

Hayden, A. H., & Haring, N. G. Programs for Down's syndrome children at the University of Washington. In T. D. Tjossem (Ed.), *Intervention strategies for high risk infants and young children.* Baltimore, Md.: University Park Press, 1975.

Hayden, A. H., McGinness, G., & Dmitriev, V. Early and continuous intervention strategies for severely handicapped infants and very young children. In N. G. Haring & L. J. Brown (Eds.), *Teaching the severely handicapped* (Volume 1). New York: Grune & Stratton, 1976.

Heber, R., & Garber, H. *An experiment in the prevention of cultural-familial mental retardation.* Madison, Wis.: Rehabilitation and Training Center in Mental Retardation, University of Wisconsin, 1971.

Horner, R. D., Billionis, C. S., & Lent, J. R. *Toothbrushing* (Rev. ed.). Bellevue, Wash.: Edmark Associates, 1975.

Ingenthron, D., Ferneti, C. L., & Keilitz, I. *Nose blowing.* Bellevue, Wash.: Edmark Associates, 1975.

Kanner, L. *A history of the care and study of the mentally retarded.* Springfield, Ill.: Charles C Thomas, 1964.

Keilitz, I., Horner, R. D., & Brown, K. H. *Complexion care.* Bellevue, Wash.: Edmark Associates, 1975.

Keogh, B. K., & Levitt, M. L. Special education in the mainstream: A confrontation of limitation? *Focus on Exceptional Children,* 1976, *8*(1), 1–11.

Kirk, S. A. *Early education of the mentally retarded.* Urbana, Ill.: University of Illinois Press, 1958.

Kroth, R. The role of the family. In A. Thomas (Ed.), *Learning and behavior problems of handicapped students in secondary school programs.* Reston, Va.: Council for Exceptional Children, 1977.

Kroth, R. & Scholls, G. *Getting schools involved with parents.* Reston, Va.: Council for Exceptional Children, 1978.

Levine, M. N., & Elliott, C. B. Toilet training for profoundly retarded with a limited staff. *Mental Retardation,* 1970, *8*(3), 48–50.

Lewis, P. J., Ferneti, C. L., & Keilitz, I. *Hair washing.* Bellevue, Wash.: Edmark Associates, 1975. (a)

Lewis, P. J., Ferneti, C. L., & Keilitz, I. *Use of deodorant.* Bellevue, Wash.: Edmark Associates, 1975. (b)

Lucky, R. E., & Addison, M. R. The profoundly retarded: A new challenge for public education. *Education and Training of the Mentally Retarded,* 1974, *9,* 123–130.

Martin, G. L., Kehoe, B., Bird, E., Jensen, V., & Darbyshire, M. Operant conditioning in the dressing behavior of severely retarded girls. *Mental Retardation,* 1971, *9,* 27–30.

Mills v. Board of Education of the District of Columbia, 348 F. Supp. 866 (D.D.C., 1972).

National Association for Retarded Citizens. *Educating the twenty-four hour retarded child.* Arlington, Tex.: NARC Research and Demonstration Institute, 1976. (a)

National Association for Retarded Citizens. *Mental Retardation News,* 1976, *25*(7), 3. (b)

Odle, S. J., Greer, J. G., & Anderson, R. M. The family of the severely retarded individual. In R. M. Anderson & J. G. Greer (Eds.), *Educating the severely and profoundly retarded.* Baltimore, Md.: University Park Press, 1976.

Pennsylvania Association for Retarded Children v. Commonwealth of Pennsylvania, 344 F. Supp. 1257 (E.D. Pa., 1971).

President's Committee on Mental Retardation. *Mental retardation: Century of decision* (Report to the President). Washington, D.C.: U.S. Government Printing Office, 1976. (a)

President's Committee on Mental Retardation. *Mental retardation: The known and the unknown* (No. OHD–76–21008). Washington, D.C.: U.S. Government Printing Office, 1976. (b)

Quick, A. D., Little, T. L., & Campbell, A. A. *Project MEMPHIS: Enhancing developmental progress in preschool exceptional children.* Belmont, Calif.: Fearon, 1974.

Reynolds, M. C. A framework for considering some issues in special education. *Exceptional Children,* 1962, *28,* 367–370.

Roberts, B. Instructional materials for severely and profoundly retarded learners. In R. M. Anderson & J. G. Greer (Eds.), *Educating the severely and profoundly handicapped.* Baltimore, Md.: University Park Press, 1976.

Robinson, H. B., & Robinson, N. M. *The mentally retarded child: A psychological approach* (2nd ed.). New York: McGraw-Hill, 1976.

Roos, P. Current issues in the education of mentally retarded persons. In W. J. Cegelka (Ed.), *Proceedings: Conference on the education of mentally retarded persons.* Arlington, Tex.: National Association for Retarded Citizens, 1971.

Roos, P. Parents and families of the mentally retarded. In J. M. Kauffman & J. S. Payne (Eds.), *Mental retardation: Introduction and personal perspectives.* Columbus, Ohio: Charles E. Merrill, 1975.

Sailor, W., Guess, D., & Lavis, L. Preparing teachers for education of the severely handicapped. *Education and Training of the Mentally Retarded,* 1975, *10,* 201–203.

Scarnati, R. A. The role of the physical therapist in special education. *Rehabilitation Literature,* 1971, *32,* 130–137.

Sigelman, C. K., & Bensberg, G. J. Supportive personnel for the developmentally disabled. In L. L. Lloyd (Ed.), *Communication assessment and intervention strategies.* Baltimore, Md.: University Park Press, 1976.

Smith, D. D., Smith, J. O., & Edgar, B. E. Prototypic model for the development of instructional materials. In N. G. Haring & L. J. Brown (Eds.), *Teaching the severely handicapped* (Volume 1). New York: Grune & Stratton, 1976.

Smith, J. O., & Arkans, J. More now than ever: A case for the special class. *Exceptional Children,* 1974, *40,* 497–502.

Sontag, E., Burke, P. J., & York, R. Considerations for serving the severely handicapped in the public schools. *Education and Training of the Mentally Retarded,* 1973, *8,* 20–26.

Stephens, B. President's message. *Education and Training of the Mentally Retarded,* 1976, *2* (1), 3–4.

Sternat, J., Messina, R., Nietupski, J., Lyon, S., & Brown, L. Occupational and physical therapy services for severely handicapped students: Toward a naturalized public school service delivery mode. In E. Sontag, J. J. Smith, & N. Certo (Eds.), *Educational programming for the severely and profoundly handicapped.* Reston, Va.: Council for Exceptional Children, 1977.

Stevens, C. J., Ferneti, C. L., & Lent, J. R. *Hand washing.* Bellevue, Wash.: Edmark Associates, 1975.

Teitelbaum, I. (Producer). *Like other people.* Northfield, Ill.: Parrenial Education, 1972. (Film)

Tennessee Chapter, American Association on Mental Deficiency. *Issues and Information,* 1976, *1* (1).

Treffry, D., Martin, G., Samels, J., & Watson, C. Operant conditioning of grooming behavior of severely retarded girls. *Mental Retardation,* 1970, *8*(4), 29–33.

Tucker, D., Hollis, J., Sailor, W., Horner, D., Kelly, P., & Guess, D. Preparing "paraprofessional" personnel for education of the severely handicapped: The teaching associate. *Education and Training of the Mentally Retarded,* 1976, *11,* 274–280.

Watson, L. S. *Child behavior modification: A manual for teachers, nurses, and parents.* New York: Pergamon, 1973.

Watson, L. S., & Bassinger, J. F. Parent training technology: A potential service delivery system. *Mental Retardation,* 1974, *12,* 3–10.

Weikart, D. P. Preschool programs: Preliminary findings. *Journal of Special Education,* 1967, *1,* 163–181.

Weintraub, F., Abeson, A., & Braddock, D. *State law and education of handicapped children: Issues and recommendations.* Arlington, Va.: Council for Exceptional Children, 1971.

Wilson, V., & Parks, R. Promoting ambulation in the severely retarded child. *Mental Retardation,* 1970, *8,* 17–19.

Notes

1. Spradlin, J. E. *The Premack hypothesis and self-feeding by profoundly retarded children: A case report* (Parsons Research Project, Working Paper 79). Unpublished manuscript, Kansas University and Kansas Bureau of Child Research, 1964.
2. Tawney, J. W. Personnal communication, 1976.
3. Adamson, G. *Training teachers of the severely/profoundly handicapped* (U.S. Office of Education, Grant No. G00–76–02994). Unpublished manuscript, University of New Mexico, Department of Special Education, 1976.

Name Index

Subject Index